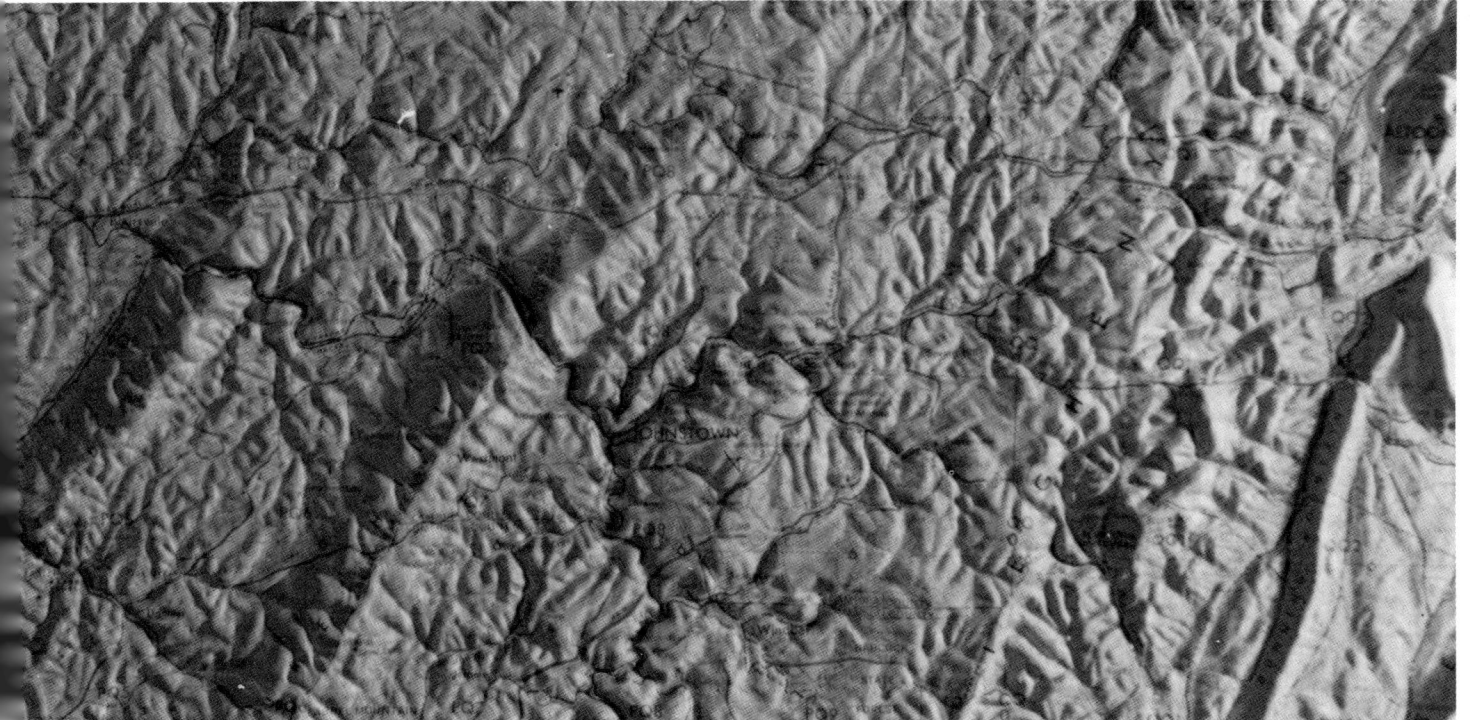

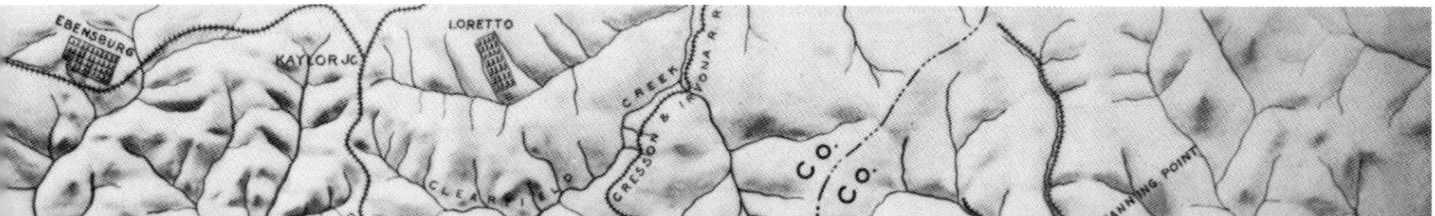

RELIEF MAP
OF THE
ALLEGHENY MOUNTAINS
BETWEEN
JOHNSTOWN ALTOONA & HOLLIDAYSBURG
1896
SCALE OF MILES

THE BED OF THE OLD PORTAGE RAILROAD. FROM THE Y SWITCHES NEAR DUNCANSVILLE TO HOLLIDAYSBURG THE HOLLIDAYSBURG BRANCH
THE NEW PORTAGE RAILROAD OCCUPIED, FOR A SHORT DISTANCE, THE BED OF THE OLD PORTAGE RAILROAD THE NEWRY BRANCH
FROM DUNCANSVILLE TO NEWRY JUNCTION IT OCCUPIES THE BED OF THE NEW PORTAGE RAILROAD.

R THE DIRECTION OF ANTES SNYDER ENG'R RIGHT OF WAY
PENN'A RAILROAD COMPANY, BLAIRSVILLE PA.
FROM THE MODEL BY
Edwin E. Howell, Washington D.C.
ORE Draftsman   E. H. BERLIN Photographer

Triumph I
ALTOONA TO PITCAIRN 1846-1996

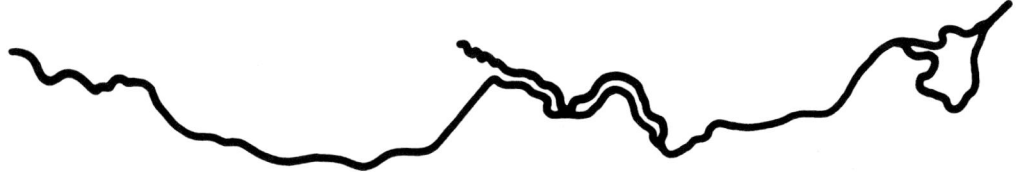

[signature] 24 Feb 2001

by Charles S. Roberts

Assisted by Gary W. Schlerf

"Books that make a Difference"

COPYRIGHT © 1997 BARNARD, ROBERTS AND CO., INC.
Manufactured in the United States of America

FIRST EDITION June 1997

All Worldwide rights reserved. No part of this book may be reproduced in any manner without permission in writing, except in the case of critical reviews.

Published by
BARNARD, ROBERTS AND CO., INC.
2606 Willow Avenue
P. O. Box 7344
Baltimore MD 21227
(410) 247-2242

Library of Congress Catalog Card No. 95-78455
ISBN 0-934118-23-X

FRONTISPIECE: The instability of the underlying rock was the bane of PRR's passage over the Great Mountain Barrier as this Horseshoe Curve scene so dramatically portrays. Once exposed to air, water and freezing action, the mountain fought back by showering the railroad with boulders large and small. The center of this scene eventually became a tourist attraction and park, but on the date of this photograph such a development seemed unlikely at best. To complicate matters, the strata abruptly varied in composition from place to place...note the difference in the cuts to the right and left of the train. Over the years, the rock wall was cut back and a bench cut higher on the mountain but the problem remains today and will stay with the railroad until the mountain erodes to a flat plain...that will be a very long time indeed. Since one can see two clamshell clerestory "PB" cars as well as two monitor-roof coaches, and the PB cars were first built in 1867, the date of this view is probably c.1870. *Hagley Museum and Library*

COVER: Bitter winter weather remains another obstacle to any mountain crossing, no less so for PRR on this or any other day. On 10 February 1968, units 6046, 2425, 2603 and 2205 with a westbounder have just topped the grade as they exit Allegheny Tunnel, PRR's first bore at Gallitzin. The summit is precisely at the portal behind the locomotives. And that blood-red keystone emblem leads the way, defying Mother Nature still another time. *The Houser Collection*

A NOTE ABOUT CREDITS: Lack of credits indicate that the subject came from the camera or collection of the author, the library of the publisher or from untraceable sources. Some material obviously originated with the railroad (e.g. track charts) so credits were not used in these cases.

Dedication

Simpson C. Roberts
1907 - 1978

Father of the author and born in Pittsburgh, the citadel of The Pennsylvania Railroad for well over a century, he was a Baltimore and Ohio Railroad traffic official for his entire career. He had the satisfaction of having a son-in-law, David M. Stern, with the railroad as a rateman.

He was the son of Charles Swann Roberts (1879-1932), who started with the B&O in 1897 at the Pittsburgh Traffic office where he spent twenty of his thirty-five years of service with the railroad.

In turn, Charles was the nephew of Thomas Swann (1809-1883) who was President of the B&O from 1848 to 1853 and led that railroad in its lunge from Cumberland to Wheeling in defiance of PRR.

All of these relatives of the author competed with PRR with ferocity and at least some success. So this dedication is really a form of a salute to "mine friend the enemy." And there is another, more personal reason.

We cannot conceive that it would be possible for anyone to have had a finer or more admirable father and we are sorry that it took so long for his only son to put such thoughts in writing.

Charles Swann Roberts
30 July 1995

Table of Contents

Chapter 1	The Situation and the Terrain	9
Chapter 2	Saga of Seven Cities	25
Chapter 3	The Philadelphia Story	31
Chapter 4	The Big Bet	39
Chapter 5	The East Slope	57
Chapter 6	The West Slope	155
Chapter 7	The Gaps	243
Chapter 8	Rip Rap	271
Chapter 9	Operations	329
Chapter 10	Color Journey	337
Chapter 11	Prelude to Disaster	385

Irony

In the mid-1970s, we created the tagline "The true railfan has two favorite railroads…the B&O and another one." This expression has appeared in print many times and has been used by other publishers and writers to the extent that it has become generic.

Yet in all that time, and with thousands of our books sold, only one individual has thought to ask this writer, "What is *your* other favorite railroad?" A gentleman asked that question at a book show a few years ago and we replied, "Well, actually, it's PRR but please don't spread it around." His mouth dropped and he said, "No, I won't, because nobody would believe me anyway."

The reason for our reticence will be apparent to a professional publisher. Any publisher's "future book" is top secret for competitive reasons and at that time our publishing house was preparing to do for the history of PRR what we were in the process of doing for B&O.

This "other favorite" selection was not feigned. No objective student of transportation history can avoid the conclusion that PRR was, and still is, awesome. In 1846 the last railroad to be chartered in the Trunkline struggle with B&O, NYC and Erie, PRR emerged triumphant just 28 years later with a dominance never lost to any challenger. PRR was literally the keystone in the march of the nation to industrial and agricultural superpower status by 1900, a lead maintained to this day.

Fundamental to this victory was conquest of the Great Mountain Barrier and the twin foes of gravity and distance. This book, first in a series that will cover the history of the entire railroad, relates the stirring saga of the fabled Pittsburgh Division from 1846 to 1996.

This magnificent story will be told in the pages to come, but first we want to provide some background to our readers.

Hopefully some of these readers will have studied our book *Sand Patch/Clash of Titans*, a work that details the contest in Western Pennsylvania between B&O and PRR from B&O's perspective. They will find some repetition in *Triumph I* simply because we had to assume there would be new readers unacquainted with the material contained in the earlier book.

Inevitably, there will be readers of *Triumph I* unfamiliar with the works, attitudes and qualifications of the author and they are entitled to some explanations. The author, now sixty-seven years of age, first started writing for publication as a journalist when he was fourteen. Of his long career as a communicator, he has spent forty years in command positions of publishing and related enterprises…not always with success, it should be said. He has been involved in mergers, acquisitions, financing and forecasting the unknowable future. Perhaps unique among writers of history, he has "been there" and understands from experience the pressures that faced the people about whom he is writing.

The cynic will say that there were not many zeros after the dollars with which the writer has had experience…the answer is that those lesser number of zeroes were just as important to the people involved as the more numerous zeroes were to, say, PRR. And precious few corporations had as many zeroes as PRR or Penn Central or, for that matter, Conrail.

Your author has also been involved in politics, sufficient to intimately know how things are really done in a republic. So as the reader considers the conclusions reached in this book, he should keep in mind that these people and institutions are being judged by a peer well aware that there are very few Vestal Virgins.

The Welsh surname Roberts appears quite frequently in PRR history. It is unlikely that the author is related to any of them.

A few minor points to the new reader. Our tradition is to use the third person as a mark of humility. In our formative years, we were taught that the use of the personal pronoun "I" was in very bad taste. To those who choose to believe it is meant in a royal sense, "Sir Charles" will do very nicely.

We have chosen to use modern spellings, abbreviations and definitions…thus Pittsburgh, Allegheny, Greensburg *et al*. The division at issue has gone by many names…we will refer to it as the Pittsburgh Division, or Pittdiv. The railroad is PRR. The merger of NYC with PRR in 1968 was actually an acquisition by PRR and the selection of the name "Penn Central" was really an amusing flashback to the early days. You see, The Pennsylvania Railroad may have been the official name, but it was widely called the Pennsylvania Central for many years. And, of course, the heart and core of Conrail is the original PRR.

The title of this introduction is apt, or at least we think so. It is ironic that a major history of PRR would be written by the scion of an old and ancient B&O family and dedicated to the father of the author.

Then again, perhaps it should have been *"Awesome."*

Chapter 1

The Situation and the Terrain

Digital shaded-relief portrayal of landforms of the conterminous United States by Gail P. Thelin and Richard J. Pike 1991, U.S. Geological Survey. Vertical exaggeration 2x.

IT IS STILL HARD TO BELIEVE that just six hundred years ago, a mere droplet in the passage of time on planet earth, no eastern or western civilization knew that the New World even existed. Nor did the peoples who populated the New World know that the rest of the globe consisted of vast continents with long recorded histories that reached back thousands of years and unrecorded heritages that disappeared in the mists of a past that was measured by hundreds of thousands or even millions of years. If one had, through some magic, published this map in the year 1500 it would have been received as fictional fantasy. And if the publisher had predicted that this slice of the North American continent would become a unified nation and an agricultural and industrial superpower in just four hundred years, he would have been a candidate for restraint or sacrificed as an offering to some appropriate deity. And if this poor soul would have postulated that this new nation would be created by a melange of humans from every conceivable race, color, religion and national origin from literally every corner of the planet, his only hope for survival would have been that his executioners might die laughing before the swing of the axe. Yet he would have been a secular prophet. Just about every description of this New World began with the adjective "Great." The Great Lakes. The Great Mountain Barrier. The Great Plains. The Great Eastern Waters. The Great Western Waters. The Great Granary. The Great Gift of Mother Nature. And she was very generous indeed, for this new nation was awash in incredibly fertile soil, raw materials beyond measure, timber, opulent fisheries, water resources, fur-bearing animals in the early days and blessed with a relatively temperate climate. But, with the perversity typical of her gender, Mother Nature rarely puts her gifts where humankind wants to use them. There are only three basic human activities…growing things, making things and carrying things. Seldom has Mother Nature been more contumacious than with her gift of the New World to the Old. For distances as vast as the prize separated production and market. For good measure, that Great Mountain Barrier added gravity to the transportation stew. To tame and harness her gifts, the fledgling United States of America entered the 1800s with an experimental republican form of government, no money, a small population, thousands of square miles of uncharted wilderness, no technological base, no significant internal transportation system, a gaggle of feisty states and city/states fighting among themselves, rich only in territory. The nation ended the nineteenth century with an astonishing twenty-five percent of world output and will end the twentieth century with the same share, envied by every other nation on earth and emulated by those who dare. This triumph is the greatest adventure story in human history.

His name was René Robert Cavelier La Salle. History knows him more simply as La Salle. Born 22 November 1643 in Rouen, La Salle emigrated to Montreal at the age of twenty-three. Having been born in Normandy, he could probably trace his lineage deep into Viking origins.

The Vikings were classic explorers and conquerors who terrorized western Europe for many centuries. Bold seamen, ferocious warriors and, perhaps above all, curious adventurers, these Scandinavians left a mark on western history indelible to this day. They would slay the men, lay the women, loot and occasionally even set up housekeeping in places that caught their fancy.

As to La Salle, surely he must have had his share of their genes. Upon arrival in French Canada, he immediately entered the fur trade. This is hardly surprising because the fur trade was the only significant industry in North America then and for some time to come. Very early on, he ventured westward into the wilderness and explored areas south of Lakes Erie and Ontario. As a reward for his various exploits, he was granted a monopoly of the trade in the Mississippi Valley.

This was an easy gift for France to give a favored son because nobody knew what was out there nor where the westward-flowing rivers like the Ohio really went. So in 1679, La Salle began a series of expeditions that entailed adventures breathtaking to behold even to this day.

Finally, on 9 April 1682, La Salle found the mouth of the Mississippi and learned that it flowed into the Gulf of Mexico. He took possession of the river, its valley and all its tributaries and named the territory Louisiana for his liege Louis XIV.

To go down the river to its mouth was one thing…to find it from the Gulf of Mexico was quite another. He mounted a seagoing expedition that missed the mouth and went too far west. Misadventures followed and La Salle was murdered by mutineers in January 1687. A rather ignoble end for a man who made one of the most pivotal discoveries in recorded history. And it was just a little over three hundred years ago.

Eleven years later Briton Thomas Savery invented a steam engine. About thirteen years after that, c. 1711, another Briton named Thomas Newcomen developed an improved engine in company with Savery.

Scottish inventor James Watt improved the Savery/Newcomen engine, receiving a patent in 1769. All of these early steam engines were used to pump water from mine shafts. Curiously, Watt's name was also used to define a measure of electrical power. Scotland was beginning to produce something more than whiskey, in and of itself no small achievement.

These developments heralded the beginning of what has become known as the Industrial Revolution, an evolutionary process that began and flowered in Great Britain. While the start date of 1760 is usually used as a reference point, important advances occurred in earlier years. Sweeping improvements in the textile industry triggered this revolution…the flying shuttle was introduced in 1733, the spinning jenny in 1764 and the power loom in 1785. Mass production of textiles ensued, costs plummeted, demand soared and the face of British society changed from agrarian to industrial in a very short span of time.

As it turned out, Britain was in the right place at the right time. The cockpit of this revolution was surrounded by tidewater and was very compact. In fact, the whole thing would easily fit inside the Commonwealth of Pennsylvania with room to spare.

The revolution fed on itself. Internal transportation needs were easily met with canals, turnpikes and rail roads. Distances were short, grades minor and the climate mild. Abundant resources of high quality coal fed an iron, and later steel, industry that soon outproduced the rest of the world combined. Since it took seven to ten tons of coal to produce a ton of iron, the iron ore was brought to the coal and much of that by cheap tidewater transport.

Wise and liberal government policies nurtured the revolution, capital formation exploded and investment was rewarded rather than punished. The factory system rapidly evolved through divisions of labor, a merchant marine was encouraged to the extent that even as late as the eve of World War I fully half of the world's trade moved in British bottoms.

The home market was soon satisfied and exports to the outer world, principally colonies and the United States, blossomed. France, once the richest and most populous European nation, dissipated her assets and colonies in a series of self defeating wars, revolutions, idiotic tax policies and unstable governments and went into an eclipse from which it has never recovered. Britain's main rival destroyed herself to the extent that even in this century the expression "égalité, fraternité, sénilité" would be the subject of sardonic toasts.

THE SITUATION AND THE TERRAIN

Spain, another continental rival, managed to steal herself into oblivion. Once this nation discovered that Central and South America had hoards of gold ready for plucking, she concentrated on "importing" it and then used it to buy whatever she needed. No need to nourish agriculture or industry. Then the gold ran out and she had nothing.

Thus, in a little over a century, Britain became the most powerful and richest nation on the planet. Then, by the end of the last century, she lost her lead to an upstart republic that started that century with nothing but a lot of empty space and a theory.

There was a price to Britain's success. The industrial revolution converted farmers into factory workers and miners to the extent that she could no longer feed herself. So Britain had to import food and the United States was the only nation with a granary large enough to meet the need. And that burgeoning textile industry gobbled huge amounts of cotton. Again, only the United States had the potential to meet the need. And the United States did come up with one solitary technological development late in the eighteenth century. In 1793 Eli Whitney invented the cotton gin which trebled the rate of seed removal from raw cotton. Production of cotton in the United States increased from 1,500,000 pounds in 1790 to 85,000,000 pounds in 1810.

On the surface, Britain's ever-growing need for food and fibre was not alarming. She would pay for it by exporting finished goods to the United States and, ultimately, invest capital in the United States to nurture the supply and take a percentage off the top for the use of her capital.

To the United States, there were some serious problems to be solved. In the South, the transportation problem was not too severe because the whole region was laced with lazy rivers flowing to tidewater. Labor, however, was another matter. The United States was entering an expansion phase and desperately needed both skilled and unskilled labor in ever increasing numbers. Immigration was the only answer, but no one would voluntarily work those cotton fields in that hot sun when better opportunities were presented elsewhere. Thus slaves were imported. Actually, in comparison to the importation of slaves in Central and South America the numbers brought into the southern states were rather small, but the whole idea of slavery would soon become an explosive and bloody issue.

And another, more subtle issue soon arose. The southern states had no significant raw materials to feed an industrial base. Consequently, they had to import finished goods from Britain. This worked well enough until the northern states decided to nourish industrial development by slapping high tariffs on imported British goods…protectionism, in other words. This process escalated until the eve of the Civil War when Abraham Lincoln rammed through a 47% tariff on British imports. Taken in combination with northern pressure to free the southern slaves without compensation, secession was inevitable. Lincoln decided to put down the "rebellion" by force and the bloodiest war in the nation's history resulted. And a most tragic and unnecessary war in this writer's view.

When Britain, in one of its "periodic fits of morality," decided to eliminate slavery, compensation was paid to slave owners and some say the total tab was some twenty million pounds. A lot cheaper than a Civil War.

In the North, Britain's voracious need for food posed a different set of riddles. From the earliest colonial days, furs were the principal export from this region and Canada. It did not take long for trappers to slaughter the fur-bearing animals east of the Great Mountain Barrier so there was no choice but to venture over the mountains to tap the vast territories to the west and north. The French were also reaching into this region from Canada; all enlisted Indian tribes as trappers and rewarded them with firearms, firewater, trinkets and an array of venereal and other assorted diseases. The cost of transportation to haul these furs to tidewater was very high, but the product was high value and the Europeans were willing and able to pay the price…indeed, they had no choice.

Food was another matter. The geologic forces that created the Great Mountain Barrier had to combat the enormous erosive power of water. Water was there first and inland water flows downhill to tidewater. The continental drifts that pushed up mountains did not impress water. The rivers simply continued to flow and wore down the surging mountains. This up and down process, incidentally, happened a number of times over millions of years. Numerous times throughout history the mountains in the Barrier were over twenty thousand feet high. Each time they were worn down. Water has always won and is winning now.

The flow of water changed the landscape in a lot of ways. A continental divide was created which ran the entire length of the Barrier. Water falling to the east of the divide flowed to the Atlantic Ocean. Water falling to the west of the divide flowed to the Gulf of Mexico. The water started the trip at the same height…the distance to tidewater, however, was vastly different.

The Eastern Waters had a very short trip and flowed with high velocity, taking with them almost all the raw materials and most of the topsoil that the mountains had heaved up from the depths of the earth.

The Western Waters had a long way to go to the Gulf of Mexico and left behind enormous reserves of raw materials and topsoil. Immense. Massive. Almost infinite.

And the size of this Mississippi basin, as we will call it for the moment, was breathtaking. Including some fecund Canadian provinces, if overlaid on Europe it would reach from the French coast deep into Mother Russia and stretch from the North Cape of Norway to the Alps.

Equally impressive was Mother Nature's gift of a transportation system. The Mississippi River and its tributaries served almost the entire basin, stretching from New York State all the way to the Western Continental Divide; from the Canadian border to the Gulf of Mexico. And we can thank La Salle for discovering where the waters flowed.

So the answer to Britain's food problem was at hand. Of course, the nation had to get farmers out there to till the soil but the lushness of the region attracted them in more than sufficient numbers.

But our fledgling republic faced another little problem. The United States did not own the western half of the basin nor the strategic port of New Orleans. The French discovered it and the French owned it.

The French penchant for making war on everyone in sight ultimately played into the nation's hands. As the result of still another disastrous war, France ceded the western half of the basin to Spain in 1762 and the remainder of her New World possessions to Britain in 1763. The final settlement between Britain and the United States as a result of the Revolutionary War gave the nation title to all the British territory save Canada.

The Spanish ignored their western basin holdings, but then the French lived up to their national tradition of self-destruction by allowing Napoleon Bonaparte to hold sway and bleed away more of their youth and treasure. In one of his transitory high spots,

Napoleon pressured Spain to cede it back in 1800. This news did not go down well in Washington. Already Americans were streaming into the Ohio, Cumberland and Tennessee River valleys and they were dependent upon free use of the Mississippi River and the port of New Orleans. This "free use" was guaranteed by a treaty with Spain signed in 1795 and Napoleon, of course, informed President Thomas Jefferson not to worry about it. "Trust me". Even the pro-French Jefferson was reluctant to put much faith in the usurper's word and, sure enough, negotiations in Paris were not bearing fruit.

In the event, Jefferson proved to be just as wily as Napoleon and after threatening Napoleon that the United States "must marry (ourselves) to the British fleet and nation" if France were to take possession of New Orleans, the usurper threw in his hand and agreed in 1803 to sell Louisiana to the United States. The last thing he needed was still another enemy.

The total price, with interest, was $27,267,622. This new territory of 828,000 square miles doubled the size of the United States at a cost of less than three cents an acre and not one drop of blood. The greatest bargain in American history. And Baring Brothers, the potent British financial house lately in the news and a firm that would play a role in American railroad affairs in the future, handled the transaction. Britain loaned money to America to pay France, a mortal enemy. It may not have been smart on the surface, but it turned out to be very wise.

Old Man River, the greatest transportation artery in the world, was now the spine of the United States just three years into the new century. Its basin contained mineral wealth beyond comprehension, a fact, by the way, not fully realized at the time of the purchase. Even the known agricultural lands, lush as they were, turned out to be only a fraction of the total available and those unexplored resources would prove to be the greatest part of the bonanza.

The Louisiana Purchase also took the western boundary of the nation to the western continental divide in the Rocky Mountains, then called the Stony Mountains, and would provide the nation with an incentive to take her western frontier to that other shining sea, the Pacific.

The downstream commerce was mostly grain, and derivatives such as flour, whiskey and animal products. Timber and coal also moved downstream; virtually all products in flatboats and keelboats constructed upstream from available timber. Width varied from ten to twenty feet, length from twenty to a hundred feet. Typical craft carried fifty or so tons and required five to seven men to handle. They were flimsy and meant to be sold for timber upon arrival downstream.

Pittsburgh and nearby cities on the upper Ohio River became shipbuilding centers well before 1800 even though 1500 miles from New Orleans. Many of these ships were oceangoing and sailed to the West Indies and Europe.

There is always a "but." Downstream was one thing…upstream was almost impossible. The rivers in the Mississippi basin were serpentine and rather narrow, precluding for the most part *upstream* movements by sailing craft. Imports of finished goods from Britain had to cross the Mountain Barrier.

Not that our stalwart forefathers didn't try. Barges or arks with keels were built and operated upstream with oars, poles and cordelling, as sailing was rarely possible. In cordelling men walked the banks and hauled the craft by ropes, sometimes gaining a purchase by taking a turn around a tree or trunk.

A rarely noted breed of boatmen evolved on the Western Waters during the first third of the 1800s; the polemen. Keelboats had walkways on each side and teams of these men would place twenty-foot long poles against shoulder pads and push from bow to stern. Each would lean forward until almost parallel with the deck and walk to the stern, then rotate back to the bow. They usually worked stripped to the waist and sometimes in loin cloths.

The work was brutal and the polemen were tough. Their exploits off-duty were legendary, as one would expect from men suffering such exhausting labor, exposure to the elements and privation.

Their reign was brief. The cost of upstream movement was very high and the rise of the steamboat shattered their occupation, although some survived until the time of the Civil War working streams too small for steamboats or in times of very low water.

The development of the steam engine changed the face of manufacturing. No longer were factories chained to water power and water wheels. Now a factory could be sited at the most economical convergence of raw materials, labor and market.

The next step was to apply the power of steam to transportation and the first application was to inland watercraft. This time the United States was the innovator and the reason was simple. Britain did not have a pressing inland transportation problem; her rivers were short and near tidewater. Not so the United States. The upstream problem in the Mississippi basin had been addressed, but there were others. The Hudson River, the only one to breach the mountain barrier, was the most significant and it was on this river in 1807 that Robert Fulton's steamboat *Clermont* proved that evaporated water under pressure would revolutionize inland passage.

The *Clermont* had a low-compression engine and would not prove suitable for Western Waters work. In fact, there were those who felt that the Ohio River was too swift and shallow for steamboat operation. Fulton, an impressive figure in American industrial history aside from this exploit, didn't believe it. The trade between Pittsburgh and New Orleans had grown so rapidly that keelboats couldn't keep up with demand regardless of cost and the opportunity for a giant step forward was golden.

Fulton and his partner Robert Livingston sent New York engineer Nicholas J. Roosevelt and his wife to Pittsburgh in 1809 to literally test the waters. By the way, Roosevelt's wife Lynda was the daughter of the famous architect Benjamin Henry Latrobe. As the reader shall see, the Latrobe name became quite famous in eastern railroad development. The United States was beginning to apply the adjective "Great" to men as well as creations of Mother Nature.

Roosevelt went downstream from Pittsburgh to New Orleans in a flatboat in 1809, measuring water depth, currents and even arranged to open coal mines for possible steamboat use. In 1810 he returned to Pittsburgh and arranged for the construction of the steamboat *New Orleans* at the mouth of a creek about a mile up the Monongahela River from its junction with the Allegheny River, the start-point of the Ohio River.

On 20 October 1811 the *New Orleans* set "sail" for her namesake port, the first trip ever made on the Ohio by a steampowered craft. The voyage was a success and the craft even survived the Great Earthquake that struck the lower Ohio and middle Mississippi region that year. Still another "Great."

Even in the early 1800s Pittsburgh was producing iron and was located near vast timber reserves so it was natural that the construction of steamboats would be centered there. Hundreds were soon plying the river, upstream and down, and the growth in trade was explosive. So, incidentally, were the steamboats. High-pressure steam engines were utilized because they were cheaper to manufacture and produced more horsepower, but they also blew up with distressing regularity.

The news of all these impressive developments *west* of the Great Mountain Barrier was not received in northeastern city/states with unalloyed joy. The exports of food and fibre were pouring out through New Orleans and southern ports. Now the *imports* of finished goods were being diverted to competing ports. The fur business was declining and what little was left was leaving through Canadian ports. The expression "withering on the vine" was heard at dinner parties, business meetings and even appeared in newspapers. The nineteenth century which had begun with so much promise was now producing alarming transmutations. And it was all happening so *fast*.

The Britain the colonists were so eager to cast out of the New World was now being called Great Britain and was in the process of crushing the French and about to impose a *Pax Britannica* that would last for over a century. Britain's internal development was exponential and those cousins were demonstrating a skill at allying science with industry.

Disquieting. Particularly in Philadelphia. Those damned mountains were not eroding fast enough. Worse, Pittsburgh saw her future in westward terms and was beginning to act as if the rest of Pennsylvania was a relic of the past.

The dilemma had its roots in Virginia and the exploits of a man named George Washington. Born in 1732 and related to British Lord Fairfax, who owned 5,000,000 acres in northern Virginia and the Shenandoah Valley, Washington hired out as a trainee surveyor at age sixteen. In 1753, alarmed at incursions into the Ohio River valley by the French out of Canada, Virginia's lieutenant governor sent Washington with a small party to the main French fort near Lake Erie with an ultimatum "get out of the Ohio country or we'll put you out." The answer was predictable and Washington came back lucky to be alive. The trip was via Cumberland, Maryland and Washington noted a number of things, principally that the Ohio country was lush indeed, that one could reach it from Virginia with just one crossing of the mountain barrier and the distance from Potomac River tidewater at his plantation at Mt. Vernon to the Ohio Valley was the shortest of any along the eastern seaboard.

The Ohio Company was formed in 1747 by a relative of Washington's to develop lands on the upper Potomac and Ohio Rivers. A small fort was built at Pittsburgh by this company. The French seized it and had the audacity to rename it Fort Duquesne. The Indians decided to back the French. In 1754 Washington began his military career by taking an expedition to "put them out", managed a small victory at Great Meadows near Confluence, holed up in nearby makeshift Fort Necessity, was promptly defeated by the French and sent packing back to Virginia a second time. The French and Indian War had begun.

There would be a third disaster. In 1755 the British decided to send an army under General Edward Braddock to deal with the cheeky French and Washington came along with some Virginia troops. This time they got pretty close to Pittsburgh before the French and Indians cut them to pieces, killing General Braddock for good measure.

Your author has been a soldier and has reviewed these two battles with a critical eye. He has concluded that the greenest platoon leader in the United States Army would not have botched as badly as Washington did on these two occasions. Yet he went on to become General Washington and the Father of his country. Of course, during the Revolutionary War the French were on the side of the colonists and the British happily continued their military tradition of tactical and strategic blundering.

Pertinent to our story, the route taken by the Braddock expedition paralleled what would become the National Road.

By 1756 the little French and Indian skirmish had engulfed Britain, France and just about every other European nation in an early version of a world-wide conflagration called the Seven Years War. It savaged three continents and resulted in abject defeat for the French everywhere including all of North America.

In 1758 the British mounted another expedition to clear the enemy out of Pittsburgh and this time chose British General John Forbes as commander. While Forbes took Washington along, he was bright enough not to listen to anything Washington had to say. Washington wanted to follow Braddock's route a second time and Forbes wasn't buying, suspecting with some justification that his recommendation was tied more to his Ohio Valley properties and ambitions than military common sense.

Forbes chose to approach Pittsburgh on an all-

Pennsylvania route that followed an Indian path through Bedford, generally following a trace that would become part of the Pennsylvania Road, the abortive South Penn Railroad and the Pennsylvania Turnpike. This route was shorter and avoided a crossing of the Monongahela River. Forbes pushed the French out and renamed the fortification Fort Pitt.

There was a lot of back and forth military action at Pittsburgh over the ensuing years, but never again was the American hold on the Forks of the Ohio seriously challenged. At least not by the British, French or Indians.

As it turned out, Washington's descendants won the first round in the cross-barrier transportation battle with Pennsylvania. At the close of the Revolutionary War nine of the thirteen original colonies claimed huge hunks of the territory west of the barrier, with Virginia being the greediest. Maryland, a tiny state which would occasionally produce something of note, refused to sign the Articles of Confederation unless all agreed to waive claims and allow new states to be formed from what became known as the Northwest Territory. In 1787, at the insistence of Virginia, an ordinance was passed obligating the Federal government to build a road across the mountains to the Northwest Territory. The money would come from the sale of wilderness land. A small sum was duly appropriated in 1806 and the final location set in 1808. The National Road would follow the Braddock military road from Cumberland across the mountains and turn left to reach the Ohio River at Wheeling, a city at that time in Virginia. George Washington and his Virginians had gotten their way and Pennsylvania would have to make do on its own.

Construction started fitfully in 1811 and Wheeling was reached by 1818, just about the time the steamboat was beginning to dominate the Western Waters. Construction of the National Road continued west through central Ohio and ultimately was extended to St. Louis.

This road was not a cowpath. The construction method employed was originated by Scotsman John L. McAdam and, by the addition of an "a", became known as a Macadam road. Actually, the first Macadam road in America was the Philadelphia-Lancaster Turnpike and it was completed in 1794.

In the case of the National Road, a strip 66-feet wide was cleared of all trees and brush, then a 30-foot roadbed was leveled and a central 24-foot road surface was installed. This roadway was built up with large seven-inch stones at the base and three-inch or smaller stones on top, sealed with stone dust and dirt. It was a super-highway for the times and, of course, was all-weather. Federal money provided for construction, but not maintenance. States set up toll systems to provide funds for the latter. No provision was made for the cost of invested capital, continuing an unfortunate trend of governmental financing of land transportation that haunts the nation to this day.

This National Road was very significant in national history for a number of reasons. First, it bypassed Pittsburgh to the south and forced Pennsylvania to connect with it via an extension of the Pennsylvania Road. Known later as Route 30 or the Lincoln Highway, this road ran from Philadelphia through Lancaster, Columbia, Gettysburg, Bedford and Greensburg to Pittsburgh.

It was necessary for a new highway to be constructed from Bedford to Washington, Pennsylvania in order to tap traffic to and from the National Road. Two rivers, the Monongahela and Youghiogheny, had to be crossed and the mountain barrier met head on.

Second, Maryland was quick to build connecting turnpikes from Baltimore to Cumberland and this route from the Ohio to tidewater was much shorter than the Pennsylvania route to Philadelphia.

Third, the cost of haulage was enormous. In this era it was far cheaper to ship from Pittsburgh to Philadelphia via New Orleans then it was to use the Pennsylvania Road!

Fourth, most of the traffic over the mountain barrier was *westbound* from early colonial days until the coming of the railroad c.1852 when the direction of tonnage movement was reversed. Only time-sensitive high-value freight traffic and passenger travel could bear the high cost of transportation.

Fifth, and perhaps most important, was the matter of highway location. The cost of constructing a highway was so much per mile. The more miles the more capital investment, so time after time the route chosen was the straightest. This approach made some sense when the route was relatively flat, but was an economic bomb with a short fuse when the route was mountainous.

Early in the last century a debate began on this very point. Opponents to the conventional wisdom postulated that the most direct route was *not* the most economical when operating costs were fed into the equation...that it was better to take the lowest *grade* route, usually along rivers that Mother Nature had provided...that it was better to go *around* a mountain than over it...that even if a summit crossing was inevitable, it was better to approach it at an angle to lower the grade. We have read the writings of many of these advocates and reviewed their financial projections. They based their calculations on four-legged horsepower, not steam locomotion. They suspected that it might be better to support the load on some sort of plank or rail, but even calculating costs on ordinary horse-and-wagon technology the arithmetic overwhelmingly confirmed their position that the straight-line approach was exchanging a short-range advantage for a serious long-range disadvantage.

The National Road was a Federal project and they did not listen. Nor, to be fair, did any other governmental body in those days. They saw what they wanted to see and heard what they wanted to hear.

For those readers who still believe that governmental bodies are citadels of wisdom and foresight, let us tell you a little story. When we were researching our book *Sand Patch/Clash of Titans*, the story of the Baltimore and Ohio Railroad's passage of these very mountains, we found this little jewel. Since we rather liked the way it was originally written, we will quote from that book. "Since B&O was building a low-grade super-turnpike from Cumberland to Wheeling, the path of the National Road could not be paralleled because of its numerous summits. B&O, however, was eager to interview the surveyors for the U.S. Board of Internal Improvements who plotted this highway early in the last century so as to pick their brains and learn from their experiences. Help was freely given, but early B&O surveyors soon became puzzled over some of the data...it seems a lot of summit elevations were at odds with their own calculations. Finally, the light dawned. The pioneer surveyors had neglected to take into account the curvature of the earth! Our precious republic was off to a great start...its national government remained convinced that the world was flat."

The National Road has been known as Route 40 for a long time and its present path over the mountains is substantially the same as when built. We have experienced its heartstopping grades and curves and, quite recently, one of the editors of this book has related the agonies of his passage. Many of the grades exceed ten percent and this introduces another factor that the student of railroading must fix in his mind.

Going uphill is a matter of economics. Apply enough power and you will get up. Going downhill is a matter of survival. Gravity has no friends.

One of the Federal objects in building the National Road was to bind the new states in the Northwest Territory to the states on the eastern seaboard through commerce and economic self-interest. Pennsylvania used similar reasoning with her Pennsylvania Road, wanting to hold her feisty Westerners within the commonwealth.

The Whiskey Rebellion in 1794 startled the fathers of the new republic and the Keystone State. These frontiersmen did not like the idea of paying a tax on one of their most profitable pursuits and responded rather violently. A combination of Federal and State troops, moving swiftly over the Pennsylvania Road, put down the revolt, happily without loss of life. The resentments, however, remained and in different forms survive to this day. As we shall see, that Eastern Continental Divide separated a lot more than water.

One has to say that those avenues of commerce, and others to come, succeeded in holding the nation together. So, no matter how inefficient, their construction has to be regarded as a success.

Ole Man River and Ole Man Mountain did not succeed in dividing the new nation.

ROBERT FULTON'S steamboat *Clermont*, seen here in a crude woodcut published in the mid-1850s, set to "sea" in 1807 on the Hudson River and this major advance in homegrown technology was quickly transplanted to the Western Waters. The dominance of the steamboat as an integral unit carrying power plant and cargo space together only lasted for about four decades and was supplanted by towboat/barge configurations which proved to be even more efficient on inland waters. The steamboat was an early terror weapon. Its propensity to explode terrorized passengers and crew; its efficiency terrorized northeastern city/states, goading them into evolving a response to this new challenge.

THE SITUATION AND THE TERRAIN

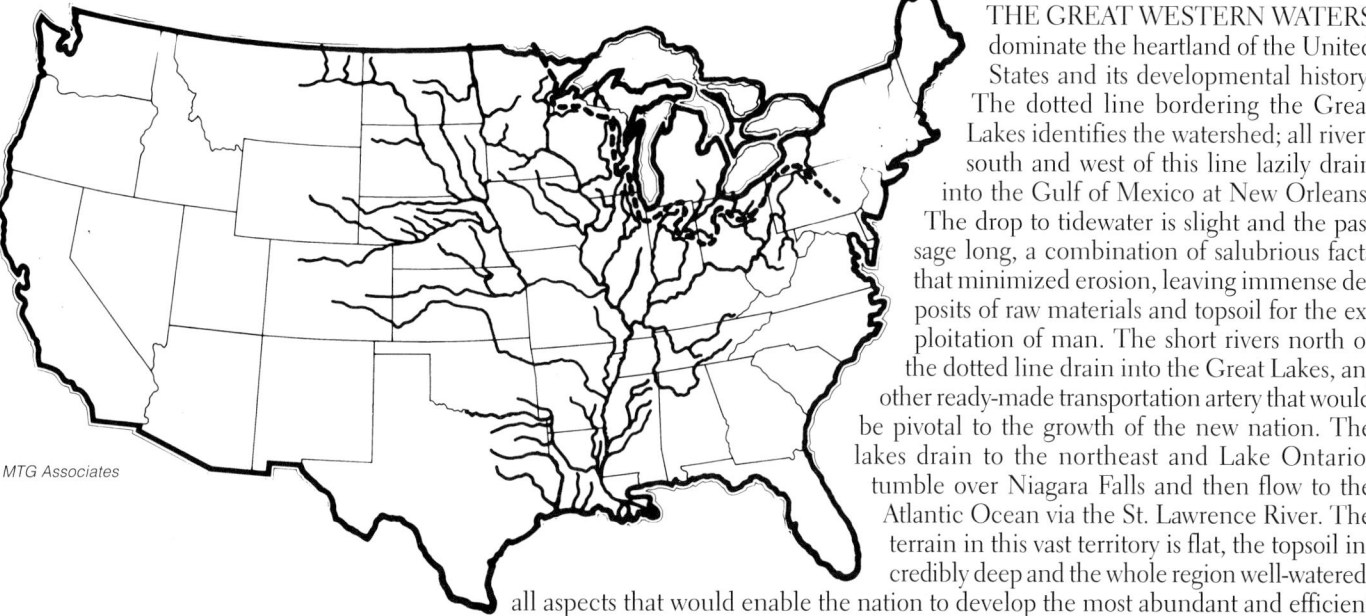

THE GREAT WESTERN WATERS dominate the heartland of the United States and its developmental history. The dotted line bordering the Great Lakes identifies the watershed; all rivers south and west of this line lazily drain into the Gulf of Mexico at New Orleans. The drop to tidewater is slight and the passage long, a combination of salubrious facts that minimized erosion, leaving immense deposits of raw materials and topsoil for the exploitation of man. The short rivers north of the dotted line drain into the Great Lakes, another ready-made transportation artery that would be pivotal to the growth of the new nation. The lakes drain to the northeast and Lake Ontario, tumble over Niagara Falls and then flow to the Atlantic Ocean via the St. Lawrence River. The terrain in this vast territory is flat, the topsoil incredibly deep and the whole region well-watered, all aspects that would enable the nation to develop the most abundant and efficient granary on the planet. Mother Nature's gift carried with it only three negatives...distance to market, winter freezing in the upper half of the watershed and the downhill flow of water. The steamboat solved the latter problem and efficient forms of transportation the former. Only ice is beyond human solution.

THE EASTERN WATERS, so impressive to early colonists, soon became a conundrum as the nation expanded westerly. All reached tidewater, but only the Hudson River was truly navigable and it ran in the wrong direction...splendid for fur-traders, useless for reaching the Western Waters. On the south flank, the Potomac River at least pointed in the right direction but the Great Falls at Washington, DC was a major obstruction. While tidal as far upstream as Washington, it was a long way to open ocean and it flowed in the wrong direction in relation to Europe. West of Washington the Potomac had at least some possibilities as a transportation artery but it swerved to the south at Cumberland and frittered away in wilderness. Yet for all that, the route from tidewater at Washington to the Western Waters in southwestern Pennsylvania was the shortest of all, a significant fact that colored much of our national history. Baltimore sat at the head of the Great Chesapeake Bay, yet the city itself was at the mouth of small waterways...Jones Falls and the Patapsco. Both were notable because their banks were steep and waterwheel factories flourished, particularly flour mills. The Susquehanna was the source of the Chesapeake estuary. This bay, H.L. Mencken's "great protein factory," alas also flowed a long way in the wrong direction. Baltimore was, however, closer to the Western Waters than her northerly rivals. The Susquehanna itself was a Pennsylvania river, but in relation to Philadelphia it not only ran in the wrong direction but was also convenient to Baltimore, an accident of geography

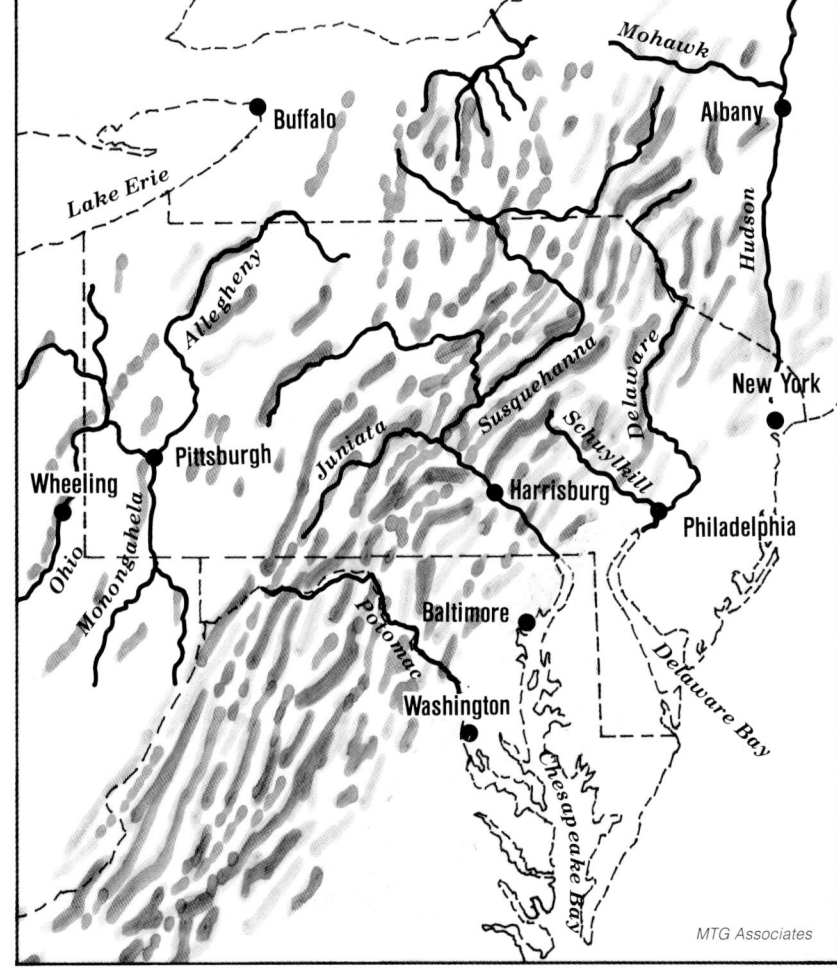

that did not warm hearts in the Quaker City. Philadelphia was not in a very comfortable position with her remaining rivers, all short and again that familiar litany...the wrong direction, true also for her Delaware Bay. Worse, she was even more distant from those Western Waters than her southerly rivals. Yet those waters originated in her own state! Frustrating.

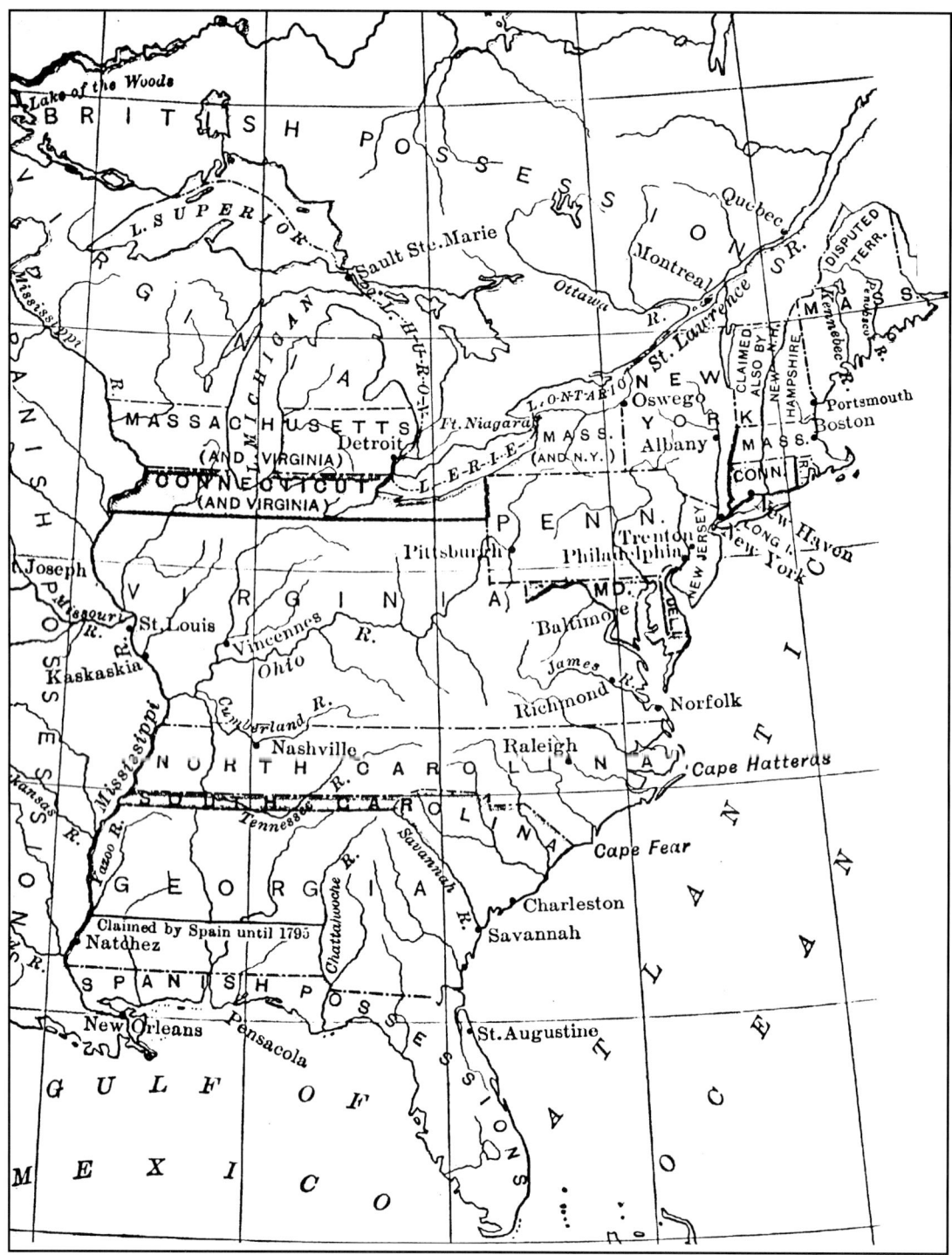

THE "UNITED" STATES at the close of the Revolutionary War and after the signing of the Treaty of 1783 with Britain had fairly well-defined outer boundaries, but inside the club it was an undignified cat fight. Not only were most of the States trying to gobble huge chunks of the lands west of the mountain barrier, they were also at each other's throats along the coast. Each state was levying tariffs at their borders and generally acting as if each was a separate nation. Indeed some were acting as if they were going to make war on their neighbors. George Washington had found it easier to get rid of the French and British than to get the ex-colonies to agree on anything. Finally in 1787 a constitutional convention was convened in Philadelphia, a new constitution drafted and ratified and Washington was elected first President of the United States. The Federal government was given some national powers, one of the most important being the right to regulate interstate commerce. That "commerce clause" has been used as a wedge to continually increase the power of the Federal government over the fractious states and would prove to be a potent factor in the transportation evolution that the nation desperately needed.

THE SITUATION AND THE TERRAIN

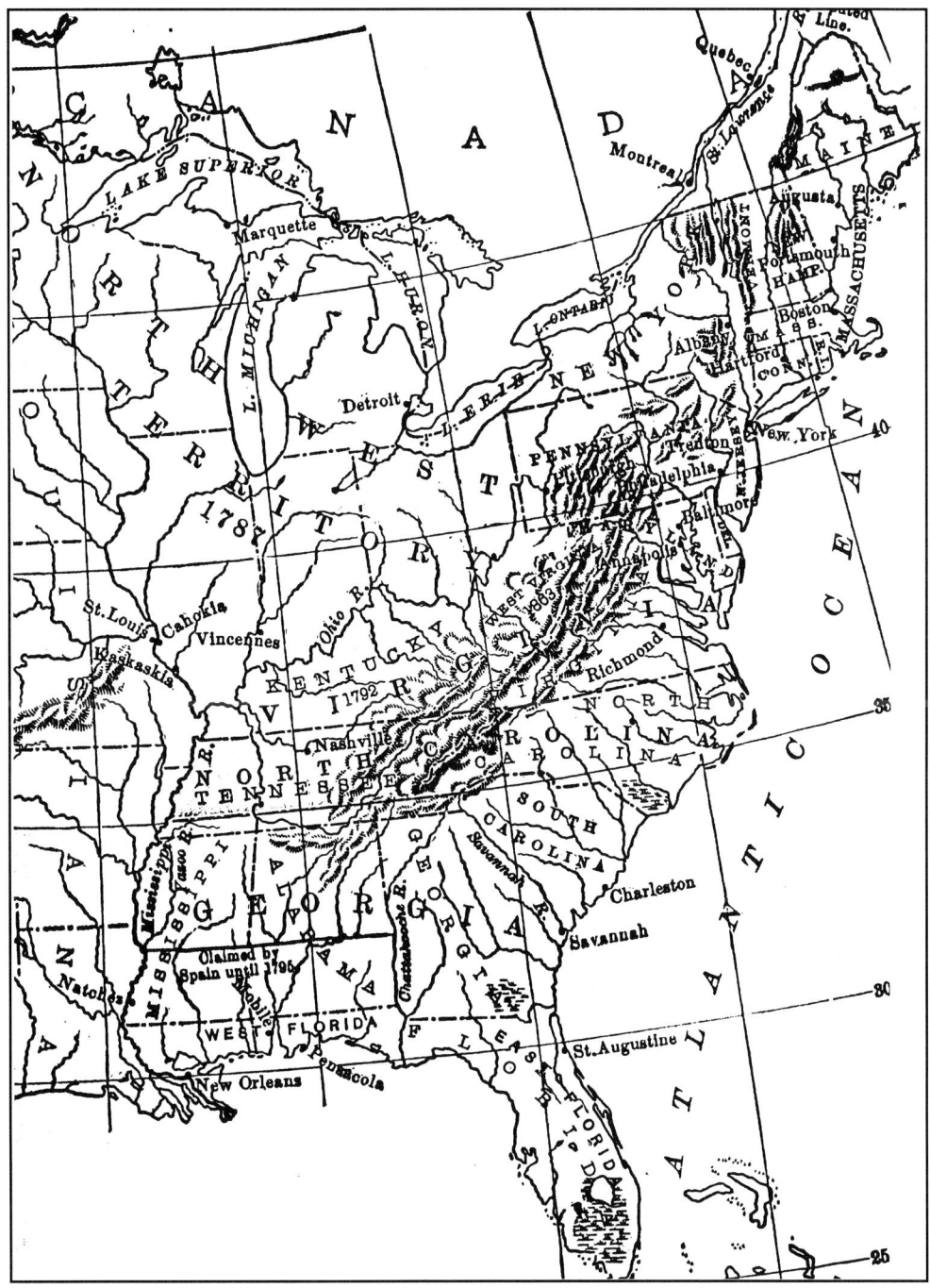

THE NORTHWEST TERRITORY was divided into five new states over the sixty-one years after it was created in 1787. The Louisiana Purchase was made in 1803 and, of course, new states were being formed in that vast region. Ohio was first in 1803, Indiana 1816, Illinois 1818, Michigan 1837 and Wisconsin 1848. In the south, Spain ceded Florida to the United States in 1821 and several new states were carved out of the Carolinas and Georgia, all east of the Mississippi River. Virginia waived her gluttonous claims, but did retain a finger pointing north with the Ohio River on the west and the southwestern border of Pennsylvania on the east. This little panhandle appears on this map to be a minor piece of territory…in fact, it would prove to be one of the most strategically important locations in the new nation's development. First, Virginia, controlled a vital part of the Ohio River itself and, second, any east-west land transportation system had to cross that panhandle to have any hope of efficiently serving most of the territory west of the mountain barrier. In short, Virginia had two locks on the gate, an advantage she retained and milked until the outbreak of the Civil War in 1861. The population of western Virginia wanted no part of the Confederacy, Virginia could not hold it by force of arms and in 1863 the new breakaway State of West Virginia was created. Of all the terrible prices Virginia paid for the sour decision she made in the Spring of 1861, a good case could be made that the loss of control of this panhandle and the enormous coal fields that underlay West Virginia was the greatest penalty of all.

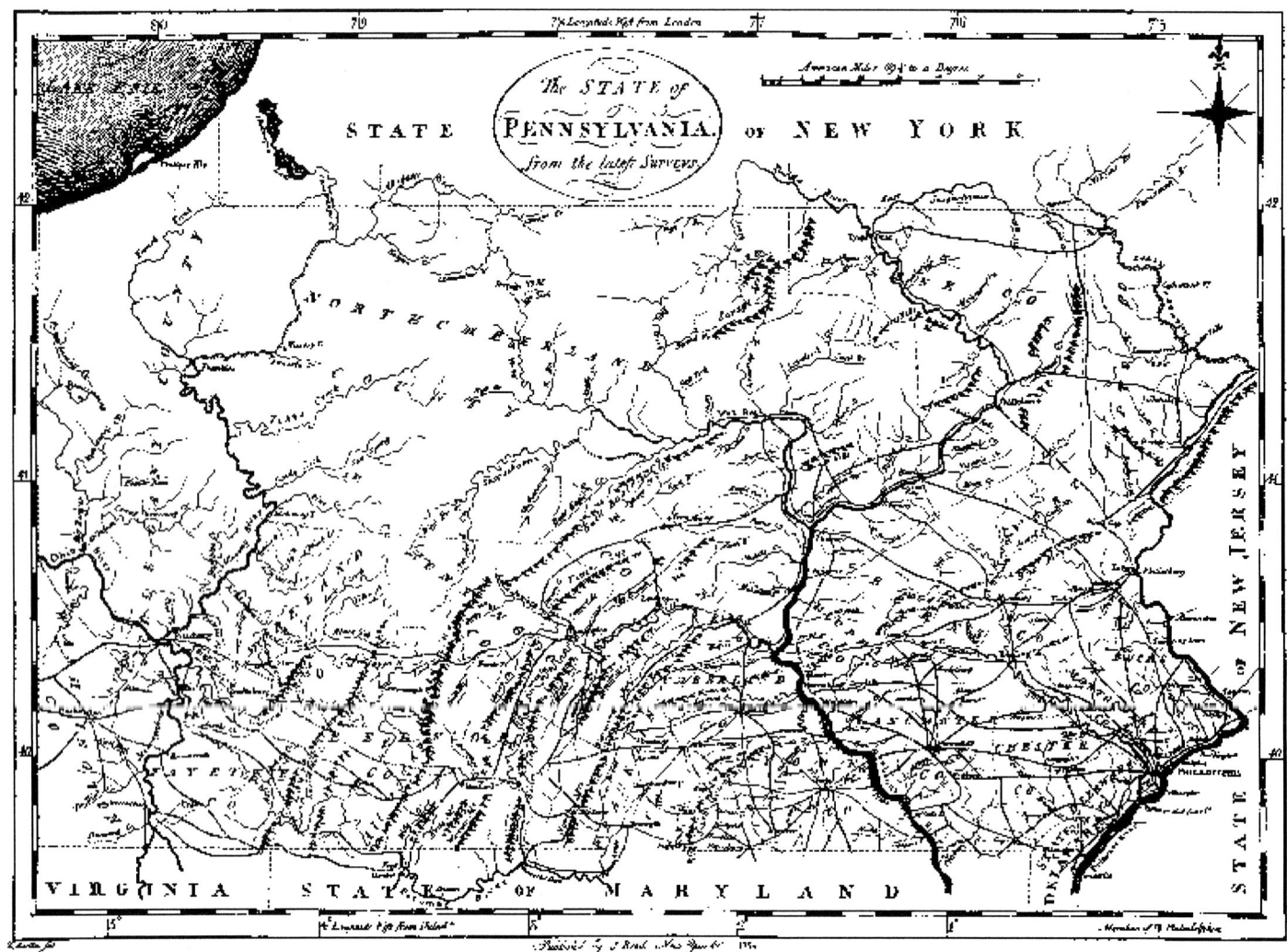

THIS 1794 MAP of Pennsylvania, we are assured by the publisher, was made "from the latest surveys." The names of the surveyors were not given. This is probably just as well because whoever drew the map certainly did leave out a lot of mountains. The rivers and streams appear to be fairly accurate, the roads suspiciously straight, the mountains pretty little shaded cones each one exactly the same. We do know some surveyors wandered into this country; George Washington was one of them. The reader will recall that the Ohio Company was chartered in 1747. Grantor King George II was quite generous. The total grant was almost 300,000 acres and included choice pieces of western Maryland and southwestern Pennsylvania. In 1752 the Ohio Company employed Thomas Cresap, Christopher Gist and Delaware Indian Nemocolin to mark a path from Cumberland to the Monongahela, a mission promptly accomplished. Pennsylvania officials were suspicious, one of them going so far as to characterize Cresap as "that vile fellow." Thus the rhetoric when two groups are competing for a piece of meat. Although 1794 was the year of the Whiskey Rebellion, we could not find the location of any stills on this map. As to the mountains, understatement by the publisher did not make them go away.

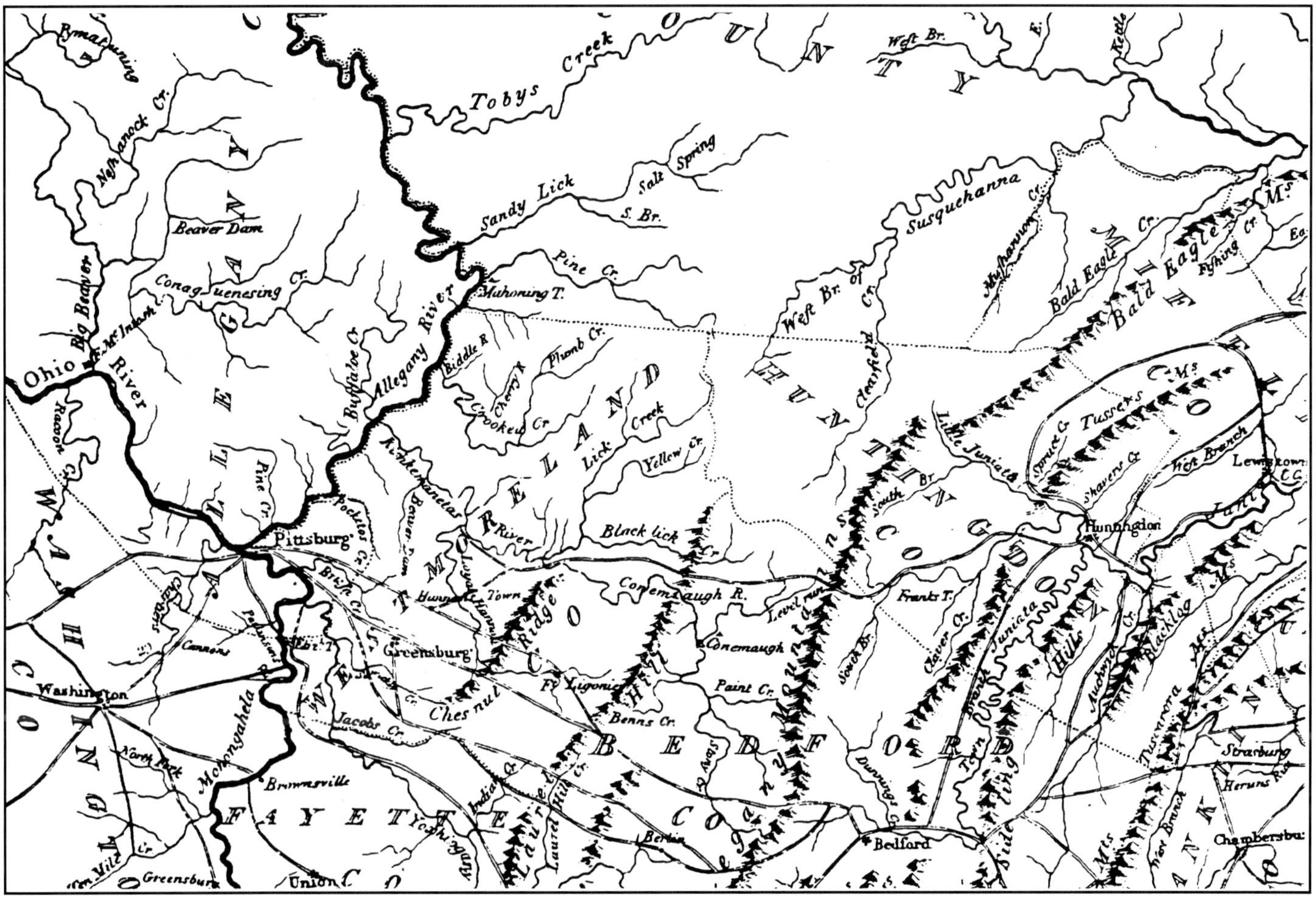

THE SITUATION AND THE TERRAIN

THIS ENLARGEMENT of the preceding 1794 map does at least bring to our attention that names had already been given to most of the prominent features, names that would resonate through the history of the transportation revolution yet to come. Chesnut (sic) Ridge, Laurel Hill, Allegheny Mountains, Bald Eagle Mountains, Conemaugh River, Juniata River, Brush Creek and so on. Not reproduced in this book is a 1755 map that presents a name for the barrier that somehow seems more appropriate than those that came down to us. The Endless Mountains.

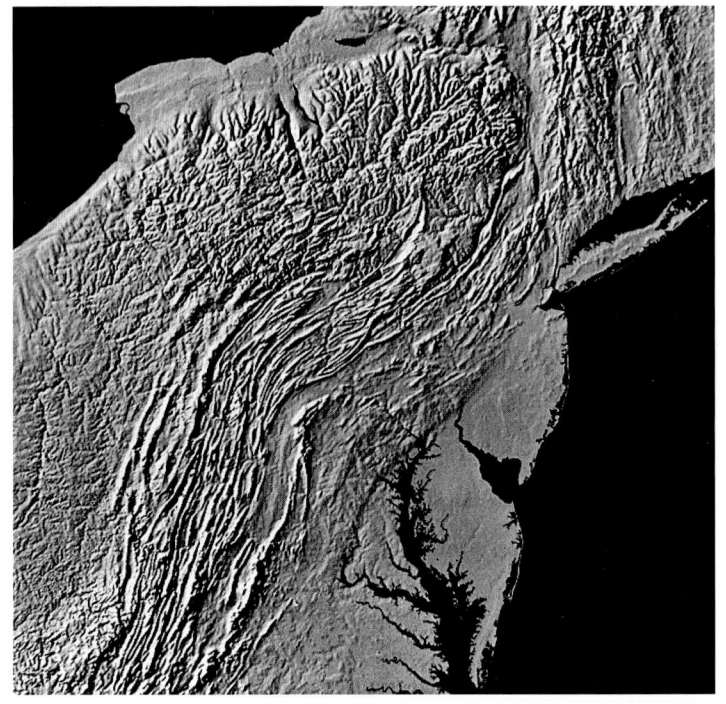

LEWIS EVANS was the cartographer of that 1755 map who coined Endless Mountains and he didn't have the advantage of seeing them from above. Perhaps he would have chosen Daunting Mountains if he had enjoyed this perspective. To east coast city/states, the choice of names was as academic as the problem was real. By any other name they would be as steep.

Digital shaded-relief portrayal of landforms of the conterminous United States by Gail P. Thelin and Richard J. Pike 1991, U.S. Geological Survey. Vertical exaggeration 2x.

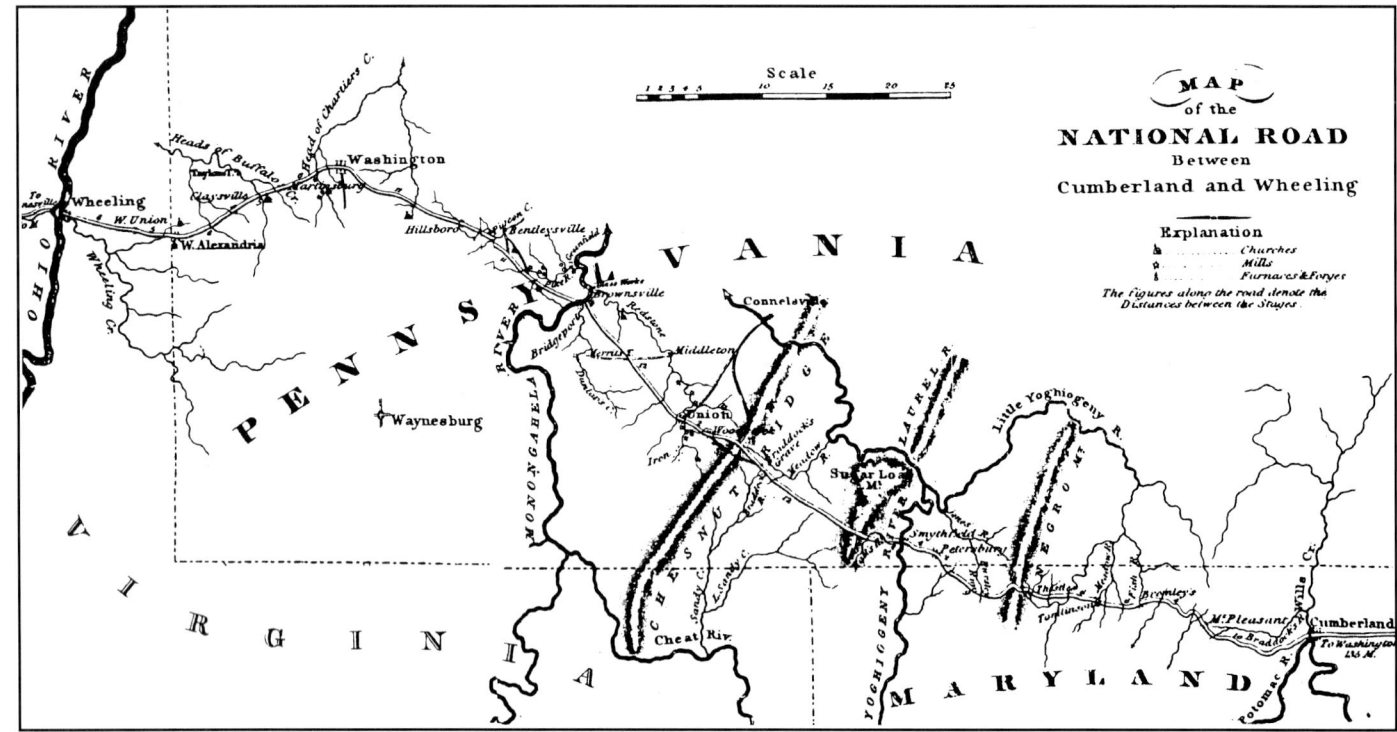

THE ECONOMIC FLAW in highway location theory is quite evident in this map of the National Road. The shortest possible route from Cumberland to Wheeling was chosen. Savage gradients were accepted, the intervening hills and mountains attacked head-on. This approach also meant that the flow of most streams and rivers was at right angles to the road, which meant a lot of expensive bridges had to be built. Now follow Wills Creek from Cumberland and trace it as it arcs southwesterly. Its headwaters are at Sand Patch, the summit of Allegheny Mountain. The cartographer did not even bother to identify it. A slight hop and the Western Waters are met, flowing downhill through gaps in the mountains on the way to Pittsburgh and the Gulf of Mexico. The "Little Yoghiogeny (sic)", by the way, was later renamed the Casselman. This was a longer route, but by taking advantage of the path carved by Mother Nature the grades were gentler.

Building any sort of land transportation passage is a bit like marriage; the initial expense turns out to be the least. Operating expenses eat you up. And then there's maintenance. The typical wagon carried a load of 6,000 pounds but some carried 10,000 pounds or a "hundred hundred" as old wagoneers liked to boast. Since wheels are round, all this weight met the road in tiny areas and pounded the pavement into atoms. This fact of life was reflected in toll charges: wheels eight inches wide traveled free; the narrower the wheel the higher the charge on a graduated scale to a charge of four cents for wheels less than four inches. Since it was estimated that about 5,000 wagons were operating on the National Road, the damage to the roadbed was horrendous. No wonder men were becoming fascinated with the idea of carrying the load on rails of one sort or another. And then there's the matter of time. Movement upgrade was agonizingly slow; downgrade equally slow for reasons of terror. The gravity coin has two sides. For all of its inefficiencies, the National Road did at least provide an avenue of commerce that would dramatically affect the development of the nation in general and The Pennsylvania Railroad in particular. That story will be told in the ensuing pages, but we do not want to leave the National Road without honoring the shades of our forebears. Copies of a statue titled the *Madonna of the Trail* are said to have been placed at various locations along this road to glorify the pioneer women who traveled it on the way west. Considering the number of inns and nubile barmaids that graced this highway and the thousands of husky wagoneers who plied it, one wonders if *Venus of the Trail* might not have been more appropriate. We shall never know.

THE SITUATION AND THE TERRAIN

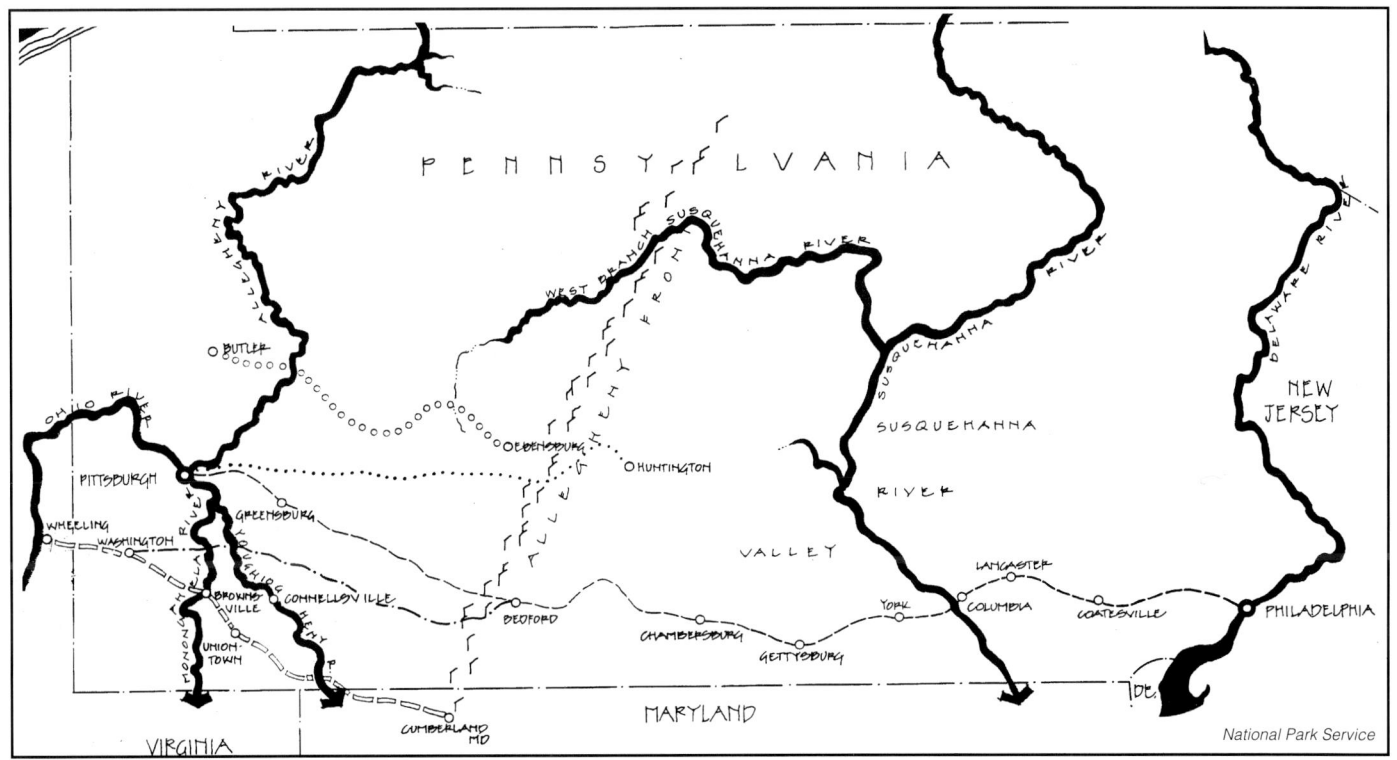

THE TRANSPORTATION MAP of Pennsylvania looked like this circa 1825. The Pennsylvania Road ran from Philadelphia to Pittsburgh through Bedford and the Bedford-Washington Turnpike connected it to the National Road at Washington. The traffic at Washington was rather evenly divided with Cumberland and was predominantly westbound. Maryland had built turnpikes from Cumberland to Baltimore (which is directly south of York) and a lot closer than Philadelphia to Wheeling and Pittsburgh. So is Washington DC. Off to the northeast is New York. These highways mark the southern approach to the Ohio. A potential northern approach is evident because the west branch of the Susquehanna had maintained a gap in the Allegheny Front, as it was becoming known, and reached tantalizingly close to the Allegheny River. A potential middle route also presents itself to Philadelphia. Southern, middle, northern. We repeat. *It was cheaper to ship from Pittsburgh to Philadelphia via New Orleans than it was to use the Pennsylvania Road.* Thanks to the steamboat, in *both* directions. This unpleasant arithmetic also applied to every other port in the northeast. Quite a challenge.

TRIUMPH I

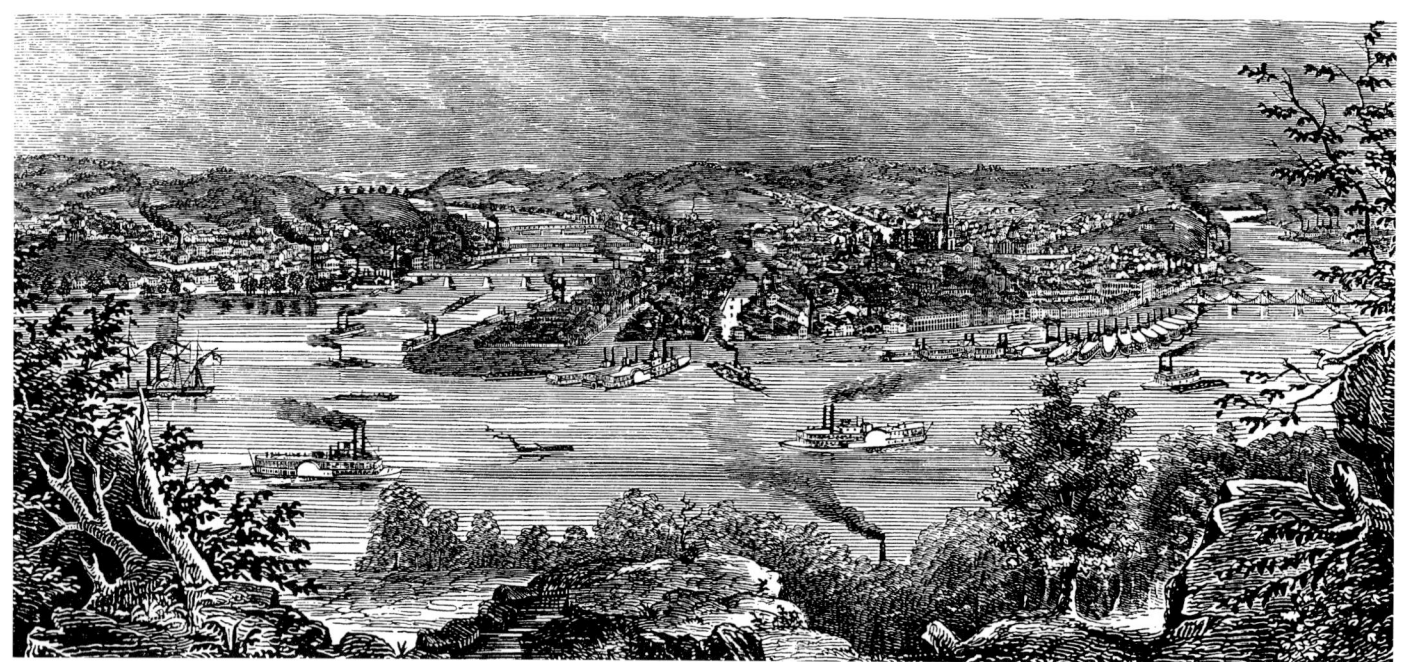

THAT THE OHIO RIVER was the commercial lifeline to Pittsburgh is manifest in this early 1850s depiction. There are steamboats everywhere, even one with a barge attached. On the far left we see an oceangoing steamer in addition to rafts and flatboats. Factories are spewing smoke, regarded then as a mark of progress. The steamboat landing is crowded with craft loading and unloading. A cathedral points its spire Heavenward indicating that at least some residents worship God as well as Cæsar. Bustle and muscle characterize the scene. The Pennsylvania Railroad is about to nudge its way into this booming city but for the moment all eyes are westward with the waters. Five bridges (one an aqueduct for the Pennsylvania Canal) are in sight, including a suspension bridge over the Monongahela which signifies that Americans, too, can innovate with technology. There is always a snake in the Garden of Eden, however, and for Pittsburgh as well as PRR it is all those hills that come right down to the rivers. One would be hard put to pick a worse location for a land transportation gateway in combination with an industrial heartland. Bottleneck and gridlock were in the future of the city and PRR.

THIS WAS THE WAY passengers and freight moved over the mountain barrier before the load was put on rails. Of course, wagons and coaches were used by man long before the building of the National Road. There was, however, one significant difference before the early 1800s. None of them had brakes. Get the horses or oxen to stop and the load would stop. That wasn't good enough in the mountains. At first freight wagoneers would chain a wheel to the body or drag a stump to slow descents, methods that were hard on the nervous system as well as the road surface. The vehicles in this scene do not have brakes, a failing that was soon corrected as a matter of survival. Now we shall see that the northeastern cities of the new nation also had a survival problem.

Chapter 2

Saga of Seven Cities

First we mold our institutions and then they mold us. At all times, but particularly in times of crisis, man looks to the past for guidance. That past which we call history is really a confusing jumble of actions taken by other men in a context not quite the same as the current situation. The estimable historian Will Durant characterized the history of man as consisting of two wars…the wars between men and the wars between the sexes. We will be so bold as to add Mother Nature to the sexual conflict. On the issue of the uneasy relationship between the secular and the spiritual he equivocated as well he should have done. What men say is interesting. What they do is important.

The affairs of man are an admixture of politics, economics, military prowess, science, the arts and the moral/religious. The predicament in which the cities of Boston, New York, Philadelphia, Baltimore, Washington DC (Georgetown), Pittsburgh and Wheeling found themselves in the first half of the last century inevitably involved all of these elements and each reacted in accordance with their heritage. The threat was palpable and prayer was not moving mountains. Revert or reach out? If the latter, how?

Let us start with Boston. When Henry VIII decided to break with the Church of Rome and establish the Church of England he certainly opened up a big can of worms. Not only did he throw Catholic and Protestant into conflict with one other, but he also created a climate that gave birth to a bewildering variety of new religious sects many of which took on the Church of England as well as the Papists. One of these splinter groups set out to "purify" the Church of England and became known as the Puritans. They were promptly run out of Britain and most ended up in New England with Boston as their Vatican and hypocrisy as the main tenet of their society.

After all, it was one of their own who described the Proper Bostonian as "sitting upon a rock, reading the Bible, sucking a lemon and contemplating adultery." Only in Salem would witchburning become weekend sport and, in the middle of this century, the birthplace of wife-swapping. Then of course, there was an influx of the Irish, Catholic to the core with no interest in rocks, Bibles or lemons and preferring to go straight to adultery without the veneers.

There is a certain poetic justice that New England was the site of the Puritan migration because the region was and is as hardscrabble as their religion. The agricultural zone is small, rocky and barren and the growing season short. Only two significant resources were present…vast tracts of timber and rivers with steep banks. In the days of wooden ships and tall masts, the timber was used to create a maritime industry. In fact, even today the timber resources in the region feed a thriving paper industry, but the day of the wooden ship has long passed.

In the waterpower era those steep river banks were an advantage and light manufacturing, particularly textile mills, provided a measure of prosperity. The rise of the steam engine, and later electricity, as power sources sounded the death knell for this aspect of their economy.

The whole region is bereft of raw materials. Everything, including lemons, must be imported either by water or over the Mountain Barrier. And there were *two* summits in their barrier. While not as high as those to the south, they nonetheless existed.

The port of Boston is small and constricted. The closeness of the port to Europe was an ephemeral advantage given that they could not economically produce much of significance.

Atlantic fishing was good and, to be fair, those Yankees did evolve an impressive educational system. Still, the Industrial Revolution largely passed them by and their merchant princes were wise enough to invest their early-earned capital in more productive climes.

People vote with their feet and New England was losing her farmers to the midwest searching for soil that would grow something other than stones.

One must give credit where due. Sitting on cold rocks does promote clarity of vision and sucking lemons does get one used to bitter tastes. These Yankees surveyed the situation early in the last century and swallowed the unpleasant pill that they were out of the running. Consequently, they did not squander their assets jousting at economic and transportation windmills.

Refer again to the map on page nine. Notice as one travels south from New England the coastal plain is widening. Not readily apparent on this map is the presence of a piedmont zone between the coastal plain and the mountain barrier. These rolling hills are not particularly high but they do present obstacles to east-west transportation lines, especially ones seeking low-grade approaches.

Now let us go to Washington DC. In this era we are really talking about Georgetown, a small river port that was tidal. Today it is part of the District of Columbia. As we have shown, the distance from Georgetown to the Ohio River is the shortest of any of the northeastern ports.

A glance at the map indicates that the hinterland (defined as the region that can be served by a port with a combination of river or overland transport) is very large. To Georgetown this is an illusion. The very large and lush coastal plain and piedmont to the south of Georgetown was readily served by rivers flowing into the lower Potomac River and Chesapeake Bay with the result that Georgetown's usefulness as a port was tied to east-west movements.

The Potomac River, while impressive on the map, is really a river of sharp contrasts. To the south it is a joy…to the west a monster. The Great Falls just west of Georgetown is a major obstacle and west of that Fall Line the river is shallow with rugged banks subject to extremes of high and low water. The closeness to the mountain barrier is a double curse. Heavy rain in the mountains has only a short run to tidewater and comes downstream with great violence. Drought in the mountains means little or no water. Neither situation is conducive to efficient and reliable transportation.

To further complicate matters, the border between Virginia and Maryland is on the south bank of the Potomac River. Maryland owns the Potomac and Georgetown was in Maryland.

Back to the can of worms. Virginia was stolidly Church of England, Maryland an English Catholic colony. It is literally true historically that these two States have been at war with one another since the earliest colonial days. By war we mean guns, invasions, raids and general unpleasantness. We will spare the reader some of the more insulting toasts that grace present-day dinner parties by pointing out that at this very moment there is a "crab war" ensuing in the lower Chesapeake Bay and weapons are being carried.

As the reader shall see as this tale unfolds, even the states in this new nation were at odds *within* their borders and Virginia will be the first but by no means the last example. What we will call the Plantation Region of Virginia was fat, rich, politically powerful and happy. They had no transportation problems, export or import. That mountain barrier was no impediment to their economy and the Western Waters no threat to their wellbeing. In their view those mountaineers in the western part of the State were crude frontiersmen, unwashed, uneducated and probably oversexed. Only men like George Washington and a few other Virginians had a vision of what might be, both commercially and nationally. That Washington was a mediocre soldier and had financial interests in the midwest did not mean that he was anything less than one of the greatest statesmen this nation has ever produced.

It was at a meeting between representatives of Maryland and Virginia over navigation rights on the Potomac River when the seed was planted which resulted in a convention in Philadelphia that produced the Constitution of the United States, a document that many feel transcends the secular and approaches the divine.

Which brings us to Baltimore and Maryland. We have already seen that the National Road provided Baltimore with the shortest practical route to the Ohio River. Some eastbound grain was moving to Baltimore, but at very high transportation cost. Baltimore's hinterland was very large and she had a few rivers with steep banks providing waterpower which nourished light manufacturing, principally flour mills and small ironworks. Thanks to the Chesapeake Bay and her relative closeness to the West Indies and South America, Baltimore was blessed with a rapidly growing export trade which included flour, iron products, tobacco and foods.

Baltimore's import trade was also booming, principally with rice, cocoa and guano, the latter a splendid fertilizer. Typical was the predominance of westbound traffic over the National Road.

Maryland was also blessed with fine river networks, tributary to the Bay, and Baltimore evolved a fine shipbuilding capability which enhanced trade.

Much of this commerce was threatened by the efficiency of Western Waters transportation.

Now we must look into the attitudinal aspects of Maryland culture. Virginia was Cavalier and Protestant. Maryland was Cavalier and Catholic. The key word is Cavalier.

Only Baltimore would produce a poet like Ogden Nash whose best lines were "Candy's Dandy, Liquor's Quicker." Only Maryland would threaten to Secede from the Union when Prohibition was passed into law. Only Maryland would produce a tradition that "Gentlemen do not lie. Except to women, or course. That doesn't count." Only Maryland would adopt an unofficial title as the "Land of Pleasant Living," which was actually written for advertising a local beer and created, incidentally, by a gentlemen still alive and whom we had the honor of meeting some years ago.

Only Maryland would adopt the philosophy that it is a gentleman's duty to wink at an ugly girl at least once a day. And only Baltimore would, early in the last century, proudly earn the title "Nest of Pirates."

We mean just that. Noting that the mouth of the Chesapeake Bay was so wide that it was almost impossible to blockade, the fine merchants of Baltimore commissioned illegal slave ships, outright pirate ships and, during the War of 1812, eagerly created a privateer fleet to prey on British East Indiamen with such salubrious results that a cabinboy's share from one successful voyage would be enough to set him up for life. It has been estimated that they took 1,700 British ships. We hope, by the way, that some local historian will try to trace back to this era and see how many Baltimore family fortunes were derived from this Cavalier source of revenue.

This privateer activity was so successful that the British were forced to react and sent an expeditionary force to Maryland in 1814. They fought their way into Washington DC, burned everything in sight and then proceeded to Baltimore to "clean out that nest of pirates." In Baltimore they were stymied at Fort McHenry and North Point, forced to retreat and endure the indignity of learning that the defense of that fort produced the national anthem "The Star Spangled Banner," surely a unique honor for the successful defense of a den of marauders.

As to Washington, DC, we want to make clear that the British burned the city, not George Washington. He died in 1799. The British did, however, burn Joan of Arc in Rouen, the birthplace of La Salle.

We hope the reader has gained an insight into the mindset of the First Families of Baltimore and Maryland and we will now proceed to the impact of the can of worms on the situation. There were alternating Catholic and Protestant monarchs in Britain, exchanging crowns and sometimes losing heads in a dizzying series of coups and countercoups. In the mid-1660s a Protestant king owed Quaker William Penn a lot of money and paid off the debt by giving Penn a choice slice of land which came out of Maryland's Catholic hide. While a map will detail this detachment later in this chapter, the essence of the grant put Philadelphia in Pennsylvania along with vital land in the southwestern part of that state and west of Maryland. In the early 1800s, as Baltimore looked upon the mercantile scene groping for a solution and seeing visions of "grass growing in the streets", the Founding Families had to face the fact that Maryland did not border on the Ohio River and, whatever she did, would have to get permission to pass from the States of Pennsylvania and Virginia. A test for the Cavalier Spirit.

Now to New York at the mouth of that fabulous river, the Hudson. Wide, deep and gentle, its path reached north almost into Canada. Its hinterland was huge and its natural harbor one of the finest on the planet. Its growth after the Revolutionary War was phenomenal, a process that continues today.

Spiritually, the typical New Yorker worshipped Mammon and commerce. Henry VIII's legacy meant nothing to them. Nor did prattlings about Puritanism or Cavalierism or Quakerism nor debates about how many angels might be tempted to dance on the head of a pin. If there was a buck in it, they were for it and willing to work and risk money to get it.

As early as 1784, George Washington wrote to Virginia's governor in regard to the trade of the west as follows: "A people who are possessed of a spirit of commerce; who see and will pursue their advantages, may achieve almost anything. In the meantime, under the uncertainty of these undertakings, they are smoothing the roads and paving the way for the trade of the western world. That New York will do the same, no person who knows the temper, genius and policy of these people can harbor the smallest doubt."

In 1822 the British consul reported to London from New York that while the trade of this city on the Hudson was growing, that of Boston, Philadelphia and Baltimore was declining.

The New England Society looked south with awe and toasted "The City of New York - the emporium of America; commerce her glory, rivalship hopeless."

A Baltimorean stated in print "The New Yorkers *deserve* success for their enterprise. There is a good spirit among the citizens to advance the business of New York. Let it be imitated - not envied."

A few sets of numbers describe the situation better than paragraphs of explanations. In 1815, exports from New York totalled $10 million for 20% of the *national* total…by 1825, $35 million for 33%. As to imports, in 1825 $49 million for more than *half*.

The western trade? Much of that trade in and out of New Orleans came through New York to and from Britain and Europe, as did cotton from the south. Can we get more of it? Let's decide and *act*.

In Philadelphia, the mere mention of the word "act" touched a raw nerve. In the late 1700s and early 1800s they had "acted" by investing in turnpikes. Pennsylvania is a very large state and Philadelphia, while on tidewater, is way off in the southeastern corner and a long way from the Ohio River at either Pittsburgh or Wheeling. The endless mountains slice the state in half. The western waters flow to New Orleans and the Susquehanna flows to the Chesapeake Bay. Only the Delaware and the Schuylkill Rivers flow to Philadelphia. Their banks are steep, fine for waterwheel industries but little else. They are also short and shallow. Furthermore, Pennsylvania is really a collection of regions, each with its own needs, dreams and agendas. Quite reasonably, each region looks to its own self-interest and rarely did those interests coincide with those of Philadelphia.

Philadelphia's hinterland is very small and the piedmont hills are close to the city, creating a mini-mountain barrier. All in all, at least in our judgement, Philadelphia's position was the worst.

Philadelphia, of course, is called the Quaker City and also the City of Brotherly Love. We have yet to fathom whether the two are related, so we will stay with Quaker. It seems to us, as an outsider, that the official designation Society of Friends smacks more of the name of a club than a religion. Whatever the merit of this view, these are certain tenets that seem to apply to its members. Pacifistic, contemplative, striving for consensus, prudence, charitable are all words that seem to epitomize their outlook. As admirable as these traits may be, Philadelphia's situation in the early part of the last century called for decisiveness and vision, two traits for which the Quakers are not noted.

Pennsylvania (literally Penn's Woods) was founded by William Penn, a Quaker. When what has been called the age of internal development dawned in the late 1700s, the Pennsylvanians reacted vigorously with the construction of turnpikes. In fact, they built more turnpikes than any other state in that era. Looking back and to be fair, we cannot see what else they could have done. But then another age began, the age of technology. Not knowing what to do, they did what they knew. They contemplated, studied, delayed and then suddenly acted and managed to put themselves in the worst of all worlds.

To blame all the errors on the Quakers is, of course, absurd. Yet we cannot help but feel that responsibility rests where power and influence lies so they must shoulder some of the censure that was to come.

On the other side of the mountain barrier, there was another contest between cities…Pittsburgh and Wheeling, one in Pennsylvania and one in Virginia. That panhandle of Virginia was a roadblock to western overland transportation expansion. Wheeling was on the National Road, farther down the Ohio River and centrally located in relation to the midwestern states. The populations of both were feisty, energetic and westward-looking. Both regarded the eastern parts of their states with disdain. The odds were on Wheeling, yet Pittsburgh won. Another fascinating part of the story of the advance of the nation to superpower status.

The news from the western waters was all bad for the eastern cities and then it suddenly got worse. Those energetic New Yorkers decided to build a canal, of all things, between the Hudson River and Lake Erie.

The canal project did not quite start out that way, however. George Washington imagined a canal from Georgetown to the Ohio River; the New Yorkers from the Hudson to the Great Lakes and, at first, to Lake Ontario. In the first decade of the last century, several surveys were made and in 1811 national financing sought. Since the national government was dominated by Virginians, the answer was predictable and a veto inevitable. They were willing to build a National Road but not a competitive National Canal.

DeWitt Clinton was the moving force behind the idea and he promptly placed the issue in the New York State legislature. This body recommended that Lake Erie be the goal in 1811. The War of 1812 delayed matters while the Baltimoreans got rich from legalized piracy. A canal bill was debated and passed in 1817 with, oddly enough, New York City and Lake Ontario interests adamantly opposed. The latter was understandable, the former puzzling, probably traceable to investments.

With that characteristic New York energy, construction started at once without the benefit of prayers. This was a bold undertaking. To build a 364-mile long canal across a largely unsettled wilderness was, in the words of historian George R. Taylor, "an act of faith, the demonstration of a spirit of enterprise by an organized government that has few parallels in world history." Well, George Washington had warned that something like this might happen.

Even though lawyers, believe it or not, did most of the planning and supervision, the Erie Canal was an instant success even before it was finished. Historian Julius Rubin, of a breed not prone to superlatives, called it "an enormous, astounding, almost unbelievable success." Local revenues alone made the canal a financial windfall and when the whole canal was opened for through traffic in 1825 the money stream can only be called a bonanza. And this in spite of its being closed because of icing for forty percent of the year.

The Erie Canal has been described as a marvelous technological feat, but that is hyperbole. There was nothing new in digging a ditch, installing locks and building slackwater dams to raise the depth of a river. It was the length of the canal and the flush of revenues and profits that attracted the eye. And this breathtaking development reduced the cost of transportation from Buffalo to Albany *tenfold*. The profits were *after* the cost of capital. Passage time was reduced from fifteen to six days. The flood of eastward traffic, principally grain, went to the Hudson and then downstream to New York. Westward trade also soared. Of equal importance, internal development along the route of the canal blossomed beyond the fondest hopes of its originators.

New York City, which already dominated national trade before the opening of the canal, saw its hinterland doubled and its commercial and financial power reach hegemony status, a position of supremacy it has never lost.

Meanwhile, over in Britain a "rail road" named the Stockton and Darlington put on a demonstration in 1824. An eight-horsepower steam locomotive pulled 65 tons of cargo for 3,000 yards at a speed of 13 mph before over 40,000 spectators. Now *this* was technological progress.

As would be expected, the reactions in Boston, Philadelphia and Baltimore varied, each according to its own heritage and attitudes, as the virulent canal fever swept the nation.

Boston, with that cold Puritan eye, immediately rejected a canal over two mountain summits and decided to wait and see if this rail road thing would provide some hope. As we have said, they were out of the running and knew it.

In Maryland and Virginia, the canal virus infected a significant number of people and the Chesapeake and Ohio Canal was founded to run from Georgetown to Pittsburgh.

Baltimore reacted in true Cavalier form. Competition with the Erie Canal and New York was impossible. To build a canal from Baltimore to Georgetown was feasible but pointless. It would be possible, however, to compete with New Orleans for at least some of the midwestern grain trade if an efficient overland transportation system could be evolved. To wait and see if this steam locomotive device would prove to be workable would involve a delay that would be too risky. Better to build a low-grade turnpike with rails and maximize the efficiency of the horse.

The best destination would be Wheeling and the best route would tap into the National Road and Maryland turnpikes to drain off traffic as work progressed. As to the mountain barrier, it was obvious that it should be crossed at Sand Patch, reach a point near present-day Connellsville and then turn west to Wheeling. One mountain crossing and the shortest distance from the Ohio to tidewater. To reach the Ohio at Pittsburgh was not a good choice. It was too far up the Ohio and surely Pennsylvania would do *something* along the same lines. As the situation developed, perhaps a branch from Connellsville to Pittsburgh would be profitable but that traffic would only be local production destined for Baltimore and south to the West Indies and South America by water.

The plan was sound and well thought out. That it did not work out that way is a subject covered in a number of books by this author, particularly *Sand Patch/Clash of Titans*.

The truly amazing thing about Baltimore's response to the crisis was the speed of reaction. From the first meeting of the Baltimore merchants to the issuance of a charter in February 1827 took just *nine days*. And these merchants decided to put up their *own money*.

Not so in Philadelphia.

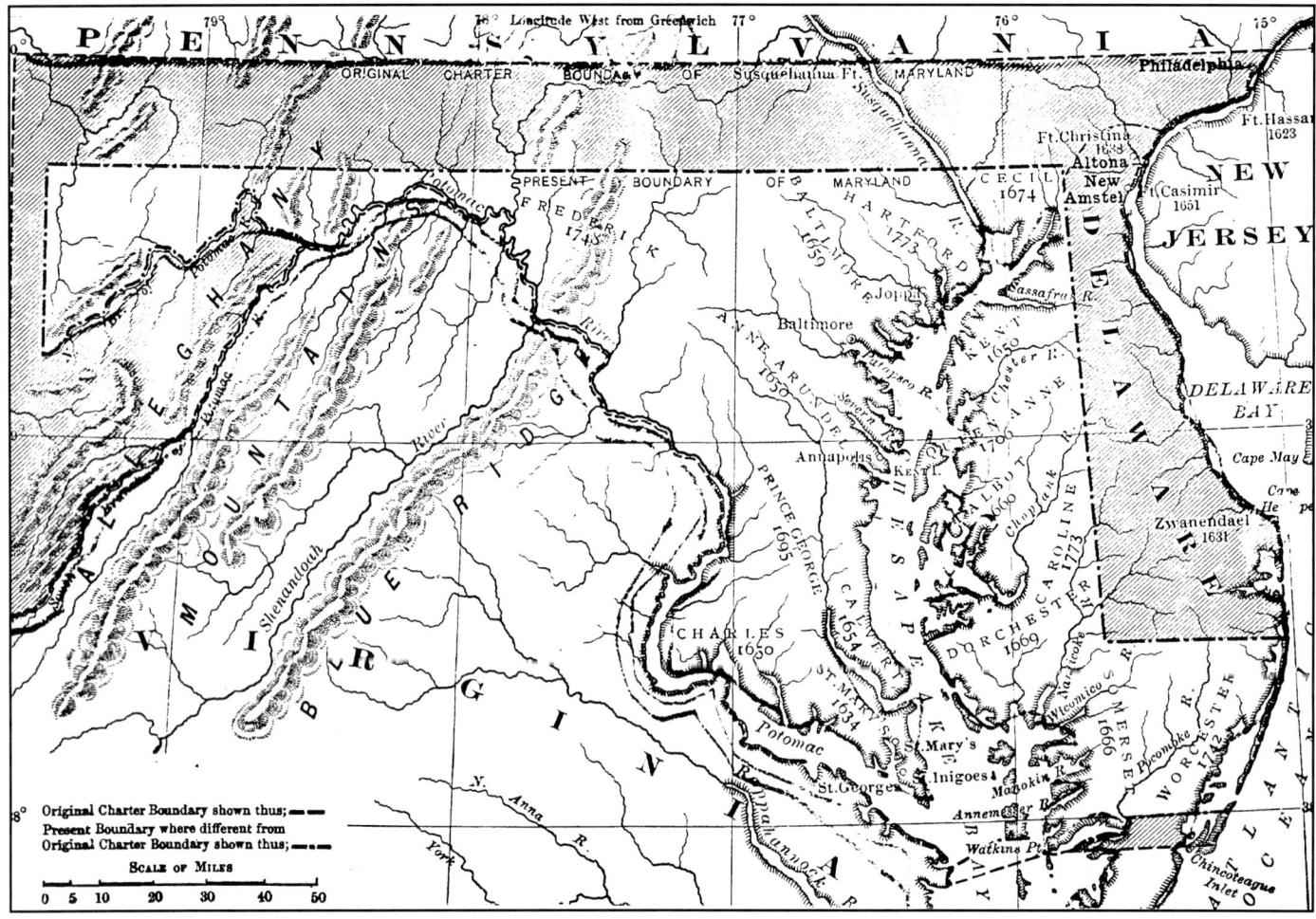

WHAT MIGHT HAVE BEEN had William Penn not loaned some money to a king and some Cavaliers been worshipping at a different altar. Even if things had been different, however, Maryland would still not have bordered on the Ohio River and would still have required the permission of both Pennsylvania and Virginia to build their railroad to Wheeling, two fatal flaws that ultimately enabled PRR to fend off a dangerous competitor and relegate B&O to a distant third place in the great trunkline battle during the middle of the last century.

Chapter 3

The Philadelphia Story

Rails and Water

King Edward VII, while Prince of Wales, visited Philadelphia about a century ago. When asked his views of the City of Brotherly Love, he is reputed to have said it was an interesting city "full of people named Scrapple who have Biddle for breakfast." Since Edward had also stated that he didn't care what people did so long as they didn't do it in the streets and frighten the horses, and had amassed an impressive list of mistresses in his day, it is reasonable to assume that the charms of the Quaker City did not impress him.

For those not familiar with scrapple, and that includes most of the normal people on earth, it is a meat concoction consisting of leftovers from the slaughtering of hogs mixed with meal and served fried. In other words, high quality garbage with a little bit of everything that no one else wants. We, by the way, are quite partial to it which in turn may say something about your author.

The Prince's reference to scrapple was apt. As we review the Great Debate about internal improvements that gripped Philadelphia early in the last century, we will have to say it had a little bit of everything except common sense.

The Prince's putdown of Philadelphia, and by extension the United States in general, also had some basis in history as well as studied rudeness. Britain invented the industrial revolution, parliamentary government, global empire building, snobbery and the railroad.

The earliest written description of a railroad was made by a Lord Guilford in 1676. It served collieries in Newcastle and consisted of beams of timber placed parallel with a four-foot gauge, just wide enough to provide room for a horse path.

Carriages had smooth wheels revolving on the smooth surface of the wooden tracks. The loads went downhill to the River Tyne and a few horses hauled the loads to destination and of course, moved the empty carriages back to the mines.

The first improvement involved the use of plate iron to cover the upper surface of the timber which not only enhanced timber life but also diminished friction. In 1766 the first rails of cast iron were made in lengths of three feet and thickness of two or three inches. Sleepers, or ties, of wood were placed under the joints and a flange was cast into the rails. Single carriages were used initially. It was soon found that the use of multiple cars spread the weight of the load, allowing the use of thinner rails.

As timber was very expensive in Britain, stone piers were introduced and sunk below frost line which, in the mild climate of Britain, was not very deep. It should be noted that the situation in Pennsylvania was the other way around; timber was cheap but the frost line ranged from eighteen to twenty-four inches, a factor in the Great Debate.

It was also determined very early on that the larger the diameter of the carriage wheel the lesser the friction and wear on the axle. By early in the last century, it was found that an edge rail rather than a flat plate required less iron and further reduced friction. The concave "flange" on the rail had obvious disadvantages so flanges were placed on the inside of the wheels.

As a curious sidenote, the British even toyed with a single-rail saddle bag design, a precursor of the monorail. While obviously impractical then and now, the attempt illustrates the urge to experiment that characterized British and later American thought.

About 1798 a high-pressure steam locomotive with a cogwheel first made its appearance at Newcastle. The design was cumbersome and it took a quarter of a century before the British designed locomotives that took advantage of what we will call the principle of adhesion. A smooth wheel on a smooth rail would adhere if enough weight was applied to the wheel, aided by the fact that the coefficient of friction of like metals is very high. This discovery, as least in our view, is one of the most significant in transportation history. It should rank with the invention of the wheel as an amazing technological breakthrough if for no other reason than it seems to fly in the face of conventional wisdom.

For all this fascinating development in steam locomotion, another aspect of railroad transportation was apparent during the time of the Great Debate in Pennsylvania. A single horse pulling a load that was suspended on rails could match the hauling capacity of *twelve* horses on a turnpike.

The "Great Debater" of the Great Debate in Pennsylvania was Mathew Carey. He was an Irish Radical, prolific writer and has been described as "the most effective political propagandist in the United States" during this era. In his native Ireland, his strident calls for revolution against the British resulted in a hasty flight to the United States to avoid arrest.

In this country, Carey provided the polemics, occult statistics and theory for what was known as the Henry Clay American System. In short, advocates of this economic plan proposed a national bank, high tariffs to encourage American industry and federally financed internal improvements.

Based in Philadelphia, Carey flooded the nation with thousands of his pamphlets, all marvels of sophistry. While there is no evidence that he coined the expression "truth is unimportant, the only important thing is what is believed," he was certainly an ardent practitioner of this questionable approach to public discourse.

Carey was a founder of The Pennsylvania Society for the Promotion of Internal Improvements, the organization which ultimately convinced the Commonwealth that the canal was the answer to Philadelphia's very serious transportation problem. Incidentally, Nicholas Biddle was one of several other founders of the Society but nowhere have we seen the name Scrapple.

An early move of the Society was to commission Philadelphia engineer William Strickland to visit Britain and submit an objective report on British experience with turnpikes, railroads and canals. Strickland did a superb job and his report clearly indicated that the railroad was the wave of the transportation future, particularly for Philadelphia in its somewhat awkward position. Since that was not what Carey wanted to hear, he began a public attack on Strickland's conclusions that ultimately convinced the Philadelphia Quakers, bankers and the State government that the world as well as the moon really was made of green cheese.

We have read almost all of Carey's writings in this era with as much openmindedness as we could muster and tried to make allowance for the uncertainties that faced Philadelphia in the context of the times. Carey was an outstanding demagogue and a skillful writer who had an almost magical talent for distorting the simplest of facts in pursuit of his vision that the canal would be the salvation of not just Philadelphia but the entire Commonwealth. He was good. He was also wrong. And Pennsylvania paid a terrible price for listening to an eloquent dissembler.

The act to create the Pennsylvania Public Works was passed in February of 1826 and work on what became known as the Main Line of Public Works began shortly thereafter. It would be another quarter of a century before a genuine giant named J. Edgar Thomson would begin to bail out the Keystone State.

Carey proselyted several themes in his pro-canal diatribes, changing them when the absurdities of some of his positions became painfully apparent to his audience.

While he was forced to acknowledge that British railroads were solving some very real transportation problems, he developed the argument that none of them were general purpose lines. Technically, he was correct. The first general purpose railroad was the Liverpool and Manchester and it did not open until 18 September 1830. That this tiny rhetorical loophole had nothing to do with the proven efficiency of the railroad did ultimately percolate through to the public consciousness, so he reversed himself by saying that perhaps here and there a railroad might be best. This switch resulted in the construction of the Philadelphia and Columbia Railroad. Left unanswered was the quite reasonable question that if a railroad from Philadelphia to Columbia over and through the foothills west of Philadelphia was a good idea, why wasn't a railroad from Columbia to Pittsburgh also a good idea?

Then there was the matter of the crossing of the mountain barrier. Carey and his colleagues wanted to bore a four-mile tunnel through the mountain. That such a tunnel had never been built in the history of mankind provoked the response that it would be as simple as drilling a well. A four-mile deep well? Even if it were theoretically possible to dig such a well, wells are vertical and tunnels are horizontal. Wells don't require roofs. Tunnels do. Wells collect water. Tunnels have to drain water.

And how is one going to get the canal to the portal of the tunnel high upon the mountain? Why, we will just build a lot of locks and float the cargo right on up. Where is the water coming from? Water flows downhill and does not form reservoirs or lakes on the tops of mountains.

Finally, Carey shrugged and said perhaps an inclined railroad would be best after all. This switch resulted in the Allegheny Portage Railroad, a subject we will explore in a following chapter.

Central to Carey's argument was the undoubted success of the Erie Canal. The Erie Canal was built through relatively flat country, only had to rise 650 feet and required only 84 locks. That the proposed Pennsylvania Canal had to rise 2,322 feet and would require 417 locks (as well as that tunnel) were facts that did not deter Carey from his pursuit of the golden fleece.

Then there was the unpleasant question: Where's the money coming from? Philadelphia bankers and merchants would not put one cent into this gigantic will of the wisp so there was no choice but to make it a State owned and operated enterprise. The bankers *would* lend money to the State simply because they could not only gouge the State through interest charges but could also leverage the creation of new money through the making of these loans. For those who did not stay awake during courses in Money and Banking, the making of a commercial loan and the required compensating deposit balance magically balloons the money supply through balance sheet manipulations. As long as things keep going up, every banker gets rich. When things go down, however, the banks collapse.

So the creation of the State-sponsored Pennsylvania Public Works resulted in a virtual explosion of State-chartered banks eager to suck on this genteel form of counterfeiting. When it began to be painfully apparent that the canal scheme was a woefully inefficient failure and was consuming more money than water, panic swept the Keystone State and the whole jerrybuilt structure came tumbling down in the latter part of the 1830s. Another amusing sidenote to this debacle: British bankers took a lot of these State loans and at one point actually owned most of the Commonwealth of Pennsylvania. To foreclose, however, would involve them in still another war with the United States and they wisely contented themselves with steps aimed at simply getting their money back.

There was another insidious aspect to the creation of the State Works. Philadelphia and Pittsburgh were eager for a trans-mountain transportation network, but the other regions of the Commonwealth could not see putting taxpayer money which would come out of their pockets into a scheme that would not benefit them. So it was necessary to promise the construction of a gaggle of subsidiary branch canals reaching into these regions in order to entice them into voting for the boondoggle. Of course, these canals required still more investment and since none of them had the chance of a harlot in heaven of becoming profitable, the bomb got bigger and bigger while New York got richer and richer.

When any human organization, and particularly governments, have blundered and the bill is coming due, the first and quite natural instinct is to cook the books and cover up. It is easier for governments to delay biting the bullet because they can tap the taxpayer to cover the losses and engage in a game of "which pod is the pea under" to hide their tracks. A private organization can also employ such tactics and do so regularly, but there is a limit to the process because they go broke when the money runs out.

Another form of corruption implicit in any governmental project is the granting of contracts on a political rather than an objective basis. The construction of the State Works was accomplished through the awardation of contracts to local firms, lawyers and politicians, a trough at which the feeding became frenzied and total investment soared accordingly.

One of Carey's cherished arguments in favor of the State Works was the developmental potential of low-cost transportation within the Commonwealth itself. Since Pennsylvania was a large state and mostly wilderness, albeit with extensive raw materials, this was an appealing theme and there was ample evidence throughout economic history to support this thesis. The key words, however, were low-cost. Carey's economic forecasts were so blatantly inflated and his cost estimates ridiculously deflated, that even after all these years your author finds it astonishing that otherwise normal and prudent people would give them any credence. In effect, Carey was proposing a gigantic subsidy program and basing it on a transportation system that could not possibly produce the desired results. All costs must ultimately be recovered and cost-shifting merely delays the day of reckoning.

The Main Line of Public Works was, of course, completed. From east to west, it consisted of an 82-mile long Philadelphia and Columbia Railroad, an Eastern Canal Division 43 miles long, a Juniata Canal Division of 127 miles terminating at Hollidaysburg, a 36-mile long Allegheny Portage Railroad to cross the mountain barrier and a 103-mile Western Canal Division to Pittsburgh. The branch canal network was extensive.

Total length of the Main Line as built was 395 miles of which 273 miles were canal with 174 locks. The prism, or cross-section, was 40-feet at the waterline, 28-feet on the bottom and the depth was four feet, the same dimensions as the Erie Canal. By 1834 the entire network was open for through traffic. Within a year it was apparent Carey's dream was in fact a nightmare.

Keep in mind that the principal reason for the construction of the Main Line was to acquire heavy eastbound tonnage moving from the midwest, diverting a large percentage of this trade from New Orleans and New York to Philadelphia. It didn't work for two reasons…transloading costs and time.

To use the Main Line, one had to haul grain by wagon to the canal, load the boat, then transfer the load to the portage railroad, then load it back into boats and finally reload it still another time into railroad cars. The traffic couldn't bear these costs. All this transloading was not only costly but also time-consuming. Time is part of cost, another factor Carey overlooked.

At each transfer point congestion was inevitable and coordination difficult to achieve in practice. The net results was that no perceptible amount of eastbound grain tonnage was diverted to the Main Line during its entire life span of some 25 years. Only when PRR was completed and operating in the early 1850s were inroads made into this eastbound traffic.

The Main Line did produce some westbound tonnage, generally high-value ladings that could carry high costs. Even in this case, turnpike transportation was usually more cost-effective and actually grew during this period.

As to Philadelphia, between 1826 and 1850 export dollar value was halved and imports barely held even. For the United States as a whole during these years, both exports and imports more than doubled.

Carey's internal development theory did bear a little fruit and Pittsburgh was the main beneficiary. Coal and raw iron moved from central and eastern Pennsylvania to Pittsburgh where it was converted into finished goods which in turn moved east to market. Soft coal moved from west of the mountain barrier eastbound. This trade was considerable and has been described as a godsend to Pittsburgh and western Pennsylvania. The cost of this transportation, however, was staggering and the losses were absorbed by the taxpayers in the rest of the State who were subsidizing Pittsburgh's growth.

The dollar amounts were not minor. Competent historians have tried to wend their way through the cooked books and the generally accepted true losses were in the neighborhood of 100 million dollars. For the record, we think even this gigantic sum is an understatement. Whatever the exact amount, the net effect was to bankrupt the State and trigger political convulsions.

New waves of politicians would be elected promising to straighten out the mess and, as soon as they looked into this financial black hole of Calcutta, would recoil with horror and temporize with more coverups in the hopes of surviving the next election. The casualty rate was high, of course, and in the meantime nothing was done simply because they did not know what to do. Burning Carey in effigy might have been satisfying but they couldn't find the money for the pyre.

The principal abscess was the Allegheny Portage Railroad, those inclined planes that crossed the mountain barrier. To be fair, in the mid-1820s even British railroads envisioned the use of inclined planes on severe grades and the Baltimore and Ohio Railroad, chartered in 1827, assumed they would have to be used to cross Parrs Ridge, a continuous hill in the Piedmont region athwart B&O's path, as well as the mountain barrier.

But nails were being driven in the coffin of the Main Line. The Rainhill Trials took place in Britain in October of 1829 and established that a general purpose railroad was feasible, not joyful news to Carey and Company.

Bad news for the Main Line came in a double dose in 1833. The B&O concluded that inclined planes were not necessary for severe grades (there is some question if the Parrs Ridge planes were even installed) and also found that steam power costs were less than half that of animal power. All this about a year before the Allegheny Portage was completed in 1834. In other words, Philadelphia had bet against technological progress and lost.

Now the reader should understand that a professional historian must resist the urge to condemn people for making wrong decisions in good faith and for guessing wrong while trying to predict the unknowable future. But it is quite proper to savagely criticize those who continue down the same path after the evidence is conclusive that a mistake was made. B&O, for example, made many pioneering errors. As soon as these blunders were apparent, however, they took immediate corrective steps and swallowed their pride.

Politicians, of course, never make mistakes and kill messengers bearing bad news. Here was the core of the problem with the Main Line…it was a government owned and operated venture. To admit error is political suicide and it is rare in history to find a politician throwing himself on his sword.

We will characterize the creation of the Main Line as a Motive Power fallacy. It would be nice to say that Philadelphia never made another one. Sadly, even the history of the mighty Pennsylvania Railroad is studded with similar miscalculations.

Perhaps it is something in the water. Or the scrapple.

"FACTS AND ARGUMENTS" was the shortened title of the 1825 booklet published in Philadelphia in which William Strickland made his case for the railway "in preference to canals" after his studies in Britain. Read by this author almost two centuries after publication, we will say without reservation that it was one of the most objective, lucid and persuasive documents ever written about transportation matters and was a marvel of reasoned arguments and prophecy. Had his recommendations been followed, his name would have been enshrined and he would have been regarded as a giant in national history. This illustration was reproduced in his booklet and the caption read: "Represents the Locomotive Steam Engine, having in tow several transportation wagons; this engine has cog wheels revolving on a rail, on which cogs are cast. As this form of rail is expensive, and liable to be clogged by mud, stones and snow, and as it has been ascertained that smooth wheels possess sufficient adhesion on smooth rails, all the engines and railways now constructing are perfectly smooth — the adhesion has been found to be 1-25th of the load." That the Factor of Adhesion of four was known to be a physical fact so long ago is astonishing. For those who are puzzled by the foregoing two sentences, let us elucidate. As rail transportation evolved, it became more convenient to express the factor of adhesion as a percentage of 100. Thus 25 into 100 equals four and the factor of adhesion would be 4.0. In more recent times as electric traction became dominant, adhesion was expressed as a direct percentage…thus 25%. The advent of new traction truck design and AC power introduces the possibility of increasing the factor of adhesion to 35%, a dramatic breakthrough which is the equivalent of a 50% increase in pulling power and *the first since c.1825*. All this is also humbling. Our forefathers were a very bright bunch of people who persevered with little or no technical training and laid the foundation for all that has followed. After all, it took almost two centuries to improve that factor of four.

TRIUMPH I

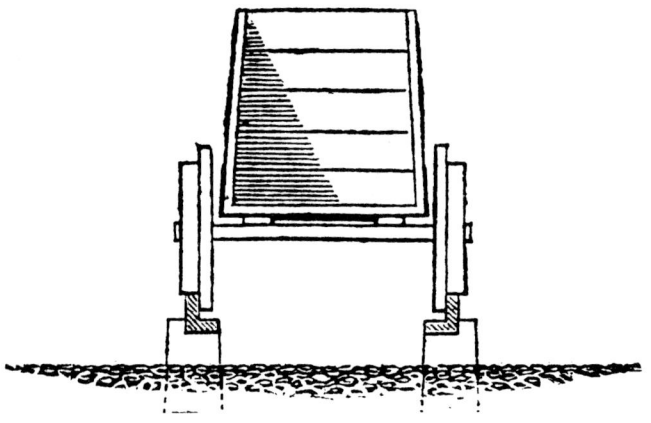

THIS CROSS SECTION was also published in Strickland's booklet to illustrate the edge-rail method and internal-flange solution. Notice that there is no fillet between the wheel and flange. We have to assume that the wheel revolves around the axle to adjust for curvature. Within the next decade B&O concluded it would be better to use a solid wheel and axle, providing for curvature with a cone-shaped fillet, and to place bearings on the outside of the wheels so that cars could be made wider. Parenthetically, the outer wheel on a curve has farther to travel than the inner wheel and the fillet increased the diameter of the outer wheel to compensate. The use of stone piers, while rational in Britain at the time, would prove to be a poor choice in the United States. B&O, to it's regret, employed this method with thin strap rail to reduce the tonnage of iron required. As long as horses pulled the load walking between the rails there was no problem, but the use of heavy steam locomotives pushing down on firmly implanted stones resulted in bending and popping of the strap rail, creating what became known as "snakeheads." The solution that evolved was the use of wood ties more closely spaced along with stronger rail. The wood ties absorbed some of the weight by flexing.

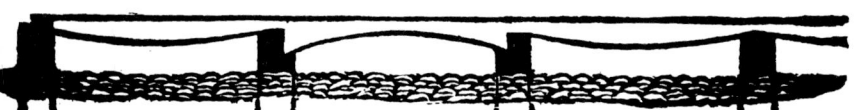

AGAIN FROM STRICKLAND'S booklet, this drawing illustrates a side view of the state of the art in roadbed design in Britain at the time. The concave and convex rails were a step forward in reducing the tonnage of iron required but the fact remained that a lot of iron would be needed to build a railroad. Carey seized on this issue, proclaiming that the need for iron would exceed the capacity of Pennsylvania ironmongers and the price of iron would soar. Worse, he opined, iron would have to be imported from Britain at great cost. Unfortunately, in this case Carey had something resembling a point and he milked it for all it was worth with emotional tirades and incantation economics. Strickland replied that the ironmongers would simply have to increase their production and this would spur internal development. If you need more, make more. If you have to import some, export more to pay for it. The British were eager for export markets and were willing to lend money to get the business. Carey's rabid anti-British attitude precluded consideration of such a rational approach and he carried the day. Actually, iron production and supply became a very serious national problem later in the century when railroad growth exploded and the issue even became one of the causative factors of the Civil War. But that is a story for another time.

THIS DRAWING of what is probably a fictional locomotive was published in a treatise in 1833 that dealt with, of all things, the reduction of friction in running gear, and implicit loss of horsepower. The aspect that amazed at least this historian was the creative vigor being applied toward solving technological problems at such an early date and that it was published a full year before the opening of the Allegheny Portage Railroad. Breathtaking progress was in the future, yet here man was fine-tuning existing designs.

THE PHILADELPHIA STORY

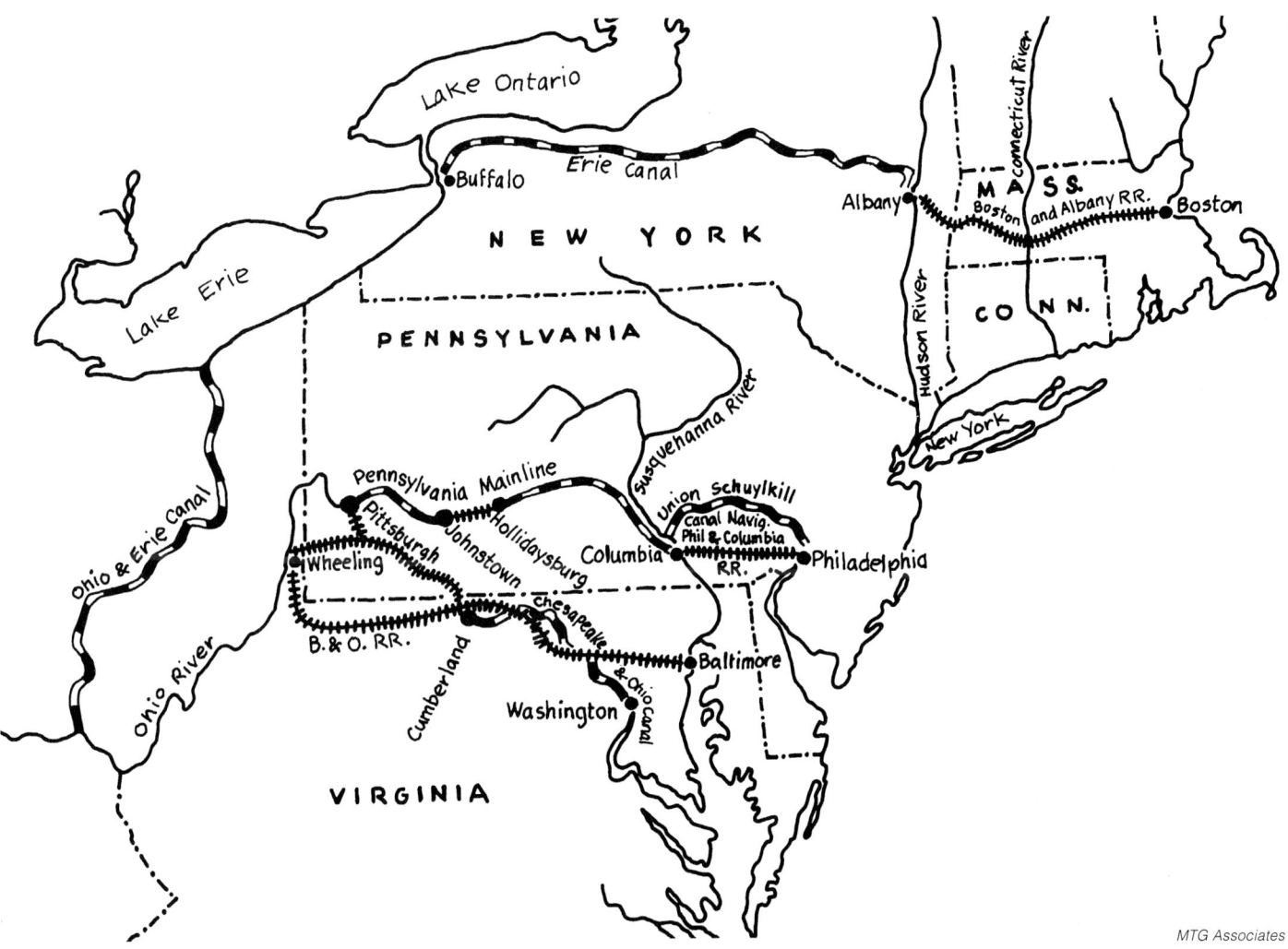

MTG Associates

HERE WE SEE the principal "trunklines" toward the middle of the nineteenth century in somewhat oversimplified form and with some poetic license. The Erie Canal and companion Hudson River were in full and profitable flower. The dour Yankees had chosen wisely by eschewing canals and building the Boston and Albany Railroad. In the midwest the Ohio and Erie Canal, built through relatively flat land, poured traffic both north and south. The trace of the Baltimore and Ohio Railroad requires explanation. The line from Cumberland to Wheeling with a branch to Pittsburgh was not built even though it was by far the best choice for B&O. As we shall see, Pennsylvania stiffed B&O by canceling their charter, forcing B&O to reach Wheeling through savage terrain and adding 80 miles in length. Note the Chesapeake and Ohio Canal. Maryland, too, contracted canal fever in this era and the net result was heartburn and serious delay for B&O. Pennsylvania was saddled with the worst of all worlds with a gaggle of canals, a short railroad and the Allegheny Portage Railroad with inclined planes that were obsolete before it was completed. The Philadelphia and Columbia Railroad was not state of the art even for the times and the same could be said for the Union and Schuylkill Canals. Only New York and New Orleans were truly booming and feasting on the explosive growth west of the mountain barrier.

37

TRIUMPH I

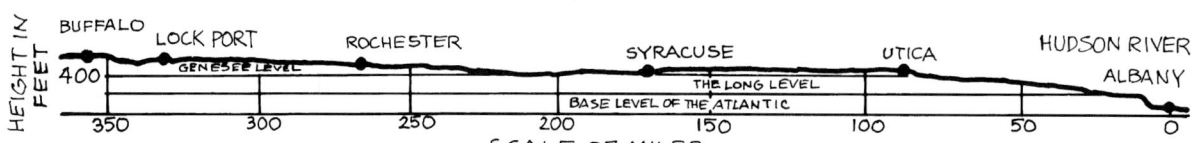

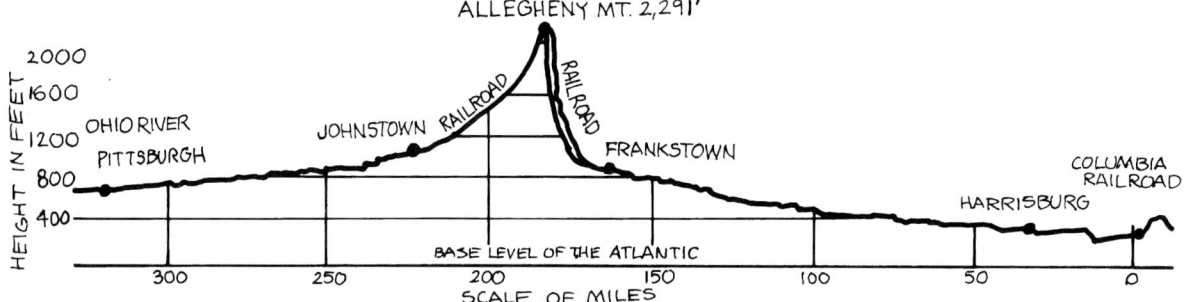

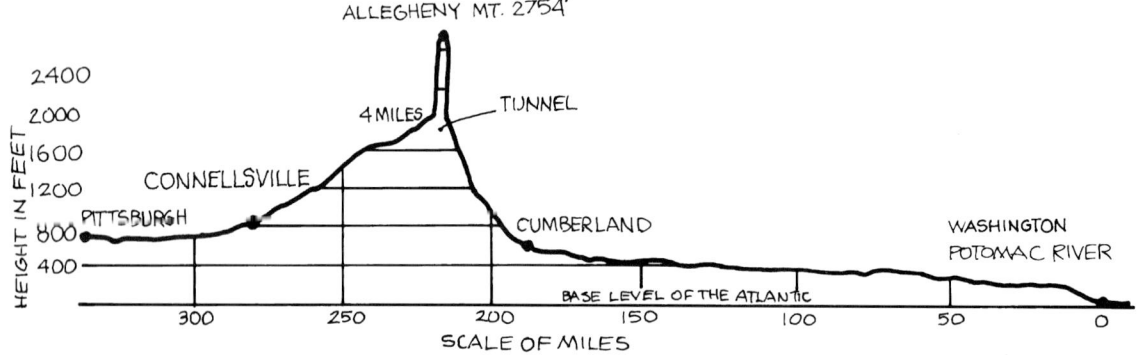

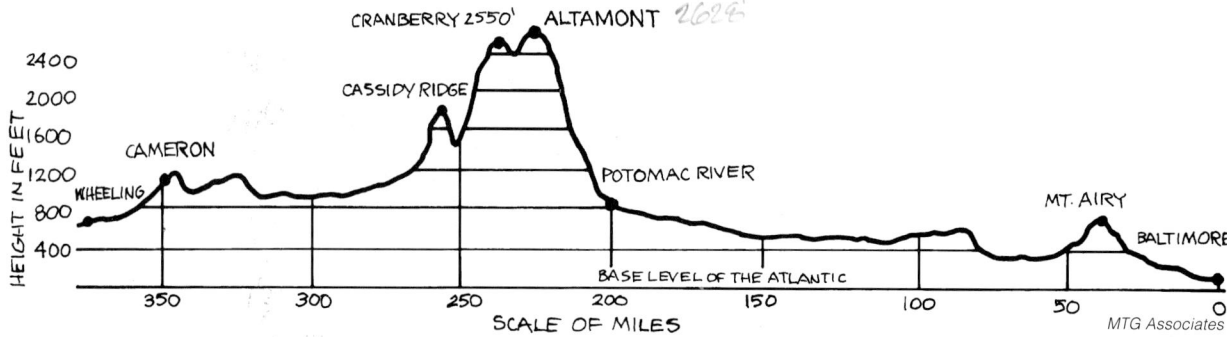

IN PROFILE the situation was even worse. The Erie Canal was in the catbird seat, awash in profitable traffic. Two long "levels" were actually flat and the rises minor. The highest point at Buffalo was only about four hundred feet higher than Albany on the Hudson River. The C&O Canal only got as far as Cumberland, which was providential because even they were planning on a four-mile tunnel to breach the mountain barrier at Sand Patch. By the by, the C&O Canal also had an alternative southerly route not shown here which would have also involved a four-mile tunnel and countless locks for which there was no water. Pennsylvania fans can take some small comfort from the knowledge that their forebears were not the only ones intoxicated with fantasy. The C&O Canal was State-sponsored and Maryland also went broke because of it. As will be shown and is vividly apparent here, Pennsylvania's decision to keep B&O out of the Commonwealth forced the latter to build to Wheeling through incredible terrain with *five* major summits, a blow from which B&O never fully recovered. The Pennsylvania Main Line, for all its deficiencies, only had one summit and the approaches in both directions were comparatively gentle, factors that would ultimately allow PRR to dominate eastern railroading.

Chapter 4

The Big Bet

Planes to the Stars:
The Allegheny Portage Railroad

The Allegheny Front ridgeline, of course, was not level. Erosion had created numerous gaps of varying altitudes, each one with individual characteristics and different sets of advantages and disadvantages for a transmontane crossing.

By 1830 in a forty-four mile stretch centered roughly on present-day East Altoona, there were seventeen named gaps from Cedar Swamp Gap on the southwest to Three Springs Gap on the northeast. However, the decision to approach the Allegheny Front with a canal narrowed the possibilities down to one, Blairs Gap just west of Hollidaysburg.

Three miles north of Blairs Gap was Sugar Run Gap, lower than Blairs and with easier, but more circuitous, gradients on both sides of the summit. PRR used Sugar Run Gap. PRR was a railroad. The State Works had to use Blairs Gap because the only practical route for a canal ended at Hollidaysburg, still another penalty to be paid by the taxpayer because their leaders had contracted canal fever.

Once the decision was made to go the canal route, Pennsylvania got off to a fast start by appointing a Board of Canal Commissioners on 31 March 1824 and the Board in turn had a bevy of axemen, chainmen and levelmen (but no engineers) in the field by 24 May. They worked hard and took 480 miles of surveying levels by 6 December.

The Board had three members, "Colonel" Jacob Holgate, James Clark and Charles Treziyulney. The reader will recall the "four-mile tunnel" scheme to which we alluded earlier. The first two members of the Board breezily recommended the tunnel in sarcastic language frequently associated with self-appointed "colonels" of dubious lineage and accomplishment. Words like "uninformed…malignant…avowed enemies of public improvements" were used to describe anyone who disagreed with them, all in the finest Carey style.

Mercifully, the man with the jawbreaker surname, Treziyulney, was not impressed with their specious reasoning nor their insults and squashed the idea in firm but moderate prose, thus leaving to history the thought that not all Pennsylvanians were bereft of brains or courage in this era. He is remembered. Holgate and Clark are not.

For all this, the problem of the mountain barrier remained. The tunnel was something *not* to do. But what *to* do?

Canal construction started quite promptly after enabling legislation was passed early in 1826 and there was general agreement that the Main Line canal from Pittsburgh would end at Johnstown, (completed by 1830), and the eastern canal at Hollidaysburg, opened in November 1832. However, it would take five years of surveys, debates and soul-searching before the final decision was made to use inclined planes over the mountain barrier.

One of the numerous plans called for a macadamized highway alongside a system of lifts and levels. Still another, favored by Moncure Robinson (who was a significant figure in transportation history for most of the last century), involved a one-mile tunnel at the summit to reduce the number of planes.

The waffling continued with teams of engineers proposing this solution or that and the politicians appointed commissions of one sort or another to "study the matter further" until finally the pressure of time forced them to do the one thing that elected officials abhor…to make a decision.

On 31 March 1831, an act was signed into law that authorized construction "without delay" of the Allegheny Portage Railroad.

Sylvester Welch was appointed chief engineer and on 12 April his locating party of two engineers, one surveyor, twelve axemen and a cook pitched their tents at Lilley's Mill (sic) at the head of the mountain branch of the Conemaugh River. The very next day they went to work moving westerly to Johnstown and in the middle of May W. Milnor Roberts began tracing the line from the mill to the summit.

Things moved with astonishing speed thereafter. Contracts for the grading and masonry were let on 29 July 1831 and by the Spring of 1832 track was being laid. A swath 120 feet wide was slashed through the spruce and hemlock forest, no small matter since this was virgin wilderness and the trees seemed to reach to the heavens. Two reasons were given for such a wide path; provision for future expansion and protection of the railroad from falling trees, the latter giving some insight into just how high the timber had grown over the ages.

By November of 1833 the first track was sufficiently completed to allow passage of the first car over the entire 36-mile length and by 18 March 1834 the road was opened as a public highway with the State furnishing the power on the inclined planes only, another way of saying bring your own horses.

One has to admire the vigor attending the construction of the railroad. At one time almost two thousand men were employed on the project. Sixty-eight masonry culverts were constructed, with a total length of 494 feet, along with 85 dry masonry drains, four viaducts, one overhead stone bridge (which is extant) and the first railroad tunnel built in America (also extant).

The railroad itself was built on stone blocks, of which 50,911 were installed. Edge rails, weighing about 40 pounds per yard, were employed and mounted in iron chairs atop the stone blocks. The rails were made in Wales in just twelve weeks, no doubt to Carey's chagrin because Pennsylvania ironmongers quoted over two years and time was of the essence. The steam engines to operate the planes, however, were constructed in Pittsburgh along with smaller iron parts such as pins and wedges. Broken stone under the blocks reached down two feet, which at the time seemed ample to combat frost heaving.

A total of ten inclined planes were needed, five on each slope. A total of 1,341,767 cubic yards of slate, detached rock, solid rock, clay and dirt had to be excavated, a very large pile indeed considering that the only tools were picks, shovels, crowbars and black powder.

Technical details of the operation of the planes and other features will be given in captions to illustrations later in this chapter. Briefly, steam engines located at the top of each plane would windlass an endless hemp rope to which cars were attached. The maximum capacity was a mere 21,000 pounds, usually carried in three cars. By March of 1835 a second track was put in service.

The planes were the most dramatic aspect of the portage, but the levels actually made up most of the mileage. These levels, incidentally, were not entirely flat as we shall see.

The builders of the portage were not totally deaf and blind to things happening in the real world and by the 1835 season three steam locomotives were on the property, by name *Boston*, *Delaware* and *Allegheny*. They could only be used on the longer levels because of weight. First to be delivered was the *Boston*, which checked in at 8½ tons *without* water or fuel. The planes could only handle 10½ tons, so four-legged horsepower was needed on the shorter levels. As we have shown, it had been established two years earlier that steam power was far more efficient as well as manureless.

For example, during the season of 1835 the *Boston*, according to Mr. Welch, performed "the labor of eighteen horses and it might do easily one-third more if it were not necessary to reserve it" for passenger trains. *Boston* averaged 52 miles a day at an average speed of ten miles per hour. On the surface this seemed like good news.

In fact, it was bad. Strickland was right, Carey was wrong and Pennsylvania was hung with a huge debt invested in an obsolete transportation network.

Nor was motive power the only bad news. The first winter was severe and most of the stone blocks heaved out of alignment. Worse, the railroad on the planes had a distressing tendency to slide downhill and buckle the track. These problems were solved by substantially rebuilding the roadbed on the planes at a price of still more capital investment.

The cost of maintenance was woefully underestimated, a syndrome that would affect all land transportation systems to come. For example, even today's Interstate Highway network is being eaten alive by staggering rebuilding costs.

From the beginning, the hemp ropes caused heartburn. They were expensive, short-lived and dangerous. Effects of weather caused rotting which weakened the fibers. Very early the engineers wanted to roof the planes, but the Legislature balked at the expense. Tarring the ropes extended life to 16 months, but at $3,000 apiece the cost was still very high.

In 1842, famous bridge builder John A. Roebling recommended the use of wire rope made by his facility in Pittsburgh. Experimentation followed but it seemed that the constant flexing made the wires brittle and subject to sudden parting, a heartstopping development on severe planes grades. It proved to be difficult and dangerous to attach hemp hitches to the wire rope and they had a tendency to slip suddenly, providing everyone with amusement park thrills for which they did not have to pay one extra cent.

Ultimately all wire rope problems were solved. They proved to be better than hemp and could pull a heavier load. However, it was not until 1850 that systemwide application took place and by that time construction of PRR was well advanced. It was hoped that the use of wire rope would allow use of locomotives over the entire length of the portage but it was very late in portage history when this actually happened.

Operationally, the portage was a quagmire from the beginning and while some improvements were made over time, the inherent weaknesses of the line's design prevented any real solution. At first, carriers provided their own horses to haul portage cars but each "train" left when it wanted, traveled at the speed it wanted and stopped when it wanted. This "do as you please" system was in true turnpike tradition, but there was no way to pass or pull off a railroad…at least not this one.

And naturally each carrier wanted his horses to go all the way through and then return as a unit. In practice it was estimated by observers that three horses were used to do the work of one. Eventually the portage evolved a system of timetables, common car design and, of course, railroad-supplied steam power. Even then the speed problem remained. In the portage's first season about fifty thousand tons of freight and twenty thousand passengers were carried, but passengers wanted speed and did not want to laze along behind a "burden" train, as they were called at the time. Carriers of high-value goods also wanted speed, but low cost was the urgent need for bulk carriers.

To be fair, this problem of varying speeds and cost control have haunted all railroads in all times. A true railroad, however, can adjust by passing, tailoring motive power to the specific need and using helpers on severe grades. On the portage the levels were too short to use these techniques and the planes were bottlenecks that could not be alleviated or bypassed.

All movements were slow and stop-and-go, with more stop than go. There were ten planes which meant ten stops, even on the downhill leg. And all this took time as well as an inordinate number of cars. If you halve the speed you need twice as many cars to carry a given tonnage in any given time. This meant car shortages which further delayed shipments. No wonder turnpike movements grew.

Then there was the little matter of cost. It was necessary to change power 33 times in 36 miles. Needed were nine locomotives, twelve teams of horses and all the stationery engines for the planes. None could "run through." All told it required 54 operating people to make a movement over the portage.

By the end of the portage's second season, the Board of Canal Commissioners made their report dated 2 December 1835 to the legislature in ebullient prose: "After nine years of unremitted toil and untiring perseverance in the construction and completion of upwards of six hundred miles of canal and slackwater navigation and nearly one hundred and twenty miles of railroads, Pennsylvania has placed herself on an eminence from whence she may view without any apprehension of successful rivalry the emulous exertions of her sister States in similar enterprises." About a month later, principal assistant engineer S.W. Roberts was quoted in a published report that the volume carried was "but a beginning of the vast trade destined to take *this route.*" The italics were those of the engineer, not your author.

Surely these gentlemen, privy to the problems of the portage, must have written these words with a lumpy feeling in the pit of their stomachs.

Mother nature replied to these paeans on 19 June 1838. A deluge in the area of Hollidaysburg caused a flood on the Juniata that swept away almost the whole of the public works from there to Huntingdon, a distance of about thirty miles, including canal, dams, locks and viaducts. It was not until late November that repairs were completed and by then the season was almost over. There were no operating problems on the portage for those five months.

At each end of the portage, of course, was an interface with a canal. While much of the tonnage was transloaded from boats into cars and vice versa by cranes and muscle power, the practice of floating the boat onto a flatcar was employed at the very beginning. Part of the lore of the portage occurred in October of 1834 when one Jesse Chrisman arrived in Hollidaysburg with a boat loaded with his wife, children, household goods, pigeons and livestock heading for a new life in Illinois. He planned to sell the boat and cross the mountains by wagon, but in the event arrangements were made to put wheels under the boat and this ad hoc vessel "sailed" over the Allegheny Front to the western waters. Mr. Chrisman disappeared from history, but the idea did not and boats were regularly carted over the portage.

The portage management did desperately try to innovate during its history. In 1843 the idea of "section boats" was tried…boats were sliced in half and carried on special sets of trucks and frames complete with cargo. While this technique was certainly something new in the way of marine engineering, it also turned to dross over time and still more acrimonious debates washed over the Commonwealth as proponents and opponents went at each other's throats.

The absurdity of the portage system was so apparent that outcrys for its replacement surfaced at the moment of its opening. In 1836 the Legislature demanded that the Canal Commissioners do another survey and engineer Charles DeHaas dutifully produced a new plan late that year. He came up with a 58-mile route with good gradients and a one-mile level tunnel utilizing Sugar Run Gap. Actually, DeHaas produced several plans and most of them were sound although compromised by the need to tie-in to canal terminals at each end. On the west end, he was so bold as to suggest taking the railroad all the way to Blairsville and abandoning the canal between that point and Johnstown. DeHaas was also quite emphatic that "bituminous coal must become an immense source of trade and revenue," a prophecy that was received by the public with incredulity.

The weakness in the DeHaas plans were political. His proposal to simply abandon the planes meant that all those employees appointed by the party in power would be out of work. No way.

About the only good that came from this process was an act passed in 1839 that resulted in the appointment of Charles L. Schlatter to make three surveys to determine if it would be practical to construct a continuous railroad from Harrisburg to Pittsburgh. Thus the famed northern, middle and southern routes entered the history books.

In 1840 an assistant engineer under Schlatter named S.M. Fox put in writing his "discovery" that a railroad from Huntingdon through Sugar Run Gap would be entirely practical and the planes should be abandoned. Poor Mr. Fox went the way of DeHaas.

The Pennsylvania Railroad, or Pennsylvania Central as it was called, was chartered in 1846 and construction on the "mountain division" through Sugar Run Gap began in 1847. Edgar Thomson, the driving force behind PRR, noted that tunnel construction would take a lot more time to complete than the lines east and west of the mountain barrier and wisely decided to use the portage as an interim connection. On the east, a short branch line was opened on 11 September 1850 from Altoona to Hollidaysburg to carry through traffic. On the west side it was very easy to connect with the portage a little east of Johnstown. This connection was never really satisfactory but it was better than no connection at all. Portage maintenance standards were abysmal and operating procedures even worse. Still, a least some through traffic managed to fitfully wend its way over the summit. PRR had begun its conquest.

By 1849 it was painfully apparent to even the most dense that the day of the portage was over. Even the governor, in his message of 1 January 1850, admitted that "The Portage Railroad, from the completion of our line of improvements to the present time, has been a serious obstacle to the business of the community and the occasion of trade seeking other channels to the Atlantic market." With PRR under construction, one would reasonably think the end of the long nightmare was in sight. One would have thought wrong.

In an act that this writer finds incomprehensible, the Board of Canal Commissioners appointed Robert Faries as engineer to come up with a plan to build a true railroad from Hollidaysburg to Johnstown through Sugar Run Gap! He dutifully came up with a plan that proved it was technically feasible to build such a railroad, albeit with gigantic fills to cross over to Sugar Run Gap, and a short tunnel. And they actually built what became known as the New Allegheny Portage Railroad, even going so far as to provide for a second track through the tunnel and do grading for a second track in most places.

In mid-1852 contracts were let and construction proceeded apace. On 15 February 1854, with their own line completed, PRR withdrew its traffic from the portage. Advocates of the New Portage were "staggered" and "stunned." What did these people think PRR was going to do? Let their own line stand idle while funneling traffic to a competitor? One cannot help but wonder what kind of stimulants these people were using.

The New Portage was actually finished and in service by 1 July 1855. The New Portage Tunnel, which we will treat in a later chapter, was finally completed by December 1856. The only traffic, of course, was that which came from the canals.

Sick of the subject, the Commonwealth put the whole "public works" up for sale in the Spring of 1855. Needless to say, there were no takers at the $10,000,000 asking price. Finally, on 15 June 1857, PRR purchased the whole thing for $7,500,000. There were no other bidders.

PRR operated the New Portage until 1 November and found that operating and maintenance costs exceeded receipts by a factor of 54%. The line was closed immediately and in 1858 was dismantled. The rails were sent to the Pittsburgh, Fort Wayne and Chicago and were laid for 82 miles from Plymouth to Chicago. Stone blocks were sent to Altoona to be used in new shops. In 1882 a three-mile branch was built to connect Bennington to the east end of the New Portage Tunnel and by 1884 a line was run from Gallitzin to Cresson. In 1898 the tunnel was widened.

The New Portage did come back to life in 1903. Inundated with traffic, PRR reopened it as a double-track bypass line to handle coal and other heavy traffic. Conrail closed it for good in 1981.

One of the most fascinating stories about the portage was related to a trip taken over it by Charles Dickens in 1842. He wrote an account of his passage.

One historian interpreted his writings as praising the line. Another regarded his musings as caustic. We have read the entire document. If Dickens had anything good to say about the portage, we were unable to find it.

Still, we have come away from our studies impressed with the portage. No matter how wrong headed, in terms of the times it was a monumental enterprise. In fact, the whole public works system was a tribute to the energy and determination of our ancestors to attack and solve a problem. That they failed is a fact of history. That they tried should be a point of pride.

TRIUMPH I

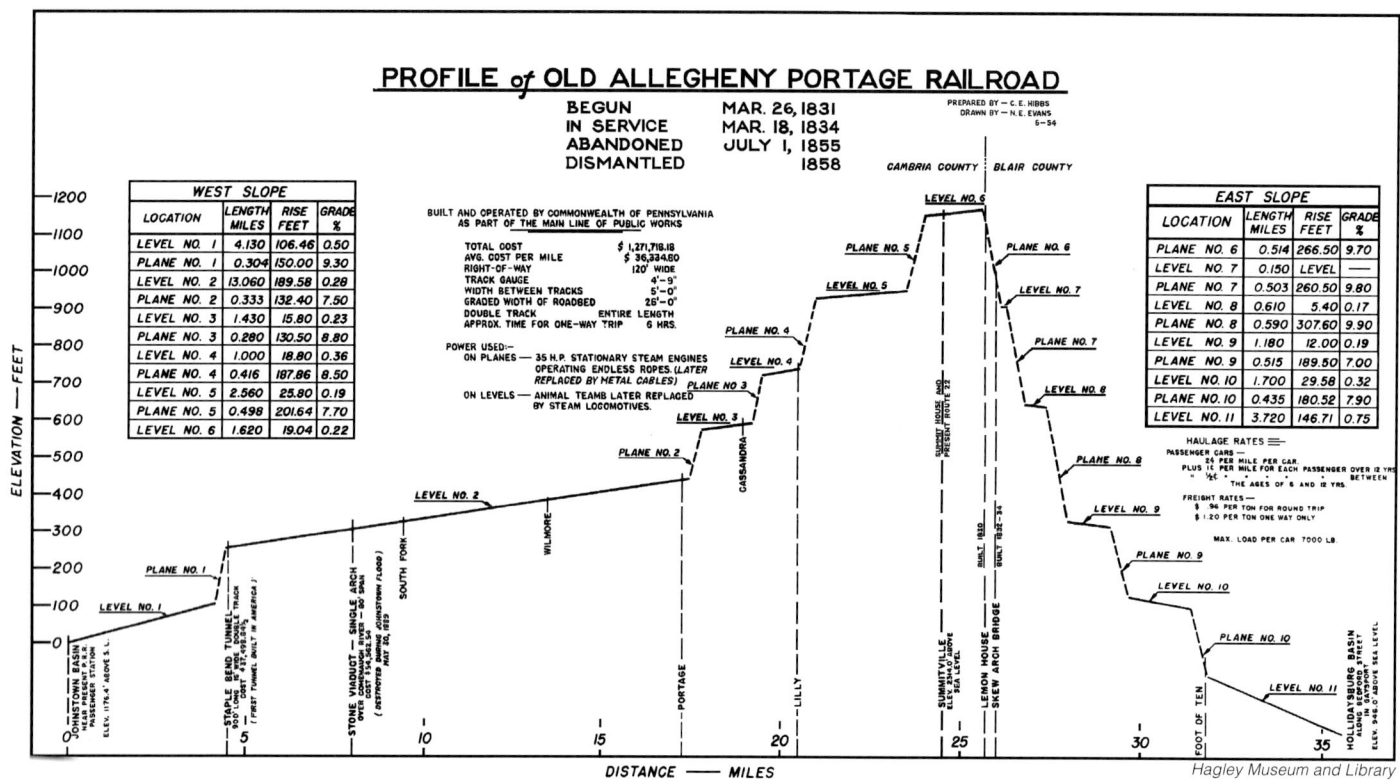

Hagley Museum and Library

THIS SPLENDID PROFILE of the Old Portage Railroad was done in 1954 and tells the reader just about all he wants to know about the technical details of Pennsylvania's bold experiment. Note that the numbering of the levels and planes goes from west to east, appropriate for a system built to capture eastbound tonnage. The western canal ended in a basin at Johnstown near the present PRR station. The OPRR began at that point with a level which ran about four miles to the first plane. The double-track Staple Bend Tunnel, built to cut off a loop in the Conemaugh River, was at the top of the first plane and was the first *railroad* tunnel built in the United States. A stone viaduct west of South Fork cut off another loop in the river. A "long level", thirteen miles in length, ran all the way to Portage where alternating and relatively short levels and planes took the railroad over the summit and down the east slope to a basin at Gaysport near Hollidaysburg where the eastern canal was met. Only Level No. 7 was actually level and it was only 0.15 miles long. Gradients on the other levels ranged from 0.17 to 0.50 percent. Nor were the plane gradients the same. The steepest was Plane No. 8 which came in at 9.9% and the mildest, if that is a proper word to describe such a savage grade, was 7.5%. The east slope of the old portage railroad roughly paralleled Old Route 22 and the west slope Route 53. The visitor will find many present-day "Planes Roads" on the west slope between Summitville and Portage. While PRR's Mountain Division was under construction, the OPRR was used as a connection. PRR's branch from Altoona met the OPRR at Duncansville, slightly west of Hollidaysburg, on 11 September 1850. On the west, PRR connected two miles east of Johnstown, about midway up Level No. 1, on 25 August 1851. The gauge was 4'9", a not unreasonable distance between the rails in the 1830s. However, that odd gauge was retained on the *New Portage Railroad* in the 1850s, believe it or not. In 1856 the NPRR spent more money to narrow the gauge to PRR's standard of 4'8½", another costly bandaid placed upon a ruptured artery. There is a joke hidden in this otherwise forthright presentation. The "approximate time for one-way trip" is stated as six hours. The *average* time was far, far higher. And a little sidenote. Plane No. 10 is long gone, but the hamlet "Foot of Ten" still exists.

THE BIG BET

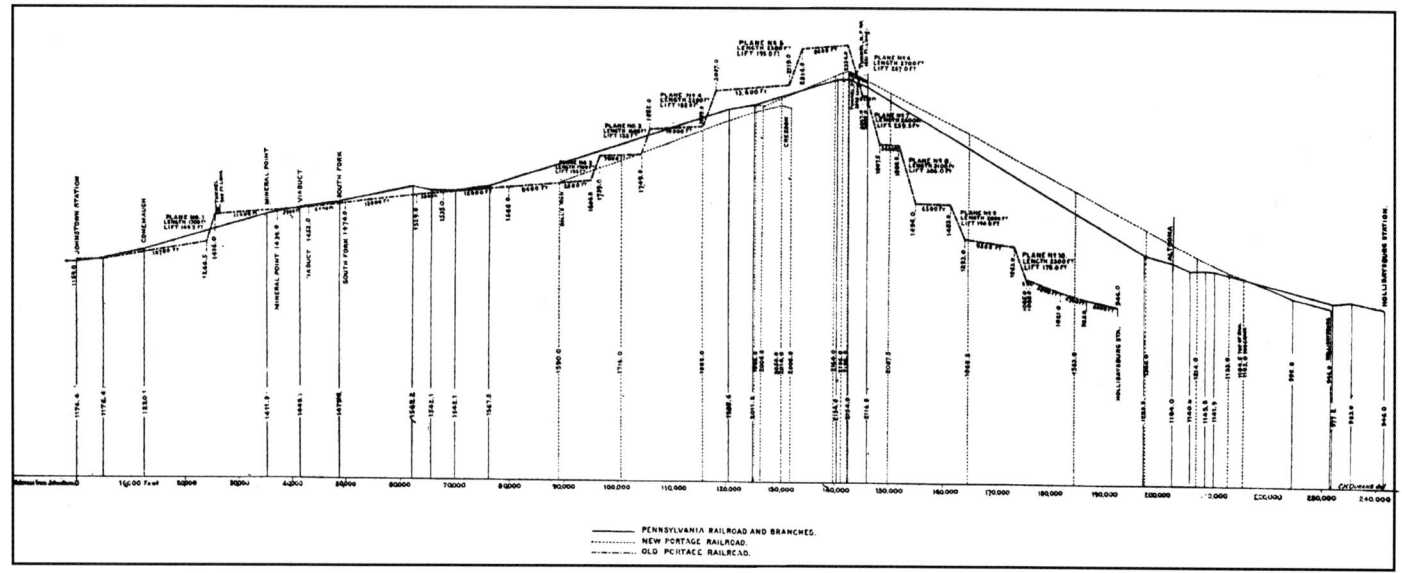

Hagley Museum and Library

THE ALLEGHENY FRONT was "conquered" three times and this profile shows the relationship between the Old Portage, the New Portage and Pennsylvania Railroads. The trace of the Old Portage is apparent and the distance from Johnstown to Hollidaysburg was 36 miles. The dotted line displays the New Portage, a 45-mile line, and the solid line represents PRR. The latter punched through the summit at a lower elevation than the New Portage at a price of a longer tunnel. Of course, on the east slope the approaches and gradients were different. PRR's maximum grade is about 1.8% against westward movements and the New Portage, taking a longer route, was an easier 1.6%. There is more to the gradient story than this, as we shall see. At the summit, each line exited at different elevations and ultimately the New Portage joined the PRR mainline at Cresson, on the west slope just west of the summit. West of Cresson the New Portage and PRR lines generally paralleled one another and ultimately PRR used portions of both the Old and New Portages. It should be noted that when PRR reopened the New Portage as a bypass for tonnage movements the volume was not sent to Altoona but rather to an expanded line to Petersburg southeast of Brush Mountain, generally along the route taken by the original canal. PRR as built lay to the northwest of Brush Mountain.

TRIUMPH I

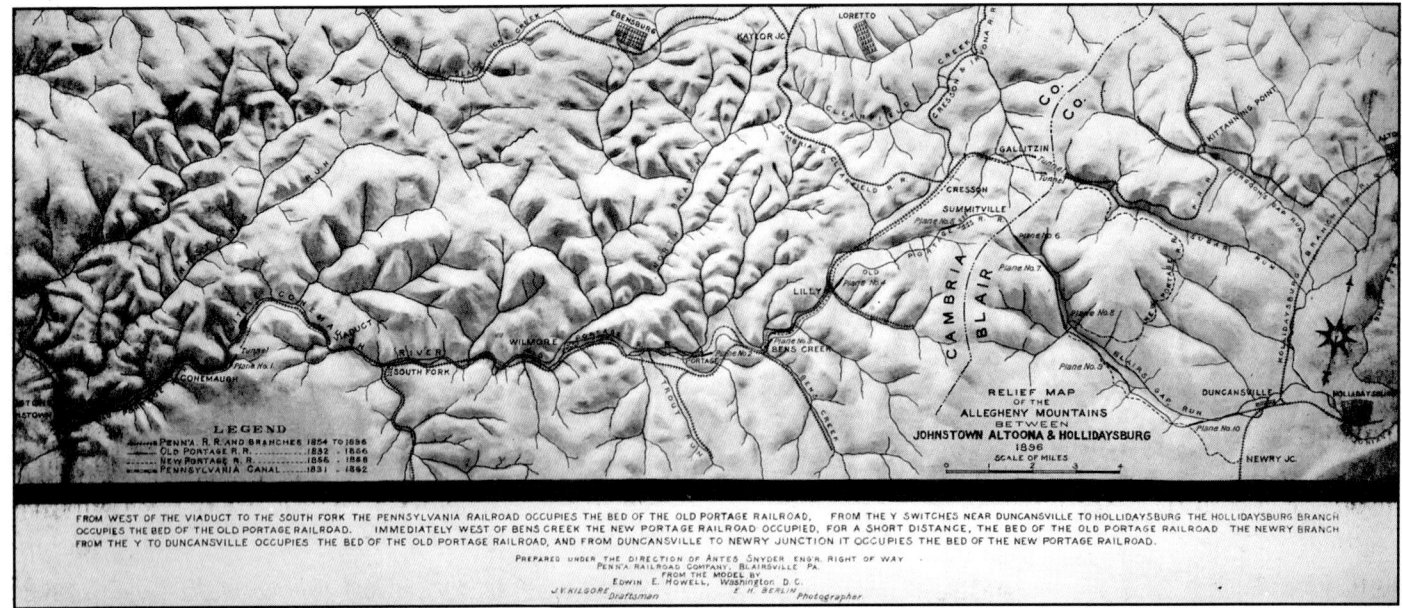

Pennsylvania State Archives

THIS RELIEF MAP was prepared in 1896 from a model and is such an outstanding portrayal of the three lines that crossed the Allegheny Front that we have also reproduced it as an endpaper in enlarged form to show small detail with more clarity. At this point in the book we are primarily concerned with the New Portage Railroad from Duncansville to the New Portage Tunnel, beginning at the wye at Duncansville. Incidentally, there is still a wye at this location although it is now a highway junction. The NPRR ran southwest to Newry Junction before turning west, gaining mileage to ease the gradient. It then ran for about five miles to Plane No. 8 where it did a 204° over a huge fill that became known as the legendary Mule Shoe. The line then dipped in and out of small canyons, gaining mileage and avoiding excessive fills.

There are seven of these "dips" before the summit is reached…the price was curvature. Compare the NPRR with the PRR mainline, noting that PRR paid most of the curvature price at what became known as Horseshoe Curve. This is as good a place as any to emphasize to the student of railroad transportation that curvature is a drag on motive power second only to gradient. As motive power technology dramatically improved over the years, trains got longer and each train was wrapped around more and more curves. The NPRR route up the east slope was a very bad actor in this regard for westbound movements and it is significant that when PRR reopened the NPRR in 1903 the tonnage was predominantly eastbound. Excessive curvature downhill actually eases the braking problem to at least some extent.

ARTISTIC LICENSE is to the artist what sod is to a doctor and ivy is to an architect. In the case of this painting, executed by N.H. Trotter in 1880, a lot of liberties were taken. First, at no point did the State Works canal meet a plane. Second, no plane was as steep as the one pictured here. Third, canal width was forty feet, not the hundred or more shown. Fourth, the galloping horses with the passenger boat and the bow wave of that boat imply a speed that was impossible. Water dynamics kept maximum practical speed to about four miles per hour. The only realistic aspect of this scene is the passing maneuver. Freight boats were required to slacken and drop their towlines to let passenger boats go by. Even that was tricky. Rudders are useless unless water is flowing by them and it wouldn't take long for a freight boat to be dead in the water. We would hazard that there were a lot of collisions. However, even if a boat sank no real harm would be done. The planned depth of the canal was only four feet, it was usually silted to three or less and the water was warm. In fact, warm water was one of the pro-canal selling points vis a vis the Erie Canal. The Erie was frozen about 45% of the year, the Main Line only 33%. In the overall transportation scheme, this difference was small change because a railroad is open 100% of the year.

THIS 1837 POSTER presents a more sedate passenger packet boat with a believable bow wave and a very interesting early passenger train. Still, to get from Philadelphia to Pittsburgh in 3½ days one had to travel by rail, canal, inclined plane and canal. To Louisville, another change to a steamboat was necessary. For the times, however, this was quick and relatively clean transportation and we must admit, Charles Dickens or no, that such a trip might have had some charms. Two years earlier, in 1835, another transportation firm advertised that the trip would take six days "with trifling fatigue." This company supplied its own rail cars between Philadelphia and Columbia as well as the portage. It is interesting, if true, that 2½ days were shaved from the journey in just two years. And the case could be made that the canal packets did give the impression of being an early form of cruise boat.

TRIUMPH I

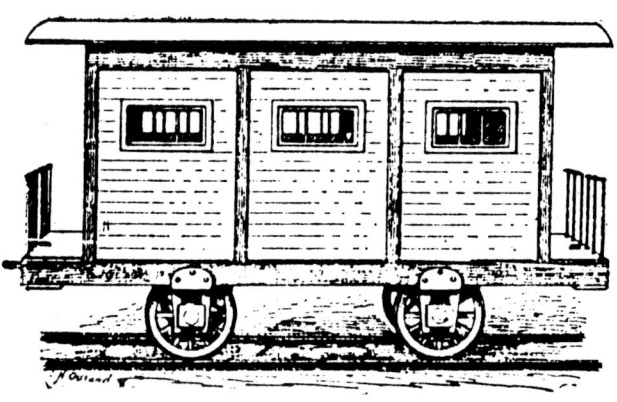

PASSENGER TRAVEL over the portage in the early days was spartan, to say the least. The left drawing depicts an 1834 passenger car with what appears to be wagon wheels, i.e. the wheel revolves around the axle. The right drawing is an 1835 model with outside bearings and we assume one-piece wheel and axle. The latter arrangement, of course, provides a wider body at the cost of curve resistance. It is interesting to note that a vestibule appears on each end and there is no apparent provision for braking. Both versions have spoked wheels to reduce unsprung weight and ease shocks on the car structure and "cargo." And the passengers must have felt like "cargo" with those tiny windows.

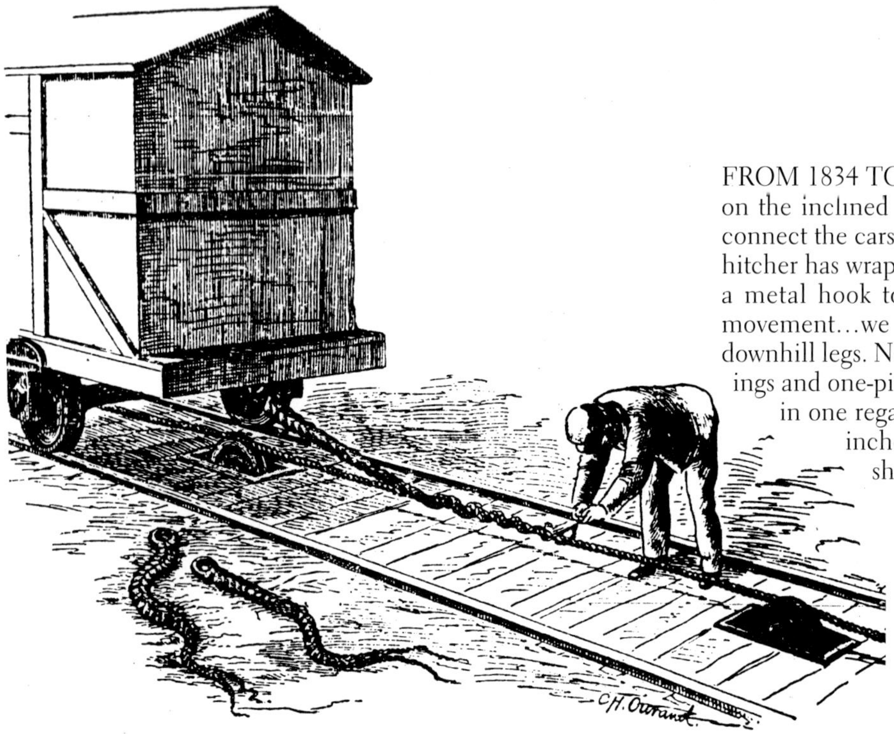

FROM 1834 TO 1848, when an endless hemp rope was used on the inclined planes, a "hitcher" employed a hemp tail to connect the cars to the cable as shown here. In this scene, the hitcher has wrapped the tail around the cable and is installing a metal hook to secure the connection. This is an uphill movement...we are unsure if a similar procedure was used on downhill legs. Notice that this freight car also has outside bearings and one-piece wheel/axle. This illustration is misleading in one regard; the hemp cables ranged from six to seven inches in diameter so were far thicker than the one shown here.

WHEN ROEBLING'S WIRE CABLE came into service in the 1848-1857 era a chain hitch was employed to secure the cars to the cable as seen here. Note that wrapping is still done and the hook used. Sudden slippage did occur, however, as we have reported. This drawing provides another view of an early passenger car with wagon wheels. The hitchers apparently assumed some legendary status during portage history and it was said they would announce their profession with pride. Of course, the crews were replaced with each change of political control.

THE BIG BET

National Park Service

AT THE SUMMIT of each of the ten planes was a "head house" that sheltered the machinery which hoisted the cars up the grade. Each station had two 35-hp steam engines. One was a backup. The steam engine operated large vertical pulleys that rotated the continuous cable through a series of sheaves. A counterweight kept each cable taut and a water brake relieved downgrade stress. The steam engine had a clutch mechanism to engage the main vertical pulleys. As mechanisms go, the equipment was apparently rather reliable. The cable, incidentally, was continuous in that one cable served both uphill and downhill legs. When one broke...and they did...both legs were in trouble. The rethreading process took time and in the interim "protection power" horses had to haul cars up one at a time. No six-hour passage today. When the cable was out of service, the downhill trip was even more exciting than usual. Sphincter muscle control was an important asset for crew and passengers alike. This illustration, which has been adapted by so many over the years that it has become a cliché, is misleading in some respects. It is unlikely that the sheds were as pictured...a following photograph will portray a probable configuration. The impression is given that sectional boats made up most of the traffic. They did not and were in fact a failed experiment. Now look at the device on the downhill side of this "train." This was an emergency braking "car" nicknamed a "buck." If a train began to run away, the wheels of the downhill car would ride up on the buck, the weight would lock the buck's wheels and force the sled-like runners of each side of the buck down on the rails. The resulting friction was supposed to bring the runaway to a stop. On a ten percent grade, and, say, a rainy day we would not care to put reliance on such an ingenious theory. These bucks were used from the very early days of the portage to the end and it has been stated that "very few serious accidents" occurred. How many is "few" and how serious is "serious?" There is ample evidence, however, that the public at large regarded the planes as unsafe. Operationally, attempts were made to balance the load by matching uphill and downhill trains to counterbalance the load and relieve the strain on the steam engines. This also doubled the load on the cable, not a comforting thought when staring at the long slide.

TRIUMPH I

THE ORIGINS OF THIS MODEL are obscure and the angle of the incline exaggerated as seemed to be the tendency in most portrayals of the portage. The indicated grade here is about 30%, an obvious absurdity. The shed structure, however, gives the impression of being more likely than the others we have seen.

Pennsylvania State Archives

THE UPPERMOST PLANE on the east slope was number six and it was crossed by this skewed masonry bridge, built circa 1832 to carry a wagon road over the tracks. This uphill, or westward, view was taken 13 May 1995. The bridge is located on the south side of old Route 22, also known as the William Penn Highway, and is maintained by the National Park Service. The path of the plane is apparent. Just out of sight at the top is a facsimile headhouse shed resembling the one pictured earlier, again maintained by the National Park Service. For those who are into fine stonework and meticulous craftsmanship, this example is worth a visit.

INNKEEPERS flock to transportation lines as sailors converge on brothels after a long cruise. Samuel Lemon started construction on this tavern just west of the shed on Plane 6 even before the portage was completed in 1834. The date of this early photograph is unknown, but it is reputed that Lemon operated a log tavern in the vicinity prior to construction of this impressive Federal-style edifice. The structure is extant, having been restored and used by the National Park Service as their headquarters.

Dick Heiler Collection

THE BIG BET

THIS ANCIENT WOODCUT shows the canal basin in Hollidaysburg and its juncture with the Old Portage Railroad circa 1842. The site was filled by PRR to gain room for shop expansion and lies just west of the shop complex.

PRR's branch line from Altoona to tie-in with the Old Portage while the mountain division was under construction ended somewhere in this vicinity. An 1855 map shows that this branch touched Duncansville and turned easterly to Hollidaysburg. PRR built a combination passenger station and warehouse in 1854 and identified it as being in Hollidaysburg. Origins of names are always interesting, at least to this writer. Duncansville was named according to the toss of a coin. Apparently Samuel Duncan and Jacob Walter owned land on each side of Blair Creek and flipped a coin on the bridge separating their holdings. Duncan won. Circa 1800 a forge in this area gave the name Iron Town to the location. As to Hollidaysburg, Adam and William Holiday founded the town in 1768. An extra "L" was added to the name over time.

Edward H. Weber

AT ITS HEIGHT after PRR reopened the New Portage in 1903, there were five towers between Duncansville and Bennington on the mainline. The first was WYE at Duncansville, or New Portage Junction on the railroad, seen here on 7 September 1962. This view is easterly and shows the line running to Hollidaysburg which is to the right. About three miles upgrade was DU and another three miles brought the line to Mule Shoe (MS). Four more miles found AH, another two miles PS and another mile the PRR mainline at Bennington. Tower records are sparse on this line and call letters changed over time...for example, early in this century WYE was SN. The ones quoted here were circa 1950. We suspect PS was just a telegraph office. Apparently all save WYE were built when the line was reopened. There were about 260 degrees of curvature in about 14 miles on the New Portage, which compares to about 120 degrees in ten miles on the mainline between Altoona (SLOPE) and Bennington. While the New Portage was less steep, the ruling grade was more severe...circa 1950 the New Portage was 2.23% westbound and the mainline 2.10%, a reflection of curve resistance and longer trains. Sadly, we were unable to find any photographs of these towers. The branch was already manual block and the principal tower was MS at approximate mid-grade.

TRIUMPH I

Hagley Museum and Library

WE HAVE ALWAYS been editorially reluctant to report on wrecks unless some significant historical point seems warranted. In the case of this unpleasantness on 6 November 1916, the anatomy of the disaster graphically illustrates that the problem of mountain railroading is not going uphill. It is going downhill. In the morning hours before dawn Extra East 2736 with 60 cars loaded with pig-iron and steel mill products in mostly open-tops was proceeding from Conemaugh to Altoona via the New Portage Branch. According to the fireman, who survived, a few miles west of Mule Shoe he noticed that the train line pressure was only 35 pounds rather than the minimum 65 pounds required by rule. The train should have been stopped immediately and the pressure pumped up. For reasons that are obscure, the train was not stopped and was running away. The operator at Mule Shoe noted that the train was going rather fast on a permissive block, but was not alarmed. A water plug was located about one mile east of MS and a westward train was laying there, presumably to take water. The conductor of that train estimated the speed of Extra East 2736 at about 50 mph and noticed that the engineer was whistling for brakes. He guessed that the train was running away and as soon as it passed, he crossed the tracks to a telephone box and called the operator at SN, located at the east end of the wye at New Portage Junction. Between MS and SN there were four light engines coupled together and moving east, by number in order from front to rear 2665, 2477, 2759 and 971. They were not in sight at SN when the warning was received, but the operator promptly reported the message to his dispatcher. These light engines were ordered to go to Altoona but the crews were close to 16 hours on duty so the dispatcher ordered them to Hollidaysburg for a crew change and emphasized that the light engines should keep moving. The SN operator, using a red lantern, signalled the crews of the light engines but none of the crews understood the meaning. Since the light engines were originally ordered to go to Altoona, they quite properly came to a stop east of SN and expected to reverse movement on the wye. Meanwhile, Extra East 2736 was plummeting down the grade. Four crewman, including the fireman, were out on the cars desperately tying down handbrakes. The fireman lost his nerve and jumped. The other crewmen stayed at their posts. Evidence showed that at one point train speed had reached 85 mph. Yet the handbrakes were beginning to bite…speed was dropping and, miraculously, the train had not left the railroad. Approaching New Portage Junction the grade was easing and the track generally straight. There was hope. Then the engineer of Extra East 2736 saw the rear markers of the 971. Hope was gone. He jumped and was killed. Only one of his three remaining stalwart crew survived. Extra East 2736 struck the light engines at a speed of about 60 mph. The wreckage caught fire, adding to the horror. This photograph, looking westward, shows the wreckage after the fire was extinguished. Seven dead…three on the extra and four on the light engines. The time of the collision was 4:55 a.m. The light locomotives had arrived four minutes earlier. An odd note…this was the first accident in which automobiles were destroyed on the way to dealerships. Gravity has no friends.

THE BIG BET

Blair County Historical Society

THE FAMOUS, or infamous if you will, Mule Shoe Curve as it appeared in 1892. Even by modern day standards with state-of-the-art earthmoving equipment, Mule Shoe is impressive. One hundred and twenty feet high at its deepest (equivalent to a twelve-story building) and sides apparently at an angle of repose, the Mule Shoe has been compared to Horseshoe Curve as a marvel of engineering achievement...in fact, in our view, the Horseshoe is a distant second. Here is a statistical comparison, with Mule Shoe numbers first: Length of curve, 2,228 feet to 2,483 feet...Curvature, 8°15' and 9°13' to 9°25'...Angular change in direction, 204° to 200°...Grade in curve, 1.68-1.20-1.37 to 1.75-1.45-1.73...Increase in elevation on curve, 250 feet to 275 feet. Even from a scenic standpoint, many of those who had an opportunity to gaze down both valleys felt that Mule Shoe was more breathtaking than Horseshoe. Since Mule Shoe is extant, albeit covered in second-growth forest, and in custody of the National Park Service, we must admit that the thought has occurred to us that conversion of Mule Shoe to a linear picnic park might be socially productive. Back to this photograph, there is a puzzling aspect. The date is given as 1892, the train identified as a photographer's special and the location as being on the Tyrone Division. There is only one problem. All historical records are unanimous that there was no rails on the New Portage from 1858 to 1903. What is the train sitting on?

TRIUMPH I

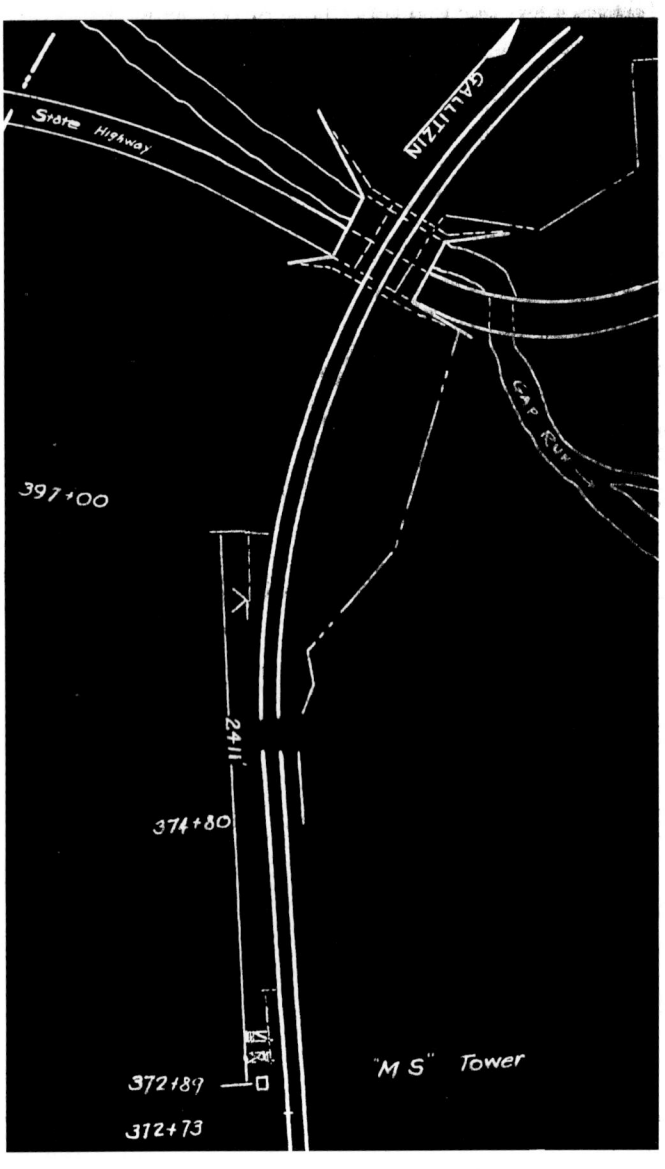

AT LEAST we can show the reader where MS tower was located, about three quarters of a mile south of the bridge over Old Route 22 (William Penn Highway). MS was taken out of service in 1925 and the distant signals removed in 1930. Even in the twenties the New Portage was seldom used because more powerful road locomotives and consequent longer train length enabled PRR to handle almost all traffic on its four-track mainline. The only through movements on the New Portage involved trains originating at Petersburg on the Middle Division and passing through Hollidaysburg simply because the route was shorter. The only real reason the New Portage was kept open was to serve as an emergency bypass in the event of derailment blockage on the mainline. During the Great Depression the westbound track and the numerous passing sidings were used to store cars. Only the eastbound main was kept open and in a minimum state of maintenance. The huge surge of traffic during World War II did result in some through movements, but even then a signalman with lanterns and a telephone threw the turnouts by hand. A 35,000-gallon wooden water tub was located about a mile east of MS with a standpipe to serve westbound trains…it was this tub at which the westbounder was sitting when Extra East 2736 flew by in 1916. It was served by a nearby small reservoir which was ultimately transferred to the city of Altoona.

THIS IS THE BRIDGE over Old Route 22 which is shown at the top of the previous drawing. The photograph was taken 6 May 1995 and is looking westerly, or upgrade. The nameplate proclaims that it was completed in 1902, obviously as part of the 1903 reopening.

THE BIG BET

Railroaders Memorial Museum

LEST THE READER think that the Mule Shoe was the only giant fill needed to get the New Portage Railroad to the summit, we present this southwesterly view of the approach to the PRR mainline at Bennington. The second track was removed in 1955 and the last in 1981. PRR management has been criticized, sometimes savagely, for keeping what appears to be excess trackage in place for too long a time. While we will not be above censuring many PRR habits and decisions, we don't think this charge holds water...particularly on the Pittsburgh Division. The enormous amount of traffic that has always transited this division fully warrants keeping a maximum amount of trackage available for the inevitable blockages. Even an interruption of a few hours can backup trains for hundreds of miles in all directions and create an operating nightmare with a very large price tag. Better too much than too little.

TRIUMPH I

FEW PEOPLE ALIVE today have ever seen virgin forested wilderness and consequently find it hard to imagine just what faced the Pennsylvanians as they gazed west at and beyond the mountain barrier in the last century. There are a few acres remaining in western Maryland and your writer wandered through them some years ago, coming away with a sense of timeless awe. We can assure the reader that this depiction, done in the 1870s before the vast forests were obliterated by man, captures the visage in all its glory and magnificence. The wilderness, as well as gravity and distance, had to be conquered to build a new nation and, of course, they were swept away in less than fifty years. But there were casualties. Did we really have to take it all?

Chapter 5

The East Slope

West Altoona to Gallitzin

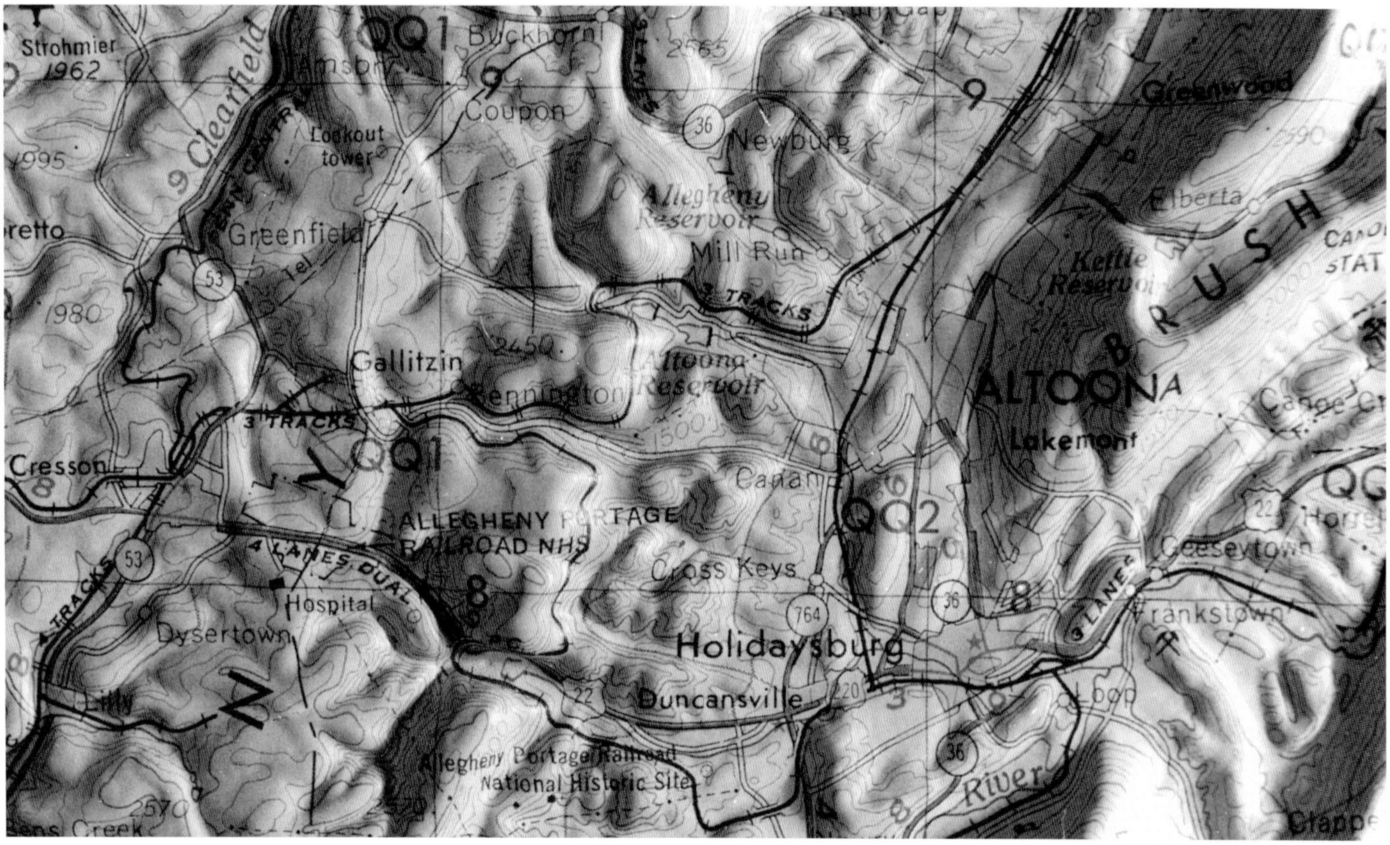

THE LAY OF THE LAND and the flow of the waters that so affected the crossing of the Allegheny Front and the transportation history of the nation is graphically shown here in a relief map originally prepared by the Army Map Service. The vertical exaggeration is three to one, necessary to give the viewer the illusion of great height when in fact the "barrier" is not all that high. The big hummer in this scene is Brush Mountain on the right, but that one was easily bypassed to the northwest or southeast courtesy of the drainage system of the eastern waters. At upper left note the Clearfield Creek…actually, even though on the western slope of the barrier, it flows to the northeast and ultimately into the Susquehanna River, thus making it an eastern water. The Conemaugh River, which originates both east and west of Cresson and is a true western water, conveniently provided canyons that presented PRR with a comparatively mild decline and, more importantly, ascent on the west slope.

The reader should trace the path of PRR's mainline beginning just below the "9" at upper right and move westerly. Note how cleverly the mainline was located relative to the terrain and the streams crossing at right angles. Sidehill cuttings were minimized and the line gently curved inward to avoid deep fills or viaducts. Until Horseshoe Curve, that is, where three choices are obvious…two moving northwesterly and one southerly. Decision time was reached at Kittanning Point, on the south slope of the mountain of the same name just to the left of Mill Run on this map. At the time of construction, the declivity moving toward "Coupon" on the map was known as Kittanning Gap. At first glance, this route appears to be far superior to any other one. The line could be easily built on the side of Kittanning Mountain until the vicinity of "Buckhorn" where it could probably cross the continental divide without a tunnel. From there through Greenfield to Cresson a gentle route is readily apparent. Mother Nature, however, put some flies in the ointment.

First, the summit of Kittanning Gap is higher than the one at Sugar Run Gap at Gallitzin and that in turn would necessitate a steeper grade on the east slope. Second, this route would be longer. Third, and perhaps most important, J. Edgar Thomson, unlike all too many of his peers, was quite capable of thinking beyond the end of his nose. He was building a railroad to capture *eastbound* tonnage and this route would involve a far longer uphill climb from Cresson to the summit. Scratch Kittanning Gap. The next hole in the hill at that time was known as Burgoon's Gap, the one running from Horseshoe Curve to Greenfield and on this map the location of a local road. There was a branch from this route known as Burgoon's South Gap, on this map a shadow pointing southwesterly to Gallitzin. Sadly, the summits of both these routes were not only higher than Sugar Run Gap but also higher than Kittanning Gap. Worse, the east slope approach was short and either one would require a very long tunnel at the summits to protect both eastbound and westbound movements. Scratch Burgoon. There was only one left, the lesser of three evils but evil nonetheless. Build two gigantic fills to get around Horseshoe Curve and two more in the area of Bennington so as to approach Sugar Run Gap, the lowest of all, at a right angle and punch through the summit with a relatively short tunnel. Three cheers for Mother Nature, the bitch. Curiously, there was a fourth possible route and it is quite apparent on this map. Simply go south from Altoona to Canan and turn west to follow the route of present-day New Route 22. This possibility fascinated your author for all too many days until it dawned on him that it was an illusion. The approach terrain is too flat and would have involved an impossible grade in the last few miles.

THE EAST SLOPE

It has been called by many names. Allegheny Front. Mountain Barrier. Allegheny Mountain. The Eastern Continental Divide. The Great Barrier. The nemesis of so many for so long.

Yet as mountains go on Spaceship Earth, the Great Barrier is a mere wrinkle and a rather gentle one at that. Man has gazed upon the Alps, the Himalayas, the Andes, the Rockies, the Cascades and dozens of others with awe and fear. These mountains reach to the heavens with jagged and malevolent visage. They are lashed by weather of savage ferocity and their very images speak of the violent tectonic forces that created them.

By contrast, the Allegheny Front is serene and docile in appearance. The summits are generally only a half-mile above tidewater and when one contemplates the mountain's east slope from the valley floor, the viewer is already halfway to the top. This is not a mountain. This is a foothill. That the approach to the east slope is abrupt in comparison to the west slope is not visually apparent and even if that were so it would still not be impressive. We have lugged ammunition up mountain slopes that make this one seem like easy duty.

Mountains, of course, are like women. They are all beautiful…it is just that some are more beautiful than others. And in this frame of reference, the Allegheny Front is a placid and tranquil siren, arcadian in appearance. The summit is enticingly rounded, the slopes soft and easy on the eyes.

Today as in yesteryear the mountain is lush with greenery in the warm season, resplendent with sparkling ice and snow in the cold months. In the early morning hours we have watched ground fog slowly drift its way down the ravines like a dance of the veils with sunlight sparkling on the wisps in ever changing patterns, an almost spiritual spectacle. If there were a beauty contest among mountains, surely the Allegheny Front would take first prize along with the Miss Personality award.

How in the name of God could anyone have called this supple mountain a barrier?

As is our wont, we tried to imagine ourselves as J. Edgar Thomson viewing this panorama a century and a half ago, plotting conquest and yet taking two whole years to just study the problem. Why so long?

It is no secret to our readers that we regard Thomson as a titan in the history of the Republic and that we worship at the feet of his accomplishments. Yet it is not as an engineer that we admire him. Actually, he was merely a competent engineer and most of his reputation in this regard evolved from applying the experience of others, a process that he freely acknowledged without reservation.

It has been said of many great leaders in human history that their early and formative years, more by chance than design, were a preparatory course that enabled them to be ready to meet a challenge when it was thrust upon them. These opportunities are usually accidents of fate and then the individual must decide for himself whether or not he should devote the rest of his life in the given cause. There can be no holding back. The commitment must be total. There can be no thoughts of personal glory or enrichment, only the accomplishment of the mission. There can also be no illusions. The chosen path will be rife with dangers and enemies, both within and without. A "go" decision is final and irrevocable. Whatever it takes to get the job done must be done without regard to false sentimentality and compassion. If you are in for a dime, you are in for a dollar.

And a vision is essential equipment. This must be a vision of what might be possible, not a wish fathering the thought. Would it be *possible*…never mind how difficult…to create a viable trunkline railroad that would enable the nation to develop its vast resources for the common good?

Thomson's early life was destined to prepare him for his ultimate role. His father, John Thomson, a competent surveyor and, by the way, a Quaker, took his son along on various jobs in the Philadelphia area. In 1827 at the age of 19, the son joined the engineer corps of the Commonwealth of Pennsylvania and assisted in making early surveys for the Philadelphia and Columbia Railroad. During the summer of 1830, he was appointed assistant engineer in charge of surveys for the eastern division of the Camden and Amboy Railroad.

Young Thomson then visited Britain to study their engineering practices, at that time the mecca of railroad development. Upon his return in 1832, he took over as chief engineer for the Georgia Railroad and spent the next fifteen years as, in effect, the chief executive of this smallish railroad.

It was in Georgia that Thomson was honed in the realities of railroad construction, operations, maintenance, administration, development of resources, financing, rate-making and politics.

And it was in Georgia that his transcontinental railroad vision was formed. This dream envisioned a railroad that would bypass the mountain barrier altogether and reach into the great granary from the south as well as extend to the Pacific Ocean through (and to) territory that actually belonged to Mexico, a slight complication that the nation solved by simply taking it all by force of arms.

Thomson was then offered the job of chief engineer for the nascent Pennsylvania Railroad. He was reluctant to take it. Thomson was happy in Georgia, had made a few dollars of what he called "nett profit" by judicious investment in real estate along the right-of-way and wasn't sure that he could transplant his transcontinental conception to a railroad that would have to cross rather than skirt the mountain barrier.

He also knew from long experience in Georgia that a railroad was an entity in and of itself and an institution that required what soldiers call "unity of command" in order to flower. He was trained and fit for such command.

PRR was organized and led by amateurs such as lawyers, bankers, speculators, politicians and others of this ilk. In order to conquer, he would have to literally seize control of the railroad by whatever means presented themselves and then orchestrate *all* the elements required to dominate the transportation scene. He would have to make himself king in order to triumph.

We have studied this man for years and have concluded that there was no ego or megalomania in his nature. No desire for riches or emoluments or a place in history. As his splendid biographer James Ward put it so eloquently, he could not even find evidence of a taste for mistresses to enliven the story of Thomson's live. His devotion to the institution was total and unequivocal. It was this characteristic, among others, that separated him from his contemporaries and made him the bane of his opponents. If you got in the way of his railroad, he cut to kill.

So Thomson had to decide. He took the job. He concluded that triumph was possible. He noted that this transmountain crossing provided the shortest route from the west not just to Philadelphia but also to New York and Baltimore. At the west end, Pittsburgh would provide a gateway to reach into the midwest from a favorable middle position which in turn had the potential of linkage into a transcontinental transportation empire. The vast mineral resources in the region west of the barrier could be tapped by PRR from a central position and this would allow the nation to develop into an industrial as well as agricultural superpower, with PRR as the literal keystone.

There was competition, to be sure, but the most dangerous was B&O and the Commonwealth had just delivered a near-fatal blow to the Mother of Railroads by cancelling its charter to build anywhere in Pennsylvania. Thus it was possible to make PRR the Father of Railroads.

And so it turned out in all respects save one. By the early 1870s PRR was the dominant railroad in the nation and for a brief moment had control of a number of railroads west of the Mississippi sufficient to create a transcontinental system. Then the financial collapse of 1873-74 put PRR's back to the wall and control was lost in the debacle, never to return. Thomson died in 1874, having achieved all he set out to do with this one exception. His railroad was in financial trouble at his death, but his successors saved it and, indeed, took it to greater heights albeit with internal rather than external growth.

So now we return to your author staring at the Allegheny Front and wondering why it took Thomson *two whole years* to study the east slope before taking action. He knew perfectly well that the whole point of building his railroad was to capture eastbound traffic and that the west slope would be an easy passage. The east slope was a necessary piece of railroad, but of secondary importance.

After all, two years is the gestation period for an elephant. Charles L. Schlatter took only two years, 1839 and 1840, to survey three different routes in widely separated regions of Pennsylvania and while, to be sure, he regretted that he did not have time to explore some tantalizing sub-routes, he got the job done shortly after the elephant was calved.

Why so long? Beauty is only skin deep. It is what was *underneath* the surface of the east slope that concerned Thomson. Here he could draw upon the experience of the Baltimore and Ohio Railroad, the pioneer trunkline that had been trying to hack its way to the Ohio River through this terrain for twenty years before PRR was even chartered and was generous enough to share their findings with all comers.

Whether with cut or tunnel, you haven't the slightest idea of what you are going to find once you slice into Allegheny geology. Worse, nothing you find is good…just varying degrees of bad.

The strata was jumbled, warped and layered with an unpredictable array of various soil and rock structures, almost all of which begin to deteriorate when exposed to air and water. Even more solid structures were split open by freezing water.

THE EAST SLOPE

There was no way Thomson could construct the east slope without cuts and he had to waste enough material from the cuts to provide fill. So he spent two years with surveyors in the wilderness meticulously calculating and planning a route that would minimize cuts, provide sufficient fill and keep costly curvature as low as possible. Gradient didn't bother him. He already knew from B&O's experience that this was a minor factor against westbound movements because those would be a slight percentage of the total tonnage, a prediction valid to this day.

Thomson was not a hipshooter. He made a fetish of calm, cool, careful and thorough planning and then, when he made his move, it was with lightning speed. If it took two years to do it right, then he took the two years.

Even with precise planning, the construction of the east slope was a nightmare. In fact, the east slope was a cross to bear throughout PRR's history and remains so today.

The east slope has been touted as an engineering marvel for generations, a reputation enhanced by the scenic grandeur at Horseshoe Curve. In our view, this is nonsense. B&O alone achieved some engineering marvels that dwarfed the east slope. The east slope was a *planning* marvel and a tribute to Thomson's genius. If, as soldiers say, strategy is merely the application of common sense to the conduct of war, then the construction of the east slope was merely the result of common sense being applied to the construction of a railroad. The less cuts and the shorter the tunnel, the less unpleasant surprises.

When violating the hillside, hope for the best and prepare for the worst. Assume the mountain is not going to like being disturbed and plan accordingly. Bite the bullet and put in two tracks at the outset, all the way up. To have to add a second track on an active single-track railroad clinging to the side of a mountain might prove to be impossible. As we will relate, PRR had an awful job adding a third and then a fourth track decades later with more modern construction equipment and after years of bitter experience. If one is looking for engineering wonders this is the operation that should be studied, not the original construction.

The years 1848 and 1849 were spent in surveying. The initial plan called for a 3,750 foot summit tunnel and a 1.74% maximum grade. Not satisfied, Thomson ordered a resurvey in 1850 which reduced tunnel length by 180 feet at the price of increasing maximum grade to 1.8%.

The final plan reduced the gradient to 1.55% on curves, a good idea that can be traced back at least as far as Schlatter's proposal and possibly back to B&O's early experience. This technique is called "compensation" and it was not Thomson's brainchild.

The location of the line took so much time that the first construction contract was not let until November of 1849. The tunnel contract was let in 1850 and the final contracts during 1851. The Mountain Division, as it was called at the time, was open for service on 15 February 1854.

Little can be found in PRR documents that gives details of the labor force that clawed the east slope from Mother Nature, unlike B&O's candid and forthright publications in that era. Almost certainly the force was heavily Irish and quarrelsome, with factions from different parts of Ireland fighting among themselves to the detriment of the work at hand. Such allusions that we found indicate that PRR's problems were similar to B&O's. B&O crushed these rebellions with a heavy hand and were frank about it. We assume Thomson was equally severe but decided to remain silent. Dead men tell no tales.

We have written several books about B&O's lunge from Harpers Ferry to Wheeling and have characterized the original construction as quick and slapdash. Not so with Thomson. He set out to build a super railroad, taking the time and investment to do it right.

The westbound track was initially laid with 56# T rail and the eastbound track with 74# U rail. Cross ties were 8" x 8" by 8½ feet, white oak, on 2½ foot centers. All rested on twenty inches of slate ballast. This was very heavy construction indeed and was typical of Thomson's obsession with quality.

Once the line was open for traffic, problems mounted. The iron rail began breaking up, particularly the U rail. Replacement of all the rail, east and west, with 83# T rail was begun in 1856 but not completed until 1859.

Apparently chestnut was used for tie replacement and this choice was found wanting. Since oak was scarce, a switch was made to hemlock and it was found to be almost as durable as the former.

The slate ballast was a mistake (we suspect it was really mostly shale) and crushed stone was substituted. A curious byproduct of Thomson's penchant for deep ballast, as related to increasing speed of passenger trains, was the reduction of dust, a bugbear to train travel in all times.

From the outset, PRR's gauge was 4'8½". We have already related that the New Portage was built to 4'9" only to have to reduce the gauge to match PRR. Oddly, in 1868 PRR widened their gauge to 4'9", a decision probably related to an attempt to mitigate car interchange with midwestern railroads employing wider gauges. It was not until August of 1892 that restoration to 4'8½" was completed throughout the PRR system.

While gauge is interesting, the deterioration of iron rail was important. Cast iron is hard but brittle. Wrought iron is flexible but soft. By the mid-1850s it was estimated that fully half of all train wrecks were caused by broken iron rail. Steel rail, both hard and flexible, was the obvious answer but the cost of crucible steel was astronomical. Thomson succeeded in getting tonnage volume on his railroad but the traffic was literally pounding the railroad to pieces.

Then in 1856 a Briton, Sir Henry Bessemer, developed his famous converter and the cost of steel dropped. Needless to say, the British would export steel but not technology. Andrew Carnegie, one of Thomson's many proteges, took his famous trip to Britain and was allowed to observe the process but not given any details. Carnegie returned and reported, feeling that we can figure out a way to do it ourselves. Thomson, an adherent of the doctrine that pioneering does not pay, was convinced and a steel industry was born centered on Johnstown and Pittsburgh. By 1868 the open-hearth process of taking pig iron and converting it into steel became workable and rapidly replaced the Bessemer method.

While the price of steel was still four times that of iron, the durability was so much greater that Thomson became a "steel rail, stone ballast" champion and continued to build his railroad so that it would become the standard against which all railroads would be measured.

Our book *West End* (Barnard, Roberts & Co. 1991), the story of B&O's conquest of the barrier, was advertised with the headline "no mountain railroad in the world combined grades, curves, tonnage and weather like B&O's West End".

Having now been a student of PRR's conquest of the barrier for some years, we will not take back a word of that statement but will provide the reader with another one.

"No railroad in the world has conquered a mountain barrier with more efficiency and handled such incredible tonnage than PRR's Pittsburgh Division." The West End is a shadow of it's former self. Pittdiv remains the world's busiest mountain railroad as it has been throughout history and will almost certainly remain so in the future.

In a 1957 article in *Trains*, the awe-struck author was impressed by "the immensity of it all." We can assure the reader that nothing has changed since 1957 or, for that matter, 1854.

This chapter, of course, concerns the east slope. For all its charms, problems and hazards, this piece of the Pittsburgh Division was always the easiest to operate simply because the enormous local traffic that burdened the rest of the division originated on the other side of the summit. To this extent, the east slope was similar to the West End where most of the traffic was through.

But before we go up the hill, let us reach back into early railroad history and set the stage with a review of the events that led to the creation of PRR. This is a subject that is awash in myths, heroes, knaves, fools and geniuses. It is also one of the greatest adventure stories in history.

As we make this passage, let us recall a description of the east slope written exactly a century ago: "In the early morning, as we ride westward from Altoona, the sun, breaking through the mists, weaves hundreds of fantastic and beautiful shapes on the mountain slopes, and gilds with its brush the distant peaks. The easy, graceful ascent, the triumph of engineering and artistic skill, is an unending source of pleasure and admiration to the traveler; and, no matter how often he repeats it, he always encounters something new in the scenery to delight him. And as he descends the mountain he sees a glory lavishly spent by nature, and here and there the Conemaugh appearing as a mirrored surface, sending upward from below the beauties of the hillsides or the swiftness of the passing train. There may be mountain scenery of far grander aspect; loftier hills with snow-capped peaks, deeper gorges and gloomier canyons; but none where sky, foliage and verdure combine with hill and stream in so many happy effects to produce the very poetry of mountain scenery!"

Thus the words of William Bender Wilson in PRR's 1896 history. One hundred and sixty-one words is worth a thousand pictures.

THE EAST SLOPE

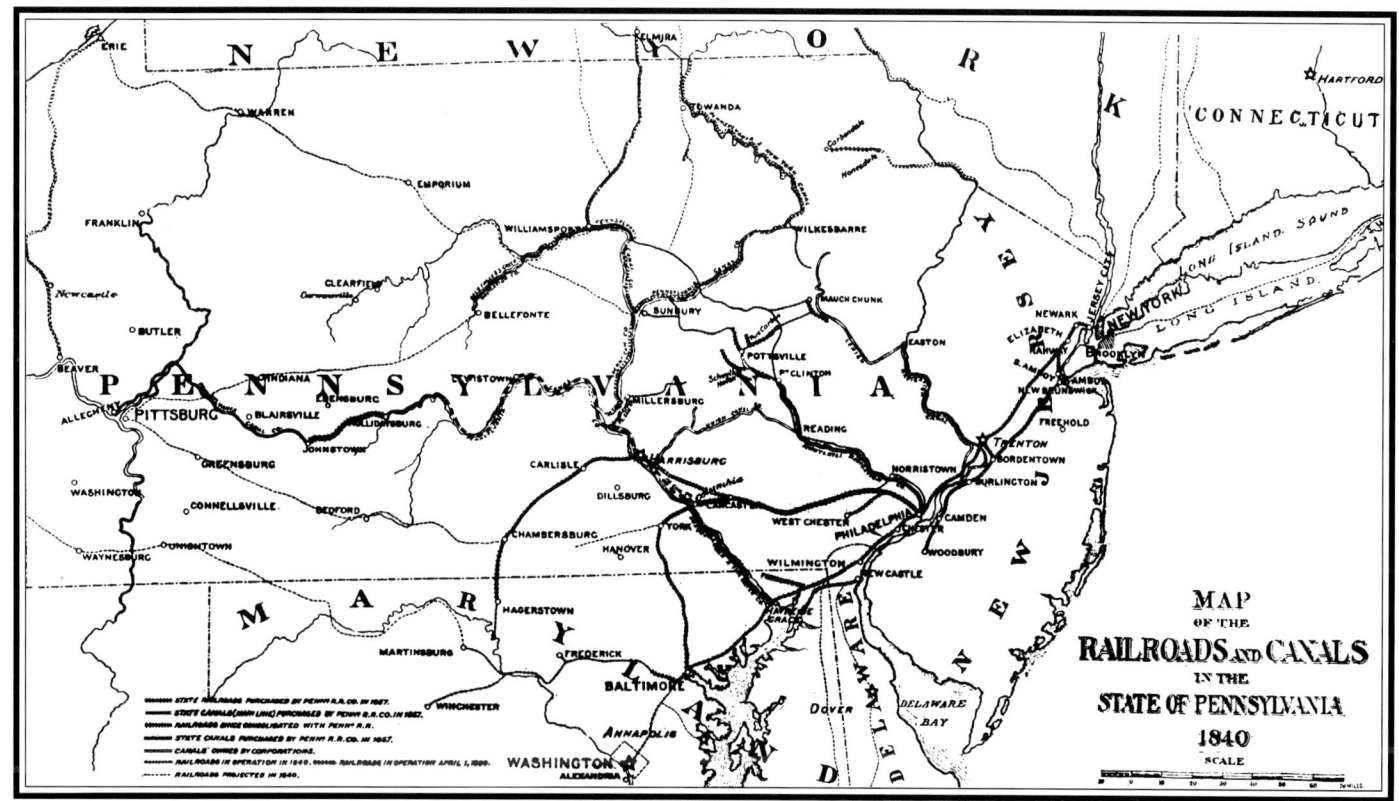

Hagley Museum and Library

THE MID-ATLANTIC transportation picture as it appeared in 1840...well, sort of. Actually, this map was prepared some fifty years later and was included in the little-known, unpublished "Watkins" history of PRR covering the first half-century of the railroad. John Elfreth Watkins was the author and he was obviously commissioned by PRR to do the work. Probably intended to be a three-volume history, it was set in type, complete with graphics, and proofs were distributed to a number of PRR executives. For various reasons, the history was never published and PRR went with William Bender Wilson's two-volume history.

This map, while useful to us as a foil to make some editorial points, is inaccurate in many ways. Nonetheless, the threat of B&O as perceived by Philadelphia was real and is manifest. B&O was chartered in 1827 and promptly received permission from both Virginia and Pennsylvania to build to the Ohio River at Wheeling following the "best route" roughly shown here. Both states granted B&O ten years to build their railroad. In 1837 both charters expired. B&O was stalled in Harpers Ferry (halfway between Frederick and Winchester) and the railroad between that place and Baltimore was a wreck. This description was charitable. B&O was the pioneer, but it paid a terrible price for its boldness. A Railroad Convention was convened in Harrisburg in early 1838 to consider renewal of B&O's charter and other internal transportation matters. Pittsburgh and Wheeling were fierce rivals, each determined to dominate trade with the midwest. Both were pro-B&O, Wheeling because B&O was its best hope and Pittsburgh because they were disgusted with the bumbling of the rest of Pennsylvania. The upshot was that both charters were renewed for another ten years, but each had the provision that Pittsburgh and Wheeling be *sole* termini of B&O. Poor B&O, from its very inception, wanted to build *only* to Wheeling for very cogent reasons. For B&O in that era, Pittsburgh was a gateway to nowhere and the evidence was overwhelming that they could never be competitive in that market no matter what Pennsylvania might do in the future. B&O had originally agreed to build a *branch* to Pittsburgh from the Connellsville area, but even that was, in B&O's view, a major and expensive concession.

We have covered B&O's predicament in great detail in our book *Sand Patch/Clash of Titans* and can assure the reader that these conflicting provisions put B&O in a very small box. They did the only thing they could do...concentrate on getting to Cumberland and worry about it then. One little bet was laid off...B&O put some money into a new railroad charter, the Pittsburgh and Connellsville, but did not want them to do anything rash like trying to build a railroad. Now back to this map, purporting to be the situation in 1840. It shows B&O in Martinsburg, a point not reached until August of 1842. Cumberland is not shown at all and the projected path of B&O goes to Uniontown when actually B&O's "best route" was to turn the corner at Connellsville and not touch Uniontown at all. Wheeling isn't even shown. Nor is the B&O branch to Pittsburgh. We can begin to see why PRR executives were dissatisfied with the Watkins manuscript.

TRIUMPH I

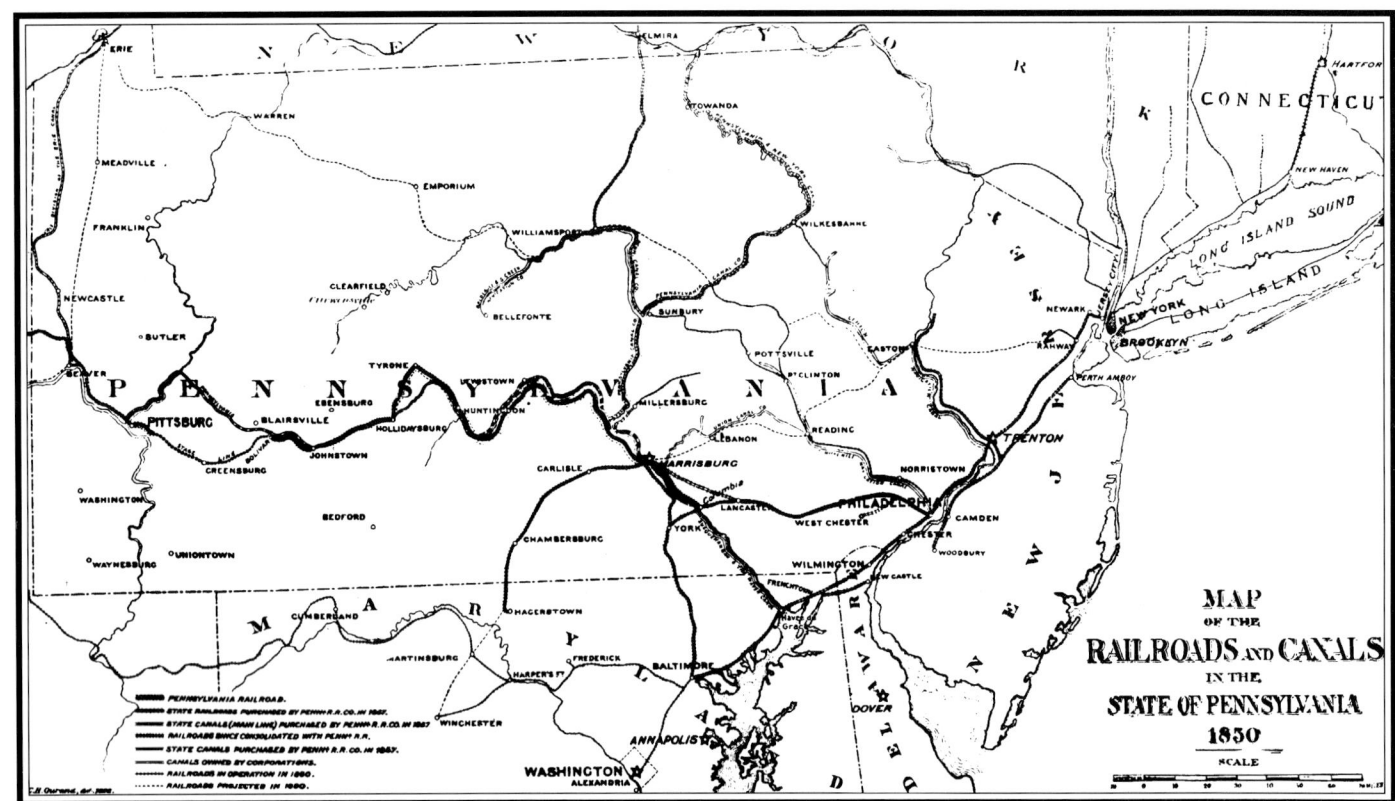

Hagley Museum and Library

TEN YEARS HAVE PASSED. A very eventful decade. In fact, in our view as an historian, the most pivotal ten years in the history of the Republic which in turn means the world. For it was in the 1840s that the decisions were made that laid the groundwork for the march of the nation to superpower status. It was not a tidy march of events, but it sure was exciting. The cast of characters reads like a Russian novel and we must confess that we are fascinated with the thought that one of our forebears was a leading actor. In one leap, B&O reached Cumberland by November of 1842. Pennsylvania was showing signs of panic and slashed State Works rates by some 25%, hurting B&O by reducing traffic received from the National Road but adding to already staggering state losses. Railroad construction was soaring and canal construction slowing. From Philadelphia's perspective, the heathens were now at the gate. Even Boston had a railroad. New York was beginning construction and, worst of all, these upstart Marylanders had actually gotten near the Pennsylvania border. New York and New Orleans had been gobbling their dinner for decades and now B&O was about to snatch lunch and breakfast while, incidentally, making some money in the process. What little prosperity they had managed to salvage was now in mortal danger. An emergency State Railroad Convention was called in Harrisburg for 14 January 1846. B&O's renewed charter was about to expire. Pittsburgh was adamant. B&O must build to Pittsburgh (or Brownsville on the Monongahela) period, no paragraph. No railroad to Wheeling which, by the way, also remained adamant that there would be no railroad to anywhere in Pennsylvania. Philadelphia was begging for a "Great Pennsylvania Rail Road" and girding for vote buying.

A true clash of titans with very high stakes and poor B&O the meat in the sandwich, forced to try to reason with several sets of village idiots. B&O could not convince any of the parties that the real enemy was not Baltimore, but New Orleans and New York. To no avail. In Richmond, controlled by fatcat plantationeers who were inclined to let those crude western Virginians do what they pleased so long as their legislators didn't linger in town too long, the situation for B&O at the moment was hopeless. One slim chance remained. If B&O could convince Pennsylvania that their best bet was to let B&O build to the Virginia border near Wheeling with or without a branch to Pittsburgh and then pressure Harrisburg to build their "Great Pennsylvania Rail Road", B&O might have a chance to persuade Richmond to let them cross to Wheeling. All sides were buying Pennsylvania legislators with abandon and privately admitted it. The machinations were byzantine and would have confused a Machiavelli. Even the bagmen were perplexed. A pro-B&O bill was defeated in the Senate on 23 February 1846 by *a single vote*. Three days later the Senate reversed itself and passed the B&O bill! Finally, on 10 April the House passed the B&O bill with some amendments which in turn passed the Senate and was signed by the governor on 21 April. The PRR bill was passed and signed on 13 April. PRR would be chartered if it could raise $3 million by 30 July 1847, of which a third must be paid in cash and if certain portions of the railroad were under contract by that date. With some difficulty and cliffhanging, Philadelphia met all conditions and on 25 February 1847 a charter was issued to PRR (it is reproduced in the back of this book). B&O's rights were declared null and void 2 August 1847. A little-noticed amendment was made to the Pittsburgh and Connellsville charter granting this railroad authority to extend its lines to the Maryland border near Cumberland. No authority was granted to go from Connellsville to Wheeling. Even the voided B&O bill contained the provision that Pittsburgh be the *sole* terminus of B&O. B&O had no choice but to build to Wheeling through Virginia and Maryland without touching Pennsylvania, a project that was widely regarded as absolutely impossible. Enter Thomas Swann and Benjamin Latrobe (one of the sons of his famous father), respectively president and chief engineer of B&O. To everyone's astonishment, including their own, they not only managed to finance and build to Wheeling but actually reached the Ohio River with a continuous railroad several months before PRR. Even Thomson was impressed. Pittsburgh interests, however, were enraged and vented their spleen against PRR, a bitterness that has endured to this day. PRR had a lock on Pittsburgh and milked it for all it was worth, a perfectly rational if brutal strategy but not one calculated to make friends. PRR shrugged, cried all the way to the bank, as the saying goes, and proceeded to build a transportation oligarchy that was, well, awesome. The linchpins in Thomson's philosophy were low cost and volume. The key to low cost was steady reinvestment in the railroad plant and to volume was to get an unshakeable grip on sources of traffic. As to cost, here is a precis of the situation at the end of 1854. Average cost per mile run on PRR - 7.05 cents; B&O - 8.97 cents; Erie - 10.30 cents. Of course, PRR had less miles to go to *any* significant destination. B&O achieved a miracle with their construction from Cumberland to Wheeling, but the piper was paid with high operating costs and longer mileage…the Erie, of course, should never have been built in the first place and in short order became a plaything of stock manipulators. Yes, a lot happened between 1840 and 1850 and with the benefit of hindsight it can be said that the nation as a whole was well served by Thomson and PRR. As to this map, the B&O wiggle from Cumberland west is inaccurate, Wheeling remains unnoticed and there is no Altoona. No map, however, could depict a thunderhead that was developing on the national horizon during the 1840s. Railroads had to have enormous tonnages of iron rail. Britain was by far and away the most efficient producer of rail and the domestic industry was not expanding at a rate to satisfy the demand. So the Federal government slapped a huge import tariff on British rail to protect and encourage production in the United States, which was another way of saving Pennsylvania because only the Commonwealth had the necessary natural resources readily at hand. The southern States also wanted to build railroads to more efficiently bring their food and fibre production to tidewater. They had no resources available to produce their own rail, but did have a highly favorable balance of trade with Britain which would enable them to easily purchase their needs. The import tax made the price outrageous and when they approached Pennsylvania producers they found that not only was the protected price cosmic, thanks to the tariff, but demand was exceeding supply and the needs of northerly railroads would be met first. The game, as Jimmy the Greek would word it in a later era, was fixed and the southerly States were the victims. This issue, among others also festering, began a process of resentment that ultimately tore the nation apart and triggered a War Between the States, to use the older form, that produced a bloodbath of historic proportions. And this convulsion resulted in cementing PRR as the dominant trunkline railroad in the nation. Quite a decade.

Proposed Routes of the Rail-road from Philadelphia to Erie and Cleveland.
EXECUTED UNDER THE DIRECTION OF THE CLEVELAND COMMITTEE.

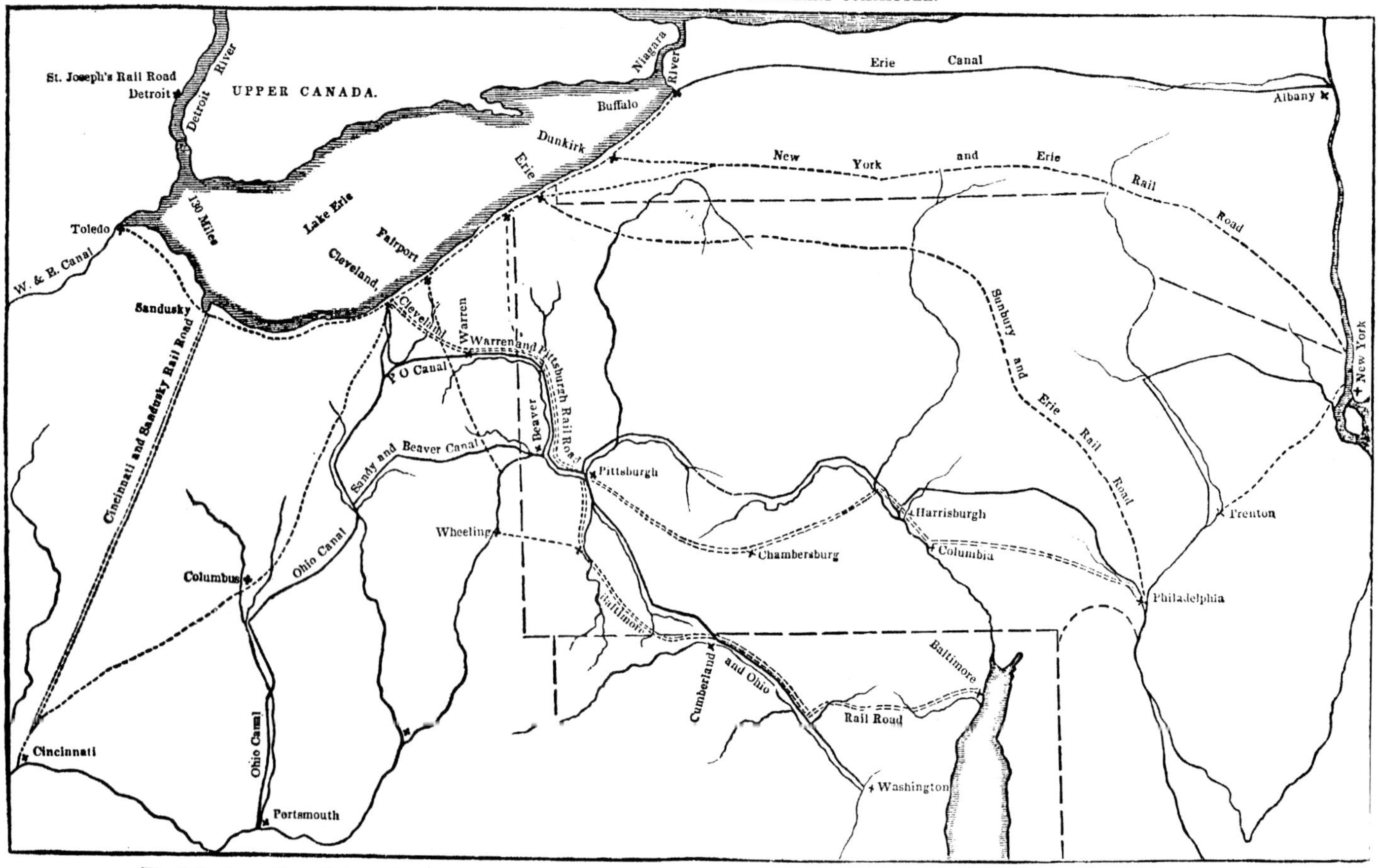

The following table will show the comparative distances of the contemplated communications from the seaboard, terminating upon Lake Erie.

Cleveland to Pittsburgh via Warren and Beaver...... 133 miles	Cleveland to Dunkirk .... 160 miles	Distance from Cleveland to Baltimore via Pittsburgh, 360 miles
Pittsburgh to Harrisburgh via Chambersburgh 201	Dunkirk to contemplated point on North River....... 485	
Harrisburgh to Philadelphia .... 98—432	From this point to New York 24	
Philadelphia to New York 100		Distance from Cleveland to New York via Buffalo and Albany
Cleveland to New York 532	Cleveland to New York 669	706 miles.

THE 1838 RAIL-ROAD CONVENTION in Harrisburg produced a lot of rhetoric and little else except for this little gem of a map that graphically displays the situation as it appeared at that time. The purpose of the map, as the heading acknowledges, was to proselyte the interests of Cleveland. They had concluded that their future would be best served by a railroad through central Pennsylvania and that entrance to New York should be the focus, with Philadelphia and Baltimore being sideshows. They were thinking clearly in Cleveland...notice that they had written-off the State Works from Harrisburgh (sic) to Pittsburgh as an obvious failure and proposed a route through Chambersburg as the answer. In the later case, of course, they were wrong but it would be several years before Schlatter's surveys would be completed and they can be pardoned for thinking that anything would be better than the State Works. This map should be studied by the serious student of this era in transportation history. There are all sorts of jewels resident therein.

THE EAST SLOPE

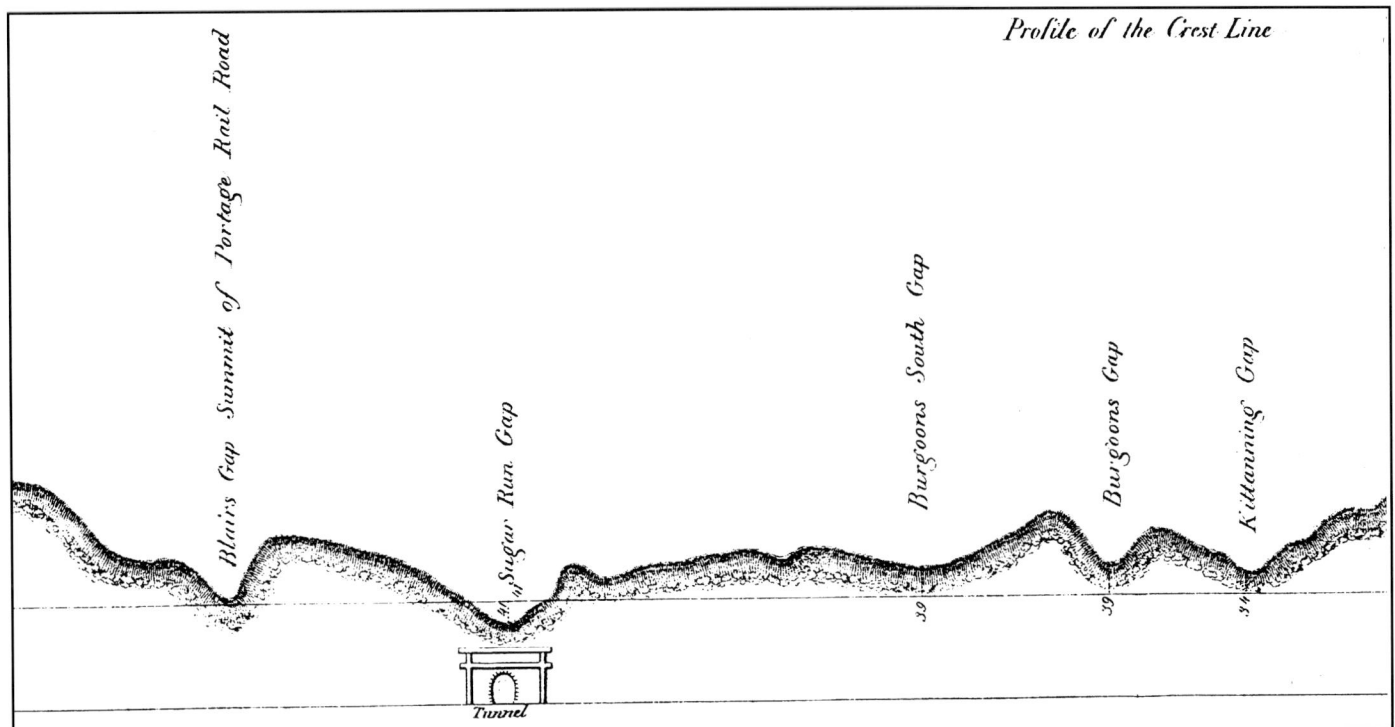

THOMSON'S VERY FIRST annual report as chief engineer of PRR was made on 12 June 1848 and upon completion of our first reading of this trenchant presentation we could immediately see why this man had all the inherent qualities needed to take him to the heights of achievement. In a mere 32 pages, and small ones at that, Thomson exhibited a firm grasp of detail, vision, reasoning and gentle persuasion, all given in a smooth prose that would have marked him as a man of letters had he chosen that profession. Devoid of the parlance that lesser men would have employed to make their case, this document is of such historical importance that we have reprinted it in full in the back of this book. Accompanying this report was a four-foot wide Profile of the Crest Line of the Allegheny Mountains that displayed seventeen gaps in a 44-mile swath from Cedar Spring Gap on the southwest to Three Springs Gap on the northeast. Since this profile is simply too large to effectively reproduce in a book this size, we have chosen to present that section pertinent to the construction of the east slope railroad.

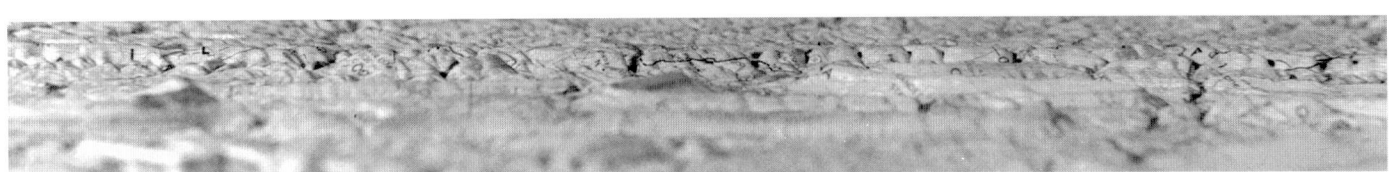

WE HAVE TRIED to give the reader another perspective on the great barrier, this time by photographing the Army Map Service relief map with only the barrier in focus. The width in this case is about 55 miles with Sugar Run Gap the dark swath precisely in the middle…the view, of course, is from the southeast and, we remind the reader, the vertical exaggeration is three to one. Even from "outer space" the Allegheny Front appears to be mild.

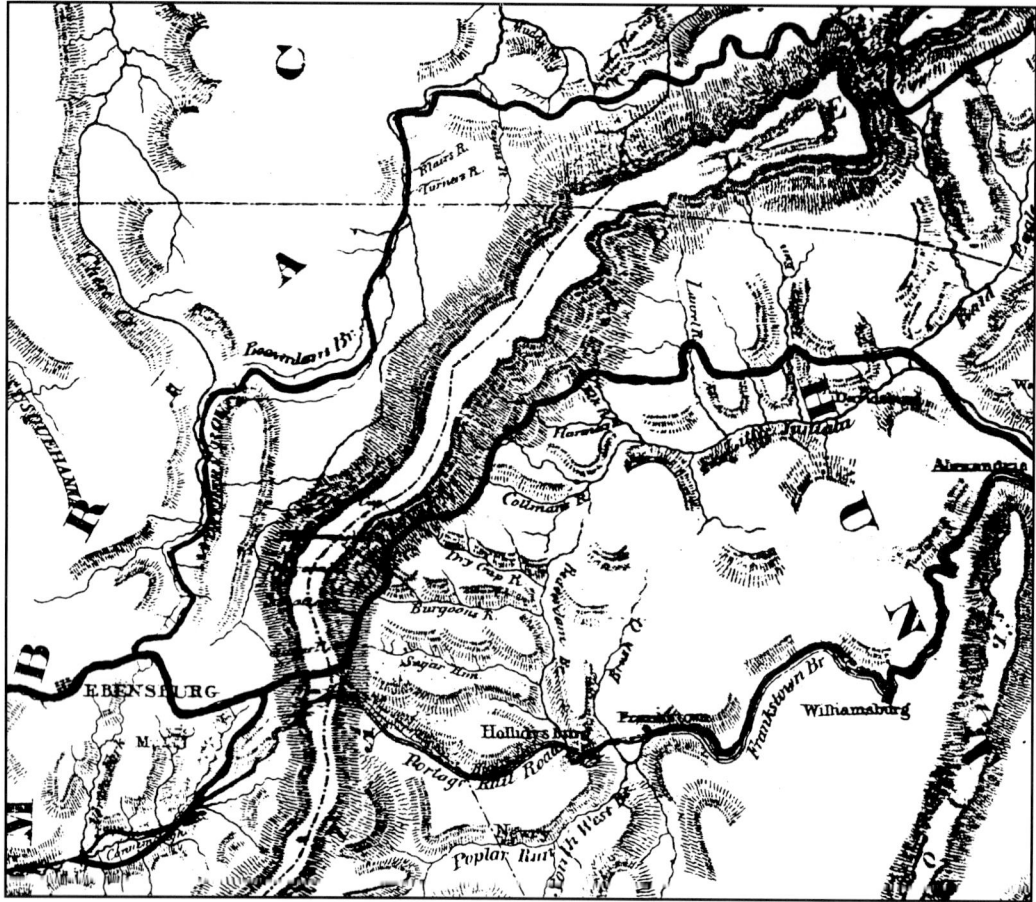

CHARLES L. SCHLATTER was one of those figures in history who appeared from nowhere, made their mark and then disappeared. Apparently born in 1807, location unknown, he was hired by the Canal Commissioners in 1839 to do his famous survey to determine if it was practical to build a continuous railroad from Harrrisburg to Pittsburgh without the use of inclined planes. That he was sometimes referred to as "Colonel" is not an appellation that would earn approbation from this author, whose opinion of self-appointed officers who never ventured anywhere near where loud noises predominate is something less than high. There is no record of his education at West Point, for the first fifty years of the last century the only engineering school in the nation, nor is there any record of prior employment by the State of Pennsylvania. After completion of his project, he apparently moved to New York and in 1855 to Georgia, in each case working as chief engineer for minor railroads. He died in Georgia in 1886. For all that, this non-entity did a job that has been described as "guided by a fine intelligence, high professional standards and an understanding of the engineering economics of railroads that would have done credit to many of his successors." Our interest here is his proposed assault on the Great Barrier, the "Middle Route" of his three approaches. He was constrained to keep the gradient on all possible routes to about 0.85% westbound. On the southern route, that was impossible; on the northern route possible but involving a path of such length that it was impractical. As we can see here on this section of the map that he submitted with his report, the only way to keep the grade down would be to slowly climb the Allegheny Front and punch through at Sugar Run Gap. The reader can easily see that this "slow climb" (the middle dark line beginning at Alexandria on the right edge) would involve heavy curvature, all too many deep cuts and fills and a number of large viaducts to cross at least fourteen streams lying at right angles to his approach. And this was to say nothing about similar problems *east* of the area shown on this map. To be fair to Schlatter, he was told to keep the grade at a certain minimum and he came up with a way to do it. When Thomson came on the scene, he could immediately see that it didn't make sense to invest a huge amount of money to ease the westbound grade when the whole point of building the railroad was to get eastbound tonnage. Surely he must have thought (but was diplomatic enough not to say in his first annual report) that here was still another example in Pennsylvania history of politicians and lawyers passing judgements on matters about which they knew nothing, a tendency all too prevalent in the history of the Commonwealth in the first half of the last century. This tendency had literally bankrupted a State that should have been the most prosperous in the nation. Thomson decided to do something about it and he did. His first step was to do the obvious…build an economical waterlevel route from Harrisburg west to a place on the valley floor soon to be named Altoona and then assault the east slope head-on, adding helper engines for the short shove up the hill. As to this map, the upper dark line represents the west end of Schlatter's northern route, which broke through the gap at upper right and ascended the barrier on its western slope to a point just east of Ebensburg. The reader should also note that Schlatter proposed two possible routes to descend the west slope, a matter to be discussed in the next chapter.

THE EAST SLOPE

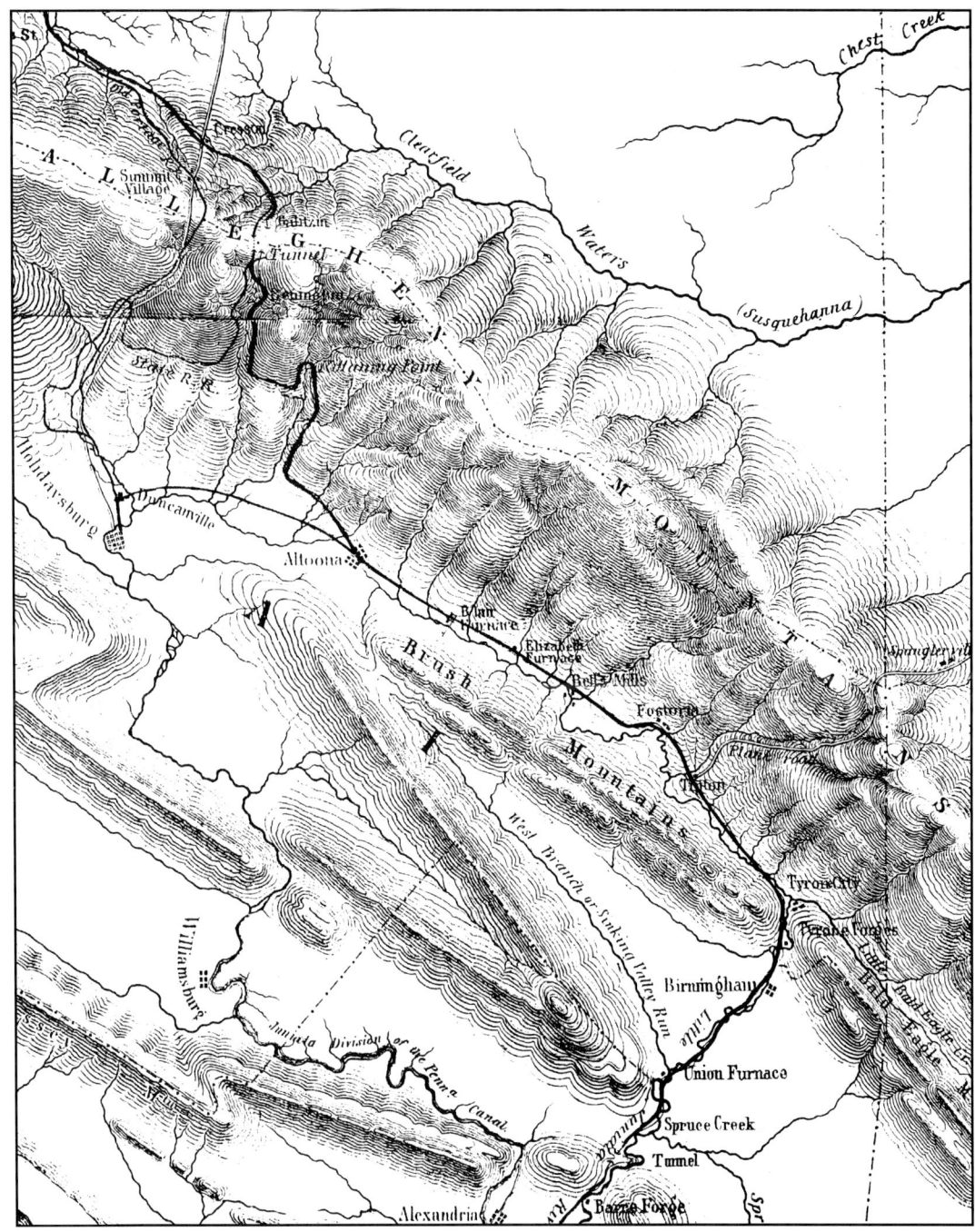

WHAT A DIFFERENCE fifteen years makes…the reader should compare this 1855 map with the preceding one. PRR as built followed the valley, eschewing the mountain slope, and a bevy of new towns had sprung up along the railroad. Obvious from their names, most of these towns boasted iron furnaces taking advantage of local ore deposits. The wood for charcoal and coal for coke, however, had to be hauled east over Allegheny Mountain. Note the plank road out of Tipton; it was built to haul lumber to the town and it was rumored at the time that there might be coal on the other side of the hill. And Altoona appears. Just four years before one lone log cabin marked the spot and it was said in 1855 to still be standing by the railroad. Another innovation from Schlatter's map was the use of contour lines, although there is a lot of reason to believe most of them were the product of guesswork. So was the spelling of a lot of place names. One name was correct, however…Fostoria was named for William B. Foster, Jr., vice president of the railroad at the time. By the way, Herman Haupt was chief engineer in 1855, another name that would take a prominent place in railroad history. The east slope west of Altoona appears to be located rather accurately, but it is the clarity of stream location at the summit that attracted our eye. The eastern waters begin well to the left of Gallitzin and the western waters at Summit Village and Cresson which means that the actual summit runs at a right angle to Allegheny Mountain. The approximate location of the real summit is marked by the turnpike known as Old Route 22, a road that did not appear at all on Schlatter's map, and at the time it was known as Laurel Swamp Summit.

TRIUMPH I

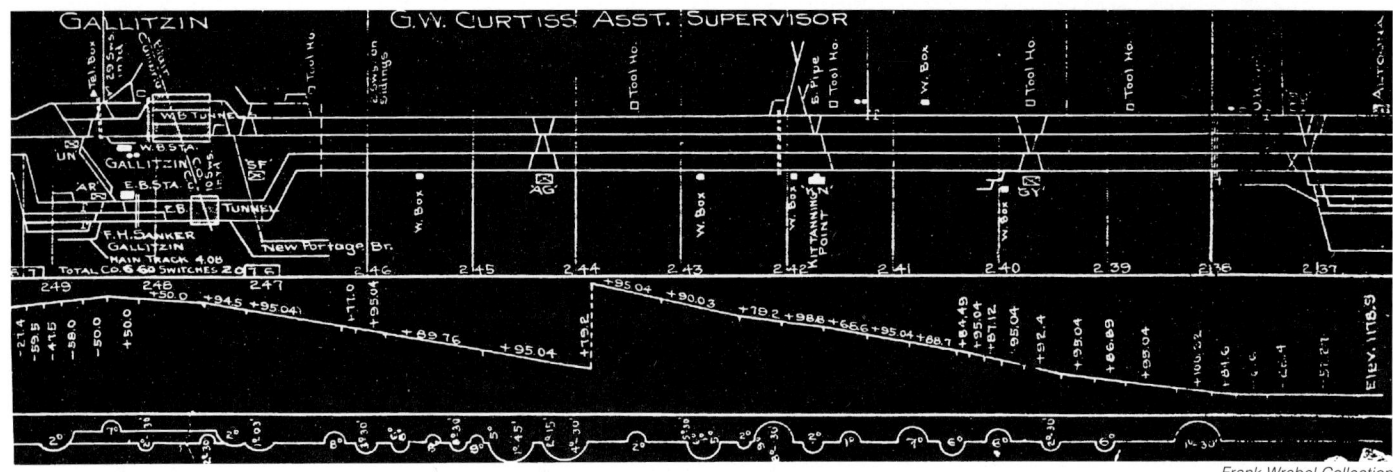
Frank Wrabel Collection

FROM 1855 TO 1910, when this track chart was published, the face of the east slope had gone from two tracks to six including the New Portage Branch, PRR had moved from challenger to supreme power, the physical plant from superior to magnificent and the traffic from dense to unbelievable. Yet for all this, the basic profile was substantially the same as when the east slope was constructed as, indeed, it is today. As we go from right to left on this chart, let us point out that Milepost 238 has traditionally been the boundary between the Pittsburgh and Middle Divisions and has always marked the beginning of the grade. Altoona itself and the latter division will be treated in another book and inclusion here is merely as a reference point. In 1910, interlockers were located at call letters GY, KN, AG and SF on the slope and AR and UN at the summit. There were five watchboxes en route and three tunnels at the summit...the middle one is the original PRR bore. One tradition has remained from the earliest days of railroading in that gradient was measured in feet per mile rather than as a percentage. A sidenote...PRR engineers had not gotten around to tracing a profile to incorporate the New Portage tunnel and line, an oversight that makes the summit crossing appear a lot better than the reality.

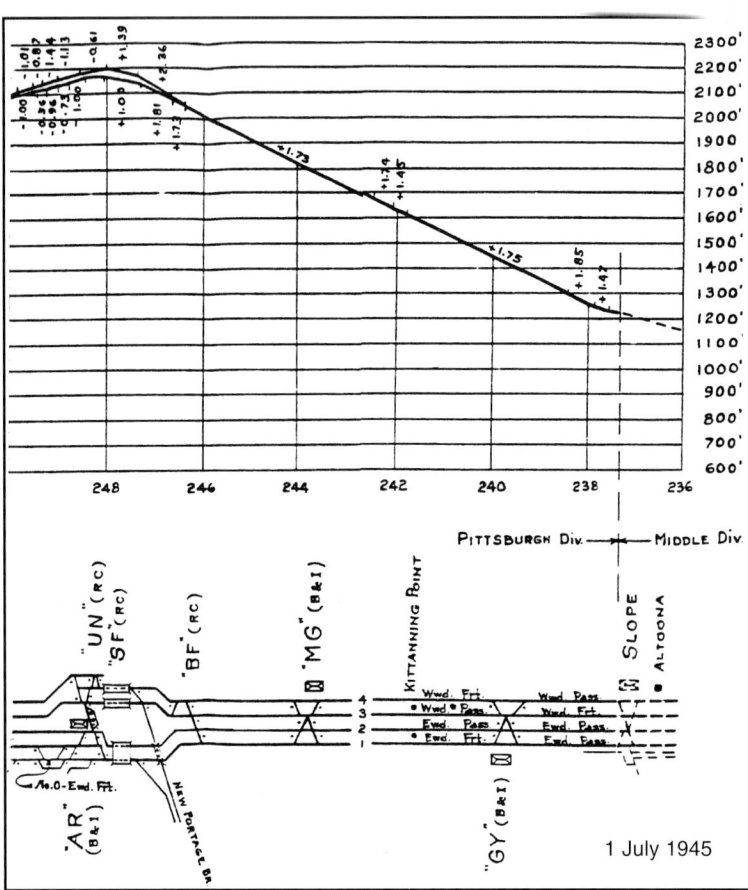

IN THE THIRTY-FIVE YEARS from 1910 to 1945, an exciting third of a century by any standards, very little of significance had changed on the east slope. Gradient was measured by percentage and that brutal 2.36% dropoff known as "The Slide" appears on the profile just east of the New Portage Tunnel, the southernmost bore. Of course, it has always been there as the crews were painfully aware. As a B&O student we cannot resist pointing out that the West End's Cheat River and Seventeen Mile Grades have over twenty miles of two-percent plus "slides", with crews desperately holding back heavy eastbound tonnage and not always with success. Worse, Seventeen Mile Grade has the Swanton Flat about a third of the way down, which is a very serious complication. Not so PRR's east slope. If the train is under control at the top, the rest of the way down is easy on an even slope without exception or wiggles. Between Mileposts 238 and 247 the profile is ruler-straight without flatspots. For those who are puzzled by the preceding sentences, let us explain that freight train air brakes can be gradually *applied* but cannot be gradually *released*. They go off all at once and it is an eternity before the system is recharged and they can be reapplied...a literal eternity for the hapless crew with a runaway. In B&O's case with the Swanton Flat, if the engineer makes too heavy an application at the summit the train will come to a stop on the flat. A release is out of the question. Cars must be braked-down by hand in sufficient numbers to keep the train under control when the release is made. This is not a problem for PRR on the east slope nor, as we shall see, on the west slope. This aspect of the design of the east slope was a

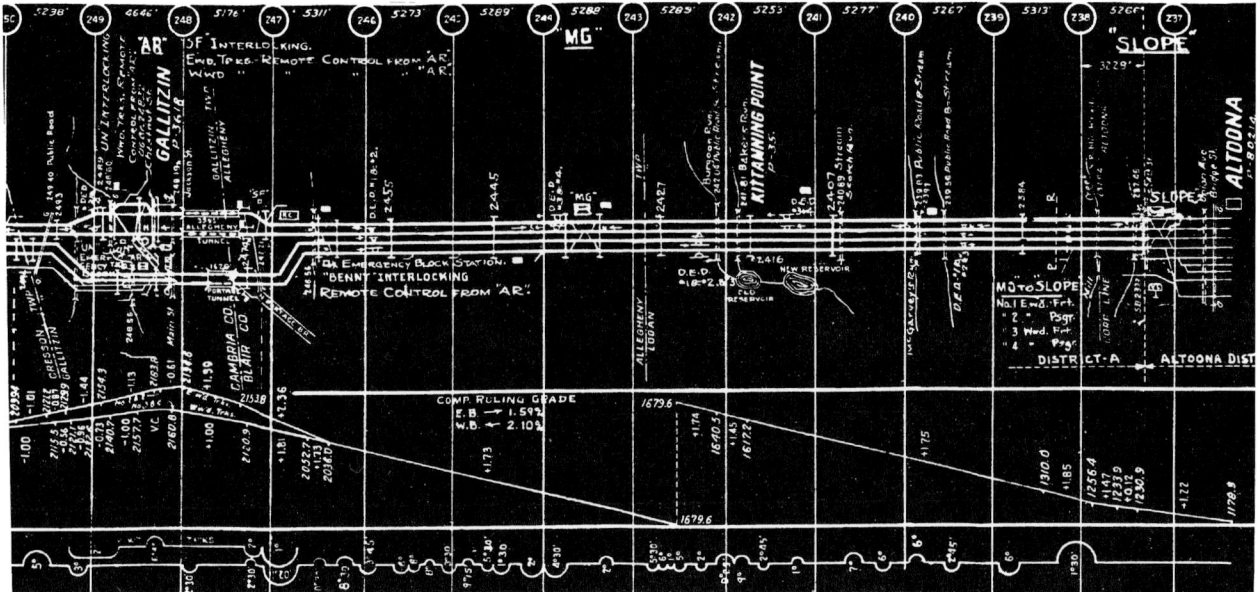

THE MORE THE EAST SLOPE CHANGES, the more it is the same. By 1958 GY was gone and there were no interlockers between SLOPE and MG. Dragging Equipment Detectors (D.E.D.) have appeared on Tracks 1-2-3 at Mileposts 239.3, 242.3 and 246…on Tracks 3-4 at 241.3, 243.9 and 249. Signal bridge locations have been added. The track numbers remain the same, although the draftsman decided to confuse the issue by listing them from top to bottom. The reference to the call letters MO alludes to an interlocker on the west slope just off the track chart to the left, a tower to be covered in the next chapter. That draftsman did decide, however, to name the tunnels. From top to bottom, Gallitzin Tunnel (the last to be built); Allegheny Tunnel (the first); Portage Tunnel. Notice that the Ruling Grade westbound is 2.10%. By the 1950s, westbound imported iron ore was moving to Pittsburgh steel mills from Philadelphia, naturally in trains of maximum length, and we assume this meant that a given train was stretched over more curvature, causing a higher ruling grade. Of course, the whole point of railroading has always been to increase car miles and decrease train miles. In our research, we have noticed that latterday commentators have suggested that Thomson might have located the east slope differently had he known that train length would increase and some heavy westbound tonnage materialize. Just how he was supposed to do that little thing, even assuming he was clairvoyant, always remained unanswered. Remove several mountains? In any event, none of his successors changed a thing on the east slope which tells us that he did the best possible job the first time.

valuable gift by Thomson to PRR and more impressive because air-braking would not be widely available for another half-century. We do not know if he had the descent problem in mind when he plotted the east slope or whether it was merely a byproduct of his concern for eastward movements, but the net result was a plus for PRR. While on this subject, let us emphasize that east slope descent has always been and will always be a dangerous game even without flatspots. In the steam era, a proper application at the summit was not a free ticket to the bottom. Trainline air leakage could stall the train during the descent. To overcome this problem, cycle braking was used. With this method, the train stops at the summit and retainers (which retain, or hold, the brakes applied) are setup on an appropriate number of cars. Then, during the descent, the train brakes are cycled on and off. While the train brakes are off and the system is being recharged, the cars with the set retainers hold train speed in check. As to trainline leakage, the pressure-maintaining braking system was evolved in the middle of this century which automatically kept trainline pressure stable. A gift of the diesel era was the dynamic brake on power units, a system which converts traction motors to generators which in turn provides braking power. Retainers haven't been used for many years and the "stop at the top" is history. What is not history, however, is the runaway. An air-headed engineer, if you will pardon the pun, can go over the top without being sure that he has sufficient brakes and/or air pressure or without being positive that his dynamics are working. He has then, in the trenchant words of a PRR operating executive, "probably eaten his last meal." There are other hazards to downgrade movements, which we will relate in captions to follow. We must confess that we have a weakness for gallows and sardonic humor. We have this vision of a runaway leaving the railroad at Horseshoe Curve in front of or on top of scores of tourists whose tickets of admission did not mention this possibility. We all pray, of course, that this does not occur and relieve journalists of a slow news day. Since this has happened to your author, we hope all readers will hear our cry to stay well away from moving trains. There are easier ways to relieve the stresses of constipation. Back to our track chart, moving from right to left, GY is still active, KN gone, AG replaced by MG, BF installed but along with SF and UN remotely controlled from AR. The two inner tracks are superelevated for passenger trains east to GY, where the changeover is shown. There are three water standpipes between GY and Kittanning Point. Still another point for those who are new to PRR practice. The mainline line tracks are numbered from south to north without regard to current of traffic. PRR just had to be different.

TRIUMPH I

GATEWAY TO THE GATEWAY and one of the few survivors. For the moment. While never to our knowledge part of the Pittsburgh Division, since 7 June 1965 ALTO tower has been the last to be seen by westward crews leaving the Middle Division and about to begin the ascent of the east slope. There has been some sort of block station and crossover in this general area since the mid-1880s, but the structure shown here was reportedly built in 1915. Here, looking east, ALTO is seen on 29 May 1970...Penn Central era but PRR origins evident. ALTO is still active at this writing and Conrail stated in the Fall of 1995 that they have "no present plans" to close it.

Edward H. Weber

Dick Heiler Collection

BY AUGUST OF 1984, the outward appearance of ALTO has changed very little, but not so the background. A new highway bridge has missed the tower and a new highrise ponders the scene. ALTO, an electro-pneumatic facility typical of PRR interlocker preference, concentrates solely on the movement of trains.

THE EAST SLOPE

Railroaders Memorial Museum

A VERY SHORT distance west of ALTO the east slope begins in earnest, true in 1854 and true today. In this photograph, looking easterly about 1870, one can fuzzily see one of PRR's classic octagon towers to the left of the locomotive. The branch to Hollidaysburg veers off to the right just behind the small, squarish office to the right of the engine. In the Conrail era known as the Cove Secondary, this line has always been active and at one time reached as far south as Cumberland in Maryland. While the railroad is cinder-soaked, we are impressed with the rail…in perfect gauge and alignment without dips at the joints. The Thomson touch.

NO VALUATION PHOTOGRAPHER has ever been nominated for a Pulitzer and the one who took this shot of the 24th Street bridge c.1920 was all too typical of the breed. The tower faintly seen through the "fog" was BO built in 1888 as an interlocker. The bridge, by the way, marks the boundary between Middle and Pittsburgh Divisions. Interlockers *per se* were developed in the 1880s and PRR installed them with weed-like fervor…twenty-one built systemwide in 1888 alone.

National Archives

TRIUMPH I

Dick Heiler Collection

BO WENT AND SLOPE came in, following PRR practice of dropping call letters and renaming interlockers when CTC was installed. The date when this structure replaced the one pictured previously is unknown, although probably in the 1920s. Also unknown is when it was converted to CTC, which proved to be a death knell because it was all too easy to operate the interlocker remotely from ALTO. The date of the transfer we know exactly. It was 7 June 1965 when SLOPE became just another name along the railroad. We don't even know the date of this photograph, but it is obviously in the PRR diesel era when the keystone was still proudly displayed. The train, of course, is eastbound. Now we will turn westbound, leave the Middle Division and venture up the hill. The first step will be a long one.

THE VERY FIRST interlocker on the east slope was GY and apparently it led a very isolated existence. The only photograph we were able to locate was this valuation picture of an octagon structure and it was taken, so the label says, in 1920. The reason for this parcity is easy to understand. The stretch of railroad from the Pittdiv boundary to GY and beyond was wilderness when built and remains wilderness today, with no attractions to lure the curious. We did find a crude photograph of a westward view of the interlocker probably taken from the home signal and it showed a typical interlocker layout with a rectangular tower.

National Archives

THE EAST SLOPE

Hagley Museum and Library

PROBABLY TAKEN in the 1930s, this splendid photograph provides an excellent reference to one of the most historically significant sectors of any railroad ever built and a visual salute to Thomson's skill at locating a line of road. Following the line uphill from the bottom, the first curve passes over Scotch Run with a fill created with waste taken from the cut just beyond. Being of mostly Scottish descent, we will permit outselves an aside. Scotch is whiskey, Scots are people. Thus it should have been Scots Run Curve. Another, smaller fill becomes evident and then the line moves west with cut-and-fill to Kittanning Point (KN). This point is *not* the one at Horseshoe Curve, but rather the one to the right. Note that the station/tower at KN still stands. It was at this point that Thomson could have gone right. Note that the trace of a branch railroad is still evident. Horseshoe Curve is traversed, with huge fills on both ends. Notice another branch line going up what was known as Burgoon's (Gap) Run (later as Glen White Run). The reader will recall that Thomson could have gone up this run. There are cars on this branch which helps date it to the late 1930s. The line moves uphill with more cut-and-fill and a kink, with much of the fill appearing *not* to be at an angle of repose. This aspect of the line's location will be an unavoidable problem from the Curve all the way to the summit. The "four-tracking" of the east slope will be treated as we go but this photo makes evident that this project was easy construction from Altoona to KN and from there on was a monster. As to the lakes, the upper body is Kittanning Reservoir and the lower Lake Altoona. They were originally built by PRR to supply water to Altoona for shop and operational use in the steam era and, after the rise of the diesel, were sold to the City of Altoona. The signals are still semaphore and there are no trains in sight, a rare phenomenon for Pittdiv and visual evidence of the severity of the economic collapse of the Great Depression. KN is slightly short of the middle of the grade, a location that made it a vital operational facility for three-quarters of a century.

TRIUMPH I

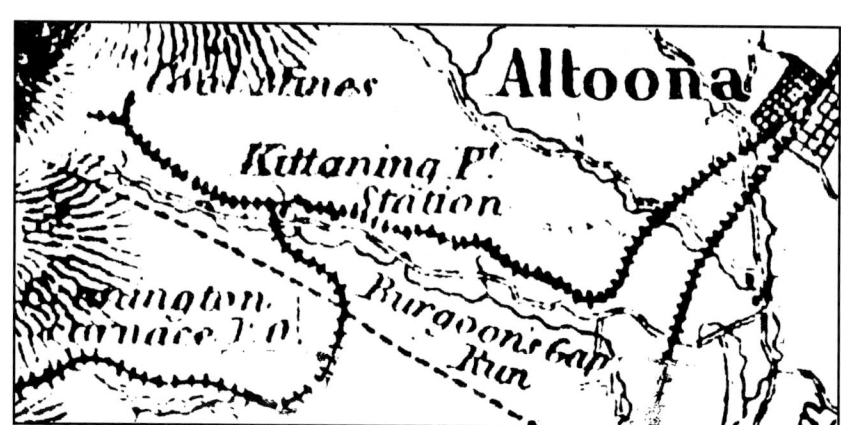

THIS 1872 MAP is included to note that the branch line from KN to some coal mines was in existence at that time.

IN ITS ANNUAL REPORT for 1864, PRR reported that a small station house had been constructed at KN and almost certainly this unknown artist's impression is of that structure. For reasons that will become apparent later in this chapter, the reader should keep that date in mind. No reference to a station at KN had been made prior to 1864 and it is obvious from this illustration that KN was a block station. PRR was inundated with Civil War and export grain traffic in the 1860-65 era and the need for block stations was urgent. Yet the most significant aspect of this nicely-done depiction is the rock structure at lower left. Docile in this scene, but not in real life.

Penn State University

THE EAST SLOPE

Railroaders Memorial Museum

THE EASY UPHILL passage on the east slope ended at KN, from both construction and operating standpoints. Every student of the east slope, including this writer, always assumed that the cut-and-fill at Horseshoe Curve was the major obstacle to Thomson's approach to the summit. Yet it was the massive spur of Kittanning Mountain that presented the most difficult obstruction. This photograph demonstrates the severity of the problem quite graphically...steep, high and unstable. In late 1852, the constructors bemoaned that the heaviest work that remained was "rock cutting, embankments and culverts" at KN. The deeper they blasted the higher it became and, unlike the Curve, the waste had to be moved west of the site in huge quantities to provide fill for the approach to the Curve, all pressing down on a culvert which in and of itself was a major construction project. At the Curve, most of the waste was simply blown straight downhill and a ledge formed that ultimately became a park. While this was not a minor operation, it was comparatively mild *vis a vis* KN. And then there was the operational problem of water supply. Steam locomotives have been aptly called "water burners." Water is heavy, flows downhill and was evaporated by steam locomotives in prodigious quantities, particularly on steep grades. Eastbound movements on the east slope did not work steam, but the westbounders sucked the tenders dry in short order. Where to add water? If one started west from Altoona with enough water to get to the summit, the weight would reduce payload dramatically and most of the water would be used to haul water. So water had to be replenished en route. On the east slope, the only practical location was KN. Where is the water coming from? The two streams at KN were far below track level and while it would be possible to pump water up, the pumps themselves would consume a large amount of water. As far as we can tell from the historic record, in the years 1854 to 1860, with very short and light trains, apparently enough water was added at Altoona to get past KN. In 1860, with a sudden upsurge in traffic and more powerful locomotives coming into service, PRR operating people were begging for water at KN. In 1861 the pleas were becoming shrill. Finally, in 1862 a 40-foot diameter reservoir was built at KN, probably fed from springs. Two plugs were installed, one at KN and the other 1,700 feet below, so two engines could take water at the same time. The story of water at KN did not end in 1862, as we shall see. Now to fuel. PRR began experimenting with coal in 1853 and by 1862 all freight locomotives burned coal...by 1864 *all* PRR engines were coal burners. If one is stopping at KN for water, it made sense to coal there also. Of course, coal was readily available at KN from nearby mines. So KN became the major east slope operating facility. But, as always, there was a nasty problem. Where is the room coming from? There was so little space that PRR had to string telegraph wire over the top of the spur.

TRIUMPH I

Gallitzin Area Tourist Council/T.C. Ketenheim Collection

TO ASSIGN A DATE to old photographs is both a burden and joy to historians, the joy emerging when a narrow time-frame can be deduced. The 751, the locomotive in the center of the scene, was reputedly built in 1865...the engine farther upgrade cannot be identified even under magnification. Of course, an octagon block station is apparent next to the station house, the latter known to have been built in 1864. The house just behind the 751 is obviously for the benefit of employees and even includes a fenced vegetable garden. All railroads provided living quarters for their people in remote locations. The big clue is the fan of the tracks, widening to the east. In 1869 a siding 1,800 feet long was built east of KN and the track relocation was done to accommodate it. Thus the probable date is circa 1870. The reader should also note that there is no crossover in sight and that the roadbed is in superb condition.

(Next Page)
PERSERVERANCE PAID OFF, for both the reader and one R.A. Bonine of Altoona when he climbed atop the cut over the Curve to take this fascinating photograph of the KN area. Time has not been kind to the image (which, incidentally, was used in a stereoscopic format) but the impact remains. We have studied this jewel under great magification and will assist the reader with observations moving from east to west. There are four tracks rounding the last curve east of KN. While this is *not* related to the "four-tracking" of the east slope, this view does demonstrate that this project was relatively easy east of KN. The four tracks pictured here were constructed to aid in the taking of water for westbound movements. One can barely see the 1862 reservoir on the hillside as the curve melds into tangent. The octagon tower and other structures are apparent. Just west of the tower can be seen the branch going up Kittanning Run. Note the structure above the roadbed with a short, steep entrance road...we suspect it is a sawmill. The massiveness of the fill and its huge culvert is apparent as is its inherent instability. No wonder this section of the east slope gave Thomson the most heartburn as indeed it gave his successors when they had to four-track through here late in the last century. There are two telegraph-pole lines, one dipping into the valley past the culvert and up to KN, the other on the north side of the mainline. There is no evidence of a coaling

THE EAST SLOPE

Pennsylvania State Archives

facility at this time, but plenty of evidence of heavy traffic. The eastbound track is brown with brakeshoe dust and the westbound white with sand, still another cross which mountain railroads have to bear. All this dust and grit interferes with drainage and hardens the substructure, requiring constant cleaning. At the very bottom of the photograph one can see a circular, stone-lined garden...a precursor of what would become a famous park. No dating joy here; we suspect late 1870s.

TRIUMPH I

Smithsonian Institution

THE PHOTOGRAPHER of this 1885 view was high in the air on something and we suspect it was the coal wharf which we will describe soon. Study the rock structure opposite the tower and then compare it to the first photograph in the KN series. A large amount of rock has been removed and this was done in 1868. This cameraman travelled in style — he had his own train. There is no crossover near the tower, but one under the train. One can faintly see the garden at the Curve and a path to it, although we don't see a road to the site. At far left the angle of the fill west of the Curve is very steep. At lower right one can see a fence line, apparently built to warn of rock slides.

Blair County Historical Society

THE SCENE AT KN changed dramatically in 1892…a new stone combination station and tower, along with a new freight house, were constructed and this photograph shows both in 1893. At this time KN was just a block station, not an interlocker. The branch line up Kittanning Run can be seen to the right of the freight station. A mail crane is evident between the photographer and the station; the slide fence, if that is what it is, is still in place. We suspect that this fence was an early electrical line that would signal a break and alert MOW people that there were rocks on the railroad. We will see more impressive installations of this genre later in the book.

THE EAST SLOPE

Dick Heiler Collection

WE KNOW THIS PHOTOGRAPH was taken no earlier than 1900 because it was in that year that the fourth track from KN west for 3.8 miles to Allegrippus (AG) was completed. The station-tower has to be one of the most unique architectural designs in history and we will be happy to defer artistic judgement to those historians who specialize in the subject. As we shall see, there were two additional towers built to this plan on the east slope (sans station), the next one at call letters IA west of the Curve, and at AG. At far left we see the first suggestion of an overtrack coaling facility, the first but not the last we will find on Pittdiv. There is a small car positioned on the bridge over the eastbound mainline track.

Railroaders Memorial Museum

A WESTBOUND passenger train pounds by KN with a clean stack and begins to roll into the Curve on a date known only to God. A signal bridge has been installed, but KN is still not an interlocker. We know that automatic signals were installed between Altoona and Gallitzin in 1900 and improved in 1914 so a guess that the date is circa 1910 is not unreasonable. We assume that this signal bridge and the signals on the coal wharf on the left were placed primarily to protect trains coaling and watering at KN.

TRIUMPH I

Dick Heiler Collection

SIMPLY BECAUSE we can see that replacement semaphore signals are being installed, it is easy to date this photograph c.1914. And for the first time we see the lead track from Kittanning Run to the coal wharf. The cars are lettered P.R.R. and are all wooden. Steel hoppers were in service by the tens of thousands by 1914, but older cars were used in company service until they fell apart.

Railroaders Memorial Museum

NOW WE SEE how the coaling system worked. On the trestle at upper right, coal was dropped and ultimately placed in small cars which in turn were pulled over the mainline tracks and dumped into tenders. The 1862 reservoir is still in service. Eastbound trains were serviced at KN in this era, taking both coal and water even though they would use neither in the descent. This procedure made operating sense…why haul coal and move water down to Altoona when it was available halfway up the east slope?

THE EAST SLOPE

Railroaders Memorial Museum/H.G. Colyer

A BRUSH FIRE was the proximate cause for the taking of this splendid photograph of the KN complex, thus proving the axiom that it is an ill wind that blows no good. The time frame is almost certainly the early teens of the twentieth century because the original signal bridge is in service. Note that there is a literal horseshoe at the Curve. The most fascinating aspect of this scene (at least to this historian) is something that has never been in sight. The reader will recall that, in an earlier chapter, we alluded to water availability at Mule Shoe Curve on the New Portage. This water came from Blair Gap Reservoir which to this day is located alongside Old Route 22 where the highway divides just before reaching the skewed bridge near the summit. This reservoir is 1,700 feet above sea level. KN is 1,600 feet above sea level. In 1903-05, PRR built the reservoir and then laid a twelve-inch gravity pipeline to KN where water was fed to locomotives from standpipes, thus solving the east slope water problem forever. Conrail sold all of PRR's former water facilities in this area to the city of Altoona in 1981. We do not know the path of this pipeline nor whether it is still in use, but its mere existence emphasizes how important and expensive water supply was in the steam era. A major benefit of dieselization was the elimination of this cost.

TRIUMPH I

Bob Lorenz Collection

PRR's CROSSING of the Barrier may have been all-weather, but there were times when it did not seem so. This bitter scene at KN on 24 January 1936, with a brakeman protecting the rear of his passenger train, illustrates that a railroad career was not all roses and sunny skies. PRR is, however, open. The station doesn't appear to be. We do not know when KN went from block station to interlocker, but we do know that the interlocker was out-of-service on 27 March 1921 and the switches removed in February of 1922. These switches were the ones east of the station seen in photographs in this chapter. Formal abandonment was authorized by PRR's Board on 26 June 1929. The station itself remained open until 1935 to serve the coal mining community up the Kittanning Run branch. In 1940, with the mines having been closed for several years and there being no need for passenger service, the station was closed. On 22 July 1940 an Authority For Expenditure (AFE) in the amount of $887 was requested to remove the station because it was becoming an eyesore "not in keeping with the scenic beauty" of the area. An article in *TRAINS* magazine, issue January 1941, contained a photograph of the station taken a few months earlier. We assume the station was razed in 1941. The reader, of course, will decide whether KN station was a jewel or grotesque. It was certainly different.

THE EAST SLOPE

Dick Heiler Collection

THE READER WILL RECALL that as early as 1872 there was a branch from KN to some coal mines up Kittanning Run. The earliest name that we have been able to apply to this line was the Altoona Coal and Coke Company, an unincorporated entity. The branch ran 4.6 miles to "Coupon," a town mentioned on a relief map earlier in this chapter. This photograph, which appeared in the *Altoona Gazette* in May of 1899, purports to show a train on that railroad, although the lettering on the tender is obviously retouched. It has been reported that there were four switchbacks on the line and, indeed, we have seen a photograph of one of them. It was said that loaded cars were wildcatted downgrade. One wonders if any of them entered PRR's mainline at KN. If so, the day was a long one. On 5 February 1905 the line was incorporated as the Kittanning Run Railroad and it's charter allowed it to go west another 5.6 miles from Coupon, although this extension was never built. In the 1900-1910 era the line produced about 30 hoppers of coal a day, much of it no doubt used by PRR at KN. The track was removed in 1917, although it was probable that PRR maintained a short stretch of track from KN for set-off purposes. We suspect that the tunnel portal seen at far left is a mine entrance. The "town" seen here is all too typical hardscrabble, yet for the times better than no town at all. All the known power was ex-PRR. This particular engine appears to be a Class I Consolidation (later H) with a straight stack and airpump.

IN 1941, during the last summer before the War, Milton A. Davis visited the east slope and one of his stops was KN. Here he caught a westbounder rounding the point with an Ils "Hippo" Decapod making "Number Ten Smoke" big time as an eastbounder grinds downgrade. A standpipe, or penstock if you will, appears just to the left of the cabin car on the descending train. There are two more standpipes between track numbers three and four out of sight behind the Hippo. A good case could be made that the Hippos were a PRR motive power mistake, yet your author must confess that they fascinated him simply because the last steam locomotive he saw in active service was an Ils on a branch somewhere south of this location in the mid-1950s. They were fat, ugly, hard-riding and the crews hated them. Yet for all that, at least to this writer they gave an impression of brute strength unrivaled by any other steam locomotive he ever saw.

Milton A. Davis

TRIUMPH I

SAME SPOT, SAME TIME. M1 6867 and a sister M1a doublehead a westbound manifest around KN...Mountains meeting Mountains, as it were. Both locomotives boast long-distance tenders, reflecting the fact that more modern steam locomotives used less water hauling water than they used in re-starting after a water stop. There was no free lunch, however. Longer tenders meant longer turntables.

Milton A. Davis

SAME TRAIN, THE OTHER END. Two on the front and two on the rear. I1s 4527 and mate try to crush an N5 cabin car against a very heavy train on a very heavy grade passing KN.

Milton A. Davis

THE EAST SLOPE

Milton A. Davis

SAME DAY, ANOTHER TRAIN, A NEW SIGNAL BRIDGE. PRR began development of its position light signal system in 1915 and eventually the new system was installed at KN, although we don't know when. The two right-hand targets are facing across the bowl of the Curve to give descending trains on the other side an "early warning" indication.

TRIUMPH I

Hagley Museum and Library

THE PROBABLE DATE for this view is the late 1930s...the KN station/tower is still standing and the connecting railroad at the bottom is still active. The latter was operated by the unincorporated Glen White Coal and Lumber Company based, curiously enough, in Baltimore. This line's origins are obscure, the earliest reference being the purchase in 1879 of a new 0-4-0 named "Irene" from the Baldwin Locomotive Works. The line ran two miles upstream to a company town named, naturally, Glen White where a tipple and coke ovens were operated and there was a lot of activity reported in the early 1900s, including the opening of a drift mine about a quarter of a mile from PRR's mainline in 1901. In the 1920s the line was extended another mile and a half to some clay pits. More interesting, a 36-inch narrow-gauge line ran from the tipple at Glen White to meet some planes which in turn brought coal downhill...shades of the Portage Railroad. Power was a mixture of ex-PRR engines, narrow-gauge locomotives and at least one Shay. By 1919 the firm employed 138 men and 25 boys under 16 and the town boasted a population of almost 200 souls. All this activity resulted in a name change; Burgoon Run became Glen White Run. Thus another little railroad wound its way west from the Curve. Nothing remains of the town or the railroad, which was torn up in 1943. This perspective gives the reader a seldom-seen view of the west side of the fill over the Run as well as a glimpse of the large culvert that was required. Also note that there is a spur on the west, or right, side of the fill. We guess that this was a PRR spur used to dump cinders and drainage-ditch tailings. In 1910 it was listed as a Shop Car track. The road that runs up the valley to the Curve area was first macadamized in 1932 and a guest house was built below the Curve with Federal "New Deal" money in 1940...just in time for the War and gasoline rationing. The park at the Curve is apparent. There are one eastbound and two westbound trains in sight, one of the latter taking water at KN with the road locomotive cut-off from it's train. When PRR began "four-tracking" the east slope, it was comparatively easy to swing from hillside cuts to valley fills from Altoona to KN as this photograph makes manifest. At KN, however, the going got rough.

THE EAST SLOPE

Hagley Museum and Library

ANOTHER PERSPECTIVE of the Curve area from a different angle, this photograph was probably taken in late 1940 several years after the preceding one. At lower right we see that the spur is no longer used as a dump and, indeed, trees are growing on the slope. PRR is now adding to the big fill west of the Curve and a ballast car is sitting on the "Glen White" wye. Many autos are parked in the lot below the Curve, a sure indication that the date was before 7 December 1941 and the onset of gasoline rationing. The KN station/tower is still there and farther down the slope a westbound road engine is making Number 10 smoke. Now let us go back to the ground and about eight decades earlier.

Dick Heiler Collection

TO KILL A MYTH is always a pleasure to an historian, a visceral reward for objective research. This photograph has been touted in many books and articles as being taken at the Curve and being the first ever taken. (To be fair, another historian did have doubts.) It could not possibly have been taken at or anywhere near the Curve. First, the rock strata in the cut is inclined upward to the right. Curve rock strata is inclined oppositely. Second, the presence of trees and underbrush to the left of the locomotive is an impossibility on the west end of the Curve in this era. And the photograph could not have been taken at KN because the mainline curved the other way.

Railroad Museum of Pennsylvania

THE CROWN JEWEL of this chapter, and perhaps the entire book, is this astonishing photograph of the Curve taken at a date so early that it is almost certainly the oldest of all. To call it historically significant is to indulge in understatement. In one glance the observer can see how Thomson and his men created the Curve. It establishes beyond question that the original location of the curve itself was well *east* of it's final path. Thomson simply dug or blew into the mountainside (in two excavations) just deep enough to provide sufficient fill to carry the roadbed...note that there is no ledge at all between the easternmost rail and the drop-off. Further, the railroad was open for traffic before the excavations had even reached the underlying rock that became the trademark of the Curve. Put differently, the original shape of the Curve was not a horseshoe but rather like a flat tire. Look at the boulder in the left excavation...Thomson simply bypassed it. The only thing Thomson pulled down was overburden...when he got to rock he let it lay, going up the hillside to get more earth. Of course,

THE EAST SLOPE

Michael G. Farrow Collection

IF THE PRECEDING photograph is our crown jewel of east slope history, this reproduction of a postcard is in strong second place. Even though the card itself was not published until the early 1900s, the original photograph was taken much earlier. There is no reservoir (1862) or station (1864) at KN. At KN one can faintly see the residue of the cut on the valley side pictured in the last photo. The hillside slash in the KN area is very raw with no apparent brush growth. This view, incidentally, illustrates just how much rock had to be removed at KN. Now to the Curve. There is no underlying rock in sight…thus this photograph was taken after the two excavations just shown were made continuous by removal of the center overburden. There is no ledge at the park, but there is evidence of some brush growing close to the tracks. Remember the trackage kink west of the Curve seen in some aerial views? There is no kink in this photograph. As Thomson and his engineers dug deeper into the hillside to lessen curvature, the radius of the curve was inevitably increased. On the east side this was accommodated by simply adding fill up Kittanning Run and moving the start of the curve at KN eastward. On the west side, however, it was necessary to cut deeper into the hillside and then swing back to move into the curve shown at lower left, thus creating a kink. To have gone deeper into the hillside would have required a slice almost as high as the one at the Curve for no real gain…after all, the kink is still there. When was the Curve eased? Obviously after 1864. Now we must speculate. It is reasonable to select a completion date of circa 1870…see the frontispiece and some photos to follow shortly. We guess that Thomson chipped away at it a little at a time as trains got longer and post-Civil War traffic boomed, much of it traceable to Thomson seizing control, through acquisition, of many midwestern railroads which in turn ballooned Pittdiv movements. Whatever the completion date, however, we have put to rest an oft-repeated assertion that Thomson did such a superb location job on the east slope that no alterations or realignments were ever necessary. The line was relocated at the Curve and he did it himself.

all this introduces the question of how long did it take Thomson to cut into the hill and relocate curve trackage westward until its final configuration was achieved. As we shall see, we must "bracket" this evolution by studying later photographs and guessing at the end-date. This photograph also demonstrates the seriousness of the construction problem at Kittanning Point. Look at the remnants of the Point to the left of the locomotive. This residue was part of the original mountain. Draw an imaginary line from the peak of this formation up the side of Kittanning Point to a point high upon the hillside, as shown in earlier photos, and the reader will see why the breach of the Point was the last to be completed. This was all rock, not overburden. Note that the "wall" on the right is sheer. Thomson did not want to take down one ton more of rock than necessary. In passing, note the "dinky" locomotive near the rear of the train. And a suggestion to erstwhile latterday archaeologists who may be tempted to do a "dig" at the Curve. Study the frontispiece of this book, this photograph and others to come in this chapter, particularly the "four-tracking" material. You will have to do a lot of triangulation to find the right area to put shovel to ground. We will also venture a little bet. There is historic gold buried under the park.

THE LENS of a camera is explicit. The eye of an artist is interpretive. This illustration by an unknown artist presents the impression of the Curve vista as he saw it. Keep in mind that the horseshoe was widely regarded as being one of the wonders of the world for many decades and this man's rendering, while technically incorrect, captures the aura of the scene with majesty.

ANOTHER DAY, another artist, another treatment. Published in 1875 and created by still another unknown artist, this dramatic rendering presents the scene in early morning with the sun still below the horizon and pinpoints of light shining from an ascending train and the structures at KN. Early light reflects from the condensate of a descending train higher up the grade and ambient light gives form to the valleys.

THE EAST SLOPE

NOW WE COME to the realism school of art and a splendid depiction. This time we know the artist's name…C. Lauderbach. Again published in 1875, this presentation captures the operational flavor of the east slope as well as the scenic beauty. A doubleheaded upgrade passenger train, with both locomotives making black smoke and trailing steam wisps from pop valves, pounds into the Curve trailing six cars, each accurately drawn. Three downgrade eastbounders are in sight, graphically displaying the preponderance of eastbound traffic. A returning light helper is in the Curve itself, followed by a freight train about to enter the kink and it, in turn, is followed by another train. Even the contours of the terrain are well done, as we are about to see.

Milton A. Davis

TWO-THIRDS of a century later, in 1941, the lens of Mr. Davis captured this scene on about the same angle as that used by Mr. Lauderbach. A toy-like train claws for the summit with the two Hippos on the rear just passing the kink. The road locomotive is about to go out of sight at the spot where IA Tower was once located on the valley side. The train is dwarfed by the overwhelming bulk of the mountain. Photography, too, is an art form.

TRIUMPH I

Railroad Museum of Pennsylvania

BOUNCING BACK in time to circa 1870, we meet an eastbound passenger train on the westbound track. The cut at the Curve is down to bedrock and a ledge has been formed in the "park" area. The reader has seen, and will see, this and similar trains a number of times in this book. It may have been a special made up just for photography or a through train stopped for that purpose. If it was a regularly scheduled train, the possibilities are few. This and other similar photos were taken at high noon, obvious from shadows. We examined public timetables, the principal one being dated June 1868, and learned that PRR moved six passenger/express trains a day in each direction over the east slope. This particular photo is the only one showing an eastbound train thus, if regular, it has to be the Parkesburg Train or the Harrisburg Accommodation. The reader should note that films were so slow in the early days that action shots were impossible…the train had to be stopped and the people standing still.

94

THE EAST SLOPE

Railroad Museum of Pennsylvania

IN A SIMILAR photograph c. 1870, we see the more typical westbound train. Again, if regular, it could only be one of two...The Baltimore Express (which ran on the Northern Central and joined at Harrisburg) or the Philadelphia Express. Of the two, the latter is the more likely. The reader should look to far left and note that the Burgoon/Glen White culvert has two bores...one for the stream and one for a road. Also note again how steep the fill west of the Curve. Of course, this culvert was extended when "four-tracking" was accomplished.

Railroad Museum of Pennsylvania

OUR UBIQUITOUS train is stopped again. Referring once more to the frontispiece, the ledge does not appear to be as wide in this photograph which implies that this is the earlier shot. Notice that PRR is adding fill to the right of the train.

95

TRIUMPH I

Railroad Museum of Pennsylvania

OUR INTREPID photographer was not deterred by snow. His determination produced this delightful product and provided proof to the public that trains could run in snowy weather. Well, not always. On 2 and 3 January 1879 a blizzard lashed the northeastern region with such ferocity that it was labelled as "fearful" and the blow to the east slope was described as "unprecedented." A huge mass of snow promptly turned to ice at Garveys Cut two miles east of KN. Four locomotives were dispatched from Altoona to break the "blockade"...then two more...then three more along with about 1,200 workmen (many from nearby mines) armed with picks, shovels and axes. Temperature dropped well below zero, accompanied by "piercing winds." For all this unpleasantness, however, the first train to break through to Gallitzin was only about nine hours late. One wonders if they are still making them like they used to. By the way, on 21 February 1880 all of the principal stations along PRR lines began to receive full weather reports from the U.S. Signal Service, transmitted on railroad wires. Perhaps this was an early start of the so-called "information age." Snow continued to fall.

THE EAST SLOPE

Smithsonian Institution

AS GLAMOUR is to passenger trains, profit is to freight trains. The fascinating thing about this photograph is the length of the train. There are 25 cars in sight and more to the rear. That is a very long train in the handbrake era, particularly on a severe downgrade. The locomotive in the foreground is apparently a helper that cut-off at the summit and is moving east ahead of the train, a scenario we have already seen. This photo was probably taken in the early 1870s...certainly the "peak" of the cut at the Curve is higher than those seen earlier and surely it must be late in the balloon stack era. All this implies that PRR was doubleheading long freight trains up the west slope and then applying brakes at the summit. How did they relieve draftgear strain on the ascent? Rear helper? Did they make severe brake application at the summit and then release some brakes to keep the train from coming to a stop as the downgrade eased? Examination of an 1874 PRR Rule Book provides some insight into these questions. Reference is made to rear helpers, so they were used this early. Brakemen were also warned to alternatively release brakes on cars descending heavy grades to cool wheels. However PRR handled this nifty little operating problem, it worked because they were able to stop the train at the Curve for this photograph. Please glance under the train at far left. PRR had added enough fill to lessen the slope, but could not add more under the last boxcar because it would have covered the "Glen White" culvert portals.

Dick Heiler Collection

IF THE HISTORIC RECORD is correct, this photograph was definitely taken after 1879 because that is the year when PRR created a park at the Curve. For many years thereafter the spot was known simply as the Flower Garden, a name that amuses this writer because B&O also had a Flower Garden at the east end of Buckhorn Wall on the Cheat River Grade. The latter's official name was Clements Fountain, the view was spectacular and even though the location has been long overgrown the name Flower Garden is still used by crews to denote the location. As to PRR, Flower Garden was used well into the twentieth century and, of course, this one still exists. Having admired the view from both of these gardens, we will have to say each is so magnificent that no comparison could possibly be fair. Back to this photo, note that there is no visible path to the site, a narrow bench has been cut high up the "wall" and the famous stone horseshoe is in place in the middle of the slope.

THE EAST SLOPE

Railroaders Memorial Museum/H.G. Coyler

THE LEAP from two tracks to four was actually done in stages; first a third track was added and then a fourth. Here we see a post-1900 photograph after all the work was finished and the mess cleaned up. From KN west around the Curve, the additional tracks were added on the valley side. As one can see, the peak of the "wall" is far higher because rock was blown down and dumped west of the Flower Garden area. Both culverts under the fills both east and west of the park were extended toward the valley; the new "Glen White" culvert portal is clearly seen here. The latter process also enabled PRR to ease the slope of the fill to something closer to an angle of repose.

THE LAST FREIGHT TRAIN we saw on the Curve had 25 cars in sight…this one has 43. The hard core doctrine of railroad operations is to increase the car miles and decrease the train miles, a fundamental tenet no less true today than it was at the beginning. The ongoing reality of railroad economics requires ever more powerful locomotives and larger, stronger cars. The longer the train the better.

TRIUMPH I

Hagley Museum and Library

WE KNOW that this photograph predates 1892 because the octagon tower is still in place at KN. Surprising, at least to this writer, is that wide-angle lenses were extant over a hundred years ago. This image has been the subject of countless postcards, but is included here to give the reader a view of how the Curve area appeared *before* three-and-four tracking construction commenced. Note that there is what appears to be a train-order signal near the shack in the Flower Garden. By the way, in this era PRR placed the hull of a canal boat in the park just west of that shack as a trophy testifying that PRR had won the War. At least PRR did not put the severed head or scalp of a "hitcher" on a pike, indicating that the fires of combat had cooled somewhat. After all, the victor can afford to be generous. The supported stick in the foreground next to the downgrade track is, we suspect, placed for the benefit of surveyors planning new trackage.

Hagley Museum and Library

NOW WE SEE the "after" image when the fourth track was finally installed. Four-tracking from Altoona to KN and from AG (Allegrippus) to Lilly on the west slope was completed by 1898. The 3.8 miles between KN and AG was done in two stages, one track at a time. This section of the project was not finally completed until 1900, although grading and track-laying were well advanced by late 1899. The waste for the fill just west of KN was, as we shall show, taken from Kittanning Run. The "wall" opposite the Flower Garden was cut back and the waste deposited at the "Glen White" fill. Moving to the "kink" area, note that a new cut was made in the side of the mountain; the waste was used both at "Glen White" and west of the kink. The kink was not entirely eliminated, however. Moving back to KN, a bracket signal bridge can be faintly seen. The four-track signal bridge was not yet in place. The ghost image at the western edge of the park represents (as we know from studying other photographs) at least one train-order signal. This photograph was probably taken c. 1901; the "browning" of the eastbound tracks shows that many trains have passed. Why was all this expansion necessary? In 1897, 826,940 loaded freight cars moved through Altoona. This is an average of 2,266 a day and 94 an hour; these figures do *not* include empty, passenger or helper movements. Three-quarters of these loaded cars were eastbound, carrying coal, coke, lumber, grain, flour, provisions, dressed beef, pig iron and miscellaneous freight. All this on two tracks over a mountain annoyed by the very presence of a railroad which persisted in taking slices out of its flanks. If one is into miracles, look to the operating people who somehow or another managed to handle all this volume, in all weather, with just two tracks.

THE EAST SLOPE

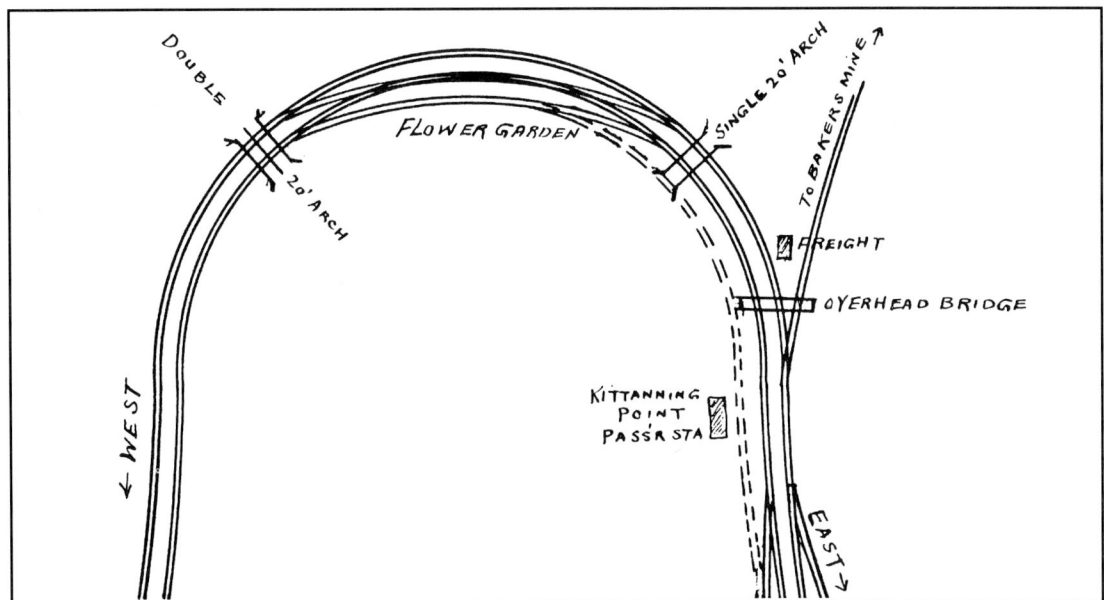

WE HAVE SHOWN "before" and "after." Now let us explore "in between." The PRR Board of Directors gave their blessing to this project on 8 December 1897 and Chief Engineer William H. Brown (another heavyweight in PRR history) okayed $675,000 on 11 December 1897 to add two tracks to KN, one from KN to Bennington, and also gave authority to doubletrack and re-line the Portage Tunnel. Contracts were let immediately. On the same day General Superintendent Frank W. Sheppard at Altoona sent a letter to Mr. Brown detailing east slope movements on the prior day, which he considered typical:

	Eastbound	Westbound
Passenger Trains	16	16
Freight Trains	62	53
"Empty" Engines	91	—
	169	69

An eastbound movement occurred on average every nine minutes...westbound every twenty minutes. The superintendent was concerned about delays. With this kind of volume, even a short delay could back up trains to infinity. He recommended a penalty against contractors of $25.00 for each delay of ten minutes or less to get their attention. We do not know whether this system was put into effect nor how many delays were experienced, but we assume Mr. Brown pointed out that the need for more tracks was urgent and everyone would have to do their best. We also assume Mr. Brown noted that the superintendent was getting nervous in the service. What did he think the engineers were going to do? Close down the railroad for a year or so? The troops got off to a fast start even though it was winter. On 15 February 1898 assistant C.S. d'Invilliers reported to Mr. Brown that two new tracks were in service as shown in the above sketch. An overhead bridge to move fill was in place at KN as shown and was producing so much fill that the assistant recommended jumping the gun by adding enough fill to provide for a fourth track. He needed authority, however, to add to the Kittanning Run culvert. We assume permission was granted. d'Invilliers also thought that enough fill could be realized from KN and the "wall" above the Flower Garden to provide for a fourth track from the garden to IA. Here he was wrong; it would prove to be very difficult to get a third track in place, let alone a fourth. The third track from "Glen White" fill to IA was placed on the hillside and a cut taken into the kink area. This cut, however, proved to be very unstable. In any event, the third track was opened and by early 1899 plans were afoot to add a fourth track on the valley side. On 11 August 1899 operating people were asked to move the three tracks at the Curve closer to the hillside and stake a path for the new "Number 1" track. A debate then ensued. Operating people knew from bitter experience that embankments, of which there was no shortage on the east slope, were expensive to maintain. Also, they wanted to eliminate the remaining curve at the kink. d'Invilliers pointed out that all this was very nice in theory, but the kink cut was so unstable and already so high that it would be foolish to tempt fate. He prevailed, at least as far as IA, and the fourth track was added on the valley side where he had at least already dumped some excess fill from KN and the "wall". Construction on the valley side was done in two "lifts," as they were called. Fill was dumped from an existing track to provide a lower-level base upon which a tram-track was built...small cars moved the fill to location. Then a second lift was built at grade. The movement of all this fill, of course, meant that main tracks had to be closed for periods of time. d'Invilliers also wanted to dig some "borrow pits" just west of the Curve; operating people were afraid they would undermine the roadbed and they were adamant. So d'Invilliers had to dig a borrow pit west of IA and haul the fill east, a process that added to the cost for the contractor. Further, the material in this pit was very hard (too bad the kink structure wasn't) and this, too, added to cost. The fourth track *west* of IA was finished 1 August 1899, but east of IA to the kink was not open until after 15 September. Being finished and ready for traffic were two different subjects and as nearly as we can tell it was the Spring of 1900 before all was finished and the operating people enjoyed the fruits of a four-track mainline from the top to the bottom of the east slope. This joyous situation lasted for 81 years; in April of 1981 L. Stanley Crane (still another giant in railroad history) pulled out Number 2 track and the New Portage as well, thus cutting east slope mainline trackage by half and picking up a lot of relay rail in the process. d'Invilliers got a promotion out of it and it was well deserved. We will meet him again in a few pages.

TRIUMPH I

Milton A. Davis

THE ONLY TRACE of the vital KN complex that remains on this day in the early 1940s is the slight dip in the treeline marking the path of the siding to the old coal wharf. Look at the cribbing under the second car, evidence that MOW concern about embankment maintenance was well-founded. From front to rear: K4, R50B express reefer, four baggage cars (B60?), PB70 combine, P70 coach, D78 diner, two Pullmans. About as pure PRR as you can get.

THE CONSTANT rain of cinders went with the steam locomotive and as a result underbrush began to flourish on the wall and embankments. Here is a 1977 scene, taken when Conrail was awash in staggering losses...note that one of the road engines has PC "worms in love" markings. The fence has been installed in the park (not far enough back, in our view) and the K4 is still resident. And there is a crowd watching the parade of trains with awe.

Jeff Madden

THE EAST SLOPE

Milton A. Davis

THE 4458, a Hippo Helper pouring sand, assists an M1a with a massive long-distance tender into the Curve in 1941. The exhausts are remarkably clean considering the strain. Note that the car against the train is an old X-23 wood-sheathed outside steel-braced box with a lot of the train hanging on its drawbar, not exactly a prime position for such an old lady.

THERE WAS SOMETHING ABOUT PRR'S five stripes that added class to an otherwise mundane diesel. In July of 1948, L1 4162 leads two E7A units and a passenger or express train into the Curve. As to the 4162, the crew was taking a rather casual view of their responsibilities. The fireman in the lead E7 is more attentive to his duty. He is inspecting the train.

R.E. Tobey/Herbert H. Harwood Collection

103

TRIUMPH I

Bob Lorenz

K4 1361, shortly after installation at the Flower Garden in June of 1957, serenely accepts the worship of visitors as she gazes at the spectacular view. (A younger reader might question why locomotives, ships, airplanes *et al* are routinely regarded as feminine. It is because they are pleasing you one minute and trying to kill you the next.) The 1361 was subsequently taken from the park and put back into steam...in the process of removal, she almost got away from the crew and was perilously close to rolling down the mountain. Point proven. She was replaced by GP9 7048 in 1985, the current reigning queen. As to the park, a joint venture of sorts between the National Park Service and America's Industrial Heritage Project (whatever that is) resulted in a breathtaking improvement that opened in April of 1992, complete with vast exhibit center, gift shop and inclined plane railway. This project involved the expenditure of almost six million dollars, far more than Thomson needed to build the whole railroad from Harrisburg to Pittsburgh. And government just can't seem to get away from those inclined planes...they're still building them. The park is now run by Altoona's Railroaders Memorial Museum with, we must say, a level of efficiency and effectiveness not usually associated with organizations of this genus. The reincarnated Flower Garden is very popular, drawing about 150,000 visitors a year. Assuming a cost-of-capital rate of ten percent, this means that it costs the taxpayer $4.00 per visitor per year...just for the sunk capital. The expenses of maintaining and operating the park are, of course, on top of that. The latter has proven so expensive that, beginning in January of 1996, an admission fee of $3.50 is being charged. PRR let visitors in for nothing and even cut the grass every now and then. As we ponder the struggle Thomson suffered to get government out of the transportation business, we will have to say that we are glad he did not live to witness this backsliding. If nothing else, the thought of building inclined planes in the 1990s would have given him a stroke. One hopes that all this does not result in another resurrection, with Mathew Carey being the star attraction this time. And another thing about the new planes. The Flower Garden is very popular with retired railroaders in the area and they visit the site frequently during the year, as old soldiers returning to the battlefield where they gave so much for so long with so much success. True, they get an annual pass for only $5.00...but it doesn't include a ride on the planes. These old-timers have to walk up. The thanks of a grateful society.

THE EAST SLOPE

Smithsonian Institution

EVEN WITH FOUR TRACKS, PRR dispatchers found it expedient to husband track by returning helpers in batches…in this case on eastbound passenger Track Two. The sign at lower right foreground reads, "Keep off the grass." Please note that the grass is cut and well trimmed.

William Brenize/Milton A. Davis Collection

IT WAS JULY OF 1953 and Mr. Davis' camera jammed at the crucial moment. Happily, his companion rushed to the fore and squeezed off this shot just in time. The two road locomotives, of course, are "Jays"…Chesapeake and Ohio designs forced on PRR by wartime exigencies. At an informal dinner party a few years ago with the then top motive power man at Conrail (with PRR experience reaching back into the forties when he started as a fireman), we were so bold as to ask him to identify the best steam locomotive in modern PRR history. After much gnashing of teeth and attempts to change the subject, he finally whispered that the Jays were the best. This gentleman, incidentally, was one of the few PRR motive power men to enjoy the respect of his peers on other railroads. Because of Jay boiler and tender length, it was necessary to increase track centers at the Curve and other locations to avoid the danger of passing trains exchanging kisses. In the case of the Curve, this was accomplished during World War II by imported Mexican laborers.

Rail Photo Service/Bob Lorenz Collection

TAKEN IN THE MID-FORTIES, Baldwin K4 5438 and Juniata T1 5508 slam a first class train through the Curve at an acceptable speed and with an abundance of drama. While an ardent admirer of so much that was PRR, this historian's worship does not extend to the railroad's motive power development prowess. Consistently throughout history, PRR did the wrong thing at the wrong time in the wrong way, doing so in distressingly large quantities and at considerable expense. The operating people paid the price, both human and capital. The 5508 is a typical example. That the "Tees" were a disaster is well known. Less well known is that they were killers of firemen. The shrouding in the cab and front of the tender were so placed that the engineer could not see nor hear the fireman in the coal bin. On more than one occasion a fireman would enter the bin to loosen the coal pile over the stoker screw as it was receding and get caught in the screw. The engineer could not see that he was in trouble nor hear his cries of distress with the net result that the fireman's remains were spit into the firebox in very small pieces. No way to die is pleasant, but this has to be one of the worst. Of course, once known the condition was corrected and PRR officialdom managed to keep this news under wraps…your author did not learn of it until decades after the Tees were scrapped.

EAST SLOPE crews were quite capable of producing translucent exhaust, even with Hippos. The 4354 in July of 1948 is coming out of the Curve with a long string of empty hoppers, passing the underbrush that has stabilized the "Glen White" fill and providing the viewer with a record of the status of the Flower Garden at that time.

R.E. Tobey/Herbert H. Harwood Collection

IF THE LAST EXHAUST was translucent, this one is transparent. With I1s 3715 on the point and another Hippo on the rear, this 1941 photograph is one of Mr. Davis's most prized. The rise between the rear and the headend of this train is about one hundred feet, which doesn't sound like much until one considers that this is the height of a ten-story building. The horseshoe has an unremarked operating benefit, aided by this rise, as we shall see next.

Milton A. Davis

TRIUMPH I

Bob Lorenz Collection

THE GRANDEUR of this 1951 scene is self-evident. Five or so years after it was taken, your author's father (a B&O traffic official to whom this book is dedicated) suggested that we travel to this area to see "how the Penn does it." B&O people usually referred to PRR as the "Penn." Throughout history B&O and PRR were antagonists, a competition made more fierce because PRR usually won. While the reference "Penn" was not meant pejoratively, it was not used in a friendly way either. Thus father and son travelled to the horseshoe and we walked to the KN area. There we observed an MOW crew doing their thing. We both agreed that there was something unusual about this crew. Finally it dawned on us that they were all white. On B&O most would have been black. Then a westbound freight went by. As the 30th or so car came into sight, we noticed that it had sticking brakes. This is not good for a lot of reasons, the worst being that it causes tread buildup which reduces flange height. As the diesel road locomotive was about where this helper set is located, we noticed that the headend brakeman started walking toward the rear on cartops. The fireman was watching his progress. When the brakeman was about a car-length from the one with sticking brakes, the fireman pulled his head in and said something to the engineer. At that moment, the engineer briefly reduced power and a ripple of slack started moving toward the brakeman. The slack and the brakeman arrived at the errant car at *exactly* the same instant with a precision that would have made ballet dancers proud. Without the benefit of rehearsal. The brakeman kicked off the handbrake and swung down to be picked up by the cabin car. Your author thought that this virtuoso performance was one of the most impressive he had ever seen, but considered it impolitic to say so. Father folded his arms across his chest with a frown on his face. Finally he sighed, "Well, at least this crew knows what they're doing." He would have preferred that they had not, but there it was. We will address other adventures that this trip produced in later pages, but wish to make two points before leaving this photograph. First, all train crews since the beginning of time have been admonished to constantly watch and inspect their trains. Nice in theory, but almost impossible in practice because the crews can rarely see much of the train. Not so on the horseshoe. Here crewmen can see every car. Second, the reader might be wondering why he is not seeing more recent photographs of the east slope. Our editorial policy is to maximize the use of color when available, so another tour of Pittdiv will be presented in a "color chapter" later in the book. The reader gets two tours for the price of one.

THE EAST SLOPE

THE ODD FLASHBACK, in this case to a location east of KN, is an author's perogative. It is the Fall of 1981 and the sun is about to go behind the barrier as an eastbound drags its feet through the ghostland of a complex long gone. It is the first three-track winter on the east slope. The eastbound passenger track is no more.

Thomas A. Biery

HALF A MYTH

We have met C.S. d'Invilliers and recorded for posterity his splendid work in doubling the mainline trackage on the east slope. He was rewarded by promotion to Engineer of Construction. On Tuesday 6 June 1905 he received the following letter from his boss, Chief Engineer William H. Brown: "We would like you to make a hasty, rough barometrical survey of the two valleys from Kittanning Point to the top of the mountain, to ascertain if it is at all practicable to build a passenger line up through one of these valleys and over the top of the mountain, or with a short tunnel, to the western slope, and then to run along parallel with the mountain to a connection with the present road in the neighborhood of Gallitzin or Cresson, so as to have an independent passenger road and keep the passengers out of the freight tunnels. If at all practicable, we would like to have the results of this examination by Saturday morning of this week."

Note that Brown wants this report four days later. We do not know how long it took Mr. Thomson to dismiss these routes, but it certainly took longer than four days. Further, had Mr. Brown ever heard of Mr. Thomson? After all, Thomson had died only 31 years before Brown wrote this letter and the east slope had only been open for 49 years.

But let us overlook all this and imagine the impact the receipt of this letter had on d'Invilliers. Brown, after all, was his boss. One does not receive future promotions by suggesting that his mentor is out of his mind as well as being deaf, dumb and blind, no matter how tempting this course of action might appear.

d'Invilliers slept on it and the very next day he replied as follows, signing off "Yours *Respectfully*" to be on the safe side:

"...I do not think it is practicable to get a line from Kittanning Point to the mountain top on a reasonable grade, even with a short tunnel."

"Some years ago, before we built the Cambria and Clearfield Railroad, we made an actual survey up Kittanning Run, thence to Dawson and Loretto, and found the best we could do was a 3% grade...then a two-mile tunnel."

"I shall be very glad to get further information by Saturday, but I do not think I can do better than send you my print of the original PRR surveys which I have found fairly accurate and which I ask you to return. I believe you can yourself ascertain just what can and what cannot be done."

On 8 June Mr. Brown responded with a short note, stating "You may drop the matter...I was afraid you did not have enough distance..." The tone of the letter was polite and indicated that Brown was a big enough man not to mind being told he was wrong, and rather tersely at that. It is interesting to note that Thomson's original surveys were still available in 1905.

If d'Invilliers had just quit while he was ahead, all would have been well. But it seems that he had developed a "secret plan" on his own a few years before which involved a route from Kittanning Point to Lilly with a summit at Blair Gap! This plan has not survived but a cursory examination of the terrain indicates that at the very least a two-mile long tunnel would be required to maintain a 2.0% grade, in addition to some massive fills.

d'Invilliers sent his "plan" to Brown on 15 June and Brown bounced it back on 16 June, reminding him that the idea was to "get rid of the passenger trains at Kittanning Point and take them over the top of the mountain instead of through any tunnel at all." In other words, forget it. Go away and leave me alone.

Apparently d'Invilliers did not have enough to do in this time frame because it is evident that he continued to work on his grand scheme. Brown got wind of it and on 9 October issued a blunt order: "...stop all work on the surveys for the passenger line over the mountains between Cresson and Kittanning Point."

d'Invilliers went from candor to kissing-up and received a well-deserved rocket. The passenger line scheme was never heard from again.

Thus a half-myth.

TRIUMPH I

Milton A. Davis

Milton A. Davis

INSTANT REPLAY or carbon copy or seeing double. All PRR historians struggle to find prose and graphics to describe the incredible volume of traffic that has always moved over Pittdiv and all find their efforts inadequate. The subject is mindboggling. The English language is a "magnificent instrument," to borrow from Barbara Tuchman, but even this versatile and supreme tool lacks sufficient superlatives. Consider these two photographs. They were both taken from the same spot within minutes of each other in 1941. At quick glance they appear to be of the same train. Not so. Two trains. And it is not enough to see it in person with one's own eyes. You don't believe your eyes! They must be doing it with mirrors. There aren't that many trains in the whole world. Look at all the Indians.

THE EAST SLOPE

Railroaders Memorial Museum

THE INSTABILITY of the cut at the kink is manifest in this impressive photograph, as is the volume of traffic and the muscle power needed to keep the railroad operating. These workmen have already manhandled many tons into the gondolas and the day is far from over. All trains in view are stopped for the benefit of the photographer, a situation which assuredly was not pleasing to the dispatchers. On the far track, or Track 1, the two brakemen are "riding out on their train" but enjoying a rare respite and perhaps trading insults with the enginemen of the doubleheaded passenger train on Track 2, which has apparently stopped just short of knocking down the signal. "Knocking up" is perhaps more appropriate because these are counterbalanced semaphores. Track 3 is occupied by a westbound freight and, of course, Track 4 is out-of-service for maintenance. The point should be made that having a four-track mainline does not mean that four tracks are always available, particularly on a mountain railroad where maintenance is an ongoing problem. The signal bridge is interesting because it has what appear to be number plates. In more modern practice this would indicate that this is a road signal, yet its location would imply that it is the distant signal for IA which is just a fraction of a mile around a curve to the right.

111

TRIUMPH I

THIS CRUDE reproduction, taken from a photocopy, is IA block station and interlocker in what some call McGinleys Curve or, more simply, the first curve west of the kink. Notice that the KN area can be faintly seen in the distance. We know, of course, that there were three such stone towers built in 1892...one combined with the KN station, one here at IA and a third at AG which we will see shortly. We also know that there were three tracks from the IA area to AG prior to the construction of the stone tower seen here and that the middle track was a westbound freight track. We do *not* know from obscure records just when this track was installed, but believe it to have been in the late 1880s. The track at left is a puzzler. It is obviously not mainline and a mast home signal is plopped so close to it that a mini-kink was created. How far around the curve did it go? There must have been a block station here prior to the construction of the stone tower, yet there is no record. We do have records that strongly suggest that the fourth track was added on the hillside, which is logical because the dropoff to the right of the tower is very steep. Perhaps the mystery track was the original Track 2 and PRR moved the mainline tracks away from the hillside from here to the Curve earlier in the nineteenth century, in which event this is another example of east slope realignment. As if all this is not enough of a riddle, glance again at the KN area. Faint though it may be, there is absolutely no evidence of any structures whatsoever! With all respects to Mr. McGinley, perhaps it should be Conundrum Curve.

Thomas A. Biery

IT IS FEBRUARY OF 1973 as an eastbounder rolls out of McCanns Curve and approaches Conundrum Curve on Track 2. The time is three years after the Penn Central bankruptcy and the deterioration of maintenance standards is painfully obvious. The locomotives are leaning to the left. With proper superelevation, they should be canting the other way. A glance ahead of the power and comparison with the last photograph will demonstrate just how much of the hillside was removed when the line was four-tracked.

THE EAST SLOPE

C.G. Corey/Herbert H. Harwood Collection

THE DIESELIZATION of PRR was peripatetic, to say the least, and was yet another chapter in its long and sorry tradition of motive power blundering. Here, in August of 1955, we see Fairbanks Morse 9491 with a westbounder passing under the home signal at MG tower. The FM opposed-piston engines, while quite effective in marine and stationary applications where output was steady and predictable, were not suitable for locomotive application. PRR dieselized late and then on a crash basis, buying everything in sight without regard to inherent quality, maintenance needs, crew training, experience of others and the rudiments of common sense. It remains an enigma to this historian that a railroad so brilliant in so many ways that their very name was a synonym for excellence could be so consistently maladroit in an area so basic to survival. The front door on the 9491 is either gone or open. Perhaps the crew blew it off in a fit of frustration.

ALL TOWERS in all times on the east slope were isolated and MG was no exception. The call letters MG purportedly stood for "Middle of the Grade," which is not quite correct because the actual middle is near the kink. Its life was short and sweet. It was built in 1944 to assist in handling bloated World War II traffic and was really, as we shall see, a replacement for AG which was located farther west. MG closed in 1978, although it was periodically reopened as a block station when needed for, say, temporary traffic surges, maintenance detours and the like. The most recent reopening was in 1994 to provide versatility when the summit tunnel clearance project was begun...again, as we shall see. This photograph was taken in February of 1972 and it is sad to behold. We have made frequent references to PRR's long and impressive record of meticulous maintenance of its physical plant. The rails in this view appear made of spaghetti, giving the impression of branchline rather than mainline trackage. Beginning with the Penn Central merger in 1968 and continuing throughout most of the 1970s, the railroad declined to the point where it was one long slow order. A rebirth was to come, but that did not appear likely in 1972.

Thomas A. Biery

113

TRIUMPH I

FOUR YEARS EARLIER, on 7 September 1968, the first little signs of decline began to appear. A weed was growing next to Track 1 and underbrush was being allowed to rise near the tower. In this book thus far, how many weeds has the reader seen?

Edward H. Weber

Thomas A. Biery

ALCO POWER passing MG westbound in 1972 is witness to a display of concave rail joints reaching out of sight. Sadly, the situation was to get far worse before the turnaround came. Today, there is a Talking Defect Detector at milepost 243.1, just east of the tower. The railroad was reborn.

THE EAST SLOPE

AT MILEPOST 244 just west of MG, and at long last, PRR swung ninety degrees and entered Sugar Run Gap to begin the final approach to the summit. This 1875 illustration shows with surprising accuracy the drama of both the scenery and the engineering accomplishment. The railroad is climbing ever higher on the mountainside at a steady pace roughly equal to the rise of Sugar Run far below. The corner was turned just to the rear of the doubleheaded, five-car passenger train. The battle, however, was not over. Two gigantic fills and a summit tunnel are between this train and the western waters. All three obstacles would prove to be daunting. The first massive fill was at Allegrippus, just west of the cluster of structures at upper left and actually out of sight in this depiction. The origin of the name Allegrippus aptly describes the nature of the problem. In February and March of 1854, PRR purchased two 2-6-0 locomotives from engine-maker Richard Norris & Sons named *Kittatinny* and *Allegrippus*. The latter, with Thomas Ridley at the throttle in March of 1854, moved onto the first fill and the embankment promptly collapsed, hurtling the engine forty feet down the hillside. Ridley survived, albeit with serious injuries, and thereafter he always referred to the location as Allegrippus in honor of both the engine and Lady Luck. That such an accident occurred within thirty days of the opening of the line was surely disquieting to Thomson, but he still allowed the name to stick. It is Indian in origin.

TRIUMPH I

Frank Wrabel Collection

IT TOOK FOUR FILLS to conquer the east slope. The first two at the Curve have always been the most famous. The second two were the most brutal. The dropoff from AG to the bed of Sugar Run is *four times* higher than at the Curve and the slope is about twice as sheer. Here is a very early "balloon stack" view of AG looking eastward, or downgrade. The fill on the left was easy...on the right, as close to vertical as one can get without the law of gravity taking over. Which it did, quite frequently. Notice that all the fill in sight on the Run side is rock, and some big ones at that. AG became a block and water station very early in history, although we suspect the latter function was more in the nature of emergency service. Note that one can faintly see a cross-track water bridge, both in this photograph and the preceding illustration. We know that a new building and water tank were installed at AG in 1866...this photo probably reflects that construction. In 1888 a two-story frame interlocker was installed here, almost certainly octagonal. Then, in the late nineteenth century things began to change at AG.

THE EAST SLOPE

THIS IS THE THIRD, and happily the last, of the three stone monolithic towers built in 1892. This view is westerly.

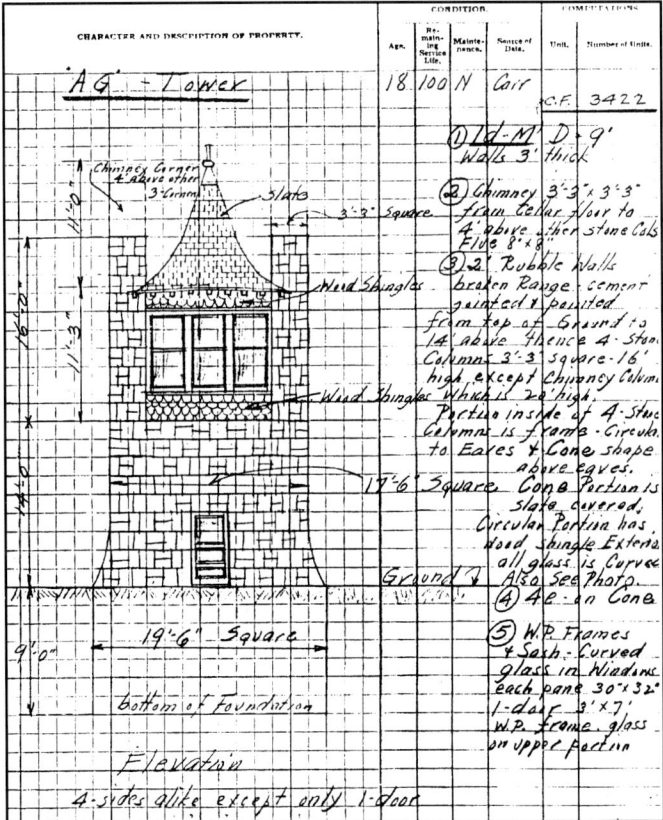

THE EASTERLY VIEW of AG did nothing to improve its appearance. A new mechanical interlocker was installed in 1899 and it was made pneumatic in 1900, surely improvements necessitated by the completion of three and four-tracking. As trains got longer, block length had to be increased accordingly and AG fell victim to this trend. The tower was closed 10 September 1931, the switches removed and stored at AG in March of 1932. Switch material was moved to Cresson in the Spring of 1933. In 1940, with the possibility of sharp growth in wartime traffic looming, operating people discussed reopening AG but concluded that the location was not the most favorable. In any event, MG was chosen and opened in 1944. We do not know when the tower was razed…whenever it was, it was not a moment too soon. We hope the stones were added to AG Fill.

IF BY SOME CHANCE there is a reader who finds AG tower and its clones to be interesting, we present here the ICC Valuation drawing and detail done circa 1918.

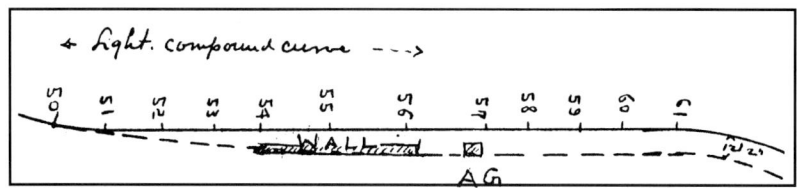

NOW LET US REVISIT JUNE OF 1899 and the three principal gentlemen involved in adding a fourth track on the upper east slope. We have already met Messrs. Brown and d'Invilliers. General Superintendent Sheppard had just been promoted and replaced by J.M. Wallis. As will be seen, Mr. Wallis may have been new to this division but he was not a parvenu in dealing with engineering types. The conflict between engineering and operating people is as old as time. The former want to build as cheaply and quickly as possible. The latter, who have to maintain and use their creations, are suspicious. At the end of the process, the engineers disappear into the sunset and leave someone else stuck with their miscues. The essence of this argument was whether to add to the valley side or cut into the hillside. Embankments were cheaper, but more costly to maintain as well as being more dangerous. The question at issue in June of 1899 was how to add a fourth track at AG. In the earlier battles the operating people usually prevailed, but now there was a new kid on the block and the engineers tested him by urging that the fourth track at AG be added to the valley side. After all, d'Invilliers opined, we put most of the third track on the hillside so let us compromise. Wallis was having none of it. Brown caved in on 15 June, stating "You may do the work on the Mountain the way Mr. Wallis wants it, if it does not increase the expense." d'Invilliers, with his usual persistence, kept at it. As the reader can see from the sketch, there was a "High Wall" at AG. We do not know when it was constructed nor just how high it was, but judging from its formal name it must have been a big hummer. When d'Invilliers went down and inspected it, he found that it was bulging in the middle. Never one to leave well enough alone, he started drilling test bores to try to find bedrock so he could propose building a new, bigger wall. Of course, he didn't find any. The whole bloody thing was fill from day one. One of these bores, incidentally, came close to undermining the wall. Finally "C.S.d'I", as he liked to sign himself, gave up and submitted this sketch for approval. All tracks were moved closer to the hillside. (The numbers are "station numbers" and are 100 feet apart.) We don't know the history of the High Wall after 1900. Perhaps it is buried under fill added later or possibly it collapsed. The reader might ask Thomas Ridley's ghost if a meeting could be arranged.

THE EAST SLOPE

Hagley Museum and Library

THE AG FILL circa 1960 remains an open sore. A fifth set-off track has been added on the valley side which reaches past the signal bridge at upper left and it is full of hoppers dumping still more fill. The cut in the hillside in this area is one that C.S.d'I had said was "practically impossible." This photograph gives visual proof of the inherent problem of maintaining embankments and fills on a mountain railroad. Notice that the drainage ditch at lower left has caused a washout. The slope is so unstable that communication wires are installed high on the hillside. In the service of our readers, we have carefully studied contour maps of this area and noted that there is no stream in the AG gap. We speculate that it was probably created by a large landslide a long time ago. If so, it was better that it happened before PRR came upon the scene.

TRIUMPH I

FOR 1972, this westerly view of the approach to AG does show that the track and subgrade are in good condition for the times.

Thomas A. Biery

Dick Heiler Collection

THE FOURTH, LAST AND DEEPEST major fill on the east slope is at Bennington Curve. The fill spans Gum Tree Hollow. On the mountain side, the fill is about 150 feet deep. On the valley side, it drops some 600 feet to Sugar Run. A minor stream created this gap. There may be a culvert underneath this mass, but we doubt it. The watershed is slight and Thomson probably decided to let absorption and evaporation dispose of runoff. Bennington Curve lies at the foot of the 2.36% "slide."

At 3:25 a.m. on 18 February 1947 Bennington Curve became the deadliest fill on the east slope. The doubleheaded eastbound *Red Arrow* left the railroad and plunged into the hollow. This photograph shows the ghastly result. Of the 276 souls on board, 22 perished and 141 were injured. Six of the dead were postal clerks in an RPO. While this train was by no means the first nor the last victim of the combination of this steep grade and sharp curve, the butcher's bill set a macabre record.

THE EAST SLOPE

THIS EASTERLY view of Bennington Curve shows the depth of both the fill and the disaster. The next photo shows that the *Red Arrow* was on Track 3 when the derailment occurred. The ICC investigation concluded that the train was moving at 65-70 mph and that this excessive speed was the cause of the accident. The speed limit approaching the curve was 35 mph and in the curve 30 mph. Surviving crew members felt that the train was travelling at 30 mph. The relief train shown here is on Track 4, which was the last to be added on the east slope and was put on the hillside at the insistence of Mr. Wallis. An eastbound freight was behind the *Red Arrow* and was the first to arrive at the scene. All four tracks were open for traffic on 19 February.

IT WAS A LONG TIME AGO and besides, as the saying goes, the wench is dead. Still, there is something about this photo and others we have seen that puzzles us. Far be it for us to question the omniscience of the ICC, but if excessive speed caused the derailment how come the train derailed while on tangent *before it even entered the curve?* Another question: if the *Red Arrow* was on Track 3, then it did not go down the "slide." As we will show shortly, there was no way in 1947 that a train could go from Tracks 1-2 to Track 3 short of MG. The "slide," we remind the reader, starts at the east end of the New Portage tunnel (Tracks 1-2). Why would the *Red Arrow* be on Track 3? PRR had a hard and fast rule that passenger trains and moving freight trains would not be allowed in any tunnel at the same time for obvious safety reasons. There was an eastbound freight (the one first to arrive on the scene of the accident) somewhere between AR and BF, so quite naturally the *Arrow* (which was running late) was switched to Track 3, probably at Cresson on the west slope. If one makes the case that the engineer was momentarily confused as to which tunnel he was in, then one would think that he would assume New Portage as usual and make a heavier brake application. All this, of course, is musing long after the event and none of it will bring back the dead. The engineer perished in the accident so he was not around to defend himself. It is easy and convenient to pin the rose on a dead man.

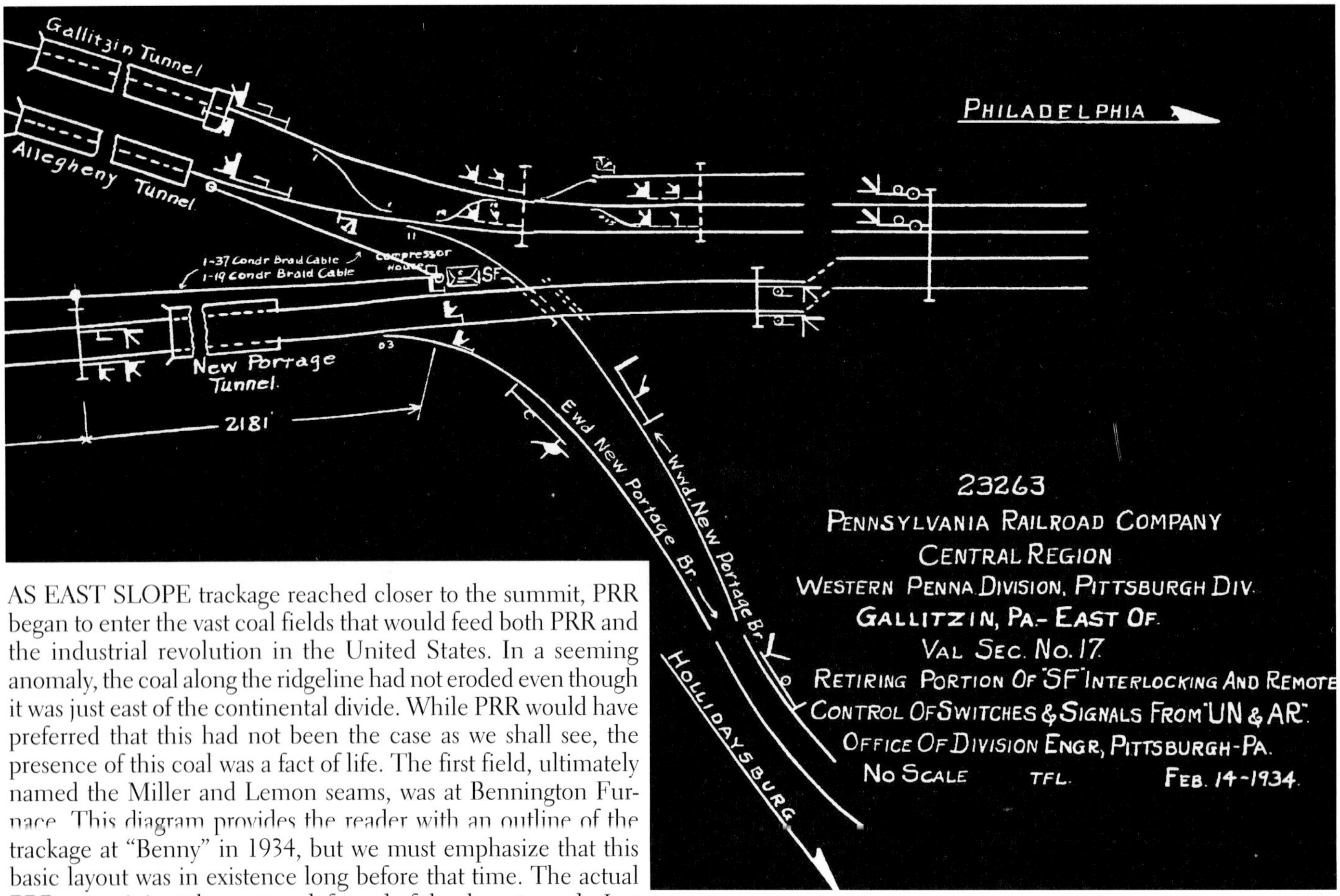
Gallitzin Tunnel
Allegheny Tunnel
PHILADELPHIA
1-37 Condr Braid Cable
1-19 Condr Braid Cable
Compressor House
SF
New Portage Tunnel.
2181'
Ewd New Portage Br.
Wwd. New Portage Br.
HOLLIDAYSBURG
23263
PENNSYLVANIA RAILROAD COMPANY
CENTRAL REGION
WESTERN PENNA. DIVISION, PITTSBURGH DIV.
GALLITZIN, PA.- EAST OF.
VAL SEC. NO. 17
RETIRING PORTION OF "SF" INTERLOCKING AND REMOTE
CONTROL OF SWITCHES & SIGNALS FROM "UN & AR".
OFFICE OF DIVISION ENGR, PITTSBURGH-PA.
NO SCALE TFL. FEB. 14-1934.

AS EAST SLOPE trackage reached closer to the summit, PRR began to enter the vast coal fields that would feed both PRR and the industrial revolution in the United States. In a seeming anomaly, the coal along the ridgeline had not eroded even though it was just east of the continental divide. While PRR would have preferred that this had not been the case as we shall see, the presence of this coal was a fact of life. The first field, ultimately named the Miller and Lemon seams, was at Bennington Furnace. This diagram provides the reader with an outline of the trackage at "Benny" in 1934, but we must emphasize that this basic layout was in existence long before that time. The actual PRR summit is at the west, or left, end of the three tunnels. Just beyond the western portals were two interlockers; AR serving eastbound movements and UN serving westbound. We shall visit them shortly. It is at Benny that the New Portage railroad and its tunnel met PRR. The flow of traffic to and from the New Portage and between Tracks 3 and 4 were controlled by SF interlocker. Note that there was no crossover capability between Tracks 1-2 and 3-4. (The fifth track to the northeast of SF is a siding which served coke ovens and coal mines.) It wasn't until the early 1940s that SF (then known as BF) became a complete interlocker between all four mainline tracks. The drafting of this diagram was done, as the caption indicates, to provide for the closure of SF and the installation of remote control from AR and UN. We will cover the evolution of SF/BF/Benny as we go. Keep in mind that it was at Benny that Pittdiv first began to receive heavy branchline traffic, sources that would become a torrent as PRR moved closer to Pitcairn. Oddly, the Benny traffic moved west. From the summit on, tonnage moved in both directions in unbelievable quantity and in addition to already staggering through traffic. There was no other trunkline mountain railroad like Pittdiv and there is no other today.

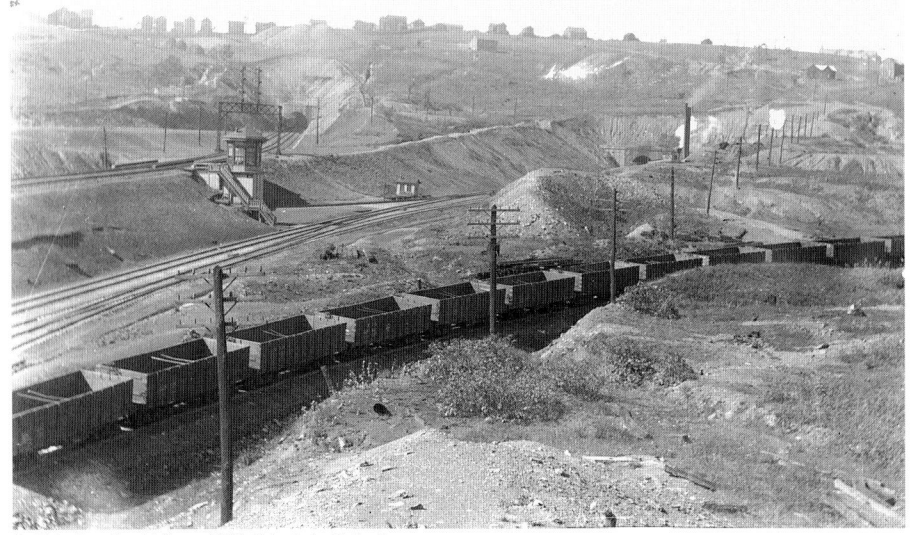

Gallitzin Area Tourist Council/T.C. Ketenheim Collection

THIS PHOTOGRAPH is in the running for the earliest known of the Benny area. It was probably taken circa 1898. The New Portage tunnel was widened in that year and one can faintly see an eastbound exiting the east portal. While the date of construction of the octagon tower is unknown, its replacement by rectangular SF was in 1901. Just to the left of the tower is an iron plate girder bridge which was completed in 1892. This bridge carries two tracks as does the New Portage tunnel. The whole scene is that of a moonscape, caused in great part by the hundreds of coke ovens in the area to the right, served by the long string of hopper cars in the foreground. While the homes on the ridgeline command an interesting view of the Sugar Run valley, the immediate vicinity is spartan.

THE EAST SLOPE

Dick Heiler Collection

THE APPROACH to Benny and the view down Sugar Run valley are the features of this misty photograph taken on 27 May 1934. The rear end of the westbound train is in Bennington Curve and the helpers are about to enter it. In the extreme lower left corner one can see hoppers on a New Portage branch train. At upper right the branch mainline can be seen wrapping around the hillside. The balance of branch trackage is out of sight below the brow of the hill. Evidence of coal mining and coke making is everywhere...note the beehive ovens just below the road engines on the westbounder. The evolution of trackage in this area is vague. We know that in 1858 a short branch was built from the New Portage tunnel on the old roadbed to serve coal mines, perhaps explaining the presence of rails in the photograph on page 53. We also know that this branch was further extended in 1882 and that a connection was built at that time to the east end of one of the PRR tunnels. In that same year a new iron bridge was erected at Benny and we assume that this was a forerunner of the one seen on the last photo. Now we should point out that Bennington Furnace was a very significant and ancient coal and coke producing area. A coke-fired iron furnace was active here in 1846, the year of PRR's birth. In the 1870s Cambria Iron Company, which we will visit when we arrive at Johnstown, acquired the works at Benny. In the 1880s Cambria operated 100 coke ovens at Benny, employed 300 men and built 95 tenement houses just north of the PRR mainline. Even in the late 1870s the mines produced 500 tons of coal a day and the resultant coke was shipped west over the summit to Johnstown. The high water mark for Benny production was reached in the 1910-1925 period, but production continued into the 1940s. The Bennington "B" mine employed 160 men that late and in 1949 this mine witnessed a rare sit-down strike of miners when some sixty men refused to leave the mine. Hunger, cold and dampness settled the strike and depletion settled the mine. Today the town of Bennington is a dump with only an abandoned cemetery bearing testimony to its lusty history. The quality of Benny coal was quite high, far superior to that available farther east in, say, the Altoona area. PRR even hauled it to Conemaugh (in Johnstown) for locomotive use. Ultimately the lush Connellsville region produced coke of even higher quality and Benny coal and coke became less popular.

Julius Westheimer Collection

THEN AGAIN, perhaps this is the earliest Benny photograph. Notes on the back of the print claim circa 1907, but that could not be right because the octagon tower is still in service. The reader will recall that it was replaced in 1901. This tower, or cabin as PRR alternatively called them (sometimes both ways in the same document), was not an interlocker. Switchtenders moved the turnout points. True interlocking came to SF in 1901. The high smokestacks at far left will be discussed later in this chapter.

Michael G. Farrow Collection

ESTABLISHING a date is not difficult for this image. During World War I PRR felt threatened by possible German sabotage and requested soldiers to provide protection. The watchtower was built to assist in this effort, so the date is 1917-18. This is the earliest photograph we have found showing the new 1901 SF interlocker, which was electro-pneumatic with nine levers. By the late 1920s, improved and more efficient power and stronger cars resulted in longer trains and the New Portage branch was being used less and less. In 1928 operating people noted that the New Portage was being used only for emergencies and to protect the odd train moving west from Petersburg through Hollidaysburg. The precipitous drop in traffic caused by the Great Depression pushed PRR to close SF as an interlocker on 5 January 1932 and operate most turnouts remotely from AR and UN. Things were not improving by early 1934 so permission was granted on 28 March to remove the tower and transfer a few more remote turnouts and signals to AR and UN. By 1937 the New Portage eastbound track was being used as a siding (known as Patch) and some signal simplification was authorized. This track was removed in 1955 and the westbound track in 1981. By late 1940 eastbound "high/wide" cars were using Track 3 all the way down to GY so it was decided to add crossovers at SF so such traffic could be diverted to Tracks 1-2. They were, of course, operated remotely from AR. There was no problem westbound that GY could not handle. Keep in mind that the versatility available at MG did not appear until 1944. By the early 1940s SF was known as BF and by 1950 as Benny. For those into the minutiae of military history, the troops guarding the area consisted of a detachment from G Company, 3d Pennsylvania Infantry. Easy, boring duty. For them, the terror part would come later in France.

THE EAST SLOPE

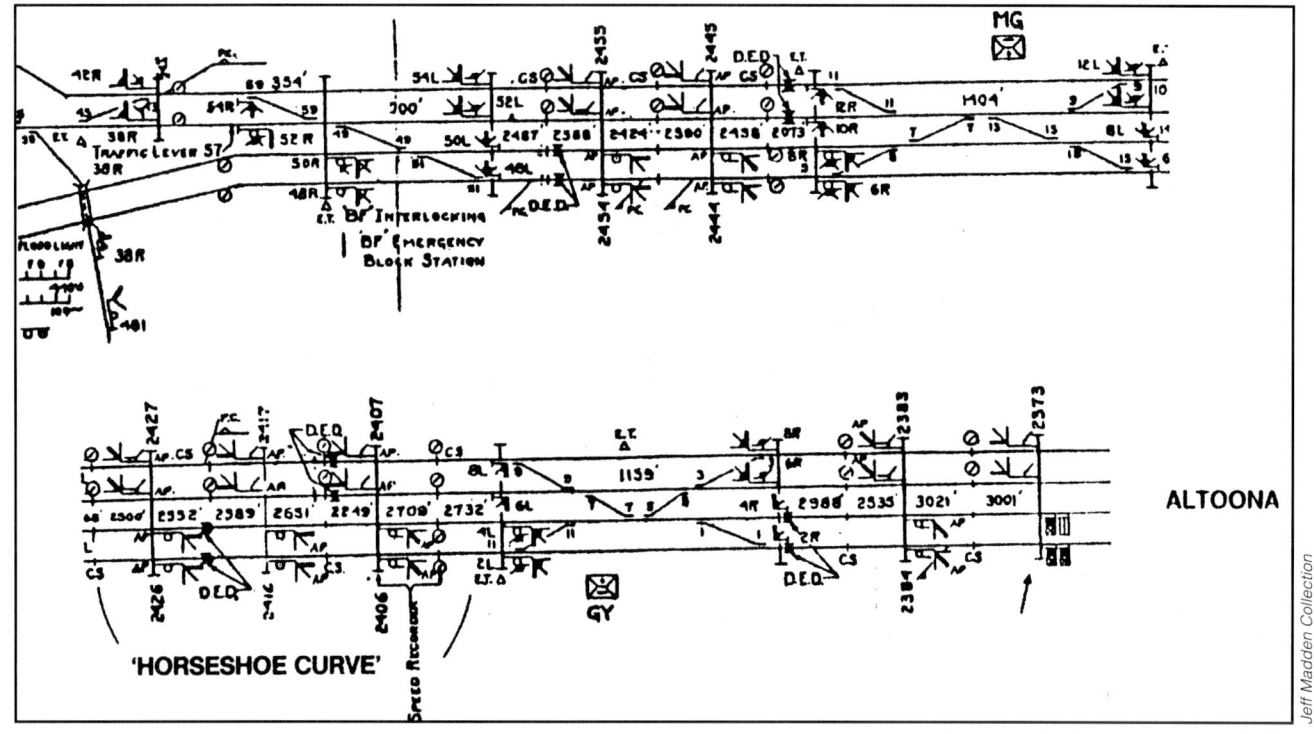

AFTER ALL THE CHANGES by 1944, this diagram represents the trackage, interlocking and signal situation on the east slope. BF, MG and GY provided dispatchers with maximum versatility in consonance with train lengths of this era. While this particular layout is dated 1948, it would be a number of years before changing circumstances would require further refinement. As the reader can see, in 1947 there was no way the *Red Arrow* could have moved from Tracks 1 or 2 to Track 3 east of the tunnels.

THE SEVERITY OF THE SCENE had improved somewhat by 15 August 1947. At least some underbrush is covering the bleak foreground. Three trains are in view, including one rounding the distant curve on the New Portage, and some coal is being moved with power on both ends. Only six months before the *Red Arrow* used this track on its way to a meeting with fate.

*Bruce D. Fales/
Jay Williams Collection*

TRIUMPH I

SOME TRAFFIC was moving on the New Portage branch in 1972. A westbounder slips under the 1892 bridge. Notice that the weeds between the rails presage an uncertain future.

Thomas A. Biery

THE 1892 BRIDGE just seen is gone, replaced by fill, and a long TrailVan train demonstrates how the nature of traffic evolves over time. The brush is now growing to the point where second-growth forest is being created. The New Portage tunnel is now single-track, although some NP Track 1 is still in place. Surely it doesn't go very far and is available for MOW and set-off purposes only. We don't know the date, but we can say that if you had come back to this spot after a hundred year absence, you would know exactly where you were. The symbol for TrailVan is TV, but it wasn't always so. Until 1970, the symbol TT was used for TrucTrain and SV for SuperVan.

Thomas A. Biery

THE EAST SLOPE

Pennsylvania State Archives

THE ALLEGHENY FRONT at the head of Sugar Run was pierced by three tunnels, two bored by PRR and a third by the Commonwealth of Pennsylvania in a last spasm of imbecility. None of the three were easy to complete or maintain. Each has a rich history, full of triumph, tragedy and even some wry humor. We have acquainted the reader with the confusing and unstable geology of the mountain barrier. Thus far we have discussed only cuts and fills. When one bores a tunnel, the effect of these unpleasant characteristics is magnified manyfold.

The very first PRR tunnel was the middle one which initially went by the name "Summit" and then "Allegheny." This early photograph is of the west portal, used because it seems nobody photographed the original east portal. The variability and virulence of the overburden is obvious. Inside the tunnel this malevolent structure assumed nightmare proportions. The goop consisted of perishable shales, fire clay, sandstone and even a four-foot vein of coal. Once exposed to air and water, the mixture became quite volatile and treacherous. Contract for the eastern approach was let to Thomas Reuther in 1851 and the work was supervised by PRR engineers Thomas W. Seabrook and Herman Haupt. The working face of any tunnel is very small and constricted, so three 6 by 10 foot vertical shafts were dug to multiply the number of active workers. From east to west, these shafts were 150, 195 and 184 feet deep respectively. Working from both ends and these shafts, there were eight working faces.

In the winter of 1853-54 a fourth 195 foot shaft with an 8 by 13 foot section was dug to speed up the work of bricklayers and masons. The second shaft from the east must have found an underground stream because steam pumps had to be deployed to remove 120 to 175 gallons of water *per minute*. The working conditions in the tunnel itself must have been horrific. It is said that some four hundred Irishmen from County Cork were sent into the bowels of the mountain during construction. One can be sure that a lot less came out alive or unmaimed because rockfalls and slides were frequent.

Daylight was first seen through the bore in 1852. During 1853 a monthly average of 2,800 cubic yards of material was removed, a rate which increased to 4,500 cubic yards by the close of the year. The roof of any tunnel or mine must be supported. Easier said than done. The vicious nature of the goop was such that it would collapse before supports could be installed. The tunnel was 3,612 feet long at completion. The first 2,770 feet from the east had to be lined with masonry. The last 800-plus feet was through sandstone so was left unlined, a decision that proved to be wrong. There was a lot of clay in the sandstone and when mixed with air and water it would swell, crack and fall in large masses. The tunnel was "made ready" by 21 January 1854 and the line was officially open for traffic the following month, but it was not really completed. Very little arching of the first 2,770 feet had been finished and the roof was supported by huge timbers. It wasn't until 17 February 1855 that arching was completed, so one may be sure that the first year of operations was single track. The last 800 feet was suspicious and 200 feet of that was timbered. Severe freezing weather in March 1856 shattered these timbers and the entire 200 feet of roof fell in. This section was hurriedly arched with obvious interference with train operations. Nor was roof collapse the only problem. Freezing in the tunnel caused heavy expense for the removal of snow and ice, so much so that in the winter of 1857-58 the west portal was closed with doors that were opened only for trains. And that last 600 feet of sandstone also proved to be dangerous. In 1869 even that part of the tunnel had to be arched with masonry. One might think all of the foregoing marked the end of PRR tunnel troubles by 1869. It was merely the first chapter in an ongoing struggle with the mountain.

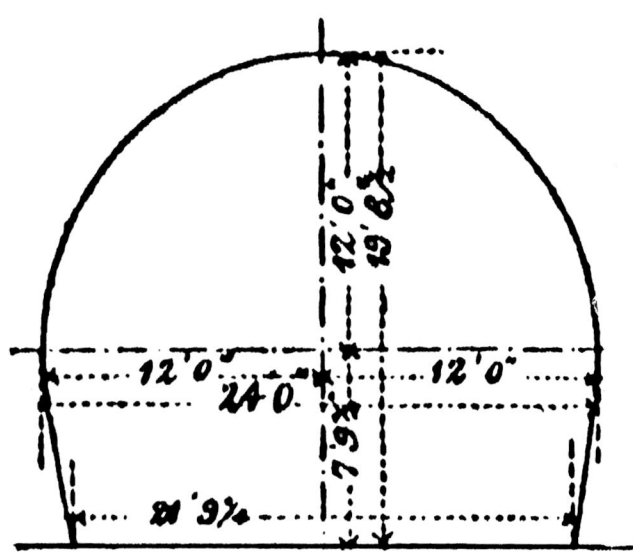

THIS DRAWING is called an "intrados," which is defined as the curve of an arch. This one, of course, is of the Allegheny Tunnel as built and is, in effect, a clearance diagram. The fit, incidentally, was very tight even for the times. The first eight feet of the arch on each side was built of cut stone 22.5 inches thick, resting upon abutments of rock of the same thickness. The first 2,770 feet of the tunnel consumed 7,700 perches of cut stone. A perch is a solid measure for stone 16.5 x 1.5 x 1 feet. By any measure, that is a lot of stone. The crown consisted of five courses of "hard burnt brick" laid in hydraulic cement. The brick was made from local clay. The tunnel consumed 6,400 perches of brick masonry. That is a lot of brick. Keep in mind that the portion of the tunnel initially arched was about a half-mile long. Remember the four-mile long tunnel scheme?

Gallitzin Area Tourist Council/Marjorie Platt Collection

THIS WIDELY PUBLISHED view of the west portal and the developing town of Gallitzin has always been identified as having been taken in the 1870s, a conclusion we are about to dispute. This photograph does provide a graphic image of the height of the overburden over the tunnel, which is about 210 feet at the topographical summit. It also shows the tight clearance in the tunnel and how little space has been provided for "springing sway." The oval sign in front of the building on the right of the track advertises "Jacob Gerhardt's Washington Hotel." Somehow we find it hard to believe George ever slept there. The more distant sign on the right nearer the tunnel portal is the more interesting one, as we are about to see. Notice that the westbound main has just received fresh new ties and the rails are "Thomson-level."

THE EAST SLOPE

Gallitzin Area Tourist Council Collection

THIS SCENE is another oft-published photograph which has been anointed with a wide variety of dates, including some contradictions from the same archive. For example, the Smithsonian Institution has two negatives, one proclaiming c.1870 and the other c.1860. The sign, to which we alluded in the last caption, directs visitors to "Gallitzen (sic) House." There is a milepost at the base of this sign in both photographs. The locomotive is a woodburner which means that the date could not possibly be after 1864 as all PRR engines were coalburners by that year and, if it is a freight locomotive, 1862. While the angle from the camera is different in this photograph, there appears to be the same number of telegraph poles in each. The surface appearance of the tunnel cut appears to be the same. So far this implies that both were taken on the same day. But this argument falls apart when the houses above and beside the tunnel cut are examined. There are houses in each photograph that do not appear in the other! We can, however, determine the earliest possible date. In 1857 a wye was installed at Gallitzin and in both photos we can see the crossover and the lead track going to the left. Now we must resort to guessing. This photo was probably taken in 1858 and the preceding one in 1859-60. One last thought: in both photos a line of houses follows the alignment of the shafts used in tunnel construction.

Blair County Historical Society

WHATEVER THE EXACT dates of the preceding two photographs, the history of PRR in the next thirty years was marked by enormous traffic growth, a large portion of which had to pass through Allegheny Tunnel. One bandaid was the development of interlockers to control both switches (turnouts) and signals. In 1888 this two-story tower was constructed at Gallitzin with state-of-the-art mechanisms. It was given the call letters UN, some say derived from tUNnel. Still, the tunnel itself had not been enlarged, as one can see, and cars were getting higher, wider and longer to say nothing of motive power improvements. The mere taking of this photograph circa 1890 must have backed up trains for miles. So Allegheny Tunnel was becoming a bottleneck that palliatives like UN could ease but not solve. Worse, the tunnel itself was giving problems. Not only were normal roof/walls/drainage maintenance riddles becoming more severe but the presence of coal underneath the tunnel roadbed was giving nightmares.

We have met Messrs. Brown and Sheppard as they dealt with expansion of trackage in the 1890s and the tunnel problem was an issue that would not go away. Brown was receiving rumors of tunnel rockfalls and he was the first to panic, requesting reports on the situation from Sheppard. The response of the operating people was amusing. In a letter dated 9 December 1897, an assistant reported to Sheppard that there had been four such incidents in the past four years. On 22 May 1893, about 1,000 feet from the west portal, small rocks fell on the north track and broke the cylinder cocks on Engine 588 (Extra West). On 21 February 1896, 700 feet from the west end, about one ton of rocks fell on the north track, blocking it for 30 minutes and causing 80 minutes of delay. On 1 March 1896, about 390 feet from the west end, two tons of rock fell and blocked both tracks for 28 minutes. On 1 December 1897, 1,200 feet from the west end, one ton of rock fell and delayed Extra 1381 East for ten minutes. The information was sent to Brown on 10 December with a laconic covering letter by Sheppard that stated, in part, that he did not think the rockfalls were alarming because "it has been coming down in about like proportions for the past 25 years." In other words, the operating people had gotten used to it and, considering all the problems they faced in keep the monster Pittdiv functioning, this was a tiny irritant. To Brown, however, the spectre of the roof caving-in on the only summit tunnel on the railroad was a matter of terror. No Chief Engineer would survive such a disaster. We must have more tunnels!

THE EAST SLOPE

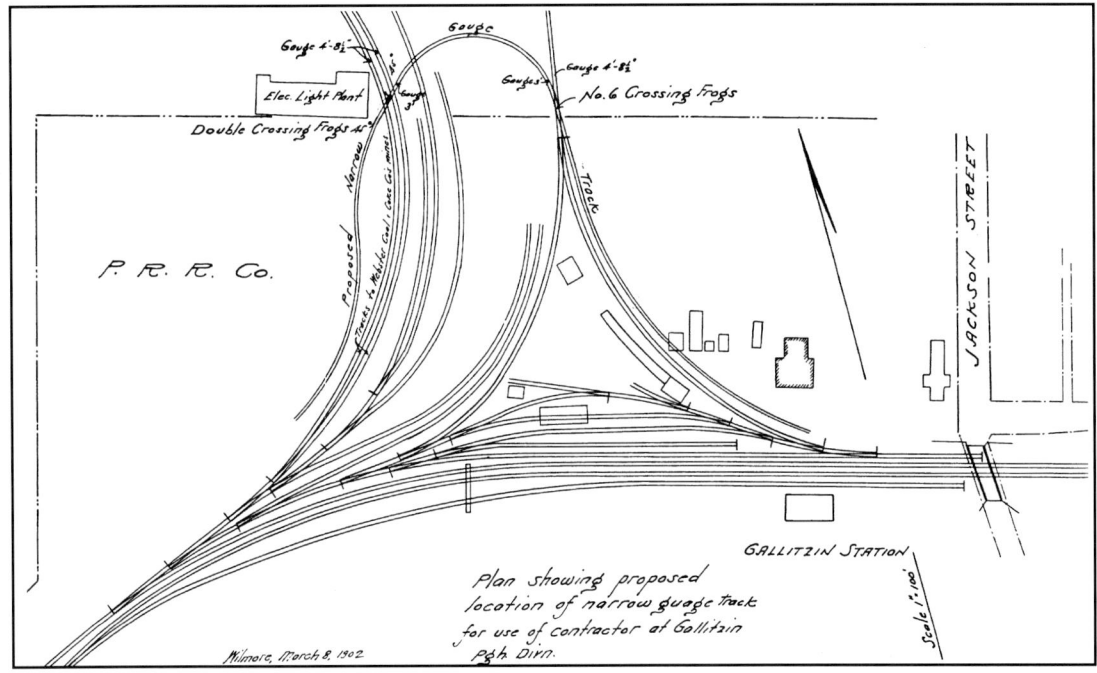

AS THE CENTURY CHANGED, four-tracking had been completed and the summit tunnel problem was crying for solution. The New Portage tunnel was to be reactivated, but that would not solve the westbound situation. Mr. Brown wrote to Philadelphia on 17 October 1901, recommending construction of a new single-track bore and single-tracking the Allegheny Tunnel. As a measure of his confidence in him, President Alexander J. Cassatt approved the plan in just a few days and on 6 November 1901 gave him carte blanche to "…construct a new…tunnel, in a location to be investigated and decided by yourself …on the lines suggested in your estimate." By 13 November an assistant reported to Brown that the north side of the original tunnel was the best location for several reasons; the south side was built-up and property acquisition would be expensive…also, material would have to be wasted on the north side in any event. Superintendent Wallis concurred on 26 November, pointing out that he had received no inquiries from property owners. As one can see from this drawing, PRR owned most of the property in the area save a few parcels around Jackson Street which was owned by a Catholic Church and School. Wallis felt that the Church would not make "exorbitant" demands and he was right. As events turned out, perhaps Holy Mother Church was a bit too easy to deal with. This drawing, dated 8 March 1902, shows the trackage situation in the Gallitzin area and provision for a three-foot narrow gauge railway to dispose of spoil. Oddly, UN tower was not shown. The Catholic Church, in the shape of a cross, appears but not the Catholic School…it is off to the right up on the hill east of the tunnel portal.

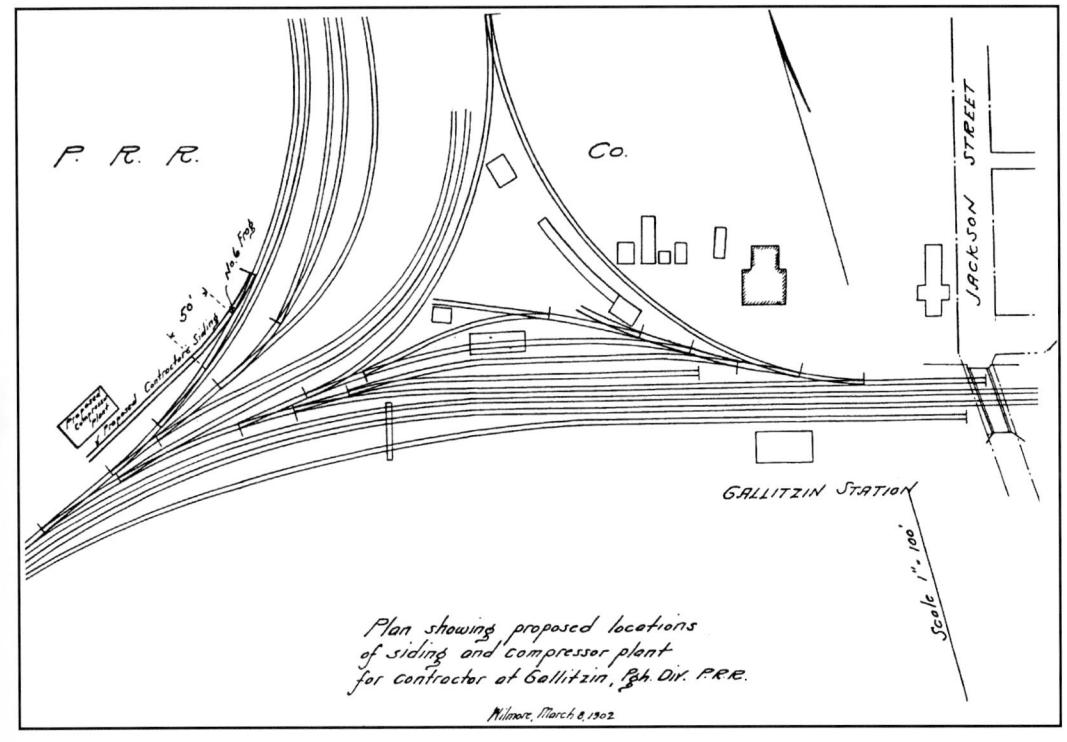

CONSTRUCTION OF THE NEW BORE, which became known as Gallitzin Tunnel, benefited from the fruits of engineering progress during the fifty years since the original tunnel was built. This drawing, for example, details the location of a compressor plant to power air hammers. Electric lights would be deployed in the bore and workmen could actually see what they were doing. Steam power could be used to transport waste and steam shovels would lift large gobs of waste with no more sweat than that required to move a few levers. Explosives, however, were rather much the same.

Gallitzin Area Tourist Council/T.C. Ketenheim Collection

THE BLESSINGS of material progress are manyfold. Here, within sight of Allegheny Tunnel's west portal in the Spring of 1902, machinery is digging away at the northern cut sidewall. The building at upper right is the Catholic School. The town is named for Prince Gallitzin, a Catholic priest of noble Russian lineage who landed in Baltimore in 1782, took up the priesthood, moved to Loretto just north of Gallitzin in 1789 to found a religious colony and rain blessings upon the poor. He died 6 May 1840, revered by all. Rain of a different sort occurred in July of 1902. A blast set-off by tunnel workers showered the central part of town with rocks, killing one and injuring one. Another blast so badly weakened the Catholic School that it had to be abandoned and the pupils housed in tarpaper covered sheds until a replacement school was finished in 1906. The science of explosive waste-removal was still in its infancy. The Gallitzin Tunnel was completed in 1904 and the Allegheny Tunnel single-tracked at once. We know less about the details of construction of the new tunnel than the two older ones; for example, we do not even know if shafts were employed. It seems, however, that the science of tunnel construction had regressed in fifty years. The Gallitzin Tunnel was inspected in early 1909 and an alarming report was made on 22 January. For a distance of about 900 feet at the east end the concrete lining was spalling off in large hunks. Closer inspection revealed that all of the concrete was disintegrating and there was a very real danger that the entire roof would collapse, taking all backing material and strata with it. In other words, a catastrophic failure that would take the tunnel back to nature all at once. The prospect that a passenger train might be in there at that moment made everyone shudder. This report was written by P. Cofrode, Master Carpenter. On 28 November 1908, he had inspected the tunnel and found that all was well. By 21 January 1909, just two months later, the concrete was soft, crumbling, shelling-off and in some cases large hunks were dangling 8 to 12 inches below the roof. It seems that the weather had been dry from 1904 to 1908 and had then turned very rainy. Remember the water removal problem at the second shaft from the east in the Allegheny Tunnel? Apparently it was flowing into the Gallitzin Tunnel, rotting the timbers that had been left in place above the concrete, softening the concrete itself and negating the concrete's adhesive qualities. Steps were taken over the next few years, but apparently new concrete was used. Then, in the summer of 1912, more distressing news was received. The concrete was beginning to deteriorate again and it was learned that coal miners had dug up to and under both tunnels. The miners had simply abandoned the workings and now the roofs were settling. In addition, water was finding its way into the mine rooms and much of it into the tunnels. Some had been found and filled with goop when the Gallitzin Tunnel was bored. The entries, however, were left open. The miners did not leave road maps behind so no one knew how serious the problem would turn out to be. PRR immediately purchased rights to the remaining coal around the tunnels and monitored mining activity in the area. This did nothing to fix the immediate problem. It was soon determined that sulphur in the drainage water, along with freezing and thawing, was doing most of the damage. Also, water was being dammed by goop and collapsed roof detritus…fine in dry weather but disastrous in wet when the dams broke. In the end, drains were drilled parallel with the bore to remove water and the roof of the Gallitzin Tunnel was replaced with vitrified brick. The reader will recall that the crown of the Allegheny Tunnel was built with brick in the first place. It was found that the rooms under the Allegheny Tunnel were some 75 feet under the floor and in 1912 it was recommended that they be filled with a thin grout to avoid "trouble…when least expected." We don't know whether this was done. If not, Conrail might find out someday. He who builds a tunnel gives hostage to fate.

THE EAST SLOPE

Gallitzin Area Tourist Council/T.C. Ketenheim Collection

IF THE WEST PORTALS of the twin tunnels were among the most photographed in railroad history, the east portals were the least. The Gallitzin Tunnel (on the right) was built for westbound freight movements and removal of smoke and gases was a significant problem on such a heavily-used line. We believe the ventilation system was installed shortly after the tunnel opened in 1904. We have absolute proof that it was active by early 1907. As with so many things in the study of history, sources of information are not where one would expect. As readers of our book *Sand Patch/Clash of Titans* are aware, B&O was considering construction of a 13,520 foot tunnel at their Pittsburgh-line summit at Sand Patch early in this century. Mr. D.D. Carothers, chief engineer of B&O, was concerned about ventilation of such a long tunnel and wrote his PRR opposite number (A.C. Shand at that time) on 16 May 1907 asking for data. A copy of Mr. Shand's reply came to our attention and the following information is extracted from that letter. The patented system was named Churchill-Westworth and consisted of two 16 by 8 foot Sturtevant fans each directly connected to a 250 hp engine. The object was to blow the smoke *ahead* of the road locomotives. Typical freight trains in that era had two up front and one on the rear, with an average speed of 11.6 mph through the tunnel. Fans running at 140 rpm produced a draft of 17-18 mph. The road engine against the train would shut down upon entering the tunnel to protect the cab of the front engine. The rear helper would continue to push, but when its smoke caught up with the road engines the gases were so intermixed with fresh air that they were unobjectionable. As one can see from this photograph, at that time no attempt was made to ventilate the Allegheny Tunnel because it was reserved for passenger trains and their speed averaged 30 mph. Two locomotive-type boilers initially provided steam to operate the system, but a third boiler was added to provide for maintenance downtime. We guess this photo was taken shortly after installation because the facility appears unsullied by grime. Notice the gob pile at upper left. As the reader has already seen, westward freight trains soon had two up front and two on the rear. We are assuming that, in this configuration, the rear helper shut down. In the first instance with the engine next to the train not working steam, available tractive power was reduced by a third. In the second and more modern instance, the scenario described would reduce power by fifty percent. Perhaps tonnage ratings were adjusted accordingly. As to Sand Patch, a new tunnel was built but not the long one envisioned. Ventilation was provided through ceiling shafts and convection. No mechanical system was employed. B&O crews had to gag their way over the top.

IF THE GIVEN DATE of 25 October 1907 on this photograph is correct, then it snowed quite early that year. At far left one can see the east portal of the New Portage Tunnel. It is higher than the twin tunnel portals.

*Gallitzin Area Tourist Council
T.C. Ketenheim Collection*

THIS 1934 PHOTOGRAPH indicates nothing much has changed in a quarter of a century. The Allegheny Tunnel is still unventilated and the Gallitzin Tunnel facility appears much the same except for the addition of two elevated hoppers at the left of the shed. It took us quite a while to determine that these cars were used for ash storage.

Smithsonian Institution

AT SOME TIME along the line, PRR added ventilation to the Allegheny Tunnel and changed the propulsion system, apparently converting to diesel. The cone-shaped duct for the Gallitzin Tunnel was original, but of course the closest one was new although built to the same general dimensions. The skeletons of Bennington Furnace beehive ovens overlook a still barren scene. Now let us venture back to the west portals of the twin tunnels.

Pennsylvania State Archives

THE EAST SLOPE

IF THE GIVEN DATE of 1907 is correct, then this photograph of the west portals of the twin tunnels is the earliest. Considering film speeds at the time, the locomotive exiting the Gallitzin Tunnel is probably stopped and posing with its stack out of the bore. The plot between the tracks is covered with grass, gardens and shrubs; it is an attempt at beautification of an inherently ugly scene that at least in this writer's view is a mark of civilized conduct.

Gallitzin Area Tourist Council
Marjorie Platt Collection

THIS CRUDE and deteriorating print does at least demonstrate that a lot of smoke can accumulate in a tunnel. The fan at the east end served only the left bore at this time. As to the right bore, one can only observe that it took a while for convection to remove the smoke. If a second section of a passenger train was following close behind, air quality at the outset would leave something to be desired.

Gallitzin Area Tourist Council
T.C. Ketenheim Collection

EXCEPT FOR THE SMOKE pouring out of the Allegheny Tunnel, a number of things changed by October of 1907. Telltales, signals and a mail crane have been added. No doubt the signals were distant for UN and the crane for the passenger station which is just behind the photographer. The snow appears to be about a foot deep, sufficient to have the railroad plowed. By summit standards, this is a light dusting. The Catholic Church is at upper left. Thankful prayers are no doubt being said celebrating the departure of the explosive experts.

Gallitzin Area Tourist Council
T.C. Ketenheim Collection

TRIUMPH I

Railroad Museum of Pennsylvania

IF THE LAST DATE of 1907 is correct, then the date of 1912 for this postcard is unlikely because there are no signals. As one can see, the garden was quite extensive, complete with crushed stone borders. The presence of a mail crane on Track 4 implies that passenger and express trains sometimes used the Gallitzin Tunnel.

WHEN THE SNOW gets over two feet deep, residents of this area acknowledge that it has precipitated. The shed between the tunnels, probably built for garden maintenance, has had the snow removed from its roof to keep it from collapsing. The railroad, of course, is open.

Railroad Museum of Pennsylvania
Gallitzin Area Council Collection

136

THE EAST SLOPE

FANS OR NOT, the passage of a Hippo produced smoke in volcanic proportions. The fireman has a mask over his face; he is still conscious and alert. By 1940, the date of this photo, the garden was long gone. The reader might think that the diesel age solved the problem of fumes, but he would only be half right. If a steam locomotive stalled in a tunnel, the exhaust could be stopped. If a diesel stalls, "shut down at once" is the rule in some bores.

Pennsylvania State Archives

A NEW Jackson Street bridge graces this aerial scene of the west portals. While the date is unknown, it is probably the early1950s simply because assignment of precious diesels to mail/express trains was seldom done until dieselization was completed. Notice how Thomson used a cut for the maximum possible distance before beginning the bore itself. The reader is reminded that the summit is at the tunnel portals. The presence of sand on both tracks beyond the summit indicates that more than one train was slipping even though the power was over the top. The road over Allegheny Tunnel runs at a slight angle. One wonders if a house was built over one of the four shafts used in tunnel construction.

THE EAST SLOPE

TV-11 punches through the Gallitzin Tunnel and closes on Milepost 248 on 8 August 1992. The suction effect of the train itself is pulling fumes from the bore. This is the last photograph the reader will see in this chapter prior to the commencement of Conrail's project to improve tunnel clearances at the summit. One should note how stabilizing underbrush has grown over the raw cuts. Sadly, it will all be removed. On 7 September 1995, TV-11 will make its mark in history. It was the first doublestack train to use the enlarged Allegheny Tunnel.

Todd Atkinson

THROUGHOUT RAILROAD HISTORY, the problem of clearances has been a bugbear that never seems to end. In the late 1980s, the rise of the doublestack configuration and continued growth of tri-level auto racks created a whole new ballgame for most railroads in general and Conrail in particular. Conrail was serving New York over ex-New York Central routes with ease, but not Philadelphia. This city, always an also-ran in the competition with New York, now faced a new challenge. Never willing to fund anything itself, the Quaker City paddled to Harrisburg and the offices of all competing railroads serving Philadelphia for help. Conrail, worthy of its PRR heritage of taking no prisoners and using any means at hand to achieve its end, attacked all of its competitors vying for doublestack access to Philadelphia. One of them (CP Rail) is Canadian owned. Conrail had already goosed switching charges for CP Rail to astronomical heights, claiming that it was their patriotic duty to stiff "foreign" intruders. At least Conrail avoided the enlistment of God on their side (as in *Gott mit uns*), keeping the argument secular rather than spiritual. This sort of gut fighting began with Thomson and explains why PRR and its successors have always been the most hated railroads in North America. The net result of this latest contest was an agreement in late 1992 that the Commonwealth would put up 33 million dollars and Conrail 45 million to improve clearances. Conrail later claimed that they had really put up an additional 19 million because of "work schedule interruptions," another example of typical PRR/PC/

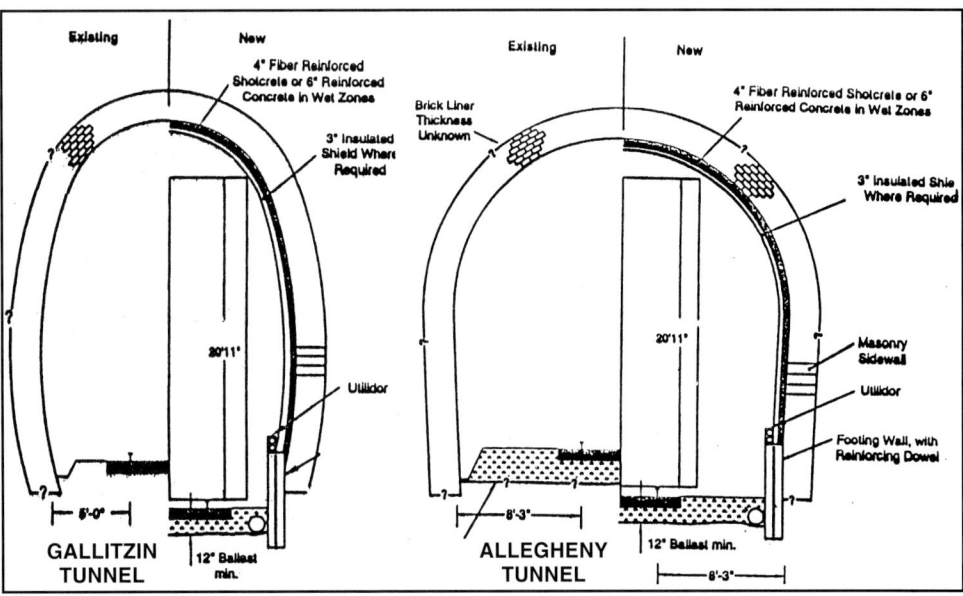

Conrail creative accounting. On Pittdiv, the major impediment was the summit tunnels. The official clearance needed was 20'8", but 20'11" was planned to allow for springing. The plans shown here reflect an early plan to drop the tunnel floor in both tunnels, maintaining single-tracks in each. Not having been privy to the discussions, we do not know why this plan was rejected. Perhaps the Catholic Church, an institution well known for its long memory, decided that this time they wanted to be consulted well in advance of the ignition of explosives. We did find one amusing note on the Allegheny Tunnel plan. Six courses of brick roof lining are shown with the note that the actual thickness was "unknown." If this latterday historian knew that there were five courses, why didn't they?

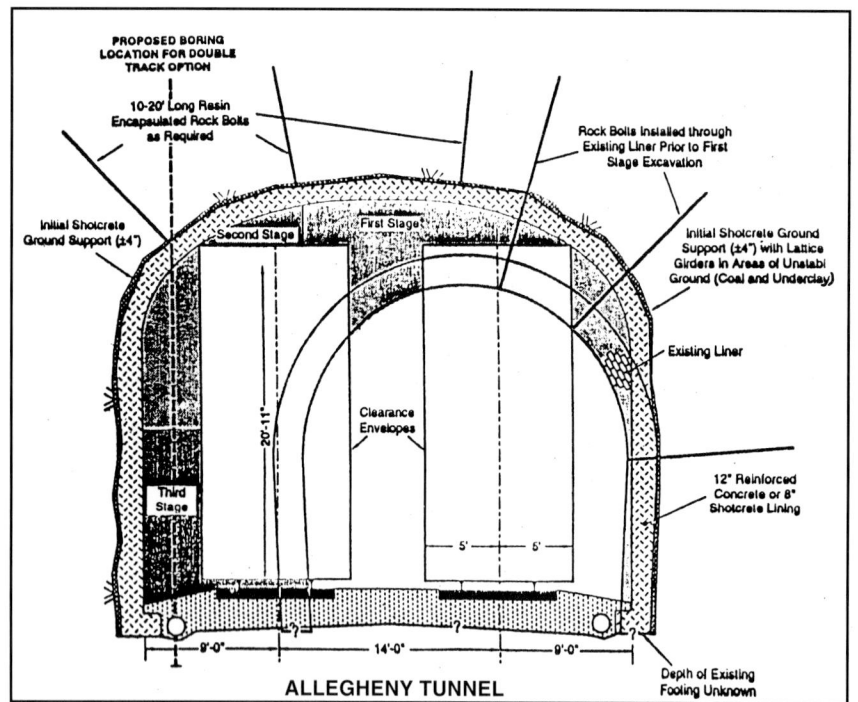

THIS PLAN, the one ultimately chosen, was presented by consulting engineers Shannon and Wilson as an option to the preceding proposal. All were presented in the summer of 1993 and acceptance must have been swift because construction started in November. It comes as no surprise to this historian that all did not go well. Perhaps the mountain was irritated because another Irishman was digging at its innards. The contractor was Monterey Construction Company and they soon found that those old coal workings were over, under and alongside the bore. Keep in mind that Monterey was enlarging the tunnel, so they found new mine rooms that earlier PRR engineers only suspected were in the vicinity. Conrail did not lose its nerve nor even consider retreating to a smaller bore with a gauntlet track. The rooms were filled with grout and only a few months were lopped off the schedule. As seen, the first train went through on 7 September 1995. The mountain lost. Again.

We will have to say that we can find nothing to criticize in the planning and execution of this project. Restoration of two tracks in Allegheny Tunnel provides versatility to meet future demands. The Gallitzin Tunnel is still in place if needed. Grown wise in the ways of tunnels, Conrail has not plugged the Gallitzin Tunnel and has left the track in place except for about 100 feet at each end. An emergency detour is readily available. We should point out, incidentally, that TV-11 is a New York train. Clearance work in the Philadelphia area was completed in time for TV-20 to arrive on 3 April 1996. The combined ports of Philadelphia/Camden now join New York as one of only two northeastern ports capable of handling doublestacks. At this time, Baltimore's position in this regard seems hopeless. Norfolk's star seems to be on the rise but we will wager that this is ephemeral. New York will remain the cock of the walk. As to the project itself, a total of 130 locations from Pittsburgh to Harrisburg, Reading and eastern Pennsylvania were improved. Thomson's legacy of engineering excellence and barefisted barroom fighting is alive and well.

THE SCENE at the twins on 6 May 1995 from the Jackson Street bridge is one of mud and progress. The reader should be reminded that history is an ongoing process and this photograph is part of that lore. Now let us go south and back in time to tell the story of the New Portage Tunnel.

THE EAST SLOPE

THE NEW PORTAGE TUNNEL'S history is just as rich as that of its more northerly twins and it seems nobody bothered to photograph the original east portal. We have already related the fantasy of the origins and construction of the New Portage Railroad and its route to the summit. Because their east slope approach from Hollidaysburg was more circuitous than that of PRR from Altoona, the NPRR could maintain a reasonable grade and pierce the ridge at a higher elevation...actually about 25 feet higher than PRR's bores. Also, the NPRR could use the lowest depression at the head of Sugar Run which in turn meant a shorter tunnel and a lower overburden (135'). Contracts for the tunnel were let to contractors Moorehead and Patterson on 29 July 1852. By the summer of 1853 they had dug into the mountain to the extent that they, too, found unpleasant surprises in the form of "perishable shale." The NPRR originally planned on a 1,800 foot bore but the presence of this unstable goop forced them to make longer cuts on both ends and reduce the bore itself to 1,620 feet, a length less than half that of PRR's tunnel. Lining the tunnel was mandatory and stone walls with brick roof was the method chosen, the same as that employed by PRR. This change involved extra costs and Harrisburg, at long last, was getting more and more reluctant to provide the cash with the result that construction languished. The contractors temporized with timber shoring. The NPRR was announced as "open" on 23 April 1855, but the tunnel itself was not ready until 1 July 1855. Optimistic press releases are not a modern phenomenon. Provision for two tracks was made. At the close of 1855 almost all of the lining was completed. However, it was not until December of 1856 that the last brick was placed. Much of the lining was installed while the railroad was in operation. Since PRR had withdrawn their traffic on 15 February 1854 and there wasn't all that much traffic, this accomplishment was something less

Pennsylvania State Archives

than heroic. PRR bought the whole bloody thing in June of 1857 and closed it down that Fall as reported. So the first stage of the tunnel's operational history lasted about two years. Forty-one years would elapse before it came back to life. The original name of the tunnel was Allegheny. PRR not only took title but also the name and gave it to their summit tunnel. From then on, NPRR's tunnel would be known as the New Portage. The town above the New Portage, by the way, is Tunnelhill...not Gallitzin. We do not know when this photograph was taken but will guess in the 1870s when PRR was using the route as a branch. The trackage is certainly not mainline...note the wiggle close to the portal. Telltales were in style at the time. Notice how different the strata compared to other photos the reader has seen of this general area. Unlike the PRR twin bores, the actual summit is not at the portal but rather well to the rear, or west, of the photographer.

Railroad Museum of Pennsylvania/Gallitzin Area Tourist Council Collection

PRR TRAFFIC continued to soar in the 1880s and the railroad was struggling to increase capacity to handle it all. By the summer of 1890, then-president George B. Roberts inquired if it would be practical to utilize the New Portage tunnel in mainline service. It seems the roof had been deteriorating for some time, periodically dropping bricks on the track. This was merely an annoyance while the line was just a branch but might be a harbinger of danger if the tunnel were to be improved. It was known that the tunnel would have to be enlarged if two-track mainline service was to be instituted and that there had been a lot of coal mining in the vicinity. It was decided to hedge by widening the arch for two tracks only at places that required immediate attention and to do so in such a manner that the line could be opened for single-track traffic on a few hours notice. A brutal depression in the mid-1890s slowed progress, but by 1898 the enlargement work was completed and the New Portage tunnel was in full service as part of PRR's two-track eastbound mainline. The two tracks ran from Benny to Cresson on the west slope by that date. Here, in near-blizzard conditions, we see the west portal within a few years of its rebirth.

141

TRIUMPH I

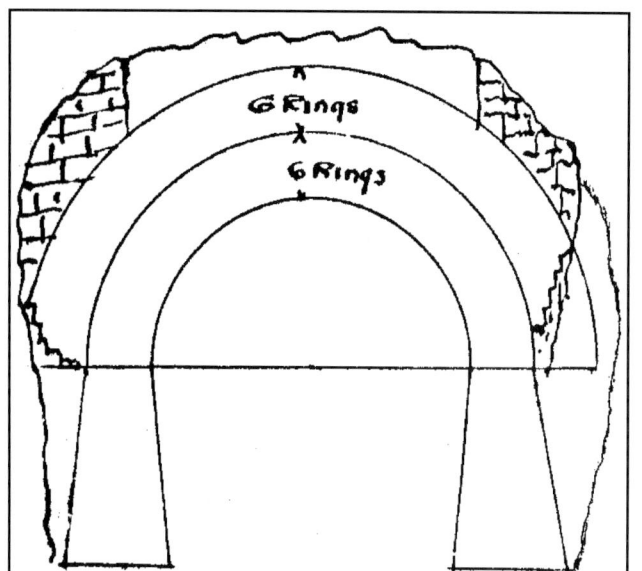

ONE OF THE GENTLEMEN employed on the 1890s enlargement and relining of the New Portage tunnel was Warren Mitchell. In 1911 he was asked to report on his experience in the bore and he stated that no serious conditions were encountered. Quite a few old mine openings were found over and alongside the tunnel. In each case, a stone wall was built about 10-15 feet away from the roof or sidewall ring to help carry the load. Shafts used in 1850s construction were found and in these cases the roof arch was enlarged to a 12-brick ring rather than the usual 6 or 7. In addition, masonry wall backfilling was done from the haunches to the 12-ring section to take care of any possible falls from the shafts. This sketch was drawn by Mr. Mitchell to illustrate the latter procedure. If perchance some presentday Conrail engineers should read this caption, we submit that sleepless nights are not warranted. We have already suggested wariness in regard to the twin bores.

BY 1934 the only significant change in the scene has been the substitution of position light signals for semaphores. Faint hints of sand on Track 2 is puzzling. Why would PRR even consider putting a westbounder on this steep grade? Perhaps it is explained by an emergency detour or an MOW train.

Smithsonian Institution

WISPS OF ICE remind the viewer, as well as the author, that the greatest enemy of man's works is water in each of its three forms. Liquid, gas, solid.

Julius Westheimer Collection

IN 1963, PRR moved New Portage Track 2 up against the north wall of the tunnel and Track 1 to the middle. The TVs of the time were called TrucTrains and, for clearance reasons, Allegheny Tunnel was used for such movements in both directions. PRR, incidentally, was an early pioneer in "trailer on flatcar" operations and while their ratemaking policy in this regard was somewhat shortsighted it has to be said that operationally the railroad was on top of the problem. Back to 1963, putting eastbounders through Allegheny Tunnel caused obvious complications so it was decided, in effect, to single-track New Portage and provide clearance. At the time, this was announced as a trial which is the reason Track 2 was not removed. This change must have been salubrious because by 1971 it is known that Track 2 had been removed. The photograph seen here, however, was taken on 3 March 1995 from above the west portal looking west.

Ice and snow attest that Spring comes late in mountain country. The scene from here to the overhead road bridge in the distance has not changed much in the last 140 years. This is the first time in this book that the reader is seeing the work of Brian Paulus, in our view one of the most brilliant railroad photographers of all time. Many more of his splendid shots will be seen in color later in the book. This particular day was not a good one for Mr. Paulus, however. His recalcitrant 300mm lens locked up for the last time while he was standing here and, as an act of final frustration, he threw it over the side and down into the cut. Then, as he departed in his truck, an unseen pole tore off his mirror. On 6 May 1995 your author almost clipped the same pole, after he had come perilously close to falling off the edge. Let the reader be warned that this location has bad vibes.

THE NOTORIOUS "SLIDE" begins here, just east of the Main Street bridge in Tunnelhill. The cars of this eastbounder appear to be plunging into a hole and that is rather close to the truth. Yet this is the easy part. The grade from here to just east of the east portal is only 1.59%. The 2.36% dropoff starts on the far side of the ridge and continues for just over a mile until the original PRR mainline is met at Benny. There was no "slide" when the NPRR was built; the gradient ranged from 1.59% to 1.50% to 1.34% to 1.50% until Sugar Run was crossed. While these numbers do not represent a mild grade, they were actually easier than PRR's approach to the summit as we have seen. The "slide" was created because the NPRR had to be dropped quickly to join PRR. Today's rules are simple. Maximum speed leaving the tunnel is 12 mph and 8 mph for tonnage trains, somewhat akin to porcupines making love. Very, very carefully. This photograph was taken by us on 6 May 1995, an hour or so before we almost took our own "slide." We studied quite a few eastbounders that day. All had helpers on the rear, but that is not mandatory procedure if all dynamics are working on the road units. It simply means power is needed at Altoona for westbound shoves. Every train we saw was completely under control and each time the inevitable slack run-in was mild. Father would have been disappointed.

TRIUMPH I

TRAIN NO. 54 Engine 5833 and 16 cars has just left the east portal on the New Portage tunnel on 25 June 1948. The lead Baldwin Centipede has just entered the "slide," We could not resist the temptation to again remind the reader that PRR motive power policy left much to be desired. The case could be made that "turkey" rather than Centipede might have been a more appropriate name. These units ended up as helpers on the east slope and on our trip with Father in the mid-1950s we saw several units resting on the loop between AR and UN. Father did manage a wry smile when he saw them. The day did have a few bright spots for him.

B&O Historical Society
E.L. Thompson Collection

APPARENTLY EVEN the New Portage Tunnel had a thing for Irishmen. The "doubletrack" decision for New Portage was easy...simply drop the tracks with an undercut. Consultants Shannon and Wilson presented this perfectly rational plan in mid-1993. Keep the railroad single-track, drop the floor about 16 inches and put in additional footings to secure the walls. This drawing, by the way, looks west. Nothing can go wrong. Contractor Frontier-Kemper dashed into the bore fully prepared to remove some perishable shale. Quite abruptly they found the floor consisted of rock so hard that diamond-tipped drills had to be used to gouge it out. By late 1993 it had taken about four months to complete the work. Of course, New Portage had to be finished before Allegheny Tunnel could be closed and schedule slippage disease set in. Still another time profanity washed the Allegheny Front summit. Conrail now has three doublestack tracks through the barrier. Curiously, the New Portage "slide" is not a factor taken into account by today's dispatchers. But it was on 9 December 1931 when Extra East 4272 (the South Fork coal train) was wrecked at Bennington. Some common criminal swine closed the angle-cock on the 12th car from the locomotive and the resulting wreck killed a member of the crew. If it were not for the slide, there might have been time to pull the air from the rear. PRR put a twelve-man special police force in the area to protect their trains. By February of 1932 nine floodlights were installed west of the tunnel and this security enabled PRR to cut the force in half. The reader should note that there are reasons why railroads are sensitive to trespassers. For example, hobos would close an angle-cock and count on trainline leakage to bring the train to a stop where they wanted to get off. The early 1930s was a Depression era.

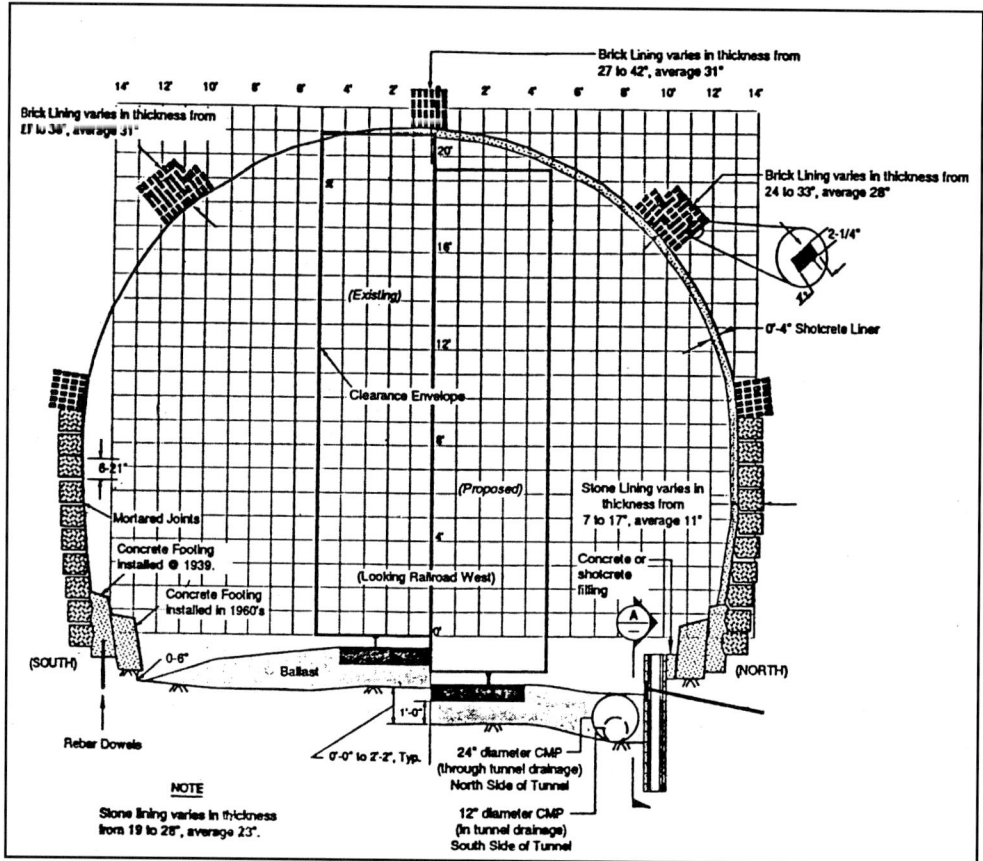

THE EAST SLOPE

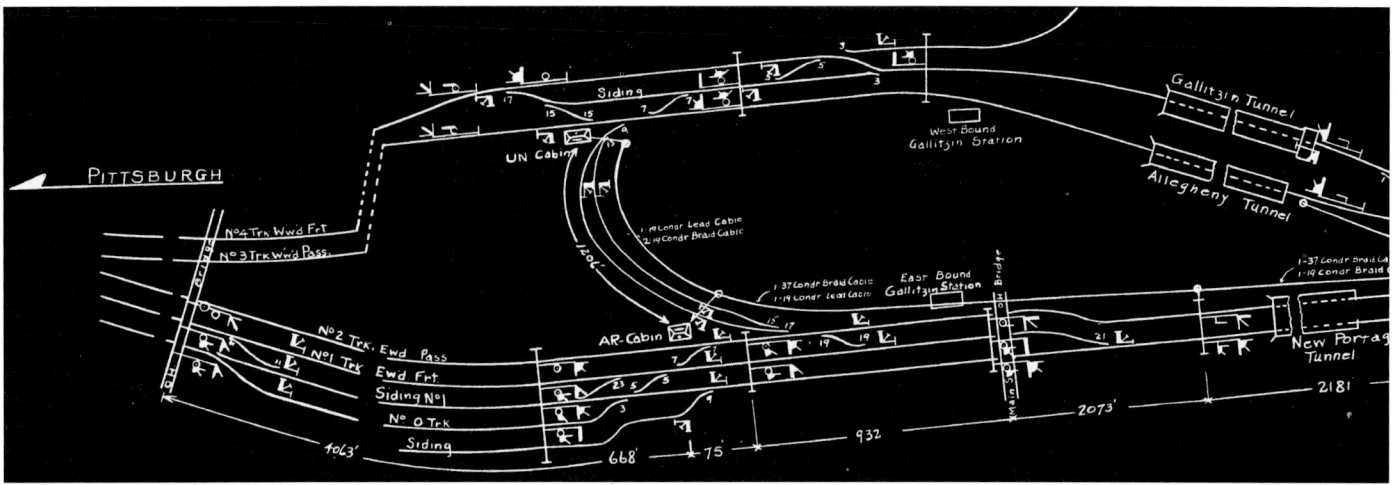

WHILE TECHNICALLY not part of the east slope, the immediate area west of the tunnels was above Laurel Swamp Summit so we have decided to include its history in this chapter. This is the track layout in 1934. The reader will recall that effective 5 January 1932 SF interlocker was operated remotely from UN and AR and that this drawing had to do with additional SF turnouts being added to UN/AR. We wish to draw your attention to the location of these two "cabins," the two stations, the overhead bridge on the New Portage line to the right of AR and the overhead bridge at far left. Notice that in 1934 signals were still semaphore. Curiously, the overhead Jackson Street bridge just west of the twin portals is not shown.

Two loop tracks run from AR to UN. Over time they were named the Altoona and Conemaugh Loops, parlance signifying that helpers were turned here for the return trip to helper stations at the bottom of both the east and west slope grades. Keep in mind that the eastbound New Portage mainline is higher than the westbound and they will not come together until Cresson, off the map on the left. There was no "slide" on this side of the summit as PRR had ample length to ease the transition and had a vested interest to do so because heavy eastbound tonnage needed all the help it could get. Also note that Track 2 and 3 are still designated "passenger," simply because the stations are on the inside.

Gallitizin Area Tourist Council/T.C. Ketenheim Collection

THIS IS A VIEW of the overhead bridge on the New Portage line, looking westward. One can see the station just west of the bridge and AR in the distance. Actually this is Tunnelhill and the bridge carries Main Street even though PRR always identified the station as Gallitzin. There are steps on both sides of the bridge and gently fenced walkways for the benefit of residents and passengers. There is a mail crane at far right, establishing that not all trains stopped here.

145

TRIUMPH I

Gallitzin Area Tourist Council/T.C. Ketenheim Collection

THE SAME OVERHEAD bridge from the west and taken earlier than the preceding photograph because there are no signals on the structure. This iron bridge was erected in 1898, the same year that the New Portage tunnel widening was completed. The station was built in 1899. Remember Messrs. Wallis and Brown? On 26 September 1899, Mr. Wallis wrote Mr. Brown a rather caustic letter in regard to this bridge in which he reminded Mr. Brown that "your engineers" provided clearance of only 19 feet and 1/2 inch at this location and that he hoped Mr. Brown understood that "it is necessary for all brakemen to be on top of the cars when starting down the mountain, and it is on that account [this is] an unusually dangerous place." Twisting the knife a little, Mr. Wallis also wrote "...you had intended *quietly* (author's italics) raising the approaches with stone, after which you proposed raising the bridge a foot or 18 inches" and "I am very desirous that this should be done as soon as possible, before we have an accident at that point." Pointedly left unsaid was "these are my troops you idiots have put at risk of life and limb and I am getting tired of waiting for the fix you promised." Here is a tiny little insight into the wars between those who create something and those who have to use these creations. The reader can be assured that such wars are in full flower throughout world society at this very moment. It is a given that without creativity and innovation there will be no progress. Since your author has usually been on the "user" end of this equation throughout his career, he can be pardoned for asking this question: why is it that these geniuses steadfastly refuse to communicate with the users, asking them about their problems, needs and suggestions? Is this a hangup of some sort that is implicit in intellectual brilliance? Or is it intellectual arrogance? Whatever it is, it should be exorcised.

SOME HOUSES have been built and signals installed since the last photograph. The practice of putting signals on overhead bridges was very common before the coming of the automobile. When the number of trucks and autos grew exponentially in the early twentieth century, the pounding on bridges like this one reverberated up the masts and into the mechanisms, causing all manner of maintenance problems.

Joanne Chester Collection

TRUE TO THE VALUATION TRADITION of taking only poor photographs, this view of the eastbound station records its appearance c. 1918.

National Archives

THE EAST SLOPE

ONLY A FLAT SPOT in the cut, at lower right, marks the location of the eastbound station as a Conrail freight gingerly approaches the "slide" on 6 May 1995. The cut itself, of course, was carved by the New Portage Railroad all those many years ago. Three tracks are now down to one. The actual summit of the New Portage is about six hundred feet behind the photographer, who is standing on the Main Street bridge. Vaguely seen in the distance to the right of the train is AR. While this legendary tower does not mark the precise "top," everyone thinks it does. So it must be true.

National Archives

WE WILL NOT HAZARD a guess as to how many towers graced American railroads through history, but we will speculate that almost everyone interested in railroading knew of AR and exactly where it was located. Where PRR went over the top. Eastbound. PRR's hottest spot. First string varsity for operators. The elite, cocky and cold. No room or time for error. Only at AR, when a derailment blocked all tracks save one, would the operator take the phone off the hook and reply to the complaints of an irritated executive, "Do you want me to move trains or make reports?" Only at AR, when informed that B&O cut-off helpers on the fly, would the reply be, "We don't." And it would only be at AR when Father and your author, looking around on the north side of the tower during the trip to which we have alluded, be confronted by a snarling operator who demanded that we leave forthwith or he would have us arrested. One did not speak to Father in that manner. Without a word and with a cold glare that had chilled his son's backbone on more than one occasion, Father pulled his business card from his wallet and gave it to the operator. In all our years of experience, we have never seen such an instantaneous change in attitude. "Oh. Oh. B&O! Come in! Come in!" We spent the rest of the day in AR and were made as welcome as visiting royalty. There were two operators on duty and both were pleasant, candid, earthy, outgoing and extremely efficient. Chit chat only when no movement was in progress. When a passenger train went by leaking steam, one of them said, "You know, we say that B&O runs steam through its trains and PRR runs its trains through steam." When the Aerotrain went on the bell, we were told to watch carefully because this train was a moving disaster that rode so badly passengers and crew alike had to hold on to protect their kidneys. Sure enough, the product of General Motors wizardry was corkscrewing so violently that it was a miracle it stayed on the rails. One wonders if they had barf bags for seasickness. Father made a note to report his observations in Baltimore. Father also commented later that in all his years of railroad experience, he had never seen so many trains in his life nor had he ever observed a more professional display of railroading skill. Keep in mind that he was watching the enemy in action and had found the experience sobering. After all, he and his father and his forebears had spent their careers warring with PRR and he could see that any future victories would be hard won. Within a year or so, PRR announced that they would acquire New York Central and the gloom in Baltimore was palpable. As to AR, we finally had to leave. One of the gentlemen gave me a recently outdated employee timetable which still rests in our library. Only now has it occurred to us that we were probably one of a select few non-PRR people to witness AR in action. There will be no more. AR closed for good in September of 1995.

TRIUMPH I

Edward H. Weber

LOOKING EAST, here we see AR on 7 September 1962. Not published is a photo from the same angle taken in 1953. The differences are slight, so this is the way AR appeared at the time of our visit. With one exception: there were weeds in the plant in 1962, but not 1953. Our tactical "spook" instructors used to emphasize that one should be alert for the "little changes" as they are often harbingers of things to come. The presence of weeds was, indeed, a sign of insidious deterioration. There is a significant change from the preceding photo, however. AR now has a flat roof. PRR was not the only railroad to put flat roofs on structures in snow country, a tendency that we find puzzling. AR's birthday is no puzzle. AR, along with UN, was built in 1899 and both were equipped with new mechanical interlocking mechanisms. The next year PRR completed its new pneumatic automatic block signaling system from Altoona to Gallitzin and AR was enlarged accordingly. There are those who speculate that the call letters AR were taken from poRtAge, which may be correct but we find this reasoning a little strained if not farfetched.

BY 29 MAY 1970, the weeds are gone but the rails are bow-legged. PC Engines 3201 and 3165 are moving an eastbound at about 25 mph. The year 1970, of course, was the year of Penn Central's collapse. PRR always did everything in a big way and this financial disaster was the largest in American corporate history to that time. We have studied this unpleasantness in detail and, for whatever it is worth, have concluded that it all would have happened anyway. The rot began in the 1880s when PRR initiated various stratagems to contain rate wars. It is said that the 1887 ICC act was actually written by a Broad Street law clerk and sent to Congress with instructions to pass it. The "community of interest" ploy, an attempt to "rationalize" competition, also had its roots in the 1880s. All these machinations, spearheaded by PRR as the dominant railroad in the nation, were in reality a grand design to let the national government be the arbiter of transportation policy and PRR was serene in the conviction that they could control the camel that they were letting into the tent. PRR was a Republican railroad in a Republican State and the Republican Party was in absolute control of the nation from the start of the Civil War until the onset of the Great Depression. The Republican Party, however, was not a monolith and was quite capable of progressive mutation. It was a coalition at its beginning in 1854 and has always had a populist liberality growing in its soul. In reality, then and today, it is the party of the little guy and devoted to maximum freedom for the individual. The Grand Old Party was not going to let anyone push it around and that included PRR. PRR wanted rate regulation and it got it. PRR, along with budding trusts in other fields, wanted to control all railroading and the GOP said NO. Furthermore, the GOP said, we are going to protect and nuture your competition. Free and open competition is the path to economic Heaven and maximum human freedom. Freedom yes, license no. PRR was taken aback by this turn of events but decided to feed the camel rather than throw it out. The camel's appetite was such that it then began to devour PRR. The railroad was being eaten to death by rate regulation, subsidized competition, voracious unions, inevitably high terminal costs, relatively short hauls, profitless passenger service and railroad competition on all sides with deep-seated hatred of Broad Street arrogance. Government was kill-

Edward H. Weber

ing the golden goose and PRR was the fattest. In the 1900s PRR saw rate-protected earnings soar, but into the 1910s the tide had turned and PRR began to slowly implode. The railroad went from being the hunter of railroading to the hunted. PRR management was not up to the challenge, preferring to hunker down and stonewall. At the close of World War II, PRR was in desperate shape. Still wedded to rate regulation and afraid of change, they mounted one last counterattack. Acquire New York Central and count on cost reduction to save their hides. The concept almost worked, but the camel was still greedy. Yet the Penn Central collapse was the event that finally satiated the camel. Society could not survive without a Penn Central and in one of those turnabouts that a versatile, free and open system of governance is quite capable, the fetters of regulation were torn off, the camel was castrated and a new entity named Conrail gathered to its bosom the best of the wreckage. A turnaround was achieved that was as dramatic as the collapse. From ashes to triumph took just ten years. Last year marked PRR's 150th birthday. The next 150 years are going to be equally fascinating.

THE EAST SLOPE

Thomas A. Biery

THE OLD AND THE NEW in 1976, Conrail's birthdate. Engine 2364, still in "worms" livery, and mates roar by AR and prepare for the descent to Altoona as a helper set lingers on the loop. The open field behind the tower was once home to a huge coal wharf, built in 1905. The wharf itself measured 28 by 144 feet and it boasted a 358 foot approach track. It was still there in the mid-1950s when we visited with Father, yet we have been unable to locate a photograph of it. While born in 1976, it took Conrail another five or so years to stop the financial bleeding. During that five years unsung heroes by the score rebuilt the railroad from the ground up. A man named L. Stanley Crane, retiring from the Southern Railway, decided to take on the awesome task of restoring the old PRR to its rightful place as the dominant railroad in the northeast. His almost miraculous achievement ranks him near Thomson and a few others in history as a man of the hour that this nation and its institutions bring to the fore in times of crisis. This observer of history regards the emergence of men of Crane's caliber as living proof that the framers of the Constitution of the United States were divinely inspired. There is virtually no limit to the heights to which a free people can aspire nor any goal that they cannot reach nor any diversity of interest that cannot be overcome by unfettered and open debate. By studying the past all of us can face the future with equanimity because we know that the giants of the future are sure to appear when they are needed.

ANOTHER DAY, another mineral train. On 9 August 1992, AR clears one more eastbound, probably the South Fork coal job. Before we go farther west, we would like to pass along an item in history that struck us as being rather fascinating. There is a private club in Philadelphia named the Union League. It was in this club that Republican Theodore Roosevelt, fresh from his 1904 presidential victory, announced to his audience of movers and shakers that he was going to put teeth into national regulatory authority over railroads and industry, much to the chagrin of those PRR people who were present. It was here that Roosevelt's "square deal" campaign began and he threw down the gauntlet in blunt, unequivocal terms that stunned those PRR chieftans who had invited the camel into the tent. It was on 4 May 1988 in the same club and probably at the same podium that Stanley Crane recited the history of the final dissolution of that apparatus in regard to railroads and described his own role in that counterrevolution. It was Teddy's nephew Franklin Delano Roosevelt, a Democrat, who launched the "new deal" in 1932 in response to a devastating economic collapse that must be laid at the feet of that same Republican Party. The second Roosevelt was called a "traitor to his class," whatever that means, and we doubt that he was ever invited to speak at the Union League. It is a certainty that the first Roosevelt meant to curb, not destroy, overpowering concentrations of power and it is equally certain that the second Roosevelt wanted to rejuvenate a failed system. With the best intentions, both failed. Teddy's approach ultimately ground PRR into the ground and Hitler, not FDR, pulled the economy out of the pits. Surely by this point the reader will be able to relate to the axiom that "if you want to screw something up, get Government in it."

Todd Atkinson

TRIUMPH I

Jeff Madden

WESTBOUNDERS did pass AR and here is the proof in a photograph taken in 1993, probably related to Allegheny Tunnel enlargement. We do not want to leave our favorite PRR tower without recording a few more thoughts. No doubt the reader has guessed that the Roberts family has always been Republican. To the author's horror, he learned a few months ago that his new daughter-in-law is a Democrat. After reprimanding our son and reminding him that while Republican men will go out with Democrat women, they will not marry them, we found ourselves in the awkward position of trying to convince an already-married Irishwoman that she must change. Try that sometime. The reader must understand that to be a Republican in Maryland is a form of masochism because the standard election day taunt is, "Hi. It's good to see a Republican alive on election night."

In 1965 we had been posted to Philadelphia to turn around a recently acquired subsidiary. We were asked to address some sort of chamber of commerce function which included many Philadelphia elite. After handing out the usual good neighbor pap, we decided to wrapup by saying, "My wife and I are living in Devon and will have to say that we have not found your city to be a hardship area. We are lonely Republicans from Maryland and are finding it difficult to adjust to the fact that we are now surrounded by those who have already been converted. You all can accept that I have been raised in that classic tradition of Love all things, hate but three: Hate sin, Roosevelt and the Pennsylvania Railroad Company and not necessarily in that order." For an impromptu ad lib, it drew an ovation and a host of PRR executives with whom we chatted for almost half an hour in one of the more delightful conversations of our career. Five years later when Penn Central went down, there was no one more sad than Father. "What a shame to destroy such a splendid railroad." He did not criticize Stuart Saunders other than to observe that such a monumental merger should have been led by a man with more real railroad experience. In the event, it took just such a man to bring order out of chaos.

As to the Union League, that little speech resulted in an invitation to join the club. Membership rules required that one had always voted Republican with one exception…it was OK to have voted for Roosevelt in 1932 because everyone was in a state of panic in that year. Sadly, we had voted for Lyndon Johnson in 1964. That we later wished that we could have reversed that vote was of no avail. The name Union means just that, incidentally. Preservation of the Union as in Civil War. We have been guests in at least three such clubs and there may be more. We have already addressed the question of "irony" in the introduction to this book and want to point out that we are directly related to U.S. Grant's mother, who was a Simpson. You cannot be more Unionist than that, but it wasn't enough to cancel out that mistake in 1964.

At this point the reader might ask what all this has to do with a history of PRR. The answer is everything. A railroad by its very nature reaches across many political jurisdictions and the political tides flow back and forth in response to concerns of the moment as well as the shifting winds of public opinion. Once a railroad is in place it cannot be moved. This aspect of railroading is unique in transportation and industrial evolution. Tidewater shipping can change ports of call with comparative ease; airlines can select airports almost at will; trucklines can choose a different highway net; farmers can move to greener pastures; people go with the flow and opportunity; factories can be easily moved from here to there; money and paper capital slither around with mercurial velocity; traffic patterns change almost daily in response to new, maturing and dying markets. It was PRR president George Roberts who opined in the 1880s that railroading was already infinitely too complex to be subject to the control of any czar, no matter how wise. This from a man who was King of the largest and richest of them all. And like it or not, the taproot of PRR and PC and CR is and always has been in Philadelphia. Not New York, Not Washington DC or Baltimore or Boston or Norfolk. Philadelphia.

Decisions made, right or wrong, in the boardrooms, clubs and alleys of Philadelphia have had massive impact on the industrial and political development of this nation. This historian has noted that the question "What is Broad Street going to do?" had permeated the deliberations of all and sundry for a century and a half. Simply to ask that question is an acknowledgment of vast power and influence. For those who chafe under this fact of historic life, and we remind the reader that we are descended from and related to those who fought it for generations, we will respond that better Philadelphia than New York or Washington DC. For all their warts and failings they remain, at heart, our kind of people.

THE EAST SLOPE

Gallitzin Area Tourist Council/T. C. Ketenheim Collection

THIS VIEW, looking east from a point west of AR, was taken on 29 August 1952. There were car inspectors buildings built in 1908 and 1910 in this vicinity which means that each train was carefully examined before starting downgrade. The last ridge before the east slope begins is apparent in the background, as is the last cut. AR is snuggled to the left of the home signal. The standpipes emphasize the importance of water supply in the steam era. In the Gallitzin area alone, we have found records of the following: 1900, new water tub...1902, 20 *million* gallon reservoir and 400-thousand gallon reservoir with a 3,000 foot 12" feeder pipe...1910, 500-thousand gallon brick reservoir. As we shall see, all this was a drop in the bucket compared to the needs farther down the west slope. Before we take that trip, however, let us return to the area just west of the twin tunnels.

Gallitzin Area Tourist Council/T. C. Ketenheim Collection

TAKEN FROM OVER the twin tunnel portals, this westward view was shot within a few years of the opening of Gallitzin Tunnel in 1904. The westbound passenger station can be seen on the left just the other side of the Jackson Street bridge. The bell tower at far left boasts a fire bell, certainly a necessity for a town adjacent to heavy steam locomotive traffic. The water tub at extreme left is not PRR, however. It supplied water to the hotel just east of the station and several other buildings. The PRR mainline bends to the left in the distance and pierces the same ridges seen in the last photograph. This ridge is the true Continental Divide, not the one through which the tunnels were bored. Water draining to the right in this scene flows to the Atlantic Ocean. The original UN tower rested about where Track 4 passes the cars on the sidings. The signal bridge is distant for the new UN, which is on the other side of the true summit.

151

TRIUMPH I

A CLOSER VIEW of the westbound station, taken c. 1907. It is a combination station, witness the two-door express car. The other boxcars on that siding serve the Gallitzin Bottling Company, either purveyors or brewers of beer. Judging from the number of cars, business must be good. Our 1910 track chart shows that two PRR water tubs were just behind the station.

*Gallitzin Area Tourist Council
T.C. Ketenheim Collection*

THE BEER was certainly cold on this October day in 1907. There is a Chestnut Street subway under the tracks in this area, probably constructed c.1910. It is still in service.

*Gallitzin Area Tourist Council
T.C. Ketenheim Collection*

Gallitzin Area Tourist Council/T.C. Ketenheim Collection

AS SEEN BEFORE just across from the westbound station, this building was the home and office of the Track Supervisor. The tentative date of this photograph is 1908. In 1910 George Ehrenfeld was the supervisor and, assuming he lived here, we note that PRR people lived in comfort. As we shall see, there is an Ehrenfeld just east of South Fork farther down the west slope and we wonder if there is a connection. A.J. Spiegelhalter was the foreman in this section and George H. Angus was in charge of the section next west that included UN, both in 1910. A label on the back of this photo carries the name J.G. Angus of 316 Craig Street, Gallitzin. One wonders if there is another connection.

THE EAST SLOPE

THE BACK of the westbound station c.1918, complete with dobbin and wagon.

National Archives

Edward H. Weber

SANS DORMERS, the westbound station on 7 September 1962 does appear to be adequately maintained. Curiously, we don't know when this station was built nor when it was razed. An ICC report suggests a date of 1870, but we find that hard to believe since, as we have shown, a frame combination station was built in 1864 and pictured earlier in this chapter.

THIS IS A WESTBOUNDER entering "UN cut" and it has just exited the Gallitzin Tunnel on 6 May 1995...Allegheny Tunnel was still under reconstruction. The signal bridge has been moved into the curve and is now the home signal for UN. The power in sight is the helper, which may cutoff at UN or Cresson or Conemaugh or may even go through to Pittsburgh. Diesel units with large fuel tanks provide an almost incredible operational versatility and when this is combined with, at long last, the abolition of the "hundred mile division and crew change" relic of a bygone era, the net result is a material improvement in productivity and competitiveness.

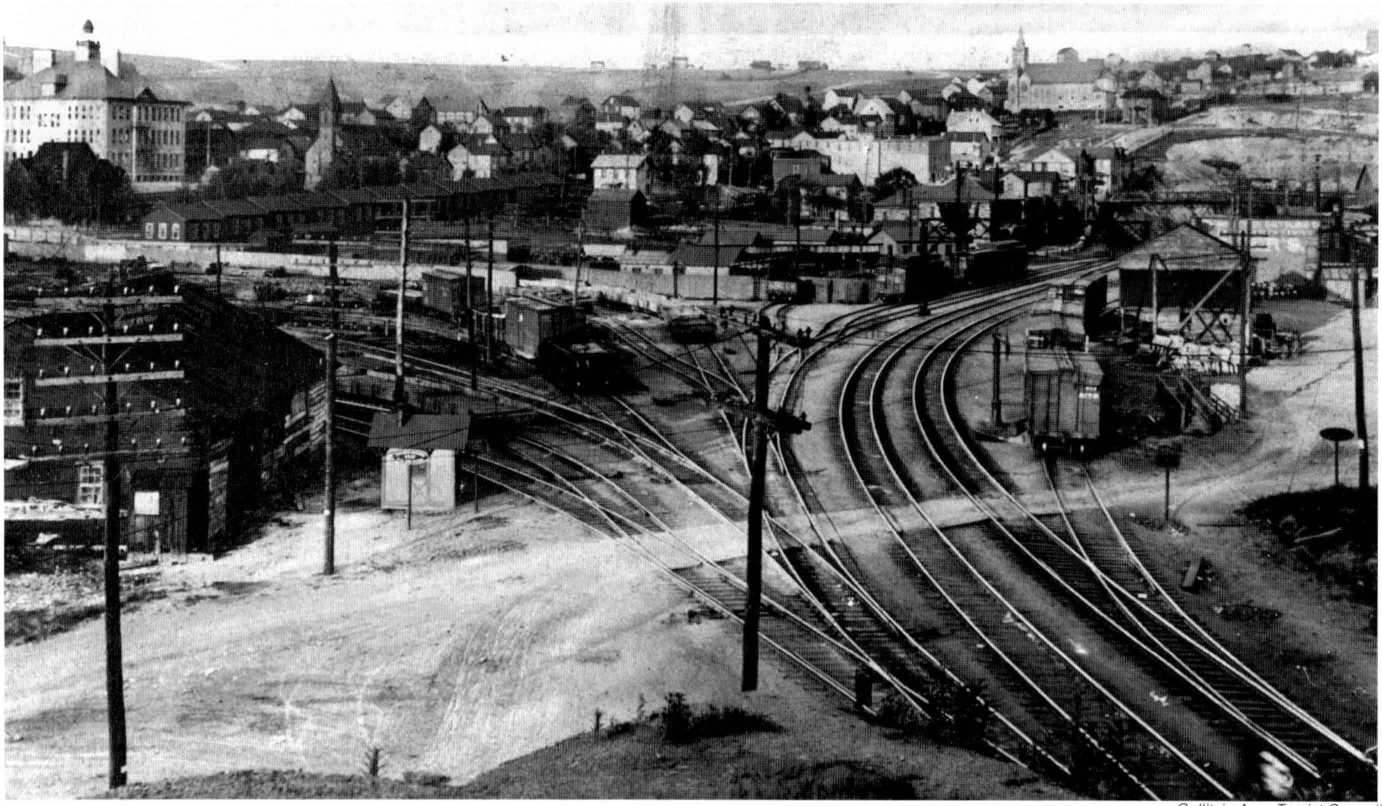

Gallitzin Area Tourist Council

A BACKWARD LOOK and back in time from the top of "UN ridge" in 1906. We can be sure this date is accurate because those tarpaper shacks in sight at upper left are those that housed the Catholic students so rudely evicted from their nice school building. They were to return to a new school in 1907 after a four-year absence. The Chestnut Street subway has yet to be constructed. The Jackson Street bridge is barely in sight at upper right as is the UN distant signal bridge. There is a standpipe next to Track 3 to the left of the string of boxcars on the "bottling" siding. The traces of the 1857 wye can be seen and that frame building appearing just beyond the left leg of the signal bridge may be the 21 by 60 foot engine house built for an MOW engine in 1863. There are vague references to a "paper" railroad named the Gallitzin and Hastings to be built to serve the vast coal deposits north of town but no evidence exists that it was ever constructed. Service of these deposits would be achieved out of Cresson as we shall see.

National Archives

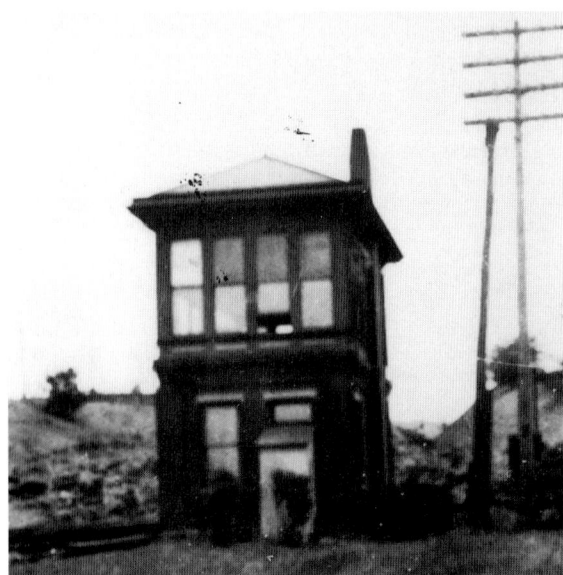

THE NEW UN as it appeared c.1918 at the west end of the cut through the Continental Divide. We have seen the first UN which was demolished to make room for Gallitzin Tunnel's Track 4. The latest and last UN was built as a twin to AR in 1899. We do not know the precise date of its demise, but have some evidence that the tower itself was gone by 1942 and the location was regarded as an emergency block station as late as 1948.

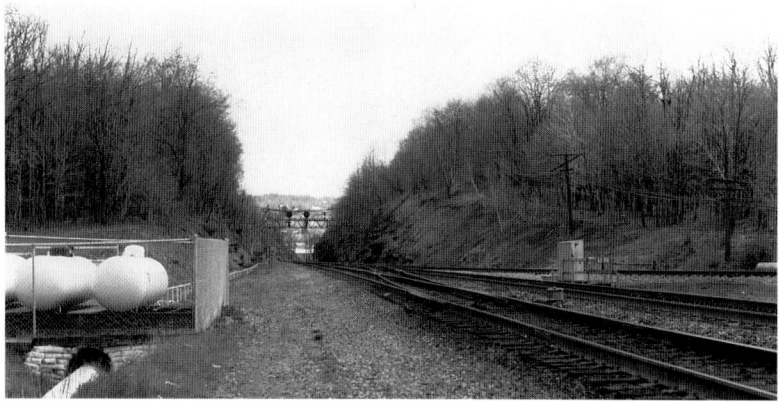

UN AND UN CUT on 5 May 1995, with the loop track to AR seen on the right, appears a little lonely. This is a very historically significant location yet nobody has ever paid any attention to it. Her twin AR was always in the limelight and poor UN never even achieved the status of bridesmaid. Well, she can take some solace that AR is also now just a placename.

Chapter 6
The West Slope
Gallitzin to Johnstown

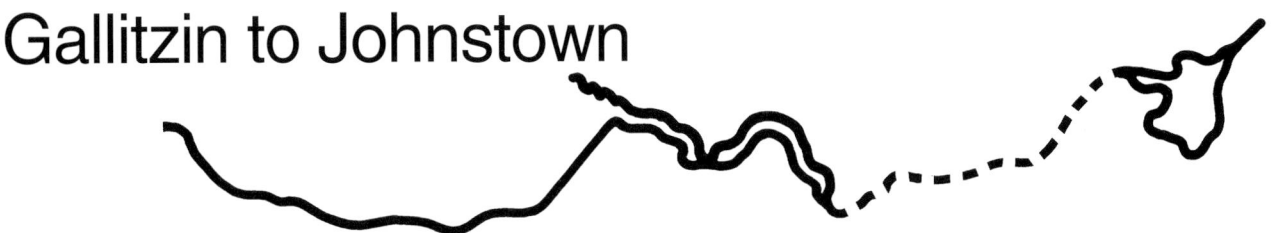

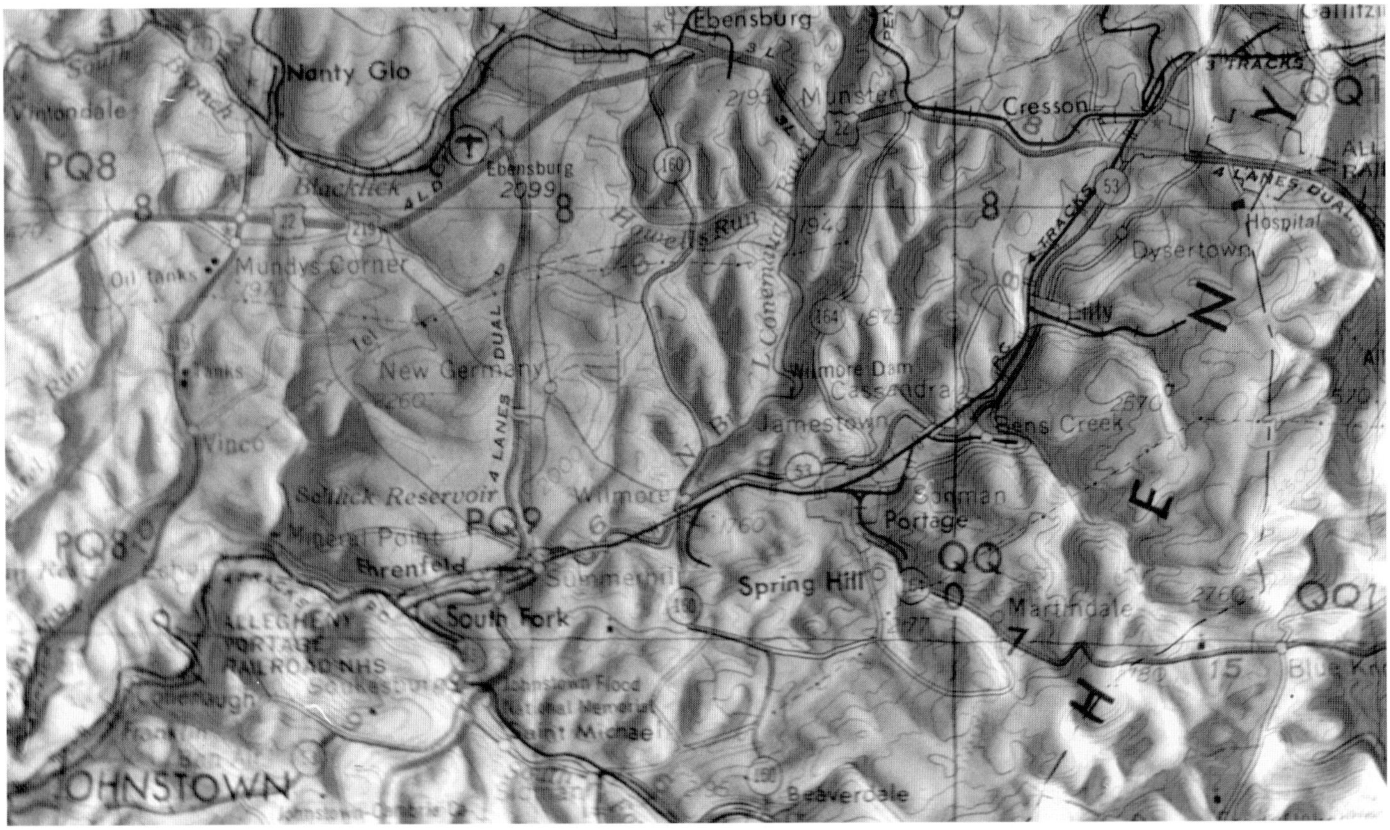

IF SIMPLICITY OF TERRAIN characterized the East Slope, jumbled confusion was the hallmark of the West Slope. Again we can thank the Army Map Service for this relief map and remind the reader that the vertical exaggeration is three to one. Also, let us point out that this particular reproduction is meant only to give the reader an overview of the West Slope. Far more detailed maps and illustrations are to follow in this chapter. From upper right to lower left, the general path followed by the Original Portage Railroad (OPRR), the New Portage Railroad (NPRR) and PRR is quite apparent. They were all laid on top of or alongside one another in such a haphazard manner that no historian, including this one, has been able to sort it out with precise clarity. We hope, however, that the reader will agree that we have done the best job to date. This transportation route of a little over 25 miles is the most significant artery in the history of the United States and, by extension, in world history. It is the most gentle eastbound grade reaching to the summit of the Mountain Barrier. It is also centrally located which in turn means that it is part of the shortest route from the west to the dominant city and port of New York as well as to the lesser city/ports of Philadelphia and Baltimore. Of course, there were other alternative pathways by land and water but none could efficiently compete in terms of distance and grade with this lone crossing. Further, this route and its western extensions ran right through the middle of a cornucopia of agricultural and mineral riches that provided the seed for an explosion of development that lifted the United States from a curious conglomeration of somewhat idle dreamers into a superpower of gigantic proportions, open-handed generosity, astonishing maturity and an intrinsic goodwill unparalleled in the history of this contentious planet. The miracle of adhesion made it possible, but it took giants with vision to make it a reality. And by giants we do not just mean those names recorded in history books. It takes everyone working together to get the job done, no matter how high or low his social or economic or educational status. Your author has spent a lot of time out on a lot of railroads and for many years has fallen into the habit of saluting the crews as they pass by. This is now a reflex action and is meant both as a mark of respect and a "thank you" for doing their "bit" in the service of something larger than themselves. So as the reader ventures into the story of the West Slope, he should always remind himself that this great adventure story carries with it the heritage of the unsung who are the true heroes of any saga in any time.

THE WEST SLOPE

Let us recall the words of William Bender Wilson's 1896 paean to the mountain crossing in the last chapter where we noted that his one hundred and sixty-one words were worth a thousand pictures. Only forty-one of those words referred to the West Slope and they were somewhat forced for the simple reason that there are no grand scenic overlooks or dramatic vistas or views that inspire the heart to poetry.

Elsewhere in his tome, Wilson wrote, "From the conception of the road the Allegheny Mountain was a formidable barrier, but a barrier that American pluck and American energy overcame. By utilizing the resources of nature the genius of man reclaimed the mountain wilderness, subdued the wild and fierce obstacles in mountain fastnesses, overcame mountain heights, bridged valleys and streams, and, supplanting the silence of solitude, made the glens and gullies and hilltops resound with the hum of industry and the notes of moving traffic, and created in the Pittsburgh Division of the Pennsylvania Railroad a powerful agent in the development of the Commonwealth."

It is a tribute to Wilson's literary talent that he could craft with at least some eloquence a word-picture of the West Slope that was accurate without being maudlin. The essence of the West Slope's role in history had to do with muscle, not gentle beauty; conquest, not submission; exploitation, not preservation.

With the advantage of another century of observation, we would edit Wilson's last sentence to read thus: "...a *decisive* agent in the development of the *United States*".

What little comeliness that may have been present in the valley of the Conemaugh River before man chose it as the prime transportation route west was soon swept aside, buried and altered almost beyond recognition. Even today the battle scars of this conflict are evident. Gob piles, mountains of raw mine tailings, strip mine wastelands and, above all, cinder beds of untold depth that came from the stacks of millions of steam locomotives that rammed their way upgrade with unimaginable tonnage on their drawbars…these are the legacy of the West Slope.

So, too, the graveyards stand as monuments to the price paid on the railroads, in the factories, in the forests, and deep in the mines of this region. This is also flood country, so many of the victims just disappeared in torrents of unleashed water with no headstones to mark their demise.

It has been said that nothing in the cosmos has any value except that which men put on it. By that measure, the West Slope and its environs is sacred ground indeed because the price was blood and sweat, tragedy as well as triumph.

But through all the mists of history, it is the triumph implicit in the West Slope that shines through to this historian. The ravages of Mother Nature, the blunders of fools, the misjudgements of men of goodwill and the accidents of fate were all surmounted by Wilson's "pluck and energy."

The East Slope has always basked in the sunlight of glamor, glory, fascination and the adulation of uncounted thousands upon thousands of supplicants from all walks of life in all times. As Americans surged westward from their enclaves on the east coast to reach the promised land, it was quite natural for their vision to be eternally focused on the setting rather than the rising sun. The future lay in the womb of the west, on the other side of the mountain barrier, ultimately all the way to that other "shining sea."

Transportation tenacles were conceived in the east and built westward. Hordes of people, both native-born and immigrants, went west chasing the golden fleece of a better life and boundless opportunity as well as that elusive but nonetheless compelling concept of freedom. So, too, did the investment money move west in search of fabulous possibilities of gain.

There is only one problem with this obsession with westbound worship. It is all wrong. Everyone is looking the wrong way. The view should be from west to east, not the other way around. It was not the conquest of *any* east slope that was significant. It was the *west* slopes that were the key to triumph. The essence of the story is put succinctly in the standard railroad rulebook: "Eastbound trains are superior to westbound trains of the same class."

The truly heavy volume has always been *eastbound*, true from day one to today. It is the comparatively gentle *west* slopes that made it all possible.

This myopia is not limited to PRR's crossing of the barrier. Your author has also written major histories of B&O's conquest of the barrier (the books *West End* and *Sand Patch*) and noted the fascination with east slope grades such as Seventeen Mile, Cheat River and Sand Patch. The grades facing the tonnage, such as Cranberry, Newburg and Deer Park, were in many cases virtually ignored by most earlier historians or, at best, mentioned in passing with a yawn. We have corrected this misconception in these books and will do no less for PRR.

The East Slope is *interesting*. The West Slope is *important*.

Curiously, long before any European inspected or surveyed the valley of the Conemaugh the Indians had a path from Johnstown to the summit along this very route and also had another one along Stony Creek south from Johnstown. Yet the Indians did not venture west from Johnstown through what we will call the Gaps, or at least no evidence has been found to this effect. Why? The State Works went through with a canal and PRR with a railroad, following the flow of the Conemaugh. Did the Indians know something we have yet to discover? After all, they were at it for thousands of years and we for only a few centuries. Perhaps PRR will find out one of these days. Maybe our predecessors had solved the riddle which asks whether the Mother in Mother Nature is a noun or an adjective. Too bad they did not record their history.

We will, however, take this opportunity to simplify some usage. Technically it is the Little Conemaugh River from the summit to the confluence with Stony Creek at the "stone bridge" in Johnstown and the (Big) Conemaugh from there west. We are just going to call it the Conemaugh, as a noun. That this placid little stream could suddenly turn into a raging killer might qualify it for use as an adjective, but we will pass on this temptation.

Now we must ask the reader to bear with us. The history of the West Slope is as confusing as it is important. As is our format style, we will give detailed history of each segment from east to west linked to graphics as we go. In this section we will give an overview of those historic developments that tended to have an effect on the slope as a whole. On occasion we will mention an event and promise more detail later.

And we wish to remind the reader that none of the events in this or any other history occurred in an isolated vacuum. There were other internal and external influences that bore on certain decisions and all of these must be weighed in the context of the times and the pressures of the moment. Wiser men than this author have noted that much of mankind's halting progress has been characterized by matching mistakes…if one side makes less mistakes than the other, he wins. Lady Luck also plays a role that should not be underestimated, and when grasped by the nettle can be honored by the appellation "noun." PRR got lucky on more than one occasion and perilously close to blowing it on others.

The first phase in the development of the West Slope was, of course, the OPRR. This subject has been thoroughly covered in Chapter 4 and we refer the reader to it, particularly pages 44-46, and the 1896 "model-map" on the endpaper. Later in this chapter we will reproduce a map that vaguely traces the route of the OPRR.

The OPRR ran from the summit to a basin and connection with the State Works Canal in Johnstown at a site now covered by PRR's passenger station.

The second phase was the construction of the original PRR mainline, in some places alongside and in other places crossing over the OPRR. The valley of the Conemaugh is not wide and shoe-horning was necessary. That PRR had an alternate possibility will be discussed.

The South Fork of the Conemaugh flows into the latter at, believe it or not, South Fork. OPRR built what became known as the Big Viaduct west of this point to provide an approach to the famous Staple Bend Tunnel, done to avoid a loop in the Conemaugh.

Now the story is about to get complex, so the reader should get a good grip on what is being said. If it slips away, the author has full sympathy because he too found himself babbling by taking the word of earlier historians who, in the event, didn't do their homework.

Conemaugh is also a *placename*. The location of the *place* Conemaugh is about three miles *east* of the PRR station in Johnstown. It is on the Conemaugh *River*.

Back to PRR and Thomson. He was building a railroad from Harrisburg to Pittsburgh and PRR's charter contained a provision demanded by Pittsburgh interests that construction begin at both ends. This may have made political sense, but it was engineering and financial stupidity all too typical of the epistles that flowed from Harrisburg. Very early on Thomson concluded that he would have to buy most of these clowns to get them off his back, but at this stage in the history of PRR that solution lay in the future.

So Thomson was building his railroad in pieces. One of those pieces ran twenty miles from the *place* Conemaugh *west* through the Gaps alongside the canal. This section was opened to Lockport (midway between the Gaps) on 25 August 1851. At the *west* end of this section PRR traded traffic with the canal. What to do at the *east* end?

Thomson cut a deal with OPRR and connected with

THE WEST SLOPE

that railroad at the *place* Conemaugh *west* of the Staple Bend Tunnel, also on 25 August 1851. On that date PRR also built a little passenger shed at Conemaugh.

Thomson, of course, continued to build PRR east from *place* Conemaugh along the *river* Conemaugh and reached the Big Viaduct in April of 1852. He immediately made a connection with OPRR at this point and closed down the *place* Conemaugh connection. Thus OPRR's Plane No. 1 was avoided. Please return to page 45 for clarity.

It is five miles from *place* Conemaugh to Big Viaduct along the *river* Conemaugh. Thus the gradient was mild.

By 10 December 1852 Thomson had completed PRR to the extent that an all-rail line was open from Philadelphia to Pittsburgh, although with the proviso that he was using OPRR to crest the mountain barrier and much of the mainline west of Johnstown was single-track. As reported, on 15 February 1854 PRR was completely finished. Yet even the latter date is questionable because we have seen a report from engineer William W. Wright that the West Slope was finished and "ready for cars" on 1 December 1854, almost ten months later.

This fudging of dates seems of little moment today, but it was a big thing in the early 1850s. The eyes of the nation and the civilized world were glued on the race to the Ohio River, B&O to that river at Wheeling and PRR to the upper reaches at Pittsburgh. PRR bragged that they got there first in late 1852 and B&O sneered that their railroad was not continuous and, besides, Pittsburgh was a backwater. B&O reached Wheeling and was open for traffic on 1 January 1853. No PRR people were invited to the lush celebratory party held in Wheeling during that month. There was no shortage of ardent spirits and no mention that B&O's switchback crossing in the Board Tree Tunnel area was something less than a poor carbon copy of OPRR's planes.

The two heroes of the moment were Thomas Swann (to whom your author is related) and Benjamin Latrobe, B&O's chief engineer and Thomson's opposite number. Benjamin was the son of a famous father to whom we have referred in these pages. Thomson admired both of these B&O figures and even went so far as to name a town on Pittdiv after Benjamin.

As to that Wheeling party, Benjamin cautiously noted that B&O had won a battle but a war was yet to be fought against some very redoubtable foes including a tough nut named Thomson. Swann, too, was well aware of these unpleasant facts and *both* knew that Thomson held all the aces. The gentle West Slope. Only one crossing of the barrier. Shortest route to New York, Philadelphia and Baltimore. Thomson's cold, steel nerves and razor-sharp brain.

So even if one takes the true opening date of the West Slope as 1 December 1854, almost two years after B&O's victory, the conclusion cannot be avoided that B&O had won its last battle against PRR. Thomson was to lose some skirmishes against other opponents and came quite close to losing PRR itself, but he never lost to B&O again. Nor did Thomson lose to Benjamin Latrobe himself when the latter tried to elbow his way into Pittsburgh with the Pittsburgh and Connellsville Railroad.

A few paragraphs ago we left PRR at Big Viaduct. At that time Big Viaduct was the boundary between PRR's Western and Mountain Divisions. In short order Thomson eliminated this demarcation line and put assistant engineer Edward Miller in charge of the mission to complete the line from Big Viaduct to the summit. When finished, the West Slope was double-track from the summit to Stony Creek in Johnstown.

The West Slope was initially laid with 56# iron T-rail. By 1867 65# and 67# rail sections had been adopted and by 1877 67# steel rail was standard. The switch from iron to steel is a story of such importance in both PRR and national history that we will discuss it in detail later in this chapter as we enter Johnstown itself.

By 1859 all West Slope bridges were stone or iron with a few exceptions averaging ten feet in length.

The third phase in West Slope history was the construction of the New Portage Railroad. With this project, the Commonwealth left the realm of bumbling incompetence and entered the kingdom of outright insanity. With great effort and a dash of sophistry, one might make a flimsy case for NPRR on the East Slope. Not even God in a good mood nor the most eloquent spin doctor ever born could explain away this lunatic project. But it was built, as we shall show.

The fourth phase was the expansion and realignment of the West Slope over a period of about twenty years and bracketing the turn of the century. The industrial growth of the nation from the end of the Civil War until early in the 1900s was incredible and so was the growth in traffic on PRR. Further, Americans were applying science to agriculture during this time frame and were also beginning a process of wresting from Europe the lead in the application of science to industry. PRR was hard-pressed to handle this burgeoning traffic on all parts of its system (as indeed were most other railroads) and the principal bottleneck was the Pittsburgh Division in general and the West Slope in particular.

More tracks had to be added, the route shortened, curves eased, dips smoothed and all this had to be done without interfering with stupendous traffic loads. Surely the masters of PRR wondered if they had created a monster that was on the verge of eating them whole.

Of all these problems, the worst was elimination of curves and consequent line shortening. Making the line shorter increases the gradient and that was the last thing PRR needed on this of all slopes.

But PRR had to take the hit somewhere. Thomson's original alignment involved a maximum grade of 1.0%. The pill was swallowed in the six miles from Portage to Lilly where the grade (moving eastward) went to 1.05%, 1.12%, 1.18% and 1.12%. Use of massive fills at least made the grade fairly consistent and, while we do not have supporting data, it is a good bet that the reduction in curve resistance offset the steeper grade.

In this era the line went from two to four tracks and in a few places five. As to that fifth track, PRR's policy of numbering mainline tracks from south to north resulted in the assignment of number "0", thus preserving PRR's reputation for being different. How many railroads ever had a Zero Track?

The fifth phase, which essentially has continued to the present time, can best be described as one of fine-tuning. Improvements in signaling, communications, interlocking flexibility, dispatching procedures, maintenance and training all served to get the maximum efficiency out of an existing plant. Consideration was given, as we shall relate, to the addition of another main track on a different path to the summit.

A sub-phase of mild retrenchment involved removal of one track in 1981 (except between Gallitzin and Cresson). As this is being written, a surge in traffic is being reported because of completion of the 1990s clearance project and it is not impossible to think that the removed track will be reinstalled. Since the roadbed is in place, such an addition would be less than heroic.

While on the subject of clearances, it should be noted that this is an ongoing problem. For example, in 1909 PRR had to raise forty signal bridges on Pittdiv.

As to communication, PRR was vigorous in pursuit of the state of the art. The first long distance telephone call in history was placed between New York and Boston on 23 March 1884. Just twenty-eight years later in 1912, PRR announced that telephone dispatching had replaced telegraph on Pittdiv between Altoona and Pittsburgh.

PRR did not invent the radio, but was quick in seizing on this interesting technology…first with low-frequency and later with high-frequency transmissions.

The reader will notice that we have yet to comment on motive power improvements during the fourth and fifth phases. Surely the reader knows by now that we are not fans of PRR in the motive power sphere nor is this a book about that subject.

Since we have not hesitated to be sardonic, we now want to acknowledge that PRR was not always wrong. The subject is electrification of the 35 miles between Altoona and Conemaugh.

Keeping in mind that mainline electrification did not even become a subject for discussion until late in the 1800s, we know that in 1913 PRR was "considering" it and preparing "preliminary estimates." By 1914 it was "believed" that large operating economies could be realized. In 1915 PRR decided to study the "experience of other lines."

The year 1916 brought comments like "no work undertaken…beyond designing and constructing the type of electric locomotives required…continuing the detailed surveys…scarcity of labor and high cost of construction materials…desirable not to urge the improvement" appeared in PRR's annual report, followed by silence.

PRR did not sucker on this chimera, much to their credit. Neither, incidentally, did B&O.

Electrification carries with it three large negatives: enormous initial investment, lack of flexibility and high energy deliverance costs. It is a source of some puzzlement to this writer that at least two otherwise sound publications in this field were urging electrification on Pittdiv as late as 1962 and 1981, quoting "experts." All too often, "experts" avoid all the small errors as they sweep forward to the grand fallacy.

To this point we have covered in general terms and with a broad brush the physical development of the West Slope and will follow with detailed history in the balance of this chapter. Now we are going to digress and tell another story about Thomson and PRR that will give substance to our constantly repeated claim that this man was a true giant in national history.

Economics and its handmaiden Finance are subjects that have been dubbed the "dismal sciences" by astute observers for a very long time. Those who choose these career fields are disdained as odd and called "bean counters" and "number crunchers" and "boils upon the backside of progress," these expressions being among the more polite. Yet it is in precisely this area of achievement that Thomson made his greatest contribution of all.

Thomson and his Pennsylvania Central entered the year 1855 with a lot of aces but also a lot of serious problems. Being "central" was fine. Unfortunately, this position also meant he was completely surrounded by enemies with very sharp teeth.

On the south was B&O. To the east was Reading. To the north was the Erie and New York Central. To the west was a gaggle of rapidly growing independent railroads on whom Thomson and all the others depended for vital connecting through traffic. This traffic was overwhelmingly agricultural products and the Great Granary was well west of Pittsburgh. Also, the Mississippi River was not drying up and was still a potent competitive force. Nor, incidentally, were the Great Lakes and the Erie Canal evaporating at a rate faster than the inflow of "new" water.

Worse, it was dawning on a lot of people with quick brains and some capital that big money could be made by speculating in the securities of these burgeoning railroads and that a lot more money could be made from trading in the securities than could be made from the operations of the railroads themselves, lush though those earnings were proving to be.

It did not take a great leap of imagination for these "investors" to calculate that it was very easy to print securities in prolific volume and sell them at inflated prices to those whose memory of the Tulip Bulb fantasy in Europe had receded to the deep subconscious. Here, they reasoned, was something that might prove to be better than sex. There was a sucker born every minute and everyone knew one should not give a sucker an even break.

So the 1850s were marked by a vast outpouring of securities that had printers working overtime and traders in these pieces of paper getting rich overnight. The expression *nouveau riche* was creeping into American lexicon, where it remains to this day. This phenomenon also produced a philosophic division in society that also remains to this day and has been the underlying cause of so much world strife in the last century and a half.

Stated simply, the clash is over *earned* and *unearned* income and how one divides it between those who created the wealth and those who merely suck at the teat of those who, through their sweat, risk-running and inventiveness, filled the breast in the first place.

It will perhaps surprise the reader to learn that the author is and has always been in the camp of the *earned*, as have all his forebears of whatever social position. Frankly, the author's views are unimportant. No one has or ever will march to the sound of his drum nor pay heed to his opinion that unearned income is obscene.

Edgar Thomson's views, however, were the same and *his* position made history. All those enemies who surrounded him and his railroad were *unearned* people. To be sure, people like Vanderbilt and Gould were not stupid. That cognomen might well be applied to B&O's John W. Garrett, but none of the others. They knew that they had to put *some* earnings back into the railroad. But Thomson put back almost *all* of it. The railroad came first, Wall Street second. Thomson would pay dividends as rent for the use of the stockholder's money, but not enough to make the stock a football in the markets. Thus raiders were forestalled.

Thomson would borrow money, but never more than a dollar of debt to a dollar of equity. The others pumped out huge hunks of debt, thus leveraging earnings. Thomson would have none of it. Of course, Thomson had to periodically issue more stock to maintain a one-to-one balance, but since he was only paying rent to the stockholders no speculator would touch it and the stockholder base became even larger and more diverse. No raider could get his hands on a big bloc of stock and the total number of shares outstanding ultimately grew so large that no one entity could possibly find enough money to take control even if they could convince enough stockholders to try a raid.

Then there is the little matter of expense and capitalization. As Thomson poured money back into the railroad, he capitalized very little of it. He charged off as expense (thus reducing earnings) expenditures that on all other railroads would have been capitalized (thus increasing earnings).

And when Thomson ultimately went on his own acquisition binge that, in the end, created the largest railroad and corporation in the world, he did almost all of it with leases. Lease payments are a charge against earnings and are not capitalized, not then or now.

To those readers who have not grasped the import of

these "financial" paragraphs, we will offer an agricultural analogy. The essence of the Thomson philosophy was to make his railroad the low-cost producer and get a lock on heavy traffic volume. Gigantic earning resulted from this approach and he hid these earnings by plowing them back into the railroad which in turn produced even more earnings. Thus he fertilized a field that grew ever larger and more productive while his competitors were fertilizing fields with flatulence.

Also, when he wanted to do some raiding and create new industries along his lines, he worked through front-men (who ultimately became known as the Philadelphia group) and kept PRR out of it, at least directly. Andrew Carnegie will become a case in point.

So effective and socially productive was the Thomson approach that all of his successors emulated it as an article of faith and even today Conrail, facing a new set of threats, has reversed field only to the extent that they are goosing earnings to stave off a raid by making the price too high. And just maybe they can gather enough strength to go on another acquisition spree as in the days of Thomson.

As with so many things in the early history of railroading, this fundamental idea of one-to-one debt and retention of earnings in the institution was not Thomson's. B&O laid the groundwork long before Thomson left Georgia and returned to his home town. Even when Swann gave away debt securities at deep discounts to raise money to get B&O from Cumberland to Wheeling in one leap, he only compromised to the extent that he carried those discounts on his books as part of the cost of construction. Swann's successors steadfastly held to the one-on-one ratio. Then, in 1857 that vast flood of wallpaper to which we have alluded caused a crisis in the financial markets and speculators suddenly concluded that wallpaper was no more digestible than tulip bulbs had been so many years before.

In 1858 banker John W. Garrett was elected president of B&O and in short order he slashed muscle to increase earnings, drove the debt to equity ratio to three-to-one for leverage and pumped up dividends which in turn made the stock take wings. For the moment, Garrett was called the "boy wonder" of railroads.

From Thomson's viewpoint, that took care of the threat on his southern flank. From then on B&O was a mere annoyance to Thomson and when Garrett got in his way on occasion, Thomson slapped him down with a flyswatter.

The Reading would annoy Thomson and his successors on several occasions as would the Erie and New York Central. In fact, the Erie had Thomson breathing a little heavy at one time and while that will be a subject in another book in this series, it is sufficient to say here that Thomson was dealing with a full deck both in his head as well as in his hand and emerged triumphant.

By the way, the reader should be reminded that most of these railroads plus quite a few others ended up as part of PRR. It is called Conrail, of course, but it is mostly PRR.

To be sure, in the early 1870s there was a PRR "revolt" of stockholders and an "investigation" of Thomson's reign. We have read every word of the "Report of the Investigating Committee of the Pennsylvania Railroad Company" issued in late 1874 and concur with their findings that "The Pennsylvania Railroad Company is wonderfully fulfilling the objects of its creation".

It is only fair to note that PRR was at risk of failure when Thomson died on 27 May 1874 and he went to his grave wondering if PRR would survive. His protégé, bagman and frontman Thomas A. Scott, also the nominal leader of the Philadelphia Group, had speculated one too many times and the whole structure was tumbling down. To his credit, Scott succeeded Thomson and spent the next six years cleaning up the mess. Thomson did not let PRR *directly* invest in these ventures, but everyone knew PRR was behind them and the markets were unsure as to PRR's liability. These indirect investments, however, were merely the tip of the iceberg.

The big balloon was Thomson's acquisition binge. Through *leases* and *guarantees*, Thomson overpaid for all those midwestern railroads and was relying on future growth to pay back PRR through earnings. This was an innovative financing approach in those days and was done on a grand scale. In short, Thomson put out future promises in paper but little cash. In a sense, he was lending short and borrowing long. If something went wrong, he would have plenty of time to adjust. Perhaps most important of all, he sensed that the future growth possibilities in this region were almost limitless and in this he was a true prophet.

It is understandable that PRR stockholders grew "nervous in the service" because Thomson played his cards very close to his chest and had not for years even bothered to inform his Board of Directors, let alone the stockholders, just what he was doing. Thus the "revolt" of stockholders.

The results of the "investigation" revealed that Thomson was a true financial genius as well as a prophet and that PRR's future was bright indeed so long as short-term setbacks were ignored. It is a little sad that Thomson died before the report was finally issued, but we are confident he checked out knowing he would be vindicated.

There was another ratio of "one-to-one" on which Thomson put his imprimatur and this one was the most cardinal principle of them all. For every two dollars in earnings, one would go to the owners and one back into the railroad.

Even here Thomson stacked the deck in favor of the railroad itself. So carefully did he obfuscate and cook the books that in fact far more than one dollar went into the railroad and far less than one dollar to the owners.

With some experience in this field, we have tried to ferret out the "real ratio" and will tentatively pronounce that it was probably in the vicinity of three-to-one…three dollars for the railroad and one to the owners. So artfully did Thomson hoodwink his own bookkeepers and Wall Street that no one will ever really know the final ratio, just as one can only guess at how much money the Commonwealth blew on their State Works.

Let us give you two examples. In 1870 B&O's Garrett, outwitted by Thomson on still another occasion, had a tract printed in which he bleated that PRR was grossly overcapitalized and was using this capital base to block Garrett at every turn. Garrett, never one to co-ordinate his mouth and brain, also spelled Thomson's name as "Thompson" throughout this printed diatribe, perhaps trying to get Thomson to rise to rhetorical bait. Thomson ignored the challenge and belted Garrett on the battlefield still another time.

The second example is more illustrative of the Thomson theology. As we shall relate later, the Civil War produced an avalanche of earnings for PRR. PRR's *reported* earnings went from $2,296,000 in 1860 to $4,619,000 in 1865. The *real* earnings were astronomical. Even Burgess and Kennedy in their "non-political" 1949 history of PRR found it necessary to note that these earnings "would have been *considerably higher* if the management had not deliberately held them down by charging *large amounts* of additions and betterments to operating expenses." (The italics are by the author.) Even these corporate hacks, dedicated to putting a good face on all historic events, couldn't ignore these transactions with a straight face.

Why did they bring it up at all? Well, the rules of the game had changed by the teens of this century. Federal regulation was in full flower and Congress, in its wisdom, had decreed that railroad profits should be tied to a maximum rate of return on invested capital. To make this quixotic experiment work, the capital base had to be determined. Thus began the "valuation" era. Since it was obviously in the interest of all railroads to make that base as high as possible, there then began a frenzy of "capitalization" that had railroads "capitalizing" everything including desks, shovels and pencils. The "valuation" photographs and drawings shown in this book were the result of this nationwide trip to outer space. Parenthetically, it was all for nothing. The base was so high that no real railroad, including PRR, could produce a rate of return anywhere near the allowed percentages.

For PRR, however, this fantasy posed certain problems because they had been masters at hiding assets. So, with some aplomb considering the circumstances, in 1917 PRR got the approval of the Interstate Commerce Commission to "restore" all those Civil War earnings to their asset account. One has to admire something when it is well done.

And well done it all was. One can only imagine how much more difficult it would have been for the United States to reach industrial and agricultural superpower status in just a third of a century if Thomson and his successors had chosen the philosophy of the "unearned" and adopted the tempting but pernicious doctrine of gluttony today and let the future take care of itself.

You see, dear reader, PRR was a lot more than just another trunkline railroad. It was literally the keystone in the development of the United States. All that was good in American ingenuity and capitalism was embodied in PRR.

Thomson came and gazed upon the rock of Allegheny Mountain and, as St. Peter did in the sphere of the divine so many centuries ago, Thomson decided to build a secular church upon it. Both succeeded in the face of all temptation and all of mankind is the richer for their devotion to a vision that transcended the narrowness of self.

Almost all of us become part of one institution or another in our lifetimes. It is given to only a few of us to create the institution itself.

TRIUMPH I

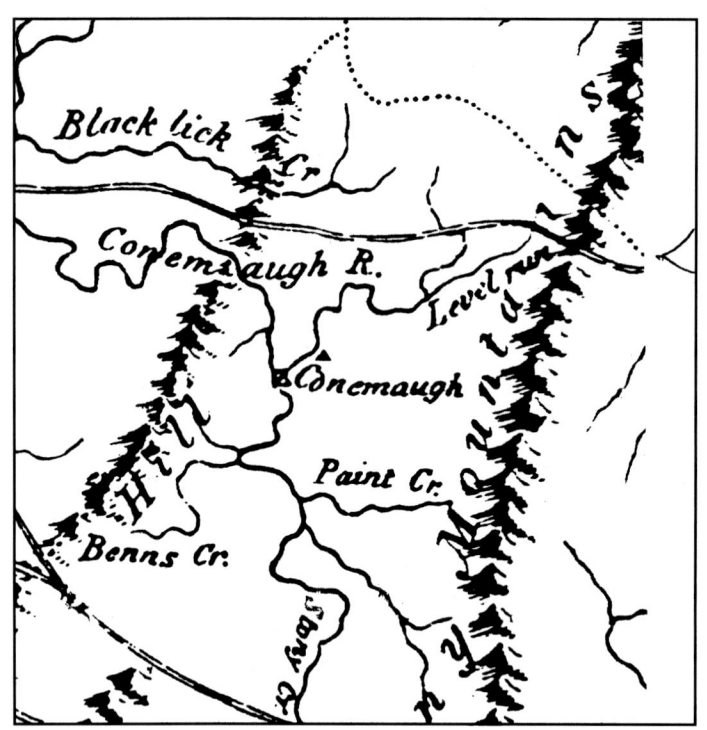

THE WEST SLOPE as it appeared in 1794, extracted and enlarged from the map on page 20. The dotted line at upper right represents the Indian path that passed through Kittanning Point and wandered northwesterly well to the north of the West Slope. This crude "highway" also avoided the Conemaugh valley although it did crest the mountain barrier in the vicinity of Gallitzin. Note that the upper reach of the Conemaugh River is named "Level run," an obvious misnomer since no waterway is level, yet indicative that the slope appeared to the mapmaker as being gentle. The trace of the river is obviously vague and no reference whatsoever is made to South Fork, an omission that suggests that the surveyor did not bother to follow the river. There is no Johnstown at this date and the location of *place* Conemaugh appears uncertain. The black triangle seems to put it at its present location, yet the box implies it being at the confluence with Stony Creek. One can see at bottom center that the "Stony" had acquired its name very early on. It seems clear that in 1794 the valley of the Conemaugh was considered to be an unimportant path west. The known Indian paths from Conemaugh/Johnstown east and south are not shown, more evidence in support of our thesis.

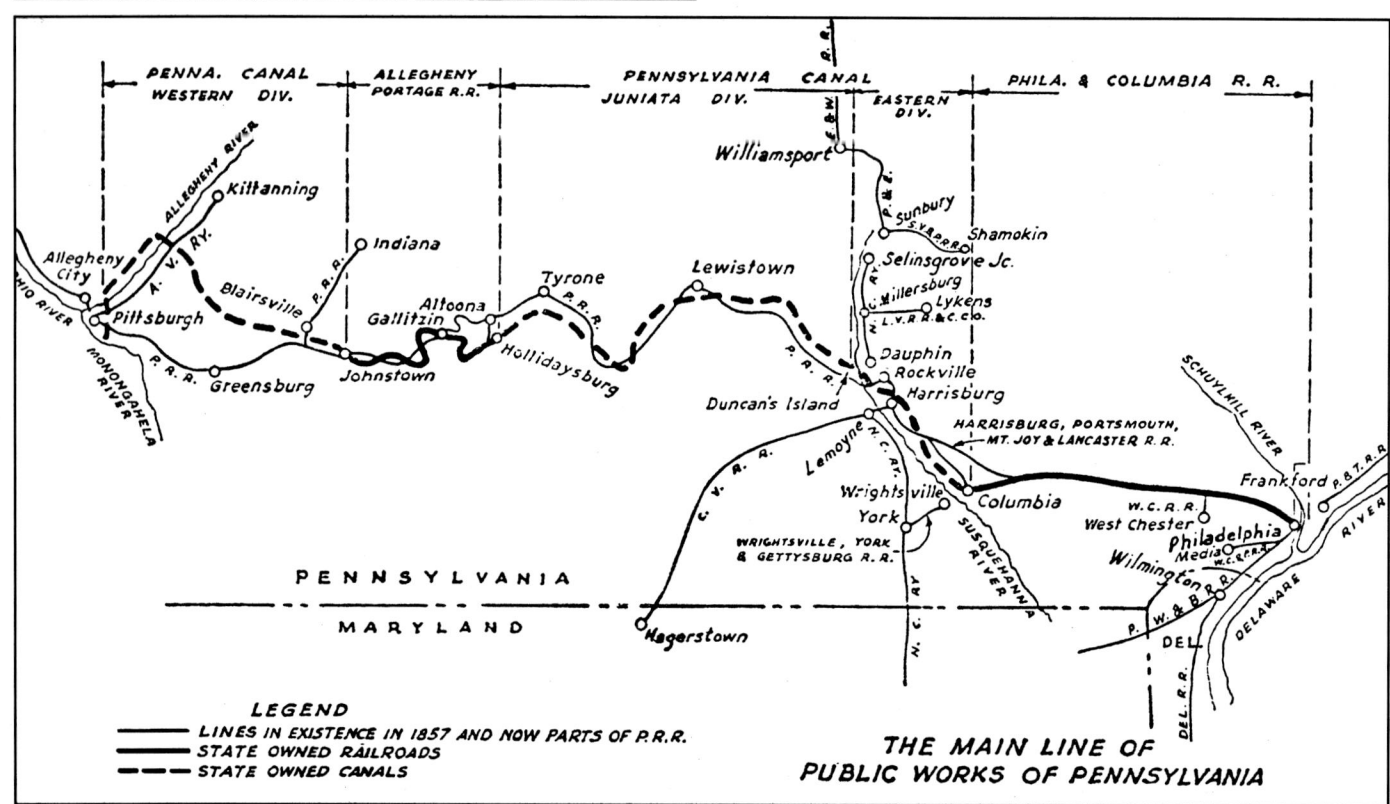

WHILE OUR FOCUS in this chapter is on the West Slope, we thought the reader might find this map useful in relating OPRR, NPRR and PRR to the broader situation in 1857. The story from Altoona east will be treated in later volumes. The reader should look to upper left and the "Pennsylvania Canal Western Division." The Conemaugh River flows northwesterly from Blairsville and is joined by Loyalhanna Creek (about which we will hear more in a later chapter) about halfway to the Allegheny River. At this point the name changes to Kiskiminetas River. The "Kiski" flows to the Allegheny River and thence to Pittsburgh. The canal followed these rivers. Initially, PRR went through Greensburg to Pittsburgh. Ultimately PRR acquired the canal as well as the Allegheny Valley Railroad (on this map running from Pittsburgh to *place* Kittanning along the Allegheny River) and built a railroad from the Allegheny River to Blairsville, thus creating what became known as the Conemaugh Division.

THE WEST SLOPE

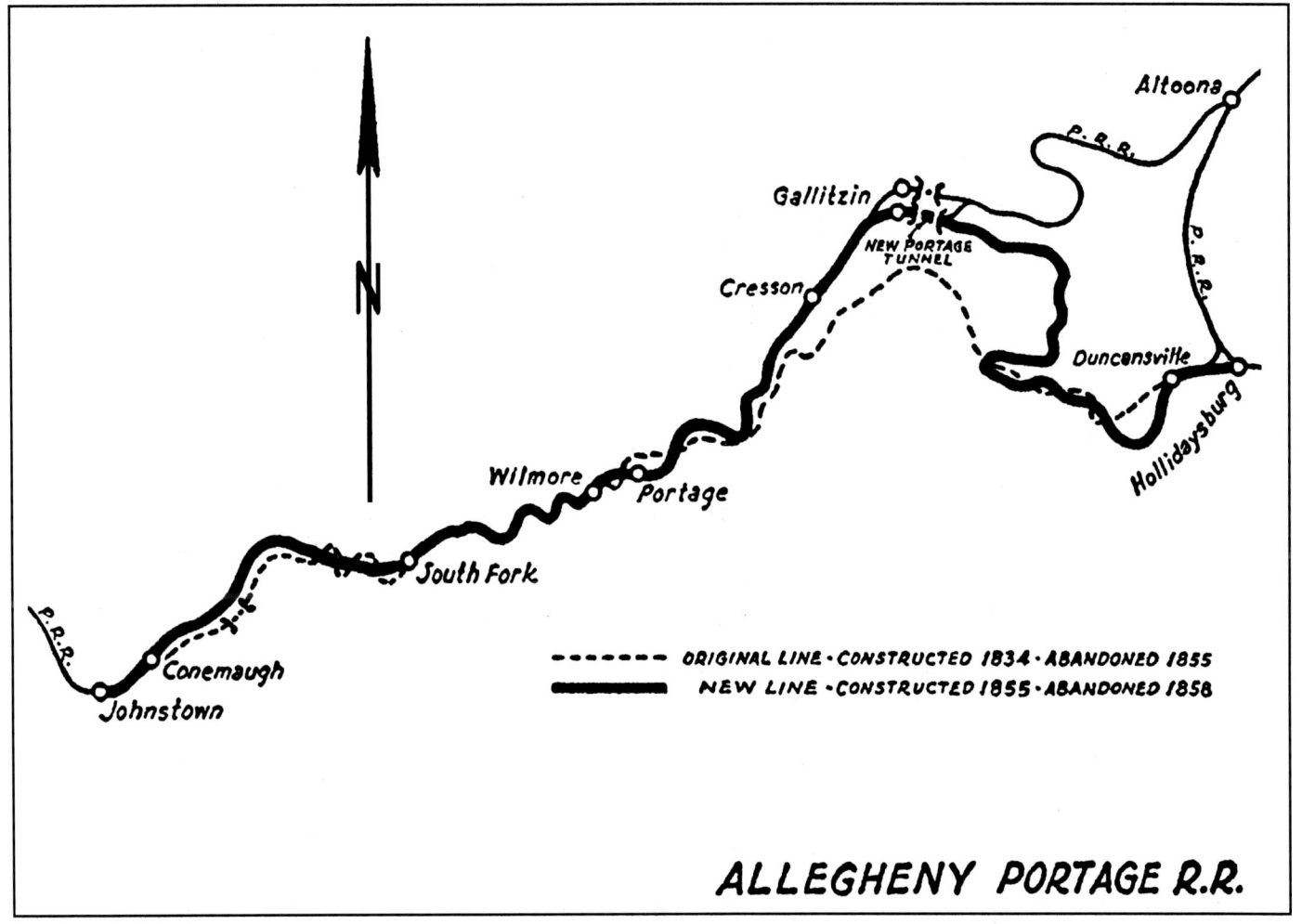

ALLEGHENY PORTAGE R.R.

THIS MAP will go part of the way toward locating OPRR and NPRR on the ground, at least in relation to one another. Sadly, PRR does not appear between the summit and Johnstown even though this depiction was prepared by the railroad. First we will try to describe the OPRR/PRR relationship from east to west. PRR was north of OPRR from Gallitzin to Bens Creek (just east of Portage) where it crossed OPRR at the foot of Plane No. 3. PRR stayed south until a river loop just west of Wilmore where it crossed OPRR twice. From this point to South Fork, PRR remained south of OPRR. West of South Fork, PRR crossed OPRR at least five times, emerging on the north side in the vicinity of Mineral Point (about halfway between South Fork and Conemaugh). From there to Johnstown, PRR remained north. Now for NPRR. From Gallitzin to the Bens Creek area, NPRR was south of but right next to PRR. At Bens Creek NPRR crossed PRR at a location *east* of the OPRR crossing referred to above.

From Wilmore to South Fork, NPRR generally used the OPRR roadbed except for a few straightened "wiggles". Remember that this was "long level" territory. West of South Fork NPRR occupied OPRR roadbed until nearing Johnstown where a short stretch of new trackage was built. All this indicates that PRR crossed NPRR eight times. In 1859 PRR, then owning the whole mess, announced that it had filled in four locations where it had crossed NPRR on bridges. This implies that the other four crossings were at grade, a situation guaranteed to give everyone heartburn. If the reader's eyes are now crossing, he should keep in mind that in 1991 the Department of the Interior surveyed the entire West Slope and concluded that there was little left that was visible and/or unaltered. We should also note that we have had access to map fragments, perhaps not available in 1991, and came away with the same conclusion. We decided that further inquiry would leave us vulnerable to a charge of masochism.

TRIUMPH I

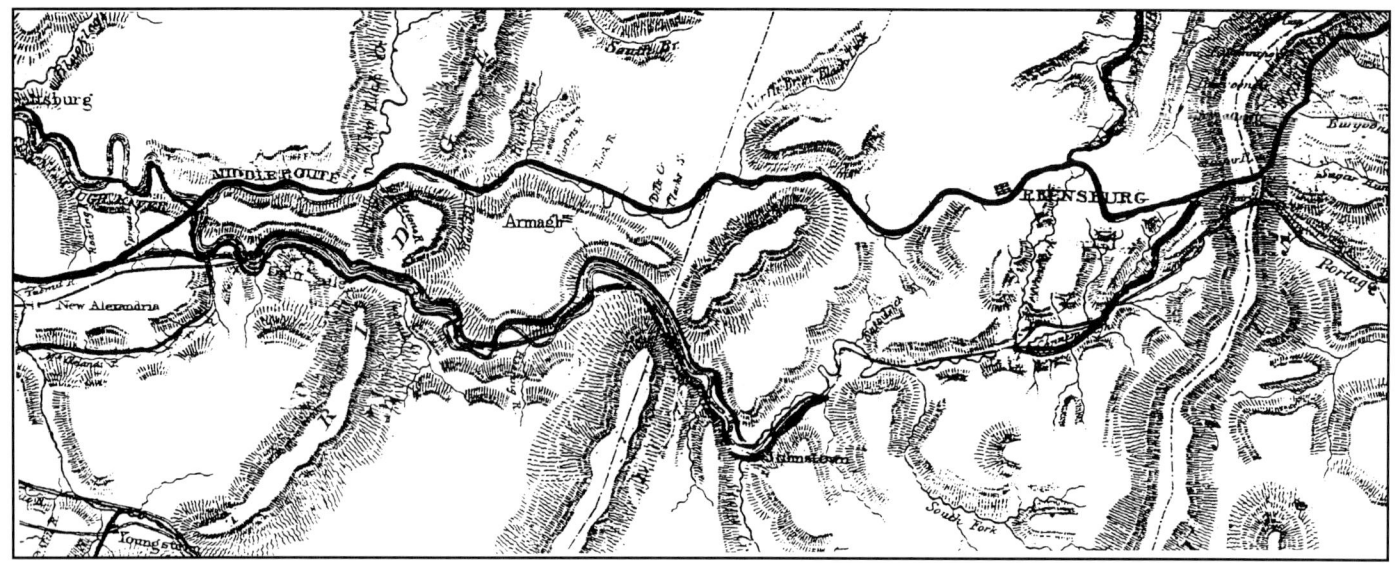

NOW WE WILL VISIT Schlatter's solution for the West Slope, keeping in mind that his mission was to determine if an all-rail route from Harrisburg to Pittsburgh was feasible subject to gradient limitations. For the West Slope, the maximum grade was not to exceed 0.85%. We have already discussed his proposal for the East Slope and Thomson's revisions. We remind the reader that Schlatter also surveyed a northern route which on this map arrives from upper right just east of Ebensburg and ends there; from there west, the "middle route" was an extension of both "middle" and "northern". West of the mountain barrier there were two choices as shown here…a southerly route paralleling the OPRR and canal, and a northerly route bypassing the Gaps. The latter passed north of Laurel and Chestnut Mountains and was shorter. As we shall see, PRR ultimately built a railroad along this general trace although it was not mainline. The southerly route, of course, used the Conemaugh Valley through the Gaps and also, one might note, employed OPRR's "long level." Schlatter proposed two lines through the Gaps, one on each shore…again, PRR built both over time. We guess that Schlatter was really showing that the canal could be avoided if that became necessary. West of the Gaps, Schlatter showed three possibilities as we shall see later in the book.

THE WEST SLOPE

HERE IS THE FACE OF PRR on the West Slope in 1855, "ready for cars" throughout its length regardless of which opening date is accepted. OPRR is now a footnote in history. NPRR has yet to appear, but it will prove to be another footnote. Thomson amended Schlatter's proposal for a maximum gradient of 0.85% and accepted 1.0%, a decision that this writer regards as sound in spite of latterday critics who bemoaned the curvature implicit in the selected route. That curvature does not show on this map and to that extent it is a public relations epistle. The line was rather straight from the summit to Lilly, but from there to *place* Conemaugh it wiggled in a manner reminiscent of the Penn Central "worms" logotype. Of course, everything is relative. Compared to B&O curvature, PRR was as straight as a saint. As to South Fork, the State Works had built a dam and reservoir upstream from the Conemaugh River to supply water to the canal west of Johnstown during dry seasons and it is not shown here. Thirty-four years later the whole world would learn of this dam. Now look just east *and* west of Mineral Point. Two loops in the Conemaugh River were avoided with deep cuts.

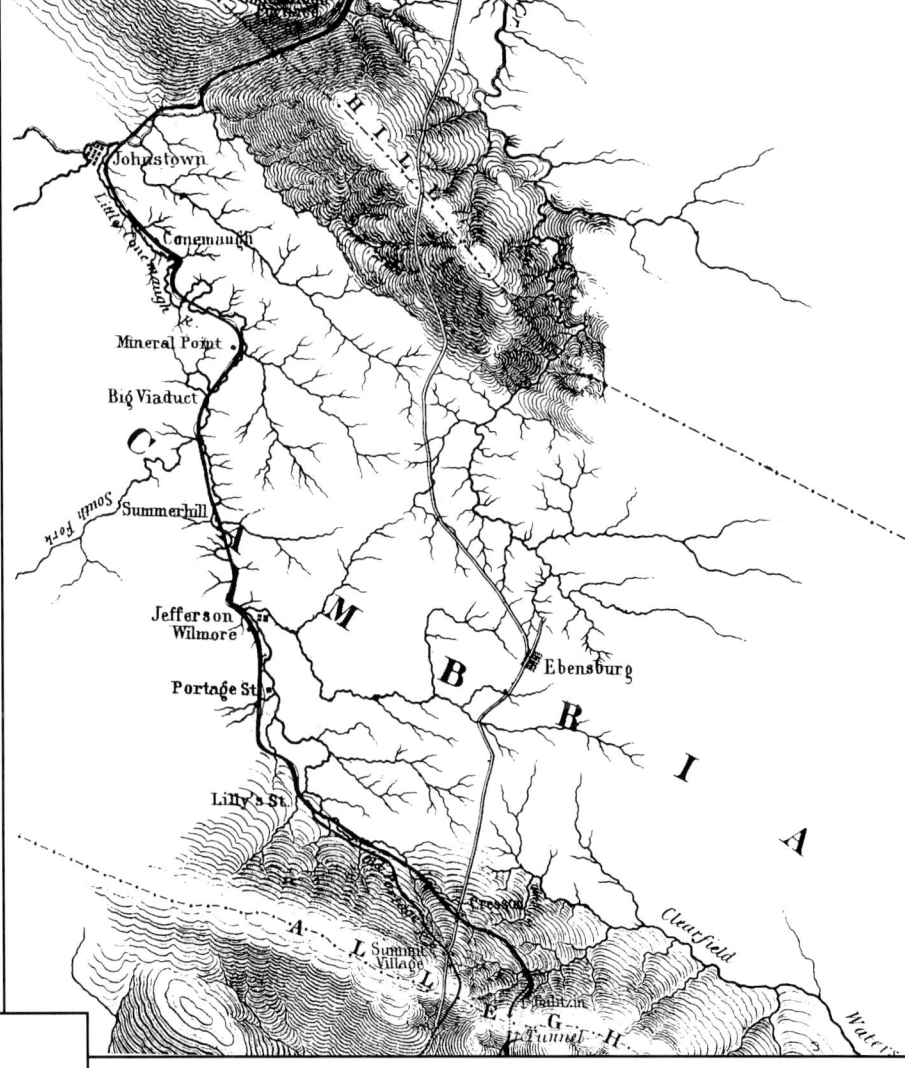

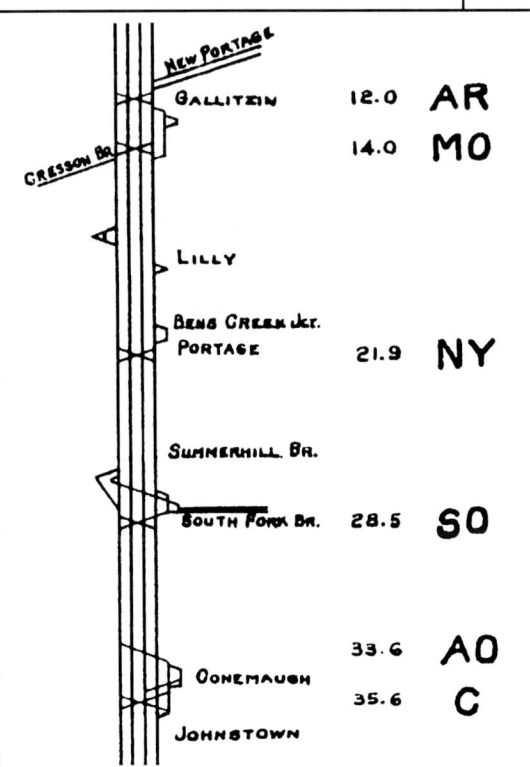

EXACTLY NINETY YEARS LATER, on 6 April 1945 to be exact, the West Slope looked like this in schematic form. Obviously, a lot of things had changed in that time span and that fascinating story is yet to be told. This drawing is presented merely as a handy reference so the reader may begin to associate place names, call letters, trackage, branches and interlockers in sequence from the summit to Johnstown.

167

TRIUMPH I

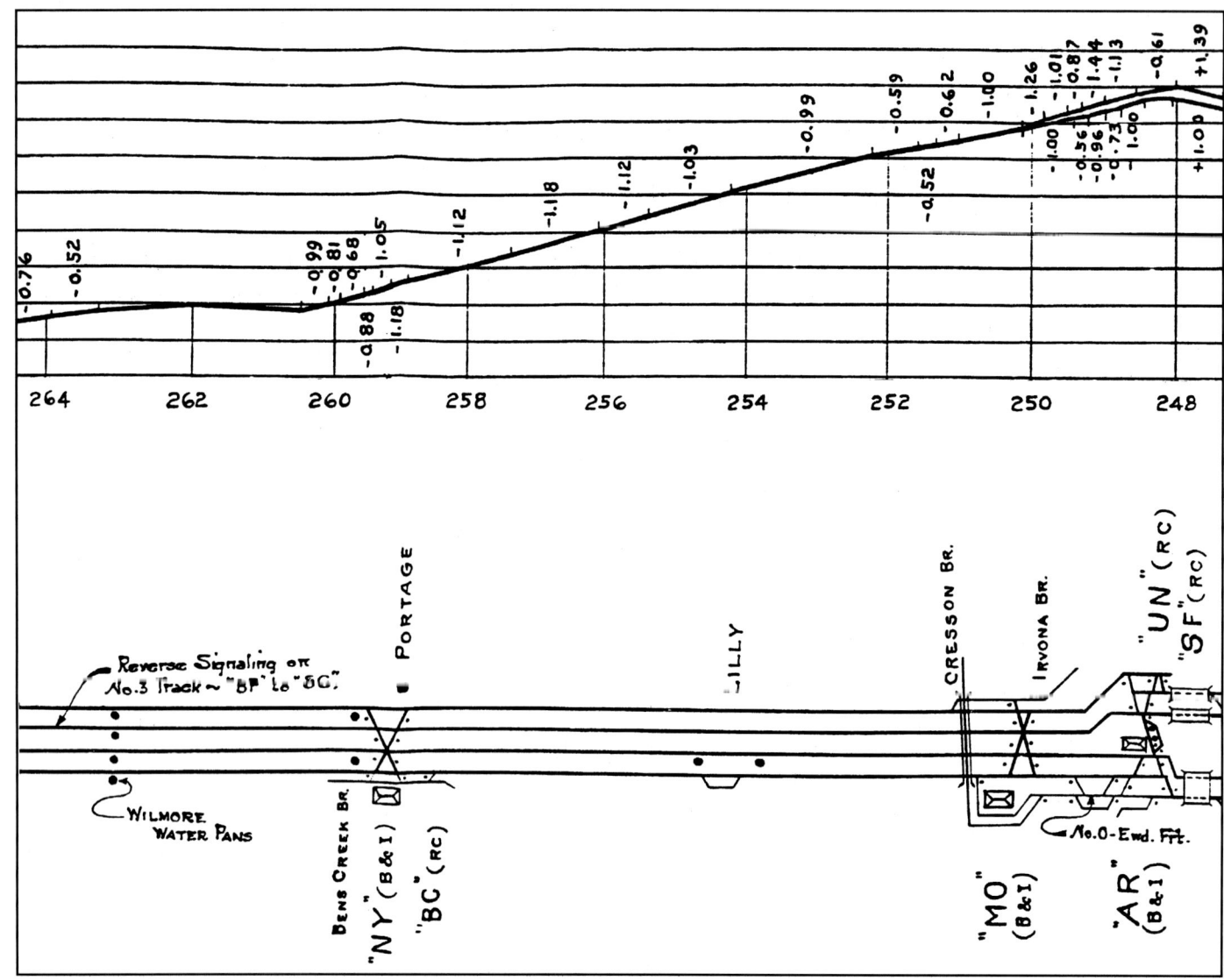

FROM THE SUMMIT TO WILMORE, this portion of the West Slope appeared as shown on 1 July 1945. If not at its absolute peak, this depiction does reflect the slope at very high tide. At lower right we see our first Zero Track and at far lower left the track pans at Wilmore, the only ones on the slope itself. This time frame is also near the high tide of steam operations so we see standpipes at Lilly and Portage. No. 3 Track is signalled in both directions from BF (Bennington Furnace on the East Slope) to Sang Hollow in the first Gap just west of Johnstown and also an historic track pan location. From mileposts 248 to 260 one finds the most severe grade on the slope. There is a mild anomaly here and it has to do with the Wilmore track pans. Such pans have to be absolutely flat yet they are shown here as being on a slight grade and at milepost 263. We have 1910 and 1950 track charts showing the pans at milepost 261 and on a 0.0% grade. And there is a slight dip between mileposts 260 and 261. On a 1992 track chart the dip is gone and has been replaced by a 0.04% upgrade. Also, the symbol on this 1945 chart is for standpipes whereas the other charts show sketches of the pans themselves. Well, everyone was busy with war traffic in 1945 and good help was hard to get. By the way, "RC" means "remote control" and "B&I" block station and interlocker. As the reader shall see, in earlier years there were a lot more of them than shown here.

168

THE WEST SLOPE

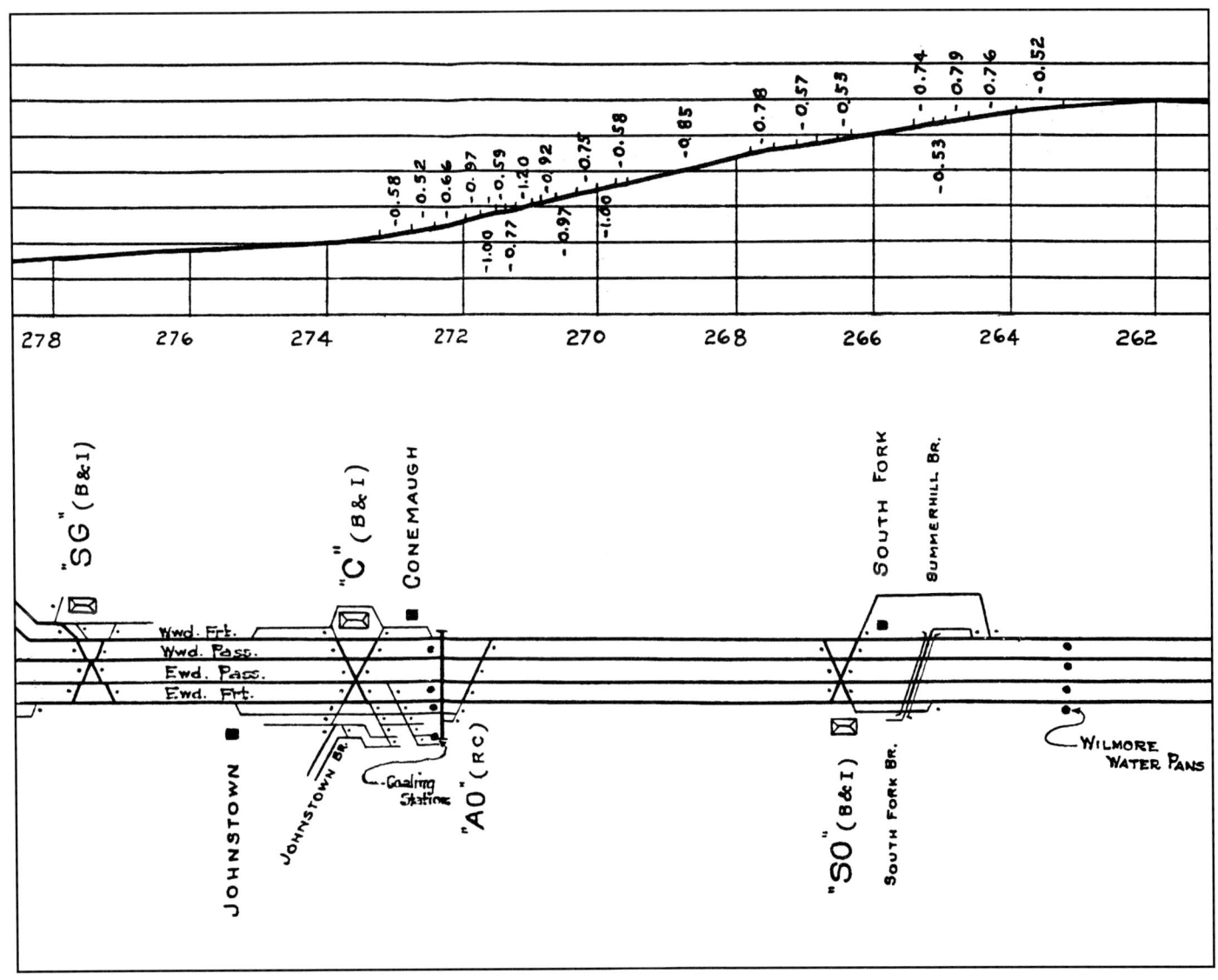

THE WESTERN HALF of the West Slope is shown here, again on 1 July 1945. We have included the Wilmore track pans on the right to ease reference to the preceding chart. We cannot be sure, but suspect the gradients (which range from 0.52% to 0.97%) are very close to Thomson's originals. That tiny piece of 1.20% just east of AO was probably created when the crossovers were constructed. Just east of South Fork there is a jumpover, and a massive coaling station at Conemaugh with the expected standpipes. We have reached beyond Johnstown into the first Gap to locate Sang Hollow (SG).

TRIUMPH I

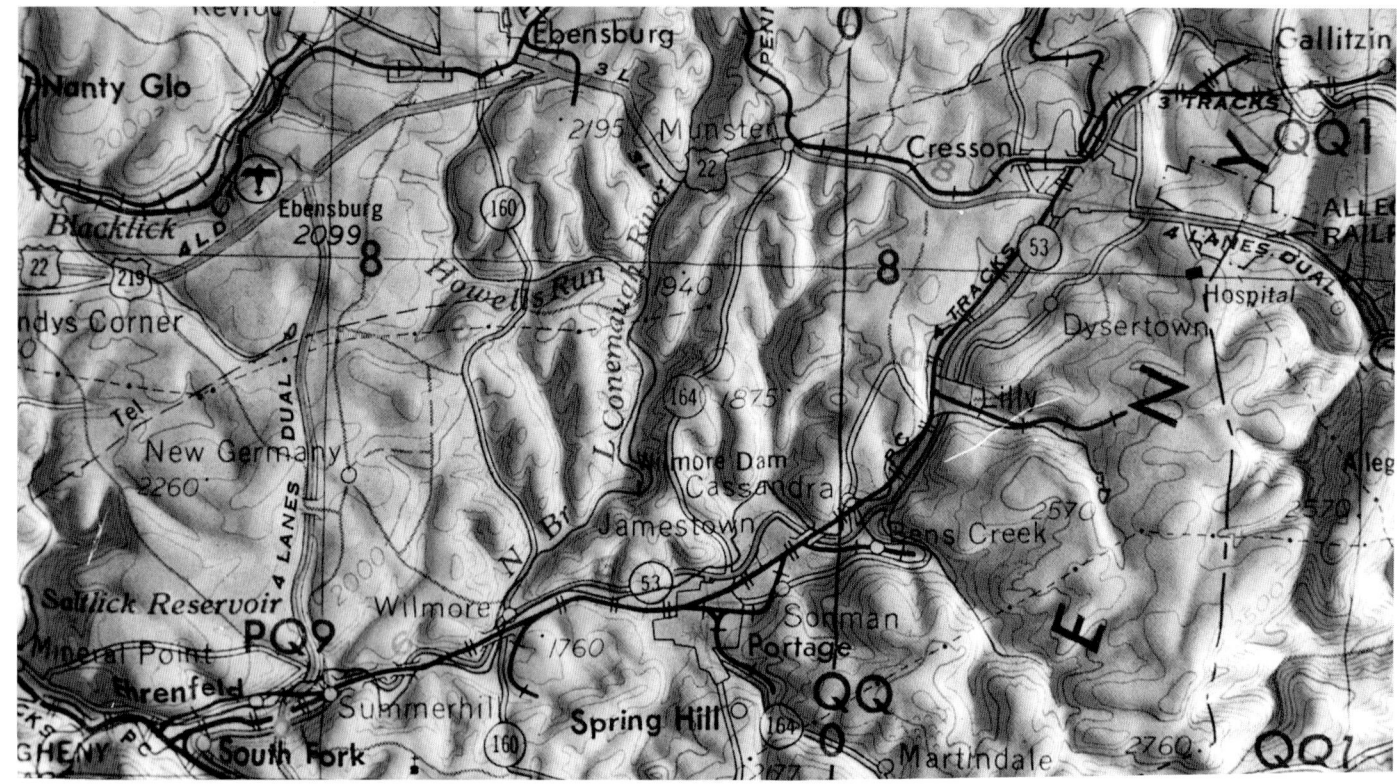

NOW LET US travel down the West Slope, adding additional placenames to this storied route and relating manmade objects to those provided by Mother Nature. Again, we owe the Army Map Service for this relief map and, again, the vertical exaggeration is three-to-one. Leaving Gallitzin, we quickly arrive at Cresson and then pass through Lilly, Cassandra, Bens Creek, Sonman, Portage, Wilmore, Summerhill, Ehrenfeld, South Fork and Mineral Point. This map was updated in 1969, hence the Penn Central references. Note that Route 53 meanders along the railroad for a considerable distance and the reader would be quite correct in assuming that significant pieces of this highway once carried OPRR, NPRR and PRR rails. There is also a plethora of "Planes" Roads in this region, all minor and unimportant except that they remind us of our heritage. Note that at Wilmore a tributary joins the Conemaugh River. The watershed of this branch reaches north to the right of Ebensburg. There is a Wilmore Dam and reservoir on this branch, clearly shown here. The reader might jump to the conclusion that this dam was built by PRR to supply water to the Wilmore track pans and he would be right. Would OPRR have been wiser to build a canal west from this point, using water from this branch and South Fork? A tantalizing question which we have no intention of exploring other than to comment that we have a hunch PRR ended up using more water to make steam than the canal would have used. To be fair, we should be reminded that this is "long level" territory. This map stops at Mineral Point at lower left. The line from there to Johnstown, and the region south from there, will be treated in another interesting context later in this chapter.

THE TWIN SLOPES in stark profile as they have been for almost a century, subject only to the qualification that the little dip in the middle of the West Slope is gone. Now we shall begin the trip down the West Slope, making our first stop at Cresson. It is less than two miles from AR near the summit to MO, the legendary tower at Cresson. Yet it is at Cresson where it first becomes apparent that the observer has entered a whole new world and that for every silver lining there is a cloud.

THE WEST SLOPE

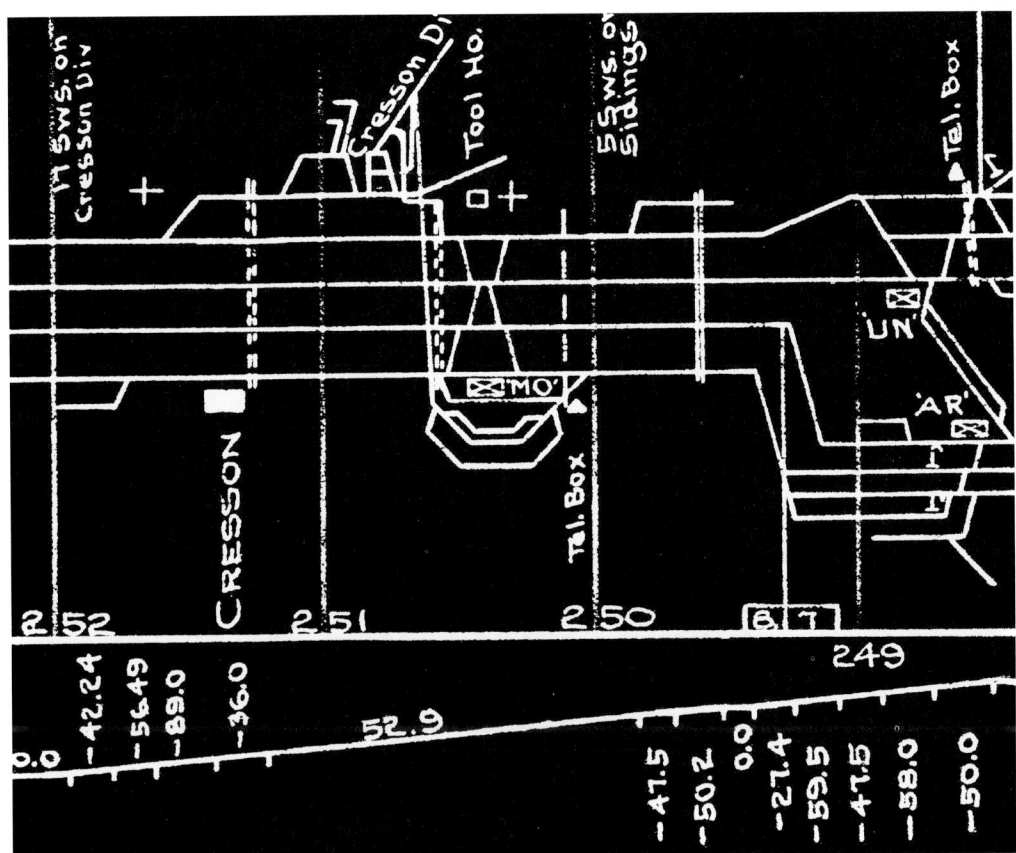

HERE WE HAVE an overview of the trackage between UN/AR through MO to just west of Cresson itself in the year 1910. May we suggest that the reader study this track chart very carefully, recalling that the mainline at AR is *higher* than at UN. While not shown on this chart, these mainline tracks meet at the same elevation precisely at the east (right) end of the MO interlocker. Also note that at this time (1910) there are only *four* mainline tracks (two eastbound, two westbound) for about a mile east of MO. Now look at top center and find the "Cresson Division" single-track line and follow it *over* the mainline tracks where it turns right, going behind MO and joining the eastbound main (Track No. 1) just east of the tower. Notice that there is an overhead highway bridge between Mileposts 249 and 250. The next photograph will show you that bridge.

Frank Wrabel Collection

THIS IS THAT OVERHEAD highway bridge, looking westerly circa 1918. On PRR it is bridge 2494 (Milepost 249.4) and it carries what is now State Route 53 overhead. The eastbound train is waiting for a proceed signal. There are now *three* eastbound tracks. The two westbound tracks are out of sight in the "hollow" just in front of the camera. The train is sitting on Zero Track. Between 1910 and 1918, PRR extended the Cresson Division track (which had ended just east of MO) all the way through to AR. The eastbound volume pouring out of the Cresson Division, added to the eastbound volume on the West Slope mainline, had created an operating problem of major consequence and the only way to relieve it was to add more trackage. Even more would have to be added later. Remember our phrase "every silver lining has a cloud"? The silver lining was the enormous traffic volume. The cloud was that all this volume was being dumped on the busiest transmontane railroad in the whole bloody world! And this was just on the first couple of miles of the West Slope. Far worse (or better depending upon the view-

National Archives

point) was to come farther down the slope. One doubts that Thomson, for all his optimistic views of future growth, had any conception of the scale of triumph that his railroad would entail, any more than St. Peter could envision that his church would encompass a quarter of the population of the world and still be going strong two millenniums hence. The secret to institutional long life, of course, is adaptation to changing circumstances and flexibility of thought. As far as the West Slope was concerned, PRR would need all the flexibility it could find.

LOOKING WEST from that Route 53 overhead bridge 2494 circa 1956, we see an eastbound mineral train on Track No. 1. The rear of the train is at MO around the curve in the distance. We would like to point out that this train is moving, unlike the one in the preceding photograph. Now let us go a few hundred yards ahead of the train, to the east.

Milton A. Davis

KEEPING IN MIND that we are now *east* of the last scene, and looking east, we see Gallitzin off in the distance, six tracks and a westbound train with a mixed consist. The vague shadow at extreme left just in front of the locomotive is from the MO distant signal bridge, which we will see next. This photograph was taken in September of 1956 and is one of the more instructive ones we have seen because it shows the relationship between the summit and the trackage emanating from it. The sixth track on far right is really a siding and thus did not have the honor of being numbered Zero Zero track. It has been gone at least since the early 1980s and a maintenance road is using the roadbed. The interlocking plant was also removed, probably at the same time. Note that there are coal *loads* moving west in this train, certainly not a typical situation.

Milton A. Davis

THE WEST SLOPE

FLEXIBILITY is inherent in this photograph of an eastbounder passing under the MO distant signal. The train is on Track No. 3 which, of course, is a westbound track. The date is September of 1956 and the number of the J1 is 6432. At this point in this work the reader may suspect that the author takes gleeful satisfaction in showing photos of Jays and constantly reminding everyone that the finest steam power ever to ride on PRR rails was *not* designed by PRR. Such needling is one of the small joys of creativity.

Milton A. Davis

THE CALL LETTERS MO for the tower at Cresson probably rank as the second or third best known in PRR history, topped only by AR and possibly ZOO. There is a mild debate over the origins of the letters, some saying from MOuntain as in the top thereof and another school saying they were derived from Mountain House, a world-renowned resort hotel located in Cresson. One historian in the latter camp contends that an original block station was opened in 1855 and was destroyed by the same rains that caused the Johnstown flood in 1889. Since there is overwhelming evidence that this tower was built in 1888 and was favored with the installation of a 22-lever interlocking machine in that year, plus the fact that few floods affect the tops of mountains, the validity of these conclusions is open to some doubt. There is no doubt, however, that the MO structure is a classic PRR design in the "Stick Style" with timber post-and-beam construction, clapboard siding on the lower story, crescent-shaped rafter ends and decorative cut-outs, all impressively Victorian. Apparently much of the switching and relay equipment is original. To us, however, the most interesting aspect to MO

Edward H. Weber

history is that Andrew Carnegie worked there as a night telegraph operator in the early 1860s shortly after he emigrated from Scotland. Whatever the questions about the beginning, there is no doubt about the ending. MO was closed in December of 1994. The building, however, is extant at this writing.

AN EASTBOUND Amtrak train was about to roll by MO on 6 May 1995. On this date the tower appeared to sport some new paint, a good sign for the future. While MO appears to be state-of-the-art today, it was not always so. A retired operator whose father and two brothers were also operators and dispatchers at MO reported in 1995 that the tower was illuminated with kerosene lamps until 1920 and heated by a coal stove until the 1950s.

TRIUMPH I

Thomas A. Biery

A WESTBOUND trailer train rolls by MO and blocks it from view in 1981, the year of the removal of Track No. 2 from this point west. We cannot quite determine whether the track has been removed by this day, but if not it does not have long to live.

Todd Atkinson

JUST EAST OF MO, all five tracks are alive and well on 8 April 1994 as an eastbound mineral train with three rare ex-Erie Lackawanna SD45-2s leading the way passes a mixed consist.

THE WEST SLOPE

THAT CRESSON was almost named Rhododendron is just one of many curious tidbits about this vicinity. The story begins with Doctor R.M.S. Jackson, a gentleman of some renown who was convinced that the medicinal qualities and invigorating properties of mountain air and local spring water made this location a potential Heaven on the hilltop. His plan was to entice the "mentally and physically diseased dwellers in those moral excrescences on the body politic (to) come and be cured by the action of God's pure air and water." By "excrescences," Dr. Jackson meant cities like Philadelphia and Pittsburgh. The good doctor chartered the Allegheny Mountain Health Institute on 29 April 1854. In spite of the doctor's unflattering references to PRR's hometown, the railroad weighed the possibility of passenger business and decided to cooperate. In the early 1850s PRR had built a combination inn and hotel at Hollidaysburg for the convenience of its patrons and named it Mountain House, a rather puzzling choice of names because it rested at the base of Allegheny Mountain. PRR had it dismantled and moved to a site southeast of Old Route 22 and the PRR mainline where it became Dr. Jackson's Mountain House. The project was an instant success. Additional structures were built over the years and sites were leased for the construction of cottages for the more affluent. This illustration, published in 1875, shows the original Mountain House slightly left of center. PRR did not, however, accede to the doctor's choice of names no matter how beautiful the shrub may be and the location was named in honor of Elliot Cresson, an early subscriber to PRR. Doctor Jackson became a surgeon in the Union army and died at Lookout Mountain in Tennessee late in the Civil War, apparently not finding that faraway peak quite as healthful as his own. The dominant building seen here was under construction in the late 1850s and we assume was opened c. 1856.

THE MOUNTAIN HOUSE in Hollidaysburg had a railroad right at its front door, a location that began to lose some charm as traffic increased. The building was placed farther away from the railroad in its reincarnation. This illustration is taken from an 1852 travel guide. The author described the hotel as "spacious and showy" and stated that it lay about a mile north of the canal basin.

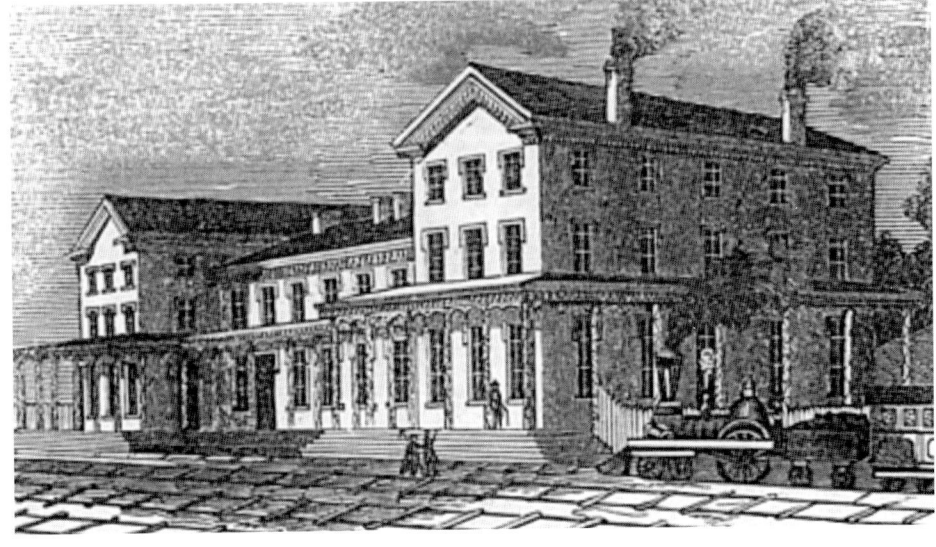

PRR OBTAINED control of the complex by 1880 and in 1880-81 this impressive structure, described as Queen Anne blended with Oriental, was erected on the site of the two older hotels. The front was 300 feet long and two 220-foot wings created quite a palatial edifice. The promenade was 1,200 feet long and 16-feet wide, graced by wrought ironwork in profusion. The hotel could accommodate 600 guests, a capacity that soon became excessive. By 1885 seashore resorts were rising in popularity and Mountain House began a slow decline. The hotel was closed in 1897, the furnishings sold at auction in 1903 and in 1916 a spark from a passing locomotive set fire to the old lady. While it did not burn to the ground, shortly thereafter the shell was converted to a barn and excess lumber removed to build still more barns. As to those cottages, Andrew Carnegie was a frequent guest and one wonders if he visited MO tower to chew the fat.

AT LEAST THE GROUNDS were being well maintained when this photograph was taken, probably in the late 1890s. This view is southwesterly, or downgrade, and the PRR passenger station can be seen on the left of the tracks in the distance. This photo was taken from the platform of a freight house, served by the siding at lower right. Technically, this location was known as Cresson Springs and the corporation as The Cresson Springs Company until its dissolution in 1911. The original plot was 300 acres and extended on both sides of Old Route 22. The PRR mainline sliced a triangle from the northwesterly corner of the property. Progress is inevitable and one cannot save everything, yet it is sad to contemplate that such a magnificent work of art could not have been converted to some socially productive use.

THE WEST SLOPE

Railroad Museum of Pennsylvania

WHEN THIS POSTCARD photograph was taken, the name had contracted to just Cresson rather than Cresson Springs. A spire of the Mountain House can be seen at upper left. This scene probably dates to the early 1900s when the resort was clearly in decline. From left to right, one finds a freight house, open shelter, station extension and the station itself. There are four mainline tracks and a siding. No siding is apparent in the last photograph.

Michael G. Farrow Collection

THE CRESSON STATION looking eastward, taken from a postcard dated 19 June 1907. We know that PRR built a passenger station at Cresson in 1859 and we are fairly confident that this is that structure. We should point out that passenger business was a large and very profitable portion of early railroad revenues. No matter how crude early trains might appear to modern eyes, travel by rail was far faster, cleaner, more comfortable and far cheaper than highway stage-coach movement. It was only later when rapid industrial development caused freight traffic to soar to predominance that passenger revenues became less important. Consequently, PRR was not being idle when they sponsored resorts such as Mountain House. Another often overlooked advantage to passenger business was that it was usually two-way. If a passenger went out, he usually came back so there were few "empty" movements. When this resort opened in the 1850s, PRR was running three trains a day on this mainline and every passenger to and from this point was gravy because the trains had to run anyway. Growth, however, presented serious operating problems because passenger and freight trains move at markedly different speeds. In fact, most of the expansion of trackage on Pittdiv, and other PRR divisions, was done to separate such movements and keep them out of the way of far more important freight trains. The creation of crossovers and later interlockers at roughly five-mile intervals on Pittdiv was also in response to this problem.

TRIUMPH I

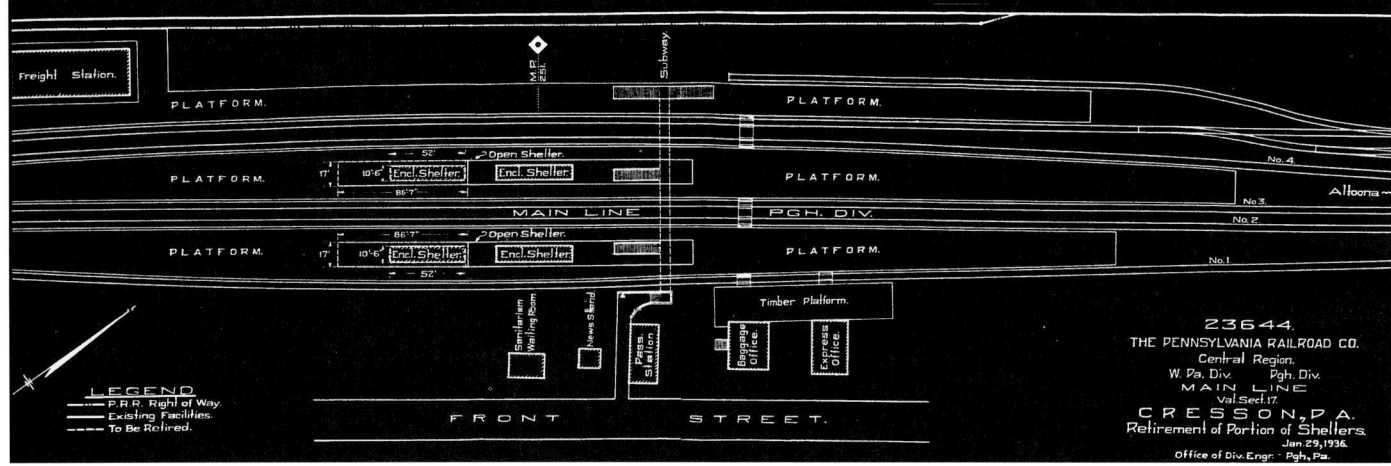

WITH THE MOUNTAIN HOUSE a dead issue and with heavy passenger traffic coming to and from the Cresson Division branch lines, PRR decided in 1911 to install completely new facilities about 1,100 feet east of the original station. This plan speaks for itself as to the details and we will shortly show photographs of the structures. Notice that Track Nos. 1 and 4 were moved outward to provide for platforms and a subway was built to lessen danger to patrons. At lower center, note the passenger station. The railroad through here is on a fill and this station was below track level. Passengers bought their tickets, went into the subway and climbed steps to the platform. An iron fence just south of Track No. 1 forced compliance. By the way, this station was meant to be temporary pending construction of a more imposing edifice...a building that never came to be. Note the "sanitarium waiting room." The automobile and bus soon took away most of the local passenger business and the Great Depression swallowed the remnants. By 1933 two of the enclosed shelters were locked and only one passenger train in each direction plied Cresson Division rails, cargo being almost entirely express. On 29 January 1936 this plan was produced to justify removal of the two excess shelters, which was authorized on 12 March 1936.

National Archives

MIRACLES DO OCCUR as evidenced by this c. 1918 valuation photograph of surprising quality. This view of the subway shelter on the northwest side of the mainline is looking upgrade. The open vestibule coach signals that this particular train is not deluxe, but at least there are some passengers. Two pretty ladies and a little girl with a whirligig all wear hats and are well-dressed in the fashion of the times. On the ground just behind the lady on the left one sees a lunchbox and food basket. Photographs in history books of this kind usually do not show people, and when they do too often they are posing for the camera. This is a casual scene of a group of normal human beings each with their untold stories, momentarily brought together on a railroad platform. Where were they going and where did they all end up? The subway, by the way, was still there at least as late as November of 1994 and still serves to keep passersby off the mainline.

THE WEST SLOPE

NOW WE ARE BACK to typical valuation quality. Track No. 1 is in the foreground, the guard fence is obvious and the subway shelter can be faintly seen at extreme right.

National Archives

THIS VALUATION photographer was fouling Track No. 4, not a healthy position on this mainline particularly while looking downgrade. Notice the end of the freight house in the distance.

National Archives

TIME WAS NOT KIND to the remaining structures at Cresson, as seen in this 7 September 1962 scene looking downgrade. The "temporary" station is in the middle and the building on the left is the baggage office.

Edward H. Weber

AT RIGHT on 7 September 1962 we find the "temporary" station and in the distance an overhead bridge with signals. Now we will embark on the part of the Cresson story that made the profits which were bled to maintain the passenger facilities.

Edward H. Weber

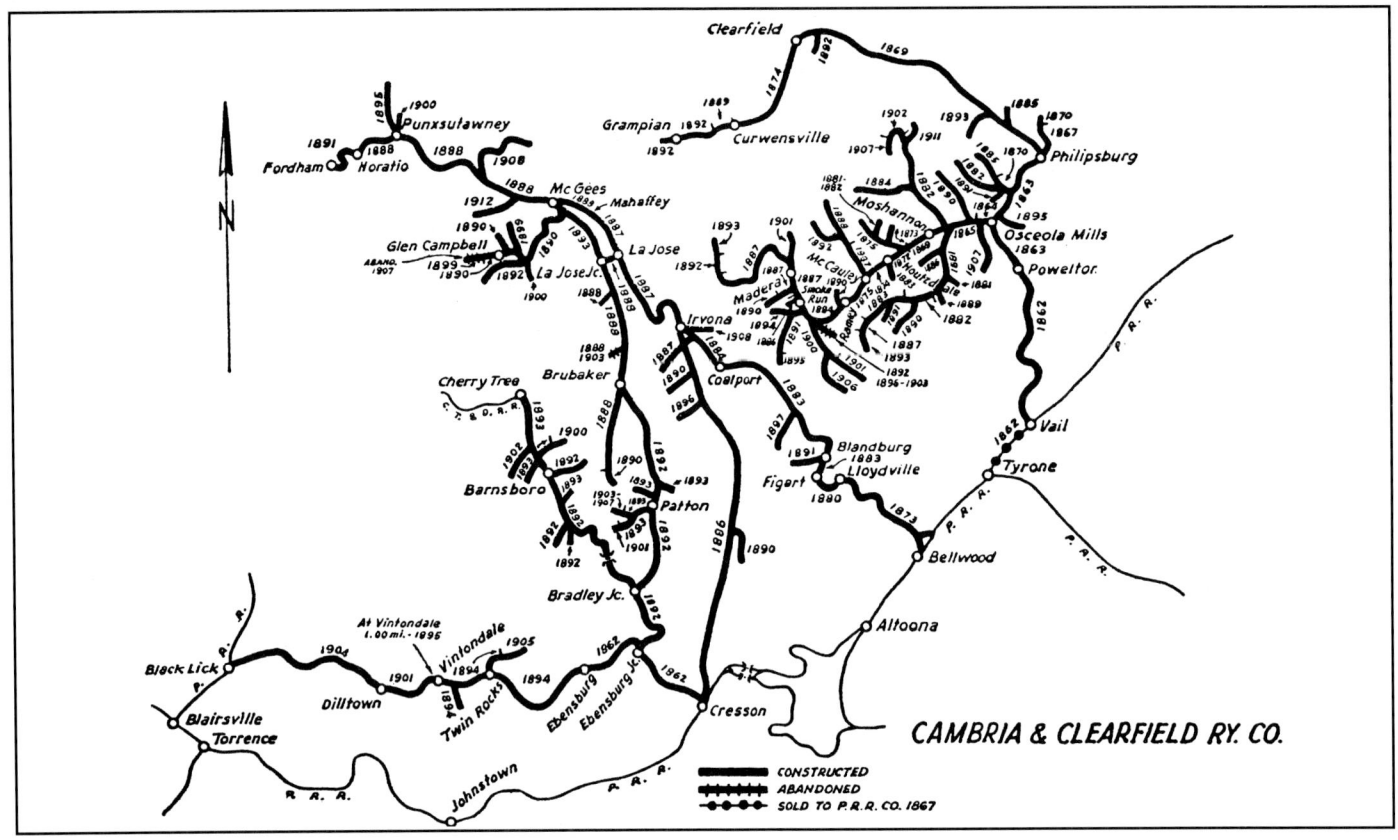

THIS SINGLE MAP, prepared circa 1945, demonstrates perhaps more than any other the immensity of PRR and the incredible industrial growth of the United States that occurred in the last half of the 1800s. There is actually a latterday historian who concluded that this growth would have happened even if railroads had never been invented because canals and riverways would have been able to provide the vital transportation. Let him look at this map. This whole region contains fabulous amounts of coking and steam coal, as well as lumber and other resources, in great quantity. The only rational way to get it to market was by rail and even PRR was hardpressed to handle the volume. The story began in a very small way. Find Cresson and then follow the line from there to Ebensburg. Had Schlatter's northern route extension been selected, Ebensburg would have had a railroad. No doubt irritated at being bypassed, the town was mollified by construction of the Ebensburg and Cresson Railroad in 1862 which traced a low summit neatly separating eastern and western waters. Incidentally, the unpublished historian Watkins gave the year as 1863 and provided PRR management with still another reason to condemn his manuscript for inaccuracy.

This branch was a backwater until vast expansion began in 1892-94. A hint of things to come was contained in an 1875 report that stated 100,000 tons of coal was mined on this short line and moved through Cresson to market. In 1886-87 a new branch was built from Cresson to Irvona, meeting a line from Bellwood. In the late 1880s and early 1890s a virtual explosion of construction took place east and west out of Ebensburg that ultimately reached all the way west to Black Lick (following Schlatter's route) and north beyond Punxsutawney. (The lines out of Vail are not part of this story, although they are also indicative of PRR growth.) As to the lines out of Cresson, the whole complex of lines became known as the Cambria and Clearfield Railway and the lines out of Cresson as the Cresson Division as we have shown. Over time the expression "Clearfield Cluster" has appeared. From now on, we will just call the railroad C&C.

We will refer still another time to silver linings and clouds.

The year 1902 is an excellent example. From the Ebensburg line, 72,905 *loaded* cars moved into Cresson. The Irvona line produced another 14,931 *loaded* cars. On a seven-day week, this was an average of 273 cars a day being dumped on what was already the busiest "slope" railroad in the world. These figures do *not* include empty movements. Since this traffic was almost entirely coal, coke and lumber, for every car out there was one back. As to "back," there was a total of 11,498 *loaded* inbound cars, 86% of which went up the Ebensburg branch. As one would expect, these loads were mostly general merchandise. Even today, these numbers are numbing. And we are just a few miles downgrade from the summit! There is a lot more to come. Now we do not know how this traffic divided between eastbound and westbound. Even if a lot of it was downhill, it still required motive power and track space. If we may paraphrase from naval history, it also needed wooden cars and iron men in profusion.

There were insidious aspects to this volume that ultimately played a major role in bringing down PRR/PC. The line hauls were rather short and the terminal costs (at both ends) very high as a percentage of the total. The investment in motive power and cars was enormous and while the traffic was captive there was also competition from other mines and railroads that tended to limit how much PRR could charge. Then there was the little matter of car supply. All railroad traffic is highly cyclical which means there are either too many or too few cars in the inventory at any given point in time. In good times, "turning" cars faster increases the supply. But this also means shorter trains moving faster. Yet the essence of railroad economics is just the opposite. Longer trains are good and speed unimportant, particularly on mountain railroads. All this is rather like dealing with women. No matter what you do you are wrong and tiny little mistakes magnify into major crises that can eat you up. As to Cresson, in 1902 there were over 500 cars a *day* moving in both directions through this junction. So much for the canal theory. Speaking of little things, we would like to note the proper spelling is "Torrance" at lower left.

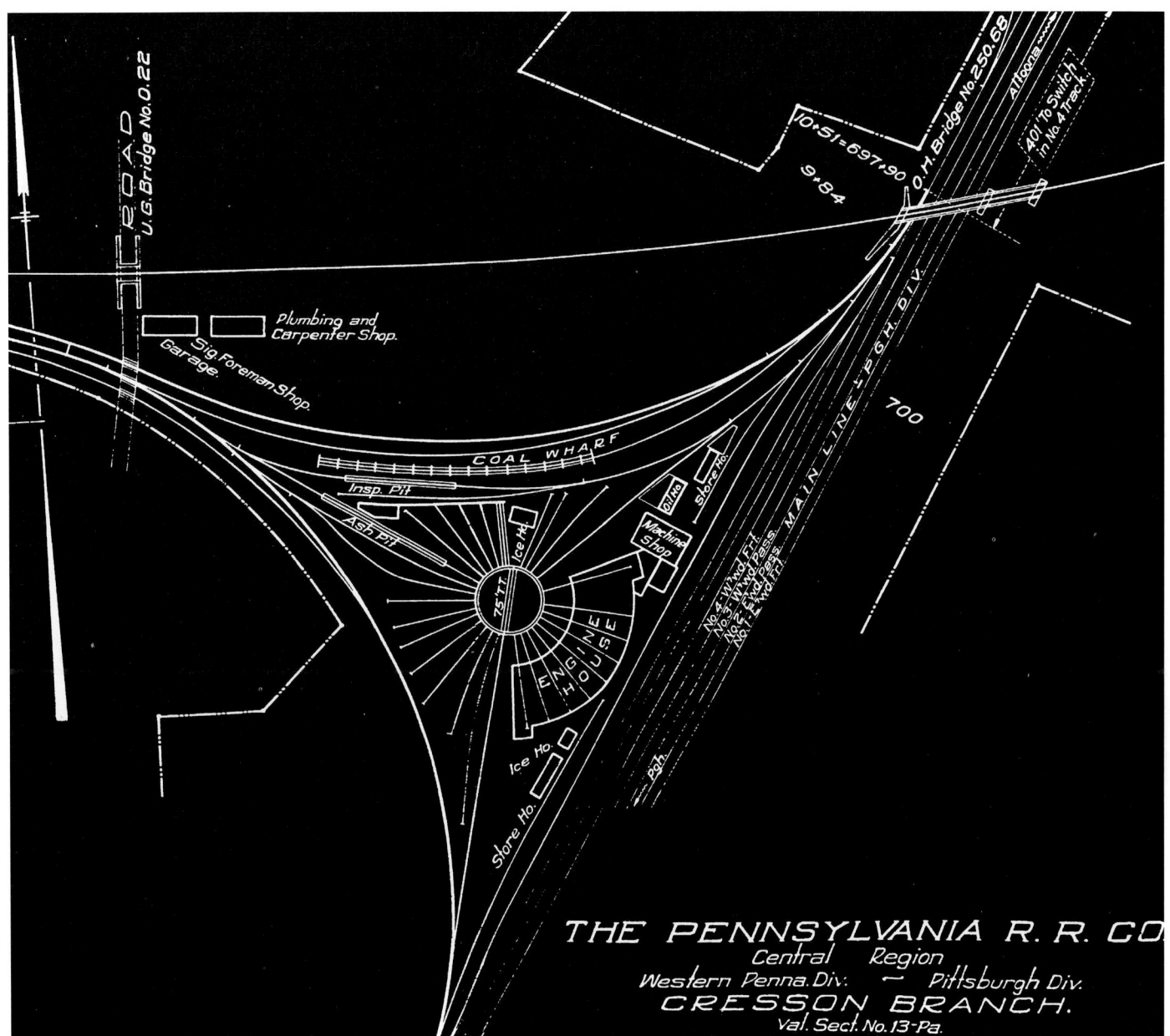

BY 1937 the nation was in its seventh year of the Great Depression and a mild recovery since 1934 was about to reverse itself. PRR was desperate to save a dollar wherever possible and the idea of the moment was to move a water station on the branch to facilitate rewatering of power on westbound empty trains. This drawing thus shows the Cresson complex as it existed in 1937. In this year, about five empty trains in winter and three in summer climbed the East Slope daily and went to the left back to the mines. Typically 9,000 gallon tenders were used and they were two-thirds empty upon arrival at Cresson. When each train stopped for water on the branch, Track No. 4 was fouled and the delay was causing overtime. The last water station prior to Cresson was Kittanning Point on, of course, an adverse grade and water was taken there only in emergency. There was a small plug about 1,800 feet up the branch from the mainline and the Bureau of New Ideas wanted to place a high-capacity water crane about 4,440 feet north of the present one. For a variety of reasons, the General Superintendent did not think this was a good idea because it would simply move delays from the mainline to the branch. We do not know how all this was worked out, but it is instructive because of the insight into Cresson and branch operations. A series of small yards up the branch performed terminal operations in both directions, the first one being at the water plug location and the next at Bradley Junction about 11 miles away. So Cresson, at least at this time, was not a terminal *per se*. The facilities shown here served branch motive power. Outbound loaded trains moving west simply entered the mainline at the bottom and eastbound loaded trains went on the "jumpover" Bridge 250.68 (at upper right) and joined the mainline east of MO. Inbound empty trains from the east travelled as described above. Inbound empty trains from the west, however, had to crossover at Lilly interlocker (about four miles west of Cresson) and move against the current of traffic until Cresson. Since the whole point of constructing jumpovers was to avoid congestion at interlockers, and there was never a jumpover in the Lilly-Portage area, it is easy to conclude that most of the traffic volume from the C&C through Cresson was eastbound. Another point should be emphasized regarding dieselization. The overwhelming advantage of the diesel over steampower was *availability*, but there were many secondary advantages and water supply was one of them. Diesels do not have to stop for water.

Pennsylvania State Archives/Tom Hollyman

THERE WAS A SMALL YARD just east of the Cresson jumpover and this is how it appeared in the 1950s. Jumpover Bridge 250.68 is at lower left. This view, of course, is eastward. The jumpover seen here was not the first structure. The original bridge was put out for bids in 1892 and completed in 1893. We shall see an image of it shortly. In 1915 PRR installed two "half-through" plate girders measuring 100 and 55 feet in length as well as a deck plate girder span 44 feet in length. Half-through girders were only used when there was a clearance problem and there certainly was just that at this location. PRR had to provide a very long approach fill to provide minimum mainline clearance and this tightness proved to be the deathknell for 250.68 during the 1990s double-stack clearance project. It was there in April 1994 and gone by May 1995. Still more clouds and silver linings. More frequent and longer trains spawned serious grade crossing problems and PRR was forced to build over/under bridges by the score. For example, Old Route 22 at Cresson had to be put under the mainline in 1909. And all these staggering traffic loads did *not* include movement of company material which was estimated, in 1910, to be about 10% of revenue tonnage with attendant empty returns.

THE WEST SLOPE

Railroaders Memorial Museum

IT IS EASY to provide a time-frame for this photograph. The ten-stall enginehouse was built in 1900 and the 1893 jumpover through-truss seen at far right was replaced in 1915. In the center can be seen the long approach fill to the jumpover as well as the ramp track to the coal wharf. Two horses are hitched to a wagon behind the trees in the center of the photograph. Codes on this and other negatives lead us to believe that this shot was taken in February of 1903.

Hagley Museum and Library

THE ENGINEHOUSE was not the only structure erected at Cresson in 1900. The building in the background at far left is a 36 by 40-foot machine shop built in the same year. We are quite sure the date of this view is February of 1903.

TRIUMPH I

M.E.570A

Hagley Museum and Library

THIS 40 by 100-FOOT CAR SHOP was another Cresson structure of the class of 1900 and is seen in February of 1903. At least in our view, architecturally this is the most interesting one of all. Large windows and clerestories were needed to provide light and this design certainly met the requirement of "function first" yet was done in pleasing form. This building was located on the C&C as will be shown. Car shops introduce the subject of railroad cars and no student of railroads is well informed until this fascinating subject is explored in at least summary form. Forty years ago your author asked Father to identify the single most serious problem faced by all railroads in the environment of those times. He pondered the question for quite a while and then replied "car shortages." Put succinctly, the cars are the point of the power and, indeed, the railroad itself. At any given point in time, there are too many, not enough, too many of the wrong kind, not enough of the right kind. Interwoven in this conundrum is the nature of traffic itself. Traffic is either captive or competitive. If captive, the railroad has the shipper by the privates. If competitive, the low-cost producer always wins. On Pittdiv, PRR was in the catbird seat on both counts. The outpouring of tonnage from the C&C was and remains captive. If the shipper wanted cars, he was at PRR's mercy. This situation was a fertile field for corruption and graft flourished. Richer shippers could purchase and supply their own cars, mitigating the problem to some extent. Other shippers had to pay off, either by "selling" shares in their enterprises to railroads and/or their executives or by "buying" cars from those in power. For example, in 1906 as a result of Theodore Roosevelt's "square deal" posture, the House of Representatives decided to open the lid to this Pandora's box. Since PRR was by far and away the richest and most powerful corporation in the nation, in reality this investigation was an attack on PRR in general and PRR President Alexander J. Cassatt in particular. PRR had owned the Senate for years, but had not gone to the expense of buying the House. There were a lot of them and the place had an uncomfortable number of unwashed Democrats. PRR reasoned that the Senate would bury any bill the House might pass or turncoat Roosevelt might propose. Remember that this was only forty years after the end of the Civil War and the triumph of the Republican Party. The United States had just become the most powerful nation on the planet. The automotive age was in the womb and the first powered flight just delivered by the Wright brothers. Never adept at public relations, PRR was beginning to brag about its supremacy in print. Not for PRR the wisdom of silence when everything is going your way. Here are some direct quotes from a 1905 epistle: "...exercises a dominating influence over the Baltimore and Ohio, Norfolk and Western, Chesapeake and Ohio, the Reading Company..." and "...unequalled in the world." The House bared its fangs and soon discovered that Cassatt and Company had mammoth coal holdings. Then the House struck the motherlode. Joseph Boyer, chief clerk to the superintendent of motive power at Altoona, admitted that he had accepted more than $45,000 in cash from certain coal companies and 11,000 shares of stock in return for supplying cars to his patrons. His salary of $2,700 a year had just somehow allowed him to become a wealthy man. Similar testimony was elicited from others plus an outpouring of complaints from less favored mining companies claiming great losses from discriminatory car distribution. Thus the groundwork was laid for the Age of Regulation and the ultimate demise of mighty PRR. To be fair, by the way, PRR was not the only sinner. Just the largest.

THE WEST SLOPE

National Archives

CRESSON WAS BUSY in other ways, as evidenced by this substantial freight-handling facility seen c. 1918. This enclosed frame freighthouse, measuring 20 by 212 feet, was built in 1910 along with the 20 by 500 foot umbrella structure on the left. Even all this was not enough to handle the traffic because a 20 by 420 foot frame transfer platform was built in 1916. This complex was located in the "high" yard behind MO tower.

A HELPER SET is eastbound out of Cresson on 13 May 1995, moving under the ghost of Bridge 250.68 and approaching MO. This photograph was taken from an observation platform recently built on Front Street to allow visitors to watch railroad activity safe from Conrail police. Funding for the platform and associated picnic areas came from a variety of national and local sources. It is hoped that the area can be turned into a railroad park and one dream involves relocation of MO tower to this area. Actual train speed is so low through this section that derailment danger is minor and we wish the townfolks good luck.

Thomas A. Biery

FOR ALL THE CHANGES over one and a half centuries, Cresson remains an important operating point on Conrail. When this photograph was taken in September of 1983 the location was known as ARCH and modern engine-servicing facilities had been in place for some years.

TRIUMPH I

PRR POSITION LIGHT SIGNALS went with the jumpover bridge and they were replaced by New York Central-style targets as shown here on 13 May 1995. This view is looking northwesterly into the servicing complex. The observation platform is behind the pickup truck seen at extreme left. The yard office in the center behind the left signal mast is believed to have been built in 1910 and, if so, is the only extant structure from the "old days."

EVOLUTION TO DATE has made Cresson a helper station as well as a supplier of branch power. And there is no shortage of power at Cresson at any given point in time as hinted in this 13 May 1995 shot. Today Cresson provides fuel, sand and running repairs with 92-day service done at Juniata Shop. On this day we came away with the impression that all the units were in first-class condition. After a long struggle with recalcitrant labor unions, Conrail along with most other railroads has negotiated run-through agreements that eliminated the ancient 100-mile division and five-man train crew. These changes, along with diesel versatility, have provided operating management with important weapons in the cost-reduction war.

A LONG EASTBOUND is literally creeping through Cresson on 13 May 1995 in this easterly view of the helper station. Notice that both sand and fuel are brought in by rail. There are now only three crew-call points on the old Pittdiv, at Pittsburgh, Altoona and Cresson. Cresson is the helper station for both the east and west slopes which is another way of saying the most important in raildom. Helpers from Cresson handle all shoves from Conemaugh (C) east and Altoona west. Organizationally, the division dispatcher has full helper-power authority from CP PITT (Pittsburgh) to and well past ALTO (Altoona). He can order helpers to shove all the way from PITT to the summit or even beyond if dynamics are not working or helper power is needed at ALTO. Usually, however, helpers couple-up at C or ALTO. Cresson itself has a branch dispatcher who handles road power for the C&C and South Fork. The former, as we are about to see, has been sold to a short-line operator but the Cresson dispatcher supplies power for certain unit trains coming from the C&C. New C&C owners supply their own power for other movements. Cresson is very quiet today, but it is an illusion. The brute force needed to conquer the mountain barrier resides there and the seeming tranquility is entirely the product of modern mufflers.

THE WEST SLOPE

HERE IS THE TRACKAGE of the C&C, or Clearfield Cluster, as of 1992. These lines were sold to short-line operator R.J. Corman on 29 December 1995. Ex-NYC and B&O lines were included in the package, some of which are not shown here. Clearfield Yard is the center of gravity and the line out of Cresson is part of the C&C's "mainline." This whole cluster is essentially a coal line with 231 miles of track. Spinoffs of this type are endemic in railroading and are basically designed to stiff unions. This whole region is awash in the skeletons of beehive coke ovens. Unit trains, as we have noted, still flow from the C&C and we should point out that PRR was an early pioneer in this innovative process. PRR was *the* pioneer in loading coal on a *moving* train. In the early 1960s at a mine in Blairsville, motion loading was first practiced and other railroads flocked to witness the procedure. Both the mine and PRR soon discovered that such loading could be *too* fast. For some mysterious chemical reason, the coal pile exploded and it was found necessary to slow up a bit. In 1967 a mine at Barnesboro on the C&C was brought on stream and it was found that a unit train could load 10,000 tons of steam coal into 100 hoppers at a rate of two minutes per car, a rate that did not produce loud noises. The cars were owned by a power company so there was no "car shortage" ripoff involved.

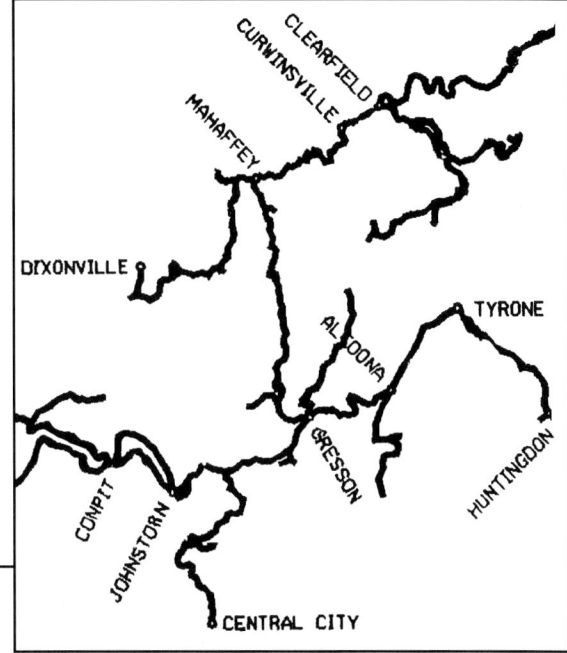

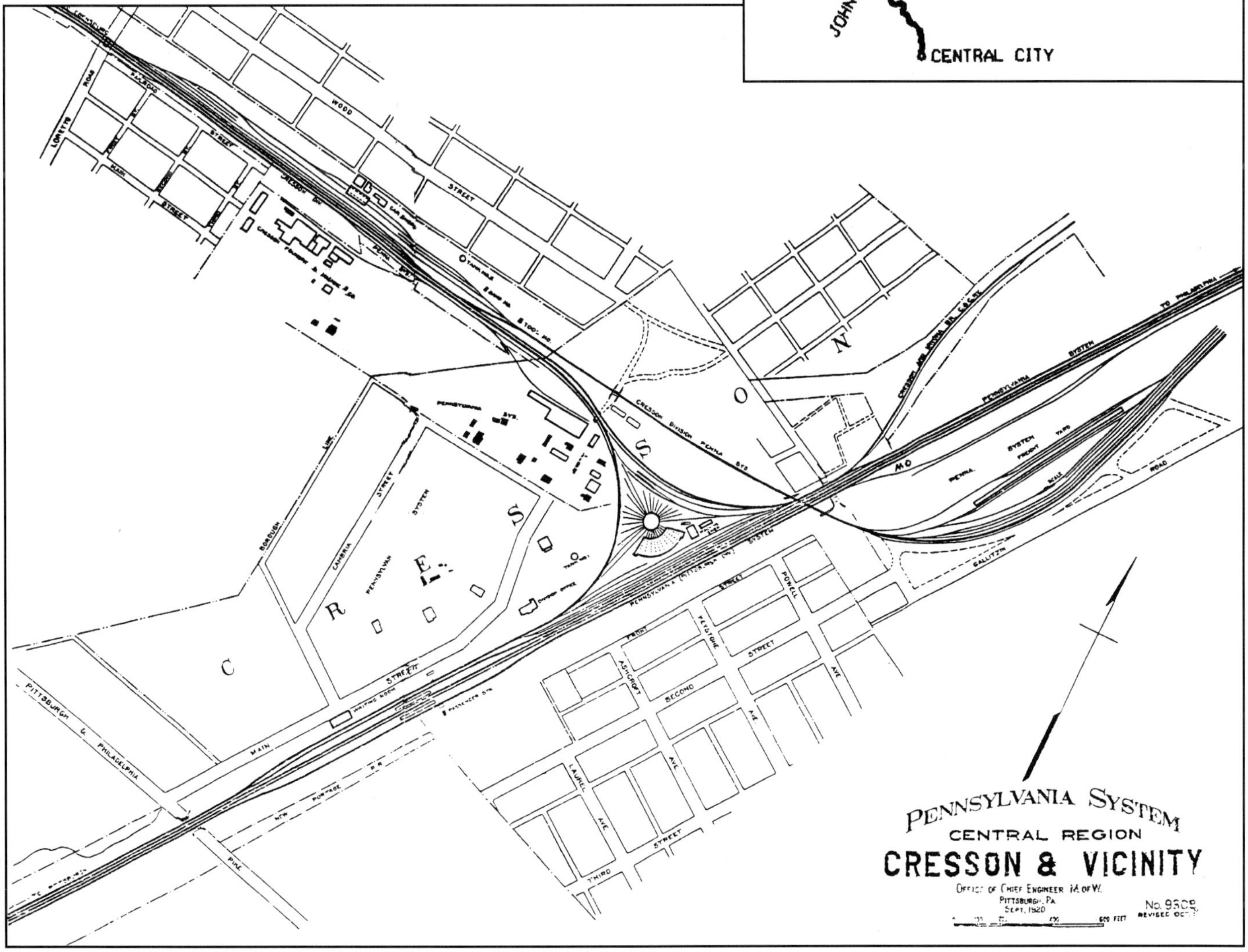

THIS RATHER FUZZY MOW MAP does at least give a general overall view of the Cresson area beyond the triangle. Note that the Irvona Branch leaves the mainline between the jumpover and MO and that the freight yard is behind (and above) MO. The car shop can be seen at upper left along with the water tank previously discussed. The "Pittsburgh and Philadelphia Road" at lower left became Old Route 22. At a right angle to this road is a strip of land titled "New Portage Railroad," a curious holdover from the old days. This map was completed in 1920 and revised to 1927. The enginehouse apparently lasted until very late in the steam era, servicing branch Consolidations on it's 75-foot turntable. Some Hippos (with *very* short tenders) inched their way up the C&C, but not in great numbers. The C&C was and remains a gaggle of severe grades in the two to three percent range rife with stories of runaways and brutal operating conditions. Now let us move downgrade to Lilly.

TRIUMPH I

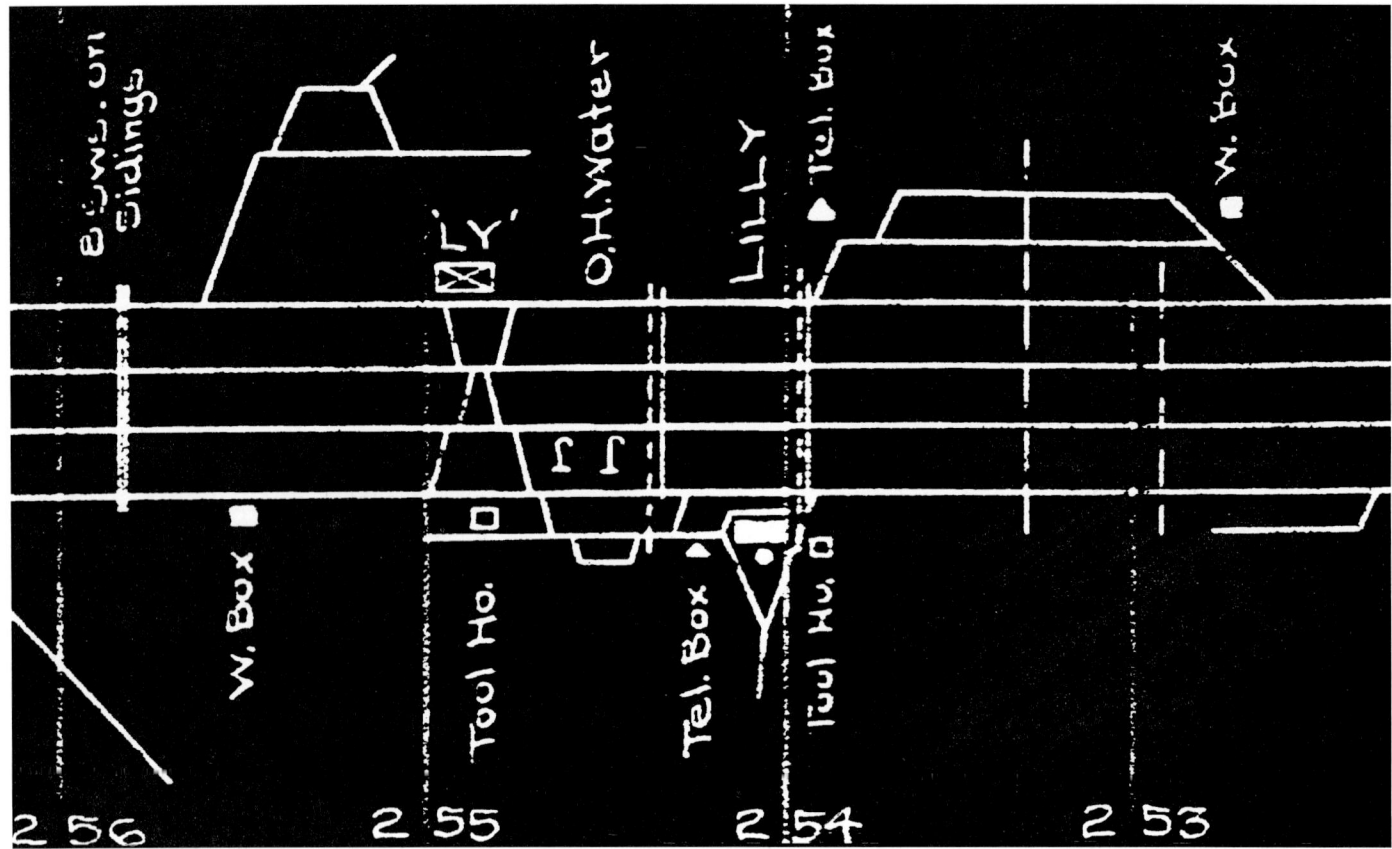

LILLY IN 1910 was considerably different than the place where Sylvester Welch and his 15 assistants pitched their tents on 12 April 1831 to begin surveying the OPRR. The Conemaugh is becoming something of a river at this location which, in 1831, was known as Lilley's Mill implying, in turn, that there was sufficient water flow to grind grain. This circumstance did not go unnoticed by OPRR or PRR. The foot of Plane No. 4 was located here and it was a major water station on PRR until the end of steam. The name evolved to Lilly's and finally Lilly. Nearby coal mines made Lilly the second source of local traffic on the West Slope, but by no means the last. Ultimately branches to mines were built on both sides of the mainline as seen here. Notice the overhead water bridge just east of LY Tower...it lasted at least until 1950 and probably into the mid-50s. In the eyes of PRR, Lilly was a water lily and little else. The first reference we have found was in 1855 and Lilly was merely described as a "water station" and "inconsiderable" at that. Taking water on a mountain grade in the steam era required somewhat more skill and forethought than the expression implies. Even moving upgrade, the crew had to stop the train with the locomotive's tender almost directly under the spout. This wasn't too easy to do, so many times the head-end power uncoupled from the train and moved forward. Did the helper also need water? If so, still another precision stop or uncoupling was required. All this took time and the track was blocked during the maneuvering. Downgrade was just as tricky. If the engineer overshot the spout still coupled to the train, he might not be able to back the train upgrade and then he was really hungup. In such circumstances, dispatchers could call upon ample reserves of profanity to describe the engineer's ancestry and intellectual capacity, at this location perhaps suggesting that a water lily could be placed upon the hapless engineer's coffin. Another more insidious aspect of "taking water" was the temptation to pass a water station and reach for the next one. If the water in the tender ran out, the engineer either had to stop at once and drop his fire or run the risk of a boiler explosion. This was a classic Hobson's choice. The wrath of the dispatcher, road foreman and superintendent in the first instance might make an explosion seem like the easier way out. Understandably, the fireman and headend brakeman would have different views of this situation. The brakeman would probably be asleep anyway, but the fireman might take one glance at the water glass and leave the premises in a hurry. So we can see that the engineer's lot was not always a happy one.

THE WEST SLOPE

National Archives

National Archives

THE LAST TOWER to be constructed at Lilly (LY) was this one, shown here c. 1918 by a valuation photographer. This tower was built new in 1899 and materially improved in 1913 with approach and route locking mechanism. The tower it replaced was built in 1884 which in turn took the place of what we suspect was a telegraph office, probably opened in the very early days. The LY seen here was closed on 10 September 1931 and removed in March of 1934. Note the gob pile in the background on the right, which shows how close the coal mine was in relation to the mainline. As we have seen, LY was next to Track No. 4.

IN 1883, a local newspaper lamented the fact that Lilly had neither a station house or a ticket agent and castigated PRR for their insensitivity. Within a few years, PRR built this combination station and freight house at a location seen earlier on the track chart. This view is valuation, taken c. 1918-20. We have reason to believe the station was out-of-service by the late 1920s because nearby coal mines were becoming defunct and PRR was understandably reluctant to provide money-losing local passenger service on the busiest mountain railroad on the planet.

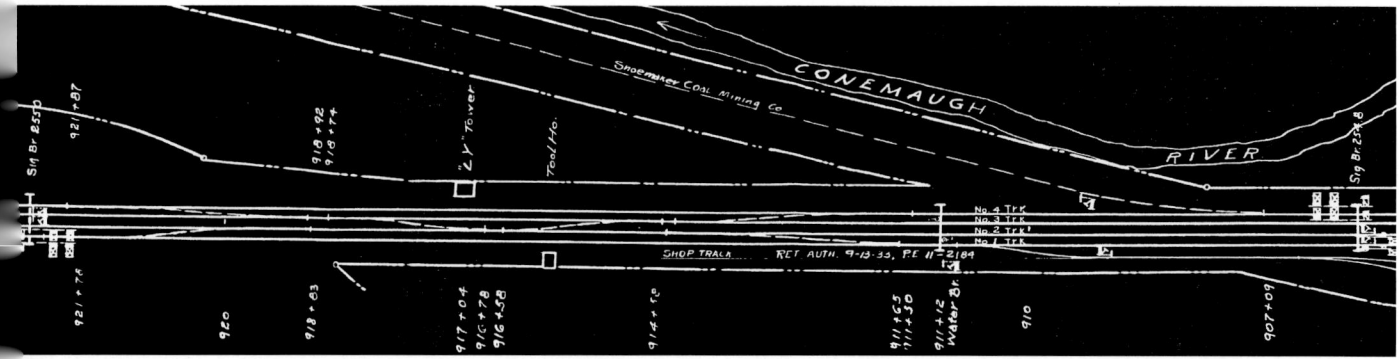

THIS MAP was prepared in 1934 to accompany a memorandum recommending that the crossovers and tower at LY be removed. Authority was granted and LY disappeared into history. It was noted that only eight miles separated MO from NY (downgrade from LY) and that the introduction of cab signals had speeded movements to the extent that this complex was redundant. The majority of coal mines on the Lilly Branch and the Shoemaker Mine noted on this map had been worked-out or abandoned. Notice how close the Conemaugh River is to the mainline. A tributary of the Conemaugh in this vicinity was originally crossed with a 19-foot wooden bridge which was replaced by an iron girder bridge in 1859 and a 62-foot stone arch in 1886. For many years PRR maintained Dragging Equipment Detectors on Tracks 1, 2 and 3 on the east end of this map and today there are "talking" detectors about a mile east of Lilly midway to Cresson which carry the name Lilly. So many times a day the airwaves carry the name of Welch's first campsite to all who wish to listen.

TRIUMPH I

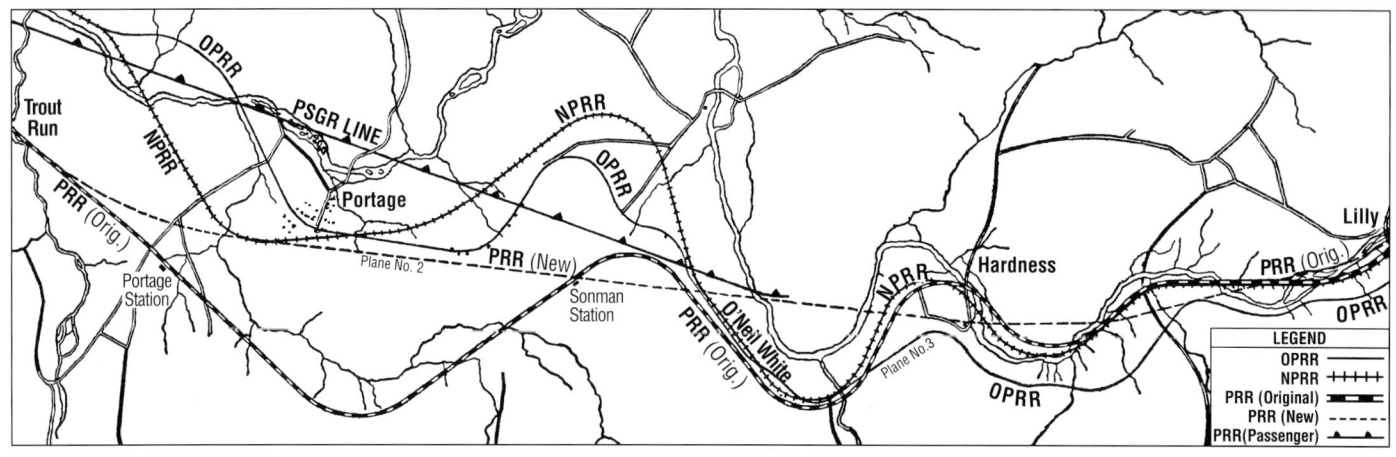

FROM LILLY WEST TO TROUT RUN, the paths followed by OPRR, NPRR, original PRR and "new line" PRR can only be described as a maze within a maze. This map, which was prepared in the mid-1890s, is perhaps the simplest rendition of a very complicated evolution. The reader should start at upper left and note the darkest "Pennsylvania Railroad" line, following its up and down route to Lilly. This was the original PRR as built by Thomson, but even this is somewhat inaccurate because some interim wiggles had been straightened prior to the 1890s. Now find the "Allegheny Portage RR" solid line at upper left and follow its circuitous route through Planes 2 and 3 to Lilly. This is OPRR. Starting at upper left in the same place, find the standard railroad cross-hatched line "NPRR" and follow its looping path to "O'Neil White" where it begins paralleling the original PRR line, crossing it near Hardness. From there to Cresson the NPRR is alongside the original PRR on the south side. Go back to upper left and find the dashed "New Line PRR." This is the "new" and present PRR mainline. Going again to upper left, notice the solid line with black triangles and follow it to "O'Neil White." This marks the location of a proposed new passenger line that was studied circa 1908 but never built. Thank God. Please note that the town of Portage is at the foot of Plane No. 2 and be reminded that the OPRR "long level" from the west ended there. When NPRR was built it was necessary to lengthen the line to ease the gradient caused by the closure of Planes No. 2 and 3, hence the meandering path through this area. We have already passed comment on the insanity implicit in NPRR's construction and merely offer this section of the line as proof-positive. One should also note that the original town of Portage was well north of the original PRR mainline and station. Rather obviously, Plane No. 2 was the reason for the town's creation in the first place and we have little doubt that a few taverns graced the fledgling locality to soothe the nerves of passengers who had, at this point, survived quite a few harrowing descents. The town, of course, expanded southerly to meet PRR's original line only to be cut in half by the "new line." At least the new passenger line wasn't built, which would have bypassed the town again. The reader should note Trout Run at far left because, as we shall see, Portage almost had to endure still another wrenching change.

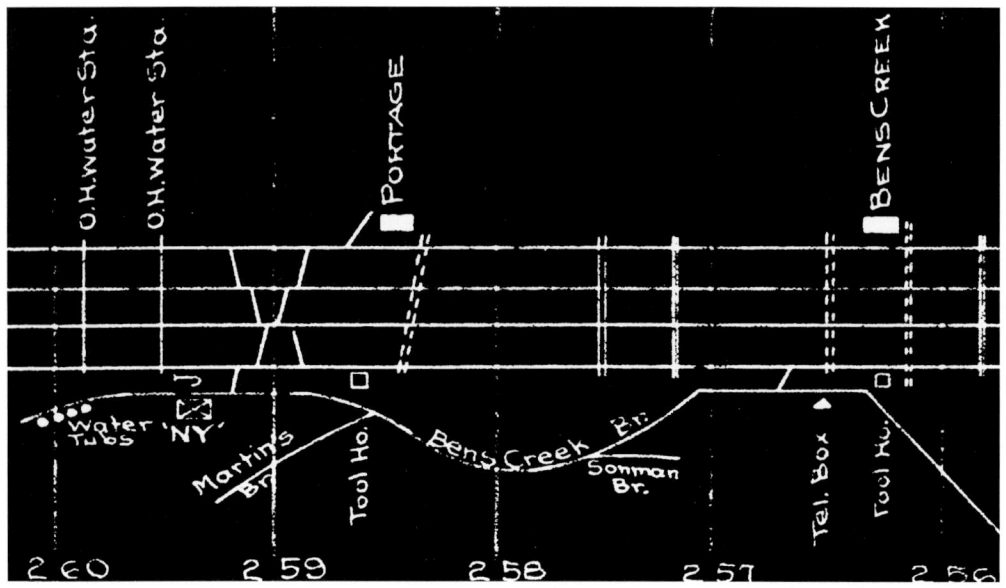

IN TRACK CHART FORM, here we see the mainline in 1910 from Bens Creek through Portage to NY Tower. Three branches have sprung forth from Track No. 1, adding still more traffic to an already overloaded mainline. There are *two* overhead water bridges just west of NY and four water tubs to satiate thirsty steam locomotives. The stations at both Bens Creek and Portage are on Track No. 4. As we shall see, most of the trackage shown here is on very high fill particularly through Portage. The main stem of Bens Creek Branch follows the trace of the original PRR mainline.

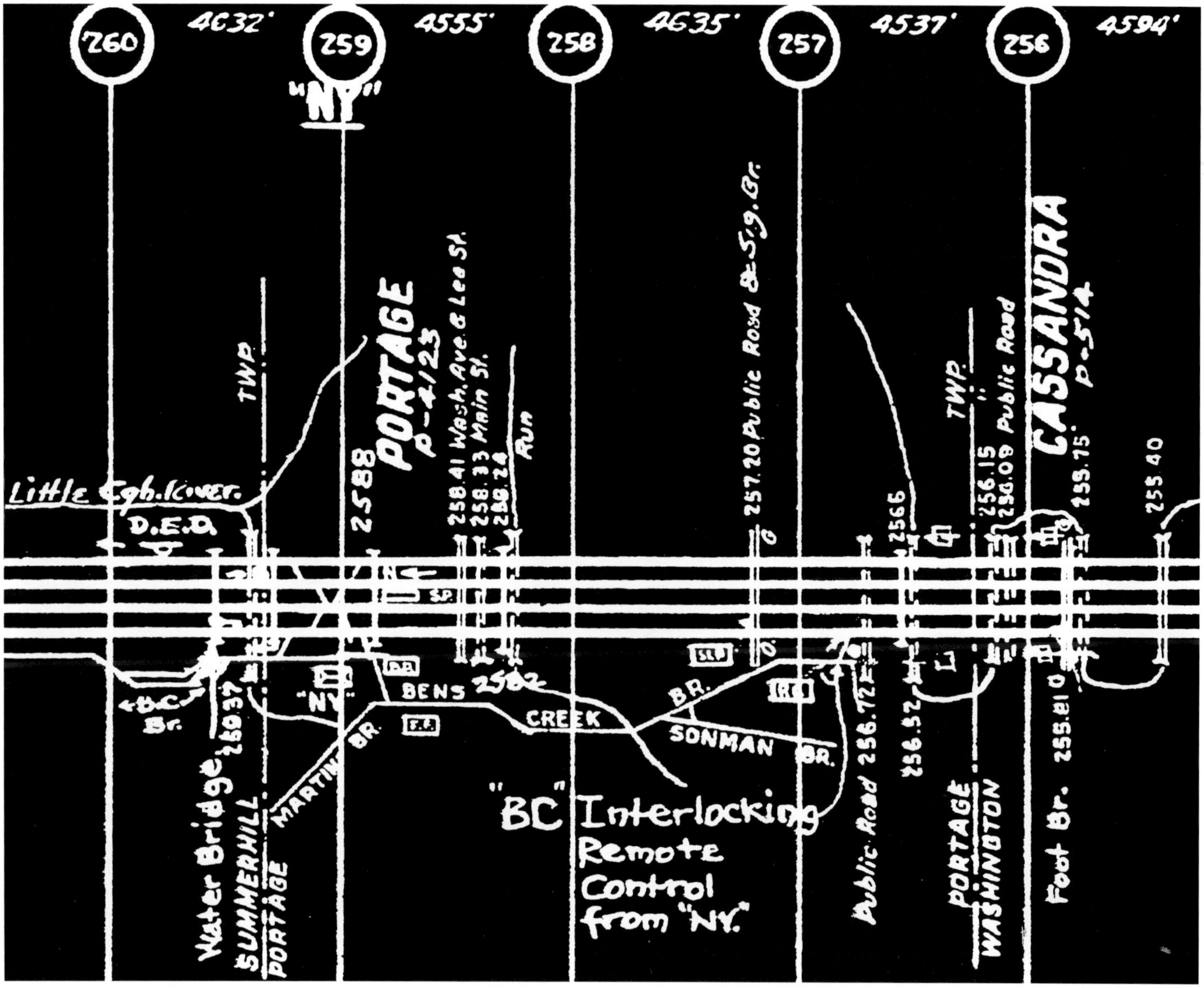

THE WEST SLOPE

LONG BEFORE this track chart was published in 1958, the town of Cassandra had appeared along with a famous footbridge. Just west of this bridge we see slide-fence symbols. At Milepost 257.20 an overhead bridge provides another vantage point. The Conemaugh River is crossed four times between 255.40 and 256.52, just slightly over a mile. NY remains alive and well, and since 1910 an interlocker has appeared at Bens Creek (BC) and then made remote from NY. One water bridge has been removed and a DED added on Track No. 4. The latter was installed at least as early as 1942 and represents still another time that PRR was willing to try anything innovative that would assist operations. Today there is a "talking" detector at NY broadcasting "Portage," just a little less than five miles from "Lilly." All three branches remain active today.

THE LEGENDARY CASSANDRA, a Trojan princess, was given prophecy powers by Apollo but then, just because she refused to sleep with him, her blessing was changed to a curse in that she would never be believed. This must have been very frustrating for her as it was for this author trying to divine why anyone would name an otherwise pleasant little town for such a tragic figure. Whatever the reasoning, PRR built this tiny passenger station circa 1913 (seen here c. 1918) almost certainly next to Track No. 4. We do know that there was a school in Cassandra and, lo those many years ago, PRR would carry children from Portage to this station for a nickel. Brutal, hardhearted PRR did that for years on this crowded mainline. Perhaps the town was well named after all.

National Archives

Thomas A. Biery

TAKEN FROM THE FAMOUS footbridge at Cassandra looking west, this photograph shows the Big Cut which resulted from the 1890s "new line" project. Overhead Bridge 257.20 can be seen in the far distance as can the Bens Creek turnout from Track No. 1 just east. This photo is dated 1978 but we are sure it is early 1980s since Track No. 2 is gone. The cabooseless train is puzzling, but probably Conrail is moving empty hoppers from here to there with special dispensation.

FROM THE SAME footbridge on 13 May 1995, two trains have just passed. The eastbound train took an interminable amount of time to clear and we had the impression with this as with all other West Slope eastbounders we watched on many trips that the addition of one more car would have caused a stall. This is, of course, smart railroading. Both trains had ditch lights and the eastbounder properly dimmed them when the westbounder was in range. We will have to say, by the way, that these lights are very effective improvements. Not only do they attract the eye, but also provide depth perception and an instantaneous indication of speed. The footbridge was supposedly built in 1928 to allow residents of Cassandra (on the right) easy and safe passage to Route 53 (on the left). We have reason to question this date.

THE NEW PRR LINE was announced as completed with four tracks from Lilly to Wilmore (west of Portage) in 1898 and this waiting room/shelter *cum* freight house was built in 1899 to serve Bens Creek. This view is eastbound through the Big Cut and we are confident that the bridge seen in the distance was a combination signal and footbridge built to serve Cassandra. The rock mounds forming the Big Cut are bald, sheer and unstable, witness the slide fences seen in previous photos. Today, of course, these humps are lush with second-growth foliage.

THE WEST SLOPE

Railroad Museum of Pennsylvania

THIS 1890s PHOTOGRAPH is one of the most frustrating as well as fascinating in this book. It is clearly and obviously associated with "new line" construction between Lilly and NY, yet we have not been able to determine from where it was taken nor the location of the valley scene. The multiple trackage running across the top rests upon a huge, *new* fill and seems to be the new mainline. The old mainline did not boast any fill of this depth. Yet if this is the case, what is the huge fill under construction at center right? This fill is aimed directly at the hill on which the photographer is standing and is *lower* than the supposed new mainline.

What is the trackage at lower right? It is far too high for the old mainline and is of such rough and raw construction that it could not possibly be mainline, new or old. It is also on a curve. The new line eliminated curves. And what is going on at lower center? Is this a quarry or is some sort of arch under construction? If the latter, it is not aligned with anything. There are more stone-laden gondolas on a siding at upper left. Are they inbound or outbound? What is going on at the far end of the "new" fill? There are a lot of cut stones on the ground and even what appears to be a greenhouse. Is the multi-story building to the left a dormitory? Back to the "quarry" area, what is the significance of the man-made wall enclosing a large area and why is it being buried by the "new" fill? Let us reach out to the faint treeline at upper right. There is a gap in the treeline roughly in line with the "new" fill. Is this the beginning of a cut? If so, which one? In what direction is the photographer facing? Shadows are an aid to photo interpreters, but there are none because this was taken at high noon. Just to complete the puzzle, what is that giant cut stone at lower right? How did that get there and why? For all the enigmatic aspects of this photograph, it is quite apparent that "new line" construction was a major undertaking by PRR and was completed in the face of the movement of staggering traffic loads. As for hunches, we suspect that this is the Sonman area and a lot of the construction is temporary in nature.

LOOKING EAST from Bens Creek toward Cassandra in May of 1995, we see the Bens Creek Branch/old PRR mainline where it joins the "new" mainline. In the distance one can see the shape of the Cassandra footbridge and see why we are content with our assertions made earlier as to its history.

TRIUMPH I

THE OVERHEAD BRIDGE from which the previous photograph was taken was sufficiently high that double-stack clearance was not a problem. The two targets are, of course, mounted on the bridge itself and the "G" informs eastbound tonnage trains to ignore "stop and proceed" rules. "Tonnage" is a relative term on the West Slope. Every single train we saw, mixed consist or otherwise, was on its hands and knees on this grade and surely qualified as G.

WE ARE NOW following the original PRR route to Sonman. Coal and PRR put this tiny town on the map and coal, incidentally, keeps it there today. The reader will recall that PRR built a station at Sonman in the early days and this is believed to be that structure. As early as 1875 about 75,000 tons of coal per year was being shipped from Sonman and in 1883 a large drift mine was opened into the Miller seam, a formation we have seen earlier. By 1919 this mine had 522 employees and 597 by 1925. Coal still pours from this area, which gives an insight to the lushness of the reserves. Today this building sits at a four-way intersection with a coal cleaning and loading facility across the street and the old PRR mainline only a few feet away. The Koza family lives here, or at least did when this photo was taken on 13 May 1995. Since the house and grounds are meticulously maintained, we like to think that this is in fact an early PRR structure.

THE AUTO is crossing the old PRR mainline, the occupants probably oblivious to the significance of just another pair of rails. This is the coaling facility at the Koza front door and the building on the left houses the hopper loading machinery. Much of this coal will go to Baltimore for export. In 1940 there was a mine disaster here and 63 men lost their lives. We should always remember that there was a price tag when we contemplate the nation's growth to superpower status.

THE WEST SLOPE

National Archives

ABOUT A MILE WEST of "Koza Corner" on the original mainline, and just east of the present-day Route 164 grade crossing in Portage, PRR built a 40 by 10-foot stone and brick-lined passenger station in 1861. *This is not that station.* The reader should be reminded that the town of Portage at the foot of Plane No. 2 was well north of this site and was described in 1855 as being "inconsiderable." As late as 1875 lumbering was the principal Portage industry and population was only about 300. The town grew south and clustered around the PRR mainline. Even in 1861 the principal reason for PRR's decision to build a substantial structure was to provide water from nearby Spring Run. There was one standpipe on the north track and two on the south track, the latter 1,500 feet apart so that road and helper locomotives could water at the same time. This length, incidentally, implies train length of 40 to 50 cars...very long for this era and indicative of the gentleness of the West Slope. One of the more amusing episodes at this water station occurred in 1868. It seems that the main water pipe had clogged and PRR replaced it with a wooden pipe which was satisfactory provided "no great pressure" was applied. How does one make a wooden pipe? When the new line was completed, the original stone/brick station was redundant and we assume promptly removed. The structure pictured here, seen c. 1918, was built as a 32 by 75-foot frame freight station in 1909. It is extant.

HERE WE SEE the Portage freight house in the Spring of 1995, looking easterly across Route 164. The original station was behind this structure. The rail line on the left, of course, goes to Sonman.

THE OTHER SIDES of the 1909 freight station in the Spring of 1995. Route 164 passes under the new line a few blocks to the right courtesy of a stone overpass completed in 1896. There is a keystone plaque on the far corner of the station with incorrect dates.

195

WITH THE OPENING of the new line another passenger station at Portage was needed so PRR built this one in 1899 on the north side of the tracks on Washington Avenue. This was opposite the location of still another 1926 station on Lee Street. This photograph was taken c. 1918.

National Archives

BY 1909 PRR concluded that a shelter was needed on the south side of the new line opposite the station just seen, so they installed this 12 by 55-foot frame building. Notice that an eastbound passenger train can be dimly seen at left approaching a signal bridge. This photo was taken c. 1918 and on the right one can see the rather bucolic nature of the surroundings. Portage was still in the process of growing south.

National Archives

PORTAGE GROWTH AND PROSPERITY enticed PRR into building this two-story brick station in 1926 on Lee Street. The prosperity part only lasted a few years and by 1933 PRR, savaged by the Great Depression, wanted to close it. Local businessmen bleated and the Commonwealth intervened with the result that the station remained open until 1954. The second story was a freight/express office and passengers used only the first floor. They had to enter the underpass and climb concrete steps to the tracks where they found a covered waiting area between Tracks 2 and 3. After several years of use as a Knights of Columbus club, the Stager family purchased it and ultimately was kind enough to allow the Portage Station Museum to take over. This photo was taken on 13 May 1995 as an eastbound trailer train passed. The museum is open to the public three days a week and is worth a visit.

THE WEST SLOPE

THIS IS THE second story of the 1926 Lee Street station, looking east on 7 September 1962 while it was still in use as a club with one lone member perched on a bench and watching the world go by. The signal bridge is in the same location as it was in 1918 and in the distance one can see the overhead road bridge at Sonman.

Edward H. Weber

COMING BACK to the original PRR mainline one more time, here on 6 May 1995 we see an old New York Central baggage car resting on a siding beside a scrap yard west of Route 164. An oldtimer told us that the car had been there for almost five years. Perhaps this is a PRR trophy. If so, it will not be the last we shall see.

National Archives

THE NY TOWER we see here c. 1918 in valuation crudity was adjacent to Track No. 1. NY's birthdate is unknown. In 1899 NY was graced with a new mechanical interlocker in common with other towers west of here. A photograph in another book claims to show NY in 1891 on the north side of a three-track mainline. Even if correct, this is not that structure. We also know that NY's westward home signal was destroyed in a derailment in the late 1980s and masts were installed as replacements. Perhaps of more interest, just west of NY Trout Run passes beneath the mainline at Milepost 259.37 with a single-span stone arch just twenty feet long. There are those who claim that this is a surviving 1851 original "virtually unaltered from its 1850s appearance." This is not very likely since the original PRR mainline was double-track and, of course, was widened to four tracks. This is probably another "Brown" stone arch built in the late 1890s. There is a remote chance that one side or the other is original since we do not know exactly where PRR added the two new tracks but after reviewing the terrain we will bet they added one on each side. To avoid future confusion, Trout Run was and is known as Trout Run. It is not "formerly known as Spring Run." Spring Run drains the Sonman area and passes beneath the new mainline just east of Route 164.

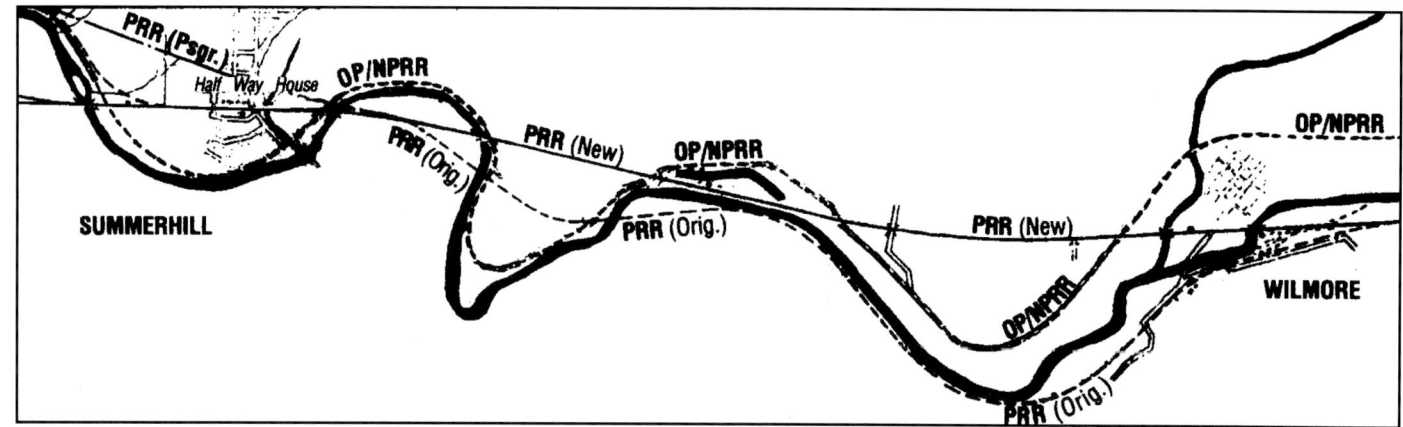

BETWEEN THE TOWNS of Wilmore (at right) and Summerhill (at left), the Conemaugh River wiggles all over the lot with a mind of its own. While this may have been "long level" territory for OPRR and NPRR, this did not mean that the railroad was straight since the river line was followed almost all the way between these two towns. At extreme upper left one may find the thick dashed line that traces OPRR/NPRR (the latter used the rails of the former). The thinner dashed line generally on the south side was the original PRR mainline. Notice that PRR crossed OPRR/NPRR at least three times. The straight line slashing through the center of this map is PRR's "new line." Oddly, there are no existing records that precisely date completion of the new line, but the time frame is 1902-1903. The third track was completed before the fourth, offering some temporary relief. By the way, this map was prepared to support the "new passenger line" to which we have referred. Note the dash-dot line at upper left by Half Way House…this is that line which, of course, was never built. While in that corner, note that the original PRR line was laid alongside OPRR/NPRR on the north side. Also notice that both the original and new PRR lines crossed the Conemaugh River seven times, a development that resulted in a lot of bridges with puzzling paternity.

So with the roads. As the rail lines were abandoned, the roadbeds were converted to highways. *Very* broadly speaking, Route 53 rests upon one or another of these lines. So do a lot of side roads. In all candor, we tried to piece together modern geodetic and old maps to produce a comprehensive master map and concluded we were wandering down the path to madness. As to the bridges, we will present images in the color chapter later in this book with as much detail as possible. Now to the towns. In 1855 Wilmore adjoined Jefferson, a hamlet of a thousand souls which apparently was swallowed by Wilmore because twenty years later there was no more Jefferson. There was a plank road from Jefferson/Wilmore to Ebensburg, Loretto and Clearfield. By 1875 Wilmore boasted a grist mill, several sawmills, several hotels and four churches with a population of 393. Summerhill in 1855 was merely a "wood and water" station with a Half Way House. (Every town from the summit to Summerhill had a "half way" sign out.) In 1875 Summerhill's population was only about 200 with a grist mill, lumbering facilities and a hopeful note that "coal of good quality exists here." Today they are pleasant little towns with friendly and polite inhabitants who are oblivious to their place in transportation history.

Before we leave this map, we want to draw your attention to the river crossing under "House" at upper left and the "double river" in the middle. When the new PRR line was under construction in 1901 Bridge No. 3 at this location was widened and a new bridge constructed just east of that point. Also, a change was made in the channel of the Conemaugh River (hence the double river.) These alterations encroached upon the pool of a dam furnishing power to the grist mill of David A. Sipe in Summerhill. Instead of just simply paying damages to Mr. Sipe, PRR forced him to sue and fought him all the way to the Pennsylvania Supreme Court *two times*, losing each step of the way. Finally, in 1909, PRR was forced to pay Mr. Sipe $14,927.28. This is merely one tiny example of the inherent arrogance which has characterized so much of the history of PRR and stains the railroad's legacy. Little incidents like this repeated time after time up to and including today make a splendid and admirable institution appear as a brutal and heartless monolith eager to step on little guys. PRR *et al* has never grasped the principle that the World is *round*. What goes around comes around.

A case can be made that buying legislators is necessary for corporate survival. Judges, however, are almost impossible to buy. Once on the bench with a lifetime appointment and no need to run for re-election, most judges become their own men and call the shots as they see them. In Pennsylvania the courts became sick and tired of PRR antics and knocked down the railroad on a host of occasions. Imagine yourself as a judge on the Supreme Court having to rule *twice* on this minor case and forced to listen to a gaggle of fat "Philadelphia lawyers" defending the indefensible. Again. We will take this opportunity to remind management that consideration for others is the keystone of gentle conduct and is a sign of great strength, not weakness.

THE WEST SLOPE

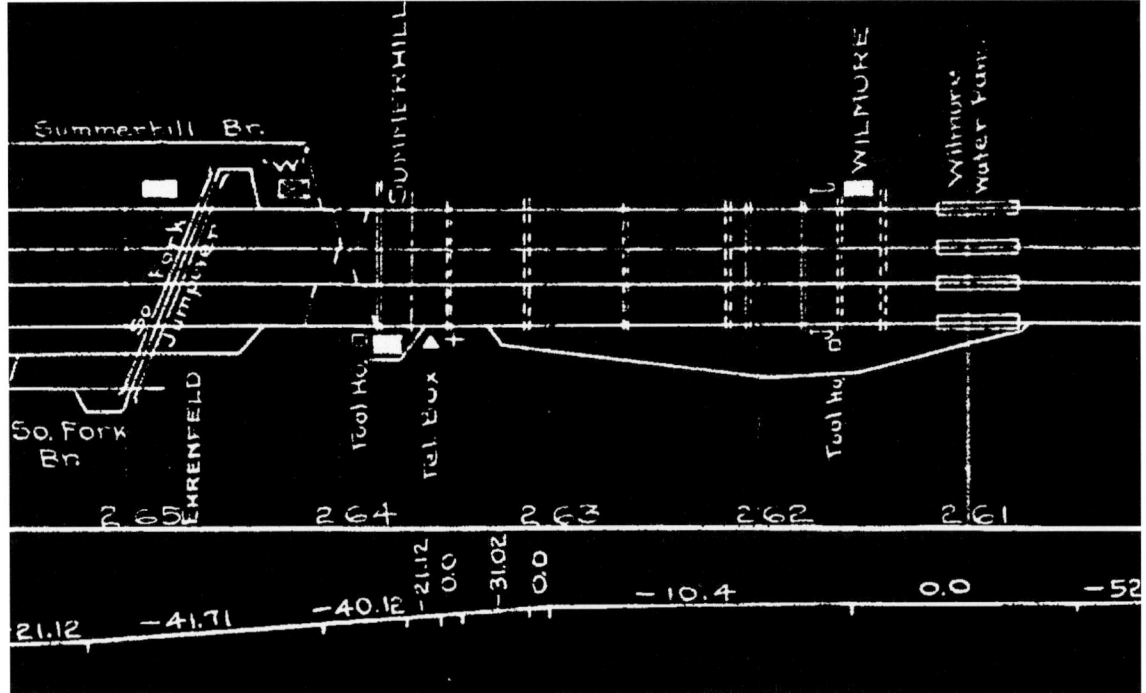

Frank Wrabel Collection

OUR TRUSTY 1910 TRACK CHART provides us with only a few historical tidbits, not surprising for a piece of railroad that was arrow-straight. There were water pans at Wilmore and we are about to explore them in detail. There was a station at Wilmore, which we shall see. There were also two standpipes by the station, serving Track Nos. 1 and 4. There was a station and siding at Summerhill on Track No. 1. Just west of Summerhill was an interlocker and W Tower, much to our surprise. We know that it was frame and built in 1905. Apparently it did not last until 1918 because we could not find a valuation photograph and this makes sense. An interlocker at this location was redundant with South Fork just down the railroad and we suspect it was an early casualty. The only three turnouts needed (from Summerhill Branch, South Fork Branch and jumpover) could be operated remotely from South Fork. W, however, is still a "live" point on Conrail. The only mild interlocker puzzle is at Wilmore. The record is clear that a new 16-working lever plant was opened there in 1897, but we suspect that it was installed to give operating flexibility during third and fourth track construction. And why was W, which after all is the first letter in Wilmore, employed west of Summerhill? This was DED territory, with one serving Track No. 3 at Milepost 262.3 in 1942 and additional ones serving Track Nos. 1, 2 and 3 at Milepost 262.9 in 1950. Another piece of trivia. PRR kept one track of the original line open from Wilmore to Summerhill as late as 1910, probably as Zero Track.

WHATEVER CHARMS the town of Wilmore may have for its residents, as far as PRR history is concerned the hamlet was known for water and water alone. Track pans on a mountain grade are a contradiction in terms. Track pans are associated with fast, level mainlines and passenger engines scooping it up on the fly. It was a measure of PRR desperation and thirst that they installed pans at Wilmore primarily for the use of freight engines. The traffic was so dense on the West Slope that, even with four tracks, PRR operating people would kill to avoid a water stop and thus keep trains moving rather than sitting even if for only a few minutes. This illustration is titled "Track Tanks near Johnstown" and was featured in PRR promotional literature to dramatize the railroad's devotion to the state of the art. Good public relations but poor history. The artist never set foot in Wilmore and got everything wrong. The terrain is impossible, the pans are on a curve and the Wilmore pans served four tracks, not two. It was, however, a nice piece of art.

199

Hagley Museum and Library

IT WOULD BE IMPOSSIBLE to overstate PRR's urgent need for clean, soft water in vast quantity as the twentieth century began, particularly between Pittsburgh and New York. Not only did the railroad need water, but so did burgeoning industry. Particularly the steel industry in Johnstown and Pittsburgh. Worse, intensive coal mining throughout the region was polluting all watersheds and this was a situation that was beyond solution at the source. (The reader should read our book *Sand Patch/Clash of Titans* with particular reference to the scheme of some energetic plotters in the Indian Creek valley above Connellsville to deliberately open some coal mines with the sole purpose of fouling a PRR reservoir with mine waste.) In 1905 PRR embarked upon a massive program to solve this problem once and for all. PRR reached into the mountains and acquired 27,300 acres of virgin watershed. In the end they created 36 reservoirs and intakes, 441 miles of pipelines and 11 pumping and booster stations which produced, by 1926, 14 billion gallons of water. Total investment was on the order of 30 million dollars. The Wilmore water pans were opened in 1902 and seen here in October of 1906 with extensive improvements in progress. The brick powerhouse on the right was new in that year and was built to provide steam for thawing systems as well as pumping power. The pans were 1,800 feet long and 800 feet were about to be paved with brick. Even this did not prove to be enough...in 1912 the pans on Track Nos. 1 and 2 were extended another 600 feet. All of these pans, of course, had to be level. One wonders if Thomson, in his wildest imagination, envisioned such incredible growth and success just thirty years after his death.

Hagley Museum and Library

AS ONE WOULD EXPECT, it was very cold at the pans on 6 February 1908. That water freezes is a reality that has closed canals, rivers and ports since time began. For a railroad that purported to be all-weather, this option was unacceptable. A gentleman named Giulio Brandimarte, a PRR track foreman and minor hero of both the East and West Slopes, first became a section foreman at the Wilmore pans in 1911. In an interview in the middle of this century, Mr. Brandimarte recalled that it was 32 below zero at the pans on a day in 1936 and it was so cold that eyelids would freeze shut if crews stayed outside too long. We have been in temperatures this low and believe every word of it. Imagine the amount of steam needed to keep the water in the pans from freezing. Mr. Brandimarte also noted that cinders from steam locomotives would bury the rails in a year if they were not constantly removed, another penalty that was eliminated with dieselization.

THE WEST SLOPE

IT WAS A LITTLE WARMER at the pans on an August day in 1940 as a freight took a drink on the fly as it drifted downhill on Track No. 4. We will see the rest of the work train on the right in the next photograph.

*Rail Photo Service
Bob Lorenz Collection*

HERE IS THE rest of that work train, engaged in ballast cleaning. Of course, the Consolidation is putting down more cinders as it goes along. The pans themselves were not immune to the black shower and had to be cleaned periodically. They were gone by 1958, much to the relief of all except the workmen directly involved.

Rail Photo Service/Bob Lorenz Collection

UPSTREAM FROM WILMORE one finds Lake Wilmore, apparent on maps previously shown and held back by this PRR dam seen on 25 March 1913. Once external combustion was gone, PRR sold this water to a steel mill in Johnstown. Since this mill has been closed for several years, we assume these waters just flow away. Curiosity question. Who maintains this dam? Is there a potential "Wilmore Flood" in the making?

Hagley Museum and Library

THE NEW LINE required a new station at Wilmore and here it is, next to Track No. 4 circa 1918. It was completed in 1904 and was extant at least as late as 1950. The "old line" 1875 freight station was reportedly still open as late as 1920. This does not necessarily mean that the "old line" was still "through" at that time. A spur could have been retained to serve the station.

National Archives

THE FIRST CURVE west of Wilmore saw this westbounder roll under a farm access bridge in 1976 led by an ex-Erie Lackawanna unit in early CR livery. New ballast has just been spread on Track No. 1.

Thomas A. Biery

WILMORE'S MAIN STREET passes under this 40 foot 1902 PRR bridge, seen 13 May 1995. The mainline runs at an angle across this structure, roughly parallel with the fence.

THE WEST SLOPE

THIS SIGNAL BRIDGE is slightly east of the Main Street Bridge just seen. Just a few hundred feet farther east of this signal is a two-span stone bridge crossing the Conemaugh River and just beyond that the water pans began. This photograph, taken 13 May 1995, hints at how much fill PRR used to raise the railroad to the required height.

THE PROVENANCE of the Summerhill station here c. 1918 is somewhat clouded. In 1862 a 12 by 15 foot passenger "room" was opened along with a 15 by 25 foot freight house. Was the "room" part of a residence? If so, this is probably that structure with the freight facility on the left. A 1920 ICC inventory, however, states that the Summerhill station, dwelling and freight station were built in 1880. We are inclined to go with 1862 since ICC/valuation dates are often merely guesses. Whatever the date, multiple tracking had brought PRR literally to the front door.

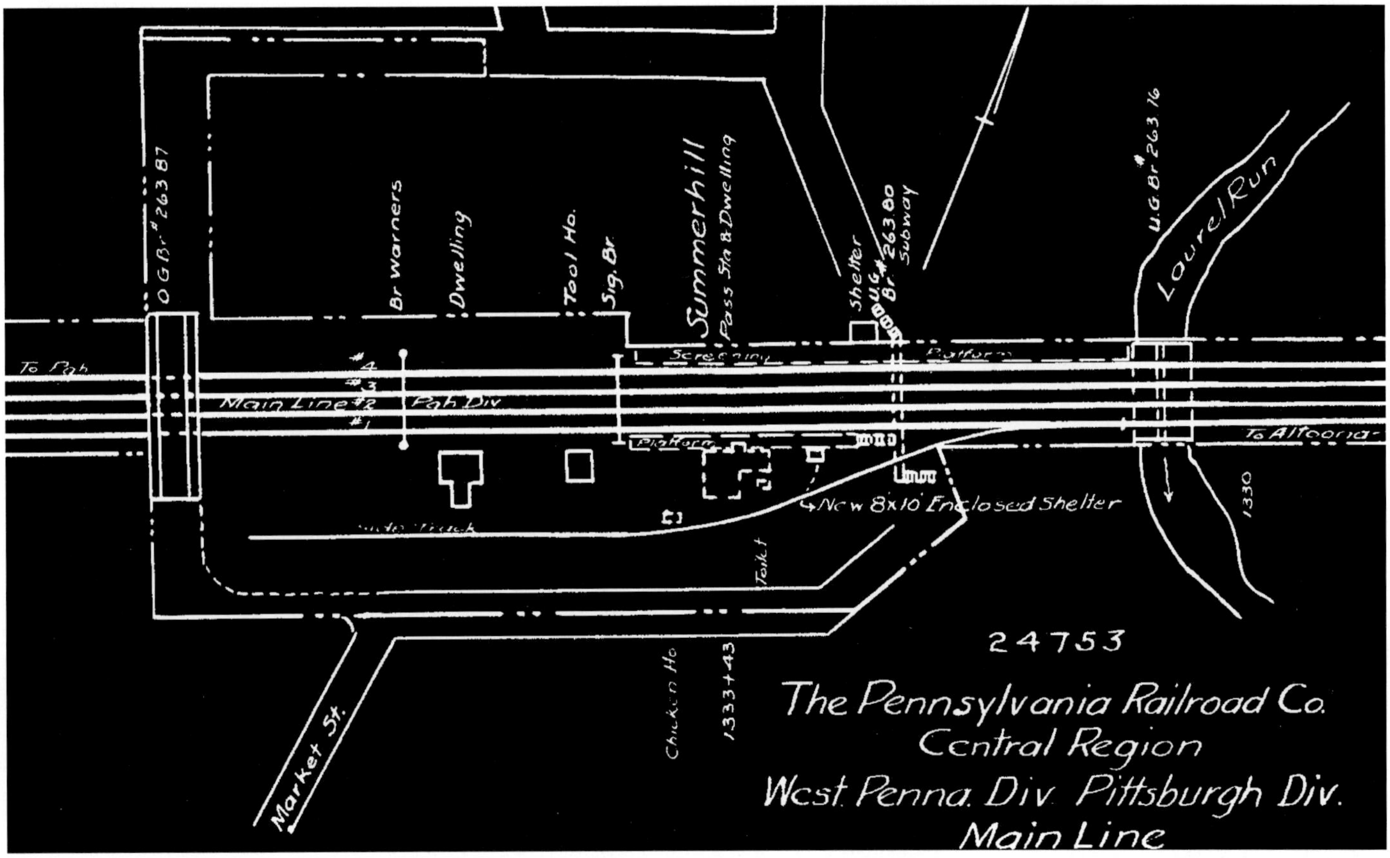

BY 1942 the Summerhill station/dwelling was so dilapidated that the Division Superintendent felt it did "not present a neat appearance along our mainline." The living quarters had long since been rented to an outside party but the income was insufficient to warrant repairs. This plan shows a proposed new eastward waiting shelter and, with dotted lines, the structures to be removed. Notice that they wanted to get rid of that little chicken house at the same time. Also note the subway east of the station. It was completed in late 1902. The paperwork in 1942 indicated that the station/dwelling was built in 1884, so there is a third possible birthdate.

Michael Smith/Aerial Views

SOUTH FORK was not even mentioned as a station on PRR in an 1855 Guidebook and by 1875, in a similar publication, the population was noted as a mere 200 accompanied by the comment that 50,000 tons of coal were mined annually. In 1889 one of history's worse tragedies would forever change the obscurity and, ironically, create one of the most lush traffic junctions on PRR's mainline. This photograph, commissioned specifically for this book and taken in the Spring of 1995, shows a gentle town of South Fork nestled in the center with only a rather wide floodplain hinting at the catastrophic wall of water that hurtled down the now-placid stream at upper right. More of that later. This view, which is easterly, shows the terrain of the West Slope all the way to the summit on the horizon. Moving up the left side, we first see a clutch of houses considered part of South Fork, then Ehrenfeld and, just the other side of a modern highway (Route 219), Summerhill. At the bottom, the PRR mainline curves toward SO Tower which is just out of sight...the four-track bridge carries SO's home signals. The single track curving off the mainline toward Ehrenfeld is notable as we shall see. The wye leading to the South Fork Branch is apparent as are the yard tracks. Here is South Fork, a cloud that turned out to have a silver lining.

THE WEST SLOPE

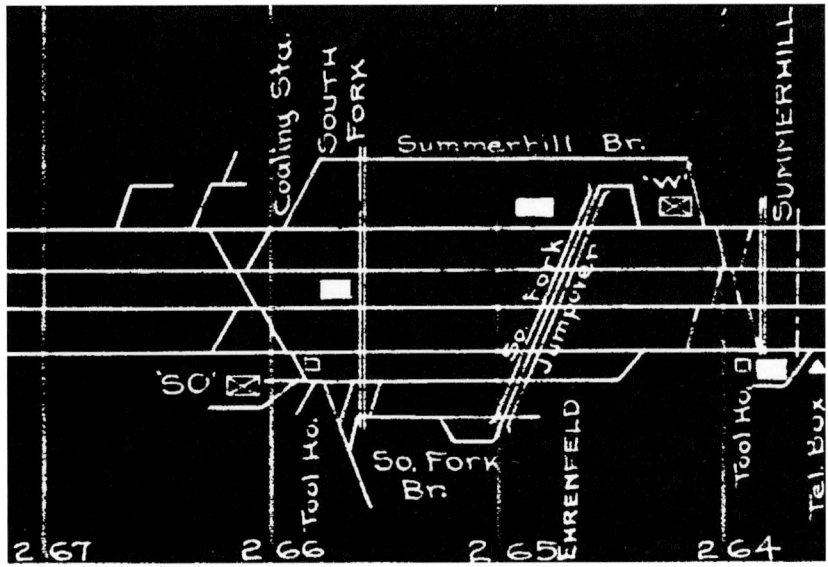

Frank Wrabel Collection

IT IS NOW 1910 and we see a track chart that reflects the numerous changes that occurred at South Fork after the flood of 1889. Moving west from Summerhill, W interlocker provides access to the mainline from the Summerhill Branch which is actually trackage built on the roadbed of the OPRR/NPRR. We are not quite sure when the rails were relaid on this roadbed, but believe it was circa 1883. We do know that the jumpover track and bridge at Ehrenfeld was completed in 1905. Ehrenfeld, by the way, was probably named for George W. Ehrenfeld. This gentleman was a well-known MOW engineer who started with PRR in 1867 as a track laborer only 15 years after his birth at Lilly. His name has been mentioned earlier in this book and the reader should know that his contributions to PRR were many and varied until his retirement in 1922. For example, it was he who designed the ballast spreader and track sweeping devices that revolutionized roadbed maintenance as seen at the Wilmore track pans. While not shown here, the rails between the jumpover line and Track No. 1 was another Zero Track, also added in 1905. Some records suggest that an interlocker was installed at Ehrenfeld in 1897 and, if true, was replaced by W. This was also the year that a third mainline track was opened between Ehrenfeld and South Fork.

The reader should note the location of SO Tower at the west end of Zero Track and the nearby coaling station. The latter served South Fork Branch motive power. The reason for what appears to be excessive trackage in the wye area had to do with turning branch passenger trains and power while avoiding interference with tonnage trains exiting the branch. The SO interlocking plant seen here was new in 1905 and was west of the original plant as we shall see.

Railroad Museum of Pennsylvania

THIS IS NOT the original SO Tower because we know it burned down and was replaced in 1877. The cross-track coaling station seen at right was built in 1881, so the date of this photograph is probably in the mid-1880s. The location, however, is east of both the present-day SO and the bridge over the Conemaugh River. Also note this tower is on the north side of the mainline very close to the Conemaugh on the left.

205

TRIUMPH I

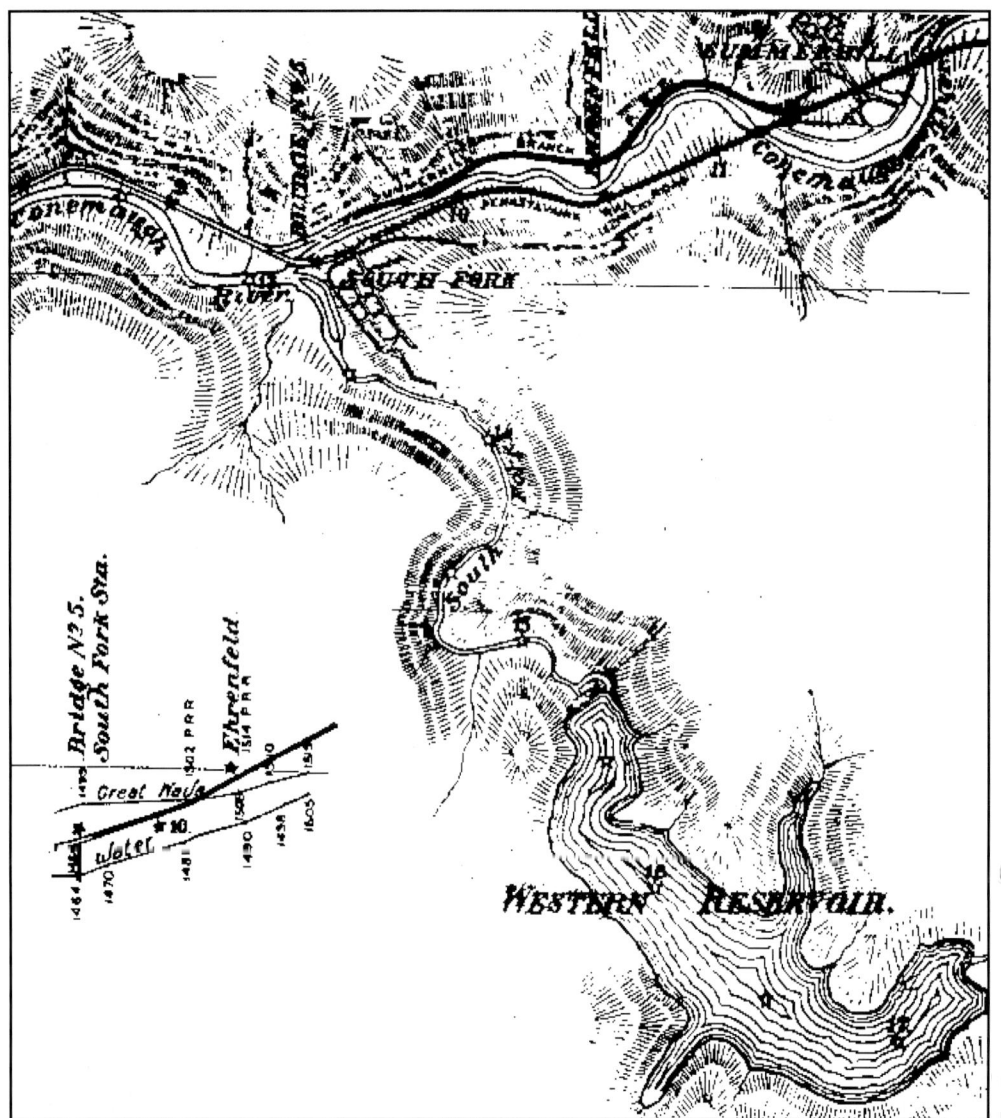

WE HAVE USED the adjective "Great" to describe much in this book and now, sadly, we must use it to record one of the most awful human tragedies in history. It is called the Johnstown Flood, but that is a misnomer. Most of the horrific damage was done by the Great Wave, a wall of unleashed water that roared down the South Fork and the Conemaugh River canyons with an awesome force that still makes one shudder. No debate here as to whether Mother is a noun or adjective…this disaster was purely manmade. This map was prepared by PRR engineers after the event to detail the Great Wave's horrendous impact on the railroad. Amazingly, a few parts of the mainline actually survived the onslaught as we shall see. Very few people did. The story began at the Western Reservoir seen here, completed in 1845 under the direction of Milnor Roberts for the State Works to store water for release in the dry season to the canal west of Johnstown, hence its name. The original dam held back 480 million cubic feet of water weighing 15 *million* tons. All evidence shows that this dam was properly and safely constructed although a small break in 1847 caused some damage. PRR acquired the reservoir with its purchase of the State Works and then sold it, title ultimately being acquired by a hunting and fishing club for the Pittsburgh elite. This club added to the top of the dam to broaden the lake and, in the process, blithely eliminated all the safety features designed by Mr. Roberts. Reservoir capacity was increased to 619 million cubic feet and 19 *million* tons. Of the latter, about 18 *million* tons would become the Great Wave. By the way, the location of the dam was at what is now known as Fishertown just southeast of Route 219. The museum at this site is well worth visiting. The dam broke at 2:45 pm 31 May 1889. Slowed by obstructions, 85 minutes later the wave arrived at the Stone Bridge in Johnstown, 13.3 miles away. The height and velocity of the Great Wave varied, of course, with the width of the canyon. Its first victim was South Fork where it was 35 feet high, lowered somewhat by the width of the flood plain seen earlier. It slammed into PRR Bridge No. 5, a double-track three-span iron structure 166 feet in length. Not surprisingly, Bridge No. 5 did not survive the impact. As shown at lower left, a huge backwave roared *up* the Conemaugh River well past Ehrenfeld taking the wreckage of Bridge No. 5 with it. Extra East 1165 had arrived at South Fork about 8:00 a.m. that morning and was held on a siding because of washouts at Lilly. Miss Emma Ehrenfeld was the operator on duty at SO which, the reader will recall, was east of Bridge No. 5. Train No. 2, the *New York and Chicago Limited*, was stopped on the mainline west of the bridge. The engineer of this train, staring up the South Fork Canyon, became nervous and moved his train, in defiance of orders to the contrary, a half-mile to the east shortly before 3:00 pm. Many passengers owed their lives to this engineer's prescience. Minutes later the Great Wave thundered into view. Engineer H.M. Bennett of the 1165 was in SO with Miss Ehrenfeld and his conductor. Mr. Bennett, the first of many heroes who would emerge that day, remembered two crewman asleep in his caboose and attempted to back his engine into the path of the Great Wave to save his comrades. The wave and debris struck first and the crewmen were lost, leaving only Bennett's nobility to history. Miss Ehrenfeld, Mr. Bennett and others made it to safety in the area of the coal tipple just shown. We assume the lady was a member of the PRR Ehrenfeld family and owed her job to this connection. It almost proved to be fatal. As to this map, the reader should note that the title "water" at lower left refers to the normal bed of the river and that the hollowed lines at upper left allude to the parts of the mainline that were totally destroyed. Stars and numbers are cross-location references.

THE WEST SLOPE

Johnstown Area Heritage Association

THE BACKWASH from the Great Wave rearranged a lot of real estate, relieved only by the fact that wood floats and upstream velocity was muted. In this photograph, we see the 1883 South Fork station where it finally went ashore. It was salvageable and, once relocated, served PRR for many years. The fate of the house at left is unknown. Actually, the backwash caused two floods east of South Fork…the uphill leg and then the downhill.

BRIDGE NO. 5 was replaced by a temporary wooden trestle until this four-span stone arch could be completed in 1890. This postcard was dated 5 December 1910. The bridge had to be widened at least once to accommodate additional tracks. This view is from the southeast, or South Fork, side. In more modern times the structure has been reinforced by poured concrete.

Frank Wrabel Collection

TRIUMPH I

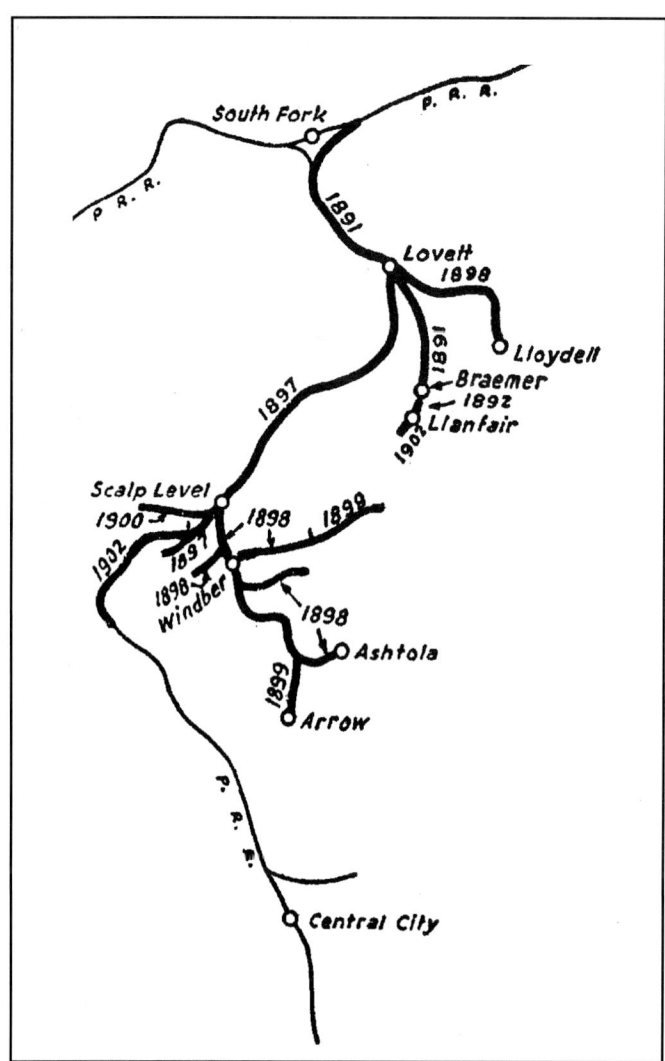

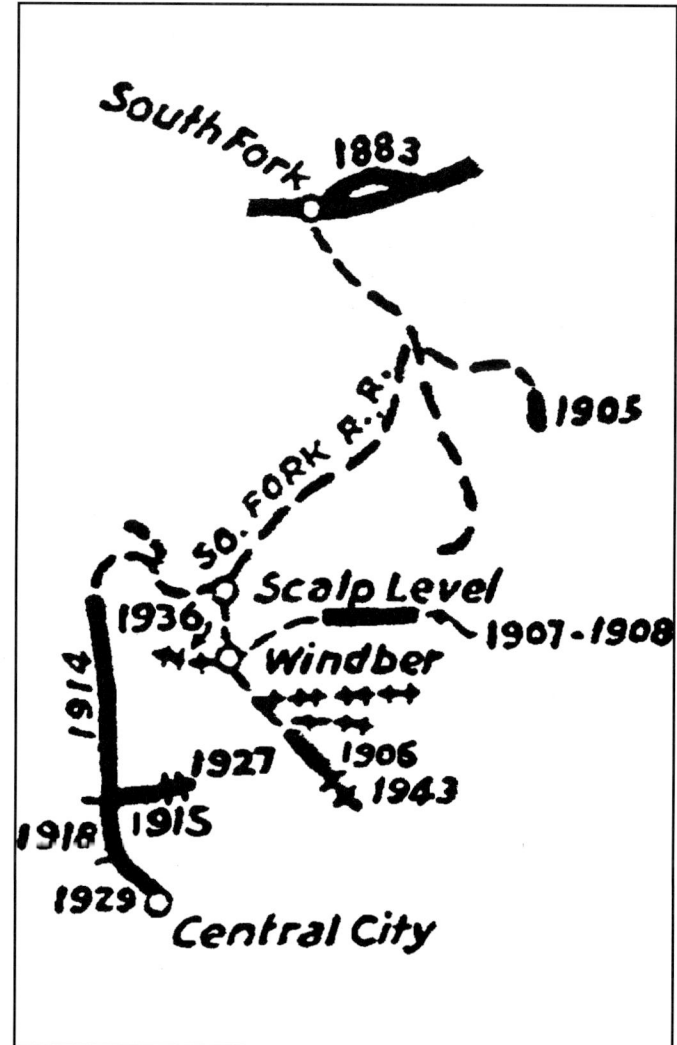

ONCE THE WESTERN RESERVOIR was emptied and all the bodies buried, PRR looked up the South Fork canyon and saw black gold. The region south of Johnstown and South Fork was home to the Somerset seam, a large bed of high quality soft coal low in ash, volatiles and sulphur. Since coal was the primary space-heating fuel in that era, this comparatively clean coal would prove to be in high demand. B&O had reached into most of this region from Rockwood in the south with their Somerset and Cambria Rail Road by 1871. B&O had a lock on most of this coal, but the South Fork area was suddenly open to exploitation and PRR lost no time in responding. The line to Lovett was opened in August of 1891 and expansion from then on was rapid. This map shows part of that history...the next will show more.

THE SPIDERWEB of rail lines continued outward as late as 1943, as shown on this 1945 map. Of course, old seams were worked-out and new ones opened as time went on, but even today very large quantities of fine steam coal meet the PRR mainline at South Fork. In 1973 there were still nineteen mines on this branch and by 1977 nine still producing. As always, PRR's gentle West Slope worked in its favor and against B&O. Ironically, much of this South Fork coal is carried to Baltimore for export.

THE WEST SLOPE

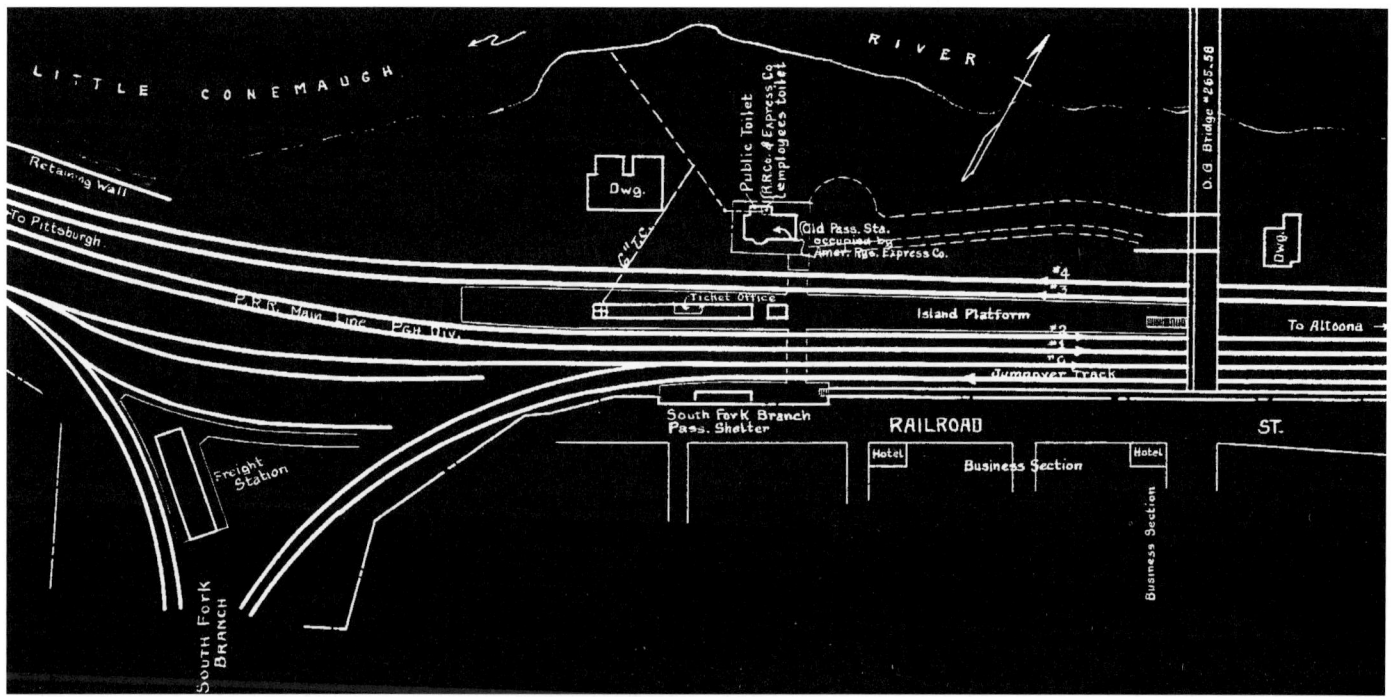

BY 1902, the South Fork branch poured 126,664 cars onto the mainline to say nothing of empty returns and 8,543 loaded cars inbound. This 1921 map details the facilities in existence at that time organized to handle this vast traffic. The steel open shelter and frame closed shelter between Track Nos. 2 and 3 totalled 293 feet in length, which gives an insight into the passenger traffic in and out of town. Both these shelters and the frame shelter on the south side for branch passengers were built in 1910. Zero track is clearly identified. The overhead bridge at upper right carried the rails of a fascinating interurban beginning in 1913. The line was chartered to run from South Fork to Portage, but funds ran out at Summerhill. A single car ran back and forth no doubt awash in passengers. In 1918 a receivership was initiated and the line emerged as, of all things, the Penn Central Railway. Harbinger of things past and to come. The lone car developed an annoying tendency to run away down the steep hill into South Fork and then slam into power poles, putting the entire town literally in the dark. In 1928 the town council had enough and placed a large bumping block across the track at town line, ending both the trolley service and the power outages. One wonders what took them so long.

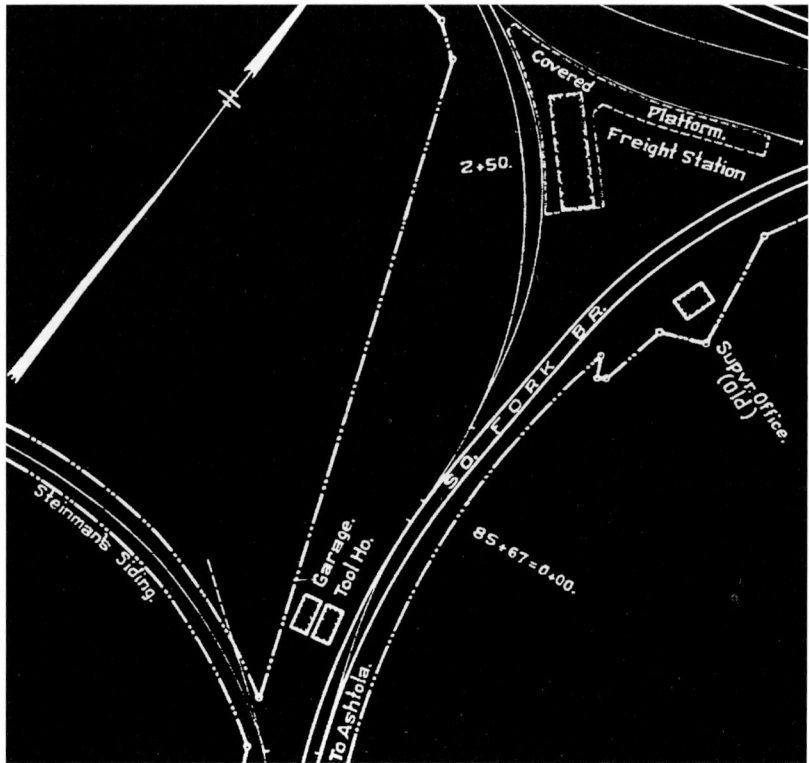

WE PROVIDE this 1935 map to show the location of the South Fork freight house and the siding reaching to "Steinman's." More on both shortly. Just off the map at bottom was a nine-track yard with a three-track 67 by 147 foot engine house erected in 1900. Traffic was so heavy that, as late as 1921, PRR had to add another runaround track to ease congestion. At that time at least 24 locomotives a day were serviced here for South Fork-Altoona turnarounds plus, of course, branch power. A number of these tracks are still in place, but not the engine house.

TRIUMPH I

THIS FREIGHT HOUSE, which we located on the preceding map, was built in 1896 to handle heavy local and transfer freight for the branch. By 1935, reduction in traffic and lack of maintenance resulted in razing. At far left, one can see miners' tenements stacked up the hillside. As we are about to see, a lot of coal was mined right at South Fork and Ehrenfeld.

THIS IS STINEMAN NO. 4 MINE (not "Steinmans') at South Fork early in this century. Located just across from the town, the company created to mine this deposit was formed c. 1867 and by the early 1900s was the tenth largest coal and coke operation in Pennsylvania. The message on this postcard, dated 31 July 1908, was from a lady visitor to South Fork who noted that two of her relatives worked "two miles underground" in a Stineman mine. While we doubt that the coal face was that far beneath the surface, the reference still shows just how extensive were the coal deposits in the immediate vicinity of the town. There was another very large mine at Ehrenfeld on the Summerhill Branch which was loading over sixty cars a day even in the 1970s. By the way, the Ehrenfeld jumpover was removed between 1958 and 1973.

THE WEST SLOPE

THE VALUATION photographer who took this shot managed to make it impossible for us to straighten. Shown here c. 1920 looking westward, SO tower's size belies the traffic that it has always handled. By 1973 all of its sixteen electro-mechanical levers were still in service plus a single two-lever table machine for W. By this time the Summerhill Branch was stub-ended out of SO. The reader will note that we usually refer to branches as such. PRR began referring to such lines as "secondaries" at least by the early 1960s, but probably no earlier than 1958.

National Archives

Edward H. Weber

SO's ALUMINUM SIDING was very new when "worm" 2314 rolled by with an eastbound mixed consist on 29 May 1970. By early 1996 we received information indicating that SO was "due to close," not surprising in view of the trend of events. The mound of mine tailings on the hilltop at upper right, one of countless ones in Pennsylvania, remind us of the importance of coal to PRR and the nation.

TRIUMPH I

ONE OF THE FASCINATIONS of researching and writing history is the discovery of some previously unknown grand plan that did not reach fruition and one of the joys is telling the story in print. Following is the tale of the *Salix Summit Zero Track Line*. Please look at this relief map and go to exact center. Slightly to the right of this spot is Salix, or Salix Summit. It is at an elevation of 2,138 feet. The New Portage Tunnel is at 2,190 feet, a difference of only *52 feet*. Now let us turn the clock back to the Spring of 1905 and recall our friend C.S. d'Invilliers, or CSD. Also recall that PRR was the cock of the walk in that year and was inundated with traffic that seemingly could only go up in the future. Four-tracking of both slopes had been completed yet the volume was still growing. On the West Slope a fifth mainline track appeared to be needed. On 24 May 1905, CSD submitted a $682,300 estimate for laying Zero Track next to Track No. 1 from Summerhill to AR. Then Mr. Cassatt intervened and requested a plan to build a level line from Salix to the summit. CSD received word of this request on 4 June and responded instantly. When Cassatt spoke, you jumped. CSD pointed out that no surveys had ever been done on this route and flatly stated in his letter that "I have the original surveys of PRR made in 1852." (Charles L. Schlatter had moaned that he did not have time to survey a number of potential routes and one wonders if this route was one he had in mind.) CSD took to his horse with a barometer and reported on 8 June that the terrain was flat at an elevation of approximately 2,200 feet. He stated that "such a line is practicable and would not be unusually expensive except in crossing the valleys which would have to be done on high bridges. The worst crossing would be Trout Run." Chief Engineer William H. Brown was now in the loop and on 12-13 September it was left to CSD to precisely lay the line at an elevation that would produce a continuous grade with no descents going east. The file then ends abruptly, leaving your author to produce an explanatory scenario. To this point we are dealing with facts; the following is supposition. We have examined the contour maps in the Salix area and concluded that the Zero line was probably *not* meant to carry South Fork Branch tonnage. The climb from branch rails to the new line would have been quite severe. Accordingly, the Zero line was meant for through eastward traffic. Yet PRR rails did not reach to Stony Creek in this area; B&O's S&C occupied the only available path to Johnstown. Now glance at lower left of this map. The two railroads were next to one another in this area and at similar elevation. Since PRR controlled B&O in this time frame, there would be no question that any PRR request would be honored. Why, then, wasn't the Zero line built? Because PRR, under heavy anti-trust pressure from Washington, had decided to give up control of B&O and leave well enough alone. Besides, Cassatt's lunge under the Hudson River to reach downtown Manhattan was consuming enormous amounts of money and even PRR was feeling the pinch. Two other points should be made. From 1905 on, four tracks were capable of handling the offered tonnage so the Zero line would have been redundant. And the new passenger line that was never built, and to which we have referred in this chapter, was not a factor because Zero was to be devoted to freight only. Some interesting little tidbits came out of this correspondence. A line had been surveyed from the South Fork Branch near Lovett across the mountains to the Bedford Division, which runs south from Altoona. And another survey had been done from Salix Summit to Mule Shoe Curve. Both had been completed some years prior to 1905. Lastly, in a prior chapter we had a little fun with CSD. For all that, he was obviously a vigorous and highly competent engineer.

THE WEST SLOPE

Johnstown Area Heritage Association

BETWEEN SOUTH FORK AND JOHNSTOWN, the Conemaugh River formed two loops. The neck of the first one seen here was almost exactly one mile west of SO Tower. All three railroads (OPRR, NPRR and PRR) crossed to the north bank of the river at South Fork and returned to the south bank at a remote but legendary location that became known as Big Viaduct. Big Loop, Big Viaduct. Everyone knows that there were two Big Viaducts. The one at upper right is of course, the second one. The first viaduct fell victim to the Great Wave. As to the history of that one mile between South Fork and Big Viaduct, it can best be described as confused. OPRR and PRR were both built on the same bank and some evidence indicates that they crossed each other at grade at least four times because the OPRR right-of-way wiggled. NPRR used OPRR rails in this stretch. For those interested in digging, there might be some OPRR/NPRR relics under the surface of those wiggles which were not washed away by the Great Wave. A little curious note is evidence that the "new passenger line" that was never built was planned to cross to the south bank of the river at South Fork. Now glance at upper left. The hamlet huddled under that giant dam is Mineral Point. Considering the history of this area, they are very brave people indeed.

BIG VIADUCT was built to be eternal and this mid-1870s rendition gives the impression that, indeed, it just might be. As it turned out, human stupidity reigned supreme. Big Viaduct was designed and its erection supervised by Solomon W. Roberts of OPRR. He described it thus in his own words: "The arch is 3½ feet thick at the springing line and 3 feet at the crown; the arch-stones are of light-colored sandstone, and the backing of silicious limestone, found near the spot. The sandstone was split from the erratic rocks of giant size, which were found lying in the woods on the surface of the ground. The contract price of the masonry was $4.20 per perch of 25 cubic feet, and the work was remarkably well done. The face stones were laid in mortar made from the silicious limestone without the addition of any sand. The work was done by an honest stonemason named John Durno, who was afterward killed by falling from another high bridge." The top of the arch was about 70 feet above the normal low level of the river. The total cost was $55,000. Big Viaduct was proclaimed as being the first railroad viaduct built in the United States. Nonsense. B&O's Carrollton Viaduct was carrying trains in 1830 and Big Viaduct was probably ready for service in 1833. As to those "rocks of giant size" lying in the woods, surely the question as to how they got there crossed the mind of Mr. Roberts. Many of them measured from 12 to 25 cubic feet each. But the top of the arch was well above the surface of the river and there seemed to be nothing to fear from Mother Nature. There is every reason to believe that Big Viaduct would still be standing if it were not for the Great Wave. The viaduct's foundation rested on solid rock on one side and timber on the other. The 1847 dam break exposed these foundations and a cofferdam was built downstream, filled with brush and stone, to break the force of future deluges. This dam probably sealed the viaduct's doom because it caused debris to be lodged against the structure to a depth of about 90 feet and the weight of this water collapsed the span.

NOT SURPRISINGLY, Big Viaduct captured the imagination of early travellers. This crude, inaccurate 1852 sketch did not add to the reputation of the artist, but did serve to acknowledge that the viaduct was quite an achievement considering that it was built in the middle of a wilderness.

THE WEST SLOPE

ANOTHER 1852 ARTIST, with a similar lack of skill, rendered Big Viaduct thus. In fact, this so-called artist was more fascinated by the cut through the "western ridge" than with the viaduct itself. It is known that the Great Wave, compressed by the banks of the river, was 56 feet high when it arrived at Big Viaduct and was 90 feet high at the span. The floating detritus, backed by millions of tons of water-weight, struck the upper arch at a velocity of about 15 mph. No structure could survive such a blow. The only surprising thing to this author was that the Great Wave did not open the neck of the loop. The entire railroad from South Fork to the east end of the viaduct was swept away which proves that a lot of water plunged through the eastern cut, yet the main force of the wave went around the loop. At least at this point, Mother Nature decided that she would not allow these incompetent human beings to rearrange the path of *her* river.

Dick Heiler Collection

BY 14 JUNE 1889, PRR announced that the mainline was open for traffic with two tracks except for gauntlets over trestles like this one at the gravesite of Big Viaduct. This view is from the upstream side and if one is interested in size references, just glance at the people at lower left and atop the trestle. The remnants of Big Viaduct's abutments are apparent in the foreground. If we may be forgiven a mixed metaphor, the Great Wave made a clean sweep. That this trestle, among others, was constructed in less than fourteen days may come as a surprise to the reader, but not to this author. In our book *East End*, we studied the impact of Civil War raids and destruction on B&O's lines from Harpers Ferry to Cumberland. A railroad is impossible to destroy. The Rebels finally gave up simply because B&O repair crews would re-open the line as soon as they left. In one case, a burned trestle was replaced in thirty minutes.

TRIUMPH I

THE REPLACEMENT for Big Viaduct is seen here. Obviously a two-span arch structure, each arch 60 feet in length, this new viaduct was built for three tracks and rose 100 feet above the riverbed. Both the new viaduct and three tracks from South Fork to Mineral Point were completed in 1891. It was not, however, until 1909 that a fourth track was completed from South Fork to Mineral Point. This date, of course, is at variance with other time frames to which we have referred and is illustrative of the inherent puzzlement when assigning completion dates in PRR history. The railroad and its records were so vast that no one really knows with certainty just what was done when. Many entries conflict with other entries. This new viaduct is an example. It was built for three tracks and yet it has carried four tracks with no evidence that it was ever widened. And we are not sure if the new viaduct was built on the exact location of the original. In the early

Railroad Museum of Pennsylvania

days PRR used the original in concert with OPRR, yet they purchased land to provide for their own bridge if that should prove necessary. For those who wish to explore the history of this viaduct at greater length, be advised that it was assigned the number 218 in 1891 and that the original was also known as Viaduct and Conemaugh Viaduct.

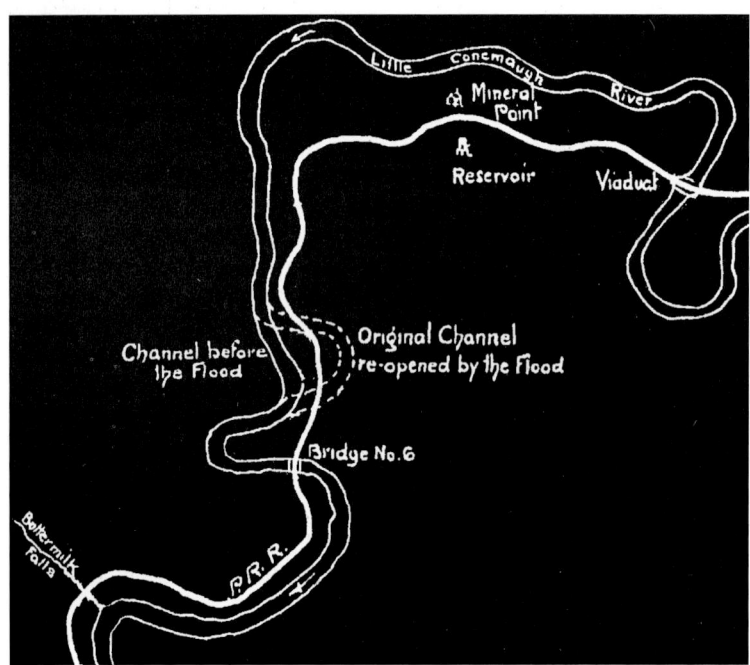

THIS THUMBNAIL sketch, crudely done years ago in conjunction with a book on the 1889 flood, shows a rough correlation between the Conemaugh River and PRR from Big Viaduct at upper right to Buttermilk Falls at lower left. OP/NPRR was always on the south side of PRR through this area. The second loop in the Conemaugh River is apparent at Bridge No. 6. OPRR's Level No. 1 and the Staple Bend Tunnel lay just to the right of this bridge, as we shall see. PRR, of course, also wanted to cut-off this river loop and did so with Deep Cut (as it became known) and a bridge. The Great Wave, after destroying Big Viaduct, roared down the river and, for a reason this writer finds puzzling, reopened the original channel which had been closed by PRR years before. PRR was unscathed from Big Viaduct to this point, but from here to the Stone Bridge at Johnstown destruction was almost total. Some of the Great Wave went through Deep Cut, but most swung around the loop and smashed into Bridge No. 6 forty-eight feet above the riverbed and level with the floor of the iron bridge. Having just taken out a stone viaduct, the Great Wave swallowed poor little No. 6 without the slightest hesitation. Actually, the water pouring through Deep Cut at a height of twenty feet above the roadbed probably crushed No. 6 before the Great Wave arrived. As one can imagine, the little town of Mineral Point did not survive the onslaught. An 1875 treatise had described the town as a source of about 3,000 tons of fireclay per year and home to 120 souls. The same publication stated that it was at Mineral Point that "the scenery of the western slope now begins to lose its tameness, and numerous beautiful vistas are opened on both sides of the road." The tameness certainly disappeared. For good measure, the Great Wave backed up Buttermilk Creek and took out the PRR bridge there with the back of its hand. The reopened original channel was again closed off by PRR, but a small pond remains on the south side of the railroad to remind us of that day in 1889.

THE WEST SLOPE

BRIDGE NO. 6 appeared thus in 1852, looking downstream with Deep Cut at right. While described at that time as a 142-foot iron bridge, its construction was probably wood with iron reinforcements. At the time of the Great Wave, it was a plate girder two-span structure with a central pier.

Railroad Museum of Pennsylvania

THE EAST END of Deep Cut, looking eastward shortly after the Great Wave had passed, displays both ravage and PRR's determination to rebuild the railroad. Looking at the base of the mountain in the background, one can see where the wave climbed up the hillside, stripping it bare. The Conemaugh River at left is now docile and the pond can be seen just ahead and to the right of the closest locomotive. The workmen are busy rebuilding the roadbed and lifting it to its former height.

TRIUMPH I

THE DEEP CUT was regarded as a significant engineering achievement when PRR originally punched through and this post-flood eastward view shows just how much rock had to be removed in order to bypass OPRR's Level No. 1 and the Staple Bend tunnel. The Great Wave scoured the walls of the cut and debris in the wave left slashes in the walls as seen about one-third the way up. Deep Cut is 110 feet from top to bottom, an impressive height that fully justified its name.

Blair County Historical Society

PRR DECIDED to replace Bridge No. 6 with a stone viaduct and, at the same time, renumber it to Bridge 219. We believe the abutments of the iron bridge were used in the new span and as evidence we offer the upper part of the far one. Note indications of scouring near the top and displaced stones, remembering that the top of the wave struck at deck-level. This photograph also corrects a common misconception about stone bridges. They are really stone veneer structures with the inside packed with fill, as shown at lower left. Also, they are *not* maintenance-free. Water gets into the mortar joints and freezes, the expansion and contraction spalling the cement. Also, the mortar and the stones themselves expand and contract at different rates, loosening the bind. Periodically these joints must be repointed. Even with that, however, maintenance costs are very low and Stone Brown's obsession with them has to be judged as wise in the long term.

Railroad Museum of Pennsylvania

THE WEST SLOPE

THE VIEW of the new "6" from the other side of the river, probably taken on the same day as the preceding photograph. To the best of our knowledge, the Conemaugh River behaved during reconstruction but one can be sure PRR was eager to get above the streambed. A total of 1,172 workmen were required to build this trestle and replace "6." One of the officers was Leonor F. Loree, who would later become president of B&O when it was under PRR control.

Railroad Museum of Pennsylvania

Blair County Historical Society

PRISTINE shortly after completion, Bridge (6) 219 with its graceful 60-foot arches is easy on the eyes of the beholder. The iron bridge was double-track and this one three-track. In 1909 the bridge was widened for four tracks, probably on the downstream (or opposite) side. Of course, there have been floods after 1889 and Bridge 219 has shrugged them off. Whether it could resist another Great Wave is a test we all hope never occurs.

Railroad Museum of Pennsylvania

IT IS POSSIBLE that this scene is west of Johnstown, but we suspect that it is east. Whatever the location, it is dramatic proof of the violence of the flood. The entire railroad simply disappeared.

THE STAPLE BEND tunnel, reputedly the first *railroad* bore in the United States, was OPRR's answer to the problem of the second loop in the Conemaugh River. This photograph of the eastern portal, of low quality even by 1920 valuation standards, is included here merely as a matter of record. The ICC worksheet with this photograph noted that a water pipeline from Wilmore for the benefit of Cambria Steel Company in Johnstown ran through the tunnel at that time, a logical proposition. Less logical is the absence of a tunnel facade which will be seen on the west portal.

National Archives

THE WEST SLOPE

WE HAVE COMPARED this late 1890s drawing of Staple Bend's western portal with a photograph taken at the same time and found this rendering to be remarkably realistic as well as artistic. It was buried in the unpublished Watkin's proof and is a tribute to the skill of an unknown artist. The tunnel was built by contractors J. & E. Appleton in 1831-32 for $37,498.84 1/4. We find that 1/4 amusing. The tunnel is 901 feet long and was bored from both ends, breakthrough occurring on 20 December 1832. It took two teams of fifty men to cut 18 inches of rock in 24 hours, which recalls again the absurdity of the four-mile summit tunnel proposal. Staple Bend was lined with cut stone for 150 feet from each end. The center 600 feet was through solid rock and did not require a lining. Plane No. 1 ended at this portal and OPRR may be pardoned for creating this Tuscan pilastered entrance to impress the eastward traveller. There is light at the other end of the tunnel, which unfortunately did not prove to be indicative of OP/NPRR's financial history. Abandoned by PRR, then acquired by Bethlehem Steel and now hidden in wilderness, it "stands alone amidst the grandeur of the mountains as a silent witness of the deeds performed by the Commonwealth in its efforts to annihilate distance." So wrote William Bender Wilson a hundred years ago.

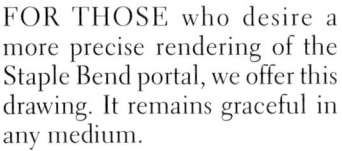

FOR THOSE who desire a more precise rendering of the Staple Bend portal, we offer this drawing. It remains graceful in any medium.

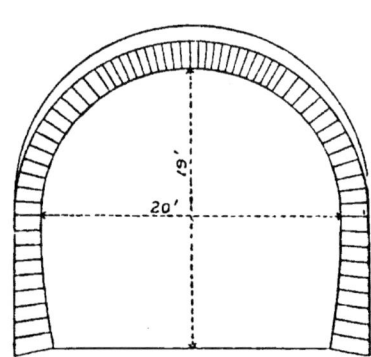

BOTH ENDS of Staple Bend have been plugged for many years as this c.1920 valuation photograph attests. Graffiti is not a new phenomenon.

National Archives

DOWNSTREAM from Staple Bend and Bridge No. (6) 219, the Conemaugh River follows a serpentine course until it joins Stony Creek at Johnstown. The loops in the river were mild and did not require bypassing. The West Slope ended at Conemaugh Station just east of Johnstown and it will come as no surprise to learn that a helper facility blossomed at this location. The first written reference to a *helper* station was in 1853 and this mediocre drawing is the earliest we were able to locate. It was included in Bowen's 1852 tour guide and his description follows: "Here's Conemaugh Station! We are down the mountain…here is a neat brick engine-house and machine-shop for…the iron nags who tug us over…the road and a characteristic water station to refresh them when they are dry." We are quite sure this drawing depicts the PRR station at Conemaugh, although its height above the rails makes one wonder how the passengers got in and out of the cars.

The following is supposed to be the first PRR timetable, commencing 31 August 1851, from Conemaugh west to Lockport. If this is so, the trains left and returned to the station building just shown. Note that the trains were mixed, carrying both freight and passengers. These trains connected at Conemaugh with OPRR and at Lockport with the State Works canal, a 16 mile one-way trip. Since OPRR passengers could connect with the canal at Johnstown, we doubt if many used PRR at this point in time. Some minor points: Rail Road is still two words, Conemaugh Furnace was *west* of Johnstown, Nineveh became Seward and the general superintendent became a significant figure in both railroad and Civil War history.

SCHEDULE No. 1
WESTERN DIVISION, PA. RAIL ROAD
ON AND AFTER AUGUST 31, 1851

EASTWARD		STATIONS	WESTWARD	
Passenger and Freight			Passenger and Freight	
Passenger Train No. 2			Passenger Train No. 1	
P.M.	A.M.		A.M.	P.M.
6:15	10:15	CONEMAUGH	7:15	2:15
6:00	10:05	JOHNSTOWN	7:25	2:30
5:35	9:45	CONEMAUGH FURNACE	7:40	2:50
5:20	9:35	NINEVEH	7:50	3:05
4:55	9:15	NEW FLORENCE	8:10	3:30
4:30	9:00	LOCKPORT	8:30	3:50
P.M.	A.M.		A.M.	P.M.

H. H. HAUPT,
Gen'l Supt.

THE WEST SLOPE

Blair County Historical Society

WE DO NOT KNOW exactly when this splendid photograph was taken, but it was in the early 1890s. The photographer was at Westmont atop a high hill just west of Stony Creek, which can be seen at bottom. The town of Johnstown is obviously on a large floodplain and PRR clings to the surrounding mountains on the far side of the Conemaugh River. The Conemaugh canyon in the distance is apparent as is the gap carved by the river. Company housing which serves the Cambria Works and PRR abounds, mostly insubstantial frame. The Great Wave roared out of the canyon just to the left of the Cambria Works at upper center. At that point it was 40 feet above the riverbed and 25 feet above PRR. The former figure is the equivalent of a four-story building, of which there are several in this photograph. It was at this point that the butcher's bill began in earnest. The Conemaugh River had been at flood stage for some time prior to the dam break and a huge pool had been created between Conemaugh and the stone bridge at Johnstown (out of sight to the left). Consequently, the widening of the canyon did not materially dissipate the wave height which had now arrived at a place where thousands of people resided and worked. One still shudders at the thought. By the by, and as we shall see, three passenger trains were being held at Conemaugh. The wave was twenty feet above the roadbed when they were struck.

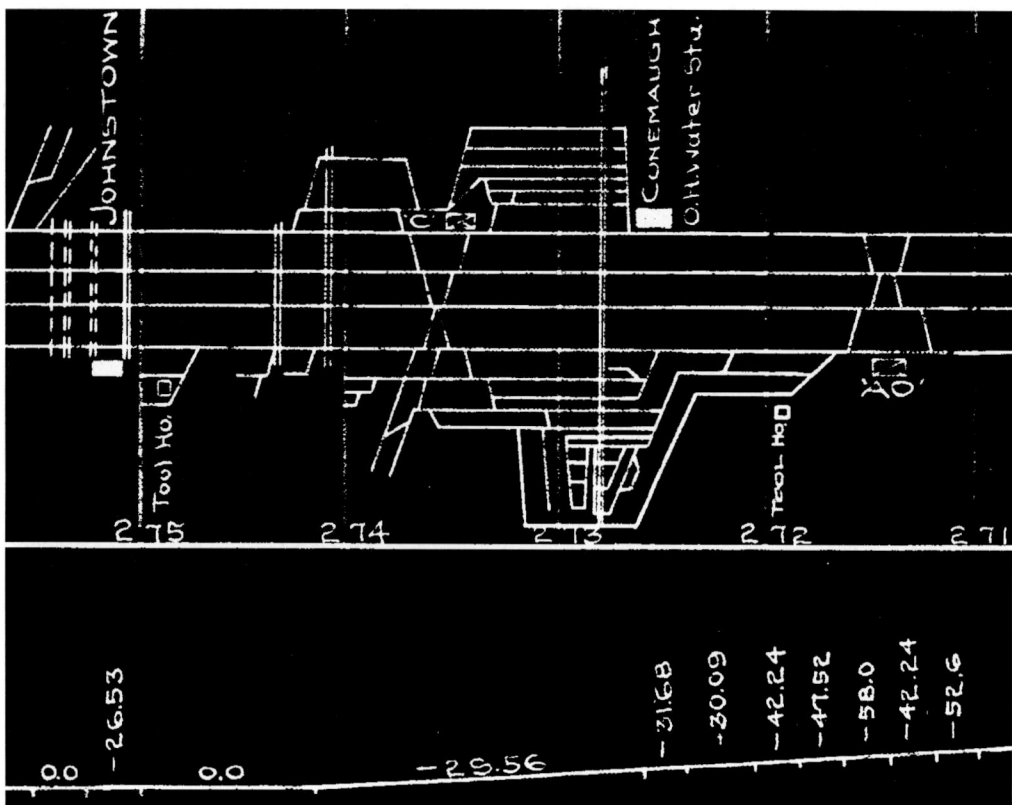

THE CONEMAUGH complex was over three miles long, from AO interlocker on the east to the passenger station at Johnstown on the west as shown on this 1910 track chart. C interlocker, on the hill-side in the center of the yard, was (and is) positioned almost exactly at the base of the West Slope as one can see from the profile at bottom. Note that the mainline is flat for over a mile west of the beginning of the grade. There are, of course, many helper stations on many railroads and, indeed, this author has written about quite a few. None anywhere in the world compare with Conemaugh, from the outbreak of the Civil War to today. The number of trains requiring help has always been little short of incredible. That the West Slope was comparatively gentle is misleading simple because the only advantage conferred is that more tonnage can be handled per train. That, in turn, attracted more tonnage. In addition, a lot of tonnage was delivered to and shipped from the trackage between Mileposts 271 and 276 which, to say the least, complicated the operational situation. For example, in 1896 Altoona handled 728,000 *loaded* cars, 27% of which were westbound. Conemaugh handled 603,000 loaded cars, 33% of which were westbound. In other words, Conemaugh handled almost as many cars as Altoona. Of course, a lot of this volume originated on the West Slope as well as at Conemaugh/Johnstown and much was through but it still had to be handled. Just five years later, Conemaugh processed 857,000 loaded cars. Indeed, Conemaugh was a very busy place Today the local traffic is minimal, but the through traffic is growing and almost all the trains have to be helped. Busy.

AO TOWER, at the east end of the Conemaugh complex, was built in 1910 principally for crossing helper locomotives returning from the summit and easing congestion at C, which is farther west. Pressed to save money during the Great Depression, PRR studied AO and concluded that most of the plant was rarely used in practice. Accordingly, in 1934 AO was closed, made remote from C and most of the interlocking crossovers removed save for one set. Even the last set of crossovers was removed years ago and AO is now only a placename on the railroad. This view is c.1920.

National Archives

THE WEST SLOPE

Hagley Museum and Library

AO TOWER was located at about the point where the mainline comes into view on the right. This photograph was taken in July of 1977 to record damage done by a flood in that month which drowned 80 people and severely damaged Conrail. The Bethlehem steel works (successor to Cambria iron and steel) appears at upper center. The ridgeline on the horizon is Laurel Hill. Westmont, from which an earlier photograph was taken, is atop this mountain. At the far right of this ridgeline one can see the gap in Laurel Hill, a subject to be covered in the next chapter. The railroad on the left bank is the Conemaugh and Black Lick, a Bethlehem subsidiary switching line with rails throughout this general area. All traces of OP/NPRR and the canal in the four miles from the Stone Bridge to AO have long since been obliterated by railroad and industrial expansion, mostly by filling-in the Conemaugh River. In 1881 PRR did cross the river and construct a branch from Johnstown/Conemaugh east for a few miles using the OP/NPRR roadbed but additional improvements buried this work. As to AO, which was on the river side of the PRR mainline, either this flood or one in 1936 would have removed it in any event.

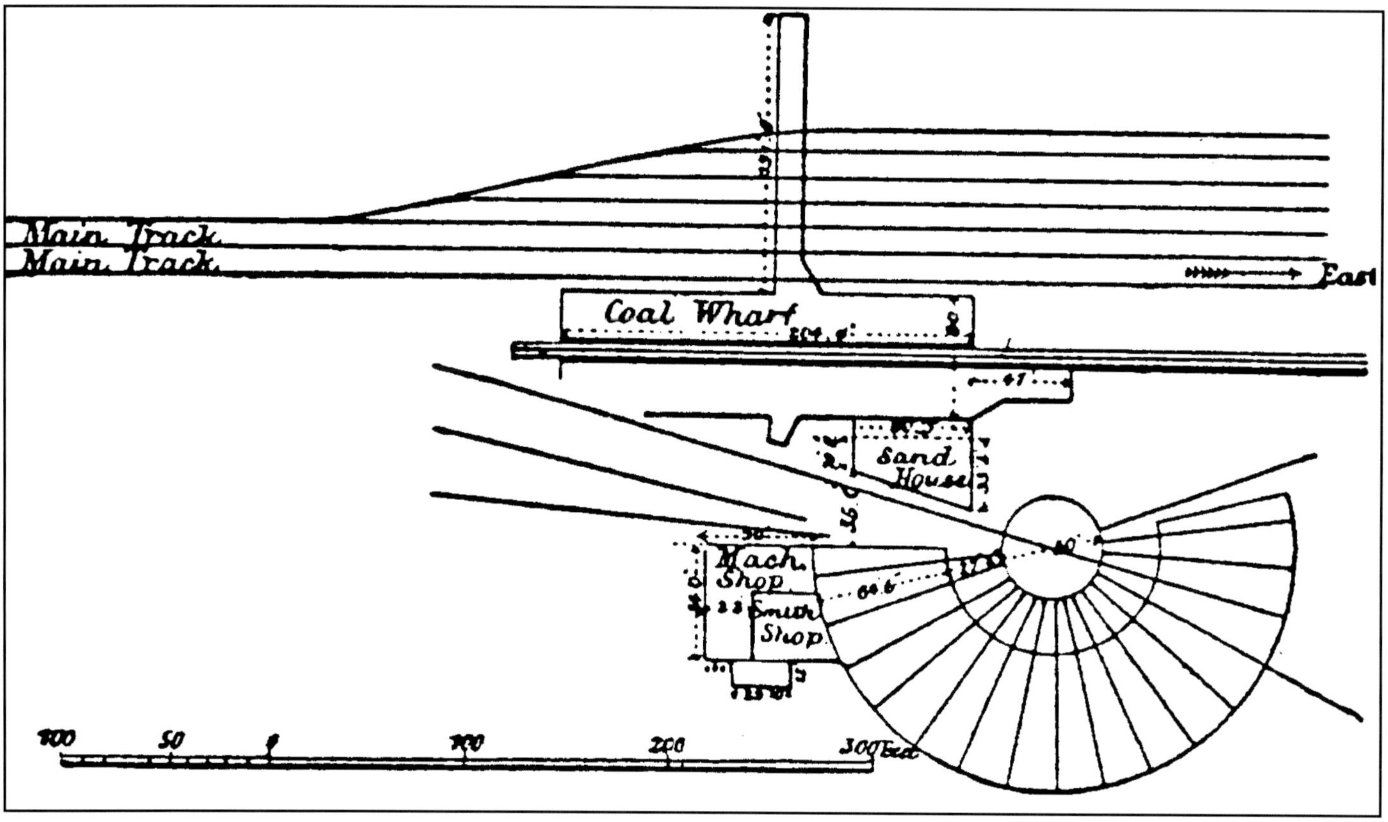

TRIUMPH I

THIS MID-1870s PLAN of the engine servicing facilities at Conemaugh is the earliest we have been able to find. We know that a nine-stall *addition* to the enginehouse was built in 1857 along with a new machine shop. There are 16 stalls shown here, which implies that the original boasted at least seven. Note that the turntable is 60 feet long. Since we know that a 50 foot iron turntable was installed in 1862, it is reasonable to assume that the original was shorter. The coal wharf is massive and typical of PRR practice. This coal "bridge" was built in 1862, was 16 feet high over seven tracks (with room for more) and consisted of small "dump-car" and "shutes" (sic). Even in 1862 it was meant to serve sidings as well as the two-track mainline which at that time was on the south side. The sand house is worthy of elucidation. The use of sand to improve adhesion was a B&O "first" and was employed at Parrs Ridge in Maryland in the 1830s. As with so many improvements in technological history, the process was evolved by an ordinary engineman. The cinders may be gone, but sand is not and ballast still requires periodic cleaning. While not apparent here, the south wall of the enginehouse is at river's edge…an uncomfortable but unavoidable location. Everything seen here, plus much else, was swept away in 1889 by the Great Wave. A new four-track overhead coaling station was not completed until 1892.

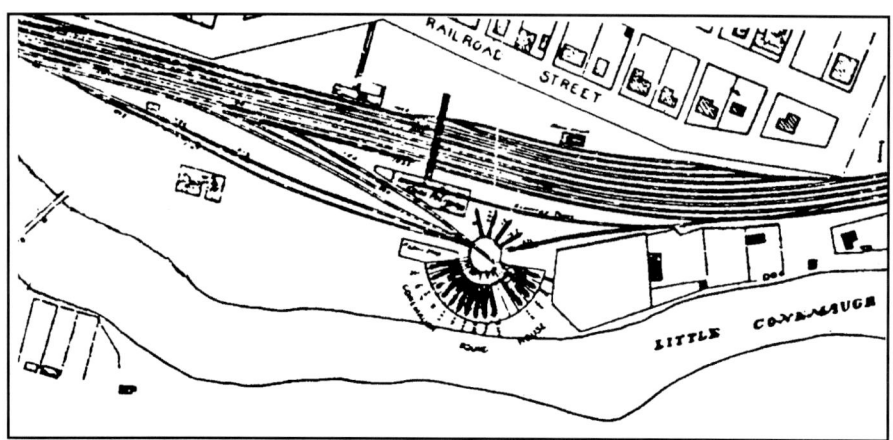

CONEMAUGH AT 3:45 pm on 31 May 1889 appeared substantially the same as in the 1870s with only the addition of four open-air engine tracks on the north side of the turntable attracting the eye. The two buildings on the north side of the tracks are, we suspect, C Tower/dispatchers office on the left and Conemaugh Station on the right. When the sun set that sad day, nothing remained. Nothing. No tracks, no buildings, no people except for a lucky few who managed to climb up the hillside or, in the case of the passenger trains stopped at Conemaugh, elected to stay in the cars. The Great Wave arrived, by the way, at 3:50 pm.

THE WEST SLOPE

Blair County Historical Society

THREE EASTBOUND passenger trains and an 18-car freight were standing at Conemaugh when the wave arrived. The first section of Train No. 8 *Day Express*, with two engines, baggage car, five coaches and one Pullman parlor car, was standing by the station. It was swept 375 feet west with one coach and the baggage car being torn from the train. Twenty-five passengers in the coach were drowned trying to escape. The second section of the *Day Express*, with one engine, three postal and express cars and three Pullman sleeping cars, was on a siding near the station. The first section apparently deflected the blow to some extent, but three women and a porter were drowned trying to climb the hillside. The Pullmans were destroyed by fire, started because a car of lime from the freight had been driven next to them and ignited for some obscure chemical reason. Mail Train No. 12, with one engine, one express car, one combine and two coaches, was behind Train No. 8. It was swept backward to the rear of the second section. A total of 30 passengers were lost from the three trains. The bodies of 17 were never recovered. Crew losses were unreported, other than the one porter. Between South Fork and Conemaugh, the following equipment was carried away, badly damaged or destroyed: 33 engines, 18 passenger cars, 315 freight cars. That hillside in the background proved to be a fatal magnet.

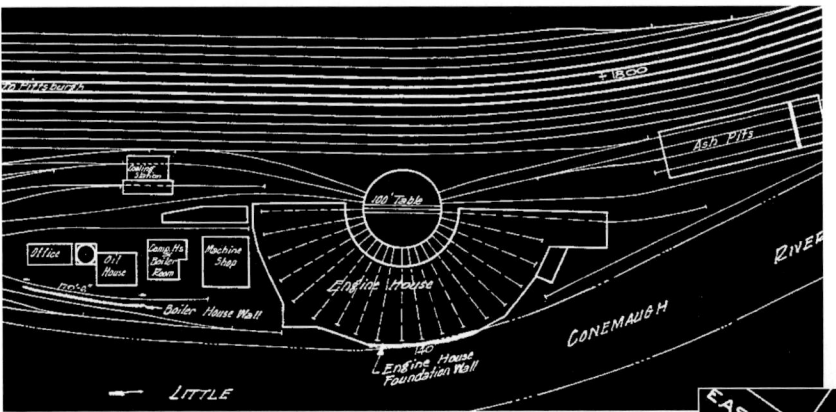

THE CONEMAUGH enginehouse had to be replaced quickly and this new structure, complete with subsidiary buildings, was completed in early 1890. Oddly, the turntable was left at 60 feet and not lengthened to 75 feet until 1899. By 1936, a 100 foot table was in place as seen here. Please note the ash pits at upper right in relation to the next plan.

THIS PLAN shows the location of the 1890 rebuilt Conemaugh station in relation to the ash pits just mentioned. By 1935, the date of this plan, the few passengers still using PRR waited at the YMCA for trains so closure was indicated. Quietly and without fanfare, PRR's station was no more. Conemaugh Station was now just Conemaugh.

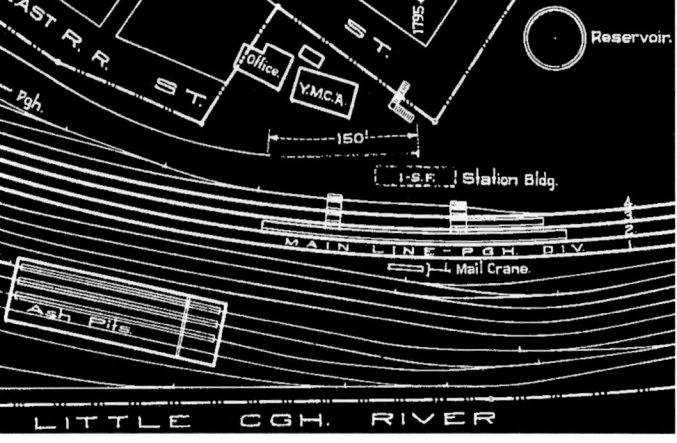

227

TRIUMPH I

THE NEW Conemaugh enginehouse is throbbing with activity in February of 1903 at the age of thirteen. That W&NBRR (Williamsport and North Branch) engine No. 10 is an 1888 Baldwin 4-4-0 moving east to its new home in northeastern Pennsylvania from original owner Elgin, Joliet & Eastern.

Hagley Museum and Library

TAKEN ON THE SAME DAY in February of 1903, from the south side of the Conemaugh River, the enginehouse can only be described as vibrant. While the south wall is close to the river, there is no more South Fork dam or Western Reservoir. Nothing can go wrong.

Hagley Museum and Library

EXACTLY ONE-THIRD of a century later, PRR's confidence in the docility of the Conemaugh River was shaken. A flood in March of 1936 reminded everyone that the "Mother" in Mother Nature can become an adjective at will.

Railroad Museum of Pennsylvania

THE WEST SLOPE

Railroad Museum of Pennsylvania

AND PEOPLE wonder why railroaders swear a lot. These locomotives were probably placed on the track nearest the river in the hope that their weight would stabilize the bank. It probably worked to some extent because they formed a wall that deflected the river away from the east end of the enginehouse. The open steel structure at right is the framework for the ashpit traveling crane. This facility was four tracks wide, three used for dumping ashes and the fourth, or closest, to hold ash cars. It was 215 feet long, big by any standard and indicative of the traffic volume moving up the West Slope. Ash disposal was still another costly burden associated with the steam locomotive.

Carnegie Library of Pittsburgh

AS TRAIN LENGTH increased, it was necessary to move coaling facilities farther east to service road locomotives and ease congestion in Conemaugh itself. In the upper center of this poor photograph can be seen a huge facility built in 1926. The location is identified as Buttermilk Falls...it is between the suburbs of East Conemaugh and Parkhill. The four-track mainline is on the hill side. Most of the other tracks were specifically installed to hold 100-car eastward freight trains free of the mainline while having their fires cleaned and, of course, fueling. The Conemaugh River was moved from its natural bed to an entirely new channel. The coaling tower is actually in the center of the old riverbed. On the other side of the river, the C&BLRR has extended the bank by fill in the other direction. So the river was not only moved but also narrowed. It did not take kindly to this intrusion. PRR was moving 7,000 cars a day through Conemaugh in 1926 and the traffic was growing. The railroad had to insult the river. It had no choice.

TRIUMPH I

THINGS DO GO WRONG on the best of railroads as this undated photograph attests. This derailment managed to close all four mainline tracks, but at least the sidings were still open. This is not, by the by, a flood picture. The slight grade through here allows PRR to drop coal hoppers under the tower by gravity, avoiding the use of a switcher.

Railroad Museum of Pennsylvania

Railroad Museum of Pennsylvania

NOW THIS *is* a flood picture. The Conemaugh River vented its frustration in March of 1936 and attempted to take back its old riverbed. This was a 250-ton mechanical coaling station capable of serving eight tracks at once.

THE WEST SLOPE

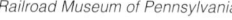
Railroad Museum of Pennsylvania

THE 1936 FLOOD took out four tracks and the Conemaugh River managed to reclaim about half of its old bed. PRR, of course, promptly counterattacked.

A STARK, LONELY SENTINEL by 4 November 1963, the coaling station lies forlorn and dismembered with no mission. Not even sand. The ridge on the horizon is the one pierced by OPRR's Staple Bend tunnel and PRR's Deep Cut, both about a half-mile to the left of the place where the mainline disappears.

TRIUMPH I

Bob Lorenz Collection

LOOKING EAST at Conemaugh on 7 August 1958, diesels dominate the scene. The helper coaling station at upper right (located on an earlier plan) dispenses only sand and the smell of coal gas is gone, never to return. In early 1969, the coaling station was collapsed with explosives and the rubble used to fill-in the old turntable, inspection and ash pits. Conemaugh, of course, remains an active helper point. The West Slope has not eroded. It's just that there are no locomotives stationed there.

THE SIZE of C Tower affirms its operational importance. It was probably the largest helper station interlocker in history. Built in 1910 as an electro-pneumatic plant with 47 levers, it is seen here c. 1920. C's operators, levermen and dispatchers had twelve front windows to observe their vast kingdom. Millions upon millions of movements have come under C's purview. Thousands upon thousands of enginemen and trainmen have sworn or cheered at the dicta issued from this building. Command, control, communicate. The visage may be utilitarian, but the power was as absolute as its home signals. Come. Go. Stop. Move. Now.

National Archives

THE WEST SLOPE

Edward H. Weber

THE WOODEN C was replaced by a brick tower, probably in the 1920s. On 30 September 1958 a westbound mixed freight derailed in the interlocker, destroyed the tower and killed an operator in an all too familiar railroad incident. This spartan concrete block structure, seen on 7 September 1968 almost exactly ten years later, was the replacement. The keystone C has been replaced by a tiny letter on a small and uninspiring rectangular black background. As we know, C controls AO and also JW to the west just east of the stone bridge in Johnstown. This is light duty since neither are interlockers. As of the Fall of 1995, C was active but closure is clearly down the road. Indeed, all manned towers on all railroads are sitting ducks.

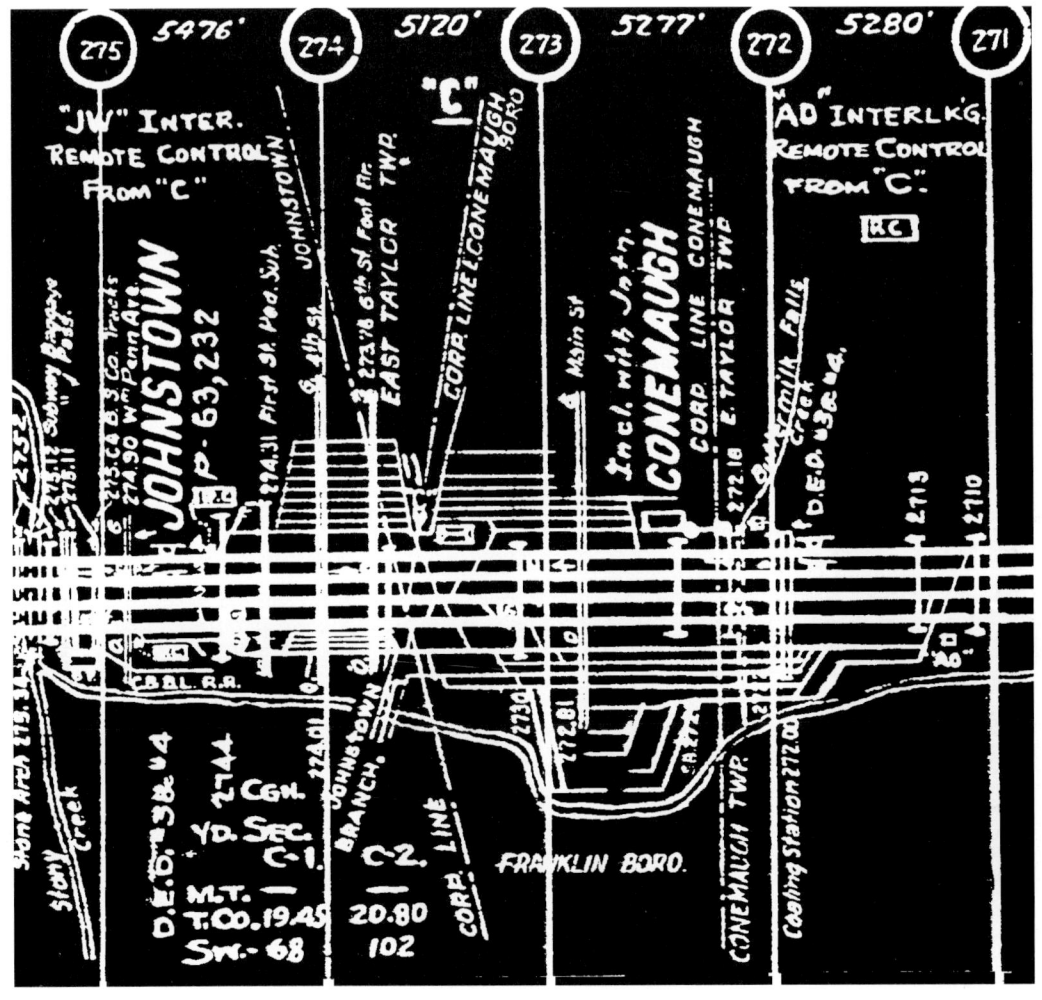

WE PRESENT this 1958 track chart under no illusion that the reader will be able to discern anything other than the most bold detail. The four miles from AO to JW and the stone bridge was a maze within a puzzle. It is still hard to believe that PRR could get it all in a narrow valley and at the same time operate a four-track mainline through the middle. Today the mainline is three-track with one interlocker and two helper pockets. C is no longer a helper station nor is it a crew-call point. Both C's rise and fall surely would have astonished Thomson.

233

JOHNSTOWN was settled by Joseph Johns, a gentleman of German extraction, about 1791. His name supplanted the Indian name Kickenapawling for this locale. One wonders if the "kicken" was meant to be prophetic. This early etching shows a gentle place devoid of significant industry. There is a canal boat at lower right with two nearby OPRR rail cars. The Conemaugh River is seen at right, flowing into the Laurel Hill gap. A canal basin appears at left mid-distance. The canal seems to flow from lower right to a connection in the center with a waterway between the basin and the river. Thus the structures in the center appear to be on what is tantamount to an island. While some details in this scene are hard to reconcile with some descriptive accounts, the overall impression is probably correct. When PRR came to town, Thomson built on the far bank of the river.

WHEN BOWEN came to Johnstown in 1851, with his biting sarcasm in full flower, this is what his artist saw. Since PRR was operating trains through this scene and into the gap at upper left at the time, and Bowen himself transferred from OPRR to PRR at Conemaugh on this trip, one would think his artist would at least have shown the railroad. The bridge carrying the canal over the river conforms to historic fact, however, and for that reason we include this illustration.

THE WEST SLOPE

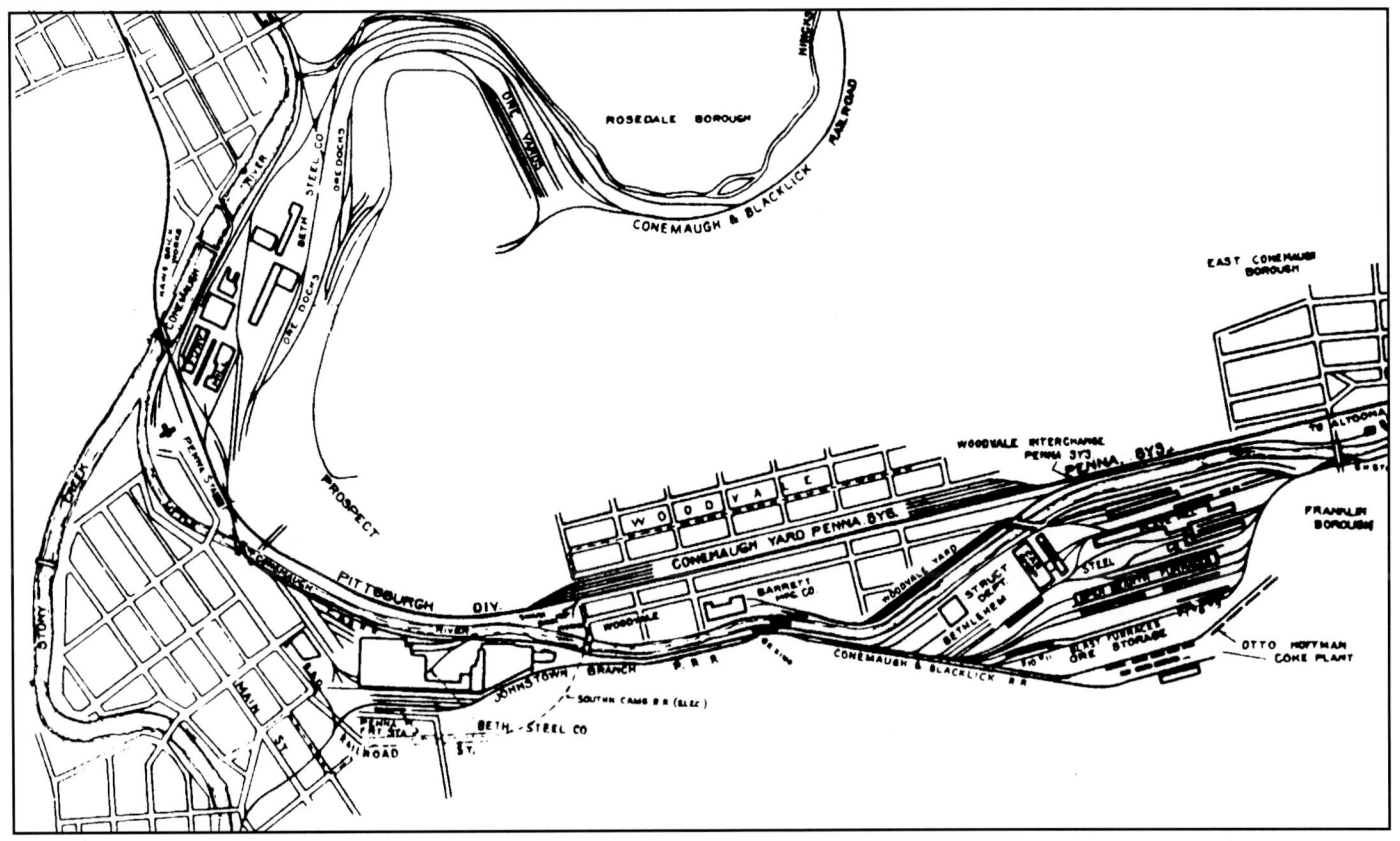

THIS PRR system map was done in 1920 and corrected to 1927. It begins at East Conemaugh on the right and extends past the confluence of Stony Creek and the Conemaugh River through the Laurel Hill gap. Please look to lower left and follow the B&O line to the PRR freight station. This building was constructed by PRR in 1896 and rests upon land reclaimed from the State Works canal basin. Note that PRR's Johnstown Branch leaves the mainline just to the left of "Prospect," crosses the river and runs to this freight station as well as a connection with the C&BLRR. The PRR/B&O connection at the freight station was installed by PRR on a "without delay" schedule in early 1897 when B&O was in receivership. In our view, this rush transaction adds credence to the Salix/Zero Track speculation given earlier in this chapter. This is where the connection with PRR's Johnstown Branch and its mainline would have been made. The reader should note the profusion of Bethlehem Steel facilities throughout this area, jammed into every piece of available land contiguous to PRR. To repeat, much of this land was cut and fill. At upper center, note that C&BLRR reached up into the hills with switchbacks. Also, notice how narrow the Conemaugh River has become in relation to Stony Creek, which is really a smaller stream.

TRIUMPH I

Carnegie Library, Pittsburgh

THE GREAT WAVE spared the Johnstown passenger station and some trackage immediately east and west of the structure because of its elevation. The devastation behind the station is painfully evident in this photograph taken shortly after the flood. The very first PRR station in Johnstown was a small rectangular structure...one must remember that in the very early days most of the traffic was handled at Conemaugh. The State Works aqueduct crossed the river in this vicinity and the PRR station was on the southern side. It was moved to this location in 1860 when the canal itself was being used by Cambria Iron Company. The octagon tower seen here at right was in place in the 1860s, which shows just how early this design evolved. In 1889 at the time of this photograph it bore the call letters Q, later changed to JW. The station shown here was built in 1883. In 1907 a 20 by 30 foot addition was made to the building and the platforms extended 200 feet. About this time PRR concluded that an entirely new station was needed and the railroad raised to a higher level. It took many years to accomplish this work as we shall see. The small switching locomotives seen in the foreground belonged to Cambria Iron, serving their works to the right of this scene.

THE WEST SLOPE

Edward H. Weber

THE NEW Johnstown Station, completed in 1917, appeared this way on 6 September 1968 looking westward. On the right, one can see just how high the mainline was raised above the original roadbed. The elevation was done with lifts of a few inches at a time over a period of seven years to avoid interference with traffic, which circa 1920 was about 200 trains a day. The passenger traffic through the station complex itself during this construction was no small matter. A PRR study done for the four months ending January 1912 showed that an average of 27 trains a day stopped at Johnstown and 386 tickets a day were sold. As to baggage, 321 pieces were handled per day. The "lifting" project also involved the construction of various bridges and over/underpasses for both railroad and public use. This is the most impressive station ever built by PRR on the lines covered in this book. Of tapestry brick on a granite foundation, with pilasters of Indiana limestone, the building is, at least in the eyes of this author, a tribute to the architect as well as the construction engineers. Johnstown deserved the best and it got it.

Edward H. Weber

THE PLATFORM layout at Johnstown was equally impressive as is seen here on 7 September 1968 looking east with the station on the right. The Penn Central had just begun and passenger business was declining precipitously which explains the grass growing on the platform.

WHEN THIS PHOTOGRAPH was taken on 29 December 1983, the station was not at its best. Happily, in 1985 the building was renovated and is now used by a local firm with Amtrak still selling tickets and passengers still boarding trains. The 62 by 45 foot waiting room is brick with marble pilasters and wainscoting, floors of terrazzo with marble borders and a vaulted ceiling. The platforms are reached through an underground tunnel. The inside alone makes this building worthy of preservation.

Thomas A. Biery

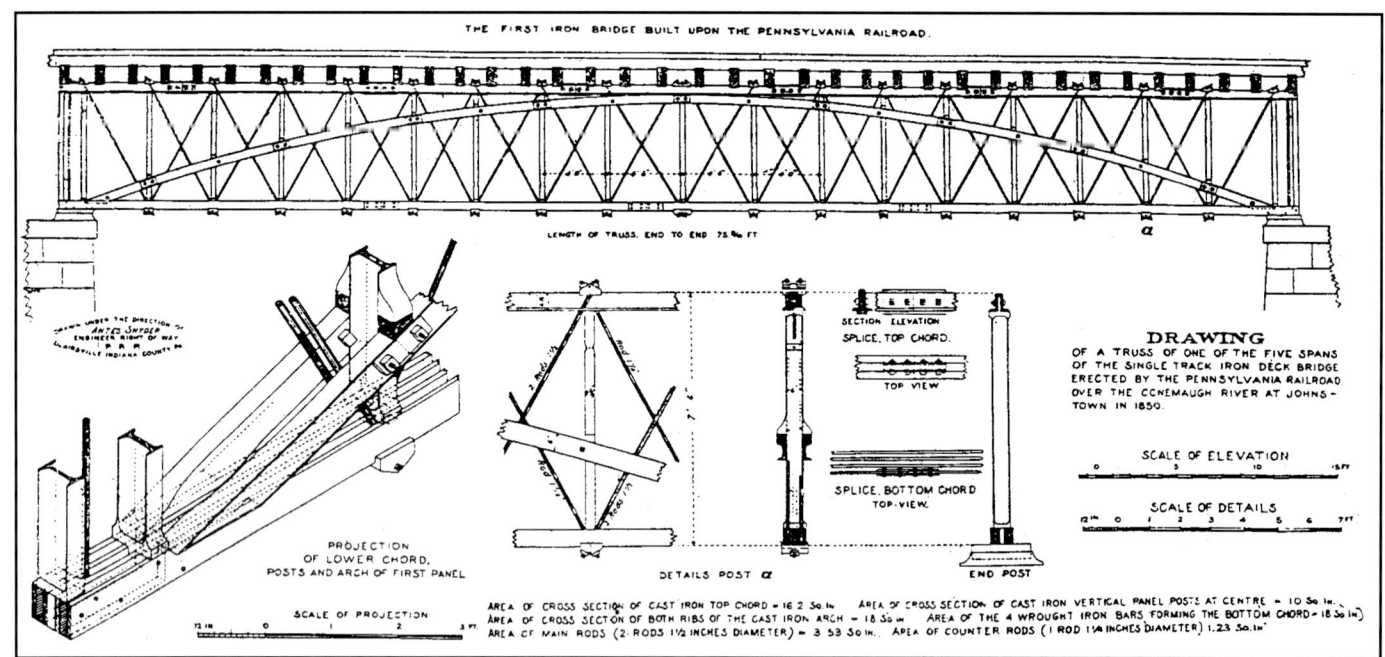

PRR HAD TO CROSS the Conemaugh River at Johnstown to gain the south bank and they did so with the first all-iron bridge constructed on the railroad. It was a single-track Pratt truss structure and the parts were fabricated in the Altoona shops. It took five of the trusses seen here to cross the river, obviously a deck design with the rails on top. Installation began in 1850 and the bridge was open for traffic early in 1851. The cast iron arch was added as a precaution even though the engineers felt the truss alone was capable of supporting a moving load of one ton per lineal foot for each track. The wrought iron bars, in tension, forming the bottom chord were calculated to handle a limited working-stress of five tons per square inch. The rods with screws were not made heavier at the thread, an error that later had to be rectified. This particular span was 76 feet long, but PRR used this design in spans from 65 to 110 feet in length on other parts of the railroad with success over the next twelve years. It is not impossible to think that this basic design was used on Bridge No. 6, shown earlier in this chapter. PRR also had to cross the canal, which at this point was on the north shore. Originally a wooden Howe design was employed, but by 1857 it was rotting and in 1859 it was replaced by a 57 foot iron span which we assume shared similar characteristics. A single-track bridge was, of course, an operating impediment and PRR installed a double-track bridge which was ready for service on 27 February 1869. As we shall see, the design was similar but without the arch. The original spans were used elsewhere on the railroad, on branches and for public road crossings.

THE WEST SLOPE

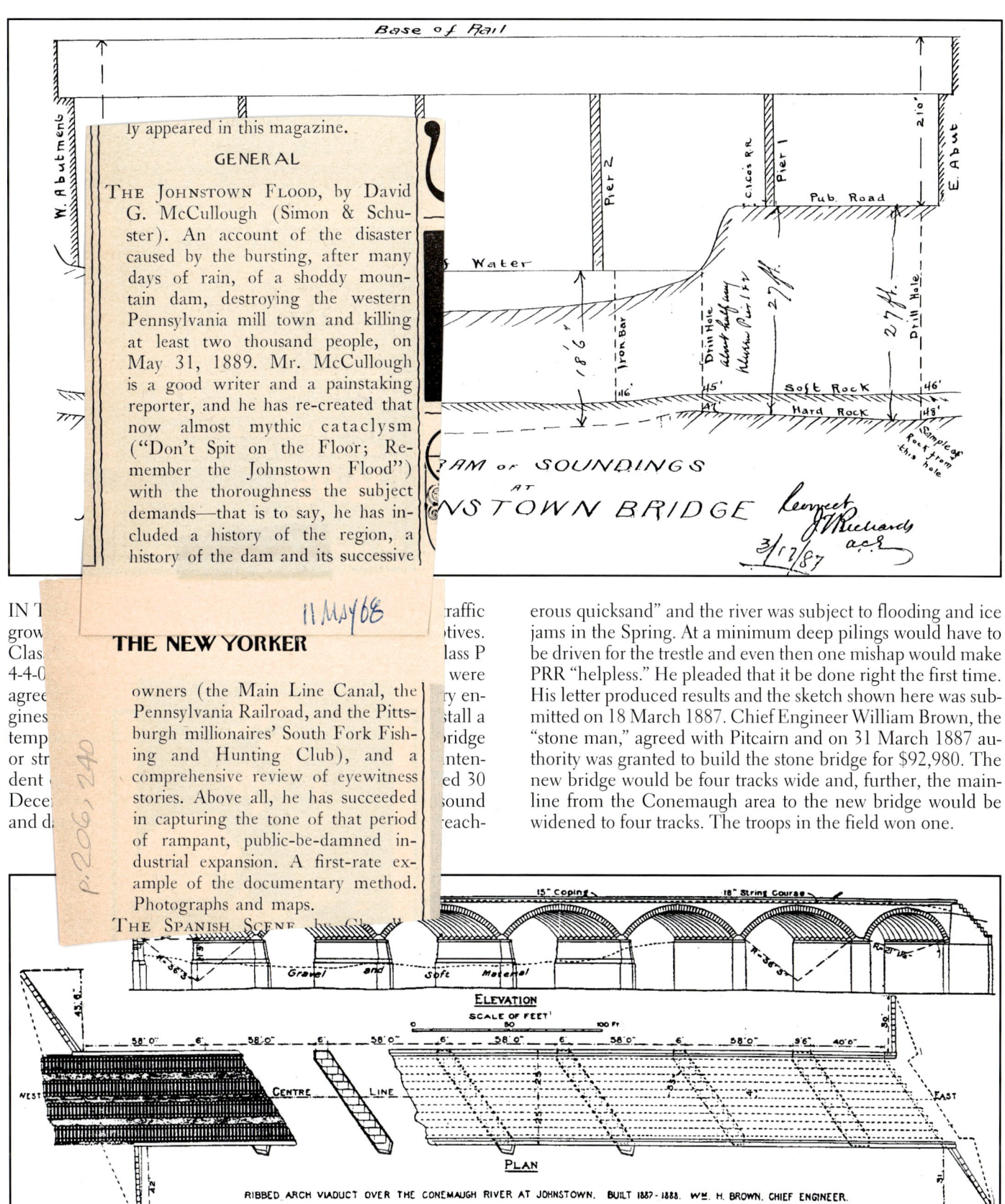

[Clipping overlay — The New Yorker, 11 May 68, p. 206, 240:]

GENERAL

THE JOHNSTOWN FLOOD, by David G. McCullough (Simon & Schuster). An account of the disaster caused by the bursting, after many days of rain, of a shoddy mountain dam, destroying the western Pennsylvania mill town and killing at least two thousand people, on May 31, 1889. Mr. McCullough is a good writer and a painstaking reporter, and he has re-created that now almost mythic cataclysm ("Don't Spit on the Floor; Remember the Johnstown Flood") with the thoroughness the subject demands—that is to say, he has included a history of the region, a history of the dam and its successive owners (the Main Line Canal, the Pennsylvania Railroad, and the Pittsburgh millionaires' South Fork Fishing and Hunting Club), and a comprehensive review of eyewitness stories. Above all, he has succeeded in capturing the tone of that period of rampant, public-be-damned industrial expansion. A first-rate example of the documentary method. Photographs and maps.

IN T... traffic grow... Clas... lass P 4-4-0... were agree... ry en... gines... stall a temp... bridge or str... nten- dent... ed 30 Dece... sound and d... reach- erous quicksand" and the river was subject to flooding and ice jams in the Spring. At a minimum deep pilings would have to be driven for the trestle and even then one mishap would make PRR "helpless." He pleaded that it be done right the first time. His letter produced results and the sketch shown here was submitted on 18 March 1887. Chief Engineer William Brown, the "stone man," agreed with Pitcairn and on 31 March 1887 authority was granted to build the stone bridge for $92,980. The new bridge would be four tracks wide and, further, the main-line from the Conemaugh area to the new bridge would be widened to four tracks. The troops in the field won one.

CONSTRUCTION of the stone bridge, technically Bridge No. 222, began in 1887 and completion was during 1888. Only the five spans on the left were over the river itself, the other two providing for surface access. When the Great Wave arrived in 1889 all seven arches were over the river. Of course, the stone bridge held. It might have been better if it had not.

239

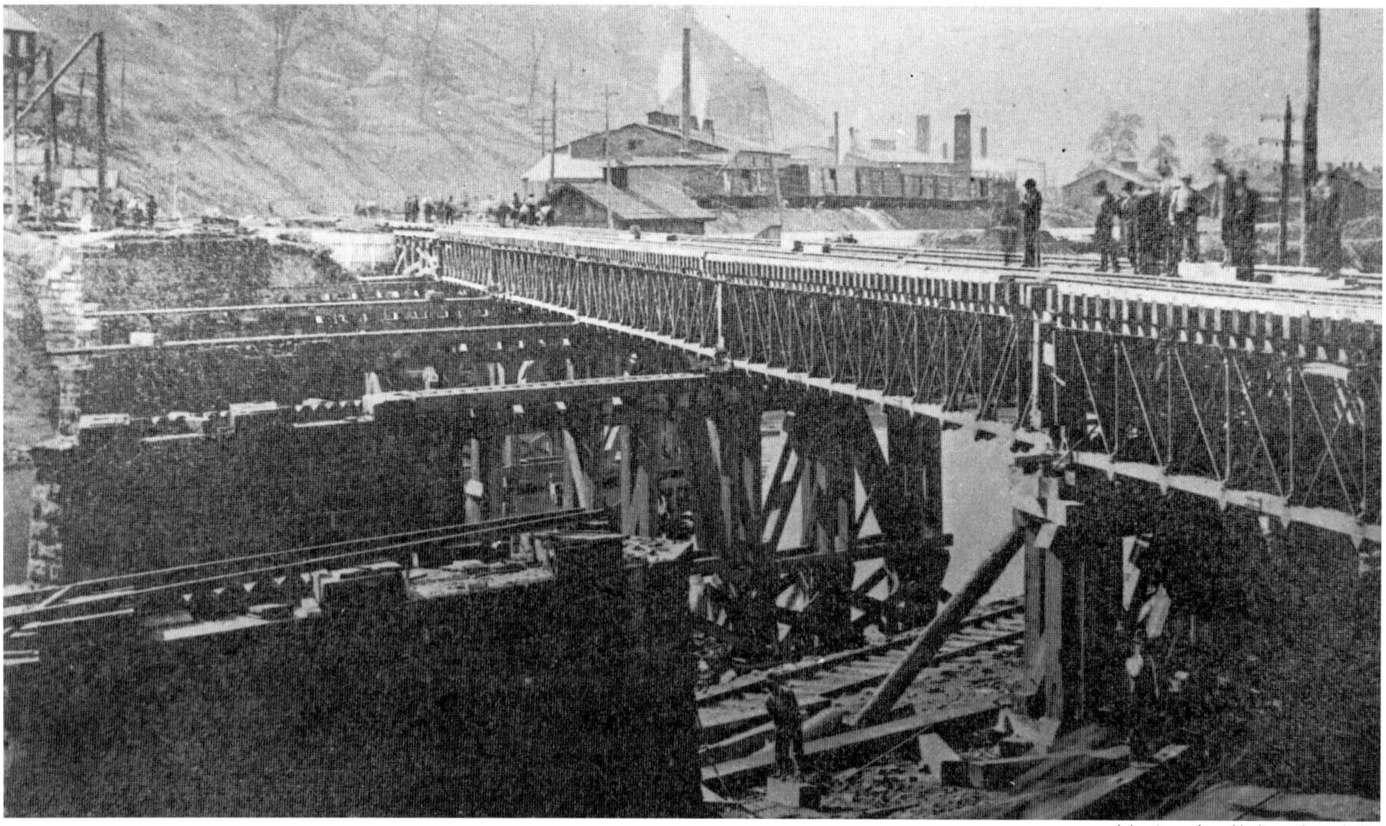

Johnstown Area Heritage Association

ON 10 NOVEMBER 1887, which was a Sunday, a large force of men amply supplied with hydraulic jacks slowly raised the existing Bridge No. 222 exactly thirteen inches and deftly moved it downstream, gently placing the truss on wooden supports as we see here. During the process the line remained open for traffic. In a long career, your author has had occasion to observe the handiwork of what we call field, or combat, engineers and have invariably come away impressed by their skill and devotion. They can do it and do it with aplomb. The trusses seen here, of course, are the second bridge at Johnstown. Eight of them were refitted and used as a bridge over the Juniata River on the Tyrone Branch.

Blair County Historical Society

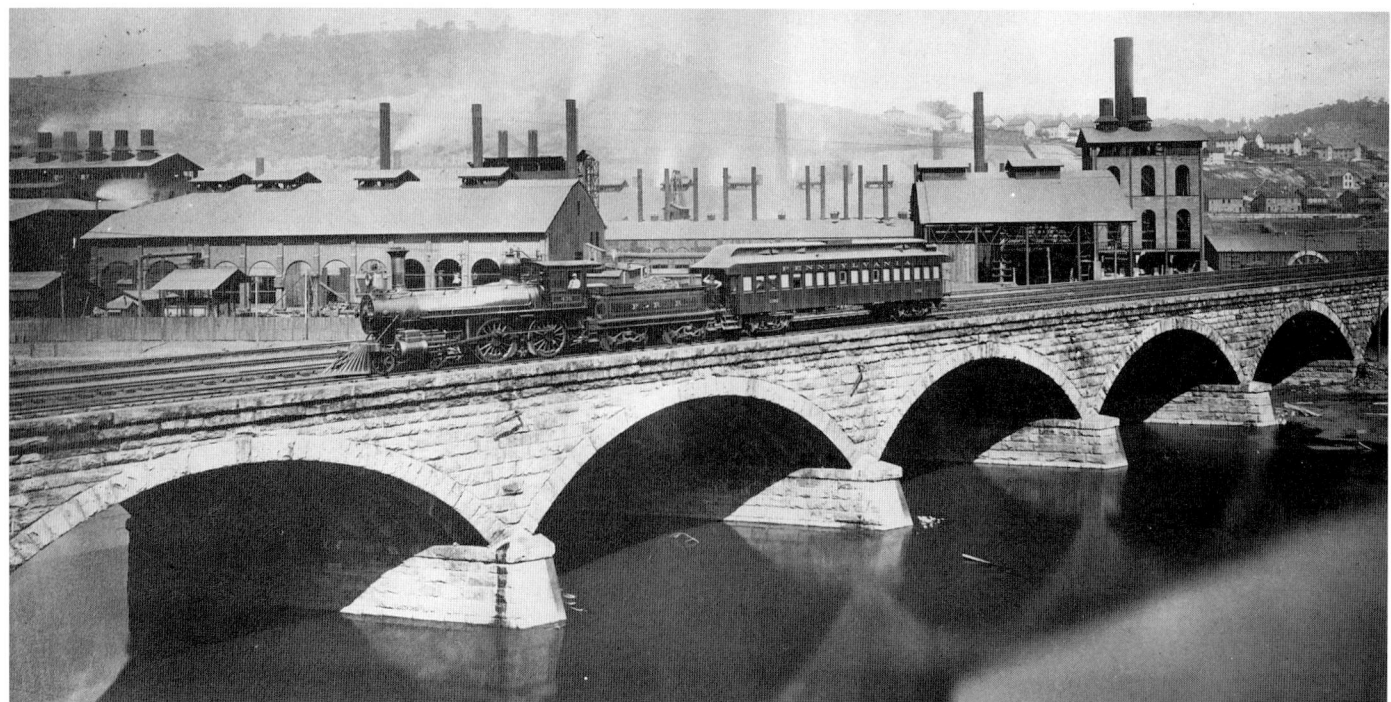

THIS PHOTOGRAPH of the stone bridge was taken c.1893 and the structure remains pristine. No sign of horror is evident.

THE WEST SLOPE

THE GREAT WAVE actually did not reach the stone bridge. As soon as it arrived at the flood plain at Johnstown it spread out over the valley floor. This dispersion created havoc. We quote from an 1889 book: "This avalanche was composed of more than 100,000 tons of rocks, locomotives, freight cars, car trucks, iron, logs, trees and other material...sliding over the ground, it mowed down the houses, mills and factories as a mowing machine does a field of grain...it swept down with a roaring, crushing sound...hurled 10,000 people into the jaws of death...so the people called it the avalanche of death." Unfortunately, the stone bridge held and this incredible mass of debris interlaced with thousands of bodies was the result. To add to the nightmare, the debris caught fire. No one really knows how many human beings perished in this calamity other than that the total was over 2,000 (not 10,000). This photograph was taken a few days after the disaster, as evidenced by the PRR trestle at the east end of the bridge. It is reproduced from the book, thus explaining the poor quality. Of all the photographs we have seen, it is this one which seems to most graphically show the magnitude of the tragedy.

ONE HUNDRED AND SIX YEARS later almost to the day on 13 May 1995, we visited the memorial park overlooking the stone bridge and took this photograph. We found the experience moving and the park a tribute to the good taste and devotion of the people of Johnstown who still pay homage to those who have gone before. Just upstream overlooking Stony Creek is an inclined plane built by Cambria Iron and opened on 1 June 1891 to provide an escape route for the citizens of Johnstown in the event of another innundation. It was used by 4,000 people during the 1936 flood. Cambria Iron sold the plane to the town for one dollar and, in 1983, over three million dollars was expended to rehabilitate it and create a tourist attraction. It is worth a visit.

PRR, IRON, STEEL AND JOHNSTOWN are synonymous. Steel historians generally agree that the modern steel industry in the United States was born in Johnstown. The iron part of the equation, however, was another matter. A Buckwalter Forge was opened on Stony Creek in 1809 and Pierson Iron Company on the Conemaugh River at present-day Franklin in 1813. Even though surrounded by raw materials in abundance, transportation costs precluded success. Only the coming of PRR and low cost haulage provided the impetus for growth. The premier company was Cambria Iron, founded in 1852 and the first large-scale integrated iron works and rail mill east of Pittsburgh. Even Cambria Iron failed in 1854 and 1855. Experiments during 1857-58 using air to remove carbon were not successful. British iron was king. Then the outbreak of the Civil War and the imposition of high "Morrill" tariffs in 1861 broke the back of British dominance and Cambria Iron flourished. Cambria Iron was the sixth U.S. plant to install the Bessemer process in 1869 and they produced steel rails in 1871. By 1873 Johnstown was the nation's steel center. Thomson's devotion to steel rails provided a handy customer as well as transportation link. This 1875 illustration shows a bustling facility and, by the way, also shows the second PRR bridge over the Conemaugh River at right. Cambria Iron enjoyed a relatively brief heyday, but the rise of the integrated steel process put the firm in an awkward position. Pennsylvania ores were suitable for iron, crucible steel and Bessemer steel, but not integrated. Great Lakes and overseas iron ore was needed and Cambria Iron (which became Cambria Steel in 1898) was not well located in this regard. Pittsburgh was closer to the former and coastal mills to the latter. Worse, Andrew Carnegie went into the steel business near Pittsburgh on PRR lines and he proved to be a ferocious competitor. Many believe that westward ore movements over the summit were a product of the mid-twentieth century. Actually, the PRR annual report for 1888 reported such movements as "heavy." Still, nearby coking coal, limestone and fire clay enabled Cambria Steel to survive for many years.

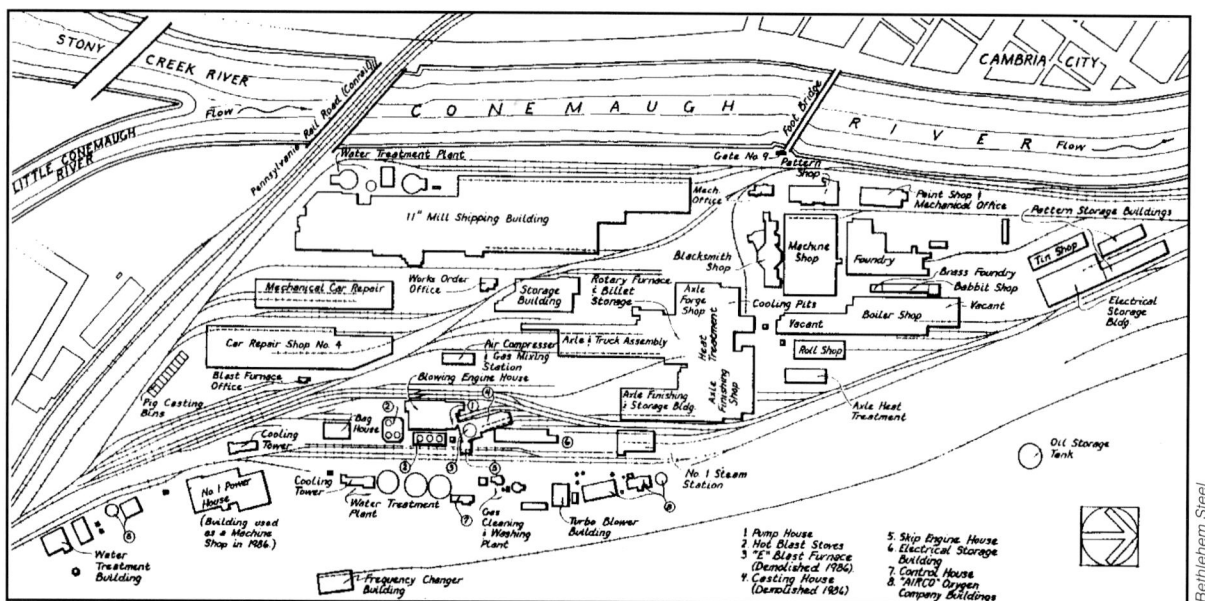

BETHLEHEM STEEL COMPANY purchased Cambria Steel in 1923 and, to be fair, tried their best to modernize and adjust to changing markets and needs. By the way, in 1925 they created C&BLRR as a common carrier to reach B&O as well as PRR rails. Here we see an active facility in 1983. For all these efforts, by the early 1990s the works were shuttered and in 1995 they sold both works and the railroad to New York-based Veritas Capital, Inc. Some Bethlehem workers with seniority work at the Bethlehem works near Baltimore and come home on weekends. We cannot leave Johnstown without noting that the 1990 census showed that this small city has the highest national percentage of residents who have not moved since 1959. Almost 25 percent. We are now leaving the West Slope and plunging into the Gaps without which PRR could not have seized its predominance. We should mention that we have concentrated on the gentle upgrade mainline. The West Slope was also gentle downgrade. There may have been the odd runaway on this slope, but we have not found any examples.

Chapter 7

The Gaps

Johnstown to Torrance

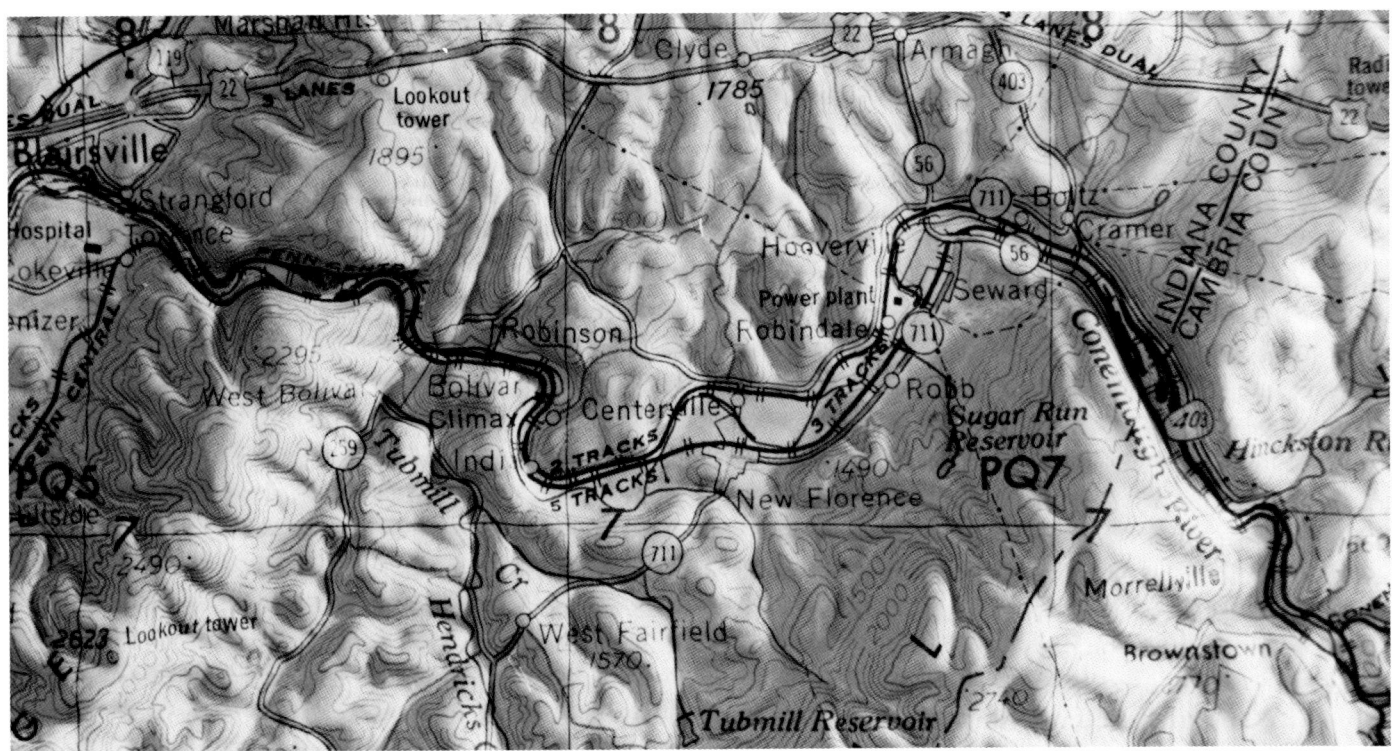

ONCE CLEAR of Johnstown and across the Conemaugh River over the Stone Bridge, PRR plunged into a gorge carved into Laurel Hill, crossed a weaving and bumpy valley and then entered another steep chasm in Chestnut Ridge. These twin gaps made possible both the Pennsylvania Canal's Western Division and PRR's mainline to Pittsburgh. To be sure, other routes were available to PRR but none were as practical as this one. The canal had no choice and traversed this sector on the north shore of the river with a slew of locks, dams and slackwater pools. PRR stayed on the south shore all the way through this region, at least initially. The meandering course of the Conemaugh River determined the route of both canal and railroad. This relief map shows at a glance that no deviation from the river valley was sensible, and none was ever attempted. Everyone had to be satisfied with the gift of the gaps, warts and all. The biggest gift was gradient. From Torrance (just under Blairsville at upper left) to Bolivar was actually downgrade for about three miles with percentages under 0.5%. From Bolivar east all the way to Conemaugh the climb was always under 0.5% and many sections were flat. PRR had to make considerable investments in grade modification, filling and curve reduction over a period of years to achieve this state of nirvana, but that the terrain allowed such improvements was a plus. The principal negatives had to do with the steepness of the sides of the gaps, particularly through Chestnut Ridge, and the circuitous path of the river as we shall see.

A handwritten, unsigned and undated letter was received in the office of PRR Lines West First Vice President James McCrea in Pittsburgh early in the month of November 1901. The writer of this epistle urged PRR to consider a wholly new mainline from somewhere in the vicinity of Latrobe, which lies west of Chestnut Ridge, straight through to Gallitzin and thence to Altoona. This proposed line would be low-grade and pass through lush coal fields.

Since no map was supplied, we must rely upon the writer's rather disjointed prose to determine the route he had in mind. There were references to slowly climbing the west side of Chestnut Ridge from Latrobe ("Latrobe is high ground") and somehow reaching the town of Ligonier (which lies about ten miles south of the Conemaugh River in the Ligonier Valley). Since Ligonier is southeast of Latrobe, one must assume that the writer was proposing a nine-mile long tunnel under Chestnut Ridge.

The writer's opening proposal was a marvel of clarity, however, compared to his plan for the route east of Ligonier. It was to parallel PRR's present mainline while at the same time reaching to the northwest on the west slope of Allegheny Mountain and doubling back to Altoona on the east side. "A dozen tunnels at Gallitzin would not decrease the grade on the Eastern Slope," he emphasized. Well, another nine-mile long tunnel just might do that little trick.

While he admitted that he had not trod his dream route "since boyhood," he was confident that "engineering science of the present day" would slay all dragons and reward PRR with a maximum grade of .95%, direction of movement unspecified. The writer signed-off by stating that it was "respectfully submitted" and that he was not "in any way interested as to property." The letter was written in a firm hand and all words were spelled correctly except for Gallitzin, which was both Gallitzin and Gallitzen. Since others had fumbled the spelling of the town, we cannot use this slight error as evidence of his mental state or sobriety.

Mr. McCrea promptly forward this proposal to Samuel Rea, then PRR First Vice President in Philadelphia, "for your information." Never one to lack a sense of humor, Mr. Rea passed the correspondence to Chief Engineer W.H. "Stone" Brown with the following memo: "It is quite evident this party has lost sight of the fact that he would have to cross Laurel Hill, one of the highest mountains in the state, by an immense tunnel, whereas our mainline goes through a gap." Actually, Laurel Hill would have been the *third* tunnel proposed. Mr. Brown filed the correspondence, where we found it almost a century later.

James McCrea became president of PRR from 1907 to 1913 followed by Samuel Rea 1913-1925, thus establishing that having a little fun with one another over a nutcase was not a bar to future promotion and that the "big tunnel" gene was not dead in Pennsylvania. The Gift of the Gaps was treasured and, indeed, Mr. Rea had played a role in exploiting them some twenty years earlier in 1881.

The passage of PRR through and between the gaps began in a most modest way. After some problems with bids, Thomson had the entire railroad from Johnstown to Pittsburgh under contract during 1850. The total distance was 86 miles and Thomson provided for a double-track roadbed for 62 of those miles. The railroad itself, however, was just single-track.

As we have seen, the 21 miles from Johnstown to Lockport (just east of Bolivar on the preceding map) was open 21 August 1851. The next 20 miles from Lockport to Beatty (the latter west of the western gap) was ready for traffic on 10 December 1851.

A second track from Blairsville Intersection (now Torrance) to Lockport was open for business in 1857. It would not be until 1862 when PRR, swollen with Civil War traffic, completed a second track from Lockport to Johnstown. Thus a gap within two gaps existed for five years, no doubt giving ulcers to operating people. And now a caveat to the reader regarding mileage. Over the years total mileage changed because of line relocation, curve reduction *et al* with the consequence of making it difficult to relate distance from one era to another. Broadly, the railroad from the Stone Bridge in Johnstown to Blairsville Intersection (Torrance) was 25 miles.

This 25 mile section of railroad, as vital as it was and is in PRR history, has languished in obscurity in comparison with the dramatic slopes to the east and the roller coaster entrance to Pittsburgh to the west.

For example, we and other historians have focused on PRR expansion from one to four mainline tracks and unfulfilled plans for several additional ones. Yet it ultimately took *six* mainline tracks to handle the volume through this area. By any standard, this was a lot of capacity for a trunkline located in semi-mountainous terrain blessed with an almost flat profile.

Why so many? Because the railroad from Milepost 275 in Johnstown and Milepost 300 in Blairsville

Intersection/Torrance was and is literally the throat of the busiest trunkline in history, in *both* directions.

We have regaled students of railroad history in this and other books that all trunklines were built for *eastbound* volume. We have also emphasized that Pittdiv was unique in that there was and is extremely heavy volume *originating* along the mainline. Big hunks of this local traffic, however, moved *west*.

The *traffic* Great Wave changed at Johnstown. For example, in 1948 there was a daily average of 72 freight trains with 5,144 cars (average 71.4 cars per train) moving *east* from Johnstown to South Fork. Coming *into* Johnstown from the west were 38 trains with 2,674 cars (average 70 cars per train). This means that there were 34 *eastbound* trains with 2,470 cars *originating* at Johnstown.

Moving *west* from Johnstown, however, there were 40 trains with 2,966 cars (average 74 cars per train). In other words, there was more traffic going *west* from Johnstown than coming east *into* Johnstown.

No wonder PRR operating men were cranky. No wonder PRR needed six tracks through "gap" territory. Incidentally, this need for six tracks continued all the way west through Pittsburgh to Conway Yard, as we shall see.

These figures include empties but do *not* include 34 passenger trains a day in each direction from Altoona through Torrance.

Later in this book we will present a schematic diagram detailing all these movements, but the essence of the story is that the traffic world changed at Johnstown.

The expansion from two tracks to six is a long and somewhat complicated story that we will relate in captions to maps later in this chapter. In general, expansion began in 1881 and was completed c. 1907. Contraction began in 1954 and was concluded c. 1980.

The reader should be warned that the history of the gaps is unusual in another sense. Placenames changed over time with confusing frequency and most of this evolution was caused by the dominance and then decline of the canal through this terrain. PRR ultimately built railroads over much of the canal bed. Towns prospered and declined accordingly.

We should note that while the State Works was a financial and transportation disaster within a calamity, the canal from Johnstown to Pittsburgh did play a significant role in Pittsburgh's industrial development, albeit at very high cost. Abundant raw materials in the region we are now entering were floated downhill to Pittsburgh with at least a semblance of efficiency and this "subsidy" proved helpful to Pittsburgh interests as well as encouraging development along the route.

The first gap was through Laurel Hill just west of Johnstown and while the slopes were steep and the flood plain narrow, there were many creeks flowing into the Conemaugh River which could be used as transportation arteries of a sort. Also, large deposits of raw materials could be reached directly from the river itself. The coming of PRR made these processes even more efficient and as a result the Laurel Hill gap became a center of industry.

The famous "12 mile" sign alongside PRR proclaimed to all observers that the shores along the river line from Conemaugh west to Sang Hollow were full of major industrial facilities.

Once out of Laurel Hill gap and into the Ligonier Valley, the nature of the terrain changed rather abruptly. There were few workable deposits of consequence along the river or south of it. For some reason, Mother Nature surrounded this sector with lush raw materials but did not deign to place any in the immediate area. Thus no branch lines sprouted from PRR in the valley and it became a traffic conduit for the canal and PRR rather than a source.

It is almost as if Mother Nature had decided that she had been generous enough for mankind in Pennsylvania and wanted to preserve at least some pristine landscape. She would provide a path, but not a playground. The result is a lovely and peaceful region with much charm and scenic beauty.

Her generosity, or capriciousness if you will, extended to the western gap through Chestnut Ridge. Here she made the slopes so steep that exploitation was impossible and, indeed, both the railroad and the canal had difficulty creating a path through this dark and somewhat malevolent gorge.

We suspect that PRR management was never upset over this paucity of local traffic. They had more than enough difficulty handling the traffic being offered to them without even more from this valley.

The reader should recall that our Indian forebears did not use either of the gaps or the valley for a trail. For whatever reasons, they decided to stay out. PRR has been there for a century and a half. Nothing untoward has happened.

The future, of course, is a very, very long time.

TRIUMPH I

THE GAP through Laurel Hill enabled man to reach massive, though finite, raw materials such as iron ore, limestone, fire clay, sandstone and some coal. Wood was abundant and reachable, so the early iron furnaces such as this one used charcoal for smelting.

WATER AND WOOD were essential ingredients for industrial development. It took about an acre of forest to supply one blast furnace with charcoal for just one day, so ironmongers had to reach ever outward until the 1880s when the original forests were swept clean. This is a waterwheel saw mill, soon to be replaced by steam power.

FROM COAL TO COKE, then to iron and steel, the Conemaugh Gap as it became known seemed to have it all. The inclined plane at upper left was probably for movement of coal. This is a c.1875 depiction, so this plane is probably not the one known to have existed c.1900 to bring sandstone to PRR for ballast.

THE GAPS

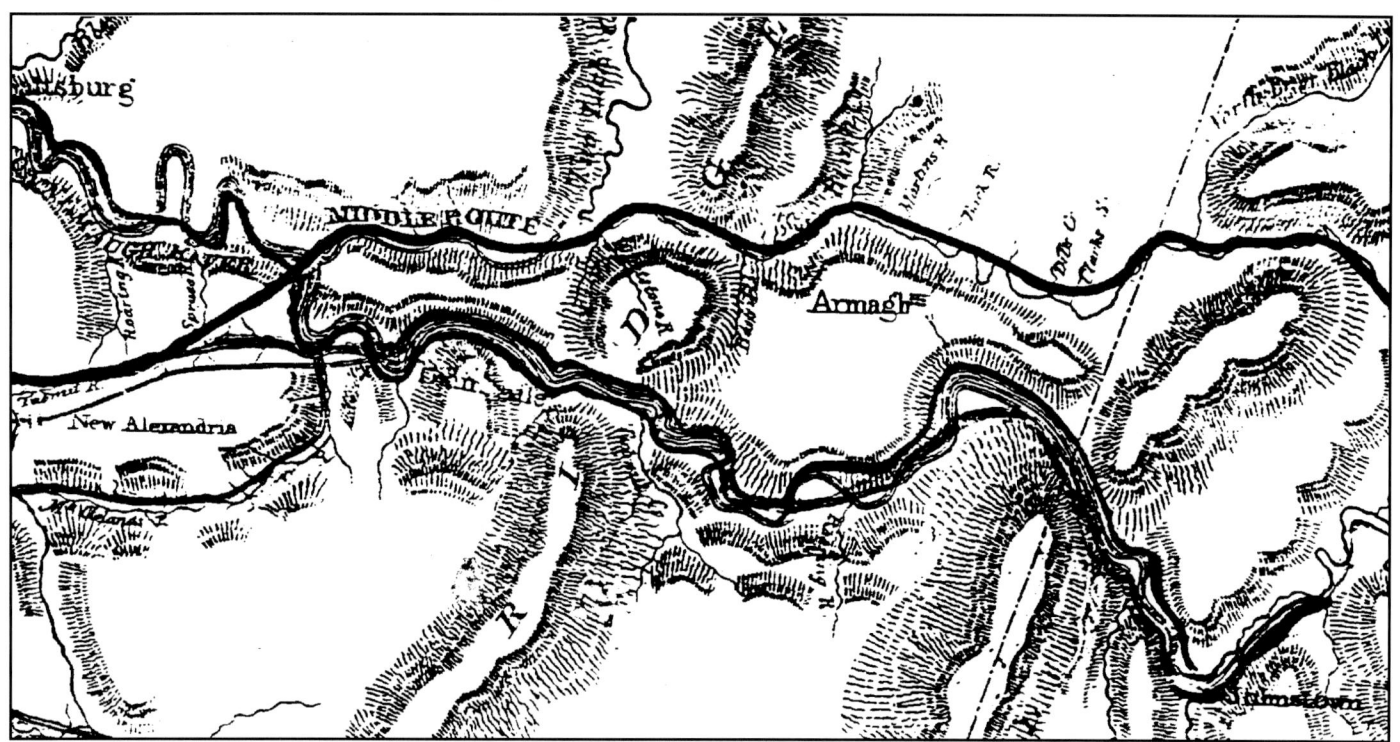

SCHLATTER presented a choice of two routes between and through gap territory as seen here. Since the canal was in existence along the north shore of the river, we assume he was proposing that it be replaced. The "middle route" across the top has, of course, been treated earlier in this book. The southern part of the huge "Reynoldsville Region" coal seam rests underneath this route, which explains why PRR reached into this area with a branch, and ultimately a through-route, in the very early days.

BY 1855, with PRR completed, familiar placenames were beginning to appear along the route. Conemaugh Furnace is seen at the western exit from the Laurel Hill gap, so named because a blast furnace has been functioning there for three years. Population was already at 500. Nineveh was merely a wood and water station for PRR at this time, and would ultimately disappear as a town. New Florence was strictly a railroad town and another wood and water station. Centreville, across the river from New Florence, boomed with the canal and would die with it. Lockport, created by the canal, was at least on the PRR side of the river and boasted a cut stone canal aqueduct. Just north of Lockport was a six-foot vein of coal which turned out to be a fringe source. Bolivar, at the eastern entrance to the Chesnut (sic) Ridge gap, had a fire-brick manufactory at this time. Inside the gap "Pack Saddle Mountain" was mentioned. Blairsville Intersection already had this name even though shown as "Blairsville Branch" on this map. The

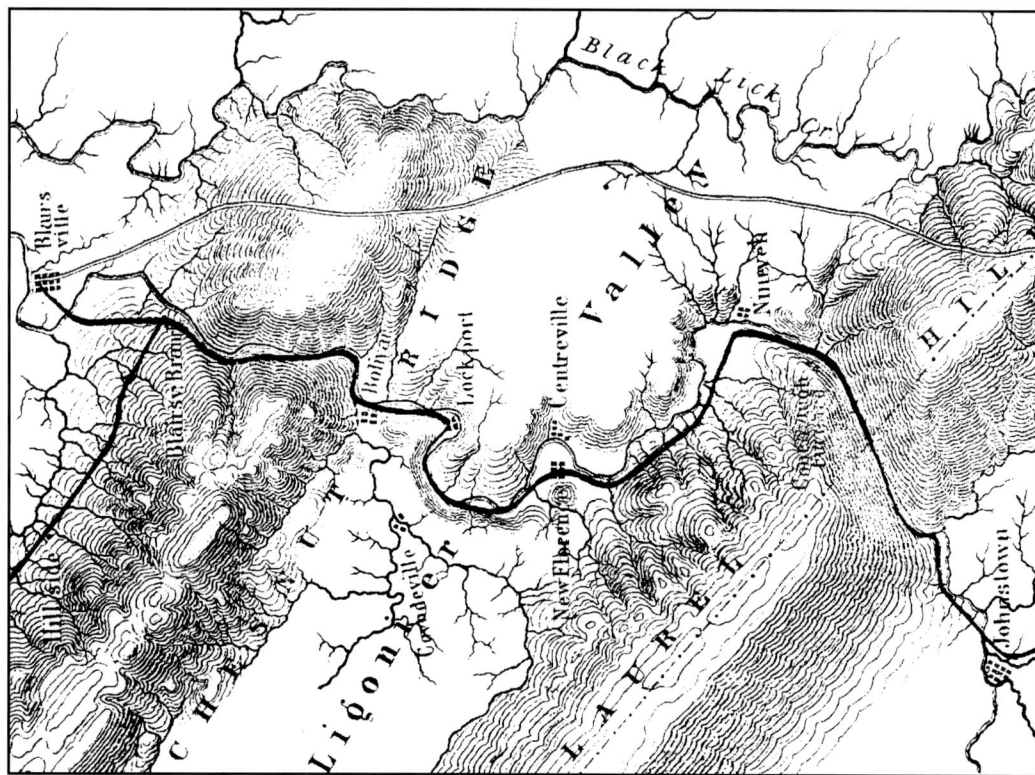

PRR mainline swings southwesterly once through the gap, with only a short branch to Blairsville to hint of future growth. The Conemaugh River now flows northwesterly, away from the original PRR mainline.

TRIUMPH I

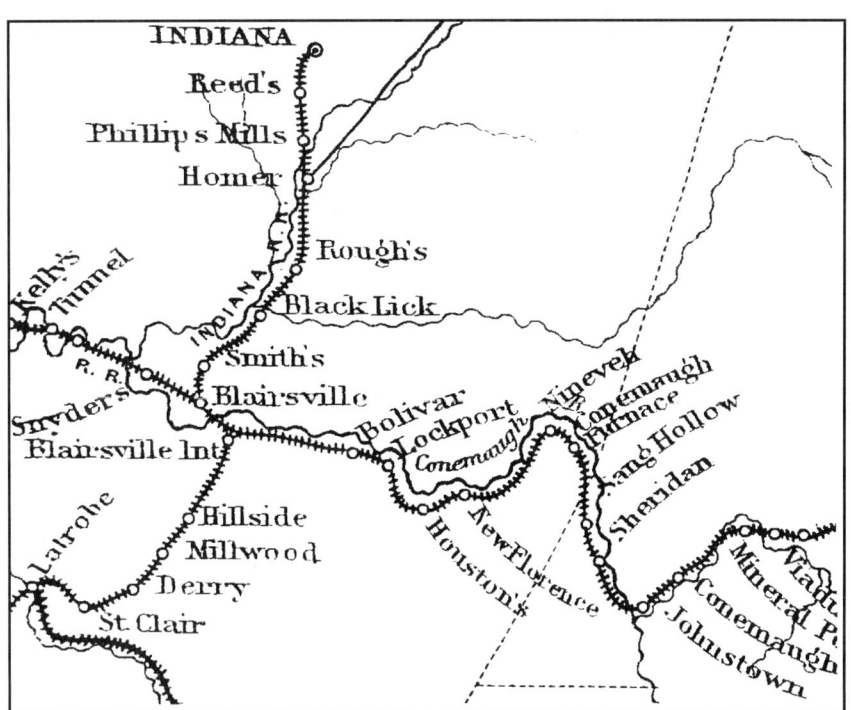

BY 1875, some new placenames were appearing. The most significant in PRR history is Sang Hollow inside the Laurel Hill (Conemaugh) Gap. At the other end, Blairsville Intersection is properly named. These two points would ultimately become important in the evolution of PRR in this area. Note the Indiana Branch at upper left. Opened 9 June 1856, this 16-mile line and its offshoots would pour countless tons of traffic onto the mainline. The railroad following the Conemaugh River northwesterly from Blairsville at left would become known as the Conemaugh Division. At lower left the mainline to Pittsburgh appears, as does a branch from Latrobe. All three of these lines would inundate the stretch between Blairsville Intersection and Sang Hollow with eastbound traffic, and the Johnstown complex combined with tonnage coming down the West Slope would do the same in the other direction. By the late 1870s the problem was crying for solution.

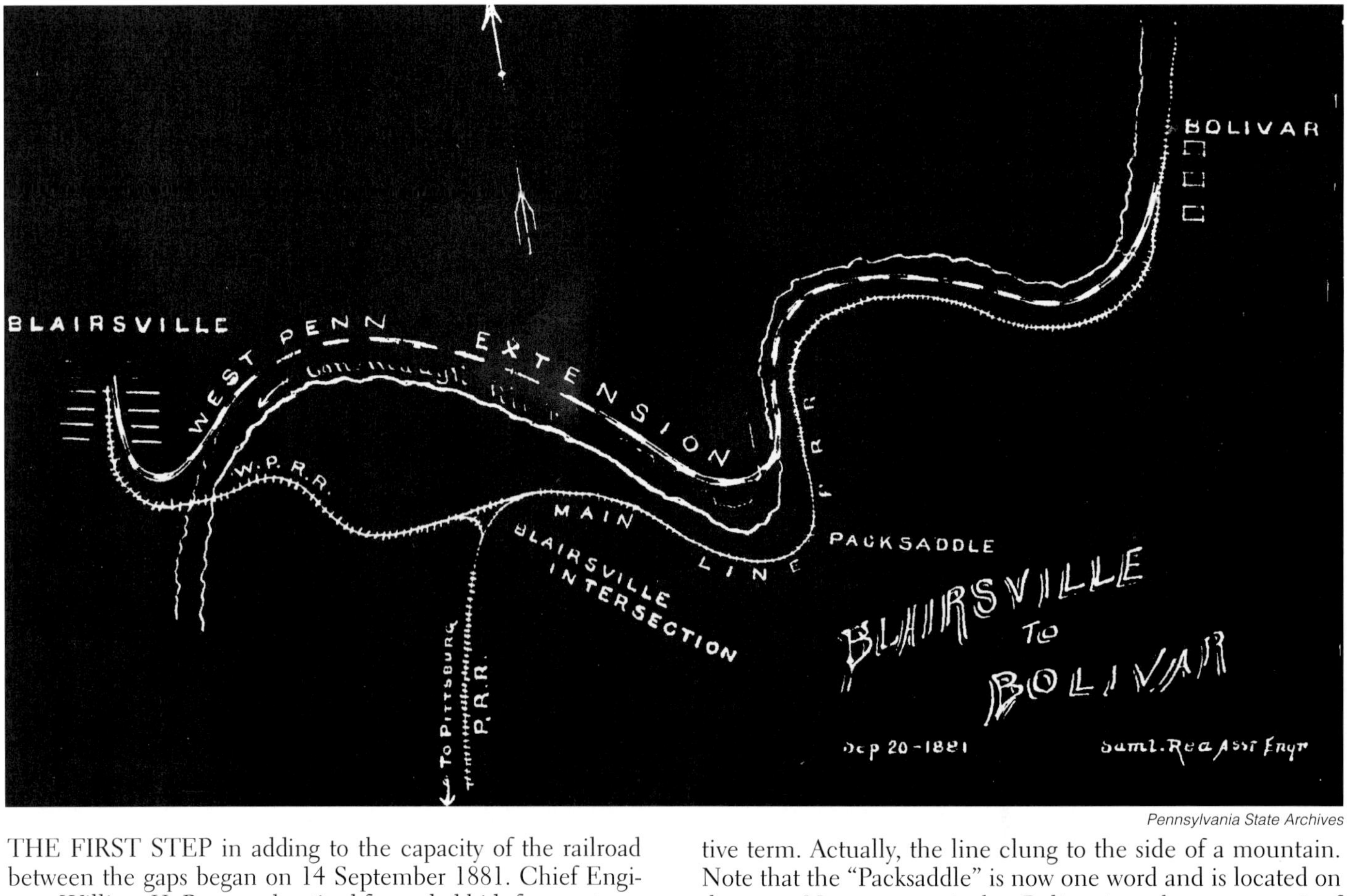

Pennsylvania State Archives

THE FIRST STEP in adding to the capacity of the railroad between the gaps began on 14 September 1881. Chief Engineer William H. Brown advertised for sealed bids for construction of a single-track "West Penn Extension" as shown here. The railroad from Blairsville to the Allegheny River to the northwest was known until early in this century as the West Pennsylvania Railroad, or West Penn...hence the name. It was, of course, controlled by PRR. This was the first rail line built on the north shore of the Conemaugh River, although considering the steepness of the slope through this gap, "shore" is a relative term. Actually, the line clung to the side of a mountain. Note that the "Packsaddle" is now one word and is located on the map. Not apparent is that Bolivar is at the eastern exit of the gap. The terrain between Blairsville and Bolivar is sheer and savage, as we shall see. This map was signed by Samuel Rea as assistant engineer. Construction of this line was apparently a testing ground for aspiring engineers. As his subsequent career showed, Mr. Rea was up to the challenge. This extension was opened 1 October 1883. By adding 12 miles to the West Penn, the grade was reduced from .99% to .40%.

THE GAPS

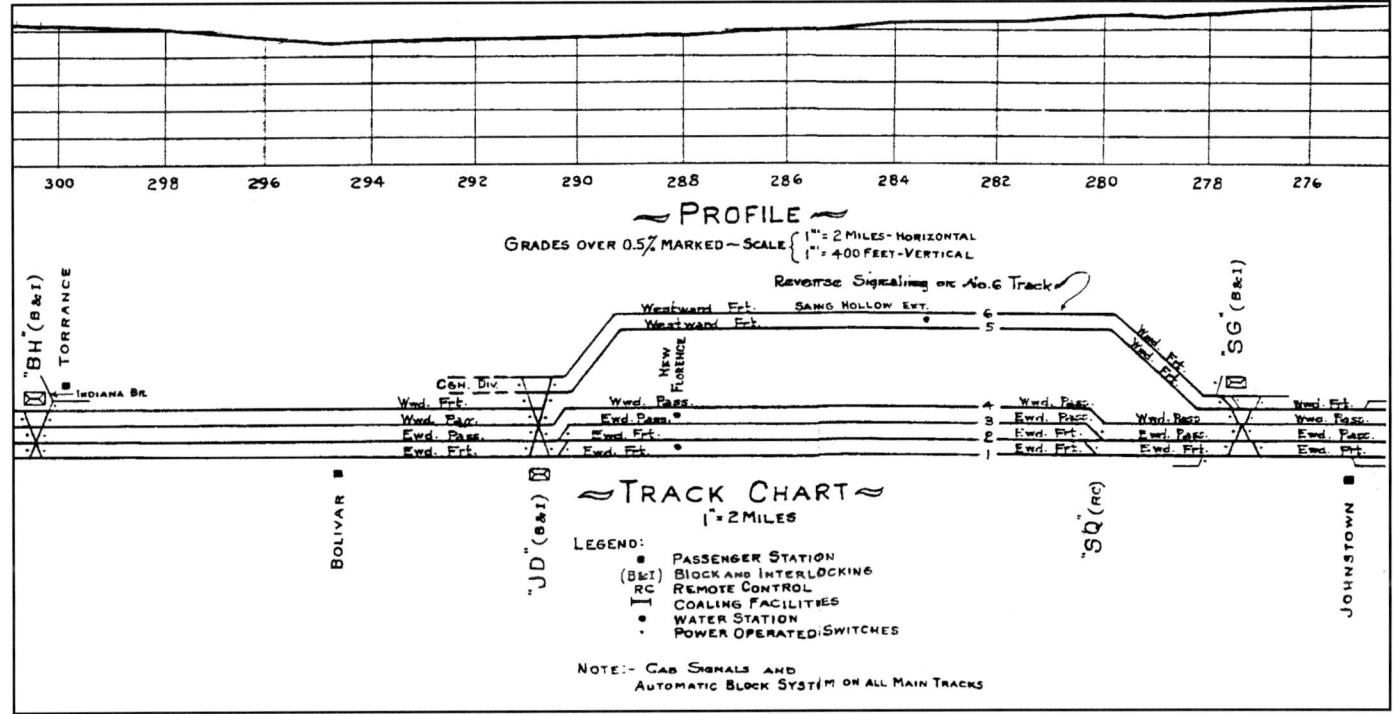

THE FINAL SOLUTION to the gap problem was six tracks, four south of the river and two north. This track chart is dated 1 July 1945, but that is misleading because almost all of the improvements were in place by 1910 and most of them were completed in the years 1895 to 1907. Amusing at least to this author, PRR did not have to assign a Zero Track since the expansion was northward. A few notes and comments: BH/Torrance is the old Blairsville Intersection; JD is Conpitt Junction; SG is Sang Hollow; the Sang Hollow Extension runs from JD to SG; the West Penn Railroad became the West Penn Division and then the Conemaugh Division by 1907. There were only three interlockers with towers and one remote (SQ) in 1945, but there were a lot more in 1910. From Johnstown west, there was SX (later SG), RU and DP on the Sang Hollow Extension and SX/SG, SQ, NR, VK, JD, VY, IJ and BH on the "mainline." SX/SG, JD and BH, of course, served both the extension and mainline. The Conemaugh Division/Sang Hollow Extension crossed the river only at Sang Hollow. Major realignments on the mainline, however, involved crossing the river at two points: Lockport and between Conpitt Junction and New Florence. The bridges required for the latter were completed c.1907. Track No. 4 was the first to go, in 1954. We are unsure when the Sang Hollow Extension was reduced to one track and the mainline to two, but believe it was circa 1981. Today the mainline is Track Nos. 1 and 2; the extension is Track No. 3. Between Conpitt Junction and Sang Hollow, both lines are at about the same level. West of Conpitt Junction, however, the Conemaugh Division and mainline rails follow different elevations.

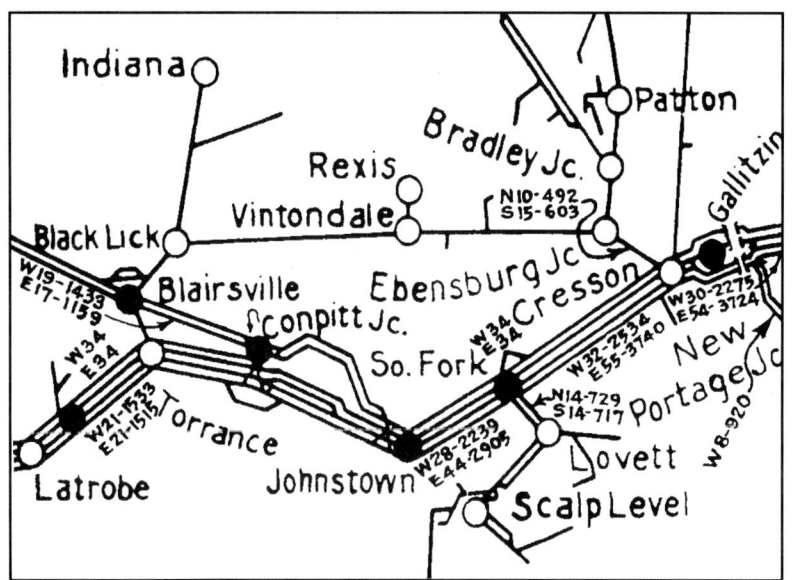

WE HAVE EXTRACTED some data from this PRR traffic-flow diagram done in June of 1948 and present the whole scene for the benefit of those who desire more precise detail. These dry statistics tell a story that is wondrous to behold. They are the average *daily* movements of trains and cars east and west (E and W) and north and south (N and S) through the area covered by this and the last chapter. W34 and E34 refer to passenger trains. The larger numbers record freight trains and cars, including empties. In 1948, and for many prior years, there were *six* mainline tracks available to PRR east of Gallitzin and west of Johnstown. The West Slope has "only" four tracks. No wonder a fifth Zero Track was considered earlier in the century. The reader can spend days dissecting and interpreting these numbers as the author has done. We offer our conclusions. The operational and engineering skill required to handle such diverse and monumental volume is in and of itself a tribute to PRR management prowess. The organizational basis for this accomplishment can be traced to Thomson's genius. It was he who installed the first line and staff structure on PRR, not hesitating to borrow from military experience and adapting it to the peculiar needs of a railroad. When we say "first," by the way, we mean the first on *any* railroad and *any* corporation in history. Thomson's mind was *open*, a characteristic all too rare in leaders of any kind, and it was this liberality in thought and willingness to take bold action that makes him such a commanding figure in national history. He was an early practitioner of a philosophy that would later be promulgated by the very army from which he borrowed. "If it works, it is right; if it does not work, it is wrong." Thomson was also open in praise. Note the town of Latrobe at lower left. We shall see an example of his generosity in the naming of this locale in the next chapter.

ONCE OUT OF JOHNSTOWN and into the Conemaugh Gap on the south shore, PRR passed through the industrial town of Morrellville. Here, on 29 December 1983, we see the westbound Amtrak *Pennsylvanian* accelerating with only three cars in tow. A far cry from the 34 trains a day in 1948, most of significantly greater length.

Thomas A. Biery

TO SPARE the reader some puzzlement, we are presenting this 1910 track chart to show the layout as it existed between Mileposts 275 and 281. As far as PRR was concerned, this six-mile stretch was known as Sheridan. Hence SX and SQ. Sang Hollow *per se* was merely a track pan location as we shall show. It was at SX where six tracks went to four with attendant operating complications. The two top tracks are the Sang Hollow Extension; the bottom three or four the original mainline. The latter was reduced to three at SQ and the extension to one at RU. The extension track crossed the river just east of RU. Later a second track for the extension crossed the river and SX was changed to SG. Some of the trackage for the extension in this area was purchased from Cambria Iron Company. An interesting letter dated 14 October 1890 from Cambria to "Stone" Brown discussed this transfer and the construction of the yard next to SX. Cambria was applauding the low-grade extension project because "all our ores from the west, which is the largest single item of our tonnage" would be handled with more efficiency. By the way, the names at the top of this chart are those of track supervisors for the section shown. William Johns covered the two miles between Mileposts 277 and 279. Was he related to the founding father of Johnstown?

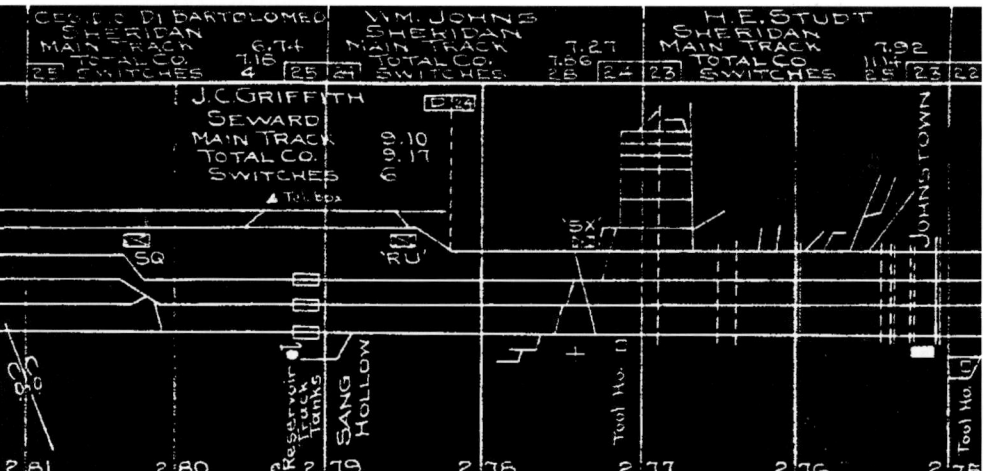

Frank Wrabel Collection

THE GAPS

Railroad Museum of Pennsylvania

AS WITH SO MANY developments in railroad history, the idea of the track pan occurred in Great Britain. John Ramsbottom, a superintendent for a British railway, designed, patented and installed the first such facility in 1860. Judging by his surname, his posterior must have been as prodigious as his imagination. Never one to pass a good idea, PRR placed its first such installation at Sang Hollow by November of 1870 as seen here. Many more, of course, would follow. The pans were 19 inches wide; the westbound pan was 800 feet long and the eastbound 1,200 feet. This view is looking west. Whether Mr. Ramsbottom received any patent royalties is unknown, but we doubt it. The tower at Sang Hollow can be faintly seen against the hillside at the end of the tangent. Also note the island in the middle of the river.

THE JOHNSTOWN FLOOD did not spare the valley west of the Stone Bridge. SX tower was spared, but not the railroad itself. This photograph must have been taken shortly after the flood waters receded because relief crews from the west were desperate to open the railroad into Johnstown and, as one can see, their work was cut out for them.

*Charles J. Burggraf
Johnstown Area Heritage Association*

251

TRIUMPH I

Hagley Museum and Library

THIS PHOTOGRAPH is supposed to have been taken in 1908-09 to record a pipe experiment of some sort. These pans were extended to 1,800 feet, probably in 1886. The water level was only six inches deep in these and all other pans on Pittdiv. At Sang Hollow all three tracks were served. The width did not provide a sufficient volume of water for following trains and by 1920 locomotives were forced to take water from standpipes at Conemaugh and New Florence (to the west). The engineers acted with commendable dispatch and the pans on Tracks 2 and 3 were widened to 29 inches. (Track 1 had been done in 1915.) Work started 6 August 1920 and was completed by 13 September. On 7 December, however, J.A. McCrea (then a vice president) noted in a sarcastic letter that no authority for this and other expenditures that year had been authorized by him as required. While he had a sense of humor with nutcases, this omission did not strike him as being amusing since the grand total was $48,478 for eight different projects. Perhaps he suggested that this amount could be deducted from the pay of the offenders, a little bit each month until the end of time. Perhaps the guilty considered tearing out the improvements, but then that would involve still more unauthorized expenditure. In any event, the Board of Directors approved the improvements at their meeting on 26 January 1921 some four months after actual completion, oblivious to the facts as are most directors in all institutions in all times. As to nutcases, the Sang Hollow pans attracted an anonymous letter in 1934, this time to President W. W. Atterbury. It seems that abandonment of the pans was under active consideration in the early 1930s and for good reason. The water for the pans was always pumped up from the Conemaugh River and required expensive treatment as well as a large staff to operate the facility. Also, longer tenders with greater tank capacity were in use and fewer trains required a drink at Sang Hollow. Apparently the writer was a disgruntled employee who, to quote from an internal memo, had "interests other than the best interests of PRR in mind." The problem with this sort of communication is that it triggers an avalanche of studies, memos and justifications that soak up management time. To the historian, however, files of this type give a fascinating insight into the situation at a given point in time and this one was no exception. Keeping in mind that 1934 was a depression year, it seems that a "daily passing-point average" of 4,852 cars, or 74% of the average for the year 1929, went by Sang Hollow eastbound! Management closed the pans for a week in November of 1933 and found that of 168 eastbound trains only 16 had to take water at standpipes at New Florence (west of Sang Hollow.) To be sure, tenders were checked at Conemaugh and eight of the engines had less than one foot of water, two of which had four inches. This was cutting it a little thin, so management decided to lengthen the pans at Saxman (just east of Latrobe and west of Torrance) to solve the problem. The pans at Saxman, and Wilmore on the West Slope, were automatic facilities which operated without attendants. A further check established that in a 24-hour period the standpipes at New Florence pumped only 6,000 gallons of water and that was for local freights, work trains, and an occasional through-freight that got into trouble. It was necessary to add tenders "larger than 7,000 gallons" to 15 K4 locomotives on Pittdiv to effect this change. On 7 December 1934 the pans at Sang Hollow were withdrawn from service. Two standpipes were installed adjacent to Tracks 1 and 3, served by a 50,000-gallon water tank which in turn was fed from a spring. Even these standpipes were gone by 1945. The salvaged parts were sent west to Saxman. Anonymous letters, of course, are part of life. The sensible procedure is to file them without comment and on this count Atterbury gets low marks.

THE GAPS

AN HISTORIANS LOT is not a happy one. We offer this c.1920 valuation photograph as an example. Notice that there are *two* sets of call letters. SG and SQ. Some things are just not done. You do not have two locomotives with the same number nor do you have one tower with two sets of letters facing the same trackage. We *know* that a new interlocker was built at Sheridan in 1899. We *know* it carried the call letters SX at least through 1910. We *know* SQ interlocker was built in 1888 and a new one in 1908 and an additional crossover was installed in 1918. We *know* SQ was three miles west of SX. We *know* that SX was changed to SG, although we do not know exactly when. We *know* that SQ was in such an isolated area that operators had to travel by train to reach it. We *know* that SQ was closed in 1931 and made remote from what was then SG. We *know* all this because we have read the bloody correspondence! Why, then, in c.1920 were there two sets of call letters on the same tower? We *know* this is the case because we are looking at the photograph right here on this page. Why? Because the valuation photographer made a double exposure.

National Archives

SG DID NOT have an identity crisis on 7 September 1968. The call letters were safely ensconced inside a PRR keystone and while the PC merger was in effect at this date, word had not gotten down to this tower. Not that anyone really cared. They were too busy moving trains and conducting the on-going battles among enginemen, trainmen and dispatchers, each with their own conflicting agendas. Only on one thing did all agree. They were led by idiots, all of whom would have difficulty finding their way to a restroom without a seeing-eye dog. Only an historian like your author, who has studied other trunkline railroads, would be able to explain to them that their middle operating management was probably the best of a very bad lot. This view is looking easterly with the Conemaugh River just behind the tower. SG was closed in the mid-1980s. Before we leave SG, we should point out that PRR expended millions of dollars raising the mainline between SG and Conemaugh. We have already referred to this project in regard to the Johnstown Station area and want to emphasize that this line-raising was necessary all the way to SG, in some cases being as much as ten feet above the old roadbed. Slag was used for fill. This project was initiated in 1909 and was not completed until the mid-teens. The problem was the grade between SG and Conemaugh, which required helpers between the two points to assist eastbound trains. The end result was a 0.30% compensated grade, which enabled material in-

Edward H. Weber

creases in tonnage per train as far west as Pittsburgh. Early planning even considered a jumpover at SG, but this was found to be impractical. Only the immense volume moved on PRR made improvements of this nature economical and adequate return-on-investment possible. From its very earliest days through to modern times, PRR was volume oriented. Sufficient volume reinforced the economic realities of railroad transportation and a large investment on just this little three-mile stretch paid off.

TRIUMPH I

SIX MILES WEST of SG on the Sang Hollow Extension, and mid-way to Conpitt Junction, DP tower held sway. It is seen here c.1920. There were two short coal mine sidings at DP and it is a measure of the complexity of PRR operations that a general manager had to write "Stone" Brown on 9 June 1900 asking who owned the sidings and who was responsible for their maintenance.

National Archives

NR TOWER was about three miles west of SQ and is seen here c.1920, snug against the hillside. It was located just across the river from DP but, of course, on the mainline. We have seen another photograph of NR probably taken c.1890 which shows the tower on the river side and on a curve. At one time or another but no later than 1910 it was moved to the hillside and, as can be seen, on tangent. The structure itself appears to be the same. NR was apparently somewhat redundant because it was closed in November of 1923 and had been in only temporary use for the prior two or three years. In 1924 NR was abandoned.

National Archives

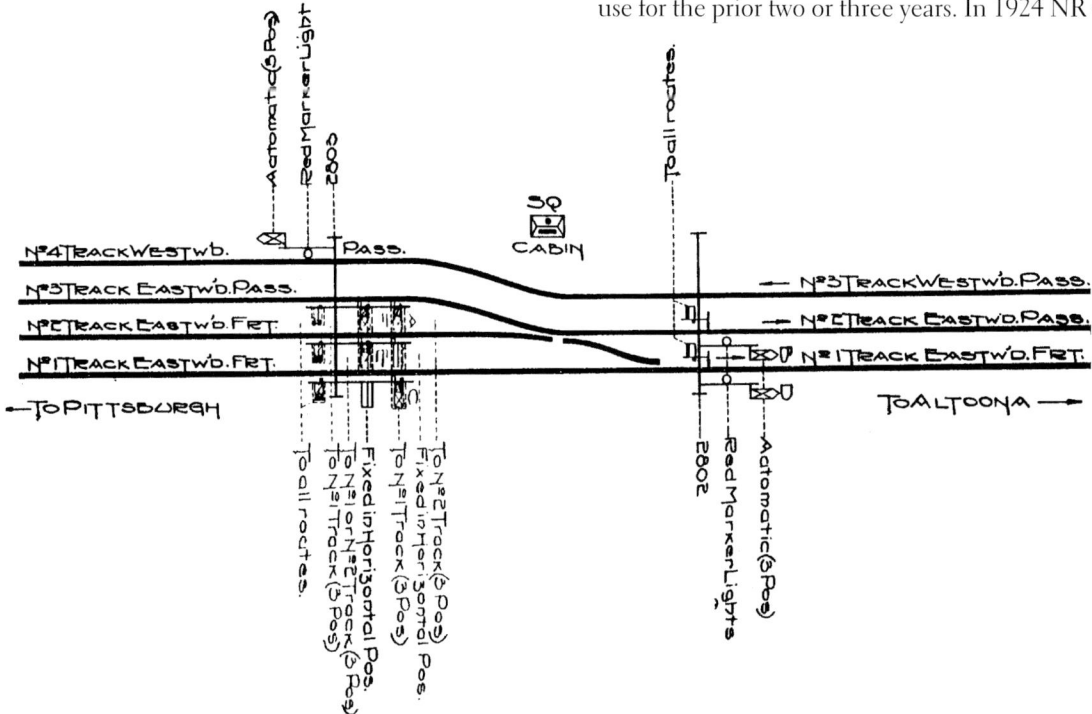

CHANGES IN SIGNALS triggered this 1912 rendition of the SQ block and interlocking station. The third track from Sang Hollow through to Nineveh to the west was completed as early as 1883 and the fourth track in October of 1907. The information about these changes was made in Pittsburgh Division General Order No. 53 dated 23 November 1912. We have already discussed the similarity between military and railroad operations and the use of the title *General Order* is pertinent. Both railroads and armies have general orders, special orders, morning reports and other similar ways of dealing with administrative details. The devil is always in the details and the promulgation of vital information to and from the field. Thus all railroads, of necessity, became paramilitary organizations because their operations are similar in so many ways. It was absolutely essential that *everyone* know that the signals at SQ had been changed. For those with military experience, the expression that there is always some poor soul who didn't "get the word" is full of dire meaning. If this were to happen at SQ, a collision could result. In the military, equal unpleasantness is the result and your author is speaking from bitter personal experience where his and, more importantly, his soldiers' lives were at stake.

THE GAPS

IN 1875, SANG HOLLOW was described as follows: "Immediately surrounding this station the scenery is picturesque and beautiful. Added to the grandeur of the mountains is the dense vegetation of the river valley, giving almost a tropical luxurance to the view." We have seen this little island earlier in this chapter and, according to geodetic maps, it still exists. It has witnessed lonely wilderness, floods, industrialization and now reversion to nature. Perhaps it will be eternal.

WE GAZED down the valley of the Conemaugh River at about the location of that little island in the Spring of 1995 and took this photograph from a roadside overlook. We had dined well in Johnstown the night before (much to our surprise) and had noted during that meal that many of the ladies of the town were quite capable of both style and class in their apparel and bearing (also to our surprise, which speaks to the inherent snobbery of a cavalier Marylander more than it does to the residents of this interesting region who have endured so much for so long with much dignity). Only moments before we had paused at the Stone Bridge memorial park and consequently we were melancholy. Yet this peaceful vista worked its magic. Almost all the land in the gap is now public and returning to forest, albeit with second growth. Both the mainline and the extension are still in place and, indeed, the forest is now beginning to grow over the tracks and create a "green tunnel." The commerce of the nation still flows and, in the case of modern railroading, in the most environmentally friendly way. High in the sky we noted a jet's contrail slowly dissipating, carrying those passengers who no longer ride through the gap. For a brief moment, all seemed right with the world.

Bob Jansen Collection

ONCE FREE of the Laurel Hill Gap, PRR wandered through a string of small towns, some of which changed names over the years. Conemaugh Furnace was overgrown with foliage by 1875. Nineveh as a name disappeared and was replaced by two towns, Seward south of the mainline and Hooverville north of it. The next town of note was New Florence, which itself went through two name changes. It was New Florence in 1855, then just plain Florence in 1875 and back to New Florence by the late 1800s. It seems that Italian immigrants were early settlers, hence the name. New Florence is on the south shore of the river opposite Centreville, the latter a canal town. There is still a Centreville today, but it is the location of a large power plant and little else. New Florence was strictly a PRR town, entirely built up by the railroad. We know that in 1860 a frame enginehouse was built to hold a supervisor's personal locomotive; in 1896 a new interlocker was installed (gone by 1910) and in 1917 a new overhead water bridge served all four tracks. This postcard view, which is looking westerly, vaguely shows the New Florence station/dwelling on the right which was built in 1850. Correspondence between "Stone" Brown and Robert Pitcairn dated 26 June 1893 shows that the structure was moved to make room for Track No. 4 and, interestingly, a new enginehouse was to be built well away from Track No. 1 to make room for a planned Zero Track. Of course, the latter was never built.

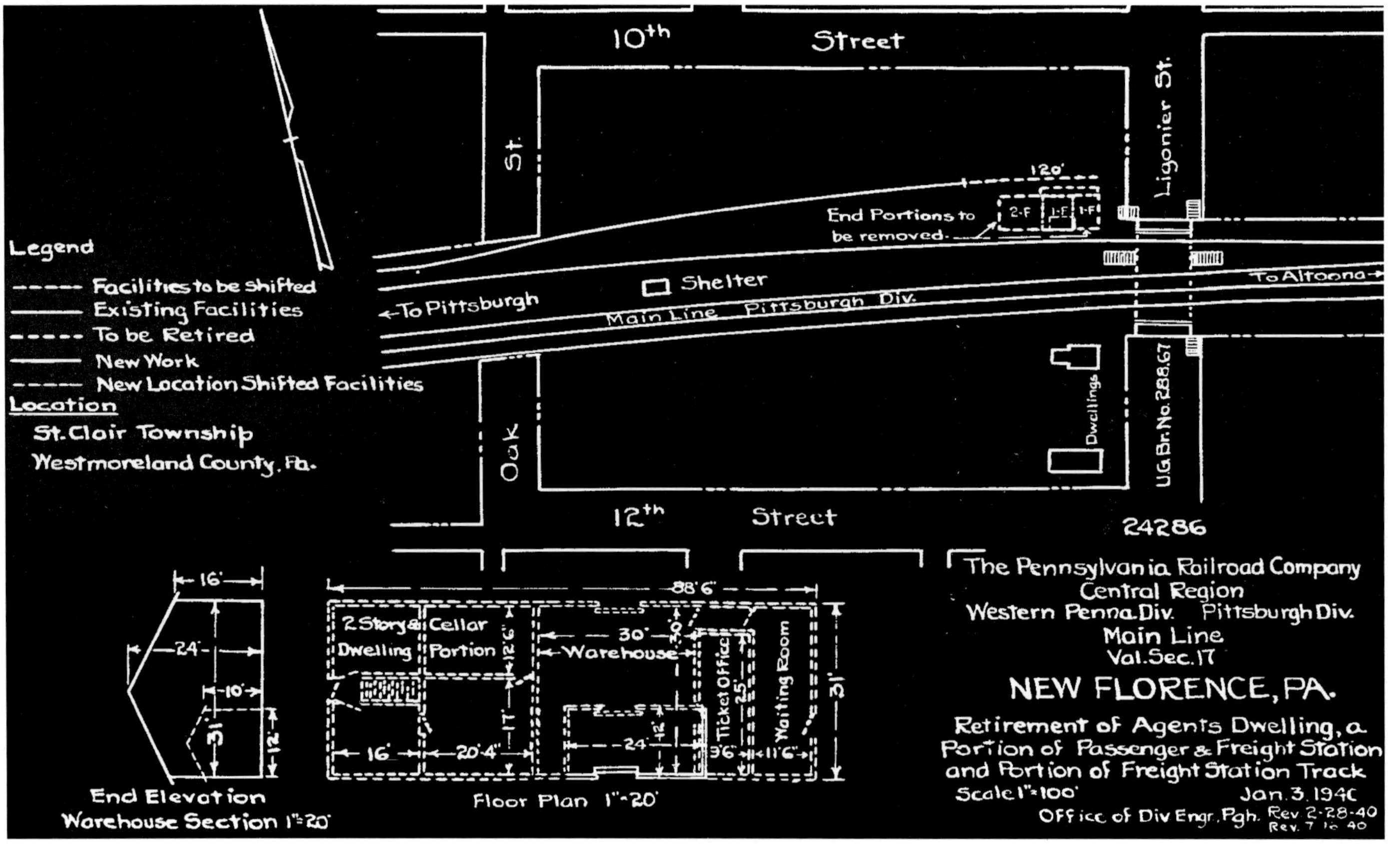

THE LIGONIER STREET underpass was built in New Florence in 1924 and the station/dwelling was raised and remodeled in that year in conjunction with that project. We have a 1920 valuation photograph of the building, too poor to reproduce here. The plan of the structure is shown on this map, which was obviously prepared in 1940 to support closing. Oddly, the correspondence states that the station's birthday was 1850 and 1868 in the same file. We suspect the earlier date is correct.

THE GAPS

HERE IS THE POWER PLANT at Centreville, seen 3 May 1995. The railroad running to the left of the giant towers and curving off to the left is the Sang Hollow Extension. The railroad running straight from upper right to upper left is the mainline. The Conemaugh River, a bit muddy this day, separates the two lines. We are about to visit Conpitt Junction which is to the rear of the photographer.

Michael Smith/Aerial Views

THE FAMOUS Conpitt Junction (JD) can be seen in the middle of this 1958 track chart which we are using because it shows the relationship between various points with more clarity than earlier ones. Track No. 4 was gone by this date, but the water bridge at New Florence was still in place. The mainline originally stayed south of the river, but it was through this area that PRR crossed the river twice in the early 1900s to both shorten the line and eliminate curvature. Earlier in this chapter we reported that the West Penn Extension crossed to the south bank at Bolivar (which lies about four miles west of JD) and joined the mainline at Bolivar Junction. The Sang Hollow Extension by name ran from SX/SG to Bolivar Junction. By 1906 PRR management decided that Bolivar Junction was not the best place for an interlocker and, in short, it was decided to build a new plant at Conpitt Junction. JD, a 35-lever electro-pneumatic facility, opened in 1908 at about the same time that double-tracking of the West Penn Extension *west* of Bolivar was completed. Electric power was supplied from a pumping plant in Lockport. Regarding mileposts, it was PRR practice to retain original milepost designations even though the distance had frequently become less than a mile. The reader should examine the numbers and distances at the top of this chart for examples of this dastardly practice which has caused so much pain to meticulous historians.

TRIUMPH I

Edward H. Weber

JD WAS STILL JD on 7 September 1968 even though the name of the railroad had changed. This is a westward view. The tower structure is original but, of course, it is resplendent in new siding

THE ORIGINAL JD as it appeared c.1920 in a valuation photograph. It is interesting that PRR was still using this standard tower plan as late as 1908.

National Archives

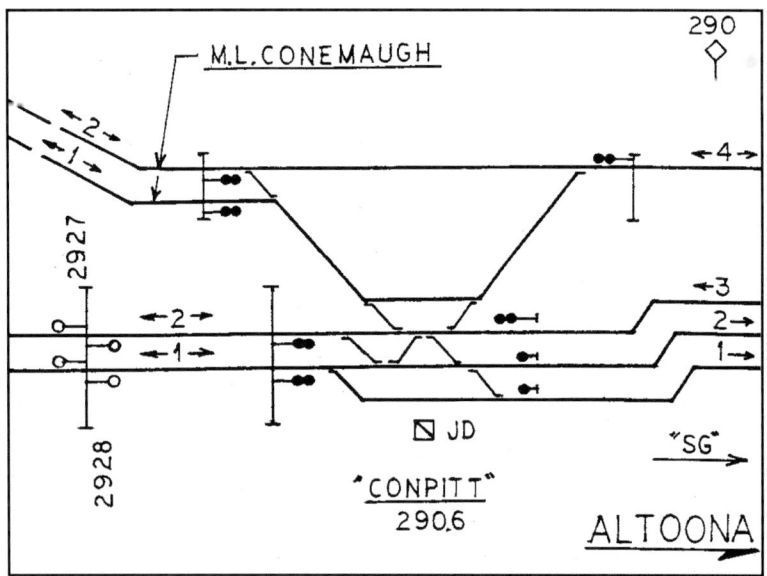

THE PLANT AT JD on 1 December 1980 still carries the name Conpitt with two "ts." Actually, when Conrail installed CTC on major portions of Pittdiv with federal money in the 1970s, call letters were changed to names effective in March of 1978 and the initials CP (for Controlled Point) came into use. Thus in 1980 this was really CP Conpit.

ONLY RELAY BOXES remained at Conpitt Junction on 7 May 1995 as an eastbounder rolls into view on the mainline. The signals are now of New York Central searchlight configuration, an irritating fact of life for oldtime PRR people who lived with the idea that God intended signals to be position lights. NYC did not lose them all.

THE GAPS

Blair County Historical Society

LOCKPORT, the reader will recall, was the westernmost terminal on PRR when Schedule No. 1 was issued effective 31 August 1851. This fascinating structure was built as a canal terminal and then became PRR's terminal. We have seen another earlier photograph (too poor to reproduce here) which shows PRR's single track right next to the building as is Track No. 3 in this c.1890s view. This building burned down c.1924 in a fire set by a drunken tramp who died in the fire.

THE OMINOUS WESTERN GAP through Chestnut Ridge looms in the background of this nicely done illustration which, in various permutations, has appeared in many places at many times. As an aside to those untutored in publishing machinations, the game is to "borrow" art, make a few tiny alterations in the scene and then claim "new" status. In this case, the two figures on the rock ledge at bottom center moved a little bit in various versions. The hamlet of Bolivar consists of a few houses, and the trace of PRR can barely be seen entering the gap on the south, or left, "shore." Without the gap PRR would have been stalemated. With it life was miserable.

259

TRIUMPH I

BOLIVAR HAD NOT grown by the time PRR was double-tracked through town as this westerly view attests. This photograph was probably taken during or shortly after the Civil War. There were clay deposits in this area and a tiny fire-brick industry did appear. The "unlimited coal of excellent quality" would prove to be something less than a bonanza and while it is true that a Bolivar Branch serving three mines was active as late as 1917, PRR would never be burdened by substantial local traffic. The rails in this scene, however, do evoke some interest. Eighty-three pound iron T-rail with wrought iron splices, measuring five inches in height, were in place between Bolivar and Blairsville Intersection on the western side of the gap by 1858. This rail replaced 64-pound rail with "chair connections" and is still another illustration of Thomson's devotion to quality.
Railroad Museum of Pennsylvania

THE BOLIVAR freight station was alive, well and modestly active in the early 1900s. This card was postmarked 1910. The passenger station between Track Nos. 3 and 4 was probably built in 1890. We are looking westerly. VY Tower, with a 20-working lever machine built in 1902, rested on the north side of the tracks a few hundred feet to the east of this complex. The lack of a valuation photograph indicates that VY was gone by c.1920, but we know the freight station was extant at that time because we have a valuation print too poor to reproduce.

THE GAPS

CONEMAUGH DIVISION rails cross the river on this bridge to gain the north shore preparatory to entering the gap. Bolivar and West Bolivar are to the left, Robinson to the right of the photographer. In the few minutes we were here on 7 May 1995 four trains passed, including the one on the mainline seen at left. The original West Penn Division crossed the river at this point and perhaps on these piers.

IT IS EASY to forget that every inch of PRR was inspected by watchmen around the clock many times a day. They searched for anomalies that could affect safety and this included passing trains. This rustic watchbox was at Bolivar and is typical of the breed. Complete with lawn, hedge and shrubbery. For all the rough and tumble, this was in many ways a gentler time.

National Archives

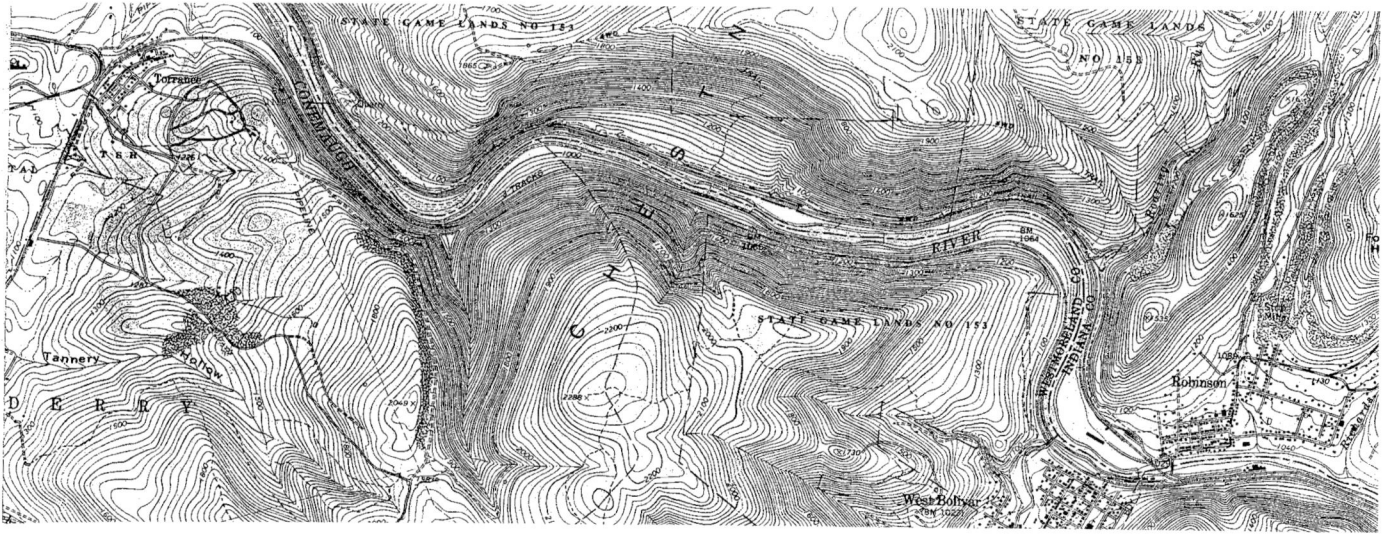

IT IS ONLY about five miles from Bolivar to Torrance. That the distance is short is about the only good thing that can be said about the gap through Chestnut Ridge. The sides are savagely steep as this contour map makes all too clear. They are also very high. And, in common with the geology of the region, the sides are unstable. The river is subject to flooding and by the time the water pouring down the west slope reaches the gap there is a lot of it and it is traveling fast. No wonder the Indians went around to the north. To be trapped in the gorge by a sudden flood, which could arrive without warning, was an automatic death sentence. There are two loops in the gap, the western one being the famous Packsaddle…so named, it is said, because it resembles the accoutrement used by travelers since time began. Normally, loops provide flood plains. Not here. The water moves too fast. As far as PRR and Thomson were concerned, it was essential to place the railroad high up on the hillside to gradually raise it so that the exit at Torrance would be at an acceptable level. Because the river was going down while the railroad was going up, the result was a gentle grade well away from the river itself. The trick for PRR was to avoid sliding down the slope, not, as we shall see, an easy thing to do. Only in one place (southeast of the Packsaddle) was there a fairly gentle plateau on the south "shore" and it was only about three-quarters of a mile long. Even this slight respite was denied PRR on the north shore. As we leave this map, let us point out that there has never been a road through this gap…only a railroad. This is an untouched and inaccessible wilderness, awesome and forbidding at the same time.

TRIUMPH I

THE UBIQUITOUS BOWEN visited the gap during his 1852 trip and described it as "high, bold, precipitous and rugged" as well as "frightful." His artist's rendition seen here obviously did not result from personal observation because there were no such solid rock ledges in the gap or, as claimed, at the Packsaddle. Bowen did give the impression, however, that he was happy to get out of the gap no matter how scenic or grand it may have been.

WITH MORE accuracy and artistic skill, this 1870s illustration of the Packsaddle comes closer to the mark. We have found references to a 109-foot embankment in this area and believe the train in this scene is passing the cut from which the fill was gouged. As with the one at Bolivar, this art was reproduced in many subtle variations. The gap has inspired almost as much literary eloquence as Horseshoe Curve. An 1875 writer said, "...scenery is unsurpassed...picture after picture of nature's beauty...in the autumn, when the leaves have taken on the bright tints which, like the song of the swan, presage their death, the whole landscape is a panorama of gorgeous loveliness." We find here a reference to "death" and, in the preceding quote, to "frightful." We encountered the same sort of allusions in our book *West End* when travelers were describing Seventeen Mile and Cheat River grades. In fact, we have experienced similar discomfort on occasion. Clinging to the side of an unstable mountain with a very heavy locomotive leading the way produces uneasiness that is only partly ameliorated by the grandeur of the view.

THE GAPS

Railroad Museum of Pennsylvania

THIS IS ONE of the more fascinating as well as instructive photographs in this book. In one scene is captured the abyss, the solitude and the untamed nature of the gap as well as its conquest by PRR (seen atop the Packsaddle plateau at upper right) and lastly the tenuousness of the canal along the shore. While the canal is abandoned and overgrown, one can make out the towpath, lock, lockhouse, lockkeeper's dwelling and the entrance of the canal into a slackwater pool.

TRIUMPH I

Railroad Museum of Pennsylvania

THE STRATA in the Packsaddle sloped toward the railroad, adding to the woes of PRR. Early annual reports were awash with moans about slides all along the mainline but particularly in the Chestnut Ridge gap. This stunning photograph of the inside curve west of the plateau shows an almost perpendicular bare-rock cut plus the end of a fitted-stone retaining wall that looks like it reaches to the stars. And the fall-off to the right of the tracks seems to plunge straight down into the bowels of the earth. A trip through here was fearsome indeed for passengers and crew alike, to say nothing of the construction men who were told to fit a railroad along the side of this mountain. The tribulations on the east slope were nothing compared to this challenge. It does not appear to have been possible, and to attempt it could have been regarded as foolhardy. Yet Thomson and his men found a way. Worse was yet to come. As the nineteenth century aged, PRR needed *four* tracks through here, and two on the other side of the river! Impossible. No way.

THE GAPS

Pennsylvania State Archives

HAVING CONCLUDED that it was impossible to put four tracks on the south side of the gap, we found that this photograph and supporting historical facts brought into question our capabilities in the field of civil engineering prophecy. Still, it was not easy. On 19 September 1904 W.W. Atterbury, as PRR general manager, wrote "Stone" Brown and informed him that all four tracks between Bolivar and Blairsville Intersection would be in service by noon on the 21st day of that month. This grand opening lasted a few weeks and then two slides blocked both new tracks until 30 April 1905. Mother is an adjective on occasion. While we have no details regarding this construction feat, we do have some evidence that a few things went wrong. On 14 November 1903, the concussion from a blast set-off by contractor Thomas McNally Company shattered two glass lights on each side of the main door of Pullman observation car "Justitia." Since this car was on feature train *Pennsylvania Limited*, it is reasonable to assume that this mishap attracted the attention of higher management. Shades of Gallitzin. This time no one was hurt. Repairs cost $11.10, of which 50 cents was for labor at a rate of 25 cents per hour. Forty years later we got a job as a drug store clerk at the same hourly rate. Who was overpaid and who underpaid?

Pennsylvania State Archives/Tom Hollyman/PRR

WHILE NONE of the passage through the gap was easy, the last mile or so at the west end was slightly less perilous. This 1950s air view illustrates the relationship of the mainline and the Conemaugh Division as well as defining the reason for the West Penn Extension. The mainline (on the left) spins around the point at upper right at a relatively high level and then enters Blairsville Intersection/Torrance on the far side of the mountain. The low valley can be seen in the distance. West Penn rails had to climb very sharply to reach the mainline at Blairsville Intersection, thus limiting tonnage. The only answer was to ease the grade by lengthening the approach and the only place to put it was on the north, or right, side of the river. As we have seen, the extension joined the mainline at Bolivar and later at Conpitt Junction and Sang Hollow. This heavy investment was made, of course, to benefit PRR traffic. Two passing thoughts regarding the gap. This is snow country and the white stuff is drawn to cuts and fills. And the Packsaddle was always a source of concern. In 1936 PRR was tempted to eliminate watchmen by utilizing slide fences. MOW Engineer J.M. Fair hastened to emphasize that the problem involved slips as well as slides and that this proposal would not be wise. Reduction to two tracks on the mainline and one on the Conemaugh Division provided relief by keeping the tracks in the middle of the roadbed.

THE GAPS

Railroad Museum of Pennsylvania

BLAIRSVILLE INTERSECTION (BH) is seen here as it appeared in 1923, looking easterly. The four-track mainline curves to the right and enters the Packsaddle inside the western gap. There is a loop track running around the station on the left, although the eastern leg is not discernible. This track was originally a wye, but by 1918 it was changed to a loop. The eastern leg was the original branch to Blairsville which lies about four miles to the left. When the West Penn Extension was completed to Bolivar/Conpitt Junctions, this leg became part of the Indiana Branch, following the old high-grade approach to BH. By 1945 the eastern leg was reduced to a siding, although the westbound track was still in place. All was gone by 1958. The passenger station was built in 1898 and all the other facilities were in service by 28 February 1905, including a subway to reach the island platforms. Here is a little insight into the reason for the construction of the West Penn Extension and easing of the grade. In 1901 122,556 *loaded* cars moved east through Bolivar Junction and 67,984 west. For that number of eastbound cars to climb to BH from Blairsville would have severely crimped the operating department and made the extension quite viable almost regardless of investment. In that same year, 15,001 loaded cars moved west to Blairsville and 4,526 cars east through BH. Quite aside from through traffic, BH was a busy place.

THE STATION at Blairsville Intersection had an attached freight house in the rear. This is a stone structure and sports a weathervane on the roof. We suspect that this vane gave warning to MOW people when it began to snow with the wind blowing into or, worse, across the gap.

National Archives

TRIUMPH I

National Archives

BH INTERLOCKER was located just west of the station on the north side of the mainline, making this c.1920 valuation view looking west. This tower was opened in 1905, replacing an 1896 structure. In the 1978 CTC/naming project it became CP PACK. The name of Blairsville Intersection also changed to Torrance effective 26 April 1925. In the late teens the construction of a large state hospital north of the mainline was being proposed and Francis J. Torrance was chairman of the building commission. Apparently this gentleman was highly respected and PRR officials wished to rename the place in his honor. Mr. Torrance wanted none of it and urged that Woodbury be used. PRR used Torrance anyway, saying that the railroad could use any name it wanted. The grounds of this hospital, by the way, sprawl for hundreds of acres north of the mainline and one must traverse the complex to reach Torrance.

IT WAS A VERY PLEASANT DAY on 7 May 1995 when we were ensconced on the overpass at Torrance looking west at an approaching train with a consist of trailers. Notice the discolored area just east of the turnout. The train, giving every appearance of being completely under control, passed under us and entered the curve into the Packsaddle. We then noticed that all the cars were swaying once they passed that dark spot. When the train entered the curve, centrifugal force dampened the sway. We were not alarmed until a rogue car came along, bouncing from side to side with such vehemence that we thought it would leave the railroad. Our loyal readers will recall our experience, related in the book *West End*, when a train did just that with us standing right next to it on the ground with a 400-foot drop-off behind us. Happily history did not repeat itself, but we reported our observation to Conrail operating management. They responded instantly. It seems that 30 cars of a westbound coil-steel train had derailed here shortly before and the dark spot represented an irregular cross-level. The ballast was retamped and the soft spot eliminated. As the reader shall see, later the same day we had another interesting experience at Latrobe. This is a good time to correct our personal historical record in regard to mishaps. Our long-standing reputation as a Jonah is not justified. All those colleagues and comrades-in-arms who so named your author, even to the extent to refusing to get on an airplane if we were on board or standing near us when live ammunition was being used, completely miss the point. *Not one single person ever got a scratch when in our company.* We walked away from every single landing and every "friendly fire" unpleasantness. Scared to death, yes. Harmed, no.

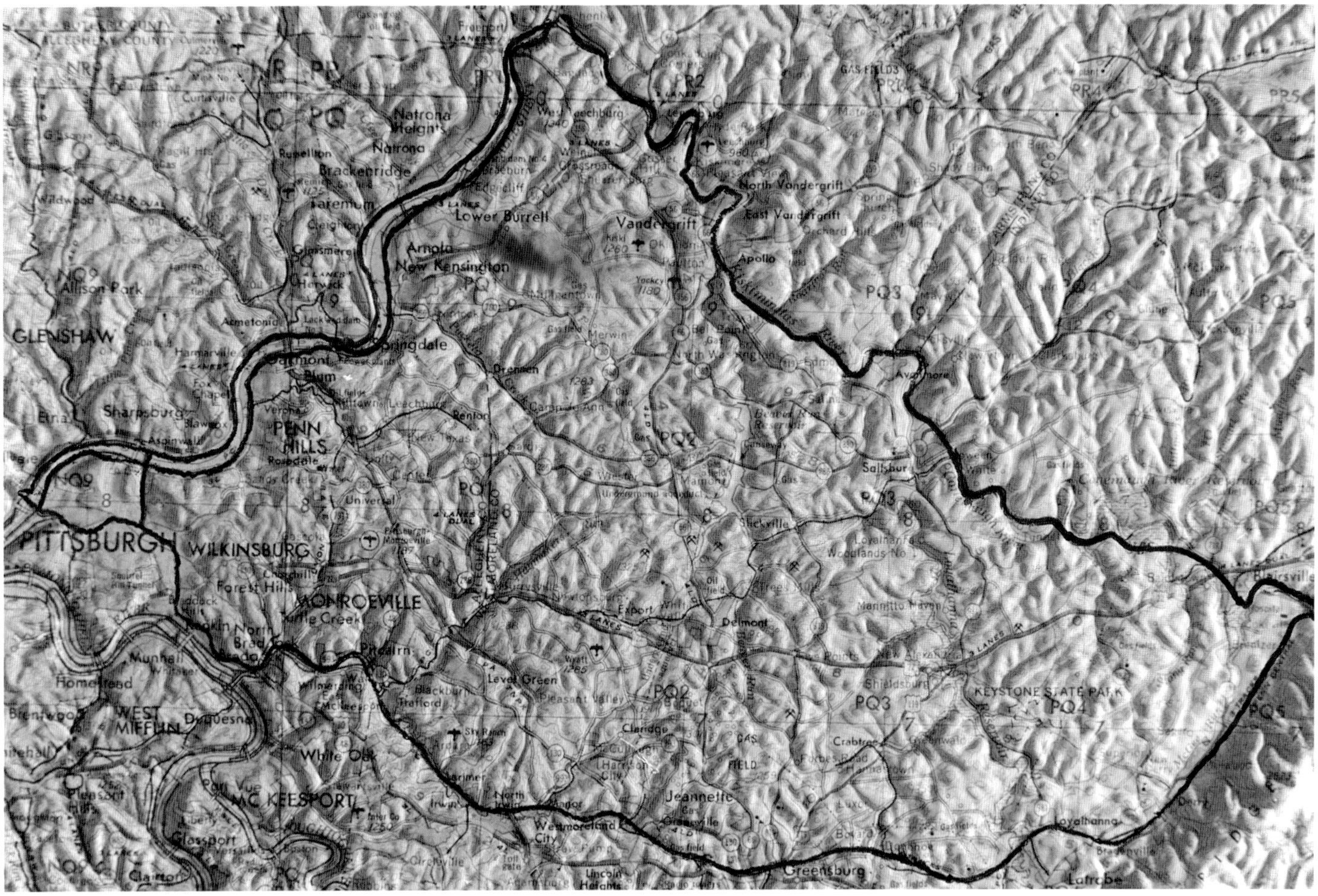

THE GAPS

IT IS NOT the purpose of this volume to explore the history of the Conemaugh Division, PRR's roundabout route from Blairsville Intersection to the Pittsburgh region. This subject will be covered in another book. We do, however, consider it important that the student understand the relationship of this route and its characteristics to the mainline. Succinctly, the Conemaugh Division is longer and suffers from severe curvature, but the grades are so slight that they are not worth mentioning. The division forms the top two legs of the "triangle" seen here. It follows the course of several rivers to Pittsburgh. The mainline is the bottom leg. As the reader shall see in the next chapter, the name "roller coaster" is apt. We have already treated the geologic aspects of this region and present this relief map to dramatically illustrate the nature of the terrain. Lumpy, bumpy, jumbled and bewildering. A natural maze.

THE TOWN of Blairsville appeared this way to an early artist in the canal days. This side trip from Blairsville Intersection was done to remind the reader that the western division of the canal followed the Conemaugh River, moving away from the PRR mainline.

TRIUMPH I

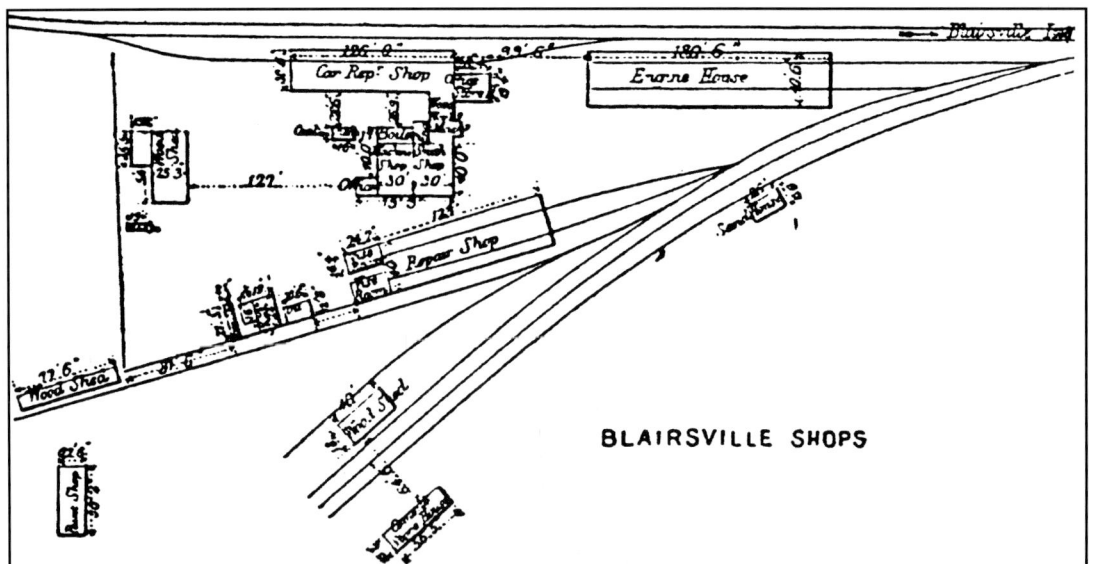

THERE WERE SHOPS at Blairsville in the 1870s, as seen here. The line to Blairsville Intersection runs to the right at upper right of the map.

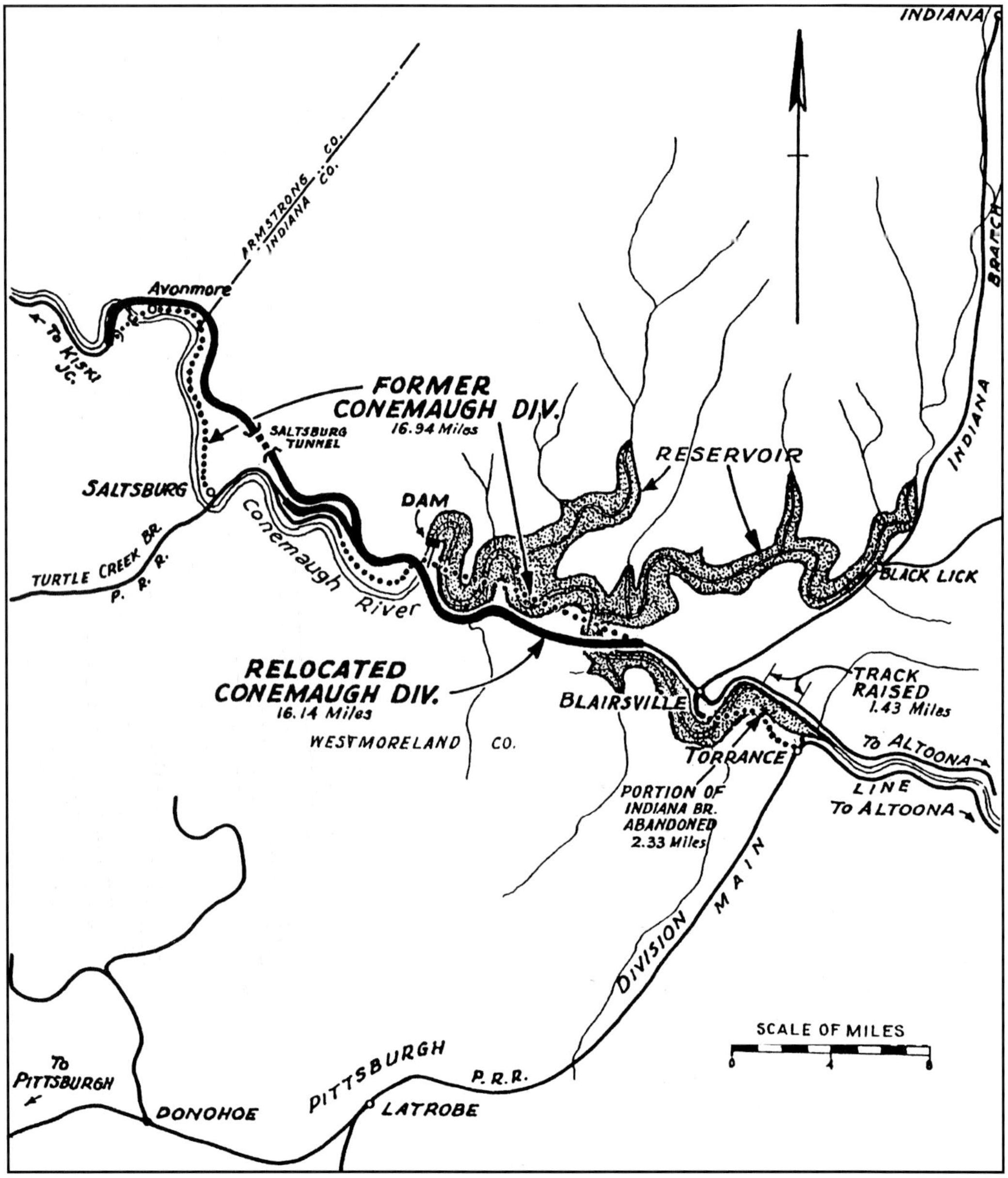

THE CONEMAUGH DIVISION benefited from a major line relocation in conjunction with Federal construction of a flood control dam and reservoir. Started in April 1946, the new PRR line was opened for traffic in September of 1950. The total cost of the project was $45 million, of which $17 million was expended for railroad relocation. Of the latter, PRR put up only $1 million. The line was shortened, curvature materially reduced and grades eased. PRR and CR always seem to come out rather well when government money is involved. The reader might note that the connection at Torrance was severed during this period. Major portions of the canal, as well as a number of PRR bridges and some towns, were "drowned." The reader may have the impression that the Conemaugh Division is redundant and some idle recent press reports suggest abandonment is under consideration. If this is so, why did Conrail put in 50,000 new ties in the Spring of 1996? The Conemaugh Division is vital and viable.

Chapter 8

Rip Rap

Torrance to Pitcairn

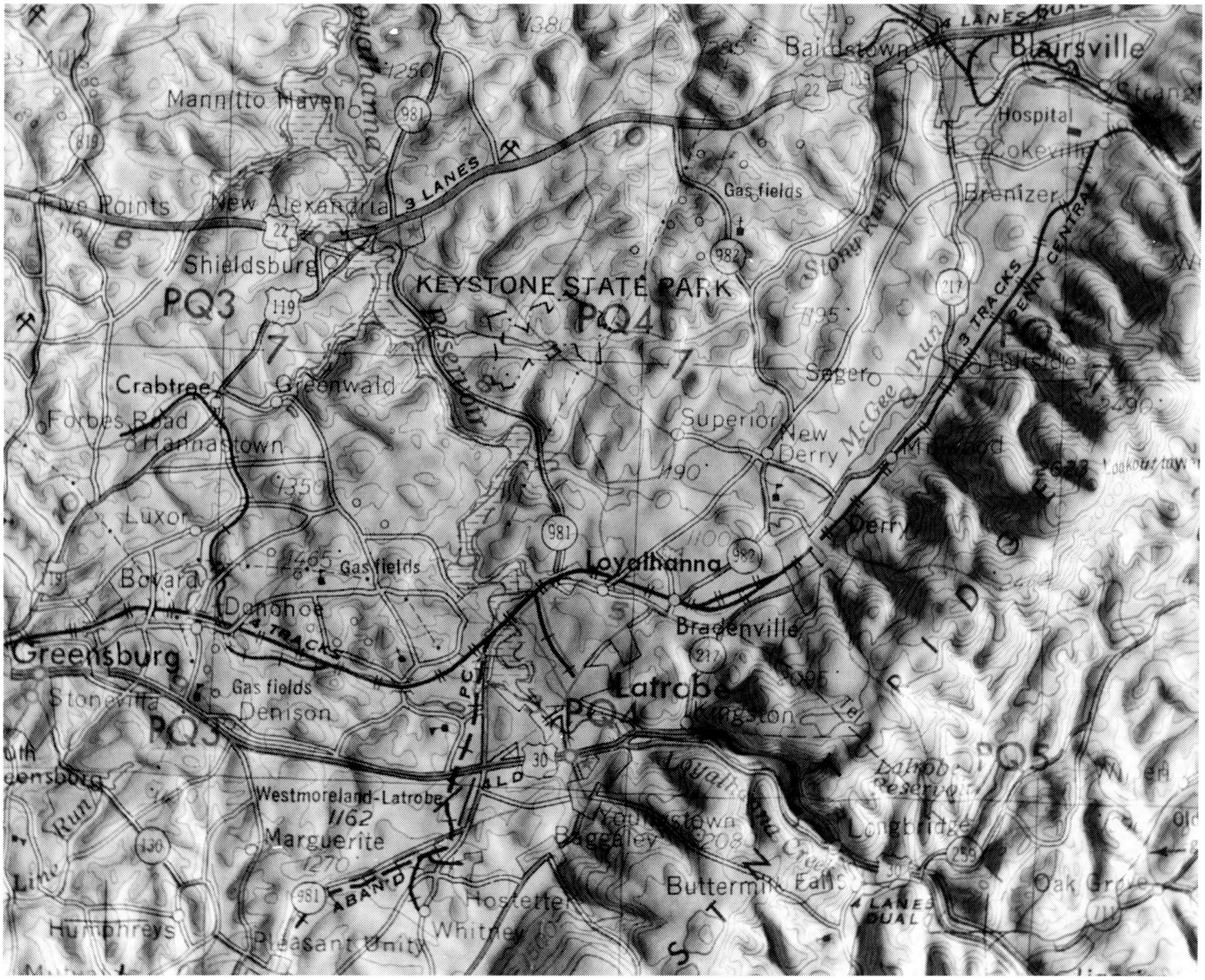

ONCE HAVING LEFT the "Packsaddle Gap" and turning the corner to Torrance, seen here at extreme upper right, PRR runs alongside Chestnut Ridge for a little over six miles to Derry. The looming and confused hulk of the ridge is quite apparent, but the mountain is no longer an obstacle for PRR. Oddly, the line is climbing westbound with two slight dips enroute. Just west of Derry the railroad moves away from the ridge and enters Latrobe, crossing Loyalhanna Creek at a right angle. The dip

271

here is quite deep and, as we shall see, a serious operating problem that has never been solved. The railroad climbs to a summit midway between Latrobe and Greensburg…it then drops to Greensburg and crosses Jacks Run. This second dip is also severe and, unfortunately, not the last one on the way to Pitcairn and Pittsburgh. Loyalhanna Creek and Jacks Run are names that sound innocuous and, as waterways go, they are minor. The valleys that they formed were shallow, but to PRR they were burdensome. The Loyalhanna, by the way, begins to the southeast of Ligonier (at lower right), flows through a gap near Latrobe and wanders north to meet the Conemaugh River northwest of Blairsville. At that confluence it becomes the Kiskiminetas River which in turn flows to the Allegheny River and thence to Pittsburgh where it joins the Monongahela to become the Ohio River. The Conemaugh Division follows the Conemaugh and Kiskiminetas Rivers. As to the latter, we interviewed several natives of the area to learn how it is pronounced. Each pronounced it differently, but all agreed that Kiski would be sufficient.

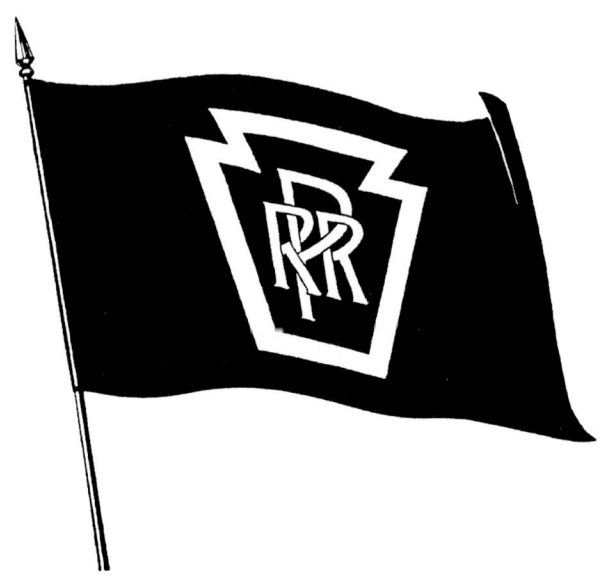

RIP RAP

We have taken the reader on a fascinating trip through time and space along the mainline of the world's premier railroad from Altoona to Torrance. We have climbed the East Slope and the West Slope. We have recorded the conquest of the Great Mountain Barrier in both directions, a story studded with the highest of drama in every sense of that word.

We have also taken a trip through the Gaps, although in all candor this section of railroad is enlivened mostly by the fearsome Packsaddle. The twenty-four miles between Johnstown and Torrance, and indeed the Conemaugh Division, are rather anti-climactic. Except for some impressive engineering achievements, the Gaps are dull. The railroad through here is merely a conduit and approach to the Barrier.

Even Charles Dickens seemed to enjoy his canal trip from the Packsaddle to Pittsburgh. Of course, he traveled down the Conemaugh River to the Kiski and the Allegheny rather than cross-country to Pittsburgh. Pretty scenery, gentle hills, burbling water. To be sure, in his *Tale of Two Cities* he began with an allusion to the best and worst of times in his opening paragraph, but obviously he was not referring to two American cities and a railroad that hadn't been built.

As to PRR, once free of that dreadful mountain and brutal Packsaddle, it must have seemed that the rest of the way to Pittsburgh was easy. Here the sun always shined, the best was yet to be and there were no dragons. A state of nirvana had been reached and arcadia had been found.

Now PRR entered territory rich with triumphant American history as well as raw materials. Americans needed the British to push out the French and, once accomplished, promptly threw out the British. Driving out the Indians was then a simple matter. Mother Nature remained annoying, but one would just have to learn to live with her. Not easy, not predictable, but possible. Her occasional tendency to eat her own children was puzzling, but surely the tranquil region west of Chestnut Ridge was exempt from her furies. And it was just so. Her damage had already been done. The ambush had been laid eons before. Now she could just sit back and laugh as PRR tried to figure out how to build and operate a railroad through this labyrinth of tangled little hills and wandering streams.

There is, by the way, a growing philosophical debate bubbling up in Western thought as to the nature of Mother Nature, if one will pardon the play on words. From the Renaissance to recent times, Western culture has been comforted by the conviction that Mother Nature was governed by an Ultimate Order. Now a new Chaos Theory is emerging, which states that Mother Nature not only does not give a damn (we've always known that) but that she is totally out of control and letting things happen at random.

It is not our role here to comment on the validity of either theory, but we will have to say that proponents of Chaos should take a look at PRR's mainline from Torrance to Pitcairn and Pittsburgh for fodder. What did she have in mind? Answer: nothing.

Because you see, dear reader, once west of Torrance the worst (not the best) was yet to come. It was *possible* to build a railroad through here, but *impossible* to operate it with any degree of efficiency.

Now we must explain why we named this chapter "Rip Rap" rather than the traditional "Roller Coaster." Railroads, like all institutions, develop their own parlance and much of it is peculiar to regions of the country. Rip Rap is a southern expression used to describe an up and down profile that makes train handling a nightmare.

One slight miscalculation on the part of the engineman and the train will rip in two or rap together with a slam. Sometimes both at the same time. Hence Rip Rap.

One doubts if any PRR man ever heard of this description, but they certainly understand the meaning. In the era of short trains, there was no problem. As trains got longer, the difficulties mushroomed.

Picture oneself as an engineer with a long train proceeding downhill. There is slack in the train, usually about a foot per car. If that slack surges toward the engine, there will be a rap that will not do any good and may even pop a car off the rails or, worse, collapse it. The answer is deceptively simple. Apply the train brakes and keep the train stretched out. This is called "stretch braking."

Now your engine has proceeded through the dip and is starting up the next grade. More and more of the train is moving upgrade, less and less downgrade. Release the brakes? If you release them too soon, the rear of the train will rap. If too late, the front of the train will rip from all the strain. Another deceptively simple answer. Leave the brakes on and pull against them. Pull against your own brakes? Add to the strain? What about fuel economy? In steam days this procedure wasted water and fuel. Now the reader can see why there were so many water and fuel facilities on PRR.

Did the diesel solve this problem? It helped because the diesel was a simpler piece of machinery to operate and, of course, the dynamic brake was useful. Unfortunately, the diesel also allowed longer trains. And fuel economy became such a pressing issue that stretch braking was outlawed. Does the reader still want to be an engineer?

Your train has now gone over the next summit and started downhill. In an ever-changing tableau, the rear of your train wants to go backwards and the front forward. Talk about strain on the draftgear. Rip. And keep in mind that a train is like a chain. It is only as strong as the weakest link.

If you have survived all this, you are now back to where you started…proceeding downhill. Between Pittsburgh and Torrance, there are three big dips and a host of small ones. Between Pitcairn and Torrance there are "only" two big ones. Pitcairn itself is at the bottom of the third one. Not exactly a great place for a yard, but PRR didn't have any real choice at the time.

Let's go back to train handling. In a perfect world and with great skill, you as engineer have avoided damaging surges and run-ins…rip and rap. By the way, you haven't done this alone. This is helper district territory and much of the time there is an engine on the rear. *Both* engineers have to do it just right. (If the reader is thinking that mid-train help is the answer, let us just say that no one in the east has ever succeeded with this technique in any meaningful way. Helpers up front? Rip.)

Now we have referred to "perfect world" in the preceding paragraph. We gave you a "solid consist" train of coal or grain or ore or stone. Each car weighs and handles about the same way. You have graduated. Now you're going to get a "mixed consist" train, with loads and empties and a host of cars made to entirely different specifications according to the whim of the designer. Each one will handle quite differently and with an independent mind of its own.

The yardmaster will put this train together for you. Until very recent times, no yardmaster in the world ever made a single extra switching move to "build" a train that would handle well out on the road. He put them in the train the way he received them and as long as it got out of his yard in one piece his job was done. Load, empty, overload, long, short, heavy, light, wide, narrow, stable, unstable, rigid, flexible…they were just cars to him and if all of them didn't get to the next yard that was somebody else's problem. In this case, *your* problem as engineer over a piece of railroad known alternatively as the Roller Coaster and Rip Rap. The pay is good, but you will earn every penny of it.

It was not until the 1970s and 1980s, with long-overhang TTX and topheavy grain cars scattering trains all over the landscape, that operating managements forced yardmasters to adjust consists so they would track well.

If the reader had become an engineer during this time-frame, he would have been lucky in another way. Schools for engineers came into vogue. It still blows this author's mind that railroads took so long to come to the conclusion that training and education might be useful. One of the unsung pioneers in this endeavor, by the way, is an editor of this and other Barnard, Roberts books. Also by the way, a recalcitrant holdout in this noble venture was, believe it or not, Norfolk and Western. What did they care? All they did was load coal and let the trains drift downhill. Why train anyone?

Let us revert to the Rip Rap. Any train that ventured forth across this profile was totally dependent upon the skill of the engineman. While the advent of the diesel allowed a poor engineer to become a fair one, the element of skillful train handling was paramount.

As will be shown in this chapter, PRR lavished all that it could in order to improve the Rip Rap and, indeed, much progress was made. In the end, however, the 1958 "Ruling Grade" numbers succinctly tell the tale.

Eastbound, the *ruling* grade was 1.56% from Pitcairn through Conemaugh all the way up the gentle West Slope to the summit. Westbound ranged from 2.10% to 2.19% with the worst on the Rip Rap.

Some of the dips were long and some were filled and much curvature was eased, but still the nemesis remained the Rip Rap. Not the mountain.

Then again, perhaps we should have called it "The Big Dipper."

RIP RAP

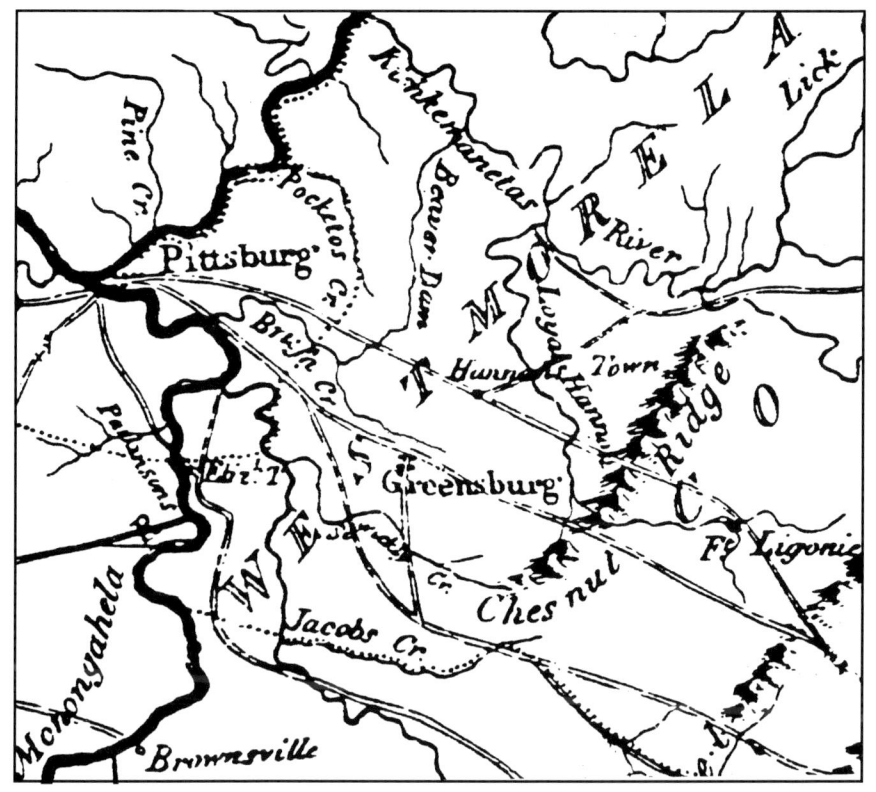

THIS ENLARGEMENT of a portion of our 1794 map shows nothing of the hodgepodge of hills in the region, but does present existing "highways" that go straight from place to place without any regard to gradient as we have discussed earlier in this book. Some creeks appear, although not all of the ones that would ultimately haunt PRR. For example, Turtle Creek is not shown. It is interesting to note (in the center) that there is a Hannas Town at a road junction, from which Loyalhanna Creek must have derived its name. The road net would prove helpful to PRR as they built through the rip rap, as they could be used to bring materials to the worksite and would provide traffic which PRR could bleed-off while the railroad was under construction.

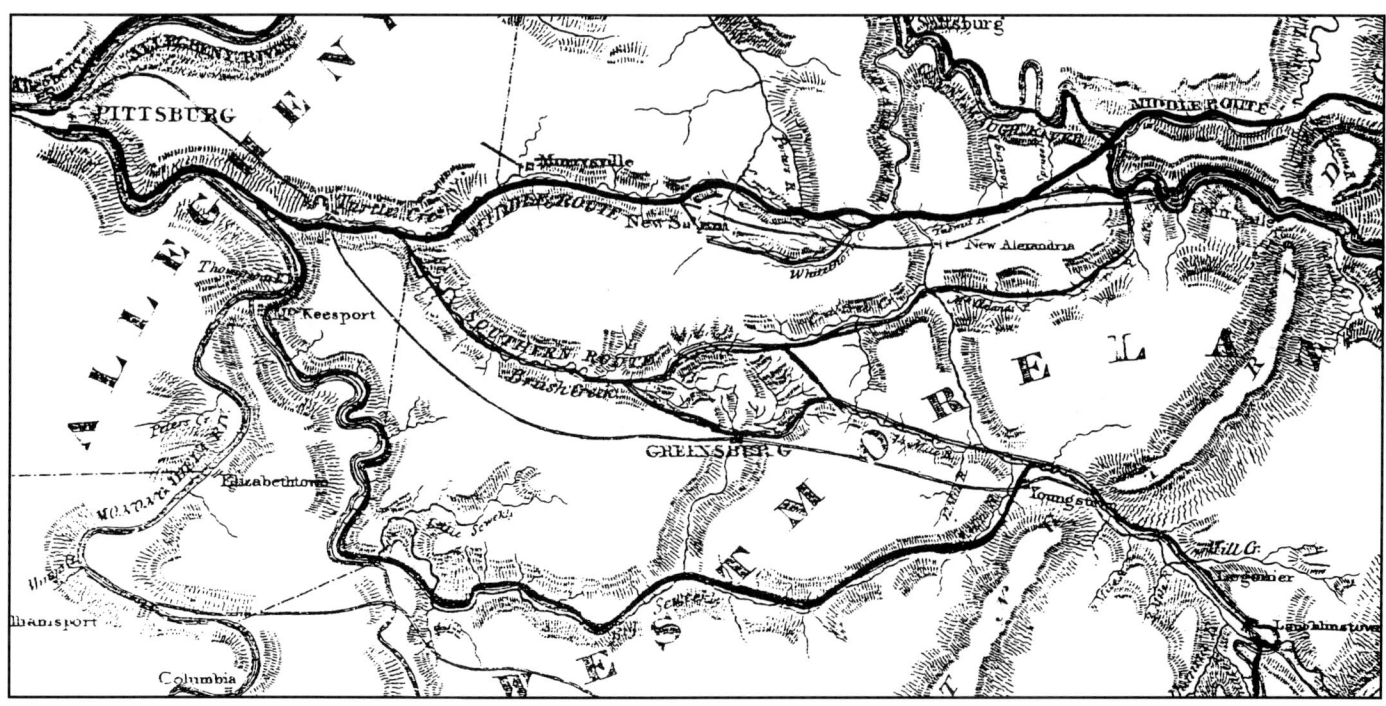

IT IS HARDLY surprising that Schlatter's three routes began to converge as Pittsburgh was approached. What startled this author, however, was the number of alternative sub-routes offered by Schlatter and that Thomson evolved his own path utilizing just selected segments of the original proposal. Thomson, once out of the Packsaddle, chose to go southwesterly along the west slope of Chestnut Ridge and this avoided at least some of the jumbled hills. Schlatter didn't even consider this possibility.

Thomson then turned westerly near Youngstown on this map (later Latrobe) and followed a path south of Schlatter to Greensburg. West of Greensburg Thomson generally followed Schlatter until nearing Pittsburgh when he went away from the Monongahela River and entered downtown by paralleling an existing highway. One can argue endlessly about the Thomson approach, but this historian's view is that the old Giant selected the marginal best of a very bad lot.

275

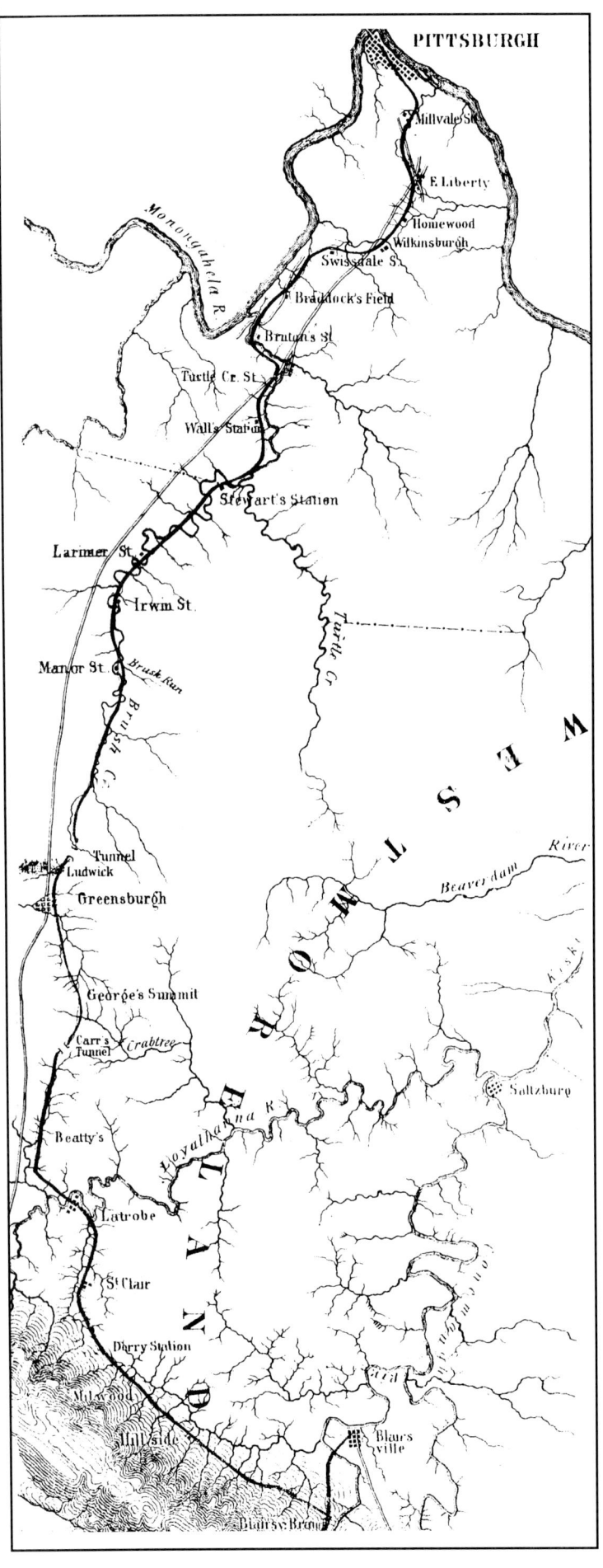

THOMSON HAD TO CROSS an almost incredible number of small creeks and runs in order to get from Packsaddle to Pittsburgh through the Rip Rap, as this 1855 map so eloquently attests. His decision to take this route was not taken lightly. A cursory glance at this map suggests that Schlatter's path through Blairsville and aiming directly at the valley of Turtle Creek was the best one, with far fewer streams to cross and only one serious dip over the Loyalhanna. Indeed Thomson did survey this route in "more-minute" detail and in the process dispensed with three tunnels as well as having "greatly softened in its asperities" the precise path located by Schlatter. (We should remind the reader that Schlatter was in a hurry, constrained by certain requirements and acknowledged that he did not have time for fine-tuning.) But there was a price tag to the Schlatter approach and it was higher gradient. Thomson chose the route seen here, even though longer and bumpier, for the reason given plus it did "not present quite so rough a surface as that by Blairsville." This was understatement at its best. Having to choose between the devil and the deep blue sea, he went with the devil. Now the reader should follow the Thomson route. From the Packsaddle all the way to the vicinity of Swissdale, he always followed the valleys. When moving from one watershed to another, he did it with the shortest possible tunnel. Only at Swissdale did he depart from his pattern and leave the Monongahela Valley. The best approach to Pittsburgh would have been to stay on the Monongahela River bank and enter the city on a mild downgrade. Yet Thomson climbed uphill to the tableland between Wilkinsburg and East Liberty and then descended to the city along Liberty Street. By doing so, he created a new summit, another big dip and a longer railroad. Why? Pittsburgh interests were virulently pro-B&O and anti-PRR, so they gave the river route to Pittsburgh & Connellsville as we have related in *Sand Patch*. It ended up in B&O hands. The PRR charter required that 15 miles be placed under contract from Pittsburgh east in a short time frame. In July 1847 that was done, although it was a sham. The year closed with only a few contractors actually working and by the end of 1848 virtually all of the contractors had opted out. Actual work did not resume until the summer of 1850. In other words, the wise money said the fix was on. The contracts had been let, the charter requirement fulfilled, the line located in the heart of Pittsburgh alongside a bustling highway to satisfy vested real estate interests and PRR was as pure as the driven snow. When it dawned on Pittsburgh interests that only $7,498 had been expended on actual grading during 1848 and that they had been outwitted by Philadelphia lawyers still another time, the reaction must have been explosive and the rages wondrous to behold. Here are some little excerpts from PRR in 1848. "The prompt beginning of the construction of PRR at the Pittsburgh end did much to modify…the unfriendly feelings which divided us from our Western fellow-citizens…have been allayed…by calm reflection…measures are now in progress in Pittsburgh which is hoped will lead to a large subscription from the citizens and authorities of Allegheny county." Prompt beginning? Calm reflection? Even after 150 years, this pap makes your author want to gag. And notice that little blackmail touch. Send us some money and we may build the railroad in your town, if and when we get around to it. The scenario probably played out along these lines. Build that railroad from Swissdale to Pittsburgh as originally planned or else there will be another Whiskey Rebellion that will not be bloodless. PRR decided to submit and accept the additional summit and dip. Years later Grandfather was in charge of the B&O traffic office in Pittsburgh and family lore relates that those "hate PRR" fires were still burning and B&O picked up at least some "spite" traffic. By the way, Swissdale later became Swissvale.

WE ARE REACHING ahead to 1872 simply to give the reader more placenames as we relate the story of the building and expansion of the Rip Rap. We have already taken the reader from Conemaugh to Lockport. On 10 December 1851 the railroad was open to Beatty and by the end of that month from Pittsburgh to Turtle Creek. The gap of about 25 miles was covered by wagon and stagecoach lines. PRR was, of course, single-track with some passing sidings. During 1852 the line from Turtle Creek to Radebaugh was completed in July and from Radebaugh to Beatty on 10 December. By using the OPRR, this gave PRR an all-rail route from Philadelphia to Pittsburgh. Or so the advertisements said. Actually, at this point in time the line from Philadelphia to Harrisburg and from Hollidaysburg to Conemaugh was *not* owned by PRR. The construction process was slowed by money shortages, wars between men in the laboring parties and heavy construction problems. Just west of Greensburg a 2,600-foot cut was required which was 74 feet deep and there were numerous high embankments and deep rock cuts of lesser dimensions for over 10 miles. As always, the strata was unstable and the headaches severe. Double-tracking was achieved by fits and starts, being completed between Altoona and Pittsburgh (except for the bridge over the Conemaugh River at Johnstown) by 1 January 1863. The severity of the work, particularly in the middle section of the Rip Rap, has been described as "unparalleled in Pennsylvania for the necessities of the heavy work required." The addition of third and fourth tracks through this brutal region, along with various line relocations, reached well into the twentieth century. Even by 1911 the work still had a few minor exceptions. Throughout this book we have regaled the reader with PRR's engineering difficulties and accomplishments. East of Derry PRR triumphed. West of Derry the victory was less complete. Note that the railroad from Swissvale to Pittsburgh along the Monongahela River is the Pittsburgh and Connellsville. And a last parting shot at the canal proponent who maintains that the coming of the railroad was not a pivotal event in the development of this nation. Even the State Works did not consider building canals in this lush but tortured region. That *would* have been absolutely impossible.

National Archives

APPROACHING MILEPOST 304, Hillside comes into view. By 1855 PRR maintained a wood and water station at Hillside. The water part of the equation lasted quite a while, culminating in a 50,000 gallon replacement water tub in 1913 and a four-track overhead water bridge in 1917. HM tower seen here was built as a mechanical interlocker in 1900 next to Track No. 1. At this point PRR had already crossed eight streams since leaving the Packsaddle. One of them was named Harbinger, which certainly was prophetic. Scores more would be traversed before Pittsburgh was reached.

National Archives

AFTER TURNING the corner at Torrance/CP PACK and proceeding a little over a mile southwesterly along the flank of Chestnut Ridge, PRR reached the thriving town of Gray. Gray? Yes, there was and is a Gray at about Milepost 302. Current maps show a clutch of a few houses. Early sources make no mention of the place, but there was sufficient passenger traffic to cause PRR to build this small and charming station supposedly in 1915 and seen here c.1920.

National Archives

JUST NEXT DOOR TO HM on the west was this interesting combination freight and passenger station. Its birthdate is unknown, but we suspect that it was very early. In 1867 the woodshed adjacent to the north track was dismantled and the annual report infers that the materials salvaged were used to construct a two-story station/dwelling next to the south track. There is a Great Bear Cave near the Hillside station. It contains numerous and immense chambers with countless passages complete with legend. It was said that a young girl was absconded by gypsies and escaped into the cave, became lost and perished of starvation with her bones being found years afterward. According to Sipes in 1875, this cave is a natural wonder of wonders and he devotes almost a full page to extolling its virtues. We suspect his advocacy was meant to draw excursion traffic. If so, it didn't work. No resort center developed, probably to the relief of PRR. The last thing the railroad needed was passenger trains stopping and laying over on this busy mainline.

National Archives

RIDGEVIEW PARK is located at Milepost 305 and it was just that...a small park is still located just south of this structure seen c. 1920. Both the station and a short siding were adjacent to Track No. 1, the latter we assume to hold a passenger coach for visitors. We have no images for Millwood, which lies about three-quarters of a mile west of Ridgeview Park. Millwood was described as "inconsiderable" in 1855 and remains so today. True, a combination freight/passenger station was built in 1887. It enjoys a tiny footnote in history as the location of overhead plate girder Bridge 305.57. As part of the 1990s clearance project, the tracks under this bridge were lowered three feet...the first undercut west of the summit. If the reader has the impression that the first six miles west from Torrance/CP PACK is bucolic and gentle, then he is correct. Next, however, is Derry. From there west, trouble looms.

National Archives

IT IS AT DERRY that McGee Run, flowing down from Chestnut Ridge, turns right and parallels the PRR mainline to the Conemaugh River at Blairsville. All the streams PRR had to cross to reach Derry are tributary to McGee Run. Derry is the first summit on the Rip Rap and it is here that the mainline begins its first dip down to Latrobe. Originally this location was known as Derry Station because the original town of Derry was located at a crossroads about a mile northwest of this site. The initial town, now a hamlet, still exists although it is now known as New Derry. (This is all wrong. It should be Old Derry.) PRR, of course, made the true "New" Derry because it was an obvious place for an important wood and water station to service helpers. In 1860 PRR constructed a station, foremen's house, 15 by 20-foot building to house trainmen stopping over, an ice house and other buildings pertinent to operations. A YMCA also appeared in this time frame. We believe the station seen here c. 1920 was the 1860 structure.

In 1865 a sand-drying house appeared. Derry grew like topsy and PRR expanded its facilities over the years until Derry became a vital operating point on the railroad. Its population in 1875 was 300. By 1955 it was 3,752. Coal mines and coke ovens blossomed in the vicinity and the presence of clay in conjunction with the foregoing created a pottery plant that ultimately became a porcelain insulator unit of the Westinghouse Electric Company. Derry also became the eastern end-point for commuter operations out of Pittsburgh as well as the east end of helper limits out of Pitcairn. Trackage grew in all directions, somewhat awkwardly because the actual summit ran right through the middle of the yardage with the result that it was downhill on both sides. In fact, the station seen here was located near the summit. The overhead bridge at upper right was built in 1892. There is also a face-off in this photograph. The headlights of a truck are staring into the eyes of a horse *cum* wagon. We all know who won.

THERE WERE FOUR HOTELS in Derry by 1875 and apparently this was one of them, seen c. 1920. Since this is a valuation photograph, it is possible that PRR owned it and, if so, used it for crew housing. This size of the building implies that PRR needed a lot of beds which in turn indicates just how sizeable was the railroad's presence in Derry.

National Archives

TRIUMPH I

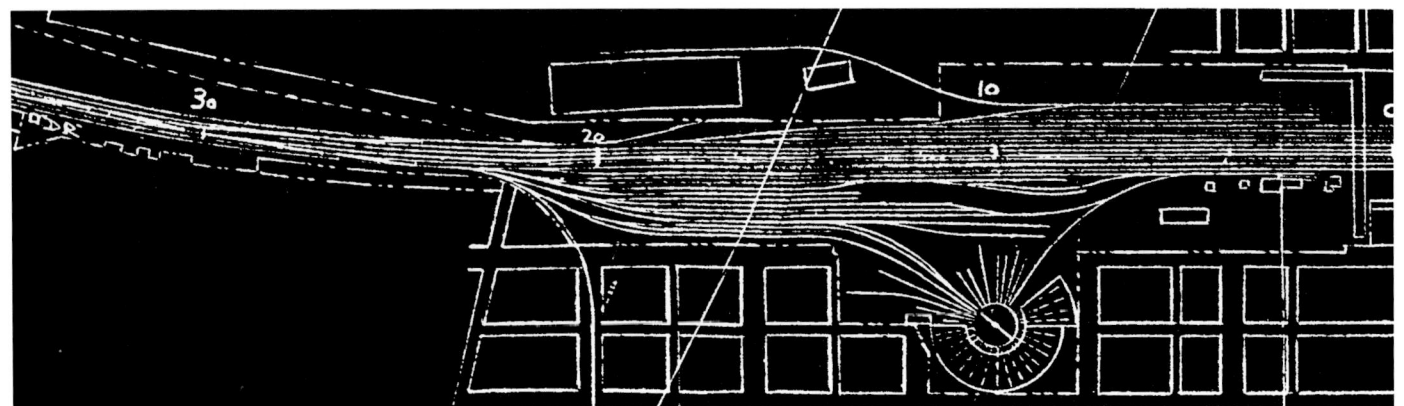

THE DATE OF THIS MAP is uncertain, but a count of the enginehouse stalls establishes that it was before 1917. The actual summit is just to the left of the enginehouse. At far left we see DR tower (although not in its original location) and at far right (split by a white vertical line) we find the station. The large pottery plant is at upper center. The amount of trackage alone signifies the importance of Derry in PRR's scheme of things. In August and September of 1904, with PRR adding mainline tracks in profusion and wanting to construct a Zero Track to Bradenville (about two miles downslope toward Latrobe), the pottery plant wished to talk about encroachment. "Stone" Brown and our friend CSD were handling this matter. Also involved was the possibility of a jumpover and, to complicate things, a planned "electric" railroad (to run from Derry to Latrobe) wanted to build a power plant on pottery premises. Compromise was the order of the day. PRR shifted its mainline tracks southward and the jumpover was shelved. As to the interurban, we don't know nor care what happened.

Railroaders Memorial Museum

WE KNOW that this enginehouse, seen here 1903-06, was built in 1888. Surely it was not the first one, although it may have been the first with a turntable. The length of the table in this scene is possibly 75 feet because one of that length was installed in 1906 along with a 100,000 gallon water tub in this vicinity. Somewhere in Derry there was a coal trestle, which was extended by a healthy 130 feet in 1915. There is a possibility that a water bridge was built in 1910 although this reference is vague.

IN 1917 PRR replaced its old enginehouse at Derry with a brick and concrete 15-stall facility with a 100 foot turntable. It was still rather clean when this photograph was taken c. 1920. By the way, throughout history PRR and B&O competed for "firsts," one of the few contests usually won by B&O because it was the oldest true railroad. A decade or so ago it came to our attention that B&O had scored again with the first female engineer to put a locomotive into a turntable pit. Since Father had gone to his reward by that time,

National Archives

we have no way of knowing what his reaction to that development might have been. Chuckle or cry?

RIP RAP

National Archives

THE FIRST INTERLOCKER at Derry was opened in 1889. The DR seen here c. 1920 was an electro-pneumatic 29-lever plant built in 1910. There is some evidence that the first two plants were located near the station in "downtown" Derry. The newer tower was soon moved west to the location shown on the Derry map, on a curve for better visibility and versatility. This location meant that all the turnouts in the plant were curved, a design and maintenance matter of significance.

Edward H. Weber

DR WAS ALIVE and well on 22 November 1960 when Mr. Weber took this eastward-facing photograph. At its height DR served six through-tracks, including (from south to north) the freight line from Bradenville, four mainline tracks and the Bradenville Branch. With the arrival of CTC in 1980, everything was removed. Today there are just two mainline tracks and memories.

Edward H. Weber

DERRY did get a new station to replace the 1860 structure and we see it here on 4 August 1960 in an eastward view. After suffering heavy commuter losses for years, PRR finally managed to end this burden from Pittsburgh to Derry in November of 1964. Chestnut Ridge is clearly seen in the background giving an impression of serene docility. The mountain has never been as gentle as it appears here. And the rickety overhead bridge on the left was replaced with a modern structure that spanned multiple trackage, most of which would disappear.

WE WERE ATOP the new overhead bridge at Derry when we took this eastward photograph on 7 May 1995. As far as the railroad is concerned, Derry was no more and the visage was empty and forlorn. So was the track empty. There were plenty of trains that day in both directions. That they were not on film is a measure of your author's incompetence as a photographer. There is a slight historical mystery in this view. Down the tracks about a mile, on a slight curve, there was a quarter of a mile of absolutely flat mainline in 1910. We have seen hints that some track pans were located at Derry in the very early years, yet only this spot was flat. We know there were pans four miles to the west at Saxman, as we shall see. Saxman is not Derry and over five miles separates the known from the possible. Were there pans there or were there not?

JUST TO THE RIGHT of the preceding view, these two cabooses are the only visible evidence that Derry was a thriving railroad town for well over a century. In a sense, they are headstones in a cemetery.

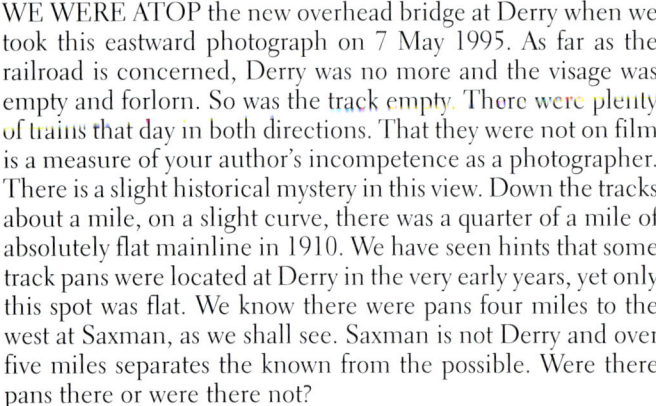

THE WESTWARD VIEW from the overhead bridge is no less forlorn. Only a setoff track breaks the monotony. Around the curve there is another one serving Track No. 1. In a few years the open areas will return to nature with second growth. In a few centuries man will have forgotten why Derry was founded and assume that New Derry came later. There is something else about a half-mile on the other side of the curve in the distance. It is the beginning of a railroad specifically designed by PRR to eliminate two of the big dips on the Rip Rap. On current geodetic maps it carries the name "Old Railroad Grade." As with Old and New Derry, this is a misnomer. It should be "New Railroad Grade." We are about to relate that fascinating story.

RIP RAP

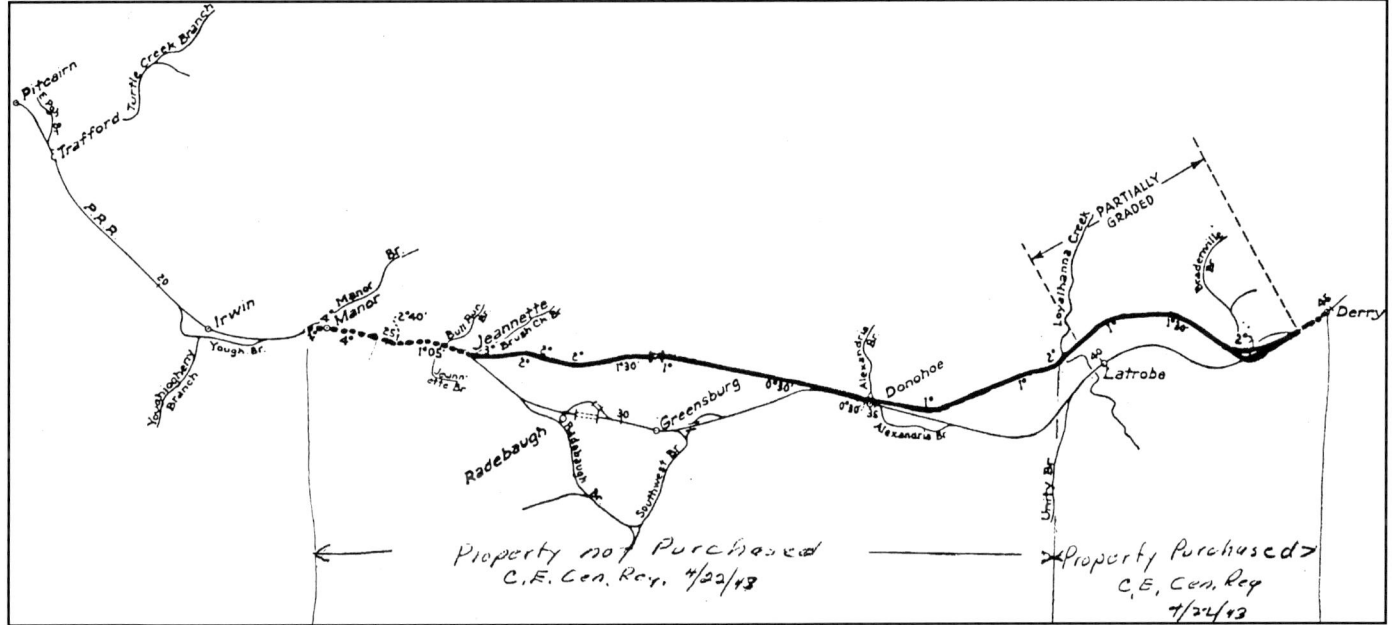

WHEN THIS PUBLISHING HOUSE decided in late 1991 to take on the project of creating the first complete interpretative history of PRR, we anticipated that it would be a daunting task if for no other reason than we noted that no one else had ever dared to do it. What we did not foresee was all the amazing revelations that we would uncover, and in many cases stumble upon, in the process. At Derry we found still another one. Prior to 1903 our friends Stone Brown and CSD were actively planning elimination of the twin dips at Latrobe and Greensburg. The earliest letter we discovered was dated 3 June 1903 and it contained references that indicated such planning had been conducted *before their time on the railroad*. Further, to leap ahead, the map seen here was prepared in 1943 as part of a study to see if the project should be completed! Now let us inform the reader how we decided to present this complex tale to minimize confusion. The thin line on this map from Derry to Manor generally represents the railroad as built (with improvements) and we will take the reader on a tour through history for this segment later in this chapter. Our purpose here is to relate the Derry-Donahoe-Jeannette (DDJ) story. The underlying purpose of the DDJ line, which was to have been double-track, was to minimize helper service for freight traffic. The thick black line shows the DDJ route. The dotted line from Jeannette to Manor was a major line relocation project to be done in conjunction with the DDJ. As the penciled notes on this map show, property was purchased from Derry to Loyalhanna Creek and it was "partially graded." Actually, the grading was almost completed. The reader might also note that the DDJ was to return to the original line at DR interlocker in West Derry. As we tell the tale, we will be showing more detailed maps prepared earlier than 1943. Also note that the new and old lines meet at Donahoe and that curvature was almost entirely eliminated.

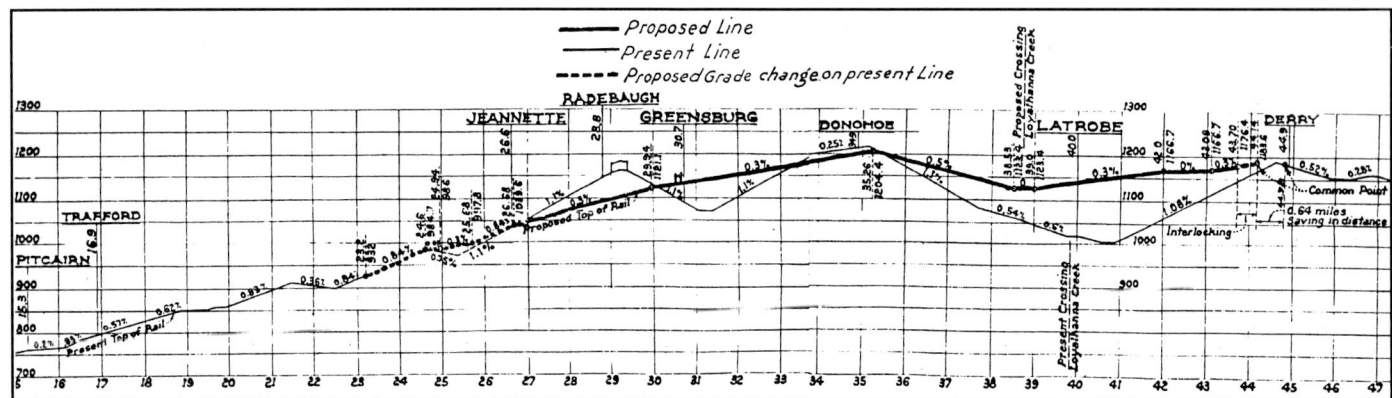

THIS PROFILE was part of the preceding 1943 map. As the reader can see, DDJ would have removed the dip at Greensburg. To do the same at Latrobe would have required more fill than there was in the whole world and side-slopes that would have covered most of the county. The eastbound grade would not have exceeded 0.3% from Jeannette to Derry, replacing grades in the 1.1% range. Westbound gradient was reduced to 0.05% for the three miles east of Donahoe. (The miles shown at the bottom are measured from Pittsburgh.) Helper miles would have been materially reduced, but not eliminated. Shoves would still be needed to get *to* Jeannette. The length of the helper grades would have been markedly shortened, however. A 1927 study showed that eastward help for tonnage trains from Trafford to Derry would be reduced from 28 to 18 miles. Westward help from Latrobe to Donahoe and Greensburg to Radebaugh Tunnel totaled 7.5 miles and would probably be unnecessary with the DDJ.

Now to the history of the project. In 1903 Stone and CSD were considering several approaches to the dip problem, including a cheaper line from Beatty to Derry. (That Derry jumpover was really meant to be a "cut-under" at DR.) A new line from Latrobe through Derry to Millwood was also being considered. The intent was to lower the Derry summit with a deep cut, an approach that Stone canceled in 1903 by telling the potential contractors that "the matter is off, and nothing will be done until the line is relocated." The urgent need for four tracks was pressing and Stone finally got permission from Philadelphia to expand to four from Latrobe to Derry. Plans and paper whizzed back and forth. In early 1904 CSD submitted plans for the segment from Loyalhanna Creek to Derry and on 26 January 1905 sent 39 plans for the whole stretch from Radebaugh to Derry. The project then went on hold, probably because PRR was awash in expensive expansion and was getting tight on money for investment. A plan was prepared in May of 1906 but it was pigeonholed until September of 1912 when it was revived for an odd reason. PRR was running out of locations to waste slag, mill refuse and cinders and it dawned on everyone that a fill from Derry to the creek would kill two birds with one stone. (West of the creek was not a problem as the cut-and-fill needed was evenly balanced.) It took until 23 June of 1918 for PRR's Board to authorize the purchase of land for this dumping enterprise. To be fair, there was a Great War and the equivalent of a nationalization of railroads between 1912 and 1918, a time that tried men's wallets as well as souls. By 1920 the wasting was well under way and in 1923 the Board okayed a "new line." DR was busy moving waste in and the empties out. Then the volume of waste fell and the project dragged on. Finally the only waste being received was from PRR, mostly cinders.

Also during the 1920s PRR was weighing the so-called Sam Rea Line, a massive project that would have created a whole new railroad from Lewistown (east of Altoona) straight through to Ohio, bypassing Pittdiv and Pittsburgh itself. The Sam Rea line would have removed big hunks of traffic from Pittdiv. Also, plans for electrification of PRR were underway in the 1920s. Thus it was easy to defer the DDJ in 1930. The Great Depression put a lot more than DDJ on hold and then, in an act that this author still finds puzzling, PRR leapt into electrification of many eastern lines. We will study the Sam Rea Line and electrification in later volumes. In 1936 then President Clement asked for an investigation of electrification and revision of Pittdiv. It took until 1939 for this study to be completed and in it was postulated the effect of electrification on DDJ. Since electric (and diesel) locomotives can exceed their continuous load rating for short distances, the helper savings on DDJ over steam would reach the vanishing point. Dead again. Why did the subject come up in 1943? We are confident it had to do with the wartime excess profits taxes which allowed railroads to deduct certain maintenance and improvement expenses. Even with tax credits, the numbers did not work. Finally, in 1955 PRR wrote off its investment in the DDJ for a tax credit. Poor DDJ. Always in the wrong place at the wrong time. We cannot help but wonder, however, how many millions upon millions of dollars would have been saved if Stone and CSD had been allowed to build it during the first decade of this century. Even in the diesel age, money would have been saved. We also contemplate with amusement what some future observer will think a thousand years from now when he discovers this huge embankment all alone out in the field. He will probably find taxpayer money to excavate it and then write a "publish or perish" treatise on his findings. No doubt he will conclude that "more research is warranted" and then apply for another grant.

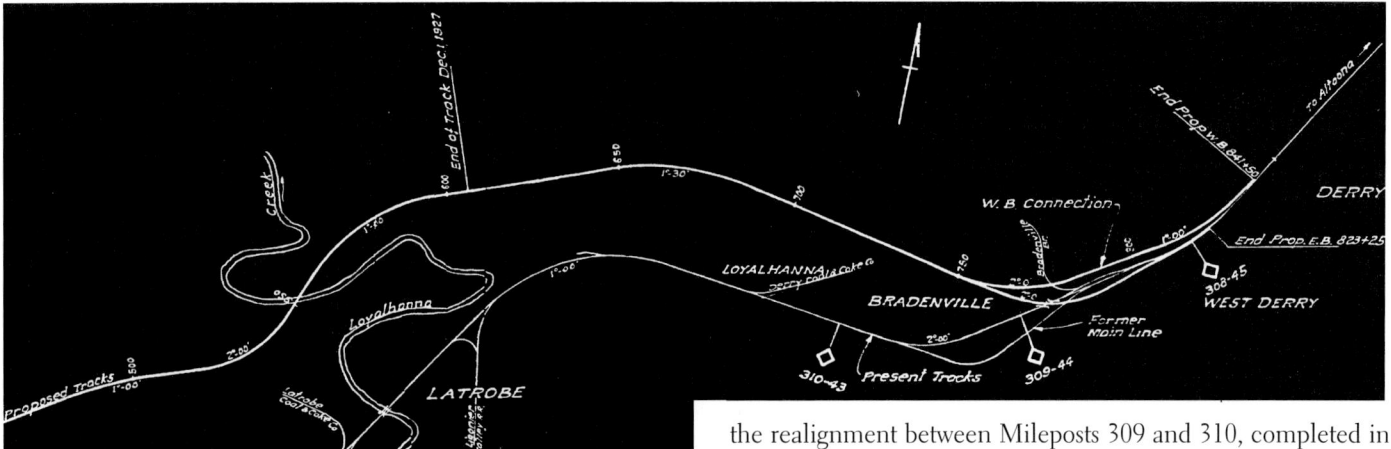

THIS MAP was prepared in 1927 as part of a status report regarding DDJ and is included because it presents an overview of the original mainline with clarity. The reader should compare it to the two track chart sections about to be shown. Moving west from Derry, one can see the planned connection with DDJ. Also note the realignment between Mileposts 309 and 310, completed in 1904 to eliminate two curves and reduce remaining curvature. (As to this and other dates, the reader is warned again that the records we have reviewed are incomplete and often contradictory.) We also caution that PRR expanded from two to three and four tracks over a period of many years and, of necessity, this was done a bit at a time. It was crucial not to interfere with existing traffic, a principle that complicated construction. And as is apparent, the respite from branch and on-line traffic ended at Derry. From there west to Pittsburgh, such volume resumed in full force. The reader may wonder why line relocations such as DDJ were kept so secret. The answer is property purchases. Once an owner learns that a railroad needs his land, the price soars.

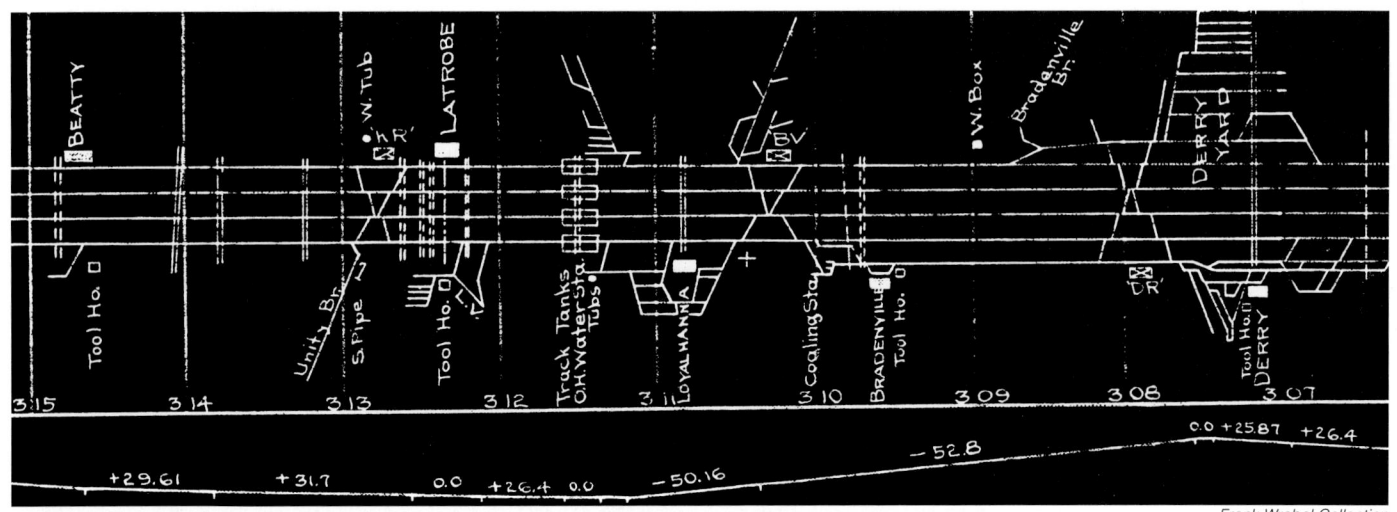

Frank Wrabel Collection

THE SITUATION in 1910 with four mainline tracks and a fifth "freight line" from Bradenville to Derry is seen here. Note the coaling station at Milepost 310; the water pans *and* overhead water station at Milepost 311.5 (Saxman); branches and sidings everywhere. The latter were due to grow.

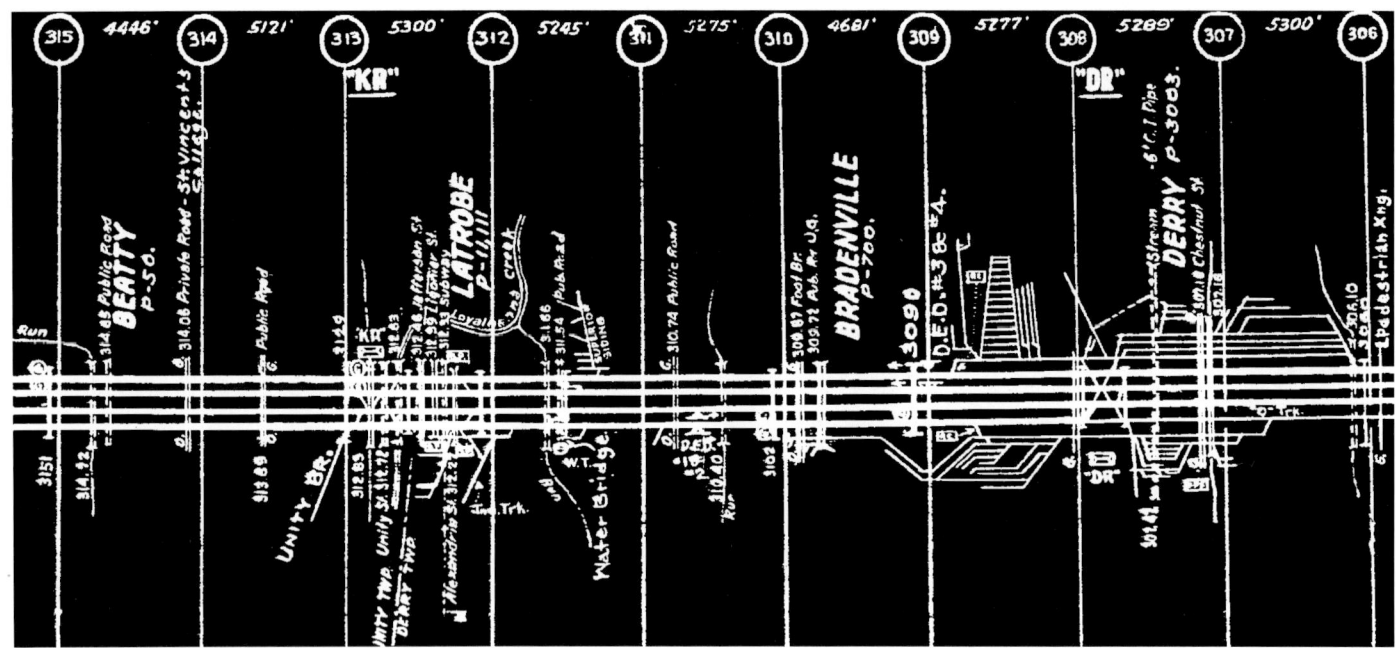

BY THE TIME this track chart was issued in 1958, a lot of things had changed from Derry to Beatty. From Mileposts 306 to 309 there had been a vast increase in yard trackage. On the north side just west of DR, much of the trackage was created to handle waste-cars for the DDJ as well as to service coal coming from the Bradenville Branch. On the south side, a mini-yard had been built to process other local traffic. Both of these yards were technically "flat" in the sense that they were not "gravity" as in hump. Another misnomer in this case because they were on a 0.95% slope! Tie them down tight, lads. We have already noted that the Derry yard was draped over a summit. By 1958 the decline in passenger traffic had allowed PRR to reduce to three mainline tracks east of Derry, but not west. Notice that a pedestrian bridge was necessary at extreme right and that the water pans were gone at Saxman; the water bridge, however, remained. Today there are just two mainline tracks through this sector, with two setoff tracks at DR as mentioned and the single Unity Industrial track in Latrobe.

BRADENVILLE, curiously enough, has some inferential American history associated with it, but not under that name. When PRR first arrived, the town was named St. Clair. Intrigued by the possibility that sainthood had been conferred on a local resident, we researched the subject enough to learn that this was far from the case. Arthur St. Clair was a Scotsman of uncertain origins (as, indeed, most of us are) who became a lieutenant in the British Army and fought under the famous General Wolfe against the French in Canada. So far so good. His reward was a thousand acres in the vicinity of Fort Ligonier (we have referred to this town in the last chapter) and command of that garrison. He took his acreage in a circle overlaying Chestnut Ridge rather than in the fertile Ligonier Valley and thus acquired an estate consisting of barren rocks and stones as well as a reputation for being somewhat odd. He espoused the American cause during the Revolution and became a Major General in the Continental Army. He fought well in several battles, but then surrendered Ticonderoga to the British in 1777. Charges of cowardice, treachery and incapacity were not sustained by a court of inquiry, the latter no doubt nervous about another Benedict Arnold. He fought some more without incident and was ultimately rewarded with the

(continued on next page)

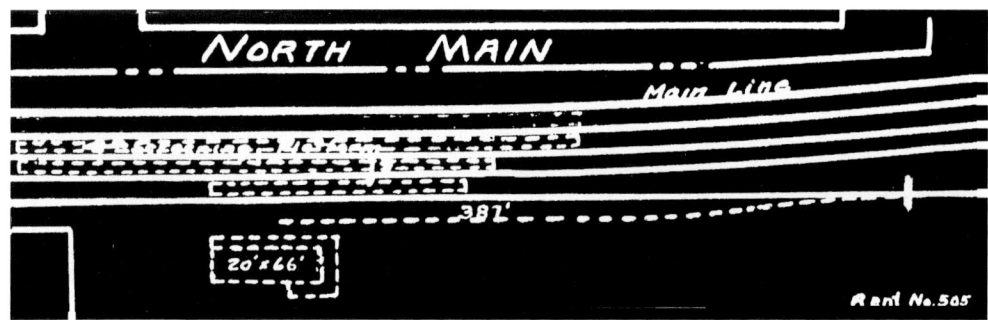

FOR THOSE who might care, here was the location of the Bradenville Station. The fifth track at lower right was the pull-in track for Derry Yard, as seen on the 1958 track chart. About a mile west is Loyalhanna, about which we can offer nothing.

WE ARE NOW arriving at the water station at Saxman (spelled Sauxman in some documents) at Milepost 311.5. That was the location by 1910, but the original location was at Milepost 312, closer to the bottom of the dip at Latrobe. Water pans were installed at a very early and uncertain date. In 1903 grading for two additional tracks from Latrobe to Derry on the old line and the elevation of tracks through Latrobe to ease the depth of the dip was well underway. Water pans must be level so it was necessary to move the pans east and raise the existing tracks several feet. The old pans were moved and lengthened. A water bridge was also installed, as seen. We found no plans or photographs of this facility, but did find some interesting supporting data and this tender plan. This 1879 arrangement was the culmination of much experimentation and shows a newly designed scoop that was capable of a filling rate of three gallons per linear foot of tank at 60 mph with a tank width of 19 inches. In one trial it was found that 3,300 gallons of water could be lifted in 1,000 feet at 68 mph. At these speeds the shock on the mechanism

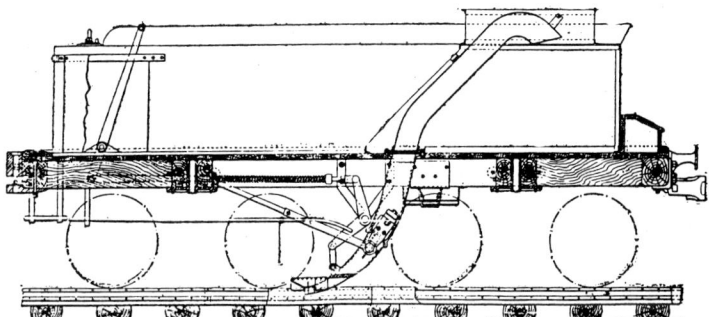

was obviously severe, yet this problem was solved with this new device. The older scoop could only lift half that amount of water. The pans themselves were fitted, inside and out, with inclined plates to lift the scoop if the fireman dropped it too soon or raised it too late. We can see a lot of interesting possibilities in either eventuality but cannot supply factual data.

(continued from last page)
governorship of the territory northwest of the Ohio River. In 1791 he commanded an army against the Miami Indians and lost 600 of his men in a pitched battle with them. In modern-day terms, that is the equivalent of losing an entire maneuver battalion in one action. And that against mere "savages" unassisted by Frenchmen. St. Clair escaped unscathed and, wonder of wonders, managed to avoid censure still another time in spite of a horrendous butchers bill. He resigned his commission in 1792 and then lived in poverty amongst his rocks and stones, dying in 1818. He was buried in Greensburg without a tombstone, an oversight corrected by Masonic friends in 1832 after they were absolutely certain he was dead. The town remained St. Clair at least until 1875, but ultimately was renamed Bradenville. Sadly, Bradenville became merely a minor point on PRR and today is regarded as a suburb of Latrobe. The station seen here c. 1920 was built in 1902 on a siding. Freight service was suspended on 16 November 1932 and passenger service 10 February 1933, yet it was not until 1954 that the structure was retired. Bradenville also boasted BV tower, a 48-lever mechanical interlocker built in 1904, and also a four-track overhead coal tipple supported by timber trestling. The yard seen at Bradenville was removed at an unknown date and a strip mine took its place.

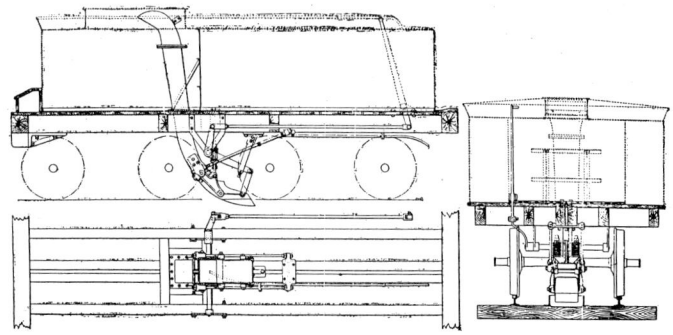

THE SCOOP DESIGN evolved, as evidenced by this 1894 plan. The chute is now almost vertical, the only change we can divine. The water station at Saxman also evolved. In 1911 the pans on Track Nos. 3 and 4 were widened to 29" and by 1920 all four pans were 29" wide and 1,800 feet long. The year 1934 saw Track Nos. 1 and 2 pans lengthened to 2,200 feet (with parts from Sang Hollow which was closed that year) to enable freight trains to operate through to Conemaugh. Put differently, pans at Saxman and Wilmore were sufficient. The pans, with attendant water bridge, lasted as late as 1950 and the bridge was extant in 1958, although surely it was removed shortly thereafter. The flat spot is still there.

LATROBE, at the very bottom of the first dip on the Rip Rap, is another one of those towns that owes its very existence to the coming of the railroad. In this case, the town also owes its name to a railroader. With full knowledge that PRR was coming, civil engineer Oliver W. Barnes was given the task of laying out a town in 1850. Thomson decided to name the town in honor of his close personal friend and adversary, Benjamin Latrobe, Jr., who was the son of the famous father mentioned earlier in this volume and who, *at the moment of the naming of the town*, was engaged as one of a two-man team with your author's relative Thomas Swann in building B&O from Cumberland to Wheeling in defiance of PRR, Thomson and the Commonwealth of Pennsylvania. The B&O's story is told in our book *West End* and PRR's here. Later Benjamin Latrobe would tangle with Thomson with the Pittsburgh and Connellsville as related in our book *Sand Patch*. Perhaps the reader might appreciate that when your author visited Latrobe in the Spring of 1995 for the first time in his life, it was with a sense of irony as well as respect for those big men who accomplished so much in so short a lifespan. Since we have competed quite fiercely with opponents in a long career, and have come to admire those of quality, we can fully understand Thomson's admiration for a noble foe and his decision to honor him in so permanent a way. Neither Thomson or Swann had cities named for them...only Latrobe. The story of these men and their impact on history is even deeper than that. We have alluded to Thomson's application of line-and-staff managerial techniques to railroading. Actually, there were three pio-

neers in this endeavor...Thomson, Latrobe and Daniel McCallum of the Erie Railroad. Thomson was the first to enunciate the concept in December of 1857, but full credit for the contributions of the other two gentlemen was given by Alfred D. Chandler, Jr., in his insightful work *The Visible Hand: The Managerial Revolution in American Business* (Harvard University Press 1977.) Here we see Latrobe as it appeared to a very poor artist in 1853. The hotel in the background was the brick Gilcrest House, obviously built in anticipation of a lucrative trade. The hope was not in vain. By 1855 population was growing and numerous firms in manufacturing and trade were blooming. Roads diverged from Latrobe in every direction, serving a rich agricultural and mineral region. Even colleges had arrived by 1875. In 1955 Latrobe was home to a variety of metal firms and was thriving. An odd note: the first professional football game was played in Latrobe in 1895. Something for everyone.

THIS EASTWARD VIEW of the Latrobe station complex, taken from the north side, is from a postcard carrying a 1910 postmark. The height of the embankment shows that PRR had eased the dip but built the station structures at the original level. Sparse records indicate that both the station and embankment were completed in 1903. It is known, however, that the shelters were not finished until 1906. An ICC completion date of 1908 is clearly wrong. We know that the original water pans at Latrobe were located a few hundred feet east of the station at Milepost 312 and that they were installed new in 1887. As shown, they were moved east to Saxman. One would think that water supply at Latrobe would have been easy, yet it wasn't. By 1862 the problem was so critical that a 600-foot well was drilled in this vicinity and water pumped up to track level. The move to Saxman ultimately solved this nasty problem. The reader will recall that Saxman was gravity-fed. One might ask why PRR did not build a higher embankment. The conundrum was the bridge over Loyalhanna Creek which lies about a half-mile to the rear of the photographer in this scene. To raise that bridge would have been very expensive indeed. As it was, the selected height presented difficulties with the connection with the Ligonier Valley Railroad and industrial sidings, which lay to the right of this view, as well as the Unity Branch on the far side

Bob Jansen Collection

of the creek. Latrobe was one of the focal points of the dispute in 1851 which led to Thomson's ascension to control of PRR. While this subject will be thoroughly treated in another volume, suffice it to say that PRR was out of construction money in that year and was stalled near Latrobe. Thomson talked Barnes into an independent real estate development venture for the entire tract and giving PRR land for station grounds, water facilities, enginehouse operations and a right-of-way. In addition, of course, for naming the town for Benjamin Latrobe. Thomson was quite a salesman.

THE STATION building appeared this way c.1920. A tunnel from the rear of the station under the mainline allowed passengers and express/mail personnel to reach the eastbound tracks.

National Archives

THE LATROBE STATION, looking west from the westbound platform, on 29 May 1970 appeared thus.

Edward H. Weber

THE LATROBE STATION has become DiSalvo's Station, which is really a restaurant. As one can see from this photograph taken 7 May 1995, the proprietors not only restored the station but have materially improved it.

THE SOUTH ENTRANCE to DiSalvo's is as grandiose as the main structure just seen. In our view, this represents preservation at its best. Regrettably, on 7 May 1995 we did not have time to enter this appealing establishment. Since Italian cuisine is our favorite ethnic choice and we find "Mediterranean Types" an enchanting race, perhaps we will revisit Latrobe some day when properly dressed.

The station sign at upper right is PRR with keystone, overlooking still another caboose. We experienced an interesting event in Latrobe on 7 May 1995 which we will relate later in the book.

THE FREIGHT HOUSE at Latrobe, seen here c. 1920, must have been on the south side of the mainline. Certainly it must have been in connection with the Ligonier Valley Railroad. By the way, PRR acquired a portion of that railroad when it ceased operation in 1952. There is still an industrial lead at Latrobe, utilizing old Track No. 2.

National Archives

THE STONE BRIDGE over Loyalhanna Creek has a touch of mystery in its history. Sound sources say that the "original" stone viaduct was double-track, askew, built by contractors Clark and Company and consisted of *three* arches of 45 feet each. PRR's annual report for 1901 states that a *new* four-track bridge will be required. Yet we have correspondence dated 10 August 1901 that clearly states that masonry was being placed on both sides of the original viaduct to provide for four tracks. There are only *two* arches seen here and only *two* in place today. Since we are quite sure the location did not change, we guess Stone Brown decided to rebuild the entire structure. The track elevation at Latrobe triggered quite a debate with operating people who wanted provision for a fifth track east of the viaduct to provide for LVRR passenger trains using the new station and to avoid use of the mainline for drilling industrial spurs. They didn't get a Zero Track, but did receive a long lead at a lower level as seen on the 1910 track chart.

Todd Atkinson

RIP RAP

THE LOYALHANNA crossing has only one change since early in this century. The mainline has been raised a few feet and a parapet built to contain the roadbed. It is seen here on 7 May 1995.

National Archives

KR TOWER was located just west of the Loyalhanna crossing and is seen here c. 1920 with "valuation focus." A 20-lever tower was installed here in 1897 and this 14 by 32-foot mechanical interlocker was built new in 1904 with 48 levers to serve four tracks.

Edward H. Weber

(at right)
KR NEEDED PAINT on 22 November 1960 but it wasn't until 1964 that relief arrived in the form of aluminum siding, along with removal of the bay window. All was well until 1971 when a massive derailment completely destroyed the plant. Short of money, PC did not replace the interlocker and the building itself was demolished in 1980 when a CTC interlocker was installed. The point is now known as CP TROBE.

BEATTY is a placename that appears frequently in PRR history yet, as far as we can determine, its only significance was as a reference point. PRR reached "Beatty's Station" on 10 December 1851 and was stalled there until late 1852. Located only two miles north of the Greensburg Turnpike, it was a cargo and passenger transfer point to the turnpike for about a year. Once that mission was redundant, Beatty just drifted away. This octagon tower, supposedly at Beatty c. 1880, appears to be a telegraph station serving only two hand-thrown turnouts. The presence of three tracks is puzzling for this purported date and we suspect that the third one is merely a lead for a siding. Note what appears to be a station and waiting room in the distance. The closest train obviously serves the photographer and the more distant one is making a station stop. Based on curvature this is an easterly view. Note the deep fill, characteristic of the Rip Rap. The gruel at Beatty is thin. We know that an interlocker was under construction in 1889 and that it was expanded from six to fourteen levers in 1897. Since there was no tower or interlocker in 1910, we are confident that this scene was victim to curve elimination completed from here west to Donahoe in 1906. We have no call letters to offer.

Railroad Museum of Pennsylvania

TRIUMPH I

THIS IS CLEARLY the Beatty Station c. 1920. Why, then, are there only two mainline tracks? We have no explanation. Beatty remains a point on the railroad at roughly Milepost 314.8, but there is no town *per se*. The same is true for Carney just west of Beatty. There are a multitude of gas wells surrounding both of these locations, as well as the remnants of strip mines. When we arrive at Milepost 317.9 history gets more interesting. Here, at Donahoe, we find the westerly summit of the Latrobe dip. The grade is called Carney Hill.

National Archives

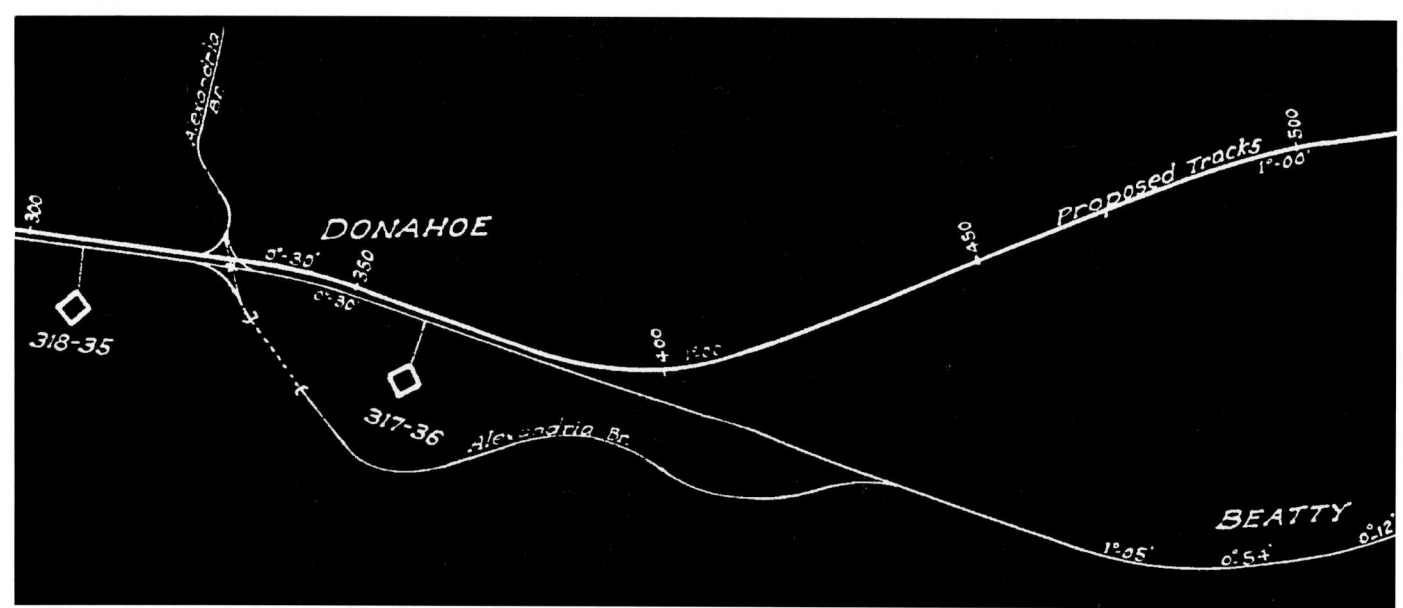

THIS 1927 MAP, the eastern portion of which we have seen earlier in regard to the DDJ, clearly shows the location of the original mainline from Beatty to Donahoe. The Alexandria Branch line on the bottom *cum* tunnel is the original; the straight line above shows the path of relocated four-track main which went in service in 1907; the "Proposed Tracks" represents the DDJ. A completely new four-mile long railroad was built from Beatty to George (slightly off the map on the left) and from there to Southwest Junction as we shall see. Contrary to lore, the tunnel was not abandoned and in fact was in service as part of the Alexandria Branch well into this century. This is the famous Carrs Tunnel.

CARRS TUNNEL was the first bore on the Rip Rap and, at the beginning, gave PRR every impression that it was at a lucky location through solid rock. Certainly this photograph gives that appearance. Sadly, this was an illusion. The 825-foot tunnel was opened in 1852 and tunnel disease began its slow but inexorable trip toward reversion to its original state, peppering the railroad with rockfalls. Arching became essential, a tricky feat considering the volume of traffic moving through it. It was not until 1870 that the arching was finally completed. By the way, this photograph carries an 1875 date. As the tunnel is not arched, that could not possibly be correct.

Smithsonian Institution

Blair County Historical Society

THE APPROACH CUT to Carrs Tunnel was an engineering monster in and of itself, deep and with steep sides. Since this line was single-tracked in 1907 and arching was completed in 1870, this photograph could have been taken at any time in a 37-year span. We suspect, however, that c.1893 is about right.

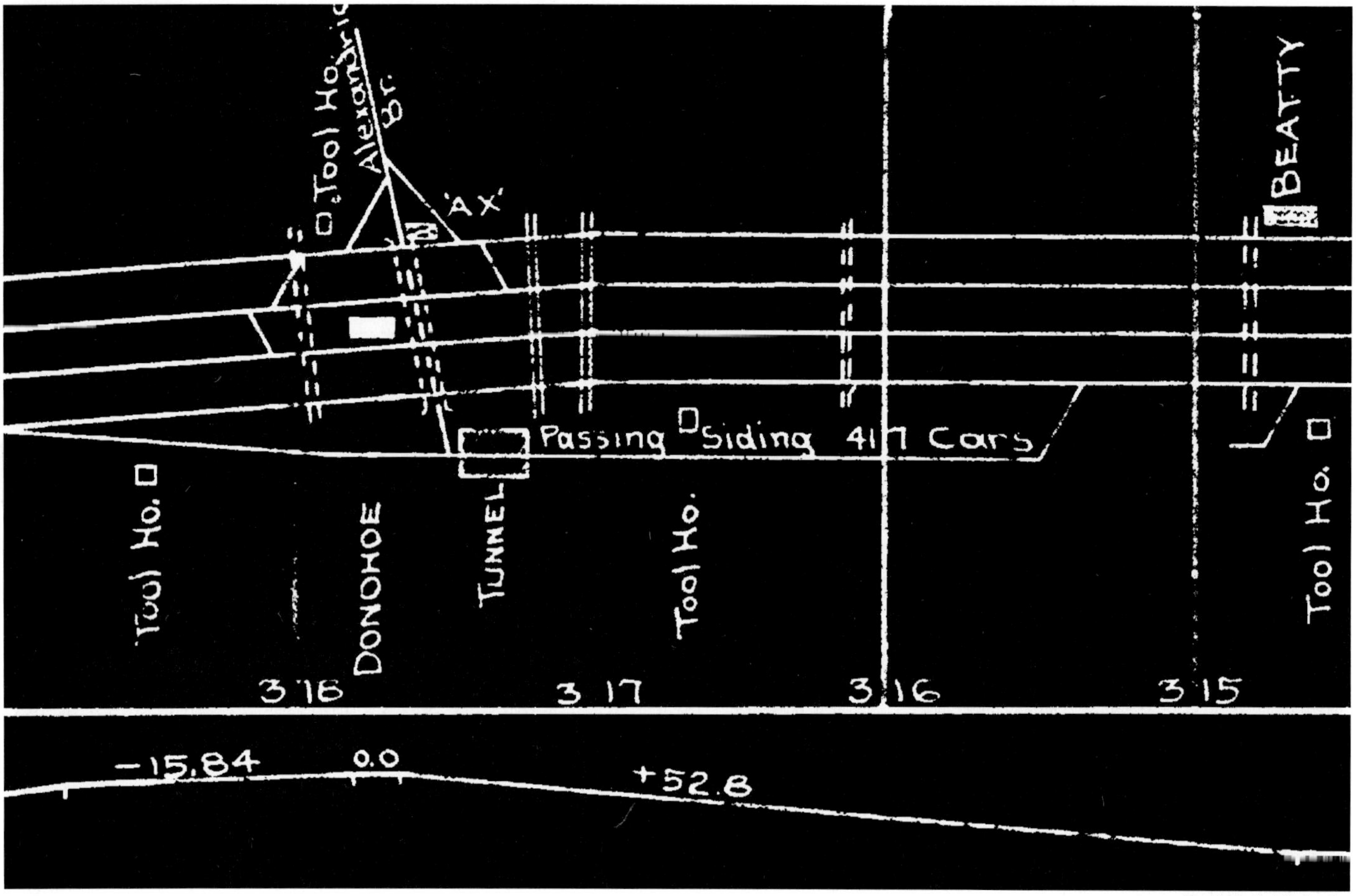

TRIUMPH I

Frank Wrabel Collection

FOR MANY YEARS, the original line was regarded as a fifth track (but not Zero) as seen here in 1910. Notice that it was almost four miles long and reached to the west well past Donahoe. As late as 1958 the line was active as part of the Alexandria Branch from Donahoe to near Beatty and two mile-long sidings were in place east of the tunnel. We know that a new passenger/freight station was built at Donahoe in 1890 and we see a station here between Track Nos. 3 and 4. One wonders if it was moved c. 1907. AX Tower is also seen, but curiously its interlocker does not reach Track No. 1. Today one finds only two mainline tracks and an abandoned tunnel. That short stretch of 0.0% grade remains at the summit, whether aid or hindrance to train handling an open question.

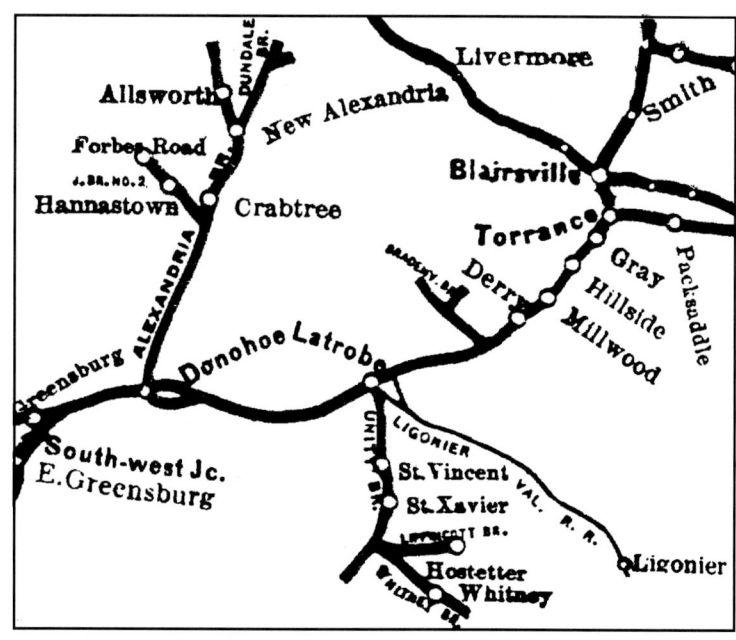

THE RESPITE from branch line traffic on the Rip Rap was short-lived. The influx began to rise with the Bradenville Branch at Derry, the Unity Branch and Ligonier Valley Railroad at Latrobe and the Alexandria Branch at Donahoe. This 1941 map shows just how extensive was the trackage from these points. The farther west, the larger the increase in volume. For example, in 1903 the Alexandria Branch poured 40,086 *loaded* cars onto the mainline and received 3,085. As always, empties effectively doubled this volume. At Donahoe, at least it was downhill in both directions. We will soon visit Southwest Junction (at lower left) near Greensburg. As we shall see, in comparison the Alexandria Branch was a yawner.

RIP RAP

National Archives

THE DEMISE of this tower at the Donahoe summit, a seemingly minor incident in transportation history, was in fact symptomatic of the disease that brought down mighty PRR. During the second and third decades of this century, the three basic trunklines were in a cost reduction war and PRR was losing. B&O and NYC were winning in spite of their inherent disadvantages and in the face of PRR supremacy in every category save one. PRR had all the advantages including shortest city/pair distances, superb physical plant, meticulous maintenance, incredibly competent engineering skills, probably the best operating management, the economic benefits that flow from enormous volume, financial and managerial skills and strength beyond compare, brutal legal prowess in defense of their turf, political power and influence and superlative capabilities in so many aspects of railroading that it would be a chore to list them all. We have carefully studied PRR financials and drawn upon fine works by other observers of the scene. The conclusion is inescapable. PRR's vulnerable heel was motive power. Their policy throughout history (and we suspect it is true today) was marked by the worst of all hindrances in human affairs. A closed mind, worsened by the deadly sin of believing their own propaganda. Nothing is more impenetrable than a mindset that we can do no wrong and its handmaiden of denial of facts no matter how stark. We shall explore this aspect of PRR history in more detail in later volumes. Pertinent to this caption, Philadelphia had noted that their two rivals were besting PRR in transportation expenses. They were not amused and ordered the Central Region (which then included Pittdiv) to slash and slash now. Comply or die. WA was found wanting and was offered as a sacrificial lamb to the competition, being abandoned at 12:01 pm Saturday 13 June 1925. WA's movements were henceforth handled by KR in Latrobe. By the way, we know that the tower had call letters AX as early as 1905 and in 1910, but by c. 1920 it had become WA as seen. For decades after 1925, B&O and NYC generally continued to beat PRR in transportation ratios so the closing of WA and other charades didn't have the slightest impact on history.

WE HAVE INUNDATED the reader to the point of boredom with tales of the immense local and branch traffic volume that cascaded upon the Pittdiv mainline throughout most of its history. One can be pardoned for thinking that, at long last in our journey, the flood was easing. Actually, the crescendo lay west of Donahoe. The name Southwest Junction sounds innocuous enough until one studies the maps to follow. It was at this junction that the plethora of PRR lines serving the Connellsville coal region first met the mainline. The reader of *Sand Patch* knows, at least in capsule form, the impact of this incredible resource upon the industrial development of the United States and western Pennsylvania. The reader of future volumes in this series will receive further illumination. Sufficient for the moment let us study this 1910 track chart. Southwest Junction lay at the exact *bottom* of the second big dip. What a lovely place to receive all this tonnage. Uphill in both directions and, by the way, a large portion of these cars moved west as well as east. Note that the SW interlocker was double, or mirror image. There were *two* plants at SW, *both* on grades. And a duckunder, an underground version of the jumpovers we have seen at Cresson and Ehrenfeld/South Fork, for westbound movements to the branch. The track and plant arrangement seen here lasted at least as late as 1945. By 1958 it was all gone except for an eastbound track alongside Track No. 1. In its heyday SW was quite a place.

Frank Wrabel Collection

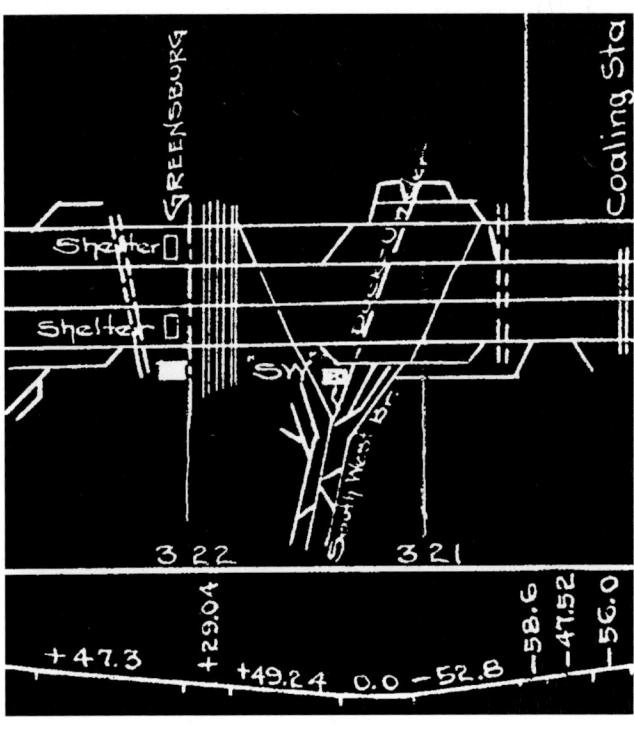

295

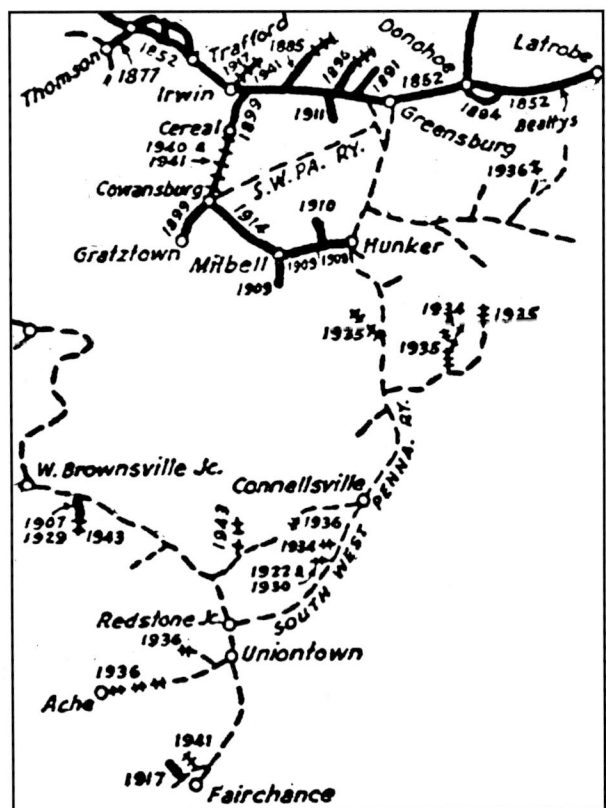

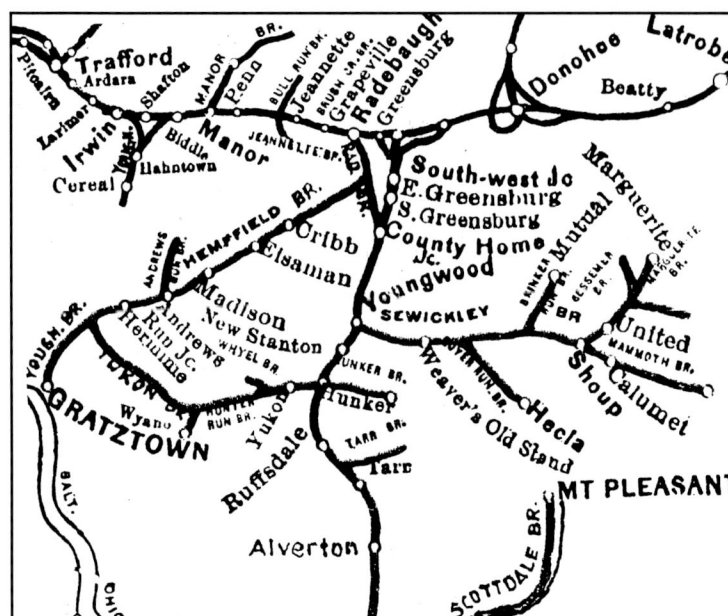

THIS 1941 MAP is included to give an overview of the northern portion of SW territory, with particular attention drawn to the line reaching into Radebaugh from County Home. Radebaugh, as we shall see, is the second summit on the Rip Rap. Shortline operator SWP, based in Youngwood, is moving lumber, newsprint, pipe, coal and some miscellaneous business over the remnants of the branches in this area. For example, in October of 1996 SWP moved a coal train over a circuitous route on ex-B&O and ex-PRR lines that ended up interchanged at Greensburg. Far less than the glory days, but better than no trains at all.

THE GAGGLE of feeder lines that emanated from SW Junction went under the collective name of Southwest Pennsylvania Railway and reached, as one can see in this 1945 depiction, as far south as Fairchance and west to Brownsville. (The crosshatched lines represent abandonments.) Of course, many other railroads served this region in competition with PRR, principally B&O and NYC's P&LE. In broad terms, B&O worked from the south, NYC from the north and PRR through the middle. In recent years ownership of most of the lines still extant in this whole area passed to Fayette County and are operated by an entity known as the Southwest Pennsylvania Railroad.

THE AMOUNT OF SMOKE that must have invested SW Junction surely was the cause of the valuation photographer's poor focus in this c. 1920 shot of SW Tower. He couldn't wait to get out of that sinkhole. Little wonder. In 1903, 120,224 *loaded* cars came off the SW and 21,414 cars went in. As usual, plus empties. SW Tower was definitely in place as late as 1955. Also in that year we see PRR referring to branches as secondaries.

National Archives

ONE WOULD THINK that Greensburg was so named for the verdant surrounding countryside, but actually the name was selected in honor of Revolutionary General Nathaniel Greene. Since the general was one of the best officers in the Continental Army, one would have thought that the "e" would have been included. It is possible that the burial of Arthur St. Clair in Greensburg was annoying to General Greene, but we have found no way to confirm this supposition. The town was laid out c. 1785 but, in spite of its resources, languished for lack of transportation until the arrival of PRR. This 1852 illustration shows a pleasant little town located upon a small hill. Unfortunately for PRR, this site was awkward because the railroad had to bore a tunnel to get through the hill to get out of the valley of Jacks Run. Thus PRR needed a tunnel at the *bottom* of two grades, an unusual and irritating situation that turned out to be doubly expensive because parts of the town were over the tunnel and had to be purchased when the railroad was widened to four tracks as we shall see. Prior to PRR's arrival, Greensburg enjoyed a resort trade from Pittsburgh's wealthy who wished holidays away from the smoke and bustle of that thriving city. In a few short decades, the smoke from PRR locomotives and the burning of soft coal for space heating made Greensburg worse than Pittsburgh with a doleful effect on the tourist business. Greensburg did enjoy a measure of prosperity commensurate with its position as a major railroad junction and became home to some light manufacturing.

Pennsylvania State Archives

THIS IS THE EAST PORTAL of PRR's tunnel under that "small hill" in Greensburg. Early accounts say the bore was 300 feet long, others 284 feet. Whatever the length, it was built for two tracks with masonry lining and was ready for service in 1852. The second track was not actually installed until November of 1859, just in time for Civil War traffic. It is known that the mainline was elevated on fills on both sides of the tunnel to minimize the depth of the dip and the length of the tunnel itself. A deep cut was also needed, as this photograph attests. Naturally, both the embankments and the cut were a constant source of maintenance problems. West of this small hill was Ludwick, where PRR constructed a brick warehouse, enginehouse, wood/water station, etc. When PRR sponsored the Southwest Pennsylvania Railway in the 1870s, Ludwick was to be "SW Junction." For a lot of local reasons, it did not work out that way and SW Junction was placed east of Greensburg rather than west. The date of this photograph is uncertain but judging by the wooden rail joiners it is quite early and we would guess early 1860s.

TRIUMPH I

Railroad Museum of Pennsylvania

THE FIRST Greensburg Station was opened in 1860 just beyond the west portal. It was a 55 by 29-foot brick structure and was indeed handsome. It was also long in coming. For eight years PRR was pummeled with complaints about the temporary building used as a station in the interim. In 1857 one complaint bemoaned that it would "scarcely be a protection for another winter." Three more winters were to pass. Two small notes: the crude road crossing the tracks is Harrison Avenue and there is no steeple on the church in the background at upper right. The given date on this photograph is 1869.

Pennsylvania State Archives

THIS TURGID PRINT of the west portal and the Greensburg Station was taken from atop the fill some time after the preceding photograph. It shows the small hill in better detail. The label says c. 1870.

AS THE TOWN grew over the tunnel, a retaining wall became necessary. Here we see a westbounder preparing to make a station stop c.1893. The sidewalls of the cut are now overgrown with vines and grasses. Notice the early train order signal adjacent to Track No. 1.

AT SOME POINT in the history of the station, a shelter was built over the platform serving the eastbound track. Westbound passengers had to stand in the rain or snow. Note the overhead road bridge between the station and the portal, which carried Pennsylvania Avenue.

Frank Wrabel Collection

GREENSBURG continued to encroach on PRR and snuggle closer to its mainline. While the date of this postcard is unknown, we know it was taken between 1891 and 1909. The former date is when the Pennsylvania Avenue overhead bridge was erected and the latter when PRR tore the roof from the tunnel, creating an open cut. Note the large new office building just behind the station, with the church steeple peeking over the roof. There is a reference that states the tunnel was deroofed in 1892 and we cannot say this is impossible, but the 1909 date was also given in the same source.

TRIUMPH I

A NEWSPAPER ACCOUNT in the early 1900s alluded to the crowded conditions prevailing in the old station as follows: "The men's waiting room at 9 am any weekday will be found packed with all nationalities and the combination odor of pipes, garlic, limburger, beer, etc., is strong enough to upset a locomotive." Also " the women's waiting room was frequently crowded by men." We find nothing amiss here except being shocked about the beer at 9 am. One should never consume alcohol before noon on workdays. As in the 1850s, PRR was unmoved by such complaints and waffled because they saw no accident reports indicating overturned engines. The decision to build a new station was directly related to the urgent need to widen the railroad to four tracks. That having been decided, PRR came to the sensible conclusion that it was wise to lessen the dip by materially raising the mainline. Here we see the new station complex shortly after completion in 1911. Notice that the raised mainline has effectively eliminated that small hill. GU Tower, incidentally, was abandoned at the same time and its functions assumed by SW. Now let us backpedal a bit. On page 237 we awarded the new Johnstown Station the nod as "most impressive" station on the line from Altoona to Pitcairn. That Greensburgers might take umbrage to this reference is under-

standable and we hasten to say that our opinion is subjective and that the contest was very close. Recalling the comparison of statistics for the four months ending January 1912, we find that Greensburg sold more tickets (58,013 to 47,121) and served more trains (5,365 to 3,339.) However, much of Greensburg's traffic was commuter and Johnstown's was through. Actually, the winner in all categories was East Liberty and no one would nominate *that* station for an aesthetic prize. For the unmollified, we promise many color views of Greensburg later in the book.

TIME and the vagaries of railroad economics were not kind to the Greensburg Station. On 29 May 1970 she appeared a little threadbare and lonely.

Edward H. Weber

RIP RAP

THE REDUCTION of the small hill was a major undertaking as this c. 1920 valuation photograph makes quite evident. The train on the left is a size-reference that tells it all.

National Archives

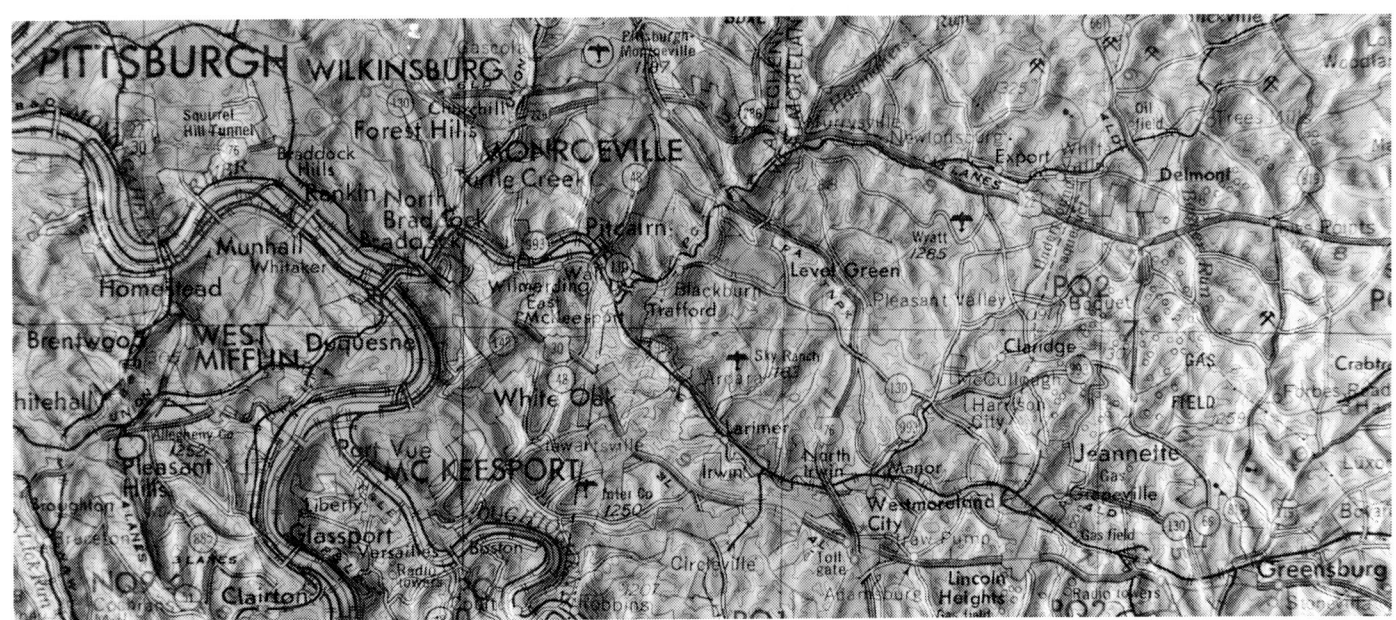

THE LAST LAP on the Rip Rap from Greensburg to Pitcairn, in relation to the terrain, can be seen with clarity on this relief map. Even with a vertical exaggeration of three, the jumbled hills give an impression of mildness which is far from the case insofar as PRR was concerned. Most of the placenames on PRR west of Greensburg are quite apparent except for one of the most significant…Radebaugh and its summit slightly west of Greensburg at lower right. We have taken PRR into downtown Pittsburgh at upper left to show the plateau beginning at Braddock Heights (Swissvale.) One might notice the references to gas and oil fields which pepper this region. While these resources will not be a subject in this book, they hint at the natural opulence of this part of Pennsylvania that played such a primary role in PRR's and the Commonwealth's rise to dominance. To say nothing of Pittsburgh in its contest with Wheeling.

TRIUMPH I

BRUSH CREEK begins its long trek to the Gulf of Mexico atop a hill just a little over a mile west of Greensburg. This minor little hillock has never had a name, in common with the other thousands of hummocks that dot the landscape in western Pennsylvania. If it were not for PRR the hill would have remained unknown and unnoticed. Unfortunately for PRR, this hill was in the way so, over time, it acquired two railroad names. The first was Barkleys Summit, also spelled Barclays in early literature. In short order the name evolved to Radebaugh, source unknown to us. By any name, however, this pimple became a boil on the backside of PRR that was not finally lanced until 1965. Two tunnels were drilled to lower the summit to manageable proportions. Tunnel/tunnel/trouble/trouble. We will posit the case that these two tunnels gave PRR more heartburn than the three at the Allegheny Summit. We present this map to give an overview of the location of these two tunnels in relation to each other. The short tunnel is the original, the longer one the "new" bore. This "Proposed Tracks" represent, of course, the DDJ, a solution that never was as we have seen. As we proceed with our story, let us make a few points. The curve that ended at Milepost 323-30 was eliminated in 1892. The "No. 4" at the east end of the old tunnel is a track number. The "Radebaugh Branch" that joins the mainline at Milepost 324-29 is really part of the Southwest Pennsylvania Railway Company lines. The call letters at this junction were RG, now known as CP RADE.

Jeff Madden

THIS IS A 1960s view of the east portal of the original tunnel. It was opened in 1852 and contained two tracks. The tunnel was 450 feet long and was masonry lined at the beginning. It is located between two knobs. The entrance cut, not apparent here, was deep, steep and unstable. The construction of this tunnel, and indeed the entire railroad from Beatty to this point, triggered the palace revolution that brought Thomson to full power. PRR was running out of construction money and Thomson was demanding borrowing power to produce funds. This tale will be told in another volume, but the upshot was a Thomson victory over near-sighted Philadelphia dilettantes who were losing their nerve. The assistant engineer in charge of construction from Beatty to Radebaugh was C.P.B. Jeffries. Thomson himself, of course, was Chief Engineer at this time. Jeffries did a fine job and this tunnel is a tribute to his skill. Generally, the tunnel remained in service until the Noah-like rains of Hurricane Agnes collapsed a portion of it. We will show a 1977 color photograph later in the book. When the new tunnel was opened in 1898, the original was abandoned for a few years. Early in this century, it was restored as a single-track westbound freight line as Track No. 4. When the mainline was reduced to three tracks, it became Track No. 3 until Agnes struck.

302

THE WEST portal of the original tunnel is seen here late in the last century. The overburden is the low point between the two knobs. Jeffries minimized the length of the bore at the price of very deep cutting to the portals on both sides. Here we have still more graphic evidence of the instability of the terrain. Note the telltales anchored in the hillsides.

Blair County Historical Society

WE INCLUDE this 1958 track chart to demonstrate the location of the original tunnel in relation to gradient and the summit. At this time, the original bore carried Track No. 4. The approach to the summit was quite steep on both sides. The actual summit was west of the tunnel, good planning considering the predominance of eastbound tonnage at the time of construction. The original line topped at 1,171 feet...the new bore at 1,164 feet. As will be seen, the new tunnel was not quite the panacea that these elevation numbers imply.

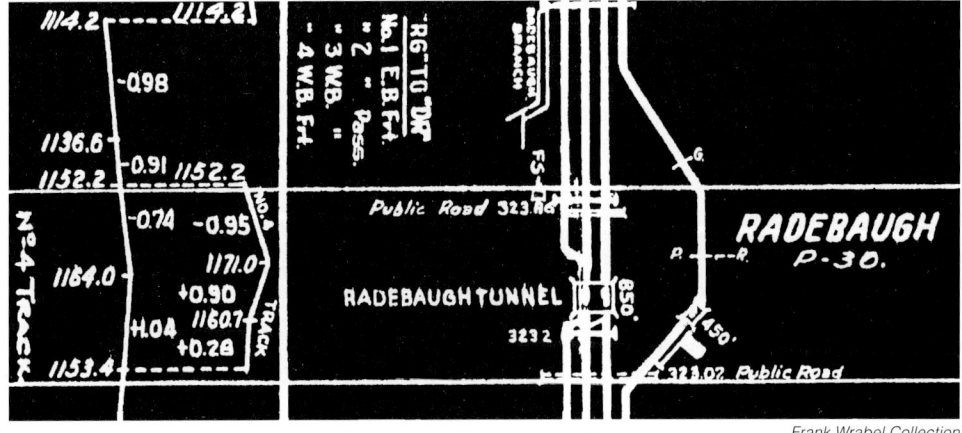

Frank Wrabel Collection

TRIUMPH I

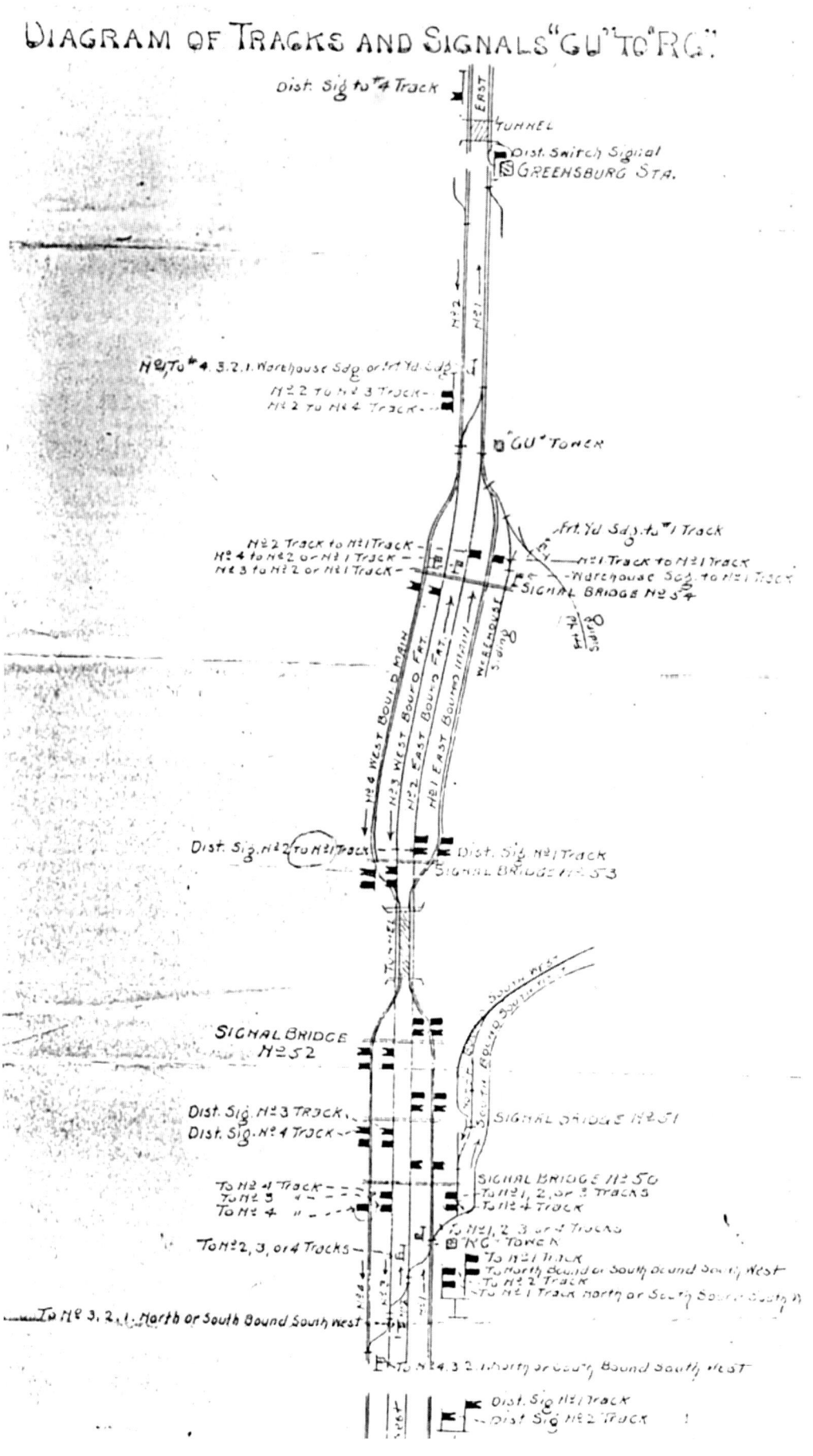

WE KNOW the new Radebaugh Tunnel was under construction in 1896, although the start date is uncertain. It was masonry lined, 850 feet long and, unfortunately, only double-tracked. We can give the opening date with great precision. It was Sunday 10 April 1898 just after the passage of Train No. 302 (east) and Train No. 3 (west.) As is seen here, both tracks were gauntleted and the old tunnel line abandoned. This sketch (dated 4 April 1898) and accompanying correspondence is one of our most satisfying finds in researching the history of Pittdiv. Starting at the top, the line from Greensburg to GU Tower was still double-track. The warehouse and freight yard siding from GU enables us to pinpoint the location of the "lost town" of Ludwick. The summit is just east of the new tunnel. RG Tower stands west of the new tunnel where the Southwest Pennsylvania Railway joins the mainline. RG had been handling the enormous traffic from this line since it first opened to Connellsville in 1873. (To have put this traffic on the mainline at Ludwick below the summit and east of the knobs would have been, to say the least, unwise.) The provenance of this sketch and the story behind it is fascinating. To begin, let us dismiss arguments that a four-track tunnel would have been best. An arch would have been essential to support the weight of the overburden and such an arch would have been so high that it would have been easier to create an open cut. To have dug such a cut for four tracks would have required excavation comparable to removing the entire hill. The problem confronting PRR engineers was how to safely signal the gauntlet tracks. Electrical signaling was a young science in the 1890s and the first debate was whether to employ mechanical interlocking or electro-pneumatic systems, the latter at triple the capital investment. Either method involved intricate wiring of great complexity utilizing something called electricity which, by the way, is still not entirely understood by scientists. One little design misstep and a tragic collision inside the tunnel would result. Parenthetically, *to this day* modern signaling systems deploy false clears. Quite aside from the human problem of misreading or misunderstanding by the crews. Plus, of course, mechanical failure such as broken rails, dragging equipment and so on. The chances of such mishaps may have been small statistically, but the enormous volume on Pittdiv made them probable. In the event, and with some trepidation, PRR engineers went with the most expensive solution. Now we will introduce the name of a gentleman familiar to us but not to the reader. He was R.L. O'Donnel, assistant superintendent of Pittdiv, second in command to Superintendent Robert Pitcairn and assigned the task of coordinating operations with Stone Brown. The written exchanges between O'Donnel and Brown are measured by the score and we have read them all. Our favorite is a "personal" letter dated 4 April 1898 from O'Donnel to Brown. In journalistic jargon, "personal" means off the record. The subject was changeover day at Radebaugh. Brown was queasy and had wired O'Donnel on 2 April seeking reassurance. O'Donnel wrote "...we are firmly of the belief that we can make all the connections of all tracks within three hours after we begin..." Brown wanted to do it piecemeal, O'Donnel all at once. "We would not regard it as practicable or safe to put the track in piecemeal, as the governing feature of this entire revision is the system of signals that must go into effect at the same time that all the tracks are put in operation in order to operate the trains through the tunnel safely. We do not want to teach our men to run on the gauntlet tracks without signals for even a very short period of time." For many paragraphs, O'Donnel detailed his plan and attached this sketch. As to detention of trains, O'Donnel wrote "We are just a little surprised to find you dubious about our ability to take care of this track in one day. We do not like to do any braggadocio business, but we want to say that if we delay trains more than three hours...we will be glad to have you tell us the next time you see us. (Don't write us: it looks too cold in black and white.)" To calm Brown, O'Donnel pointed out that if something went wrong he could always run passenger trains down the branch from RG to County Home Junction and up to SW. A General Order was issued on 5 April 1898 over Pitcairn's signature and O'Donnel had his way. Nothing went wrong. Not then, anyway. A lot went wrong in the future.

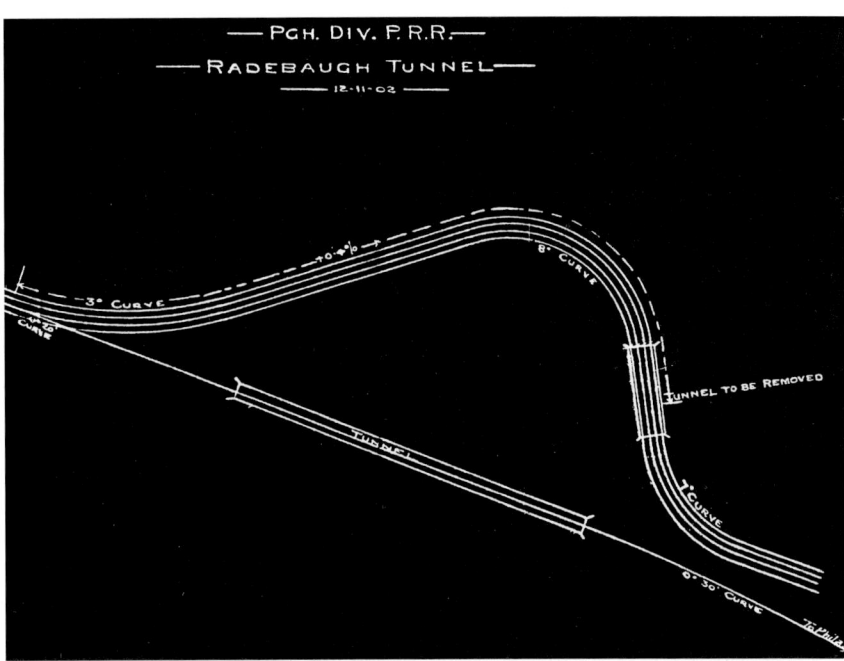

GAUNTLET TRACKS are fine in theory and nightmares in practice. No matter how it is sliced, two tracks cannot do the work of four. The convoluted interlocker trackwork alone is very costly to maintain. Most of the frogs and points are non-standard and have to be made to order. Rail renewal is complex and expensive. Tie replacement requires non-standard lengths. Pushing tracks as close to the tunnel walls as possible reduces the size of drainage ditches to the extent that heavy rains create flood conditions inside the tunnel. When two trains enter the tunnel in opposite directions, neither crew can be visually certain that they will clear in spite of the assurances of signal people that nothing can go wrong. The complex trackwork in the interlockers is an open invitation for derailments and all too frequently the invitations were accepted. Within four years of opening, relief was essential. The possibility of the DDJ solving the problem by bypassing both tunnels turned out to be a non-starter. The first step was to reopen the original tunnel with a single track. This map, dated 11 December 1902, presents a more dramatic solution that was seriously considered. Tear the roof from the original tunnel, widen it to take four tracks and lower the floor to achieve a 0.4% grade. Under this plan, the new tunnel would be reduced to a single track. The curvature problem, however, remained and this solution was shelved, as was a bypass to the south of the knob. O'Donnel, who by this time was Pittdiv superintendent, and Brown decided to eliminate one of the gauntlets (between Track Nos. 3 and 4) and make do while praying for the DDJ.

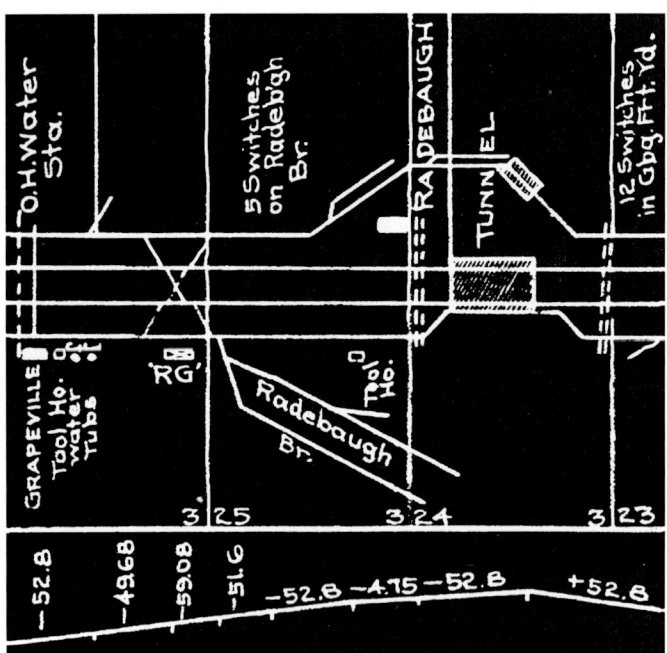

Frank Wrabel Collection

SEEN HERE IN 1910, the interim solution at Radebaugh lasted for many decades. Minor changes in the RG interlocker were made in 1920, 1924 and 1934, involving for the most part turnout changes. Unremarked on this track chart but nonetheless real was the staggering volume coming from the Radebaugh Branch. In 1903, for example, 124,329 *loaded* cars came from this branch at RG and 8,503 entered it. Tragedy also stalked this section of railroad. On 10 March 1906 a westbound work train and an eastbound "milk" train collided near RG. The work train was carrying about 75 Italian laborers and a number of flat cars loaded with pipe destined for the water line PRR was building from Indian Creek to Pitcairn. In our book *Sand Patch* we have told the story of the adventures of this pipeline and it was a bit of a shock for us to learn of this accident. The collision killed three workmen outright and injured scores more, some fatally. Pipe and men were hurled in all directions. The survivors were enraged and attacked the crew of the milk train, yet there is no evidence that these men erred. Since the pipe train entered the mainline from a siding, we wonder if there was a signal malfunction. The Italians were employees of a Philadelphia pipe manufacturer and were referred to by assigned numbers rather than names, making identification somewhat awkward. That fellow human beings were regarded as mere numbers does not speak well for the Quaker City mentality. Even as cannon-fodder infantry we were addressed by name. If perchance there are gravestones in a Greensburg cemetery with just numbers, we now know the source. Sadly, the terror of this incident was a straw in the wind for Radebaugh. Tunnel disease set in and we have found references in 1911 and 1912 to "unfortunate experiences" with the roof of the new Radebaugh Tunnel akin to those already related at Gallitzin.

Jeff Madden

THE EAST PORTAL of the new Radebaugh Tunnel is seen in the early 1960s. The extra rails are guard rails.

CERTAINLY LATE in life, this westerly view of the new Radebaugh Tunnel shows the 160-foot height of the overburden. The guard rails are still in place.

RIP RAP

IT TOOK JUST 11 days to daylight the Radebaugh Tunnel in 1965. Earthmovers removed the overburden to within 12 feet of the roof while traffic was still using the tunnel. The track was then removed in panels and the roof blown down. The original tunnel and the branch were used for traffic with chaotic results. More than 700,000 cubic yards of earth, rock and a coal seam were taken out at a cost of $2,000,000. PRR paid the whole tab on this improvement. On 4 June 1965 at one minute before 3 pm the mainline was back in service. The sidewalls of the cut were kept well away from the tracks and, further, the cut was benched. We will see other views of the cut in color.

THE INTERLOCKERS and signals controlled by RG required so much electricity that a power plant was necessary. This view is c. 1920.

National Archives

A HALF-CENTURY later and light years in photographic quality, RG presented this appearance on 29 May 1970. We will show this facility in color later in the book.

Edward H. Weber

TRIUMPH I

AT LEAST RG was not afflicted with heavy passenger traffic. This photograph of the shelter was taken on 22 November 1960. The train in the background is on the branch. None of the railroads shown on the cars are still in existence, which is sad in a way.

Edward H. Weber

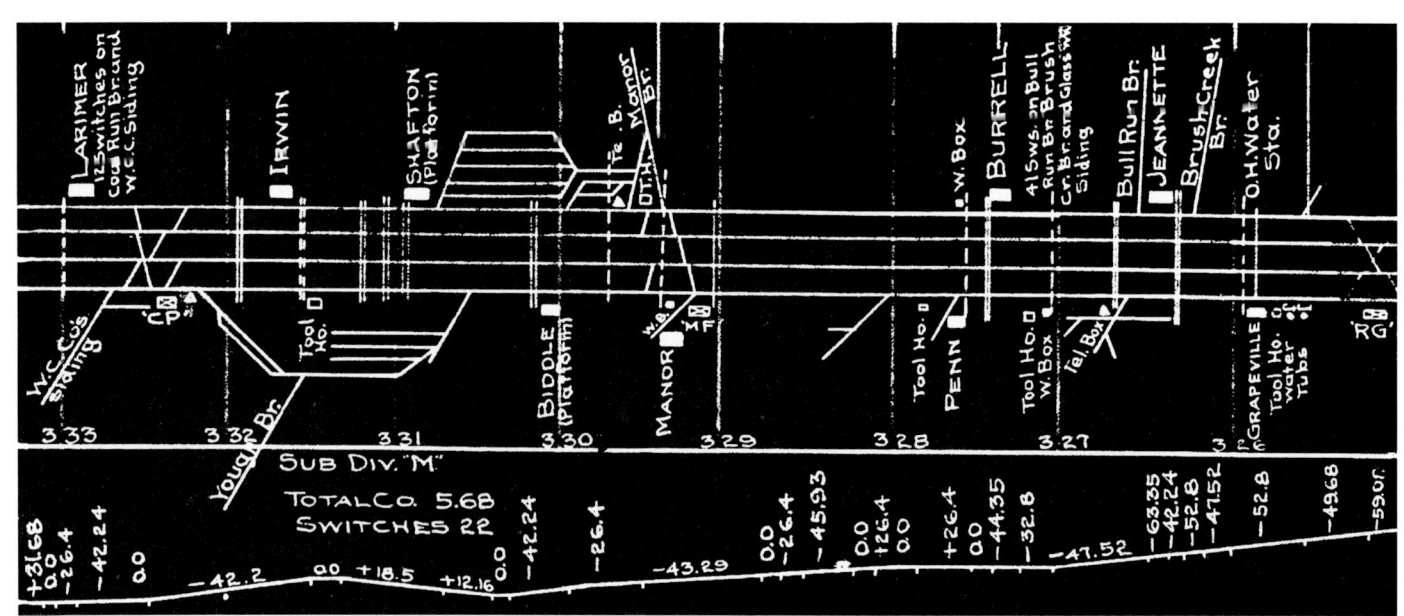

Frank Wrabel Collection

EVEN THE DOWNHILL slope from RG to Larimer had a nasty little bump-and-dip at Shafton/Irwin in 1910, just enough to ripple slack. Over the next fifty years the dip was slowly filled so that it was almost level, as it is today. When built, PRR crossed Brush Creek twelve times between RG and Larimer, but this had been reduced to five times in seven miles by 1910 because of line-straightening. Grapeville is the first point west of RG, another case of a town moving to the railroad. Grapeville originated on the turnpike one mile south of PRR. In 1872 a tiny 38 by 21-foot frame combination station was built and in 1873 a water station was established. By 1888 a third track was completed east and west of the town and the overhead water station seen here was opened in 1896, ultimately served by a 50,000-gallon steel water tank. Another overhead water station was built sometime after 1910 about a mile west at Jeannette, which we shall see. The eastbound drill for tonnage trains had the road power taking water at Grapeville and the helpers at Jeannette. By 1933, heavier power and larger tender cisterns allowed the majority of trains to run from Pitcairn to Latrobe without stopping for water and the water station was closed on 29 March 1933. A water tub at Portage was destroyed by fire on 31 August 1933 and the Grapeville tank replaced it. As we move west to Larimer, the reader might wish to refer to this chart as we go.

GRAPEVILLE soon became a mere suburb of Jeannette. The combination station located here was built in 1889, closed on 1 February 1932 and demolished in October of 1936. When Mr. Weber toured the railroad in the early 1960s, Grapeville remained a commuter stop but was without a shelter or even a sign. Today the name does not even appear on track charts.

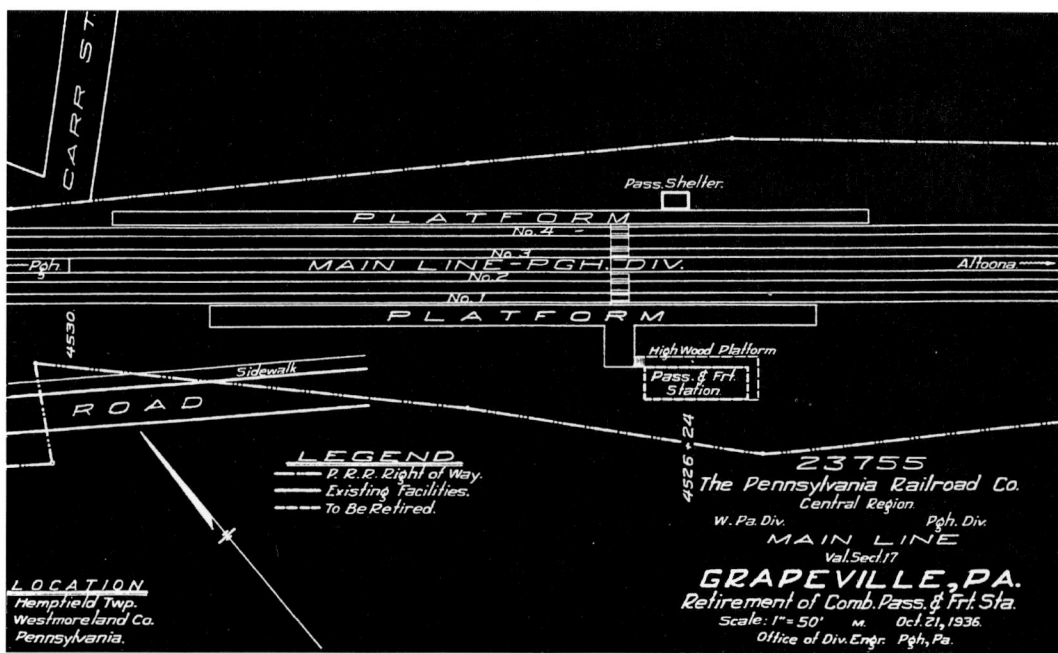

JEANNETTE was named for the wife of the founder of a glass works at this location and, in short order, the town became known as the "Glass City" because of the rapid growth of this and other competing firms. This expansion started in 1889 and in that year PRR built a combination passenger and freight station to serve the sudden "new town." We believe, but are not positive, that this eclectic station is that building. A rubber company was also located here. The presence of high quality coal spawned a lot more than the iron and steel industry in western Pennsylvania. Glass, rubber, concrete and related industries require high heat in production processes. By the way, your author's great-grandfather was an artisan glass blower and early union activist in the Pittsburgh area in this time frame and a lone piece of his work survives. A few miles north of Jeannette is Bushy Run Battlefield Park where, in 1763, Colonel Henry Bouquet defeated Ottawa Chief Pontiac who was leading a confederacy of seven Indian tribes. This action relieved Fort Pitt which had been under siege for several months. We wish to remind the reader that this whole region has been soaked in the blood of noble warriors of divers origins and the sacrifices of brave men on all sides should be remembered with respect.

TRIUMPH I

THE JEANNETTE STATION still retained an aura of dignity on 22 November 1960 even though the freight station and part of the platform roof had been removed. The steps to Second Street are still in place. This view is westerly.

Edward H. Weber

BY 1971, the dignity was waning, the platform shrinking and the paint flaking. The steps to Second Street were still in place, but they would disappear by the following year. The cut at right acquired the name "Deadman's Cut," a chilling cognomen that speaks to the dangers implicit in railroad operations.

Jeff Madden

SUBJECTIVE as it may be, we find the Jeannette station a felicitous architectural gem so have decided to include this rare rear view, taken in 1971 when she was not at her best.

Jeff Madden

RIP RAP

National Archives

THE SEVENTH STREET BRIDGE in Jeannette was looking down its nose at an ancient slide-valve locomotive with a box headlight on this day c. 1920. Look to the right of the engine and one will find a retaining wall that PRR had to build to contain the cut. There were three branches emanating from Jeannette, Brush Creek and Bull Run on the north side and the Jeannette Branch on the south. The track on the left led to the latter, which survives today as an industrial lead. This bridge is at Milepost 326.50.

THE WATER BRIDGE at West Jeannette which, the reader may recall, served eastbound tonnage train helpers is seen here in a westerly view in 1957. Its life was literally draining away. It would be gone the following year.

Jeff Madden

TRIUMPH I

Edward H. Weber

RECOLLECTING that the DDJ was planned to rejoin the original mainline at Jeannette, we now move slightly west of that town to Penn. As inconsequential as Penn may seem on the surface, its location is significant in history because of the character of the coal deposits which were first reached at this point. These coals were perfectly suited for the manufacture of illuminating gas, having a rich proportion of volatiles, and as soon as PRR was open to Penn the movement of these gas coals to eastern cities soared. In 1875 the shipment by just two Penn companies, which employed 600 men, reached 300,000 tons per year. This prosperity continued until the advent of electric power generation later in the century. In 1859 a combination station was built here, soon followed by an overhead coaling station in 1863. Demand for gas coal declined as rapidly as it had climbed and was extinct well before the time Mr. Weber took this sad photograph of the Penn shelter on 22 November 1960. One must remember that it was not until 20 December 1879 that Thomas Edison first introduced his incandescent light bulb in Menlo Park NJ.

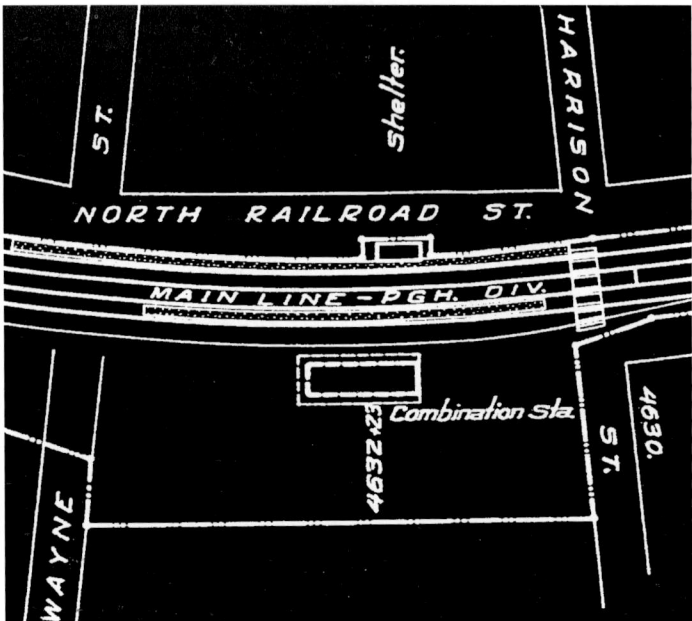

ACROSS from the shelter at Penn just seen, in 1893 PRR built a new combination station which survived until closure in 1932 and demolishment in 1936. The reader has seen the photo credit "Jeff Madden" several times in this book, particularly in the Jeannette area. His grandfather owned a foundry in Penn until it burned in 1949 and was relocated to Manor one and a half miles west.

312

AS MINOR as Manor may be in the PRR scheme of things, its very name reflects a link deep in the history of the Commonwealth of Pennsylvania reaching back to Quaker William Penn and his charter from Charles II of Great Britain. This royal charter vested absolute ownership of the entire state to Penn and his heirs. On 4 July 1776 the landscape changed and Americans no longer bowed to the throne. What about title to the land? Much of it had been sold and settled by others prior to 1776. Should title be wrested from them? Hardly. What about the lands held by Penn's heirs? Briefly, in 1779 the Pennsylvania Legislature purchased much of Penn's land but allowed his heirs to retain title to numerous "manors" throughout the State, totalling over a half-million acres. There may have been a revolution but there would be

Edward H. Weber

no land reform. This little village of Manor lay in the middle of one such vast tract, whence its name. While on the subject of William Penn, we should point out that there is a portrait of him hanging at Christ Church College at Oxford University along with many others of England's "greats." Penn is portrayed with a breastplate of steel, the only one so armored. That a pacifist should be pictured as a warrior is as incongruous as would be a portrait of a PRR president smiling, and equally as jarring. As to Manor on the railroad, as we have shown there was a Manor Branch and a yard complex reaching west to Shafton on the north side. Traffic was controlled by MF Tower which was placed in service on 28 September 1913, replacing an 1887 22-lever plant nearer the Manor Branch. This interlocker existed to route trains to and from the Manor Branch (opened in 1885) as well as the Youghiogheny Branch which was located between Shafton and Irwin to the west. MF was rarely used to reroute mainline trains and was accordingly closed in 1932, its functions being handled remotely from CP at Larimer. Today there are no crossovers from CP RADE to CP TRAFF (Trafford) at Milepost 336.5. As to stations, a combination structure was built in 1875 (an ICC, and consequently uncertain, date) and we believe this is the one seen here on 22 November 1960.

SHAFTON, another minor point on PRR, did have a few interesting characteristics. The Manor Branch yard entered the mainline to the right just behind the photographer and, on the left, still another Zero Track is clearly seen. This track connected at CP(Larimer) to the west and served the Youghiogheny Branch as well as acting as a freight bypass. The last mainline dip before Pitcairn was just east of this point, as seen on the 1910 track chart shown earlier. Over the years it was filled to the extent that it was almost gone by 1958 and today it is hardly noticeable. This c. 1920 photograph looks west at overhead Bridge 330.69. Note the telltales. Today the Pennsylvania Turnpike soars over the mainline just to the east, reminder of so much in transportation history. Four tracks between Manor and Shafton were ready for service in 1900. In 1901 a new 48 by 147-foot brick enginehouse with a slate roof was built somewhere in this vicinity. Just on this one subject we have read three letters between Messrs. J.M. Wallis, W.H. Brown and R.L. O'Donnel. As we wind down this volume, we wish to comment that we have read reams of correspondence between these gentlemen and others whose names appear throughout this book and others we have researched and written. Perhaps only a fellow historian can appreciate what we are about to say. Even though most of these men were all long dead before we were born, one comes away with the feeling that you knew them

National Archives

intimately…that they were close personal friends even though they were adversaries of some of your own ancestors…that you have been given a rare privilege to look into their lives by reading letters that they never thought would become part of a significant history book read by thousands of people. While we can offer no insight into the validity of nether world theory, we can only hope that somehow we will enter an eternity where we can meet these men and listen to their stories while sitting at their feet. They were a great bunch of regular guys. And, as Father would have worded it, even the cads have their story to tell.

Railroad Museum of Pennsylvania

THE IMMENSITY of the cut at Irwin, so apparent in this undated photograph, merely typifies PRR's determination to make their railroad a super-efficient purveyor of transportation. The village of Irwin was founded by John Irwin in the late 1700s. His father-in-law John Scull built a home here in 1794 and had founded the Pittsburgh Gazette in 1786, which was the first newspaper in this region. The town itself was not laid out until 1853 and obviously was spawned by the arrival of PRR. In just two years Irwin was shipping 30,000 tons of gas coal a year to Philadelphia and New York. By 1875 these shipments had soared to a million tons annually and over a thousand workmen were employed in mines in a ten-mile radius. The original PRR mainline dodged around this hill with two reverse curves and at a lower level. The four-track improvement seen here opened in 1900 and included a deep fill on the far side of the cut beginning at the station seen on the left, this view being eastward. As with so many improvements on Pittdiv, the increased gradient was more than offset by curve reduction. Note that the side-slopes have been set back almost to the angle of repose, particularly on the right. Let us remind the reader that four-tracking of PRR on Pittdiv and elsewhere was primarily done to separate freight and passenger trains, each moving at different speeds. Usually, as in this scene, the passenger tracks were in the middle. That this gigantic dollar investment in passenger business was in place just as the automotive and air ages were about to begin merely illustrates the perils of technological commitments. Yet if society in its wisdom forces freight traffic back to railroads, PRR's successors may be only too glad that a century ago this marvelous pathway was carved into the terrain. At this point, and using this photograph as a foil, we would like to emphasize an aspect of curve reduction that is little-remarked yet nonetheless real. Fast trains require superelevation to keep the train against the inner rail in curves. Low speed trains, usually far heavier, must avoid putting too much weight on the inner rail in curves. Readers of our book *West End* know that this riddle almost killed your author at a sharp curve on B&O's Cheat River Grade in 1979 when an inner rail rolled over. As we repeat our constant admonishment to stay well away from moving trains, let us direct the reader back to this photograph. Generally speaking, on Pittdiv the two middle tracks were used for passenger trains and the two outer ones for freight. Beginning in the vicinity of Radebaugh and westward from that point to Pittsburgh, that pattern changed because of commuter traffic. Loading large numbers of passengers in the middle was time-consuming and dangerous, as well as expensive in terms of facilities such as subways, guard fences and so on. Taking 1945 as an example, at RG the two inner tracks were freight and the two outer passenger. Thus in this photograph the coal drag is on the eastbound passenger track assuming, of course, that the 1945 assignment was in effect at this earlier date. Yet the superelevation is slight on Track No. 1 as well as the other three tracks. This is an unheralded reward associated with gentle curvature.

THE STATION AT IRWIN, seen here shortly after opening in 1900, sits atop the large fill created by PRR. Notice that the roadway is unpaved and that a horse-and-buggy has just exited the underpass. PRR was in no rush to open a station here in the early days. In 1857 Irwin was merely a water point and even that was closed in that year because of water scarcity. In the same year an old woodshed was converted to a freight warehouse but pleas for a passenger station were ignored. Finally, in 1859 a small station was built and a 35 by 143-foot combination station was constructed in 1877. The water station was re-opened in 1865, but apparently it did not last long. PRR did deign to install a sand-drying house in that year. Irwin was a minor power-point in those days, with a frame enginehouse being built in 1862 with room for a princely total of two engines. It was replaced with a brick 32 by 64-foot enginehouse in 1867. Still, when PRR finally gave Irwin a nice station they did have the good taste to surround it with some pleasing grounds and shrubbery.

Frank Wrabel Collection

A CLOSER view of the Irwin station complete with passenger train shows that at least some traffic was generated, although proximity to Pittsburgh suggests that it was mostly day-trippers and commuters. Notice that the train is on Track No. 4 next to the station. Another aspect of commuter operations is frequent stops, each one closing down the line for a given period of time. No dispatcher wants to have heavily loaded freight trains behind such passenger movements, stopping and starting again and again. Particularly on the Rip Rap. Once a drag is stopped on a grade, the crew might not be able to get it started again in one piece thus triggering new waves of delay and profanity from divers sources.

TRIUMPH I

AUTOMOBILES of commuters clogged the Irwin parking lot on 22 November 1960, with nary a horse in sight. The height of the hill in the background is apparent, another of those bumps on the Rip Rap that gave PRR indigestion.

Edward H. Weber

THE IRWIN FREIGHT STATION seen here c. 1920 was more impressive than the converted woodshed used in 1857. We assume this was built in 1900 because combination stations were employed prior to that time.

National Archives

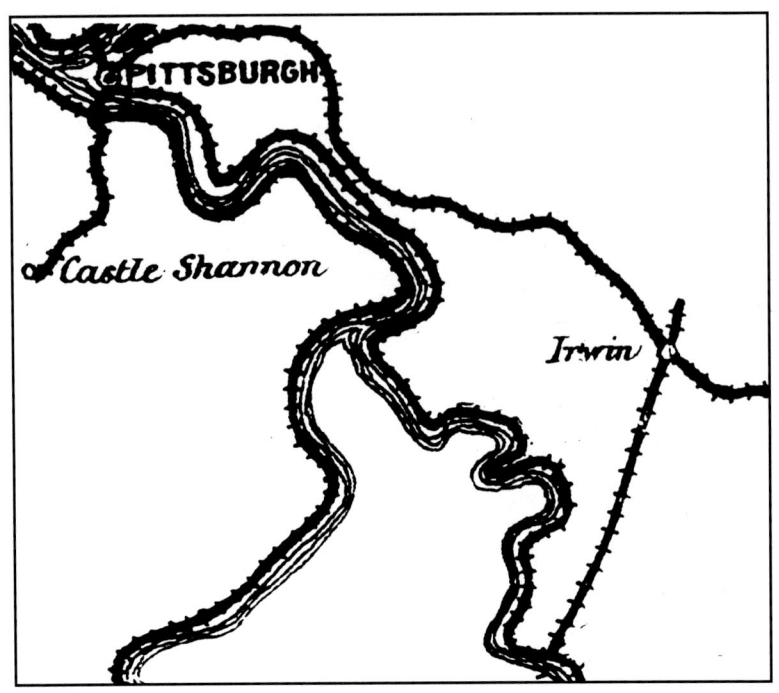

THIS 1878 MAP shows the Youghiogheny Branch running south from Irwin to the river of the same name, the primary source of the gas coal to which we have referred. The railroad along the rivers is the Pittsburgh, Washington and Baltimore, B&O's subsidiary in Pennsylvania...better known as the Pittsburgh and Connellsville.

RIP RAP

Edward H. Weber

CP TOWER at Larimer was a major interlocker on the Rip Rap because Zero Track from Shafton rejoined the mainline here and passenger/freight track assignments were shifted again. Track Nos. 1 and 2 became freight and Track Nos. 3 and 4 became passenger, involving many crossover movements. For example, an eastbound passenger train moved from Track No. 3 to Track No. 1 at CP; a westbound freight moved from Track No. 3 to Track No. 2 and so on in a dance of the wolves. Each such crossover, of course, increased running time and fuel consumption. We see here still another Rip Rap cut and a brick tower. The history of the tower is confused. Records show that a 24-lever interlocker was installed at *Irwin* in 1897 and was replaced by a brick tower in 1900. Other records show a new brick tower at *Larimer* in 1910. We also know that four-tracking was complete to Larimer from the east in 1900. A solid fact is that this photograph was taken on 22 November 1960. The plant appears to be in splendid condition.

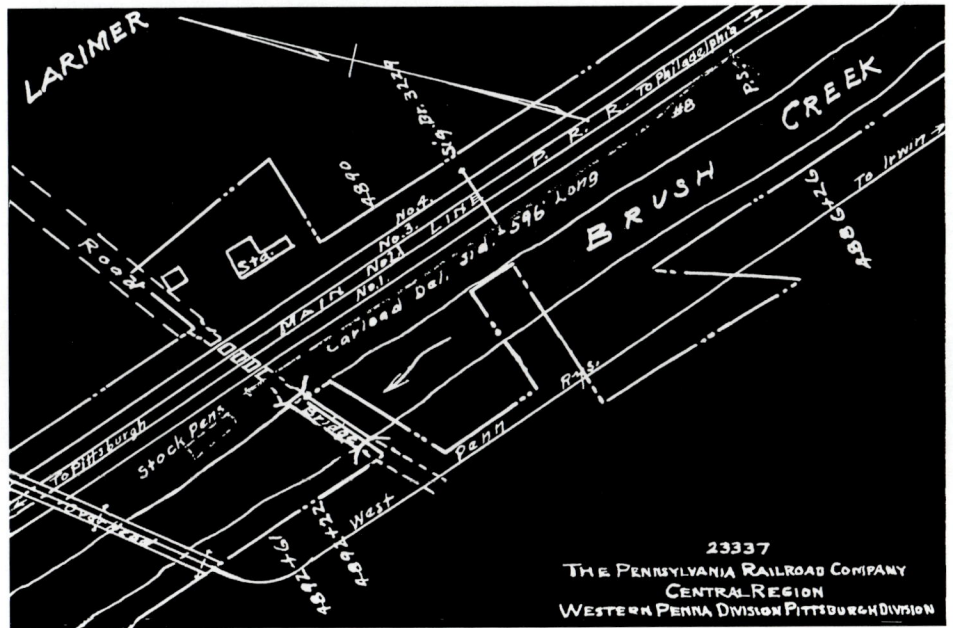

LAR[IMER]... Larimer Station in 1855, apparently there never was a station building *per se*. In 1929 a letter referred to a passenger waiting room measuring only 10 by 15 feet and a 10 by 12 foot shelter, both on the north side of the tracks and seen here along with a stock pen and carload delivery track. There had been a tiny warehouse next to the siding, but it was torn down in 1928 and the business referred to Irwin. This map was prepared in 1934 to support closure of the remaining facilities, yet we came away with the impression that PRR wasn't quite sure just where Larimer was.

[Note: INTERURBAN ON PRR LAND]

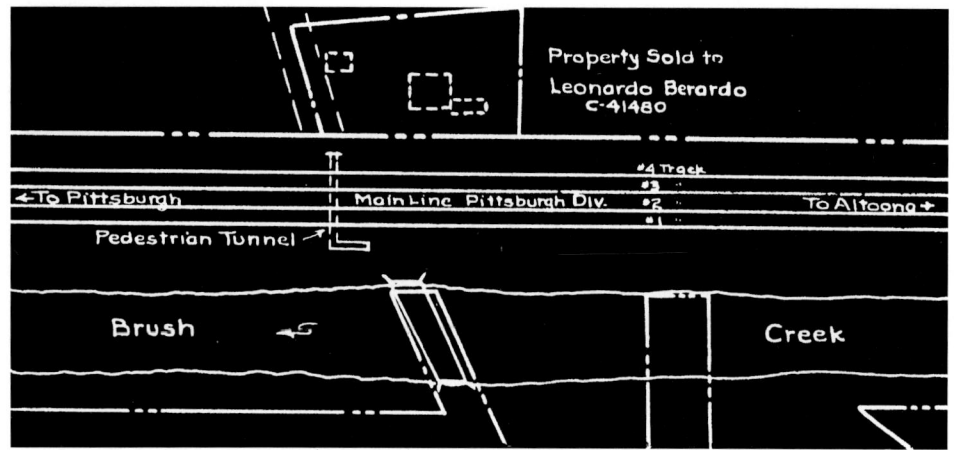

IT SEEMS PRR lost track of the buildings at Larimer to the extent that facilities that were supposed to have been closed in 1934 were still there in 1940 when this map was made. To confuse matters more, the land under the buildings had been sold in 1937 and, further, information surfaced that the passenger facilities were ordered closed in 1928. One thing is certain. Mr. Weber went to Larimer with his camera in 1964 and found neither a shelter nor a sign. To us, the interesting thing about Larimer is Brush Creek. It not only runs straight through on this map, but also runs straight for a quarter of a mile in both directions. A glance at a Geodetic map suggests that PRR filled-in the stream bed while four-tracking and that part of the village north of the tracks rests on that fill.

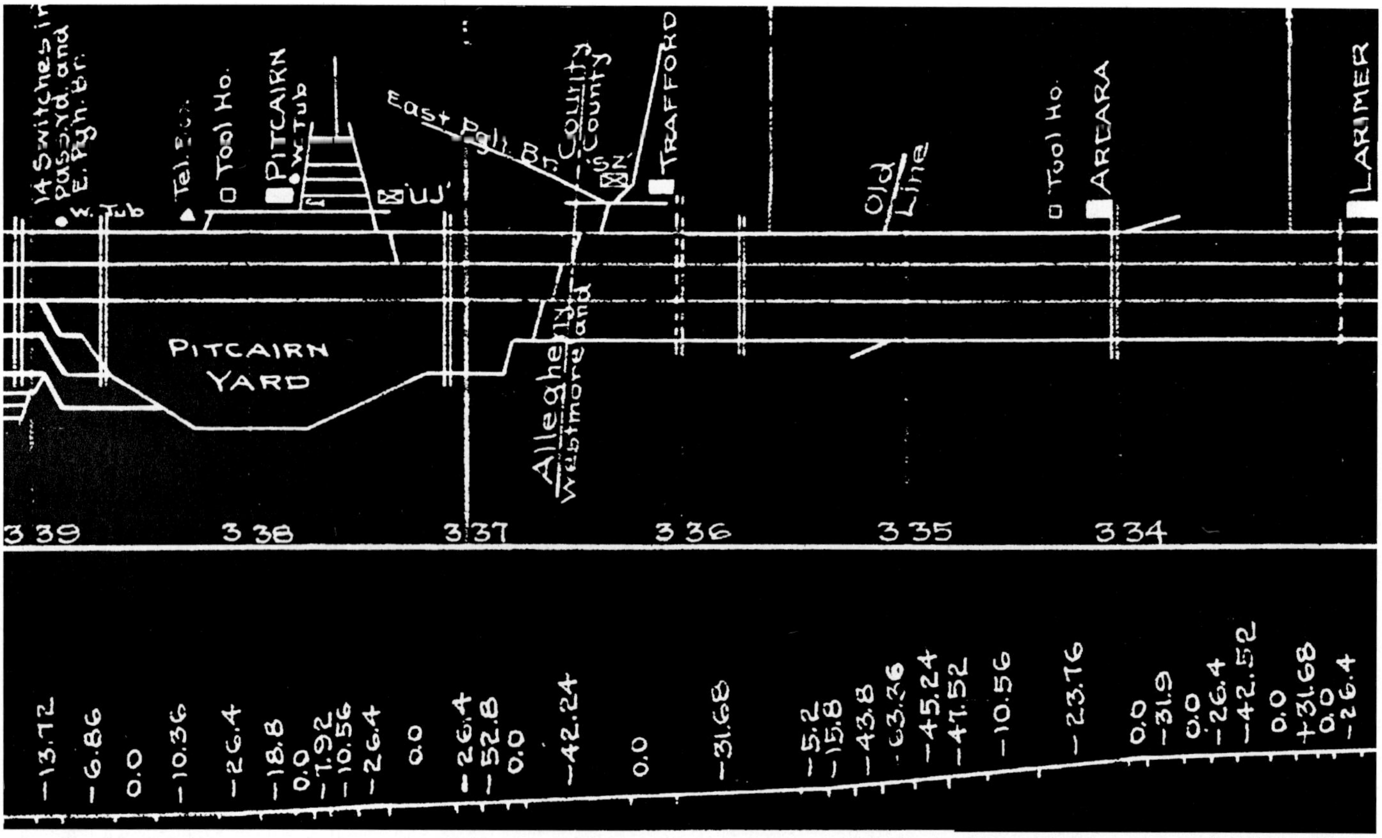

Frank Wrabel Collection

AS WE SLIDE downhill toward our final destination at Pitcairn, let us clarify the location of certain legendary points on Pittdiv. Moving west from Larimer at the right, we first come to Ardara. A tiny place of no consequence in PRR history except for one item as we shall see. Then, just west of Milepost 335, note the "Old Line" stub. We enter Trafford at Milepost 336 and SZ Tower, which we shall visit. Now the reader should restudy the 1855 map on page 276 and note the locations of Stewart's and Wall's Stations. The huge Pitcairn Yard stretched *between* these two points, beginning at Milepost 337 (Stewart) and ending at Milepost 339 (Wall.) Ultimately, this yard reached to SZ on the east and Wilmerding on the west. Again, we will study this vast complex. Now go back to "Old Line" at Milepost 335. By 1875 this vicinity was known as Carpenter. It did not show as a placename in 1855.

RIP RAP

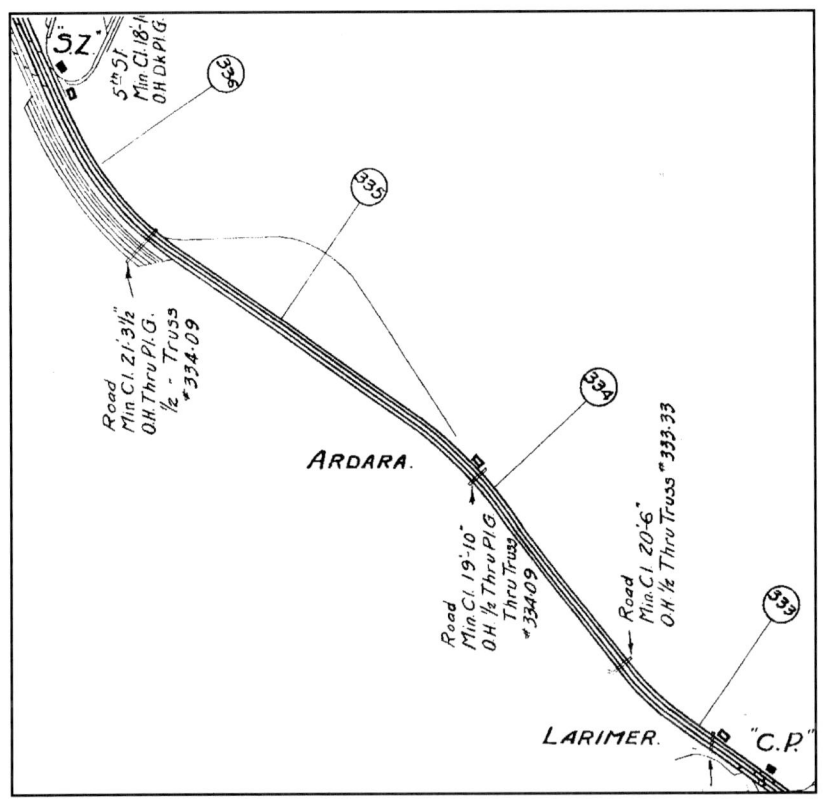

THIS 1927 TRACK PLAN shows the path of the original PRR mainline between Ardara and Milepost 335.5. It is interesting that a single track was still in place in that year. Today a public road rests on most of the original roadbed. Notice that the old main does not connect at Ardara. This little gap represents the tunnel we are about to see.

E. Roy Ward Collection

Railroad Museum of Pennsylvania

THE ORIGINAL PRR mainline wandered along the Brush Creek valley, trying to dodge hills wherever possible. A cut was required at the Ardara "gap" just shown and it was duly built for a single track. As can be imagined from this photograph, that single-track cut was a bugbear. By 1861 a second track was essential and the decision was made to cut-and-cover. During the summer and autumn of that year, this tunnel was built with 6,000 cubic yards of masonry and 800,000 bricks. It was 550 feet long and cost $25,000. When the new line was nearing completion and some tracks were in service, the Carpenter Tunnel was abandoned in 1904. Considering the cleanliness of the portal and the character of the rail and ties, we suspect that this is an early 1860s photograph. We know from later photographs that a lot of rotten rock piled onto the roof. We are confident this is the east portal. The cut-and-cover procedure was not unique to PRR. As *West End* readers know, B&O's Hitchcock Tunnel on Seventeen Mile Grade was similarly built. A color photograph of the cut will be shown later in the book.

319

TRIUMPH I

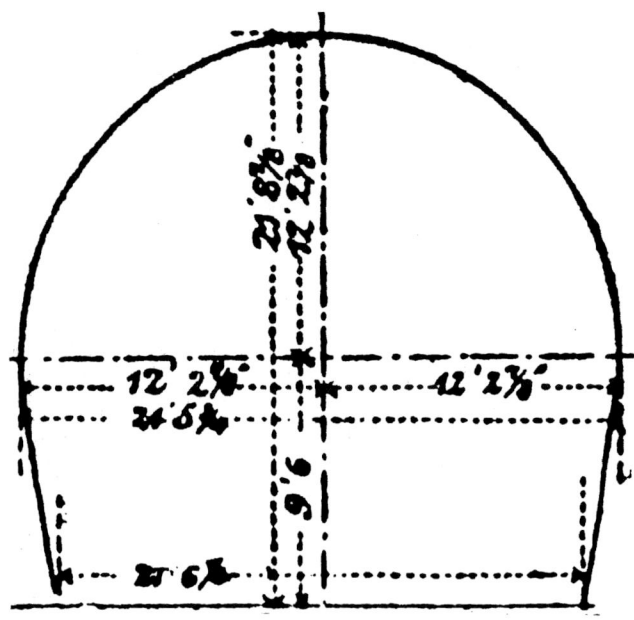

THE DIMENSIONS of Carpenter Tunnel were quite generous for the times as this "intrados" indicates. What was ample in 1861 was worse than inadequate as the decades wore on and one can safely bet that PRR was only too happy to bypass this obstruction.

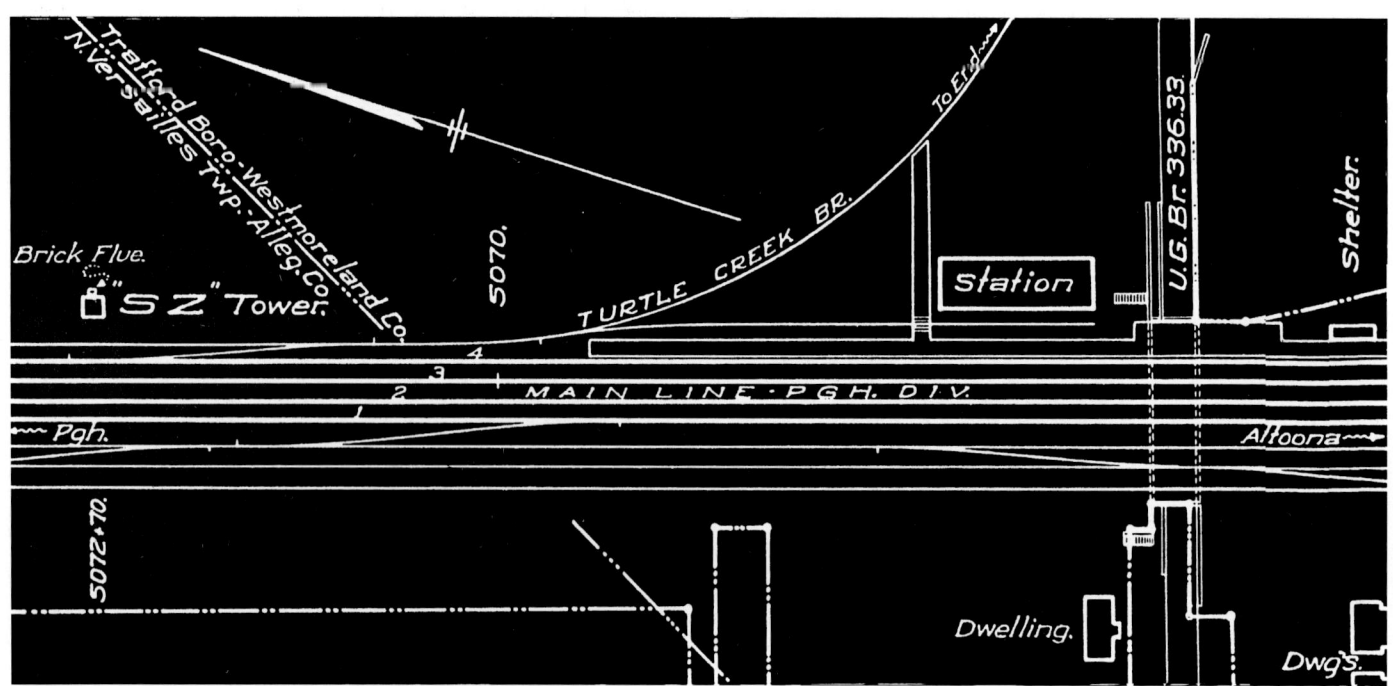

TRAFFORD had many claims to PRR fame. It was the junction with the Turtle Creek Branch, which ran for about 22 miles to Saltsburg on the Conemaugh Division, and also with the East Pittsburgh Branch as will be shown. Trafford was the location of the eastern interlocker serving Pitcairn Yard. Indeed, many yard tracks extended well east of Trafford. Three of the four main tracks seen here were ready for service on 27 November 1903. Track No. 1 was open on 1 November, but because of a right-of-way complication at Stewart it was necessary to use a temporary track until the end of the year. Note the Pitcairn Yard trackage on the south side. This map was dated 20 December 1935 and was prepared to show the addition of a brick flue at SZ Tower on the left. As will be seen, the station at upper right enjoyed a sunken track.

E. Roy Ward

THE YARD TRACKS were full when this eastbounder was accelerating just east of SZ on a cold and snowy day in 1965. She is moving without caboose to pickup the rest of her train from the yard on the left. Steadily increasing train length throughout railroad history has had many negative effects, particularly on yards. Doubling and sometimes tripling became necessary because the classification tracks could not be lengthened beyond a certain point. The triple-rack auto cars behind the road engines introduce another aspect of railroad operations. In this era railroads were steadily taking finished-auto business away from truckers and many of the displaced drivers reacted violently. We interviewed a man who witnessed the dropping of concrete blocks from an overhead bridge near Irwin on consists such as this one. In the end, auto cars had to be totally enclosed to reduce damage.

THE BRICK FLUE was apparently still in use when this photograph was taken on 22 November 1960. This interlocker is extant and known as CP TRAFF. The reader will recall that in 1945 the two northerly tracks were passenger. By 1958 it was the other way around. There are three mainline tracks west of CP TRAFF today, the southernmost becoming the Port Perry Branch at Milepost 341.

Edward H. Weber

TRIUMPH I

THE SUNKEN siding at Trafford is apparent here. SZ can be seen just behind the cars on the siding and the home signals are overlooking a passing freight train. The date is 22 November 1960 and the supposed birthdate of the board-and-batten combination station is 1881. The position lights and bridges are gone, replaced by NYC-style signals on masts. The Turtle Creek Branch exited the mainline just this side of SZ and ran to the right.

Edward H. Weber

FAMOUS TURTLE CREEK and PRR met at the bottom of the third dip on the Rip Rap. The location began modestly, burgeoned into one of the largest and most strategic classification yards on the PRR system, declined to a wasteland and is now experiencing a modest rebirth. From the beginning the PRR mainline followed the south bank of Turtle Creek, taking advantage of the creek's floodplain. Getting into and out of that plain, however, was a problem caused by the narrowness of the gaps and the steepness of the sideslopes. The easterly gap was at Stewart, which was located slightly west of Trafford at lower right. Thomson chose to come close to the knob on the left rather than loop the mainline to the right at the confluence of Brush and Turtle Creeks. Predictably, the slope was continually slipping onto the railroad and early annual reports were a litany of woes and corrections. Stewart was just west of the knob and by 1855 was blessed with a "handsome" combination station. As late as 1901 Stewart had retained its name and, indeed, a new but modest 18 by 51-foot brick passenger station was built in that year. By 1910 both the name and the station were gone, swallowed by the expansion of what was by then called Pitcairn Yard. We have met Robert Pitcairn in this book and have no argument with the choice of name, although Mr. Stewart might not agree. Your author's mother is a Stewart but we decided not to bring this switch to her attention for fear of starting still another clan feud. To the left of center, one sees that the name Wall did survive. Actually, the nascent yard expansion began there near the westerly gap. In 1855 Wall was merely a wood and water station. By 1875 it was an eastern terminus of commuter operations from Pittsburgh, with 18 trains a day on its schedule. Rapid yard growth began in 1888 and expansion was explosive during the 1890s, continuing well into the 1920s until the entire plain was awash in trackage and associated facilities. This map was corrected in 1979 and shows that the valley was still full of tracks.

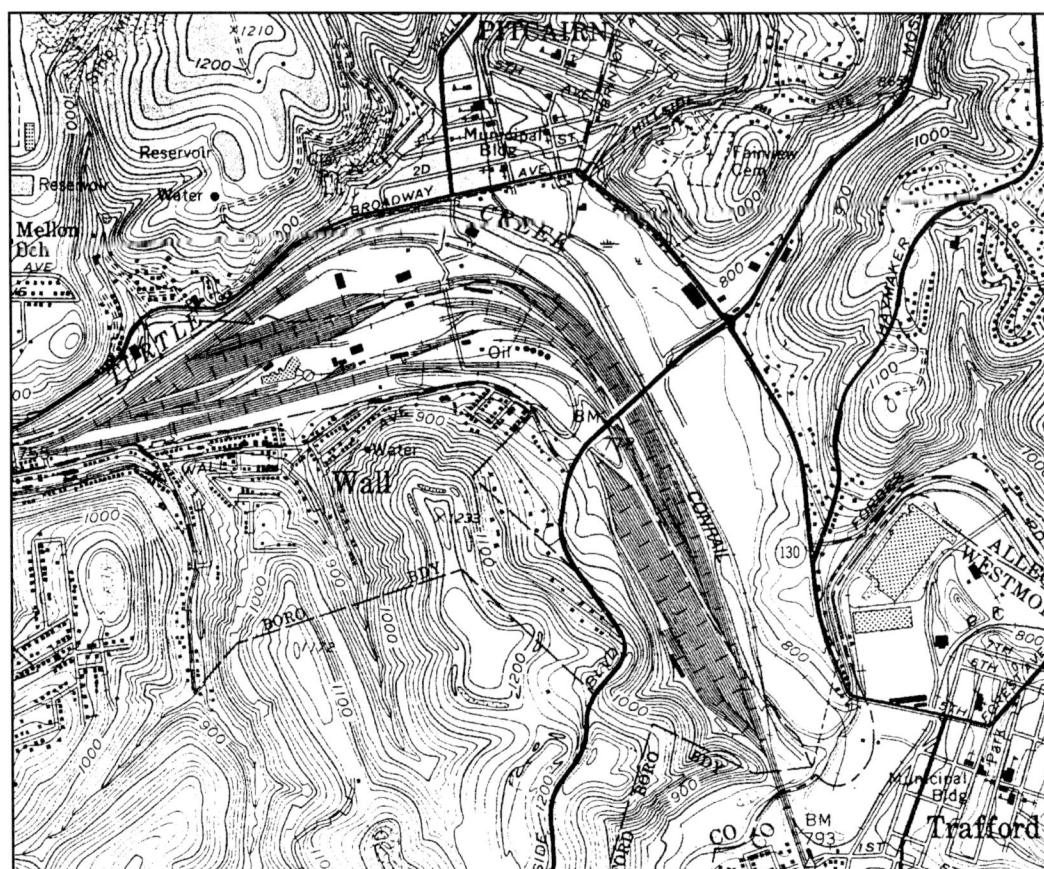

RIP RAP

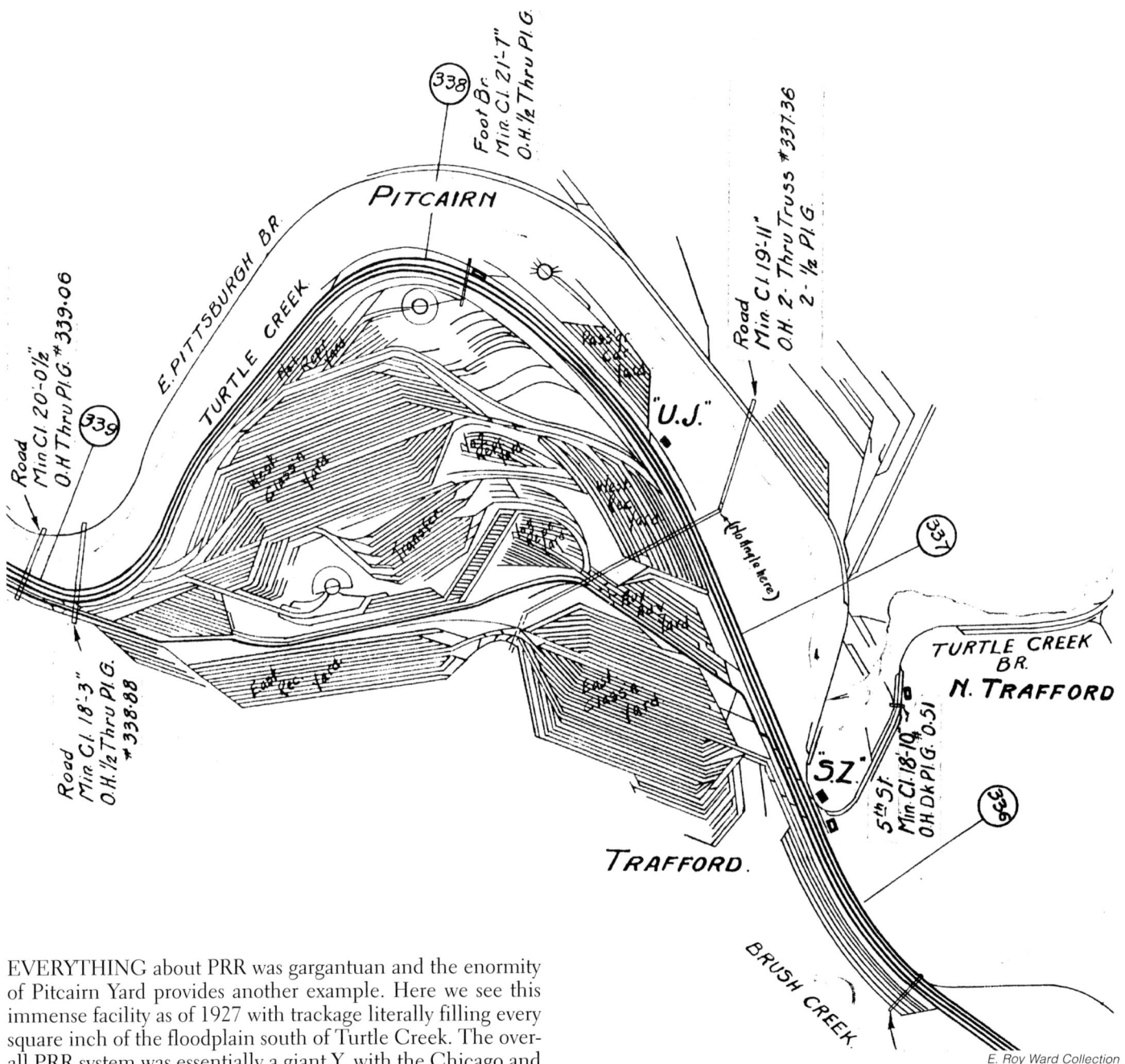

E. Roy Ward Collection

EVERYTHING about PRR was gargantuan and the enormity of Pitcairn Yard provides another example. Here we see this immense facility as of 1927 with trackage literally filling every square inch of the floodplain south of Turtle Creek. The overall PRR system was essentially a giant Y, with the Chicago and St. Louis mainlines meeting at Pitcairn. PRR's rival transmontane trunkline was B&O and its western lines met at Cumberland, a subject about which we have written three books. We can assure the reader that the similarity ended there. As weighty as B&O's problems were, they were dwarfed by those of PRR. The Pittsburgh region alone produced unbelievable amounts of *local* traffic which had to be melded with enormous *through* traffic in a physical location that can also be described as Dantesque. Yards require long, wide flat space. There wasn't any such land in the Pittsburgh region. The only candidate was the small plain between Stewart and Wall and that was squeezed between two high ridgelines with narrow entrances at both ends and was at the *bottom* of two nasty grades. Let us imagine the thoughts of a yardmaster at Pitcairn being overwhelmed by traffic from all directions 365 days a year, 24 hours a day and probably allowing himself a fantasy of sympathy with General Custer at Little Big Horn. This map is worthy of study. Begin at SZ, the eastern throat. The East Pittsburgh Branch, which served industry north of Turtle Creek, and the Turtle Creek Branch meet the mainline at SZ. From SZ west, Track Nos. 2, 3 and 4 follow the south bank of the creek. Track No. 1, however, forms a base to the triangle and runs directly to SZ. A classification yard is really two yards, one for receiving trains and another for creating new ones. In addition to eastbound/westbound receiving and classification yards, there are also three repair yards, a transfer yard and a passenger car yard. There is also an auxiliary advance yard nestled in this maze, along with three turntables and two enginehouses. Plus a passenger station facing Track No. 4 just east of Milepost 338. We will visit these facilities as we go.

TRIUMPH I

Railroaders Memorial Museum

THE ORIGINAL circular enginehouse can be seen in the middle of this northerly view taken in the 1903-06 time frame. The precise birthdate of Pitcairn Yard is vague. In 1891 the "Walls" Yard was reported as "in service" with 20 miles of track and sidings, along with two frame freight transfer buildings, each measuring a princely 400 by 800 feet opening on 1 June 1891. Also vague is the birthdate of the enginehouse, as will be seen. As to the other structures seen is this photograph and others to be shown, we can only comment that most of them were located in the vicinity of this enginehouse which, by the way, was the northernmost shown on the preceding map.

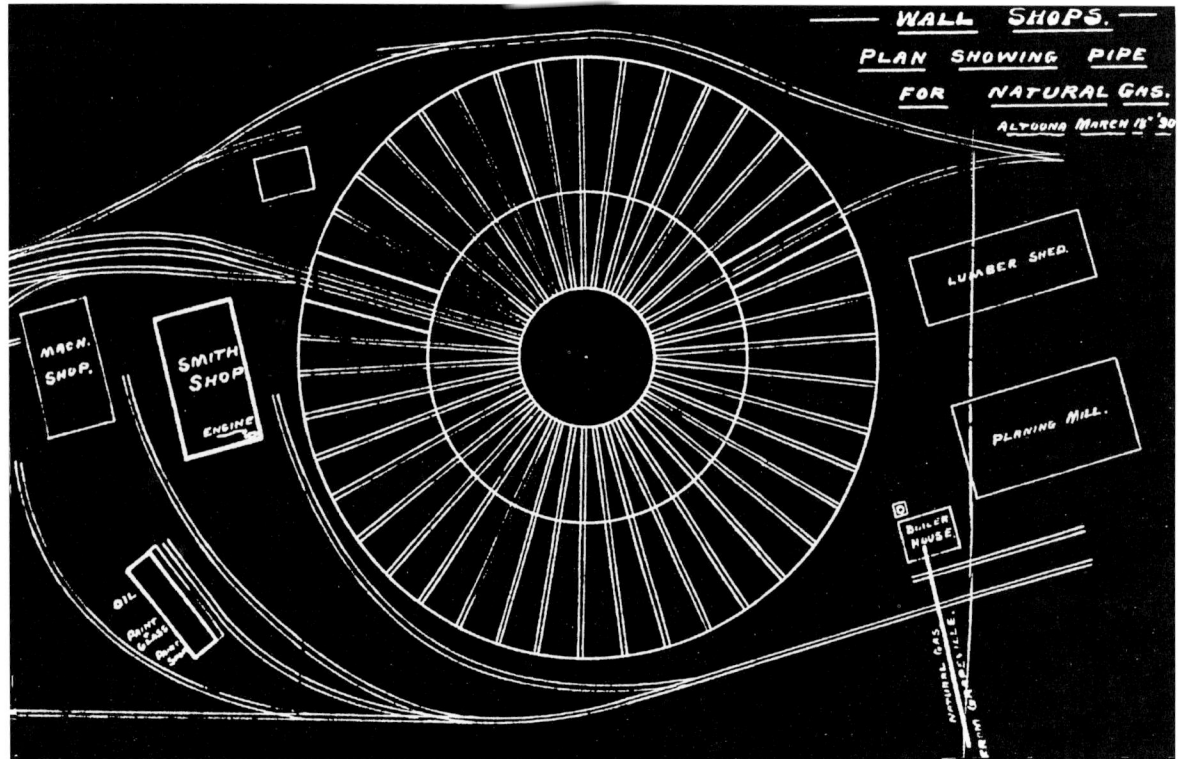

SINCE THIS DIAGRAM of the original enginehouse is dated 18 March 1890, it is reasonable for us to assume that later completion dates given are incorrect. Also apparently incorrect are varying statements that the house contained 42 and 44 stalls...there are 39 in this plan. The diameter of the house was 320 feet. The fascinating information on this diagram, however, has nothing to do with dimensions and dates. It was prepared to show the location of a natural gas pipeline to the powerhouse for Grapeville. Moreover, we have evidence that a ten-inch gas pipeline was run from these fields all the way east to Johnstown where it was used for steam generation at the Cambria Works.

324

RIP RAP

Hagley Museum and Library

THIS EASTERLY view of the circular enginehouse was taken in February of 1903, four years after the original turntable was lengthened to 75 feet. In short order the open space seen here would be filled with new buildings, including a 75 by 310-foot paint shop which was extended in 1905, 1915 and 1918. We have already referred to PRR's insatiable need for water in the steam era. As seen on the 1979 map, a 15-million gallon reservoir was constructed in 1914 on the north side of Turtle Creek to serve Pitcairn.

Frank Wrabel Collection

WHILE THE POSTMARK on this card is 1917, it was actually taken much earlier when the yard was still named "Wall." Note how the enginehouse is now completely surrounded by buildings on both sides. Crude as it is, this photograph does show the floodplain to good advantage. By 1915 Pitcairn was dispatching about 100,000 cars monthly and in 1916 this number was growing. Nearly 200 locomotives were serviced by a force of 700 men, including inspection, fire cleaning, sanding, watering, coaling, lubricating and performance of running repairs. The new 100-foot turntable was proving inadequate for new L1s and I1s engines and improved facilities were desperately needed. For example, coaling was done from a platform with a crane while out on the mainline coaling had been achieved with overhead facilities for decades. Between 1918 and 1921, almost two million dollars were invested in improvements including, as we shall see, a new enginehouse.

TRIUMPH I

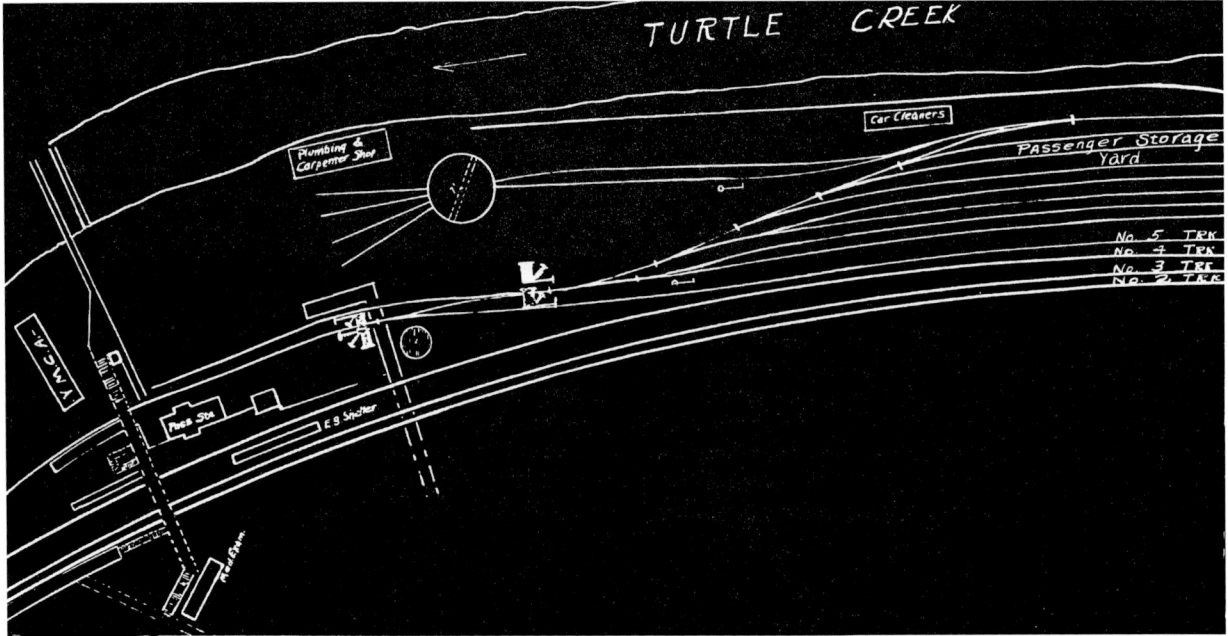

Bob Jansen Collection

IN 1922 this new brick enginehouse with 34 stalls and a 110-foot turntable was ready for service…just in time because the old one was in bad shape. The latter was used as a car repair facility for some years after 1922. The vast sea of cars in this scene is testimony to the size of what had been described as one of the largest yards in the world, with a capacity of 5,775 cars. Pitcairn was originally a flat yard and was converted to gravity (hump) in 1908. Car retarders were installed in 1929. All this was a far cry from a modest combination station, tower, office and supervisor's dwelling opened in this vicinity in 1881.

UJ TOWER, which we have seen on prior maps, was built in 1901 to control an interlocker handling movement of local passenger trains in and out of the passenger layover yard noted earlier. On 5 November 1931 UJ was closed and the movements handled remotely from SZ at Trafford. This map was prepared pursuant to that revision and had the benefit of precisely locating the Pitcairn passenger station, YMCA and short Track No. 5 which passed through this area for local trains.

THIS BRICK AND STONE combination station was built at Pitcairn in 1900 and on the day this photograph was taken there were a fair number of passengers awaiting transportation. Considering its proximity to the yard, we suspect the shelter roof was built to protect passengers from cinders as well as rain and snow. Note the passenger car at far left on Track No. 5. The postmark is 19 August 1913, Pitcairn. Postage was one cent.

THIS WESTERLY VIEW of the Pitcairn station was taken on 22 November 1960 and shows the footbridge over the tracks just west of the platform. The lack of clientele compared to the last photo is testimony to the decline in passenger traffic over the intervening years. This will be the last image in this book bearing the credit of Mr. Weber and we do not wish to pass it without commenting that this ardent student of railroading deserves the accolade "gentleman of the old school." This expression is rarely heard these days nor is he the only one to whom we will award it. Still, perhaps this mention will encourage others to emulate his conduct and encourage a return to older standards of civility.

TRIUMPH I

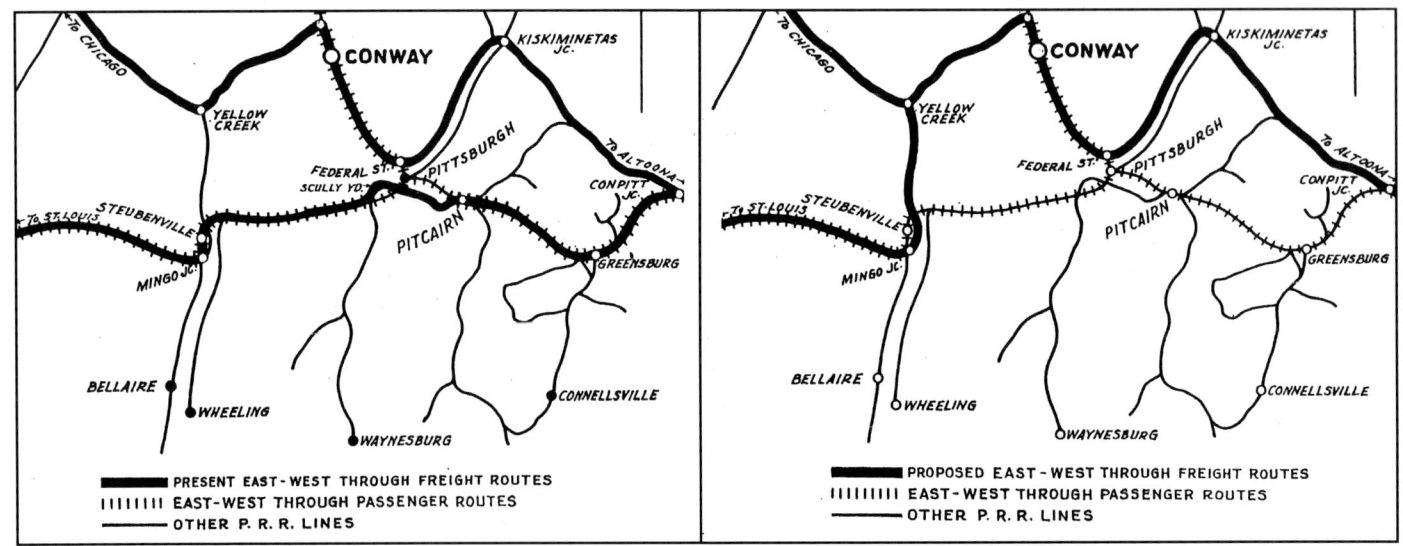

THE DEATH KNELL of Pitcairn Yard occurred in 1952 when the PRR Board authorized the investment of 31 million dollars to triple the capacity of Conway Yard northwest of Pittsburgh, which was originally opened in 1883. These maps show the impact of the planned reroutings of St. Louis freight traffic through the Pittsburgh area. While this project did not go entirely to this plan (for example, the mainline from Torrance to Pitcairn did not become just a passenger line), the effect on Pitcairn was obvious. Many years would pass before Pitcairn as a yard disappeared and that precise date is unknown to us, but its day in the sun was over. Or perhaps just beginning. In the steam era the sun seldom shined in that sinkhole. Yet, in November of 1996 Pitcairn Yard was reopened as an intermodal facility.

E. Roy Ward

PITCAIRN YARD was still active on 30 January 1965, at least to some extent. A westbound through-train is moving on Track No. 4 on the left and another is awaiting track space on the right, while a third train is moving eastbound into the yard. Now let us tell the story of James Lewis Marks. He was born in 1893 and started with PRR in 1913. He worked on many PRR divisions east and west of Pittsburgh, ending his career as master mechanic at Pitcairn. He died in 1941 and his will specified that his body be cremated and his ashes scattered at Horseshoe Curve. PRR assigned a business car and several officials to accompany his widow on this mission. At least she didn't have to walk up to the tracks. The Curve is a magical place in our national history and deservedly so. Perhaps someone will finance a memorial at the Curve, honoring both Messrs. Thomson and Marks. The creator and his servant.

Chapter 9

Operations

Throughout this book we have regaled the reader with insights into the incredible traffic volume handled on Pittdiv and in this chapter wish to provide a medley of excerpts to illustrate that Triumph is an apt name for a history of PRR and its successors.

In 1856 PRR moved 454,000 tons of freight…in 1860: 1,347,000 tons…in 1865: 2,556,000 tons…in 1869: 5,403,000 tons. The 1869 figure was *11.9 times* the tonnage moved just thirteen years before. (All these tonnages include company tonnage which was generally in the range of ten percent of the total). In 1976 144 *million* gross tons were carried on Pittdiv alone. Triumph.

In 1875 the eastward tonnage, mostly minerals and cereals, was 82.5% of the total and the westward 17.5% was mostly manufactured goods. The railroad was built to capture eastward tonnage. Triumph.

Leaping ahead to 1945 and using employees as a reference point in comparing the nation's major trunkline railroads, the numbers are thus: PRR 161,436…NYC 124,461…B&O 64,285…Erie 24,551. Keep in mind that in the 1850s both B&O and Erie were far larger than PRR and NYC was an upstart. Triumph.

Passenger traffic turned out to be a millstone that played a major role in the downfall of PRR and NYC. (B&O and Erie were luckier in that they had only a minor share of this profitless business.) Even at that PRR's struggle in this category was impressive. In June of 1948 there were 34 scheduled passenger trains in each direction. Twenty-seven of them formed what became known as the nightly "Parade" as they rounded the Curve between 10:43 pm and 3:41 am. Triumph.

Freight traffic as measured by trains is a far less reliable statistic simply because larger cars and longer trains obscure the data. Still, the net result has always been exciting. From the late 1940s through the mid-1960s a typical day saw about 100 trains. By the late 1970s through 1996, about 60-70 trains a day passed over Pittdiv. However the merger game ultimately plays out, the PittDiv plant is ready to handle additional volume and can be easily expanded if that should prove to be insufficient. Triumph.

Only in the category of motive power can PRR be described as bumbling. In January 1954 an official "modernization" treatise was issued by the railroad, attempting to explain away the rationale behind their ten-year delay in dieselizing while having to admit that "savings in operating costs gained by the efficiency of the diesel locomotive have been an important factor in the economics of railroading during the last ten years. Many wholly steam-power railroads benefited from diesel conversion before PRR started its program." Having made this admission, the document then went on to shower the reader with self-justifying statistics that can only be described as setting a new standard in sophistry. The *important* aspect to dieselization was *availability* and this wasn't mentioned at all, even in 1954! Denial of the obvious is always a fatal failing and in this case it provided a very large nail in a very large coffin. Disaster.

Yet the reaction of operating management to blundering in Philadelphia and Altoona was admirable. In the Spring of 1945 a study of train operations on Pittdiv between Pitcairn and Altoona was published. We will now quote from this report. The day under study was 6 April 1945, a Friday.

Conclusions

The principal interferences to both eastward and westward freight train movements were caused by the limitations of the plant and the operations peculiar to the railroad line over the Allegheny Mountains between Conemaugh and Altoona.

Interferences to westward movements were also found in the blocks east of Derry, Radebaugh and Pitcairn.

STUDY OF TRAIN OPERATIONS
APRIL 6, 1945

Subject

This study was made to determine what physical limitations of plant and what interferences exist in movements of freight trains which prevent higher average freight train speeds.

Scope of Study

All freight train movements in each block between block stations in the 24-hour period were recorded and analyzed. The normal time for the movement of each train through each block without interference or accident, but including time for water, coal, attaching helpers, and the like, was determined by local train dispatchers. Comparison of this normal time with the actual time developed the delays due to interferences or accidents. Average speeds in each block and delays incurred by freight trains were derived from this data.

Discussion

The main line of the Pittsburgh Division between Pitcairn and Altoona is used by through trains between those points and also handles traffic to and from connecting routes. About 50 passenger trains and 25 freight trains from Pittsburgh to Altoona, and from Altoona to Pittsburgh, constitute the bulk of the traffic, to which is added the suburban passenger service west of Derry, freight traffic via the Conemaugh Division at "JD" and connecting branches at Greensburg, South Fork, Cresson, and Gallitzin. Light helper engine movements at certain locations also greatly increase the traffic density. The variations in movements on different portions of the route are illustrated by the following summary:

	Number of Movements									
	SZ – DR		DR – JD		JD – AO		AO – AR		AO – SLOPE	
	East	West	East	West	East	West	East	West	East	West
Psgr. Trains	60	60	50	47	51	51	50	51	50	51
Frt. Trains	36	35	36	33	64	59	69	62	67	36
Light Engs. (Pushers)	3	26	1	3	2	2	2	111	89	2
Shifters and Work Trains	3	4	1	2	2	1	3	3	1	2
TOTAL	102	125	88	85	119	113	124	227	207	91

Eastward Freight Movement

In the 24 hour period April 6, 1945, the following trains were dispatched form Pitcairn to Altoona:

Train	No.	Average Initial Terminal	Average Road Time	Average Final Terminal	Average Total Time of Crews	Average Road Speed
Arranged Service	20	1'23"	7'46"	0'30"	9'39"	12.9 mph
Through Extras	3	1'22"	9'25"	0'45"	11'32"	10.2 mph
TOTAL	23	1'23"	7'59"	0'32"	9'54"	12.0 mph

Average Normal Time and Speed of Eastward Freight Trains

The average normal time required for trains to be handled through each block, if no interferences from traffic or accidents were encountered, was 4 hrs. 44 min., Pitcairn to Altoona, and the average normal speed 20.3 mph.

Between Pitcairn and Conpitt Junction, 44 miles, the time required was 1 hr. 39 mins., and the normal speed 26.9 mph., whereas with denser traffic and adverse grade conditions Conpitt Junction to Altoona, 52 miles, the time required was 3 hrs. 5 mins. and the normal speed was 17.0 mph.

Average normal speed is relatively low in the following blocks:

Blocks	Average Normal Speed	Reason
C-AO	3.5 mph	Attaching helpers, coal and water at Conemaugh
MO-AR	9.3 mph	Setting up air brake retainer valves at "AR".
MG-GY	13.7 mph	Slow speed with brakes held on by retainer valves on descending grade.
GY-Slope	13.7 mph	Slow speed with brakes held on by retainer valves on descending grade.

Average Actual Time and Speed of Eastward Freight Trains

The average actual time for trains to be handled in each of the blocks was 8 hrs. 3 mins., Pitcairn to Altoona, and the average actual speed was 11.9 mph. In comparison with the average normal time estimated for trains to run from Pitcairn to Altoona of 4 hrs. 44 mins., the average delay incurred by each train was 3 hrs. 19 mins.

Between Pitcairn and Conpitt Junction, 44 miles, the average actual time of trains was 2 hrs. 21 mins, the average actual speed 16.5 mph, and average delay per train 1 hr. 2 mins. Between Conpitt Junction and Altoona, 52 miles, the average actual time of trains was 5 hrs. 22 mins., the average actual speed 9.8 mph, and average delay per train 2 hrs. 17 mins.

The average actual time and corresponding delays per train are high and the actual speeds are relatively low in comparison with the average normal times and speeds in the following blocks.

Blocks	Average Elapsed Time per Train			Average Speed of Trains		Total Delays Incurred
	Actual Mins.	Normal Mins.	Delays Mins.	Actual MPH	Normal MPH	
JD-SG	56	30	26	13.8	26.0	28 hrs. 02 mins.
SG-C	36	13	23	6.8	19.2	24 hrs. 23 mins.
C-AO	65	34	31	1.9	3.5	33 hrs. 27 mins.
NY-MO	42	28	14	11.2	17.0	16 hrs. 54 mins.
MO-AR	23	13	10	5.2	9.3	12 hrs. 33 mins.
AR-MG	28	17	11	10.4	17.1	12 hrs. 14 mins.

The delays incurred in the blocks mentioned above are summarized as follows:

	Equip. Failures	Open Routes Road	Open Routes Yard	Trains Ahead	Slow Speed	Road Work	Coal & Water	Helpers	Retainers	Total
JD-SG	3'35"	2'05"	—	11'27"	1'33"	1'30"	7'52"	—	—	28'02"
SG-C	2'15"	—	10'30"	8'11"	0'26"	3'01"	—	—	—	24'23"
C-AO	0'15"	—	—	1'55"	—	0'29"	6'23"	24'25"	—	33'27"
NY-MO	3'07"	2'13"	—	3'59"	1'23"	5'14"	0'58"	—	—	16'54"
MO-AR	2'59"	0'35"	—	1'28"	—	0'25"	—	—	7'06"	12'33"
AR-MG	3'39"	0'25"	—	6'18"	1'11"	0'41"	—	—	—	12'14'

Analysis of these delays discloses that the bulk of delays incurred by eastward trains occurs in two locations, JD to AO, 19 miles, where delays of 85 hrs. 52 mins. constitute 46% of all delays to all trains between Pitcairn and Altoona, and NY to MG, 14.8 miles, where delays of 41'41" constitute 23% of all delays between Pitcairn and Altoona. The total of the delays at these two locations, 127 hrs. 33 mins., is 69% of all delays incurred by eastward trains.

Interferences to Eastward Freight Train Movements
Physical Limitations and Operating Conditions

C to AO	—	Attaching helpers, coal, water and engine attention.
MO to AR	—	Setting up air brake retainer valves.
MG to Slope	—	Slow speed with brakes held on by retainer valves on descending grade.

If the normal average speed of 24 mph on the balance of the route between Pitcairn and Altoona could be achieved at these locations, the normal time required to run from Pitcairn to Altoona would be reduced 44 minutes, making the total normal time 4 hours.

Interferences from Other Trains and Accidents

JD to AO	—	1 hr. 20 mins. per train.
NY to MO	—	0 hr. 35 mins. per train.
TOTAL	—	1 hr. 55 mins. per train.

If these interferences could be eliminated, the average actual time from Pitcairn to Altoona would be reduced to 6 hrs. 08 mins., and average speed would be increased to 15.8 mph, instead of 11.9 mph which was the average actual speed on the day in question.

Westward Freight Movement

In the 24 hour period, April 6, 1945, the following trains were dispatched from Altoona to Pitcairn:

Train	No.	Average Initial Terminal	Average Road Time	Average Final Terminal	Average Total Time of Crews	Average Road Speed
Arranged Service	15	2'02"	7'02"	0'37"	9'41"	13.7 mph
Through Extras	4	1'35"	8'23"	0'45"	10'43"	11.5 mph
TOTAL	19	1'56"	7'19"	0'39"	10'00"	13.0 mph

Average Normal Speed of Westward Freight Trains

The average normal time required for the average train to move from Altoona to Pitcairn was 3 hrs. 57 mins., and the average normal speed was 25.5 mph.

Between Altoona and Conpitt Junction, 52 miles, the normal time required was 2 hrs. 12 mins. and the normal speed 23.8 mph.

Between Conpitt Junction and Pitcairn, 44 miles, the normal time required was 1 hr. 45 mins., and the normal speed 25.5 mph.

Average normal speed is relatively low in the following blocks:

Blocks	Average Normal Speed	Reason
Slope-GY	14.9 mph	Adverse grades
GY-MG	13.6 mph	Adverse grades
MG-AR	12.4 mph	Adverse grades
AR-MO	16.5 mph	Anticipated interference

Average Actual Speed of Westward Freight Trains

The average actual time for freight trains to be handled in each of the blocks was 7 hrs. 40 mins. Altoona to Pitcairn, and the average actual speed was 12.5 mph. In comparison with the average normal time estimated for trains to run from Altoona to Pitcairn of 3 hrs. 57 mins., the average delay incurred by each train was 3 hrs. 43 mins.

Between Altoona and Conpitt Junction, 52 miles, the average actual time of trains was 4 hrs. 01 min., and the average actual speed was 13.1 mph.

Between Conpitt Junction and Pitcairn, 44 miles, the average actual time of trains was 3 hrs. 39 mins., and the average actual speed 12.1 mph

The average actual time and corresponding delays per train are high, and the average actual speeds are relatively low in comparison with the average normal times and speeds in the following blocks:

Blocks	Average Elapsed Time per Train			Average Speed of Trains		Total Delays Incurred
	Actual Mins.	Normal Mins.	Delays Mins.	Actual MPH	Normal MPH	
SO-AO	29	8	21	10.4	37.7	22 hrs. 14 mins.
BH-DR	54	18	36	8.1	24.3	19 hrs. 15 mins.
DR-KR	30	14	16	9.5	20.3	9 hrs. 03 mins.
SW-RG	28	10	18	7.0	20.1	9 hrs. 33 mins.
CP-SZ	27	10	17	8.0	22.3	10 hrs. 16 mins.

OPERATIONS

The delays incurred in the blocks mentioned above are summarized as follows:

Blocks	Equip. Failures	Open Routes Road	Open Routes Yard	Trains Ahead	Slow Speed	Road Work	Coal & Water	Helpers	Total
SO-AO	—	1'00"	—	18'26"	25"	50"	1'33"	—	22'14"
BH-DR	2'14"	—	—	6'37"	22"	3'39"	6'23"	—	19'15"
DR-KR	—	10"	—	49"	—	3'51"	—	4'13"	9'03"
SW-RG	18"	25"	—	1'00"	17"	7'33"	—	—	9'33"
CP-SZ	—	3'41"	2'59"	2'42"	54"	—	—	—	10'16"

Comparison of Westward and Eastward Freight Train Operations

Trains Dispatched from Altoona to Pitcairn and from Pitcairn to Altoona

April 6th	Westward	Eastward	Inc. or Dec.
Number of Trains	19	23	(D) 4
Average Initial Terminal Time	1'56"	1'23"	(I) 33 mins.
Average Road Time	7'19"	7'59'	(D) 40 mins.
Average Final Terminal Time	0'39'	0'32"	(D) 7 mins.
Average Total Time of Crews	10'00"	9'54"	(I) 6 mins.
Average Road Speed	13 mph	12 mph	(I) 1 mph

Average of All Freight Trains in All Blocks between Pitcairn and Altoona

	Westward	Eastward	Inc. or Dec.
Number of Freight Trains	43	56	(D) 13
Normal Road Time per Train	3'57"	4'44"	(D) 47 mins
Normal Road Speed	25.5 mph	20.3 mph	(I) 5.2 mph
Actual Road Time per Train	7'40"	8'03"	(D) 23 mins.
Actual Road Speed	12.5 mph	11.9 mph	(I) 0.6 mph
Delays Incurred per Train	3'43"	3'19"	(I) 24 mins.
Total Delays Incurred by all Trains	156'30"	186'08"	(D) 29'38"

Interferences to Westward Freight Train Movements

Because of the higher estimated normal speed attainable by westward trains as compared with eastward trains they are able to absorb more delays per train and still make better actual speed on the road. Their over-all performance compares unfavorably with eastward trains, however, because of the higher initial terminal time at Altoona where trains dispatched via Hollidaysburg and New Portage Branch are adversely affected by terminal conditions. The principal interferences on the road are in the vicinity of Conemaugh (AO), Derry (DR), Greensburg (SW), and Pitcairn (SZ), where delays for various causes such as work, open routes, trains ahead and coal and water are prominent.

Summary

The long steep grades of the line over the Allegheny Mountains constitute the major cause of interferences to both eastward and westward freight train movements. Eastward trains are affected by the limitations of the railroad plant and of the operations peculiar thereto all the way from JD to Altoona. The servicing of helpers at Conemaugh engine house at the throat of the route over the mountain, the attaching of helpers to all eastward freight trains, the slow speed on the steepest part of the grade from Portage to Gallitzin, the setting up of retainer valves to hold air brakes on the descending grades, and the interferences caused by helper engines returning to Altoona, all combine to increase the average road time about 3 hours and reduce the road speed to less than 10 mph from JD to Altoona, a distance of 52 miles.

Westward trains are affected by physical limitations of the grades of the Eastern Slope which limit their attainable speed to about 14 mph, and by interference from helper engines returning to Conemaugh. Road time of westward trains would be reduced about 2 hours per train if the interference caused by the Mountain operations could be eliminated.

Westward trains also suffer interferences aggregating over 1 hour per train approaching Radebaugh and Pitcairn for work, trains ahead and open routes, and at Derry for these causes and coal and water.

Phila.,
8-8-45

(We must thank the Pennsylvania State Archives for this document, which they had the widsom to purchase at the PC auction in 1972. There were numerous exhibits. Following is a portion of one of them, included to illustrate just how dense the traffic was on Pittdiv.)

TRIUMPH I

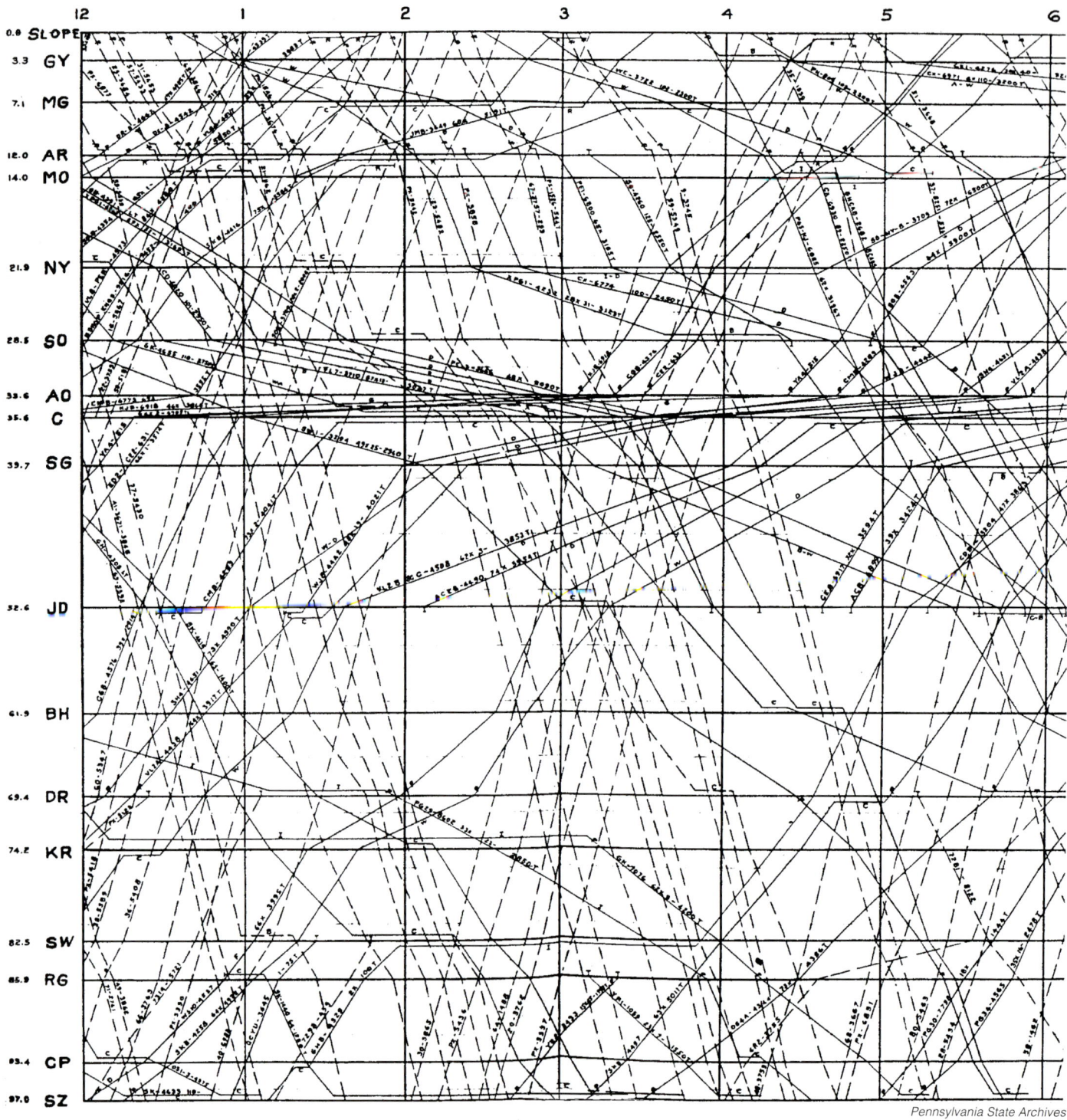

Pennsylvania State Archives

THIS FLOW CHART, which accompanied the 6 April 1945 report, covers the movements from midnight to 6:00 am that day. The balance of the 24-hour period was included, of course, but is not reproduced here. The solid lines are freight trains, the dashed lines passenger. Solid line with a P is a Pusher move. The letter codes are A (engine failure), B (car failure), C (open routes), D (trains ahead), E (held for yard room), F (slow speed), G (held for power), H (yard work), I (work), W (water) and R (retainers). The track diagram for this sheet appears on the front endpaper of this book.

OPERATIONS

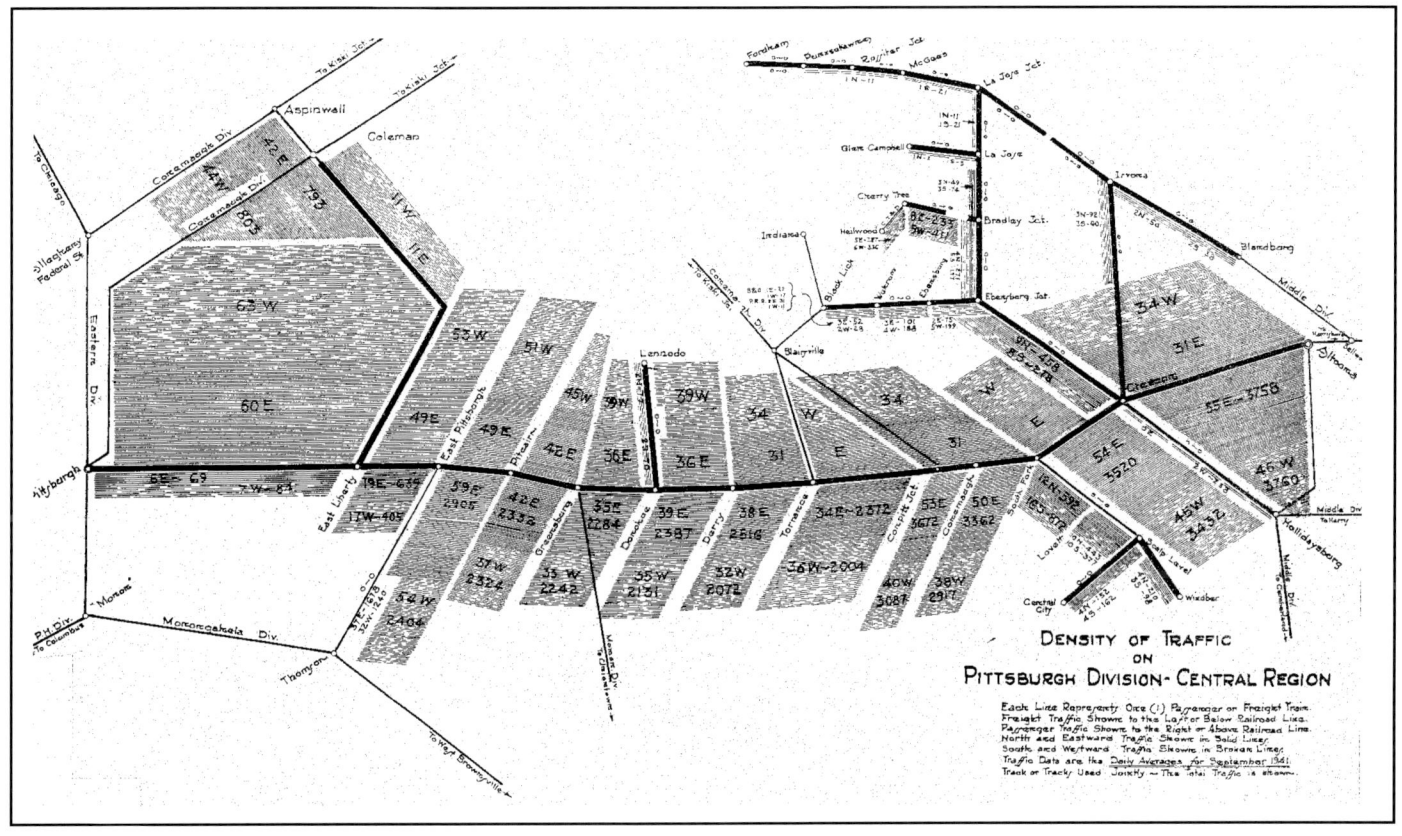

THE DENSITY OF TRAFFIC on Pittdiv appeared this way as a daily average for September 1941. Each line represents one train. Broken lines are eastward/northward, solid lines westward/southward. Passenger trains are above or to the right of the railroad line, freight trains below or to the left. The multi-digit numbers for freight trains represent the number of cars moved. Of course, this chart goes west of Pitcairn to Pittsburgh and illustrates the huge amount of commuter traffic from Derry west. PRR needed all four of those mainline tracks. The gigantic surge of World War II traffic had yet to appear.

TRIUMPH I

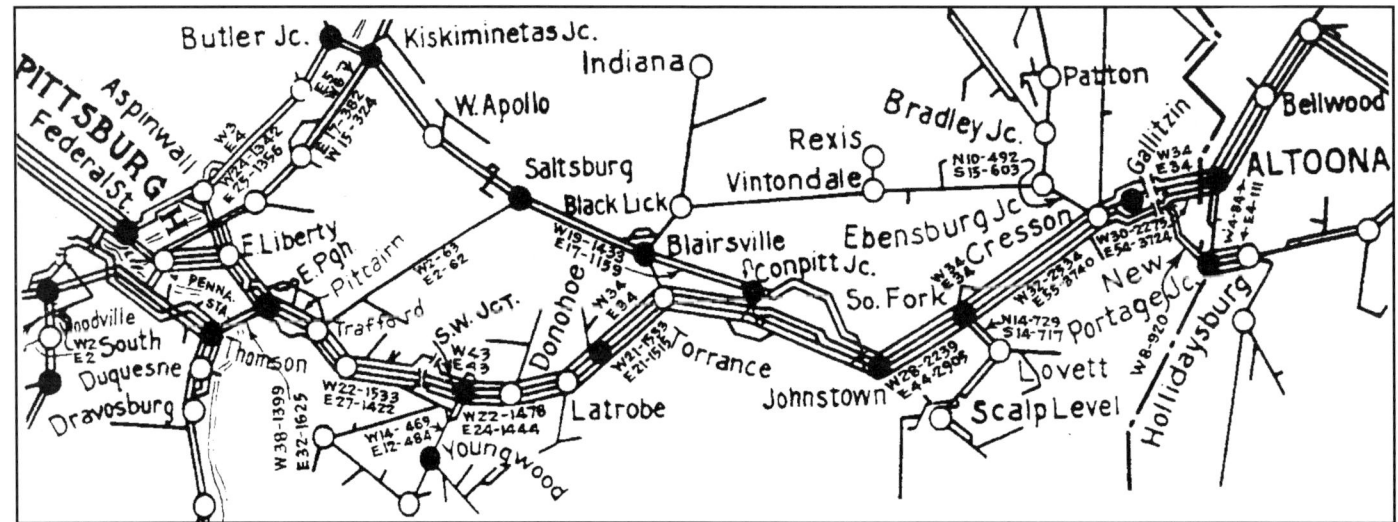

EVEN WITH THE WAR OVER, Pittdiv traffic was still immense. This chart, parts of which we have shown earlier, reflects the average daily traffic density for June of 1948. Comparison with the 1941 chart shown on the preceding page can develop many interesting tidbits of operating information. For example, eastward freight trains between Johnstown/Conemaugh and South Fork averaged 67 cars per train in 1941 and 66 cars in 1948. No improvement here.

AND THEN WE HAVE our orphans. This photograph is identified as a 1903 view at the Curve. This is impossible as there are no cuts in that area, yet it was too nice to pass up. Now let us go back to Altoona and go west once more, this time in full color.

Railroad Museum of Pennsylvania

Chapter 10

Color Journey

Michael Smith/Aerial Views

THE MOUNTAIN BARRIER looms on the horizon west of Altoona on 3 May 1995 just as it has for countless millions of years, misty and forbidding. The railroad and the town are poised for still another assault on its flanks.

REAR HELPERS lean against the train as TV-1 passes Alto Tower on 22 April 1995 and prepares to do battle against a grade that is just beginning.

Brian A. Paulus

TRIUMPH I

Todd Atkinson

THE GLOWING lights of Alto Tower are a beacon of comfort on 20 July 1995, signaling to crews and passengers alike that they are not alone on the railroad. As towers close, never to reopen, the feeling of security that they have always imparted will be gone forever.

THE BRICKYARD at Milepost 239 is the first significant structure on the trek west from Altoona and has become a haven for photographers. On 14 March 1996, a set of westbound helpers passes two eastbound coal drags and remind us of the density of traffic on Pittdiv.

Todd Atkinson

FOR ALL THE MAGIC of dynamic brakes, it is important to remember that gravity is still a vicious foe and that brake applications are not *passé*. Brakeshoe smoke is quite apparent on this eastbounder at the Brickyard on 9 April 1994.

Todd Atkinson

COLOR JOURNEY

MOVING BACK IN TIME to 25 October 1964, smoke is even more evident as a drag grinds and whines its way downhill surrounded by Fall color. Uphill and downhill tracks are obvious, the former white with sand and the latter brown with residue from glowing brakeshoes.

Michael Smith/Aerial Views

NOW THE PANORAMA of glorious Horseshoe Curve appears in the distance as we fly westward, catching up with a westbounder snaking through the Curve itself with towering mountains forming a visual bowl. The trees are just beginning to leaf on 3 May 1995 and the reservoirs starting to reflect the rays of the morning sun.

TRIUMPH I

Michael Smith/Aerial Views

BOTH THE WESTBOUND TRAIN and our intrepid photographer moved west as the aircraft approached the Curve and brought the new park facilities into sharper focus. Another Spring dawns on the eternal Curve and Kink, the latter named by this author to remind us that the mountain did not surrender unconditionally.

IN THE SAME AIRSPACE, the Curve and environs appeared thus over a half-century earlier as Fall change paints the forest and an eastbound passenger train, resplendent with red cars, drifts toward the Kink and Curve.

KITTANNING POINT and the cuts were bare when this tinted postcard was produced about a century ago. The card itself is slightly out-of-register, a flaw that does not diminish the grandeur of the scene.

Michael G. Farrow Collection

COLOR JOURNEY

THE COMPLEX at Kittanning Point at full tide with four tracks in service and the illustrious view intact is seen in this early 20th century postcard. This card was produced in Germany, a pioneer nation in the graphic arts until the advent of World War I.

A HANDSOME JAY drifts into Kittanning Point just east of the Curve, surrounded by the green jungle that has evolved in a return to Mother Nature.

"TRIPLE CROWN" Road Railer (RR261) is passing OIPI at Kittanning Point on 9 April 1994. The Road Railer experiment is another theory gone awry.

Todd Atkinson

TRIUMPH I

THREE TRAINS appear in the Curve area on this PRR public relations postcard, issued c. 1950. The artist did a splendid scenic rendition but could not resist his orders to edit-out the Kink, which is represented by a faked sidewall cut. The back of the card points out that two million passengers and 25,000 freight trains composed of nearly two million freight cars passed through the Curve in a typical year in that era. By any standard, those numbers are impressive.

THE CURVE AREA appeared thus in the late 1930s, with the Kittanning Station still in place. The back of this card is postmarked 5 August 1942 and the message reads, "Pittsburgh here I am!" A gentleman named "Ray" had arrived.

ONE CAN BE CERTAIN that there were nowhere near two million passengers on the eastbound *Pennsylvanian*, seen here passing TV-2 on 26 August 1990 at 1:55 pm. Not on that day nor in that entire year.

Eric Powell

COLOR JOURNEY

Eric Powell

JUST TWENTY MINUTES earlier, the five-car westbound *Pennsylvanian* passed on 26 August 1990, led by F40PH No. 211.

Todd Atkinson

GP9 7048 is the second PRR locomotive to rest at the Curve and is seen here on 8 April 1994, with that glorious keystone displayed with justifiable pride.

PRIDE ALSO GOETH BEFORE A FALL. The infamous Aerotrain passes the Curve on 11 November 1956.

AN EASTBOUND TOUR TRAIN paused at the Curve in early 1972 and discharged passengers to admire both the view and the K4 which was the first resident at this location. Note the three-unit Baldwin Shark helper set at distant left.

Gary W. Schlerf Collection

TO MARK THE 100th ANNIVERSARY of the opening of the Curve and the 75th anniversary of the introduction of the incandescent lamp, PRR and Sylvania Electric Products cooperated to produce what is probably the most spectacular night photograph ever taken. The cameras were mounted on a 150-foot high tower (the steps to the tower can be seen at bottom center) and the project required months of planning, 31 miles of wiring, and 6,000 large photoflash bulbs to light 2,000,000 square feet. With passenger and freight trains rounding the Curve, the button was pressed on the night of 20 October 1954 with skyrockets bursting in midair. For a railroad not known for its public relations prowess, this tribute to Edgar Thomson and Thomas Edison...bigger-than-life giants of the last century...has to be noted as a marvelous coup. Oh, to have been with Father on that tower at that magic moment.

SOME FIFTY YEARS earlier, this photograph of the Curve area was taken by an unknown cameraman and tinted by German craftsmen to produce, via what was then called the Poly-Chrome process, the postcard seen here. For its time, this was state of the art. The postmark is 27 April 1907.

Bob Jansen Collection

Michael Smith/Aerial Views

MG SITS LONELY on the mountainside as two trains pass on 3 May 1995 in a view of the East Slope west of the Curve that has to rank as a unique treatment of this section of the railroad.

TRIUMPH I

WITH BRAKESHOE SMOKE beginning to curl, an eastbound drag descends the west leg of Horseshoe Curve in the early diesel era, sporting train/phone aerials on the lead unit.

Ed Ward/E. Roy Ward Collection

WITH SHEER MOUNTAINS in the background, a westbound trailer train is about to enter MG's domain at the eastward distant signal on a snowy day in the Penn Central era.

MG WAS SETUP for a movement when this photograph was taken in the three-track era, with position lights ablaze.

Julius Westheimer Collection

COLOR JOURNEY

Michael Smith/Aerial Views

PRR TURNS THE CORNER and enters Sugar Run in its march to the summit. Here we look east on 3 May 1995, with Hollidaysburg on the right and Altoona on the left nestled in the valley. New Route 22 is apparent at lower right as is the roadbed of NPRR to the right of the highway. A westbounder has entered the Sugar Run valley, having just passed Milepost 244. Famed Allegrippus Curve is at lower left. Of all the scenes in this book, it is this one that most dramatically illustrates how small the railroad and how large the Mountain Barrier.

Brian A. Paulus

TRAIN NO. 44 *Pennsylvanian*, drops down Sugar Run on 12 February 1995. By the way, this train number is "Sunday only."

TINY AGAINST THE BACKGROUND, a mixed freight descends on 29 January 1995.

Brian A. Paulus

347

TRIUMPH I

CABOOSES were still in vogue in July of 1986 when a mixed consist eastbound dropped through Bennington Curve, with pushers counteracting gravity with their dynamics.

Kurt R. Reisweber

RED-NOSED AMTRAK ENGINE 588 is passing a freight at "Benny" on an unknown date with four mainline tracks.

Ed Ward/E. Roy Ward Collection

Eric Powell

AT THE SAME LOCATION, but with only three tracks, two SD40-2s on the front and three on the rear ease a drag through CP BENNY at 5:00 pm 26 August 1990.

WHILE THE DATE IS UNCERTAIN, the era is not. Three Penn Central trains pass just east of the summit tunnels with underbrush creeping toward the tracks.

Ed Ward/E. Roy Ward Collection

COLOR JOURNEY

THIS MAGNIFICENT VIEW of the summit and the West Slope beyond was photographed on 3 May 1995, with an eastbounder exiting the New Portage Tunnel and well into the Slide.

Michael Smith/Aerial Views

A CLOSEUP of the east portals on the same day with the same train shows clearance work in progress. The east portal of the middle tunnel is being extended, wisely in our view. Note at extreme upper left the New Portage line west of the summit and approaching AR.

Michael Smith/Aerial Views

TRIUMPH I

WITH EXHAUST SMOKE reminiscent of the steam era, a westbound approaches the east portal on Track No. 2 on 5 January 1995 with sufficient snow to remind the reader of the elevation of these parts.

Brian A. Paulus

NINETY-TWO CARS of black diamonds, seen from directly above the New Portage Tunnel, are moving down the Slide very carefully on 13 March 1995.

Brian A. Paulus

THREE BALDWIN SHARKS with empty hoppers on the drawbar and led by that red keystone grind uphill toward the east portal on 25 October 1964 with Fall change enlivening the scene.

COLOR JOURNEY

Michael Smith/Aerial Views

THE TWIN BORES AT GALLITZIN, with the Jackson Street Bridge crossing the westbound tracks of the mainline, were abuzz with clearance construction when this photograph was taken on 3 May 1995. Notice the red caboose in the green patch on the left between the bridge and the "new" portal. This is N5C PRR "cabin car" 477951 built in 1942 and donated to the town in 1991 for use as a gift shop and display facility. Happily, a red keystone is prominent on each side.

THE KEYSTONE had been replaced by worms on these locomotives, roaring westbound through a rather barren scene on 8 May 1970.

BLACK HOPPERS AND BLACK SMOKE billow forth from the "new" tunnel on 26 August 1990. This empty train had a lot of power…an SD40 and two GP40s leading and two SD40s on the rear. The hoppers on the left are empty, but note that the ones on the right are loaded with ties.

(BELOW)
THIS HISTORIC PHOTOGRAPH was taken on 6 May 1995 from the Jackson Street Bridge, with typical smoke and waterlogged clearance activity. Why historic? This is one of the very few photos taken by the author that was considered good enough to publish.

Eric Powell

(BELOW)
CAPI (Camden NJ to Pittsburgh) came very close to nicking some icicles on 25 January 1995, illustrating still another hazard of mountain railroading.

Brian A. Paulus

(LEFT)
A NEW DAY DAWNS at Gallitzin as TV-99 roars out of the wider and higher Allegheny Tunnel on 12 December 1995 with doublestacks. The original facade was retained and the icicles in the Gallitzin Tunnel can multiply at leisure.

Brian A. Paulus

COLOR JOURNEY

WESTBOUND BAPI (Baltimore-Pittsburgh) punches through at UN on 3 March 1995, passing the loop track to AR on the right.

Brian A. Paulus

Brian A. Paulus

MOVING TO TUNNELHILL and the New Portage line, we see 110 cars of coal dive into the Slide on 18 March 1995 with whining helpers on the rear. For all the tonnage, drags are relatively easy to brake because that weight is evenly distributed throughout the train. That is small solace, of course, if the train gets away from you.

THERE WERE "ONLY" 94 cars of eastbound coal entering the New Portage bore on 24 March 1995, with twin SD40-2 helpers holding back their share. Here we see the west portal at an angle seldom photographed, a tribute to the skill and determination of Brian Paulus who is, in our view, the finest railroad lensman of this era.

Brian A. Paulus

TRIUMPH I

WITH PASSENGERS AND CREW a lot warmer than Mr. Paulus, Amtrak No. 42 has just passed AR on 14 February 1995 and is about to enter the Slide.

Brian A. Paulus

AR WAS ALIVE AND WELL on 10 March 1995 when the 6372 led 76 cars of "east" coal through the plant with the loop track to UN in the background.

Brian A. Paulus

UNUSUAL IF NOT RARE, *westbound* MAIL-9 passes AR on 24 February 1995. The train crossed over at MG and came back at MO, a diversion probably caused by clearance tunnel construction.

Brian A. Paulus

COLOR JOURNEY

E. Roy Ward

SPANKING NEW "Yellowball" H43 hoppers, rolling behind two single-stripe PRR EMD units, entered the MO interlocking plant circa 1965 with Gallitzin bright on the horizon.

Ed Ward/E. Roy Ward Collection

FROM THE SAME vantage point on the Route 53 bridge, we see new and old Conrail livery on a three-unit helper set in April of 1978 with snow accenting Gallitzin as well as the railroad.

Pennsylvania State Archives

JUST TO THE SOUTH of the preceding scenes, one finds the Lemon House and OPRR. We have visited this location earlier in the book. This colorful painting was created by nineteenth century artist George Storm and has at least some elements of technical accuracy.

TRIUMPH I

LOOKING WEST from the Route 53 overpass in July of 1969, a multi-unit eastbounder is approaching with a keystone on the nose.

E. Roy Ward

EIGHT YEARS LATER almost to the day, and after earthshaking transportation tumult, a "nose job" has produced a new (and mercifully shortlived) hood emblem. The rest of the scene is the same, however, on 27 July 1977 and the roadbed appears to be properly maintained.

ON A WINTER DAY described as colder than a whore's heart, westbound EDPI-1 (Edgemoor-Pittsburgh) with 109 cars rolls past MO on 11 February 1995. In the parlance of the railroad history publishing profession, this photograph is an example of "perfect Paulus composition".

Brian A. Paulus

COLOR JOURNEY

LIGHT POWER is moving west into Cresson from the Irvona Secondary and on the mainline on 13 November 1990 with the blind eyes of MO surveying the scene.

E. Roy Ward

THE CRESSON JUMPOVER was also blessed with power on the same day as a westbounder passes MO on the mainline.

E. Roy Ward

Michael Smith/Aerial Views

THE JUMPOVER WAS GONE, but the track to the Irvona Secondary was still in place on 3 May 1995 when this splendid air photograph of the Cresson area was taken. Gallitzin can be faintly seen at extreme upper right.

TRIUMPH I

A WESTBOUNDER punches into the Cresson scene, which is cluttered with cars and power, on 8 April 1994. In their last days, the jumpover's position light signals stare at the ordered confusion.

Todd Atkinson

E. Roy Ward

REMINDING THE READER that it snows in this country, a removal train is departing Cresson on 2 January 1977.

Todd Atkinson

THOSE ICICLES we have seen must be removed and, here at Cresson on 10 April 1994, we see an ancient PRR four-bay hopper used in that service. The word PENNSYLVANIA can be seen on the side of the car, peeking through overlaid paint and reminding us of past glory.

Gary W. Schlerf

THE CRESSON SCENE on 18 August 1975 can only be described as desolate, particularly with that Penn Central green on the office building. Comparing this with "rebirth" photos of Cresson shown in this book, one comes away impressed with the managerial prowess of Conrail leadership.

COLOR JOURNEY

Todd Atkinson

LOOMING OUT OF THE BLIZZARD, an eastbound roars by that office building at Cresson on 8 March 1995 with headlight and ditch lights piercing the gloom. Mercifully, the building is now as white as the snow.

THE MAINLINE is now gently descending the West Slope through historic Lilly, winding its way to the right on its way to Johnstown. Note the overhead bridge in the center of this photo, taken 3 May 1995.

Michael Smith/Aerial Views

Todd Atkinson

THAT OVERHEAD BRIDGE at Lilly enabled Todd Atkinson, another skillful railroad photographer of note, to catch the eastbound *Broadway* on 9 March 1995 just six months to the day before its last run. We confess that we are partial to dramatic snow shots and this has to be one of the very best.

Brian A. Paulus

FROM "LILY SNOW-WHITE" at Lilly to blue and black. On 18 March 1995, the 6079 and friends move 110 cars of coal upgrade at a crawl.

Todd Atkinson

MANY ARE THE VIEWS looking *west* from the Cassandra footbridge, but the east has seldom been done. Here, on 21 July 1995, an SD60M rolls around a gentle curve and is about to enter tangent, surrounded by a sea of sparkling white ballast.

Todd Atkinson

BLUE WOULD NOT have been our choice of color for a caboose, but then again no one would give an award for aesthetics to Conrail. Westbound empty hoppers at Cassandra in July of 1986.

ALL MAINLINE TRACKS were full at Cassandra on 14 March 1996. The three trains were eastbound and Amtrak No. 46 was gaining. It is not easy to get multiple trains on a single photograph and luck is an important ingredient. Todd Atkinson is another "comer" in railroad photography and the reader should note the frequency of his byline in this book.

Kurt R. Reisweber

SONMAN AND "KOZA CORNER" from the air on 3 May 1995, with the path of the original PRR mainline slashing diagonally across the view. The new mainline can be barely seen at lower left. The huge coal pile is obvious evidence that mining is still alive and well.

Michael Smith/Aerial Views

Michael Smith/Aerial Views

FROM PORTAGE to the summit in a single easterly view taken on 3 May 1995, clearly showing the new and old PRR mainlines as well as Sonman and even the Big Cut at Cassandra. The depth of the new mainline fill is impressive even from this altitude.

Brian A. Paulus

THE WILMORE water pan flat-spot is under the wheels of Amtrak No. 43 on 15 April 1995 as she races west over the Route 53 underpass.

Brian A. Paulus

SUMMERHILL was host to 104 westbound empty hoppers on 17 February 1995. Position lights indicate that Track Nos. 1 and 2 are clear for at least two blocks.

ON 18 MARCH 1995, five units lead ALPI (Altoona-Pittsburgh) with a healthy 144 cars over a three-arch stone viaduct just east of Summerhill at Milepost 263.59. The span has been improved with concrete deck and spandrels. The east arch originally provided for a wagon road. The bridge and cut are "new" line. Date of construction, however, is uncertain…possibly opened in 1888 to replace an iron bridge, according to 1887 and 1888 annual reports.

Brian A. Paulus

A WESTERLY view of the same viaduct on 25 February 1995 shows PIEN (Pittsburgh-Enola). Just south (left) of this viaduct is a single-span stone arch that was "original" PRR and which now carries Route 53. Where, then, was the iron bridge mentioned in the last caption? Please reread page 198 and join the ranks of the puzzled.

Brian A. Paulus

COLOR JOURNEY

E. Roy Ward

A HUGE MOUND of mine tailings frown upon an overpowered westbounder at South Fork on 27 May 1984.

SNOW HAS softened the Ehrenfeld manmade mountain as TV-1 passes on 10 March 1995.

Brian A. Paulus

E. Roy Ward

PASSING AT SOUTH FORK on 27 May 1976 one sees a westbound trailer train and eastbound Amtraker.

A DRAG moves east through South Fork on 10 March 1995. Note the benches in the hill at upper left.

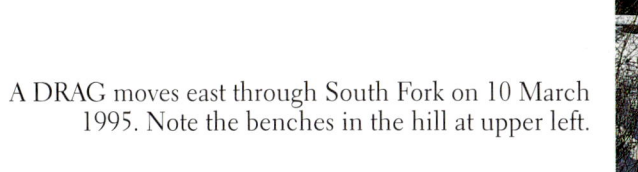

Brian A. Paulus

363

TRIUMPH I

Michael Smith/Aerial Views

LEGENDARY BIG VIADUCT, buried in the wilderness, is seen here on 3 May 1995. The river has yet to punch through that narrow neck, but there is no guarantee that it never will.

IT TOOK FIVE units to get this drag to Big Viaduct on 3 May 1995 and it is a long way to the summit. This view is downstream and the neck is at lower right.

Michael Smith/Aerial Views

GRAIN STILL MOVES east on Pittdiv, but it is a tiny fraction of today's total tonnage compared to the early years. This scene, taken in July of 1986, shows the Bethlehem Steel facility at Mineral Point at upper right. The helper has just come into view.

Kurt R. Reisweber

THE CREWS could enjoy delightful Fall foliage at Staple Bend in October of 1985, including those aboard the caboose. The leaves would soon be gone as well as the "cabin car". The leaves would come back. The caboose would soon be gone forever.

Kurt R. Reisweber

AS WE ENTER the Johnstown area, an eastward glance dramatizes the ruggedness of the terrain and the Conemaugh River canyon.

Michael Smith/Aerial Views

E. Roy Ward

COAL, STONE, SCRAP AND STEEL fill a colorful fall spectacular at Conemaugh in October of 1989 as an eastbound mixed races into the West Slope grade.

Brian A. Paulus

HELPERS SHOVE an eastbound drag on 18 March 1995, passing more of the same awaiting power. Ubiquitous rust is beginning, as always, to eat away at the hoppers on the right.

AS AN ARTIST with the telephoto lens, Brian Paulus has few peers. With exhaust heat shimmering, an eastbounder passes C Tower on Track No. 1 with the Johnstown skyline in the background. The signals are lit for an approaching westbound running on track No. 3 which didn't quite make it for inclusion in this photograph, appropriately for April Fool's Day in 1995.

Brian A. Paulus

TRIUMPH I

WE COULD NOT RESIST another opportunity to snipe at PRR motive power blundering. Two Centipedes, a single-striper and a five-striper, at Conemaugh on 24 July 1952.

E. Roy Ward Collection

THE CAMBRIA STEEL COMPANY at Johnstown, seen on a postcard carrying a date of 18 November 1908.

Frank Wrabel Collection

THE JOHNSTOWN STATION on a postcard issued shortly after opening.

TV-22 HAS CROSSED the Stone Bridge and is approaching the Johnstown Station on 11 March 1995. The Memorial Park to flood victims can be seen just beyond the highway bridge at lower left.

Brian A. Paulus

COLOR JOURNEY

MIXED FREIGHT with steam up front moves west across the Stone Bridge. This 1920s postcard was produced in the United States. World War I put an end to German graphic arts dominance.

AS WE ENTER the first Gap, we look up Stony Run. The bottom photograph on the opposite page was taken from the top of the incline seen at middle right. The Memorial Park, in arrow-shape, is just below and the station to the left of that.

Michael Smith/Aerial Views

WE LOOK EAST AGAIN, this time from the middle of Laurel Hill Gap. The island at upper middle survives. The overlook where we mused can be found just below center. The valley no longer throbs to industry, but trains still pass in profusion.

Michael Smith/Aerial Views

SG STUDIES an eastbounder on 16 December 1984. The only thing missing is a red keystone.

THE SANG HOLLOW water pans, alongside that little island.

THERE WERE STILL three tracks on the south bank when Mr. Reisweber, who has the agility of a mountain goat, snapped this splendid photograph of a westbound in May of 1977.

ANOTHER HIGH SHOT, this time by Mr. Ward on 27 May 1984, illustrates just how convenient was the Laurel Hill Gap for PRR.

A JAY is rolling westward in 1945 with a coal train and is approaching the bridge to the Sang Hollow Extension about a quarter mile west of SG.

Robert S. Yagodich Collection

THE MAINLINE turns a corner at Seward, now free of the Laurel Hill Gap, and on 13 May 1995 we see an eastbound PIEN with 151 cars on Track No. 2.

Brian A. Paulus

THE POWER PLANT just east of Conpitt Junction is certainly spectacular from any angle. This eastward view, taken 3 May 1995, shows the Sang Hollow Extension on the left and the mainline at upper right. The junction lies to the rear of the photographer.

Michael Smith/Aerial Views

LED BY A NEW SD60M, a westbound merchandiser streaks into the Conpitt Junction plant on 6 April 1995. The condensate from the massive generating plant is actually several miles away. Note the NYC-style signal. A little-remarked aspect of railroad signaling is lens design, the art of projecting a tiny light source for a maximum distance.

Brian A. Paulus

TRIUMPH I

E. Roy Ward

CONPITT JUNCTION on 27 July 1978 watches an eastbounder rumble through a weed-infested roadbed. There are four units on the headend during this unhappy time, but one doesn't know how many are operating. Operating men had to put extra units on each train to allow for breakdowns out on the road.

TRAIN NO. 40 passes over the Conemaugh River at 8:58 am 13 May 1995 at Lockport. A bit different from the first PRR train to reach here.

Brian A. Paulus

DEEP IN THE LIGONIER VALLEY, two westbounds grace the Conemaugh River on 1 April 1995.

Brian A. Paulus

THE DOGS OF WAR move east at the same location on 2 March 1991, the tanks in desert camo and destined for a conflict on the other side of the world.

Brian A. Paulus

COLOR JOURNEY

Michael Smith/Aerial Views

THE CONEMAUGH was muddy when this eastbounder crossed it on 3 May 1995.

Michael Smith/Aerial Views

THE PACKSADDLE is as grim and forbidding on this day in May of 1995 as it was when PRR first ventured into its confines. The setting sun is tinting the Conemaugh an ominous pink in this westerly view.

E. Roy Ward

A WESTBOUND TV on 20 March 1979 rushes to escape the Packsaddle.

ON THE SAME DAY, a mixed scurries toward the Ligonier Valley.

E. Roy Ward

TRIUMPH I

ON 19 MARCH 1982, a year in which Conrail was at last making some money, a westbounder is passing another cliff in the Packsaddle.

E. Roy Ward

E. Roy Ward Collection/Patrick Yough

WHILE BLAIRSVILLE is not on our tour, we could not resist this photograph of the original "West Penn" 1850s station taken 8 April 1990. The building is now a residence and is meticulously maintained.

E. Roy Ward

A STRING OF ROADRAILERS are passing Torrance on 30 March 1994, with Track No. 2 in unimpressive condition. Note the train on the setoff track which then served a quarry.

RIPRAP ON THE RIP RAP near Hillside on 2 February 1994. There had been a slip along the Monongahela River and this stone train was carrying riprap to stabilize the embankment.

E. Roy Ward

COLOR JOURNEY

E. Roy Ward

MOVING EAST PAST DR and about to enter Derry on 2 November 1977, we see a mixed with the latest paint scheme on the lead unit.

E. Roy Ward

A PLACID SCENE at Bradenville on 12 November 1994.

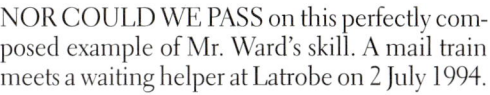

CREASED OR NOT, we could not resist this early 20th century postcard of the Latrobe Station which was, incidentally, produced in Great Britain rather than Germany.

NOR COULD WE PASS on this perfectly composed example of Mr. Ward's skill. A mail train meets a waiting helper at Latrobe on 2 July 1994.

E. Roy Ward

373

TRIUMPH I

MIRACLES DO HAPPEN and this photograph of a westbound empty hopper train approaching the Latrobe Station on 7 May 1995 is evidentiary. We were not planning to take this train, but the sudden burst of smoke and fire caused us to try a quick snapshot which obviously, and much to our astonishment, resulted as seen. A minisecond later the flames soared even higher and as the cab went by we tried to signal the crew that they were on fire. We don't know the appropriate hand-signal for that eventuality so tried to point in an excited way. If perchance a crewman should read these words, we were *not* giving the finger. As the locomotive passed, the fire went out and, as we learned after reporting the event to Conrail management, the engine arrived at destination with no discernible damage. Since we witnessed the volcano-like proportions of the fire, that seemed to us a miracle second only to the fact that we actually took a stunning photograph. Also, we thought for a second that the hummer was going to blow up in front of us and will confess that "Oh, no, not again. I'm getting a little old for this sort of thing" did dance through our mind. What went wrong? Succinctly, and after soliciting professional views from a number of sources, the only explanation we can offer is that it was another GE unit acting up. They are all smokers but this was a bit extreme.

E. Roy Ward

THE 7776 ON ITS MAIDEN RUN crosses the Loyalhanna on 21 April 1976, passing KR at extreme left. The nation's 200th birthday and Conrail's birthdate.

ACCENTED BY SNOW, a westbounder on 1 February 1978.

E. Roy Ward

THE CUT AT CARNEY on 14 June 1991.

E. Roy Ward

E. Roy Ward

DONAHOE SUMMIT on 20 August 1977.

IRON ORE BEING SHOVED at George on 5 July 1985.

E. Roy Ward

THESE UNUSUAL dragging equipment detectors offered a digital display to the crew. They are seen at SW Junction 15 October 1983.

E. Roy Ward

375

TRIUMPH I

Michael Smith/Aerial Views

THE "SMALL HILL" at Greensburg is not very apparent from the air, but is real nonetheless. The station complex and the terrain to the east on 3 May 1995.

THE GREENSBURG STATION, pristine shortly after opening on a postcard printed in Pittsburgh, which is a commentary on graphic arts history. Note the automobile.

Kurt R. Reisweber

AN EASTBOUND TV glides past the station in March of 1996 as renovations are in progress.

TWIN SD40-2 HELPERS press hard against the rear of a 75-car drag on 13 May 1995, moving at such a high rate of speed that passengers awaiting arrival of the *Pennsylvanian* decided that it was the better part of wisdom to distance themselves from the coal dust emanating from the train.

Brian A. Paulus

THE RADEBAUGH CUT in March of 1977 with two helpers shoving an eastbound over the summit. This photograph is also a study of the strata on the Rip Rap.

Kurt R. Reisweber

A WORK EXTRA at Radebaugh on 29 October 1981. RG, its plant and the branch to Connellsville are at upper left in this westerly view.

E. Roy Ward

THE EASTBOUND *National Limited*, and a local at RG, in March of 1977.

Kurt R. Reisweber

E. Roy Ward

THE ORIGINAL TUNNEL at Radebaugh, sad and lonely in March of 1977.

RG ON 25 January 1978 sees an eastbounder with a smoking unit taunting the snow.

TRIUMPH I

A WESTBOUND Flexi-Van Mail Train passes the forlorn Jeannette station in August of 1971, exiting Deadmans Cut. The station was still active as a freight agency in that year and the freight station was just to the right of the B&O boxcar.

Kurt R. Reisweber

BOTH STATIONS were long gone when this eastbound doublestacker slid through in March of 1996. The freight station was on the left and the passenger station on the right just ahead of the lead unit.

Kurt R. Reisweber

FOUR TRACKS filled the deep cut at Irwin on Independence Day of 1966 when a keystone led the way east.

E. Roy Ward

BOULDERS in the drainage ditch and overhanging strata catch the eye as two trains pass near Larimer on 24 June 1989.

E. Roy Ward

COLOR JOURNEY

CARPENTER TUNNEL was located at Ardara and the cut now boasts the public road seen here as a helper set moves west on 22 April 1995.

E. Roy Ward

LOOKING WEST at Trafford c. 1960 with two examples of PRR power.

E. Roy Ward Collection/Bob Reid

IN SAME YEAR, one-stripe PRR Fairbanks-Morse power moves west.

E. Roy Ward Collection/Bob Reid

A RED-FLAGGED PC unit moves east with train through Trafford on 31 December 1976

E. Roy Ward

TRIUMPH I

AS DUSK SETTLES IN, dwarfs and targets emit their messages at Trafford on 15 December 1967.

E. Roy Ward

A LEADEN SKY overlooks a fast moving westbounder throwing snow showers at Trafford on 29 January 1986. The two SD60s are ex-EMD demonstrators.

E. Roy Ward

NOW CP TRAFF with NYC signals irritating PRR purists, an eastbounder plunges through on 13 June 1995. The PRR signal bridge was removed for the clearance project on 27 August 1994.

Steve Raith

COLOR JOURNEY

Michael Smith/Aerial Views

THE BOWL at Pitcairn, looking east on 3 May 1995.

THE SAND TRACKS at Pitcairn on New Year's Day in 1977 found at least some units at rest although a far cry from steam days.

E. Roy Ward

E. Roy Ward

THE SUMMER OF 1969 found this lone New York Central F on the table at Pitcairn with a forlorn engine house in the background. One year later the largest bankruptcy in the nation's history would take place which makes this scene rather sad and prophetic.

381

TRIUMPH I

A MEDLEY OF COLORS and livery at Pitcairn on 1 November 1976 with the westbound hump facility in the background.

E. Roy Ward

Bob Jansen Collection

SEVENTY-SIX YEARS EARLIER the passenger station added some muted color to the Pitcairn scene.

Steve Raith

PITCAIRN is not bereft of traffic and activity, however, as this eastward view taken on 16 May 1995 attests.

EVEN AS LATE as 1968, Pitcairn was active and graced by a keystone.

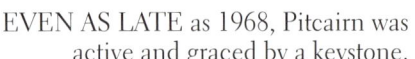

E. Roy Ward

COLOR JOURNEY

Steve Raith

THE COMPLETION of the clearance project was celebrated in a grand ceremony at Pitcairn on 28 September 1995. The "ribbon" being broken proudly states "Pennsylvania is open for business." Noting the mundane slogan, choice of venue and lack of a crowd, we guess that Conrail deliberately wanted to understate the importance of the event for reasons that we have yet to divine.

THE FIRST TOWER west of Pitcairn was WG at Wilmerding, seen here on 18 August 1969.

Ed Ward/E. Roy Ward Collection

E. Roy Ward

THREE ABREAST at Wilmerding on 16 November 1988.

383

TRIUMPH I

R TOWER at East Pittsburgh rested west of WG and represented PRR's entrance into the vast Pittsburgh industrial region as evidenced by all the fascinating elements in this scene.

Ed Ward/E. Roy Ward Collection

Michael Smith/Aerial Views

THE VISTA in this scene where PRR met the Monongahela River and the Edgar Thomson Works of the Carnegie Steel Company portrays the focal point of America's railroad and industrial history. Here the three trunklines met and clashed. We have led the reader along PRR to this point. B&O came down the river from upper right and the Pittsburgh and Lake Erie (New York Central) up the river on the left bank to do combat with Andrew Carnegie and each other. Thomson, Vanderbilt, Carnegie and Garrett. Three giants and a dwarf. Four men primarily responsible for the rise of the United States to superpower status by the year 1900. We have told parts of this grand adventure story in this and earlier books. God willing, this house will complete this tale in future volumes. Oh, what a saga!

Chapter 11
Prelude to Disaster

On 15 October 1996 the railroad earth shook when CSX and Conrail announced that they had agreed to a "merger of equals."

On 4 March 1997 another earthquake rattled the dishes when the news broke that the merger of equals, or MOE as we shall refer to it, was dead and that CSX and Norfolk Southern had agreed to jointly buy Conrail for an astronomical price and then dismember it, with CSX generally taking ex-New York Central lines and Norfolk Southern ex-PRR trackage including the crown jewel Pittsburgh Division.

The latter drama we shall call LEM, short for "lemmings who do not read history and thus are doomed to repeat it." To call these developments pivotal is an understatement. For us, in the throes of a major history of PRR, to ignore them was out of the question.

Some historical background is essential to the telling of the tale. Norfolk Southern was the result of a merger of Norfolk and Western Railway and Southern Railway in 1982. PRR controlled N&W early in this century, sold their shares and then reacquired them. PRR milked N&W for many years until Penn Central was created in 1968 and the ICC forced PRR to sell their N&W shares as a condition of merger approval. Norfolk Southern has been courting Conrail for many years, making numerous puny offers that insulted everyone's intelligence.

And there is CSX, descended from Chesapeake and Ohio Railroad. C&O was also controlled by PRR from 1900 to 1909. C&O acquired B&O in the early 1960s and merged with "Seaboard/Family Lines" in 1980.

Now to Penn Central. The concept of combining PRR and NYC, the two largest trunklines in the nation, into one entity was the brainchild of PRR President James M. Symes. He announced his goal in 1957. Symes was the last of the breed of PRR "up from the ranks" leaders and one of the best. It was also Symes who dragged PRR into dieselization.

Stuart T. Saunders, who came from N&W, was given the task of executing this grand plan. The operation ended in a startling collapse and Saunders bore the blame, quite unjustly in our historical view. He was a scapegoat for those special interests who put so many constraints on the merger that success was impossible.

Conrail was formed in 1976, combining the wreckage of Penn Central and five other bankrupt northeastern railroads. The Federal government poured billions of dollars into the rebirth and it was a long time coming, but come it did and the money was fully repaid. *Central to the creation of Conrail was recognition of the cold fact that the nature of northeastern railroading was such that only a unified system had a chance of survival.* Since MOE preserved Conrail intact, it was a sound plan. Since LEM fragments Conrail, it is fated to failure.

The MOE and LEM drama has three leading actors: David M. LeVan, Conrail…John W. Snow, CSX… David Goode, Norfolk Southern.

LeVan and Goode are career accountants. Snow is a lawyer. Snow and LeVan have some slight operating experience, but only briefly and at the highest level. Goode has no operating experience whatsoever.

None of the three have any discernible marketing or engineering experience. Snow has an impressive dossier in regard to politics and is very well-connected in Washington DC. As we shall see, *very* well. As to the rise of these gentlemen to the top of the tree, as it were, we can only suggest to the reader that *HMS Pinafore* be revisited. If one wishes to become ruler of the Queen's Navy, never-ever-ever go to sea.

Now to events. In September of 1996, the Conrail Board of Directors met in a secluded resort in Ligonier PA and unanimously decided to seek a merger with CSX.

Why? Conrail had a lock on northeastern railroading, was operating profitably with a respectable operating ratio around 80%, was offering truly seamless service between the St. Louis and Chicago gateways to New York, Philadelphia, Boston and Baltimore.

The railroad was operated by a very effective management and was enjoying some traffic growth. Financing was solid and, quite contrary to claims made during the battle that was to come, shippers were generally satisfied with the service offered. Arguments about rates, of course, were ongoing as always throughout history, but Conrail was winning across the board thanks to new regulations which allow railroads to recover the cost of providing service and the cost of capital, reckoned to be about 11%.

It is true that CSX was nibbling at

the old Erie mainline in the Meadville area and Norfolk Southern was continually knocking at the door. So what? Stockholders were happy, creditors serene, labor relations under control and the roses were blooming. Why sell?

The reader will find that this unanswered question will merely be the first in this chapter. LeVan, however, had received his marching orders and met with Snow in Crystal City VA near Washington DC in early October.

A deal was cut and the papers drawn in an astonishingly short period of time. We will spare the reader most of the details of this proposal, but give assurance that we carefully studied it with an open mind and concluded that it was in the best interests of all concerned, including the national interest.

There were *real* consolidation economies envisioned and the possibility of *real* service improvements. Since the CSX offer was mostly stock, the owners would benefit from increasing earnings as they were made manifest. By using stock, the bugbear of a huge debt burden was avoided and, of course, stock swaps are tax-free.

Since CSX/CR would be end-to-end in the east and most western lines were in close proximity, initial capital expenditures (reckoned at $70 million) were more than adequate. Of that figure, $25 million would be deployed to raise the low ex-PRR Susquehanna River line about sixty feet to meet the ex-B&O line at Perryville MD thus offering doublestack service to Baltimore and taking freight traffic off the Amtrak mainline.

The headquarters of the new railroad would be in Philadelphia, a central and sound location. Draw a marketing and operating circle around Jacksonville and one gets ninety percent water and scrub pine. Do the same at Philadelphia and one covers the heartland of eastern railroading.

Father would have smiled.

Norfolk Southern did not, however. They reacted swiftly and ferociously, made a higher all-cash offer and challenged the merger in every court in sight. They spent millions in advertising and set standards in sophistry that recalls Mathew Carey at his worst.

Why? We can only say that we have searched in vain for any rational explanation of Norfolk Southern's bizarre behavior.

We did consider that NS is desperate in one regard. Deregulation in the electric power generating industry and the effects of new clean-air regulations will gut their coal revenues over the next decade whereas Conrail will take a smaller hit at worst and might even post a few minor gains. But this class of revenue is low-margin and hardly justifies the price paid.

We also considered that the merger mania sweeping the railroad industry might be giving Norfolk Southern a lonely feeling. West of the Mississippi two huge systems have evolved: Union Pacific, headed by Jerry Davis, and Burlington Northern/Santa Fe, led by Robert D. Krebs. (Unlike their eastern counterparts, these two men are hardened operating people.) Since we are not fully conversant with the history and evolution of railroading west of Old Man River, we will accept on faith that the creation of these systems was in the public interest. We want to note, however, that it is a different world west of the river and a totally distinct one east of it.

One could hardly miss industry-wide chitchat that the trend of events is leading toward the creation of two gigantic megasystems blanketing the entire nation. We did note that Krebs was making public utterances in reference to "Burlington Norfolk" shortly before MOE was announced. Even giving that all these things come to pass, the question remains that none of it excuses the rich price paid.

And it is rich indeed. While calculations vary, most observers feel that CSX and NS paid about $4 *billion* too much. Not contested is that the acquisition was the costliest in history and so was the bond placement needed to finance it...$4.3 billion for NS and $2.5 billion for CSX. Bond ratings for both railroads, of course, declined.

The debt load for these railroads is now so high that one wonders just how "megasystem" financing will be managed. Also begging is the question of whether creation of two megasystems is in the national interest.

Perhaps the tulip bulb growers of the world could stage a comeback in alliance with wallpaper manufacturers.

By late April of 1997, teams negotiating the splitup concluded that *cost-cutting alone could not justify the high price.* Since we had come to that conclusion by 10 March, we can be pardoned for wondering just what part of the galaxy these people came from.

Of course, we were not alone. There were a number of voices in the wilderness with far more impressive credentials than ours questioning the sanity of all concerned. If some are so blind they cannot see, it follows that there are some who are so deaf they cannot hear.

Quite adept at press release artistry, they announced that the way to the golden planet way out there in space was via the conquest of the trucking industry with intermodal operations. Lack of knowledge certainly did not prevent them from coming to some rather sweeping conclusions. We offer the reader two lessons.

First, the CSX "Iron Highway." The goal is to capture short-haul truck traffic with an overpowered slackless dedicated easy-load train. Those close to this project cautioned Snow that this "dawg might not hunt." It won't even sniff. There is no way any railroad can compete for short-haul time sensitive traffic. Trucks have virtually all the advantages in this market.

But even with a suspension of the

transportation laws of economic gravity, the Iron Highway will fail out on the railroad. Signal respacing has been accomplished to favor long trains. Short trains take up a lot of track space. We have a vision of a score of tiny Iron Highways saturating a mainline for 500 miles.

Second, let us gaze upon United Parcel Service, a transportation giant that has become an oligarchy of vast proportions.

UPS over-the-road haul is done by truck so long as the driver and rig can go out and back in one shift. Rarely do drivers layover. This works out to about 250 miles. And those drivers must not exceed the prevailing speed limit. They are timed in and out to ensure compliance, a policy that would earn them the Good Corporate Citizen Award if there was such a thing.

A haul over 250 miles goes by rail. There are cases where rail service is not available in which event teams of drivers are employed. In those instances 500 miles is the absolute maximum. Put simply, short hauls go by truck and long hauls by rail because transportation economics so dictate.

Now we would like to share some little jewels that we have selected, in no order of importance, from the MOE and LEM discourse.

ITEM: An NS advocate *seriously* alluded to NS efficiency by pointing out that, at the end of every run, excrement is removed from the locomotive and carefully bagged and tagged. As we read their press releases and ads, we will have to say they recycled every ounce.

ITEM: The Triple Crown roadrailer operation is jointly owned by Conrail and NS. North-South traffic moves through Hagerstown to near Harrisburg, thence to destination.

Now we introduce the subject of "divisions." On interline movements, which railroad gets what percentage of the revenues?

This has always been a very important subject in railroading, rife with conflict. For example, Stanley Crane had to convince southern railroads that Conrail had to have a larger share in order to survive.

NS wanted to build a new intermodal terminal near Harrisburg and split the cost with Conrail. Conrail balked, saying that their small share of such revenues was not adequate. Now NS will own these lines and will build the terminal. *The dollars are the same dollars.* NS will be merely taking money out of one pocket and putting it into another with no cost reductions.

Another begging question is the validity of the road-railer concept itself. To us, it does not meet minimum standards of common sense. Where is the net gain?

Please tell us about the rabbits again, George.

ITEM: In a brave announcement that NS will now make war on the trucking industry just two days after LEM was made official, they complained that Conrail service on the busy New-York Chicago route operates today on a 30-hour schedule which is six hours longer than in 1960. Shocking. When the Conrail senior vice president for operations pointed out that these schedules are precisely designed to meet *customer* arrival and departure needs, and that the 1997 trains pull twice the tonnage of the 1960s variety, the headline was very small.

Why power a train to arrive hours earlier so it can sit in the yard?

ITEM: The officer just mentioned, of course, is history. New owners immediately lop off management to gain a momentary surge in earnings. That the people thrown on the street were the very ones who made the property valuable in the first place does not enter into the equation. An inevitable sag occurs. The brains are gone and the limbs hang limp.

Burlington Northern is an excellent example. Krebs, a man *with* operating experience, now admits in public print that it will be another five years before the consolidation tree will produce more fruit.

ITEM: The president of a midwestern trucking firm with a 2,000 tractor fleet servicing the northeast yawned when the breakup of Conrail was announced. He ordered another 100 trucks.

ITEM: A CSX spokesman likened MOE to the sexual chemistry of man meets woman, a glance across a crowded room and all that jazz. Look at the well-turned traction motors on that.

ITEM: After 26 years of deficits, Amtrak has announced their intention to lease 600 freight cars and start hauling time sensitive, high-value freight in competition with railroads like NS and CSX. Jim Hill was supposed to have said that passenger business was as worthless as "teats on a bull." Another history lesson that had to be re-learned. How does this bode for northeast corridor freight traffic?

ITEM: We listened very carefully to see if we could discern any complaints from NS and CSX shareholders, questioning the wisdom of the gross overpayment for Conrail. We didn't hear a sound.

ITEM: Transportation costs as a percentage of gross domestic product dropped from 15% to 8% as the result of deregulation. The reduction of inflation in the economy during the last decade or so has been much discussed, but we have yet to see any recognition given for this remarkable achievement.

ITEM: The three railroads spent about $80 million in the fight, about $10 million more than the initial MOE consolidation would have cost.

ITEM: The Surface Transportation Board has replaced the ICC as the final arbiter of railroad mergers. During the MOE fight, however, only *one* member was actually seated. Her name is Linda Morgan. During the fracas Morgan made some public comments that convinced everyone that the STB would not approve MOE. It turns out that while LeVan and Snow were busily negotiating in the early days, the well-connected Snow said that he did not think regulatory approval could be obtained. How did he know?

And where is Morgan's certificate of election that gives her the *sole* power to make such a sweeping decision well in advance of any review of the evidence? The law says *three* people make such decisions. Three. Not two. Not one. If this were a matter pending before a court and a judge made such statements, talk of impeachment would be in the air. "Recuse" would be demanded at a minimum. In future volumes we will follow Morgan's career with interest.

ITEM: While LeVan was talking with Snow, Snow was meeting with Goode in a series of discussions that even Snow later admitted could be labeled as "betrayal." Apparently LeVan has never read *The Prince*.

Very early in this book, we cautioned the reader that there would be very few Vestal Virgins.

LeVan came close. Reports indicate that he will leave the stage with about $22 million in benefits, mostly the exercise of stock options.

This means he fought to the very last round to keep Conrail intact when it was in his own best personal interest to do the opposite.

This is called loyalty to the institution and selfless performance of duty as seen. Surely Thomson would have applauded.

Just as surely, Father would have cried.

A Call for Vigilance

A Conrail charter amendment was necessary for MOE to go forward, the so-called "opt-out" provision. A stockholder vote was necessary and the proposal was overwhelmingly defeated.

Conrail stock had become a plaything for speculators who were interested only in the maximum price here and now without any regard to the future. This is a timeworn story, but there was a new element in this struggle that we find alarming.

More and more of the shares of all corporations are being held by non-profit, non-taxpaying institutions. In the opt-out struggle, huge systems like the California Public Employee's Retirement System voted against the amendment, being interested only in the highest possible price for its shares without any regard for the future impact on the railroad industry or society as a whole or the national interest, let alone the railroad itself.

Then we read that consideration is being given to pass Social Security funds to Wall Street and the "markets."

This is an emerging issue of staggering implications and it is happening by default. *The trend is markedly toward quasi-government ownership and control of the private economy.* This is a movement toward socialism by the back door without any open debate whatsoever.

We can only hope that our "call to arms" is heeded by those in power. And, yes, we would warmly welcome the odd Democrat into the discussion. They come in handy every now and then.

Please help us help you by completing the following and mailing it to us:

- [ ] A documentary VCR tape based on this book is in production. Check if you wish to be advised when it is available.
- [ ] Advise when future volumes in this series are available.
- [ ] Send literature concerning your other books and projects.
- [ ] I have PRR/PC/CR photographs and/or archival material and would be willing to cooperate with you on future projects.

Please give us your opinion of *Triumph II* expressed on a scale of 1 to 10 with 10 being the highest.

COMMENTS:

NAME

STREET

CITY ———————— STATE ———— ZIP ————

PLACE STAMP HERE

BARNARD, ROBERTS & CO., INC.

Publishers

2606 Willow Avenue

P.O. Box 7344

Baltimore, MD 21227

Musings

As we venture into the realm of commentary, let us emphasize some fundamental tenets. Neither the author nor this house has any material tie of any kind to any of the railroads involved in this or, for that matter, any book bearing the Barnard, Roberts imprint.

As journalist/historians we answer only to our readers and that glorious First Amendment. As historians, we answer only to posterity.

Merely as a tiny example of our fierce independence, in the Spring of 1995 when we requested permission from Conrail to enter their property for the purposes of photography, we were told that such permission would be granted only if we submitted our manuscript for their approval. We suggested that Conrail perform an anatomically impossible feat and took the photographs from the air. No one tells us what to do, say or write.

The writer of interpretative history has a duty to his readers to be *critical*, and even sarcastic when the negative evidence is overwhelming, but a professional historian should never become *hypocritical*.

We must admit that had we been in the position of so many of these historic figures, we probably would have made the same decisions and taken similar action. The reader alone must decide if we have stepped over the line to hypocrisy in some cases.

However, we would never have countenanced bald-faced propaganda nor engaged in personal invective as typified by the Mathew Careys of history. One can disagree without being disagreeable.

We have had a little fun with some people in this and other books. The reader must keep in mind that many of them are not here to defend themselves. And, as any journalist knows, there is joyous glee in knowing that we will probably have the last word. The only antidote to this inherent arrogance is to maintain a sense of humor and retain the capability of laughing at our own foibles and weaknesses.

EARLY PAGES

In *Irony* on page seven the gentleman who was so astonished at our "other favorite railroad" was Michael O'Loughlin of Falls Church VA.

Throughout his life, Father was not Father. He was Pappy and we were Butch.

CHAPTER 1

The United States reached industrial and agricultural superpower status by 1900. In that year, in the face of enormous industrial growth, 85% of all workers were still engaged in agricultural pursuits. By the year 2000, only 3% will be so employed.

In 1950, 73% of the nation's employees worked in manufacturing and production. By 2000 only 15% will be so engaged. The readers should ponder the implications of these numbers.

The Endless Mountains are still called just that.

CHAPTER 2

One cannot ignore the impact of the spiritual upon the secular in human history. It is all of one piece.

CHAPTER 3

Scrapple is also known as Pennsylvania Paté. There are two basic recipes for this delightful concoction…Pennsylvania and Delmarva. Delmarva is ambrosia, Pennsylvania mundane. There will be no editorial compromise on this issue.

CHAPTER 4

In Pennsylvania an anti-Masonic movement began in the late 1820s, revolving around the Big Bet, and it permeated Pennsylvania politics for twenty or so years.

Jesse Chrisman may not have disappeared from history after all. There is a town of Chrisman in east central Illinois.

The father of an ancient colleague of the author was a PRR MOW man on the East Slope and gave several "portage" stones to his son. They rest on the son's farm near Baltimore.

Charles Dickens also looked down his nose at Pittsburgh as follows: "Pittsburgh is like Birmingham—at least its townspeople think so. It is distinguished by the great cloud of smoke hanging over it. The similarity ends there." Thus another tale of two cities. By 1900 Pittsburgh had swamped Birmingham.

CHAPTER 5

Beginning on page 109, we began making references to the original Thomson surveys being in existence. Other sources establish that these surveys were in safekeeping in the middle of this century. We will continue the search.

The gentleman of "Flights Folly" was William Flight, division superintendent in this time frame. He came out of Erie Lackawanna and assumed this office in 1977.

On 29 November 1925, Extra East 1262 with 58 cars ran away and derailed at the Seventeenth Street bridge. This particular "flight" created a mass of wreckage. The incident was the basis for a ballad, "The Altoona Freight Wreck."

Harry C. Eck, a nationally known motive power officer and one of the editors of this and other books, studied our pages on the wreck of the *Red Arrow* and came away convinced that excessive speed was the fundamental cause. "Even if the lead locomotive lost a tire, it would not have plunged across the tracks and down the embankment so far."

Another editor, Eric Powell, visited

the AR area in 1990 with his father and also met a snarling employee. "Unfortunately, neither one of us had a B&O business card."

The Eastern Continental Divide separates a lot more than just the eastern and western waters. There is a sea change in outlook and attitudes as the mountain barrier is crossed. The frontier ethos begins here. The westerners look east and see rich, effete snobs sipping tea and fine wines while living off the sweat and enterprise of others. They pose as intellectuals and so conduct themselves that they give the impression that their status has been ordained by God.

In the other direction, the easterners see lower classes of obscure and unimportant lineage who could not possibly produce anything of real importance.

There is just enough truth in these perspectives to create caricatures that haunt the nation. Let us remind our brethren of British heritage that Scotland's poet Bobby Burns was a peasant.

The Jackson Street bridge is almost precisely at the summit. If this bridge is named for Andrew Jackson, our first western president of ferocious comportment, it is apt.

CHAPTER 6

In mid-September 1996, workmen attempted to move MO Tower to a new site and it started to fall apart. What to do now?

Cresson was the birthplace of Admiral Robert E. Peary, discoverer of the North Pole. From cold to colder.

There are those who feel that the change from "branch" to "secondary" had to do with signaling capabilities.

On page 162, our reference to the possibility of Conrail doing some raiding turned out to be something less than prophetic.

Our reference to dining in Johnstown could be regarded as being condescending. It was meant as a compliment.

That it took 85 minutes for the Great Wave to reach the stone bridge was taken from PRR records. It does seem like a long time.

It was our original intent to thoroughly examine the subject of the conversion from iron to steel and its impact on railroading in a chapter entitled "A Spongy Residue." We decided to defer this amazing topic to a future volume.

CHAPTER 7

At least one commentator has stated that "Torrens" and "Torrance" are the same. He is wrong. Torrens was a small station near Pittsburgh.

On 14 October 1856 near Bolivar a rifle ball was fired through a mail car on Mail Train West, narrowly missing the agent. A stone had been thrown at a moving engine several weeks earlier and a watchman in that area had been killed shortly before that. These incidents were reported to the PRR Board on 29 October and a stop to these outrages was ordered. Of course, they go on to his day.

CHAPTER 8

Confession is supposedly good for the soul. We always put our feet on that ground about which we are writing. We want to see the terrain with our own eyes and listen to the people with our own ears. For a variety of reasons, we did not get west of Latrobe. Our soul is now refreshed.

CHAPTER 9

The splendid *Study of Train Operations April 6, 1945* is one of the most thorough reports we have ever read. It is also a classic statement of the obvious. What did Philadelphia think was causing the delays? Little gnomes and elves? Those in the field always shudder when an epistle is received from headquarters. Thousands of manhours right down the tube for no productive purpose whatsoever.

BEHOLDEN

Any writer who edits himself has a fool for an editor. In the case of this work, the manuscript was submitted to four independent editors. With bared fangs, they descended upon this magnificent prose with savagery and no consideration whatsoever for the author's feelings. Years ago a meticulous study of editors was completed and the conclusion announced that, indeed, editors were human and should act that way more often. Not in the case of *this* book. Criticism was delivered with a meataxe and praise with an eyedropper. Treachery was the name of the game.

Eric Powell of Speedway IN was the worst of the villains. About to graduate as a Journalism major, he described this writer as a "literary genius" for an earlier book. When invited to edit this manuscript, he was downright obsequious. Then, when he gets his hands on the copy, he blithely announces that in college he was known as the "slasher" and proceeds to prove that he is a monster. That we accepted almost all of his changes should not be allowed to obscure the fact that he shows no respect whatsoever for the elderly. We are determined to get him to do a book for *us* and then we will see who has the sharper knife.

And then there is Harry C. Eck whose own *Modern Locomotive Handbook* (Railway Fuel Association) has sold so many copies it should be on a bestseller list. He was bitten by a traffic man while a young child and has continued his practice of taking revenge on this lowly descendant of such people by going so far as to refuse to sign-off on certain passages unless they were changed! Thank God.

Gary W. Schlerf was a true gentleman who almost perfectly disguised his disdain for our pretensions. We will respond similarly with his *Triumph* book.

David W. Messer, still another *Triumph* author, confined his contribution to making a series of improvements of such perfection that he could not possibly know how humbling they were to this writer.

Responsibility still remains where power lies. There were a few cases where we refused to submit. Blame for those rests upon the shoulders of the author. All conclusions and interpretations are the sole province of the author. Ire should be directed to the author and the author alone.

In the early stages of research for *Triumph I*, Herbert H. Harwood, Jr., played a very helpful role. That we later had a parting of the editorial ways does not reduce the author's gratitude.

The photographers and contributors to this book are legion. Perhaps credits alone do not do justice to their openhanded cooperation and selfless attitude. Our thanks are heartfelt. Each one deserves far more than the brief mention given here.

Now we shall leave the realm of the editorial and enter the kingdom of art, design, typography and reproduction. In this sphere there is no question that this book is a ten across the board.

As with all of our books for many years, Walsworth Publishing did the pre-press, printing and binding. The devotion of Suzanne Rhodes is approaching the legendary. A new name now appears, Jenny Shoemaker. This lady was posted to our project in place of Jan Maxwell, who was promoted. Where does Walsworth find so many peerless people? Do they have scrapple in Missouri? To our fellow easterners, we should say that we have never found a comparable source on this side of the summit.

Thunder Grafix, Ltd., of Columbia, MD was responsible for typography and page design. Roberta Poling was the lead, ably backed by partner Marsha Harding Stepowany. The relationship began about two years ago. It was immediately apparent that two professional perfectionists were locked in a creative struggle without precedent in our fifty years of experience. The net result was a book so close to impeccability that it moved a competing publisher to pass unsolicited praise.

There are 688 illustrations in this book. We found it necessary to change the layout in only four cases and three of those were simple transpositions. This performance is as mindboggling as the history of PRR. It should be noted that Poling is from west of the mountain barrier.

Michael T. Goorevitz of MTG Associates produced the splendid cover design and much inside art. Those veteran readers know what we mean when we say we have found a replacement for Warren Somerville of Somerville Studios.

If *Triumph I* should turn out to be, in the words of one of our editors, "the best railroad history book ever written," we wish it noted that it was the product of many, many hands and minds. We do nothing alone.

CENTRAL RAILROAD

AN ACT

TO INCORPORATE THE

PENNSYLVANIA RAILROAD COMPANY,

PASSED APRIL 13, 1846.

WITH A SUPPLEMENT.

PHILADELPHIA:
"NORTH AMERICAN" PRINTING OFFICE, N. E. COR. FOURTH AND CHESNUT STREETS.
1846.

Section 1. *Be it enacted by the Senate and House of Representatives of the Commonwealth of Pennsylvania, in General Assembly met, and it is hereby enacted by the authority of the same:* That Thomas P Cope, Robert Toland, William M Meredith, A S Roberts, John K Kane, John B Myers, Henry Welsh, John M Atwood, Henry D Gilpin, John A Brown, George Cadwalader, Thomas M Pettit, George W Toland, A J Lewis, A G Ralston, David S Brown, William C Patterson, Henry White, James Magee, Hugh Campbell, Henry M Watts, Gideon Scull, Charles S Wood, J Fisher Leaming, Thomas C. Rockhill, Thomas P. Hoopes, Robert Allen, Alexander Fullerton, John Welsh, junior, Alexander Osbourn, William Reynolds, William S. Charnley, B. M. Hinchman, Townsend Sharpless, C. G. Childs, Charles Humphreys, Thomas Tustin, Thomas Robbins, William Musser, Robert Steen, Edward Siter, Charles Macalester, Joseph R. Evans, Edward Duff, Henry M. Phillips, Elhanan W. Keyser, Hyman Gratz, John White, John J. Ridgway, Walter R. Johnson, Elliot Cresson, Josiah Randall, J. Rhea Barton, John Swift, George Campbell, G. R. Childs, Hugh Catherwood, Horn R. Kneass, James Steel, James M. Davis, Joseph A. Clay and William P. Smith of the city of Philadelphia, Thomas Sparks, Thomas M'Cully, Isaac W Norris, George M. Stroud, George N. Baker, James Martin, E. A. Penniman, Abraham Helfenstein, Philip M. Price, John J. M'Canen, George W. Carpenter, John S. Littell, Samuel C. Ford, Benjamin Crispin, Nathan Trotter, Jacob Broom, Thomas D. Grover, John Naglee, Archibald Wright, Edward F. Gay, William S Hallowell, William English, Joseph Lippencott, Robert Flinn, Jr., Christopher Mason, John T. Smith, Charles Brown, John Miller, Michael D Whartman, John S Cash, Joseph Baker, Mitchell Bomeisler, Samuel Jackson, Peter Rambo, John Robbins, George Shetsline, Samuel Ovenshine, James Eneu, Jr., Henry Manderfield, David F. Condie, Benjamin L. Berry, Joseph Diamond, William Laughlin, and Levi Strickland, of the county of Philadelphia, Samuel D. Ingham of Bucks county, Joel K. Mann, Charles Kugler, of Montgomery county, H. Jones Brooke, of Delaware county, Thomas S. Bell, Francis James, Robert Parke, of Chester county, Alexander L Hays, Emanuel C. Reigart, John N Lane, Reah Frazer, Benjamin G. Herr, Edward Davies, Reuben Mullison, Bernard Flinn, Samuel Shoch, John F. Huston, J. S. Clarkson, Frederick Hipple, Reuben Hause, of Lancaster county, Henry Flannery, Henry W Smith, J. Pringle Jones, Henry A. Muhlenburg, Michael K. Boyer, John S. Heister, William High, William Heidenreich, Charles Keely, J. Glancy Jones, of Berks county, Levi Kline, of Lebanon county, Valentine Hummell, senior, William Ayres, Jacob M Haldeman, James M'Cormick, James Peacock, Henry Buehler, John C. Bucher, Simon Cameron, David R. Porter, of Dauphin county, Benjamin M'Intyre, Robert Elliott, James M'Farlane, George Stroop, Robert S. King, Findley McCown, Hugh R. Wilson, Henry Fetter, and Jacob Keiser, of Perry county, James Mathers, Andrew Parker, of Juniata county, Abraham S Wilson, James Criswell, Reuben C. Hale, Francis W. Rawle, Moses Montgomery, Joseph Milliken, Joseph Ard, Joseph Kyle, David Zook and Wm. Reed, of Mifflin county, John G. Miles, John Kerr, A. P. Wilson, Edwin F Shoenberger, Benj Leas, John M'Canan, John Long, Brice Blair, Thomas E. Orbeson, Edward Bell, William Williams, and John Porter, of Huntingdon county; James Irvin, James T. Hale, W. W. Houston, James Potter, Abraham S. Valentine, Henry Brokerhoff, William [illegible]. Reynolds, and Daniel Ulman, of Centre county; A. K. Wright, A. B. Reed, J. W. Smith, of Clearfield county; John Linton, W. A. Smith, John Mathew, John Fenlon, Peter Livergood, Edward Shoemaker, Stephen Lloyd, and Richard Lewis, of Cambria county; James Clark, George Mulholland, Jr, David Ralston, Daniel Stanard of Indiana county; John Hill, J. R Logan, John [illegible]. Laird, Henry M'Bride, Joseph Harvey, Hugh Irwin, S. L. Carpenter, F. J Cope, Richard Coulter, of Westmoreland county; Jesse Carothers, Joshua Hanna, Harmar Denny, Thomas Bakewell, John Bigler, William Wilkins, Wilson M'Candless, William McKnight, William Eidebann, C. M'Gee, William Larriner, James Marshall, John T. Wilson, William R. Vankirk, Samuel Walker, E. Percival, Andrew Bayne, John Hay, H. G. Roland, Hiram Hultz, and Samuel W. Black, of Allegheny county; Michael Doudel, Samuel Wagner, Charles Weiser, Daniel Hartman, A. C. Ramsey, of York county; Jacob Mechling, John Bredin, of Butler county; Robert H. Hammond, Jesse C. Horton, J. M. Pollock, John Forsyth, A. Jordan, C. W. Hegins, Samuel Hepburn, and E. Greenough, of Northumberland county, Ner Middleswarth, Robert Cander, Henry Snyder, John L. Watson, and Robert Stoys, of the county of Union; David Leech, Philip Klinginsmith, and Lewis Bremseman, of Armstrong county; Henry Allen, John P. M'Glachery, David Norwood, Samuel Vanhorn, William Maginness, James Stewart, James Culbertson, Joseph Pollock, and Alva Leonard, of the county of Beaver; George Chambers, Frederick Smith, and William Baker, of the county of Franklin; Thomas H. Sill, Giles Sanford, John H. Walker, C. M. Reed, C. M'Sparrow, George Seldon, and John Galbraith, of Erie county; Joel B. Curtis, Samuel Goodman, David Cortney, R. W. Cunningham, and John Hoge, of Mercer county; Thomas Ringland, John Wishart, T. M. T. M'Kennon, A. W. Acheson, James Gordon, and John Grayson, of Washington county; Morrow B. Lowry, J. Porter Brawley, and Joseph Patton, of Crawford county; Abbot Green, William Cameron, Nathan Mitchel, Levi B. Christ, Joseph Casey, Henry C. Eyer, of Union county; William Donaldson, Joseph Paxton, of Columbia county; be, and they are hereby appointed Commissioners, to do and perform the several acts and things hereinafter mentioned, that is to say, they, or such of them as shall act in the premises, not less than twelve, shall before proceeding to the performance of their duties, be respectively sworn or affirmed before an officer competent to administer oaths, well and truly to perform the duties enjoined upon them by this act and as soon as conveniently may be, and within three months next after the passage of this act, shall procure and open suitable books at such proper times and places as they may designate, in the cities of Philadelphia, Lancaster and Pittsburgh, and in the boroughs of Harrisburg, Lewistown, Huntingdon, Greensburg, Bloomfield, and Blairsville, and at such other places as they may deem expedient, of which times and places at least thirty days previous public notice shall be given, in not less than three daily newspapers published in Philadelphia, and in not less than two daily or weekly papers in the other places named, if so many are therein published, in which books they shall enter as follows: "We whose names are hereunto subscribed, do promise to pay to the President, Directors and company of the Pennsylvania Railroad Company, the sum of fifty dollars for each and every share of stock set opposite to our respective names, in such manner and proportions and at such times not exceeding five dollars per share, in any period of sixty days, as shall be determined by the President and Directors of said company, in pursuance of an act, entitled 'An Act to incorporate the Pennsylvania Railroad Company.' Witness our hands and seals, the

day of one thousand eight hundred and " And at the times and places so designated and named in the public notices to be given as aforesaid, the said commissioners by themselves, or by committees to be by them appointed, shall attend and furnish to all persons duly qualified who shall offer to subscribe an opportunity of so doing, and it shall be lawful for all such persons, and for all firms, copartnerships and bodies politic and corporate, by themselves, or by persons duly authorized, to subscribe for shares in said stock, and the said books shall be kept open at least six hours in every juridical day for the term of ten days, unless the whole number of one hundred and fifty thousand shares shall have been sooner subscribed, and if at the expiration of ten days the said books shall not have the whole number of shares aforesaid subscribed therein, the said commissioners may adjourn from time to time, and transfer the said books elsewhere, until the whole number of one hundred and fifty thousand shares shall have been subscribed, of which adjournments and tranfers the said commissioners shall give such public notice as in their opinion the occasion may require, and when the whole number of shares before mentioned shall have been subscribed, the books shall be closed. *Provided,* That no subscription for such stock shall be valid unless the party or parties making the same shall at the time of subscribing pay to said commissioners five dollars on each and every share for the use of the company. *And provided further,* That if more than one hundred and fifty thousand shares shall have been subscribed within ten days and before the closing of the books as aforesaid, the commissioners shall reduce the subscriptions pro rata as near as practicable, in such manner as to them may appear equitable, until the number of shares do not exceed one hundred and fifty thousand, but no subscription for ten shares or under shall be so reduced.

Section 2. That when fifty thousand shares or more of the said stock shall have been subscribed, and five dollars paid on each and every share as aforesaid, the said commissioners, acting in the premises as aforesaid, or a majority of them, shall certify to the governor, which certificate shall be be verified by the oath or affirmation of at least two of said commissioners, the names of the subscribers and the number of shares subscribed by each, and that five dollars

on each have been paid; whereupon the governor shall, by letters patent, under his hand and the seal of the commonwealth, create and constitute the subscribers, and if the subscription be not full at the time, those who shall thereafter subscribe to the number of shares aforesaid, their successors and assigns, into a body politic and corporate in deed and in law by the name, style and title of "The Pennsylvania Railroad Company," and by the said name, style and title, the said subscribers shall have perpetual succession with all the privileges, franchises and immunities incident to a corporation, and be able to sue and be sued, plead and be impleaded, in all courts of record and elsewhere; and to purchase, receive, have, hold, use and enjoy, to them and their successors, lands, tenements and hereditaments engines, locomotives, cars, goods, chattels, and estate real and personal, of what kind or quality, soever; and the same from time to time to sell, exchange, mortgage, grant, alien, or otherwise dispose of; and to make dividends of such portion of the profits as they may deem proper, and also to make and have a common seal, and the same to alter and renew at pleasure, and also to ordain, establish, and put in execution such by-laws, ordinances and regulations as shall appear necessary or convenient for the government of said corporation, not being contrary to the constitution and laws of the United States, or of this commonwealth; and generally to do all and singular the matters and things which to them it shall lawfully appertain to do for the well being of said corporation and the due ordering and management of the affairs thereof. *Provided,* That nothing herein contained shall be so construed as in any way giving to said corporation any banking privileges whatever, or any other liberties, privileges, or franchises but such as may be necessary or convenient to the procuring, owning, making, maintaining, regulating and using said rail road, the locomotives, machinery, cars and other appendages thereof, and the conveyance of passengers, the transportation of the mail, and of goods, merchandize, commodities and things thereon. *And provided further,* That said company shall not purchase or hold any real estate except such as may be necessary or convenient for the making and constructing of said railroad, or for the furnishing of materials therefor, and for the accommodation of depots, offices, warehouses, machine shops, toll houses, engine and water stations, and other appropriate appurtenances, and for the persons and things employed or used in or about the same. *Provided,* That the whole amount of debts or other liabilities of said company, including loans, shall not at any time exceed one-half of the amount of capital actually paid in. *And provided further,* That no part of the capital stock or other funds of the company shall be at any time, directly or indirectly, loaned to any director, officer, or agent of said company.

Section 3. The said commissioners or a majority of them, acting in the premises as aforesaid, shall, as soon as conveniently may be after the said letters patent shall have been obtained, appoint a time and place for the subscribers to meet in order to organize the said company, and shall give at least twenty days previous notice thereof in the various papers before mentioned, and the said subscribers when met shall by ballot elect, by a majority of the votes present, to be given in person or by proxy, thirteen directors, all of whom shall be citizens and residents of this commonwealth, and shall be owners respectively of at least twenty shares in the stock of said company; the said directors and those thereafter to be chosen in pursuance of the provisions of this act, at their first meeting shall choose by ballot one of their own number as President of said Company, and the said President and Directors shall conduct and manage the affairs and business of said company until the first Monday of June then next ensuing, and until others are chosen, and may make, ordain and establish such by-laws, rules, orders and regulations, and do and perform such other matters and things as are by this act authorized.

Section 4. That the stockholders shall meet on the first Monday of December in every year, at such place in this Commonwealth as may be designated by the by-laws of the Company, of which at least twenty days previous notice shall be given in three or more daily newspapers published in the city of Philadelphia and elsewhere as the board shall direct, and choose by a majority of votes thirteen directors, qualified as provided in the preceding section for the year ensuing, who shall continue in office until the next annual election, and until others are chosen; at which annual meeting the said stockholders shall have full power and authority to make, alter or repeal by a majority of the votes given, any or all such by-laws, rules, orders and regulations as aforesaid, and do and perform every other corporate act authorized by their charter. The stockholders may meet at such other times and places, and they may be summoned by the President and Directors in such manner and form, and giving such notice as may be prescribed by the by-laws; and the President, on the request in writing, of any number of stockholders representing not less than one-tenth in number and interest, shall call a special meeting, giving the like notice and stating specifically the objects of such meeting, and the objects stated in such notice and no other, shall be acted upon at such meeting, nor shall any business be transacted at any such special meeting, unless a majority of the stock shall be there represented; but the meeting may adjourn from day to day, or until such times as a majority in interest shall be present.

Section 5. That the elections for directors provided for in this act shall be conducted in the following manner, that is to say: At the first election the Commissioners shall appoint three stockholders, not being candidates, to be judges of the said election, and to hold the same; and at every succeeding election the directors for the time being, shall appoint three stockholders who shall not be directors nor candidates, for the like purpose; and the persons so appointed by said Commissioners and Directors, shall respectively take and subscribe an oath or affirmation before an alderman or justice of the peace, well and truly, according to law, to conduct such election to the best of their knowledge and ability, and the said judges shall decide upon the qualification of voters and when the election is closed shall count the votes and declare who have been elected; and if it shall at any time happen that an election of directors shall not be made at the time specified, the corporation shall not for that reason be dissolved, but it shall be lawful to hold and make such election of directors on any day within three months thereafter by giving at least ten days previous notice of the time and place of holding said election, in the newspapers aforesaid, and the directors of the preceding year, shall in that case continue in office, and be invested with all powers belonging to them as such until others are elected in their stead. In case of the death, resignation or removal from this state of a director, or a failure to elect, in case of a tie vote, or in case any one of them ceases to be qualified to act as a director in the manner hereinbefore provided, the vacancy may be filled by the board of directors. At all general meetings or elections by the stockholders, each share of stock shall entitle the holder thereof to one vote, and each ballot shall have endorsed thereon the number of shares thereby represented, but no share or shares transferred within sixty days next preceding any election or general meeting of the stockholders shall entitle the holder or holders thereof to vote at any such election or general meeting; nor shall any person or party, females excepted, residing within ten miles of the place appointed for any such election or general meeting, be entitled to vote by proxy. No person shall represent by proxy more than three absent stockholders, nor shall any proxy be received, or entitle the holders thereof to vote unless the same shall bear date, and have been duly executed and acknowledged before some person legally authorized at the place of executing the same, to take such acknowledgments, within the three months next preceding such election or general meeting, and every such proxy received and voted upon as aforesaid, shall be retained and filed amongst the papers of the company until after the next annual election or general meeting, subject to the inspection or examination of any stockholder who may desire it.

SECTION 6. That the President and Directors for the time being are hereby authorized and empowered to exercise all the powers granted to the corporation. They shall meet at such times and places as shall be by them deemed most convenient for the transaction of their business, and when met, seven shall be a quorum; the President, if present, shall preside at all meetings of the board, and when absent, the board shall appoint a President pro tem. They shall keep minutes of their proceedings fairly entered in a suitable book to be kept for that purpose; they shall choose a secre tary and treasurer, and may appoint or employ all such officers, engineers, agents, superintendents, artizans, workmen or other persons as in their opinion may be necessary or proper in the conducting and management of the affairs and business of said corporation, at such times, in such manner, and under such regulations as they may from time to time determine; they may require security in such amounts as they may deem necessary, of each or any of said officers or other persons by them appointed or employed, and generally to do all other such acts, matters, and things, as by this act and the by-laws and regulations of the said company they may be authorized to do. The treasurer of said company shall enter into one or more sureties, satisfactory to the President and Directors, in a sum not less than thirty thousand dollars, conditioned for the faithful discharge of all the duties of his office while he shall continue to hold the same, and for faithfully accounting for and paying over according to law and the by-laws of the company, all moneys that may come into his hands as treasurer aforesaid, and for the payment to his successor in office, or other person authorized by the President and Directors to receive the same, the balance of all such moneys, and in like manner for the delivery to said successor, or other person authorized as aforesaid, all books, papers, documents, accounts and property that he may have or hold by virtue of his office, and the bond or bonds of the treasurer shall be renewed at least once in every two years.

SECTION 7. The President and Directors shall fix the amount of salaries and wages of the several officers, engineers and agents employed by them, but no Director shall be allowed any compensation but the President, whose salary shall be fixed by the vote of a majority of all the Directors.

SECTION 8. That the President and Directors first chosen shall procure certificates or evidences of stock for all the shares of the said company, and shall deliver one or more certificates or evidences, signed by the President and countersigned by the Treasurer, and sealed with the common seal of the corporation, to each person or party entitled to receive the same, according to the number of shares by him, her, or them, respectively subscribed or held, which certificates or evidences of stock shall be transferable at the pleasure of the holder, in a suitable book or books to be kept by the company for that purpose, in person or by attorney duly authorized, in the presence of the President or Treasurer, subject, however, to all payments due or to become due thereon; and the assignee or party to whom the same shall have been so transferred, shall be a member of said corporation, and have and enjoy all the immunities, privileges and franchises, and be subject to all the liabilities, conditions and penalties incident thereto, in the same manner as the original subscriber would have been. *Provided*, That no certificate shall be transferred so long as the holder thereof is indebted to said company, unless the Board of Directors shall consent thereto.

SECTION 9. The capital stock of the company shall be called in and paid at such times and places, and in such proportions and instalments, not however exceeding five dollars per share in any period of sixty days, as the directors shall require, of which public notice shall be given for at least three successive weeks next preceding the time, or times, appointed for that purpose, in the newspapers last above mentioned; and if any stockholder shall neglect to pay such proportion or instalment so called for, at the time and place appointed, he, she, or they, shall be liable to pay, in addition to the proportion or instalment so called for, at the rate of one per cent. per month, for the delay of such payment; and if the same and the additional penalty, or any part thereof, shall remain unpaid for the period of six months, he, she, or they, shall, at the discretion of the directors, forfeit to the use of the company all right, title, and interest in and to every and all share or shares, on account of which, such default in payment may be made as aforesaid, or the directors may at their option cause suit to be brought before any competent tribunal for the recovery of the amount due on such shares, together with the penalty of one per cent per month as aforesaid; and in the event of a forfeiture, the share or shares so forfeited, may be disposed of at the discretion of the president and directors under such rules and regulations as may be prescribed by the by-laws. No stockholder shall be entitled to vote at any election, nor at any general or special meeting of the company, on whose share or shares any instalment or arrearages may be due more than thirty days next preceding said election or meeting.

SECTION 10. That dividends of so much of the profits of said company as shall appear advisable to the directors, shall be declared in the months of May and November in each and every year, and be paid to the stockholders or their legal representatives, on application at the office of said company, at any time after the expiration of ten days from the time of declaring the same; but the said dividends shall in no case exceed the amount of the nett profits actually acquired by the company, so that the capital stock shall never be impaired thereby; and if the said directors shall make any dividend which shall impair the capital stock of the company, the directors con senting thereto, shall be liable in their individual capacities to the said company for the amount of capital stock so divided, recoverable by action of debt, as in other cases, and each director present when such dividend shall be declared, shall be considered as consenting thereto, unless he forthwith enter his protest on the minutes of the board, and give public notice to the stockholders of the declaring of such dividend. *Provided*, however, that after bona fide contracts shall have been made for the immediate construction of fifteen miles of road at each end thereof, a sum equal to five per centum per annum on all capital stock of said company actually paid in, shall be estimated and credited to the several holders thereof on account of the amounts payable by them respectively for stock subscribed, and shall so continue to be estimated and credited until one hundred miles of said railroad, that is to say, fifty miles thereof commencing at the city of Pittsburgh, and extending eastward; and fifty miles thereof commencing at the easternmost terminus of said road and extending westward, shall be completed and in use—which said estimates and credits shall be estimated and considered as part of the cost of construction. And provided further, that no dividends of profits shall be made until one hundred miles of said railroad shall be completed and in use as is specified in the foregoing proviso; and if any loan of any part of the money received on the subscription to the stock be made to any officer, stockholder or agent of the said company, or to any other person or corporation, it shall be deemed and taken as a violation and forfeiture of the charter authorized by this act, to be ascertained and declared as provived in the twenty-fourth section of this act.

SECTION 11. That the president and directors of said company, shall have power and authority by themselves, their engineers, superintendents, agents, artizans, and workmen, to survey, ascertain, locate, fix, mark and determine such route for a railroad as they may deem expedient, not however passing through any burying ground or place of public worship, or any dwelling house, without the consent of the owner or owners thereof, and not, except in the neighborhood of deep cuttings or high embankments, or places selected for sideings, turn-outs, depots, engine or water stations, to exceed four rods in width, and thereon to lay down, erect, construct and establish a railroad with one or more tracks with such branches or lateral roads as are hereinafter mentioned, and with such bridges, viaducts, turnouts, sideings, or other devises, as they may deem necessary or useful, beginning at and uniting with the western terminus of the Harrisburg, Portsmouth, Mountjoy and Lancaster railroad, in the borough of Harrisburg. *Provided*, said Harrisburg, Portsmouth, Mountjoy and Lancaster Railroad Company shall be subject to, and consent to, the same rate of tax on tonnage for the use of the State, as is provided to be paid in this act by the Pennsylvania Railroad Company; and in case the said Harrisburg, Portsmouth, Mountjoy and Lancaster Railroad Company should not agree to comply with these conditions within three months after the distance of fifteen miles from Harrisburg westward shall bona fide be put under contract, the said Pennsylvania Railroad Company are authorised to connect their road with the Columbia Railroad, at or near the borough of Columbia, in Lancaster county: and thence by such direct practicable route, with moderate gradients, as will, in the opinion of the said president and directors, most conduce to the public interest and the interests of said company, having due regard to economy in the construction, maintenance and management thereof, and terminating at such point or points in, at, or near the city of Pittsburgh, or other place in the county of Allegheny, with authority to extend said road, or a branch thereof, to the town or harbor of Erie in the county of Erie, as to the said president and directors may seem most advantageous or expedient, and in like manner by themselves, or other persons by them appointed or employed as aforesaid, to enter into and upon, and occupy all land on which the said railroad or depots, warehouses, offices, toll houses, engine and water stations, or other buildings or appurtenances hereinbefore mentioned, may be located, or which may be necessary or convenient for the erection of the same, or for any other purpose necessary or useful in the construction, maintenance or repairs of said railroad, and therein and thereon to dig, excavate and embank, make, grade, lay down and construct the same; and it shall in like manner be lawful for the said company, their officers, agents, engineers, contractors or workmen, with their implements and beasts of draft or burden, to enter upon any lands adjoining, or in the neighborhood of the said railroad so to be constructed, and to quarry, dig, cut, take and carry away therefrom any stone, gravel, clay, sand, earth, wood, or other suitable material necessary or proper for the construction, maintenance or repairing of said railroad, or for the construction of any bridges, viaducts, or other buildings which may be required for the use, maintenance, or repairs of said railroad: *Provided*, That such compensation shall be made, secured, or tendered to the owner or owners of any such lands or materials as shall be agreed upon between the parties, or in such manner as is hereafter mentioned: *Provided further*, That the timber used in the construction or repair of said railroad, shall be obtained from the owners thereof only by agreement or purchase.

SECTION 12. That when the said company cannot agree with the owner or owners of any lands or materials, for the compensation proper for the damage done or likely to be done to, or sustained by, any such owner or owners of such lands or materials which said company may enter upon, use, or take away in pursuance of the authority hereinbefore given, or by reason of the absence or legal incapacity of any such owner or owners, no such compensation can be agreed upon, the court of Quarter Sessions of the proper county, on application thereto by petition, either by said company or owner or owners, or any one in behalf of either, shall issue their precept to the sheriff of the county, commanding said sheriff to summon twenty discreet and disinterested persons, freeholders of said county, to act as jurors, and to meet at such convenient place near the premises as in the said precept or by the said sheriff may be designated in not less than ten nor more than twenty days, giving such reasonable notice as the court may direct to both parties, by publication or otherwise, whose duty it shall be to ascertain and report to said court whether any, and if any, what damages have been or may be sustained by the owner or owners of said land or materials, by reason of the construction of said railroad, or by reason of the materials used or taken away in manner aforesaid; and if twelve or more of the said jurors attend they shall be empanelled, and if twelve do not attend, the sheriff shall forthwith, or as soon thereafter as practicable, summon others to attend on a day by him fixed for that purpose, and the said twelve jurors being so empanelled and having been first sworn or affirmed by said sheriff or his deputy, faithfully, justly and impartially to decide, and true report to make concerning all the matters and things to be submitted to them, and in relation to which they are authorized to inquire, in pursuance of the provisions of this act; and having viewed the premises they shall estimate and determine the quantity quality and value of said lands so taken or occupied, or to be so taken or occupied, or the materials, so used or taken away, or to be so used or taken away, as the case may be, and having a due regard to and making just allowance for the advantages which may have resulted, or which may seem likely to result to the owner or owners of said land or materials, in consequence of the opening or making of said railroad, and after having made a fair and just comparison of said advantages and disadvantages, they shall estimate and determine whether any, and if any, what amount of damages have been or may be sustained, and to whom payable, and make report thereof to the court, and if any damages be awarded, and the report be confirmed by said court, judgment shall be entered thereon, and if the amount thereof be not paid, execution may issue thereon, as in other cases of debt, for the sum so awarded, and the cost and expenses incurred shall be defrayed by said railroad company. *Provided*, That if said report be not confirmed as aforesaid, and justice may seem to require it, a new inquisition may be ordered by said court. *And Provided further*, That any owner or owners or other party applying for a review shall be liable for the costs of the proceedings prayed for, in case a report more favorable be not obtained upon such review. *And Provided further, nevertheless*, That nothing herein contained shall authorize the said company to enter upon any lands or take any property without making compensation to the owners of said property or giving adequate security therefor. *And be it further provided*, That in all cases where the parties cannot agree on the amount of damages claimed, either for land or materials, the company shall tender a bond, with sufficient security, to the party claiming the damages, the condition of which shall be that the company will pay, or cause to be paid, such amount of damages as the party shall be entitled to receive, after the same shall have been agreed upon by the parties, or assessed by the provisions of this act. *And provided further*, That in case the party or parties claming damages refuse to accept the bond as tendered by the company, the company shall in every such case present their bonds to the Court of Common Pleas of the proper county, and if the court approve of the security, shall direct the same to be filed for the benefit of those to whom it is given, which bonds shall be answerable, as all other debts for the amount of the damages assessed, if the same be not paid in a reasonable time after such assessment.

SECTION 13. That whenever in the construction of said road or roads, it shall be necessary to cross or intersect any established road or way, it shall be the duty of the President and Directors of said company so to construct the said road across such established road or way, as not to impede the passage or transportation of persons or property along the same; or when it shall be necessary to pass through the land of any individual, it shall also be their duty to provide for such individual proper wagon ways across said road or roads from one part of his land to the other.

SECTION 14. That in all suits or actions against the said company the service of process on the President, Secretary, Treasurer, Engineer, Agent, or any Director of said company, shall be good and available in law; but no suit or action shall be prosecuted by any person or persons for any penalties incurred under this act, unless such suit or action shall be commenced within twelve months next after the offence committed or cause of action accrued, and the defendants in such suit or action may plead the general issue, and give this act and the special matter in evidence, and that the same was done in pursuance and by authority of this act.

SECTION 15. That if any person or persons shall wilfully and knowingly break, injure, or destroy the railroad hereby authorized, or any part thereof, or any edifice, device, property, or work, or any part thereof, or any machinery, engine, car, implement, or utensil, erected, owned, or used by the said company in pursuance of this act, he, she, or they so offending, shall forfeit and pay to the said company three times the actual damage so sustained, to be sued for and recovered with full costs before any tribunal having cognizance thereof, by action in the name and for the use of said company.

SECTION 16. That if any person or persons shall wilfully and maliciously remove, or destroy, any of the company's constructions, or place designedly and with evil intent, any obstruction on the line of said railroad, so as to jeopard the safety or endanger the lives of persons travelling on or over the same, such person or persons so offending shall be deemed guilty of a misdemeanor, and shall on conviction be imprisoned in the Penitentiary for a term not less than three months nor more than three years. *Provided*, That nothing herein contained shall prevent the company from pursuing any other appropriate remedy at law in such cases.

SECTION 17. That the said company shall not prevent any person or persons, being the owner or owners of land bordering on or adjacent to said railroad, from making lateral railroads and connecting the same with the railroad of the company for the purpose of transporting thereon their produce or other material, being the products of said land, the said connections being made at the expense of the person or persons wishing the same, and according to the directions and subject to the approval of the directors of said company or their authorized agent. And it shall be lawful for the said company, in the manner and subject to the conditions and provisions hereinbefore provided, in relation to the main line of their railroad, by this act authorized to be made, to make such lateral railroads or branches leading from the main line of their said railroad to such convenient places or points in either of the counties into or through which the said main line of their road may pass, as the president and directors may deem advantageous and suited to promote the convenience of the inhabitants thereof and the interests of said company.

SECTION 18. That in times of war, invasion, or domestic insurrection, the said company shall carry and transport, or permit to be carried and transported, on said railroad, any troops called into service by any competent authority, their ordnance, munitions and military stores, at one half the usual charge, for the time being, for carrying and transporting other passengers and freight.

SECTION 19. That at each annual meeting of the stockholders of said company, the president and directors for the year preceding shall lay before them a full and complete statement of the affairs of the company for the year ending on the last day of October immediately preceding; exhibiting under the various appropriate heads the amount of moneys received, and from what sources; the amount disbursed, and for what purpose; the balance remaining with the company; which statement shall be accompanied with a report of the acts and proceedings of the company for the same period, with such further information as may be requisite to convey to the stockholders a full knowledge of the affairs and condition of said company. The said statement and report shall be published as soon as conveniently may be in pamphlet form, and in such newspapers as the stockholders or president and directors may designate, and a copy thereof shall be transmitted to the governor and to each branch of the Legislature at its next annual meeting.

SECTION 20. That if any increase of the capital stock shall be deemed necessary in order to complete or improve the said railroad or appurtenances, it shall be lawful for the stockholders of said company at any annual meeting, or at any special meeting convened for that purpose in manner as aforesaid, to increase and dispose of any additional number of shares, not exceeding fifty thousand, so that the whole amount of said capital stock shall not exceed ten millions of dollars, and receive and demand the moneys for the said additional shares, in like manner and subject to the same conditions hereinbefore provided for the original subscriptions, or as shall be provided for in the by-laws of said company.

SECTION 21. That upon the completion of said railroad or any part thereof, the same shall be esteemed a public highway for the conveyance of passengers and the transportation of freight, subject to such rules and regulations in relation to the same, and to the size and construction of wheels, cars and carriages, the weight of loads, and all other matters and things connected with the use of said railroad, as the president and directors may prescribe and direct. *Provided*, That the said company shall have the exclusive control of the motive power, and may from time to time establish, demand and receive such rates of toll, or other compensation, for the use of the said road and of said motive power, and for the conveyance of passengers, the transportation of merchandize and commodities, and the cars or other vehicles containing the same, or otherwise passing over or on said railroad, as to the President and directors shall seem reasonable. *Provided, however, nevertheless*, That said rates of toll and motive power charges so to be established, demanded or received, when the cars used for such conveyance or transportation are owned or furnished by others, shall not exceed two and a half cents per mile for each passenger, three cents per mile for each ton of two thousand pounds, for freight, three cents per mile, for each passenger or baggage car, and two cents per mile for each burden or freight car, every four wheels being computed a car; and in the transportation of passengers no charge shall be made to exceed three cents per mile for through passengers and three and a half cents per mile for way passengers.

SECTION 22. That all tonnage of whatsoever kind or description, except the ordinary baggage of passengers loaded or received at Harrisburg or Pittsburgh, or at any intermediate point, and carried or conveyed on or over said railroad more than twenty miles, between the tenth day of March and first day of December, in each and every year, shall be subject to a toll or duty for the use of the commonwealth, at the rate of five mills per mile for each ton of two thousand pounds, and it shall be the duty of said company between the twentieth and thirtieth days of July, and between the first and tenth days of December, in each and every year, after thirty miles or more of said railroad shall have been completed and in use, to cause to be made out and filed with the Auditor General, a true and correct statement, exhibiting the amount of such tonnage so loaded or received, and the distance so carried or conveyed, during the respective periods intervening between the said tenth day of March and the twentieth day of July, and between the said twentieth day of July and the first day of December, in each and every year; which said statement shall be verified by the oath or affirmation of the receiving or forwarding agent or agents, or other proper officer or officers of said company having knowledge of the premises, and at the time of filing said statement or on or before the said thirtieth day of July and the tenth day of December in each and every year, the said company shall pay to the State Treasurer the amount of said toll or duty so accruing, for the use of the commonwealth, during the respective intervening periods before mentioned. *Provided*, That if it shall hereafter be deemed necessary or expedient, the Governor may appoint one or more State agents, not exceeding three, who shall have the right at all times to travel free of charge on or over said railroad between Harrisburg and Pittsburgh, in the cars or other vehicles of the company used for the conveyance of passengers, and at all times during the usual hours of business shall have free access to and liberty to inspect and examine all such books, accounts, way-bills, bills of freight, manifests and other papers of the company, as may be necessary and proper to enable the said agent or agents to ascertain and keep a true and correct account of all such tonnage so loaded, received, carried or transported on or over said railroad, during the periods aforesaid, and the Legislature hereby reserves the right to adopt such additional measures to secure a faithful compliance with the condition of this proviso as may hereafter be deemed right and proper.

SECTION 23. That if the Legislature of this State shall at the expiration of twenty years from the completion of said railroad, make provision by law for the re-payment of the said company of the amount expended by them in the construction of said railroad, and in the construction of permanent fixtures, and all other appurtenances for the use of the same, together with all moneys expended by said company for repairs, attendance and otherwise, for the purposes of said railroad, with interest on such sums, at the rate of eight per cent. per annum, after deducting the amount of tolls and other revenue received by said company for the use of the same, then said railroad, with all its fixtures and appurtenances, shall vest in and become the property of the people of this State. But if the Legislature shall not, at the expiration of the said period of twenty years, claim the said railroad, and so forth, as aforesaid, then the said company, with all its said rights and privileges, shall continue for another period of twenty years, subject to the claim of the Legislature as aforesaid at the expiration thereof, on the same terms and conditions as aforesaid, and so on, from twenty years to twenty years.

SECTION 24. That it shall at all times be lawful for a committee of the Legislature, appointed for that purpose, to inspect the books and examine into the proceedings of the corporation hereby created, and to report whether the provisions of this charter have been by the same abused or violated, and if the officers of said corporation shall refuse to be sworn or affirmed or give evidence, or refuse to produce any of their books or papers that may be demanded before any such committee, then the legislature may, by law, declare the said charter void, and repeal the same; and whenever any committee as aforesaid shall find and report, or the Governor shall have reason to believe that the charter has been violated, it may be lawful for the legislature to direct or the Governor to order, a scire facias to be sued out of the Supreme Court of Pennsylvania, in the name of the Commonwealth of Pennsylvania, which shall be served by the sheriff of any county in this commonwealth, on the president, treasurer or secretary, at the office of the corporation, for the time being, at least ten days before the commencement of the term of court, calling on the said corporation to shew cause why the charter hereby granted should not be declared forfeited. And it shall be lawful for the said court, upon the return of the scire facias, to examine into the truth of the alleged violations, and if such violations be made to appear, then to adjudge that the said charter is forfeited; and thereupon and in case the legislature shall have power to declare the said charter void, and to repeal the same for the cause aforesaid, the railroad aforesaid, with its appurtenances and all estate, real and personal, of the said corporation, shall revert to and be vested in the commonwealth, upon the payment by the commonwealth to the stockholders, the par value of their stock. And until the commonwealth shall have made such payment to the president and directors of said company to be by them distributed among the stockholders, the rights, privileges and franchises of said corporation shall remain as though said judgment and forfeiture had not been pronounced or declared. *Provided, however*, That every issue of fact which may be joined between the commonwealth and the corporation in said proceedings, shall be tried by a jury summoned by an officer, to be named by the court from the body of the State, and it shall be lawful for the court aforesaid to require and compel the production of such of the books and papers of the corporation on such trial, as it may deem necessary for the ascertainment of the controverted facts; and the final judgment of the court shall be subject to all the usages of law as in other cases. The first twenty of the commissioners appointed in the first section of this act, or any five of them, shall have authority to convene the commissioners at such suitable time and place as they may designate for that purpose, giving sufficient notice thereof, as the occasion may seem to require. And all reasonable expenses incurred by the commissioners in the performance of the duties by this act imposed, shall be allowed and paid by the corporation out of the first instalment or payment, to be received by the commissioners at the time of subscribing as hereinbefore provided.

SECTION 25. That if the said company shall not commence the construction of said railroad within two years, and complete and open the same for use, with one or more tracks within the term of ten years; or if, after the completion the said railroad shall be suffered to go into decay, and be impassable, for the term of two years, then this charter shall be null and void, except so far as relates to the payment of damages.

SECTION 26. That if any person or persons travelling on the road of the said company, or that of any other company in this commonwealth, shall be wounded by reason of any imperfection or defect in such road, or in the machinery or cars employed on the same, or by the negligence of such company or their agents, no action brought by such person or persons against such company to recover damages therefor, shall abate by the death of the plaintiff or plaintiffs, but the same shall survive to his or her executors or administrators.

SECTION 27. The legislature reserves the right to authorize any company hereafter chartered, to connect any railroad not running parallel with the same, to be constructed by such company, with the railroad of the said Pennsylvania railroad company at such point or points on said Railroad, as the legislature may direct. Provided, that no higher rates of toll or of transportation shall be charged by said company, for persons or things having passed, or destined to pass, over such connecting road, than may be at the same time charged upon persons and things passing over the main line to and from Philadelphia and Pittsburgh.

FINDLEY PATTERSON, Speaker of the House of Representatives.
DANIEL L. SHERWOOD, Speaker of the Senate.

Approved the thirteenth day of April, one thousand eight hundred and forty-six.

FRANCIS R. SHUNK.

SECRETARY'S OFFICE,
Harrisburg, April 16, 1846.

Pennsylvania ss. I certify the foregoing to be a true copy of the original Act of Assembly, which remains filed in this office.

{L. S.} In testimony whereof I have hereunto set my hand and caused to be affixed the Seal of said Office, the day and year above written.
J. MILLER,
Secretary of the Commonwealth.

AN ACT, Supplementary to an Act to incorporate the Pennsylvania Railroad Company, passed April, eighteen hundred and forty six.

SECTION 1. Be it enacted by the Senate and House of Representatives of the Commonwealth of Pennsylvania, in General Assembly met; and it is hereby enacted by the authority of the same, That nothing in the act to which this is a supplement shall be so construed as in any wise to impair the right of the Legislature to pass such additional laws, as may be deemed expedient in furtherance of the objects contemplated by said act, and for the better enforcement of the provisions thereof; and, in case the charter of said company shall be forfeited in the manner therein provided, it shall be competent for the Legislature by law to vest the said railroad and appurtenances, and all the estate, real and personal, of the said company, in the commonwealth, or in another company to be incorporated for that purpose, upon the payment to said Pennsylvania Railroad Company for distribution amongst the stockholders, according to their several interests, the actual value of their said railroad appurtenances and other property, to be ascertained and appraised by twelve disinterested persons, acting under oath or affirmation, to be appointed and governed in their proceedings in relation thereto, in such manner as the Legislature shall by law direct. Provided, that in case the said company shall at any time fail to pay the toll or charge on tonnage, which may accrue or become due to the Commonwealth, under the provisions of said act, the same shall be and remain a lien on the property of the said company, and shall have precedence over all other liens or incumbrances thereon, until paid.

FINDLEY PATTERSON, Speaker of the House of Representatives.
DANIEL L. SHERWOOD, Speaker of the Senate.

Approved the Thirteenth day of April, one thousand eight hundred and forty-six.

FRANCIS R. SHUNK.

SECRETARY'S OFFICE,
Harrisburg, April 16, 1846.

Pennsylvania ss. I certify the within to be a true Copy of the Original Act of General Assembly, which remains filed in this office.

{L. S.} In Testimony whereof, I have hereunto set my hand, and caused to be affixed the seal of said Office, the day and year above written.
J. MILLER,
Secretary of the Commonwealth.

This reproduction of the PRR charter was taken directly from an original, but unattested, document. The original measured 5 by 8½ inches and was set in a two column format. The reproduction seen here has not been reset, thus explaining the variations in weight, alignment and spacing.

Earlier in this volume we promised to reproduce Edgar Thomson's first report as Chief Engineer dated 12 June 1848. It did not prove to be practical to include the report in this book. It will, however, be reproduced in full in a future, appropriate volume in the series.

And, yes, we do plan to reproduce the color map included in the 1855 "Guide" in a future volume. The reader has seen black-and-white excerpts from this work. An original is in the house archives.

Bibliography

BOOKS

(Act), *Central Railroad; an Act to Incorporate The Pennsylvania Railroad Company Passed April 13, 1846*, North American Printing Office (printer), Philadelphia PA 1846. Reproduced in this book.
Alexander, Edwin P., *The Pennsylvania Railroad*, Bonanza Books, New York NY 1967.
Alexander, Edwin P., *On The Main Line*, Bramhall House, New York NY 1971.
Allen, Charles, *Pennsylvania, Second Geological Survey*, Board of Commissioners, Harrisburg PA 1878.
Badnall, Richard, *Treatise on Railway Improvements*, Sherwood, Gilbert & Piper, London 1833.
Baer, Christopher T., *Canals and Railroads of the Mid-Atlantic States 1880-1860*, Eleutherian Mills-Hagley Foundation, Wilmington DE 1981.
Baumgardner, M.J., and Hoenstine, F.G., *The Allegheny Old Portage Railroad*, by the authors, Ebensburg PA 1952.
Bowen, Eli, *The Pictorial Sketch-Book of Pennsylvania*, Willis P. Hazard, Philadelphia PA 1852.
Bryant, Keith L. Jr. (Editor), *Railroads in the Age of Regulation, 1990-1980*, Bruccoli Clark Layman and Facts on File, New York 1988.
(Committee), *The Pennsylvania Rail Road...Address to Citizens*, Jesper Harding (printer), Philadelphia PA 1846.
(Committee), *Proceedings...Citizens...Great Pennsylvania Rail Road...to the People*, Steam Press (printer), Philadelphia PA 1846.
(Committee), *Proceedings...Rail-Road Convention...Harrisburg March 6, 1838*, Peter Hay & Co. (printer), Philadelphia PA 1838.
Cope, Thomas P., *Report...Delays...Transportation Westward...Spring 1836*, Philadelphia Board of Trade, 1836.
Craig, Neville B., *History of Pittsburgh*, J.R. Weldin Co., Pittsburgh PA 1917.
Crane, L. Stanley, *Rise from the Wreckage, A Brief History of Conrail*, The Newcomen Society of the United States, Exton PA 1988.
Day, Sherman, *Historical Collections of the State of Pennsylvania*, by the author 1843.
Davis, Patricia J., *End of the Line*, Neale Watson Academic Publications, New York NY 1978.
(Delegates), *Memorial...State Convention...Delegates in favor of a Continuous Railroad...Harrisburg to Pittsburgh*. Harrisburg Argus (printer), Harrisburg PA 1846.
Dredge, James, *The Pennsylvania Railroad, "Engineering"*, London; John Wiley & Sons, N.Y.; 1879.
Duane, William J., *Letters...Pennsylvania...Internal Improvement...Roads and Canals*, Jane Aitken (printer), Philadelphia PA 1811.
Faries, Robert, ...*Surveys to Avoid the Inclined Planes on the Allegheny Portage Railroad*, PA Canal Commissioners, Harrisburg PA 1851. *Report on (progress) on the Allegheny Portage Railroad*, by the author, 1851. *Reports...Allegheny Portage Railroad*, by the author, 1852.
Feibelman, W.A., *Rails to Pittsburgh*, Superior Publishing Co., Seattle WA 1979.
Fitzsimons, Gary, *Blair and Cambria Counties (PA) Inventory Historic Engineering and Industrial Sites*, National Park Service, Washington DC 1990.
Frey, Robert L. (Editor), *Railroads in the Nineteenth Century*, Bruccoli Clark Layman and Facts on File, New York 1988.
Fritz, David and Clemensen, A. Berle, *Pennsylvania Main Line Canal, Juniata and Western Divisions*, National Park Service, Denver CO 1992.
Gambrill, J.M., *Leading Events of Maryland History*, Ginn & Co., Boston MA 1903.
Garrett, John W., and Latrobe, B.H., among others, *Formal Opening of the Pittsburgh, Washington Railroad (Connellsville Route)*, by the railroad, Baltimore MD 1871.
Haney, Lewis H., *Congressional History of Railways in the U.S. 1850-1887*, University of Wisconsin, Madison WI 1910.
Hilton, George W., and Due, John F., *The Electric Interurban Railways in America*, Stanford University Press, Stanford CA 1960.
Hollis, Jeffrey R., and Roberts, Charles S., *East End*, Barnard, Roberts & Co., Baltimore MD 1992.
Johnson, Willis F., *The Johnstown Flood*, Edgewood Publishing Co., (?), 1889.
Livingood, James M. *Philadelphia-Baltimore Trade Rivalry 1780-1860*, Commonwealth of Pennsylvania, Harrisburg PA 1947.
Marshall, C.F.D., *A History of British Railways...to 1830*, Oxford University Press, London 1938.
Poor, Henry Varnum, *History of the Railroads and Canals of the USA*, John H. Schultz & Co., NY 1860.
Roberts, Charles S., *PRR Great Photos* (Series), Book 1 (Milton A. Davis) 1977; Book 2 (E.L. Roberts, Jr.) 1978; Book 3 (H.H. Harwood, Jr.) 1978; Book 4 (Bob Lorenz) 1979. Barnard, Roberts & Co., Baltimore MD.
Roberts, Charles S., *Sand Patch/Clash of Titans*, Barnard, Roberts & Co., Baltimore MD 1993.
Roberts, Charles S., *West End*, Barnard, Roberts & Co., Baltimore MD 1991.
Roberts, S.W., *An Account of the Portage Rail Road...*, Nathan Kite, Philadelphia PA 1836.
Rogers, Henry D., *Geological Exploration of the State of Pennsylvania*, 2d Annual, Packer, Barrett and Parke, Harrisburg PA 1838.
Rohrbeck, Benson W., *Pennsylvania's Street Railways*, by the author, West Chester PA 1982.
Rosenberger, Homer T., *The Philadelphia and Erie Railroad*, Fox Hills Press, Potomac MD 1975.
Schotter, H.W., *The Growth and Development of The Pennsylvania Railroad Company*, Allen, Lane and Scott, Philadelphia PA 1927.
Shank, William H., *Vanderbilt's Folly*, American Canal and Transportation Center, York PA 1973.
Staufer, Alvin F., *Pennsy Power (1962)*, *Pennsy Power II (1968)*, *Pennsy Power III (1993)*, all by the author, Medina OH.
Stover, John F., *History of the B&ORR*, Purdue University Press, West Lafayette IN 1987.
Swetnam, George, *Pennsylvania Transportation*, Pennsylvania Historical Association, Gettysburg PA 1964.
Taber, Thomas T. III, *Railroads of Pennsylvania*, by the author, Muncy PA 1987.
Taylor, Jeremy, *Conrail Commodities*, Silver Brook Jct. Pub. Co., Telford PA 1994.
Thomas, Tom, *The Evolution of Transportation in Western Pennsylvania*, National Park Service, Denver CO 1994.
Vrooman, David M., *Daniel Willard and Progressive Management on the B&ORR*, Ohio State University Press, Columbus OH 1991.
Walton, Walter F., *The South Pennsylvania Railroad*, American Society of Civil Engineers, Pittsburgh PA 1982.
Ward, James A., *J. Edgar Thomson: Master of the Pennsylvania*, Greenwood Press, Westport CT 1980.
Weber, Thomas, *The Northern Railroads in the Civil War*, King's Crown Press (Columbia University), New York NY 1952.
West, Francis R., *Report...on the Allegheny Portage Railroad*, by the author, 1851.
White, John H., Jr., *The American Railroad Freight Car*, Johns Hopkins University Press, Baltimore MD 1993.
Wilson, William Bender, *General Superintendents of The Pennsylvania Railroad*, Kensington Press, Philadelphia PA 1900.
Wilson, William Bender, *History of The Pennsylvania Railroad*, 2 volumes, Harry T. Coates & Co., Philadelphia PA 1899.
Woodward, W.E., *Meet General Grant*, Liveright Publishing Corp., New York, 1928.
(unsigned), *Facts and Arguments in favor of Adopting Railways in Preference to Canals in the State of Pennsylvania*, 4th Edition, William Fry (printer), Philadelphia PA 1 August 1825.
(unsigned), *First Annual Report Society for Promotion of Internal Improvements in Pennsylvania*, J.R.A. Skerrett (printer), Philadelphia PA 1826.
(unsigned), *Guide for The Pennsylvania Railroad*, T. K. and P.G. Collins, Philadelphia PA 1855.
(unsigned), *The Main Line of the Pennsylvania State Improvements*, T.K. & P.G. Collins, Philadelphia PA 1855.
(unsigned), *Pennsylvania Railroad 1950 Track Charts*, Rails Northeast, East McKeesport PA date uncertain.
(various) *Encyclopedia Britannica*, William Benton, Chicago IL 1967.

PRR/PC/CR PUBLICATIONS AND RECORDS

Annual Reports, 1846 to 1962.
Burgess, George H., and Kennedy, Miles C., of Coverdale and Colpitts, Consulting Engineers, *Centennial History of The Pennsylvania Railroad Company*, by the railroad, Philadelphia PA 1949.
Coverdale & Colpitts, Consulting Engineers, *The Pennsylvania Railroad Company*, 4 Volumes, by the railroad and press of Allen, Lane and Scott, Philadelphia PA c. 1947.
CT 1000: 1 July 1910, 1 Nov 1923, 1 Nov 1924, 1 May 1945 (last).
The Pennsy, various incl 11-12/62, 1-2/63. by the railroad.
Report of the Investigating Committee of The Pennsylvania Railroad Company, Allen, Lane and Scott, Philadelphia PA 1874.
Sipes, William B., *The Pennsylvania Railroad*, by the railroad, Philadelphia PA 1875.
Thomson, J. Edgar, *First Annual Report of the Chief Engineer of the Pennsylvania Rail-Road Company*, by the railroad and John C. Clark (printer), Philadelphia PA 1848.
Warner, Paul T., *Motive Power Development on The Pennsylvania Railroad System*, from articles published in periodical "Baldwin Locomotives", probably by the railroad, Philadelphia 1924.
Watkins, John Elfreth, *History of The Pennsylvania Railroad Company 1846-1896*, probably 3 volumes, set in type and proofed but unpublished, c. 1896.
(unsigned), *Conrail Coal Directory*, by the railroad, Philadelphia PA 1977.
(unsigned), *Conrail...Track Chart, Harrisburg Division*, by the railroad, Philadelphia PA 1992.
Various correspondence files, reports and memos as well as numerous employee timetables and other operating publications.

PERIODICALS

Ballash, Richard D., *Of Keystone Heritage*, The Bull Sheet, Baltimore MD 1994.
The Keystone, Summer 1986 (Ed Waytel), Summer 89 (R.L. Keyser), Summer 95 (Charles Edwards), PRR Tech/Hist Society, Upper Darby PA.
PC Railroader, Jan-Feb 1973, 3-4/73, 11-12/73, 5-6/74, 5-6/77, E. McKeesport PA.
Railfan, Mar 1993 (Doug Harrop), Carstens Publications, Newton NJ.
Railpace, May 1992 (Michael Bezilla), 12/92, 1-2-3/93, Piscataway NJ.
Rails Northeast, Apr 1976, 4/77 (R.L. Fredland), 1/80, 9/80 (Bill Metzger), 1-2/81 (Wm Lewis), 3/81 (Bob Reid), 4/81, 5/81 (Ed Spodobalski), E. McKeesport PA.
Rubin, Julius, *Canal or Railroad?*, Transactions of the American Philosophical Society, 1961.
Trains, March 1941 (Wm Moedinger, Jr.) 6/43, 4/57 (D.P. Morgan), 1/85, 11/92, 1/93, 6-7-9/95. Kalmbach Publishing, Waukesha WI.

MISCELLANEOUS

Credit for certain material such as maps and track charts have been given throughout the book. The author conducted many interviews with various sources that enjoy First Amendment protection. Note that this is an abbreviated bibliography made necessary by the sheer volume of the records that were studied.

Index

Adhesion 32, 35
Aerotrain 147
AH 51
Albany 38
Alexandria Branch 292
ALTO 72-74, 337-8
Altoona 37, 42, 45, 51, 54, 58, 68-9, 337, 347
Altoona Coal & Coke 85
Allegheny (loco) 40
Allegheny Front/Mountain 21-23, 39, 42, 46, 57, 59, 60, 67, 69, 127, 157
Allegheny Portage Railroad 33-37, 39-56
Allegheny River 13, 23, 164, 272
Allegheny Tunnel 71, 127-131, 133-40, 349, 351-2
Allegrippus AG 70-1, 81, 100, 112-13, 116-120, 347
Appleton, J & E 221
AO 169, 224-5, 233
AR 70, 122, 124, 145-50, 354
ARCH 185
Ardara 318-19, 379
Articles of Confederation 15
Atterbury, W.W. 252, 265
Atlantic Ocean 12, 17
AX 294-5
Baring Brothers 12
Bald Eagle Mountains 12
Baltimore 15, 23, 25, 27, 29, 60, 66, 140
Baltimore & Ohio Railroad 16, 30, 34-7, 61-4, 133, 157, 159, 162, 208, 212, 235, 276, 295
Barkleys Summit 302
Barnes, O.W. 288
Beatty 244, 277, 291-2
Bedford 15, 23
Bennington BF, SF 43, 51, 55, 58, 71, 100, 120-6, 134, 348, 350
Bens Creek BC 165, 170, 190-3
Bessemer, Sir Henry 242
Big Viaduct 158-9, 213-16, 364
Blair Creek 51
Blairs Gap 39, 109
Blairsville 42, 164, 187, 247, 267, 269-70, 272, 372
Blairsville Intersection BH 244, 247-8, 267-8
Board of Canal Commissioners 39, 41-2, 68
Bolivar 248, 257, 359-61
BO 73-4
Boston 25, 27, 29, 64
Boston (loco) 40
Boston & Albany Railroad 37
Braddock, Edward 14
Bradenville & Branch 280-1, 286-7, 373
Brandimarte, G. 200
Brickyard 338
Bridge No. 6 216-9, 238
Brown, W.H. 101, 109, 118, 130-1, 146, 212, 218, 239, 244, 248, 250, 256, 265, 280, 283, 305
Brownsville 64
Brush Creek 21, 302, 308, 311, 318, 322
Brush Mountain 45, 57
Buffalo 38
Bull Run Branch 311
Buttermilk Falls 216, 229
Burgoons Gap 58, 75, 88, 95
Cambria & Clearfield Railroad 109, 180, 186-7
Cambria Iron (Steel) Co. 123, 220, 223, 225, 235-6, 241-2, 250, 324, 366
Camden & Amboy Railroad 59
Canada 10-12
Carolinas 19
Carey, Mathew 32-4, 36, 40
Carnegie, Andrew 62, 162, 173, 176, 242
Carney 292, 375
Carpenter Tunnel 318, 320, 379
Carrs Tunnel 292-3
Cassandra 170, 191-3, 360-1

Cassatt, A.J. 131, 184, 212
Casselman River 22
Cedar Swamp Gap 39, 67
Central America 11
Centreville 256-7, 369
Chambersburg 66
Chesapeake Bay 17, 26-8
Chesapeake & Ohio Canal 29, 37-8
Chestnut Ridge 21, 166, 243, 245, 247, 259, 261, 264-5, 271, 275, 277, 281
Chrisman, Jesse 42
Civil War 11, 19, 36, 65, 76, 242, 244
Clark, James S. 39
Clermont 13, 16
Cleveland 66
Clinton, DeWitt 28
Columbia 15, 47
Commerce Clause 18
Conemaugh & Black Lick Railroad 225, 229, 235, 242
Conemaugh C 158-9, 164, 169, 186, 222, 224, 226, 227-33, 365-6
Conemaugh Division 164, 248-9, 261, 266, 269-70, 272, 320
Conemaugh River 21, 40, 44, 57, 62, 157-9, 164, 166, 189, 191, 205-6, 213, 216-7, 219, 223, 225, 228-31, 234-5, 238-9, 242, 245, 247, 255, 257, 269, 272
Confluence 14
Connellsville 29, 63-4, 123, 296, 304
Continental Drift 11
Conpitt Junction JD 257-8, 369-70
Conway Yard 328
Cotton 11
County Home Junction 296
Cove Secondary 73
CP BENNY 348
CP CONPIT 258
CP PITT 186
CP PACK 268
CP RADE 302
CP TRAFF 321, 381
CP TROBE 291
Crane, L.S. 101, 149
Cresap, Thomas 20
Cresson 43, 45, 58, 69, 145, 170, 171-87, 357-9
Cumberland 14-17, 20, 22-3, 37-8, 63-5, 71
Cumberland River 12
DP 244, 254
DU 51
Deep Cut 216-8, 231
DeHaas, Charles 43, 273
Delaware (loco) 40
Delaware Bay & River 17, 28
Derry DR 271, 277, 279-82, 373
Derry-Donahoe-Jeannette (DDJ) Project 283-6, 292, 302, 305
Dickens, Charles 43, 273
d'Invilliers, C.S. 101, 109, 118, 212, 280, 283
Donahoe 292, 295, 375
Duncansville 44, 46, 51
Duquesne, Fort 14
Durno, John 214
Earthquake 13
East Pittsburgh et al 320, 323, 384
Eastern Waters 12, 17, 151
Ebensburg 68, 166, 180
Edward VII 31
Ehrenfeld 170, 204, 210, 363
Electrification 160, 284
Endless Mountains 21
Erie Canal 29, 33, 37-8, 47
Erie, Lake 10, 14, 38
Erie Railroad 162, 288
Europe 13, 25
Evans, Lewis 21
Fairfax, Lord 14
Florida 19

Forbes, John 14
Fox, S.M. 42
France 10
French & Indian War 14
Frontier-Kemper 144
Fulton, Robert 13, 16
Furs 11
Gallitzin 43, 69, 128-30, 172, 351, 355, 357
Gallitzin, Prince 132
Gallitzin Tunnel 71, 131-40, 349, 351-2
Garrett, J.W. 161-3, 384
Gaysport 44
George 292, 375
Georgia 19
Georgia Railroad 59
Gettysburg 15
Gilcrest House 288
Gist, Christopher 20
Grapeville 308-9, 324
Gray 277
Great Britain 10-14, 31-2, 65
Great Debate 32
Great Lakes 17, 28
Great Meadows 14
Greene, Nathaniel 297
Greensburg 15, 271, 275, 296, 297-302, 376
Glen White Run 75, 88-9, 95, 101, 107
GU 300
Guilford, Lord 31
Gulf of Mexico 10, 12, 17, 22
Gum Tree Hollow 120
GY 70-1, 74, 125
Hannas Town 275
Harpers Ferry 61, 63
Harrisburg 42, 63, 66
Haupt, Herman 69, 127, 222
Henry VIII 25
Hillside HM 277-8, 372
Holgate, Jacob 39
Hollidaysburg 34, 39, 41-2, 44-5, 51, 54, 73, 124, 175, 347
Hooversville 256
Horseshoe Curve 46, 53, 57, 61, 75, 77, 83, 88-108, 328, 339-40, 342-4
Hudson River 13, 17, 27-9, 37-8
Huntingdon 42
IA 81, 93, 101, 111-2
ICC 148, 163
IJ 249
Illinois 19
Indian Creek 200
Indiana 19
Indiana Branch 248, 267
Indians 11
Industrial Revolution 10, 25
Iron 62, 65
Irvona Branch 180, 187, 357
Irwin 308, 314-17, 378
Jacks Run 272, 297
Jackson, R.M.S. 175
Jeannette 308-11, 378
Jefferson, Thomas 12
Jeffries, C.P.B. 302
Johnstown et al 39, 42, 44-5, 158-9, 223, 234-42, 365-6
Johnstown Flood 206, 208, 214-18, 223, 226-7, 239, 241, 251
Juniata River 21, 41
JW 233, 236
Kickenpawling 234
Kiskiminetas River 164, 272
Kittanning Point KN 57-8, 70-1, 75-92, 96, 100-2, 109, 164, 304-1
Koza 194-5, 361
KR 291
Lancaster 15
Larimer CP 308, 313, 317-8, 375
LaSalle, R.R.C. 10, 12

Latrobe 250, 271-2, 275, 286, 288-91, 373-4
Latrobe, Benjamin H. (Father & Son) 13, 65, 159, 288
Laurel Hill 21, 166, 225, 234-5, 243, 245, 247, 367-8
Laurel Swamp Summit 69, 145
Lemon, Samuel 50, 355
Ligonier 245, 271, 286
Ligonier Valley Railroad 288, 290, 370
Lilly LY 40, 100, 109, 170, 181, 188-9, 359-60
Lincoln, Abraham 11
Lincoln Highway 15
Livingston, Robert 13
Loree, L.F. 219
Lockport 158, 222, 244, 247, 249, 257, 259, 370
Louisiana 10, 12
Louisiana Purchase 12, 19
Louisville 47
Loyalhanna Creek 164, 271-2, 275-6, 283, 288, 290-1, 374
Ludwick 297, 304
Macadam Road 15
Manor MF 283, 312
Marks, J.L. 328
Martinsburg 63
Maryland 15, 26-7, 29, 30, 37
McAdam, J.L. 15
McCallum, Daniel 288
McCrea, James 244, 252
McGee Run 279
McHenry, Fort 27
MG 71, 113-4, 117, 125, 345-6
Michigan 19
Middle Division 54, 70-1, 73-4
Mill Run 57
Miller, Edward 159
Millwood 278
Mineral Point 165, 167, 170, 213, 216, 364
Mississippi River 10, 12, 13, 19
MO 71, 171-4, 181, 189, 355-7
Monongahela River 13, 15, 20, 24, 275-6
Monterey Construction Co. 140
Moorehead & Patterson 141
Morrellville 250
Mountain Barrier 9, 11, 13
Mountain House 173, 175-8
Mule Shoe MS 46, 51-5, 83
Napoleon, Bonaparte 12
Nash, Ogden 27
National Road 14-6, 22-4, 26, 28-9, 64
New Florence 247, 249, 256-7
New Portage Railroad 43-6, 51-5, 62, 70, 83, 101, 122, 124-5, 147, 155, 158-9, 164-5, 170, 190, 198, 205, 213
New Portage Tunnel 43, 46, 70-1, 101, 121, 126, 134, 141-4, 349, 353
New Orleans *et al* 12-3, 15, 17, 28-9, 34, 37, 64
New York 12, 23, 25, 27-9, 33-4, 37, 60, 64, 66, 170
New York Central Railroad 147-8, 162, 295
Necessity, Fort 14
Nemocolin 20
Newcastle 31
Newcomen, Thomas 10
Newry Junction 46
Nineveh 247, 254, 256
Norfolk & Western Railway 274
Northwest Territory 15, 19
NR 249, 254
NY 189-90
O'Donnel, R.L. 305
Ohio 19
Ohio Company 14, 20
Ohio & Erie Canal 37
Ohio River 12-5, 19, 24, 26-30, 60, 63, 65, 159
Ontario, Lake 10, 17, 28
Original Portage Railroad 155, 158-9, 164-6, 170, 188, 190, 198, 205, 213, 216, 218, 234, 355

Pacific Ocean 12
Packsaddle 247-8, 261-6, 271, 371-2
Parrs Ridge 14, 226
Penn 317
Penn, William 27, 29, 30, 313
Penn Central Railroad 148
Pennsylvania 14-6, 19, 20, 23, 27-33, 63-4, 68
Pennsylvania Public Works 24, 32-4, 38-9, 47, 64, 66, 158, 163-4, 167, 206, 235-6, 243
Pennsylvania Road/Turnpike 15-6, 23
Petersburg 45, 54, 124
Philadelphia 14-5, 17-8, 23, 25, 27-9, 31, 33-5, 47, 60, 64, 66, 71, 140
Philadelphia & Columbia Railroad 32, 34, 37, 59
Philadelphia-Lancaster Turnpike 15
Philadelphia Group 162
Pitcairn 279, 301, 318, 320, 322-28, 381-3
Pitcairn, Robert 239, 256, 305
Pitt, Fort 15
Pittsburgh 13-5, 22-5, 28-9, 33-4, 37, 39, 42, 47, 60, 63-6, 71
Pittsburgh & Connellsville Railroad 63-4, 159, 276-7, 288, 316
Pittsburgh Division 62, 70, 73
Pittsburgh, Ft. Wayne & Chicago Railroad 43
Portage 44, 170, 190, 195-7, 361
Port Perry Branch 321
Potomac River 14, 17, 26
PS 51
Puritans 25
Q 236
Quaker 28
Radebaugh RG 277, 296, 301-8, 377
Railroad Convention 1838 63, 66
Railroad Convention 1846 64
Rainhill Trials 34
Ramsbottom, John 251
Rea, Samuel 244, 248
Rea, Sam Line 284
Reading Railroad 162
Red Arrow 120-1, 125
Reuther, Thomas 127
Revolutionary War 12, 14, 18, 27
Richmond 64
Ridgeview Park 278
Ridley, Thomas 115
Roberts, G.B. 141, 150
Roberts, S.W. 214
Roberts, W.M. 40, 206
Robinson, Moncure 40
Rocky Mountains 12
Roebling, J.H. 41, 48
Roosevelt, Nicholas J. 13
Roosevelt, Theodore 149, 184
Rouen 10
RU 249
St. Clair, Arthur 286-7, 297
St. Lawrence River 17
St. Louis 15
Salix Line 212
Sand Patch 22, 27, 30, 133
Sang Hollow SG 165, 169, 248, 250-3, 255, 368
Sang Hollow Extension 250, 257, 369
Saunders, S. 150
Savery, Thomas 10
Saxman 252, 282, 285-7
Schlatter, C.L. 42, 60-1, 68, 166, 247, 275-6
Schuylkill River & Canal 28, 37
Scotch Run 75
Scott, T.A. 162
Seabrook, T.W. 127
Seven Years War 14
Seward 256, 369
SF 70-1, 122, 124
Shafton 308, 313
Shannon & Wilson 140, 144
Sheridan 250

Sheppard, F.W. 101, 130
Slide 70, 120-1, 143, 349
SLOPE 51, 74
Sonman 170, 194, 361
SN 51-2
South America 11, 26, 29
South Fork 44
South Fork SO *et al* 158, 165, 167, 170, 186, 199, 204-11, 363
South Penn Railroad 15
Southwest Junction SW 294-6, 375
Southwest Penna Railroad 296, 304
Spain 12, 19
SQ 249, 253
Staple Bend Tunnel 44, 158-9, 216, 218, 220-1, 231
Steel 62
Stewarts 318, 322
Stone Bridge 239-40, 366-7
Stony Creek 158-9, 164, 235, 241-2, 367
Stony (Rocky) Mountains 12
Strickland, William 32, 35-6, 40
Sugar Run (Gap) 39, 42, 58, 67-8, 115, 120, 122, 347
Summerhill 170, 198, 203-4, 362
Summitville 44
Susquehanna River 17, 23, 28
Swann, Thomas 65, 159, 162, 288
Swissdale 276
Swissvale 271
SX 249, 251, 253
Tariffs 11, 65
Taylor, G.B. 29
Tennessee River 12
Thomson, J.E. 32, 42, 58-60, 62, 65, 67-8, 75, 78, 90, 109, 158, 160-3, 167, 190, 244, 250, 275-6
Three Springs Gap 39, 67
Torrance 244, 248, 268, 271, 372
Trafford 52, 318, 320-2, 379-81
Treziyulney, Charles 39
Trout Run 190, 197, 212
Tunnelhill 141, 143, 145-6, 353
Turtle Creek 275-7, 320
UJ 326
UN 70-1, 122, 124, 130, 145, 153-4, 353
Union Canal 37
Uniontown 63
Virginia 14, 19, 26-30, 63
VK 249
VY 249, 260
W 199, 205, 211
WA 295
Wallis, J.M. 118, 146
Walls 318, 322
War of 1812 27
Washington PA 11, 23
Washington DC 17, 23, 25-8
Washington, George 14, 18, 20, 26, 29
Watt, James 10
Welch, Sylvester 40, 188
West Indies 13, 26, 29
West Virginia 19
West Penn *et al* 248-9, 257, 266-7
Western Continental Divide 12
Western Waters 12, 17
Wheeling 15-6, 22-3, 25, 28-30, 37-8, 61, 63-5
Whiskey Rebellion 16, 20
Whitney, Eli 11
Wills Creek 22
Wilmerding WG 318, 383
Wilmore 165, 168-70, 198-202, 362
Wisconsin 19
Wright, W.W. 159
WYE 51
Youghiogheny Branch 313, 316
Youghiogheny River 15

161 → J.E. Thomson

7 Mar 1999
6 APR

216-9
147-8

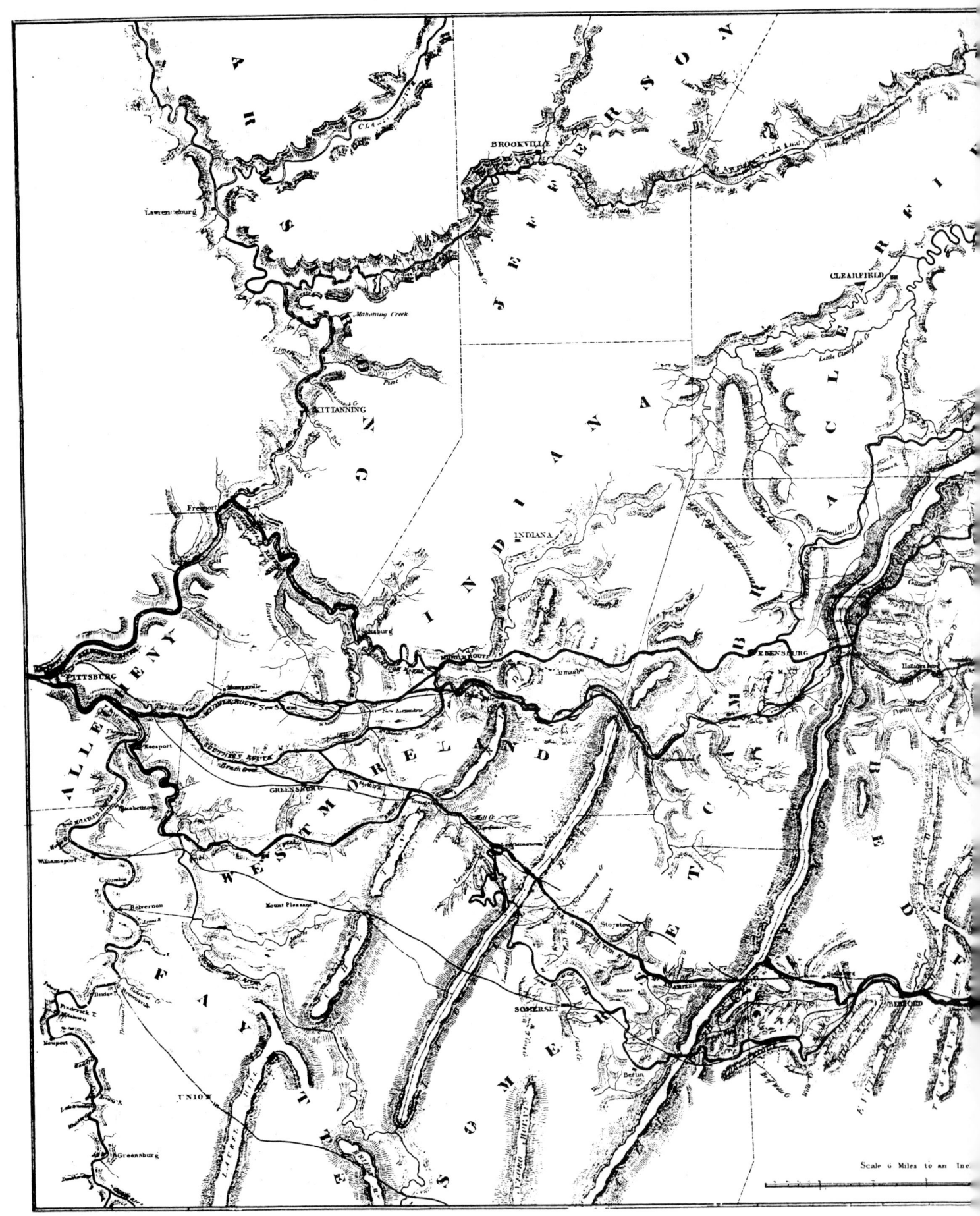